Where Nation-States Come From

Where Nation-States Come From

Institutional Change in the Age of Nationalism

Philip G. Roeder

PRINCETON UNIVERSITY PRESS

PRINCETON AND OXFORD

COPYRIGHT © 2007 BY PRINCETON UNIVERSITY PRESS

PUBLISHED BY PRINCETON UNIVERSITY PRESS, 41 WILLIAM STREET,

PRINCETON, NEW JERSEY 08540

IN THE UNITED KINGDOM: PRINCETON UNIVERSITY PRESS, 3 MARKET PLACE,

WOODSTOCK, OXFORDSHIRE OX20 1SY

ALL RIGHTS RESERVED

LIBRARY OF CONGRESS CATALOGING-IN-PUBLICATION DATA

ROEDER, PHILIP G.

WHERE NATION-STATES COME FROM : INSTITUTIONAL CHANGE IN

THE AGE OF NATIONALISM / PHILIP G. ROEDER.

INCLUDES BIBLIOGRAPHICAL REFERENCES AND INDEX.

ISBN-13: 978-0-691-12728-6 (ALK. PAPER)

ISBN-10: 0-691-12728-X (ALK. PAPER)

1. NATIONAL STATE. 2. NATIONALISM. I. TITLE.

JC311.R488 2007

320.1——DC22   2006037467

BRITISH LIBRARY CATALOGING-IN-PUBLICATION DATA IS AVAILABLE

THIS BOOK HAS BEEN COMPOSED IN JANSON AND AVENIR

PRINTED ON ACID-FREE PAPER. ∞

PRESS.PRINCETON.EDU

PRINTED IN THE UNITED STATES OF AMERICA

10   9   8   7   6   5   4   3   2   1

CONTENTS

PART FOUR
OUTCOMES: CRISES AND INDEPENDENCE

FIGURES

TABLES

ACKNOWLEDGMENTS

SO MANY GOOD FRIENDS AND COLLEAGUES have contributed so much to this book that I can only begin to acknowledge my debts to them. And none can I really thank adequately. Two friends who happen to be political scientists played such important roles in shaping this project that I must thank them first of all—Gary Shiffman and Valerie Bunce. At the beginning and end of this project they helped me reorganize my thoughts in ways that profoundly reshaped the book. In addition to Val, Cheryl Boudreau, Charles Bethel, Lauren Cole, Stephen Fish, Hendrik Spruyt, Michael Tierney, and Nicholas Weller kindly consented to read the manuscript and offered important suggestions for improvement. I also owe much to the many patient listeners who challenged me with tough questions when I presented the segmental institutions thesis in private conversations, at conventions, and in seminars hosted by Columbia, Harvard, and Princeton Universities, particularly Richard Anderson, Shari Berman, George Breslauer, Timothy Colton, Robert English, Michael McFaul, Kenneth Schultz, Kathryn Stoner-Weiss, Joshua Tucker, and Celeste Wallender. Lawrence Robertson and Kathryn Stoner-Weiss generously shared documents they had collected that I was having difficulty finding. Michael Kelley, Daniel Lake, Stephanie McWhorter, and Jeffrey Timmons served brilliantly as research assistants in the often tedious task of compiling data sets. Chuck Myers of Princeton University Press once again has treated me with the professionalism and integrity that distinguish him as one of the finest editors in the field. Finally, I have learned much from so many scholars that I cannot list here. The footnotes at least list their names, but in no way fully express my profound respect and gratitude for the giants on whose shoulders I have tried to climb in order to get a peek at the world in which we live.

PART ONE

THE INSTITUTIONAL ORIGINS OF NATION-STATES

ONE

Who Gets a State of Their Own?

A **NATION IN THE MODERN ERA** is a population that purportedly has a right to a state of its own.[1] Over the two centuries that we call the age of nationalism, philosophers, politicians, and polemicists have imagined hundreds, if not thousands, of nation-states. Indeed, a piece of folk wisdom often repeated in academic and policy communities holds that around the world today there may be as many as six to eight hundred active nation-state projects and another seven to eight thousand potential projects.[2] Yet today, only a little more than 190 nation-states have achieved the status of sovereign, independent members of the world community.[3] This begs a question: Why do some nation-state projects succeed in achieving sovereign independence while most fail?

The current configuration of borders in the world that privileges these 190 or so nation-state projects over the alternatives is something of a puzzle. Few would defend the present configuration as politically, economically, or culturally optimal. Indeed, on all continents there are competing projects to unite some states into larger states, such as a European Union or regional unions of African states; to make others smaller by granting independence to such substate entities as the Basque Country or Somaliland; or simply to decertify some nation-states and redraw borders in a more rational or efficient manner. Their proponents have made compelling cases that these new states would be superior to the current nation-states.

The question of which nations get states of their own is obviously a question of why some nation-state projects have triumphed over the empires, multinational states, and nation-states they replaced. Yet it is more complex than that. During the crises that led to new nation-states, typically there were multiple, competing nation-state projects on the table. For example, during the process that led to the fragmentation of the Union of Soviet Socialist Republics (USSR or Soviet Union) into fifteen successor

---

[1] This definition of the term "nation" derives from Max Weber's definition in "Diskussionsreden auf dem zweiten Deutschen Soziologentag in Berlin 1912": "a nation is a community of sentiment which would adequately manifest itself in a state of its own; hence a nation is a community which normally tends to produce a state of its own." See Gerth and Mills 1958, 176.

[2] Gellner 1983, 45.

[3] The United Nations in mid-2006 included 192 nation-states and recognized one other sovereign state as an observer, the Vatican City State. In addition, the Republic of China (Taiwan) constituted a potential nation-state.

states, there were proposals for dozens of alternative nation-states that would have united or divided these fifteen states in diverse ways, such as a revived Soviet Union, a Slavic union, a Turkestan to unite the so-called "stans" of Central Asia, or a Republic of Mountain Peoples that would unite communities on both sides of the Caucasus. Thus, the question of which nations get states is also a question of why some projects have triumphed over the many alternatives for unification and division that have been contending for sovereign independence.

Humanists and social scientists have devoted considerable attention to the various phenomena associated with the process of creating new nation-states, including nationalism, secessions, and state failures. The attention is warranted. The attempt to create new nation-states has been the inspiration for some of the most glorious and tragic moments of modern politics. The success of some projects to create new nation-states, such as Ireland, Israel, or Lithuania, represents the fulfillment of aspirations for self-governance that define the era of nationalism. Yet the success of nation-state projects has often been associated with violent destruction, as the breakup of Yugoslavia illustrates. The frustration of nation-state projects has often been equally costly, as the conflicts in Chechnya and Palestine attest.

The attention is also warranted because nation-states are among the most important institutions of political life; they establish fundamental parameters of both global and domestic politics. For example, in the past century changes in the configuration of nation-states have given strength to new global forces, such as the rise of the Third World following the breakup of European empires, and have changed the polarity of the international system, such as the end of bipolarity following the breakup of the Soviet Union. The changing configuration of nation-states provides the building blocks with which diplomats must seek to build peace and security even in the face of transnational forces such as terrorism. The boundaries created by nation-states define the outlines of domestic politics as well. The boundaries constrain the likelihood that democracy can succeed in a polity, demarcate the actors and preferences that must be balanced in domestic politics, and thus shape the direction policy will take.[4] For example, little imagination is needed to identify the ways in which North American politics inside and among sovereign states would have been profoundly different had the project for a Confederate States of America led to sovereign statehood in the nineteenth century.

The explanation for which nations are likely to get states of their own also has practical implications as we look ahead to the policy problems that may engage governments and the global community in the future. For policy-makers who must anticipate crises, the explanation helps to identify

[4] Roeder 1999, 2004; Alesina, Baqir, and Easterly 1999; Lustick 1990.

potential instabilities in existing nation-states. It identifies nation-state projects seeking sovereign independence that may be most threatening to the peace. Such nation-state crises have been extraordinarily destabilizing. For example, in recent decades projects to create new nation-states have been the single most common agenda of terrorists. Robert Pape recorded 188 suicide bomb attacks between 1980 and 2001. Fully 82 percent of these attacks were associated with the campaigns to achieve independence for a Palestinian state, a Kurdish state, a Tamil state, or a Chechen state, or to separate Kashmir from India. (Most of the other attacks were associated with nationalist attempts to end a foreign occupation of an existing nation-state.) As Pape summarizes, "the strategic logic of suicide terrorism is specifically designed to coerce modern democracies to make significant concessions to national self-determination."[5] Similarly, nation-state crises have been the single most common cause of internal wars over the last half-century. Nils Petter Gleditsch recorded 184 wars within the jurisdictions of sovereign states between 1946 and 2001, including 21 within their external dependencies and 163 within the metropolises. More than half of these wars, 51.6 percent, were associated with nation-state crises in which parties challenged the existing state and demanded either statehood for themselves or unification with another state.[6]

Furthermore, for the designers of transitions to peace after civil war, democracy after autocracy, or independence after subjection, answers to the question of where nation-states come from can provide guidance for the design of stable political orders in culturally diverse societies. Indeed, I argue in this book that the source of new nation-states has been a crisis of "stateness"—a crisis in which residents contest the human and geographic borders of existing states and some residents even seek to create new independent states—and that this crisis typically results from the design of their institutions. An implication of this finding is that by prudent action, governments and the global community could avoid such crises in the future, but probably will not.[7]

Patterns of Nation-State Creation, 1816–2000

The American Declaration of Independence and the French Declaration of the Rights of Man and the Citizen ushered in an age of nationalism that led to the conscious creation of nation-states. In the 185 years that followed

[5] Pape 2003, 344.
[6] Based on data posted by Gleditsch at www.prio.no/cwp/armedconflict. These figures include all cases except those listed as interstate conflicts. Also see N. Gleditsch, Wallensteen, Eriksson, Sollenberg, and Strand 2002.
[7] Roeder and Rothchild 2005.

the final defeat of the French in 1815, most existing states sought to redefine themselves by the new logic of nation-statehood, namely, that their statehood was the expression of the sovereign will of a people. More dramatically, a total of 191 new or reconstituted states joined or rejoined the international system, most with the claim that this represented the sovereign prerogative of a people to be self-governing.[8]

Although the creation and reconstitution of states around the world continued throughout the years from 1816 to 2000, as figure 1.1 shows, this process accelerated during the latter half of the twentieth century. The creation of new nation-states in the past two centuries has occurred in a few episodic bursts. Specifically, since 1815 there have been four bursts in the creation of new nation-states: the classic period, from the Congress of Vienna to the Congress of Berlin; the first quarter of the twentieth century; the three decades that followed World War II; and the decade that straddled the end of the cold war. It would be imprudent to make bold claims about trends, especially a claim that this is a declining trend. Compared with earlier decades, the decade of the 1990s was the second most intense period of transformation in the existing state system and creation of new nation-states, after the 1960s.

Decolonization represents the single most common source of new nation-states—62 percent of the total number created since 1815 (table 1.1). These 118 new states had not previously been incorporated into the metropolitan core of the governing states but remained juridically separate as colonies or protectorates. In the first and third phases of nation-state creation, 1816–1900 and 1941–1985, decolonization was the primary process by which new states were created. The second most common source of

[8] In compiling the list of new and reconstituted states I began with Kristian S. Gleditsch and Michael D. Ward's (1999) list of all independent polities that have relative autonomy over some territory, are recognized as such by local states or by the state on which they depend, and reached a population greater than 250,000 at some point prior to 2000. I have added the polities with population below 250,000. I am not, however, seeking to catalogue the list of states in the international system but the creation of new nation-states, so a few adjustments must be made. New states that result from decolonization of territory, such as Bechuanaland, not previously incorporated into the metropolitan core do not change the national character of the metropolitan core, such as the United Kingdom. I add only the new state to the list. Alternatively, secessions from a metropolitan core can change the national character of the rump state—for example, the Russian Federation is a different state from the Soviet Union. In counting rump states as new nation-states, only those rumps that constituted less than three-quarters of the population of the previous state are counted as reconstituted. With the loss of a quarter or more of its population—usually the loss of a distinctive ethnic population—the basis for the rump nation-state typically must be reconsidered. Similarly, addition of independent states to an existing state may transform the national character of the unified state. The unified state is counted as a new nation-state unless the population of one of the constituent parts that were previously independent exceeded 75 percent of the newly unified state.

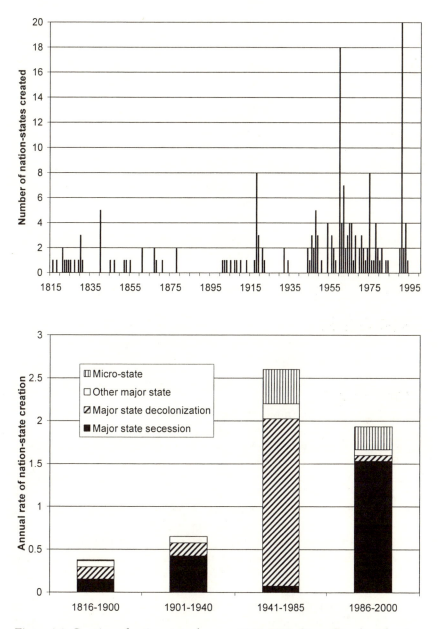

Figure 1.1 Creation of nation-states by year, 1816–2000. *Source*: Based on data in Gleditsch and Ward 1999. Also see footnote 8 in this chapter.

TABLE 1.1

Numbers of new and reconstituted states worldwide, 1816–2000

Origin of state	Examples[a]	Major states	Micro states	Total
Division of states				
Postcolonial states	Argentina 1816, Zaire 1960	97	21	118
Postsecession states	Estonia 1918, 1991, Romania 1878	50	—	50
Rump states	Austria 1918, Russia 1991	6	—	6
Postoccupation states	North Korea 1948, South Korea 1948	6	—	6
Unification of existing states	Germany 1871, 1990, Vietnam 1975	5	—	5
Newly incorporated territories	Liberia 1847, Transvaal 1852	6	—	6
Total		170	21	191

Source: See footnote 8.

[a]Examples indicate the year the state joined or rejoined the international system as a sovereign state.

new nation-states has been division of (or secession from) the metropolitan cores of states, which accounts for about 32 percent of the total. The division of the Ottoman Empire, the Austro-Hungarian Empire, the Russian Empire, the USSR, and Yugoslavia in particular stand as major sources of new states. The sixty-two states created by division of metropolitan cores include secessionist territories (e.g., Estonia in 1918 and 1991), reconstituted rump nation-states left behind (e.g., the Russian Federation in 1991 or the Czech Republic in 1993), and regimes imposed by occupying authorities (e.g., the Peoples' Democratic Republic of Korea in 1948). In the second and fourth phases of nation-state creation, 1901–1940 and 1986–2000, division or secession was the primary source of new nation-states. The remaining eleven new nation-states include five that resulted from the unification of existing states (e.g., Germany in 1990, Vietnam in 1975). Another six resulted from incorporation of peripheral regions into the international system through settlement (e.g., Liberia in 1847, Orange Free State in 1853) or recognition of indigenous sovereignties (e.g., Afghanistan in 1919, Saudi Arabia in 1932) in areas previously not recognized as falling under any sovereign authority.

These changes in state boundaries through decolonization, secession, and unification have in fact moved the world closer to the ideal proclaimed by such nationalists as Giuseppe Mazzini—a universal system of nation-states. Almost all new states have claimed to represent the sovereign will of their people to have a state of their own. For example, the acts adopted by new states to declare their independence typically predicate this act on the right of a specified people to constitute a state of its own.[9] Today, the constitutions of most states are predicated on the claim that the people, such as "the Burundian Nation" or "the Chadian people," have a right to govern themselves and to choose the form of their own government. For example, 72 percent of the 143 constitutions of major states in force in 2000 began with just such a claim.[10]

This pattern of nation-state creation sets the question I address in this book: Why did these nation-state projects achieve sovereign independence while hundreds of other projects have not?

The Segmental Institutions Thesis

The usual explanations for the success of nation-state projects begin with identities, grievances, and mobilization. A common nationalist narrative about the origins of individual nation-states celebrates the politicization of an ethnic identity and the awakening or reawakening of national identity. The narrative immortalizes bold proclamations against the oppression of overlords and the heroic mobilization of nationalist resistance on the path to independence. In the academy, these narratives have become the basis of a significant body of sociological theory that imputes prime causality to identity, grievances, and mobilization. More recently, these traditional explanations have been challenged by theories in the fields of economics and international relations that claim that economic greed, not cultural grievance, motivates nationalist resistance and that the selection mechanism of international recognition actually determines which nation-states become sovereign members of the world community.

In this book I argue that all of these elements—identity, grievance, greed, mobilization, and international recognition—must be present for a successful nation-state project. For the proponents of a nation-state project to advance to sovereign independence, all of these elements must align so that they are mutually reinforcing. Misalignment of any one element can create an insurmountable obstacle to success. Misalignment is a reason why so few projects succeed. The argument in this book turns our attention to the question, what could possibly lead all of these elements to align favor-

---

[9] Based on the author's coding of documents in Blaustein, Sigler, and Beede 1977.

[10] Based on the author's coding of documents in Blaustein and Flanz 2006.

ably? Perhaps this alignment can result from simple luck or coincidence, but that is unlikely. Rather, I argue that there is a common overarching constraint that has increased the likelihood of such an alignment: almost every successful nation-state project has been associated with an existing institution that I refer to as a "segment-state." Independence represented the administrative upgrade of this existing jurisdiction. For example, after the demise of the USSR, the successful nation-state projects were the projects associated with the first-order jurisdictions called union republics, such as Kazakhstan and Ukraine. The nation-state projects not associated with these segment-states, such as the projects for Turkestan, Idel-Ural, the Mountain Republic, or Novorossiia, failed in the 1990s. I will call this argument *the segmental institutions thesis*.[11]

This pattern, which privileges nation-state projects associated with segment-states, holds around the world and throughout the twentieth century. From 1901 to 2000, 177 new nation-states were created, and 153 of these new nation-states had been segment-states immediately prior to independence (see table 10.5).[12] That is, 86 percent of all new nation-states in the twentieth century had prehistories that looked much like the creation of independent successor states of the USSR.[13] Indeed, for the past century it would have been safe to bet a considerable sum with the rule of thumb, "no segment-state, no nation-state." No other simple rules would have yielded such a high return. For example, it would have been hard to win as much by betting on the elevation of ethnic groups to national consciousness and then statehood; fewer than a dozen ethnic groups without segment-states achieved sovereign independence in the twentieth century. Nor would it have been as lucrative to bet on the constituents of federations, since only one of those that were not segment-states became a nation-state. (These anomalies are discussed in chapter 10.) Rather than groups or territories alone, it is the unique conjunction of popular and territorial jurisdictions in a segment-state that has paved the way to independence. Thus, this simple thesis explains why, since 1815, most nation-state projects that have sought sovereign statehood have failed. The authors of most imagined nation-states, such as Kurdistan, Turkestan, Tamil Eelam, or Atzlán, have been unable to draw on the resources of segment-states.

The findings presented in this book also underscore the observation that without segment-states, nation-state projects are far less likely to produce crises in the first place. That is, the segmental institutions thesis not only

[11] Compare Beissinger and Young 2002, 30–35.

[12] The operational counting rules that establish cutoff points for gains or losses in territory or population that constitute new nation-states are described in footnote 8.

[13] See also Mann 1995, 49.

explains which nation-state projects are likely to succeed in achieving sovereign independence, it also explains which projects are likely to become an
issue in a nation-state crisis in which the issue of sovereign independence is
on the bargaining table. For example, among Africanists there have been
many who see a puzzle that Pierre Englebert has called Africa's "secession
deficit": even though Africa is plagued by weak governments, many ethnic
groups, and a high propensity to political violence, it has had fewer secessionist attempts than other continents.[14] From the perspective of the segmental institutions thesis, however, there is little puzzle: independent Africa has had far fewer segment-states than other continents. In the
twentieth century, the independent states of Asia and Europe each had
about three times as many internal segment-states. While African states
maintained twenty internal segment-states at various times (and ten of
these were South Africa's Bantustans), Asia maintained fifty-six and Europe
maintained sixty-seven internal segment-states. For this reason Africa has
suffered few attempts at secession. (The only successful secession attempt,
that of Eritrea in 1993, was initiated by one of the few segment-states on
the continent.) The segmental institutions thesis predicts that weak common-states without segment-states should not face many significant secessionist threats. In Africa, the absence of segment-states explains why alternative nation-state projects have failed to gather adherents beyond small
circles and why nationalist attachments to existing independent states have
tended to be nearly monopolistic and unchallenged.

The segmental institutions thesis also implies the counterfactual claim
that if the territorial and human boundaries defined by segment-states had
been drawn differently, a different set of national claims—or even none at
all—would have assaulted the common-states. For example, if the USSR
had preserved the Bukhara, Khiva, and Turkestan republics rather than
dividing these among five union republics, we would today be celebrating
the independence of Bukhara, Khiva, and Turkestan rather than Kazakhstan, Kyrgyzstan, Tajikistan, Turkmenistan, and Uzbekistan. Moreover, if
the USSR had created economic regions (oblasts) based on economic efficiency rather than union republics based on purported nations, as the early
economic planners advised, few if any nation-state projects would have
been able to challenge the USSR.

In short, new nation-states have mostly come from administrative
upgrade of segment-states. In explaining the origins of nation-states, the
segmental institutions thesis shifts primary focus from national identity
formation, material greed and grievance, nationalist mobilization, or international selection mechanisms to political institutions. The independence
of a new nation-state is the consequence of the failure of one set of state

---

[14] Englebert 2003; compare Beissinger and Young 2002.

institutions to keep people and territory within their jurisdiction. Creating new nation-states is an act of institutional change. That is, to explain which nation-state projects have succeeded in achieving sovereign independence, it is necessary to look to the institutions of the states that gave birth to them. In particular, it is necessary to examine what I call the segmented state and its constituent segment-states. The segmental institutions thesis explains why almost all nation-states created in the past two centuries have emerged from a crisis of stateness that has developed within this specific institutional framework. The creation of new nation-states is institutional change that responds to the failure of segmental institutions.

Some Terminology

This brief overview of the segmental institutions thesis has already introduced some terms that need more precise definitions before continuing. A *nation-state project* is a claim that a specific population (purportedly a nation) should be self-governing within a sovereign state of its own—one that may not yet exist.[15] Challengers to the status quo who press nation-state projects belong to the category of constitutional claimants demanding a greater share of an existing state's powers or decision rights. Unlike other constitutional claimants, who may be democratic reformers, civil libertarians, or corporatist groups, claimants pressing nation-state projects ultimately seek not simply to change the government or the regime within an existing state but to change the very human and geographic boundaries of the state itself. Unlike other autonomy claims, which much scholarship argues are *either* territorial *or* communal claims, nation-state projects are simultaneously territorial *and* communal.[16] Nation-state projects assert that a community of people has a right to a state of its own within a specific territorial domain that allegedly belongs to that people as its homeland.

The nation-state simultaneously defines a territorial jurisdiction (the state) and a political community (the nation). A *segmented state* (which may itself claim to be a nation-state) divides its territory and population further among separate jurisdictions and gives the population that purportedly is indigenous to each jurisdiction a distinct political status. In the terminology I develop in chapter 2, these institutions create a *common-state* that is common to the whole territory and population and separate *segment-states* for the separate territories and populations. Segment-states are not simply territorial jurisdictions within a federal state; they also contain juridically separate communities of peoples who purportedly have special claim to that

---

[15] Compare Breuilly 1994, 1, 9; Hechter and Levi 1979, 262. For alternative definitions, see Connor 1994; Haas 1986; Hutchinson 1987.

[16] A. Smith 1979, 21–22; O'Leary 2001.

jurisdiction as a homeland. For example, the USSR as a common-state was purportedly the sovereign expression of the right of the Soviet people to self-governance—that is, a nation-state. Yet the fifteen union republics, such as the Uzbek Soviet Socialist Republic (SSR), which were segment-states, also purportedly expressed the sovereign right of their respective nations to statehood and self-governance.

In an age in which almost all states are based on claims of popular sovereignty, the segmented state has been an attempt to compromise with the simple logic of the nation-state: one people, one state. The segmented state began as modern democracies extended the franchise to inhabitants of the metropolitan core, like the United Kingdom, but refused to extend it to subjects of similar strata in colonies or protectorates. Hence, a complex formula began to emerge: one nation (Britons) and many subjects outside the nation, but under one common-state (the United Kingdom), which constituted the nation-state of only some (the British). Then many of the subjects received states of their own as colonies and protectorates were permitted to develop their own governing institutions, so the formula became even more complex: many nations (British, Nigerians, and others), many segment-states (Nigeria and others), but submission to one common-state (the United Kingdom), which remained the nation-state of only some (the British). The varieties of segmented states expanded further as governments began to treat parts of the population within the metropolitan core as separate nations. Then the formula became still more complex: many nations (Northern Irish, Scots, Welsh, and perhaps English), many segment-states (Northern Ireland, Scotland, and Wales), but subsumed within one common-nation (Britons) and one common-state (the United Kingdom). All of this institutional gerrymandering defies the simple logic of popular sovereignty and in many parts of the world has led to institutions that have proved less durable than the simple nation-state.

The segmental institutions thesis leads to the view that typically only states have given birth to new nation-states. There is no spontaneous generation. As states began to turn their populations into citizens, parts of the common-state were left out, particularly parts that were inhabited by culturally distinct populations. In the age of nationalism, these territories and populations often became the bases of segment-states. When the common-state was no longer willing to accept the losses associated with maintaining these separate jurisdictions, the common-state began either to incorporate its segment-states as parts of the metropolitan core or to shed them as new nation-states. This institutionalist perspective shifts our focus so that new nation-states are not in the first instance the expression of society but an adaptation of existing state institutions to political circumstances that those institutions helped create.

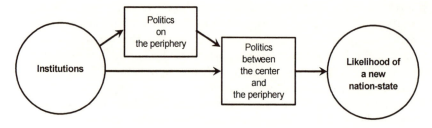

Figure 1.2 The segmental institutions thesis.

Consequences of Segmental Institutions

Segmental institutions shape politics in unique ways (figure 1.2). First, they shape the politics on the periphery in which proponents of competing nation-state projects contend to establish political-identity hegemony within a target population and within a target homeland. Second, segmental institutions shape politics between the periphery and the center in which these proponents of alternative nation-state projects seek to induce the leaders of the common-state to shower their projects with favors, including independence. In both these arenas, proponents of nation-state projects empowered with segment-states are privileged in ways that other proponents of nation-state projects can only envy.

Not all segment-states become nation-states, however, so we also need to examine the ways in which segment-states differ from one another in order to identify the characteristics that lead to independence. The segmental institutions thesis argues that variations in the institutional design of different segmented states are most important in determining whether the outcome will be a nation-state crisis and the creation of new nation-states. Specifically, the likelihood of the breakup of segmented states depends to a large extent on the combined effect of (1) the balance of leverage between segment-state and common-state leaders (that is, the coercion that each group of leaders can use against the other) and (2) the differential empowerment of the population of the segment-state in segment-state politics and common-state politics (that is, whether the population of the segment-state governs itself and participates in the governance of the common-state). An extremely volatile situation—a situation in which the failure of the segmented state and the creation of new nation-states are more likely—arises when segmental institutions create the following conditions: (1) the segment-state leaders consolidate control over politics and the expression of national identity within their segment-states; (2) the segment-state leaders are autonomous from the common-state leaders, control a greater share of decision rights and revenue streams, and dominate cultural institutions within their segment-states; (3) common-state decision making excludes segment-state publics; and (4) the common-state leadership divides or weakens. This is a mouthful and requires further explanation in later chapters, but the core insight is that the presence of more of these four conditions as a result of the design of segmental institutions moves a segmented state closer to failure and segment-states closer to independence.

The segmental institutions thesis is an extension of the institutionalists' most fundamental claim, that political institutions structure political life. Admittedly, the institutions discussed here are not the usual institutions discussed by students of legislatures, electoral systems, or bureaucracies.[17] Yet the sign of a vibrant analytic approach such as the institutionalist approach is that analysis using such an approach can be extended beyond the easy issues to those that are on the research frontier. This book presents the claim that the nation-state is one of the most important political institutions of modern life, setting the foundation for both domestic and international politics, defining the major players in both arenas, and therefore shaping the agenda in domestic and global decision making. It deserves close attention from institutionalists.

Institutionalists make a number of claims that have direct bearing on the origins of nation-states. First, political institutions influence whether the dominant claimants in the political life of an existing state are politicians speaking on behalf of national groups and not spokespersons for some other "imagined" social group such as a class. In all political systems, some politicians demand changes in the allocation of decision-making rights, but only under specific institutional constraints are the most prominent claimants likely to be those making claims on behalf of populations purportedly having a right to states of their own. Second, in polities where nationalist claims are on the table, institutions privilege some nation-state projects over others. Joseph Rothschild emphasizes that "politicized ethnicity surfaces and hardens along the most accessible and yielding faultline of potential cleavage available" and that political institutions are powerful "in affecting the configuration of ethnic groups, the cutting edge of ethnic conflict, and the very content of ethnicity per se."[18] Third, state institutions favor specific organizational strategies in pressing a nation-state project. For example, an electoral system may favor the formation of an interest group rather than a political party to press a project. The presence of segmental institutions favors segment-state governments over either parties or interest groups as the most efficient means for pressing such claims.[19] Fourth, by handing decision-making rights to some individuals

[17] See, for example, Shepsle 1989; Shepsle and Weingast 1981; Cox 1997; P. Hall and Taylor 1996.

[18] Rothschild 1981, 96, 99.

[19] Compare institutional arrangements that favor different organizational strategies in Rokkan and Urwin 1983, 140; Banfield and Moynihan 1975.

rather than others, political institutions influence the internal structure of the groups on behalf of which the nation-state projects are advanced. Political institutions affect the probability that different types of politicians will emerge as the dominant spokespersons for a nation-state project. For example, nonterritorial ethnocorporatism in the Ottoman Empire's *millet* system, which gave communal autonomy to confessional groups under their religious leaders, led to a different type of national leader in the empire than did the territorially based ethnofederalism governed by Communist Party secretaries within the USSR. And fifth, political institutions shape the issues on the bargaining table by affecting the expected net payoff to different demands. For example, segment-states lower the costs of secession by providing secessionists with a ready-made governing structure. Without segment-states, many potential nationalists are deterred from pressing a nation-state project by the overwhelming costs of creating a state de novo and so press alternative demands, such as civil liberties, within an existing state.

In short, political institutions determine who plays; distribute opportunities to act; favor some types of political coalitions, organizational forms, and strategies over others; and shape the political agenda.[20] On the *tabula rasa* of an institution-free world, politics might directly express the "objective" attributes of the population and the patterning of preferences in the public. In nationalist politics the major claimant groups might form on the basis of a so-called primordial affinity among its members. Once political institutions enter the picture, however, they help determine whether pressing a particular nation-state project is likely to be efficacious. In the competition among nation-state projects to press their claims on states, political institutions select the nation-state projects that are most likely to challenge existing states and most likely to succeed.

Politics on the Periphery

In the politics on the periphery, segment-states make it possible for the proponents of one nation-state project to establish *political-identity hegemony*. This term refers both to the relative predominance of a national identity within "the people" and to the relative empowerment of a cohort of politicians associated with that project within "the homeland." Under political-identity hegemony, intellectuals and the public at large are not torn among competing national identities. Within the borders of the homeland, the cohort of politicians associated with the project of the seg-

---

[20] Ostrom 1992, 24; Lalman, Oppenheimer, and Swistak 1993, 81; Shepsle 1989, 135–36; Tarrow 1988, 429–30; Eisinger 1973; Kitschelt 1986.

ment-state determines when and whether alternative national identities will be expressed in politics.

In the absence of segment-states, political-identity hegemony is unlikely. Intellectuals on the periphery tend to multiply the number of alternative nation-state projects. Publics have little reason to make costly commitments to one or another of these projects. For example, in the late Russian Empire in Central Asia, intellectuals propagated projects for a pan-Islamic state, a pan-Turkic state, a Turkestan, Bukhara and Khiva, Sarts versus nomads, Greater Uzbekistan and Greater Kirgizia, separate Tajik and Kazakh states, still smaller states, such as a separate state for the Kazakh Greater Horde, and various leagues of independent tribes and cities, as well as projects for a reformed but united Russia. In the absence of segment-states that propagated their own nation-state projects, alternative projects proliferated in Central Asia, intellectual fads followed one after another, and the public at large remained ignorant of most of these. Thus, most proponents of nation-state projects create no more than parlor nations—or perhaps campus nations, in recent decades. These projects, examples of which include the nation-state projects for Turkestan, Novorossiia, or Idel-Ural in the 1990s, remain the prized possessions of small circles of intellectuals who fail to fire many imaginations outside their salons or classrooms.

In the presence of segment-states, it becomes significantly more likely that a cohort of politicians associated with a particular nation-state project will establish political-identity hegemony. The leaders of the segment-state are uniquely empowered to propagate a nation-state project that can challenge the common-state. Segment-state leaders can offer special inducements for intellectuals to abandon their own favored nation-state projects and accept a second-best made real in the segment-state. Segment-state leaders can induce the public at large to make costly commitments to the nation-state project. The leaders of segment-states can make it very difficult for proponents of alternative nation-state projects to garner support. Thus, those nation-state projects whose leaders control segment-states have had greater success at expanding the membership of their imagined communities beyond a few parlors or classrooms. In the competition among the proponents of alternative nation-state projects, the leaders of segment-states have been uniquely positioned to expand their membership and press the common-state for concessions of sovereign rights.

The dramatic way in which the introduction of segmental institutions can transform politics on the periphery is illustrated by a simple comparison of Bulgarian nationalism before and after 1878. In that year, the Treaty of San Stefano granted Bulgaria political autonomy within the Ottoman Empire. From that moment forward, until the achievement of independence on October 5, 1908, Bulgarian nationalism was transformed. Prior to statehood, the Bulgarian national movement was disunited, and during the 1860s and 1870s its leaders lived for the most part in Serbia and Romania. The Bulgarian Orthodox Church leaders empowered within the Ottoman *millet* system successfully championed the cause of elevating their religious status by creating an autonomous Bulgarian Exarchate (1872), but had far less interest in a separate Bulgarian state. The creation of a Bulgarian segment-state came when the Russian Empire forced the Ottoman Empire to concede territorial autonomy in the peace treaty of 1878. Once the autonomous Kingdom of Bulgaria was established, however, Bulgarian nationalism came into its own within Bulgaria. Russia had "expected gratitude in return for its role in securing independence, helping build the new state, and strengthening it by the continued presence of the Russian army. But the Bulgars turned out to be nationalists above all else."[21] Indeed, through concerted efforts of the kingdom, the Bulgarians within seven years (1885) had forced the Ottoman Empire and the European powers to accept Bulgaria's annexation of Eastern Rumelia, and within thirty years they had won their independence.

Politics between Periphery and Center

In addition to shaping politics on the periphery, segmental institutions shape the politics between center and periphery.[22] Segmented states tend to be unstable, to suffer recurring nation-state crises, and eventually to abandon segmental institutions in either centralization or dissolution of the common-state. For example, centralization was the outcome of the early Soviet nation-state crisis that followed the creation of the USSR in 1922; this ended in the concentration of union republic powers in the hands of Joseph Stalin. In the post-Soviet experience, centralization was also the outcome of the Russian nation-state crisis; centralization began in 1993 and the pace accelerated after 1999. Yet segmented states are also likely to fail by falling apart and generating new nation-states. The dissolution of the Russian Empire in 1917 led to the independence of Finland. The dissolution of the USSR following the Soviet nation-state crisis of the *perestroika* period, from 1988 to 1991, produced fifteen successor states.

Segmental institutions create this instability because of the manner in which they distribute capabilities and shape the incentives of those empowered with these capabilities. Six consequences of segmental institutions increase the odds of dissolution and the independence of new nation-states. First, under segmental institutions, center versus periphery politics come to be dominated by bargaining between leaders of the common-state and

[21] Shaw and Shaw 1977, 2:196–97. Also see 160–62, 187–89, and 196–99. Also see Jelavich and Jelavich 1977, 128–40; Mann 1995, 49.
[22] The seminal work is Rothchild 1970.

leaders of segment-states. Segmental institutions shape center-periphery politics by permitting the leaders of segment-states to muscle their way to the head of the queue and to elbow aside other interests and other nation-state projects seeking attention and favors from common-state leaders. Cross-cutting interests that might hold the common-state together find it hard to get a seat at the bargaining table in the segmented state. This was evident in the narrowing of the circle of participants in negotiations over policy and reform in the last two years of the USSR: by mid-1991, direct negotiations among leaders of union republics (such as Boris Yeltsin for Russia) and the leader of the USSR (Mikhail Gorbachev) came to exclude the leaders of almost every other interest.

Second, under segmental institutions, the agenda of center-periphery politics increasingly comes to focus on a zero-sum conflict over allocating decision rights between common-state and segment-state governments. In this context it becomes harder to find compromises, because every gain for one side comes to be seen as a loss for the other. In the last eighteen months of the USSR more issues, such as environmental protection and economic reform, and eventually almost all issues were subsumed by the overarching negotiations over allocation of decision rights between the USSR government and the individual union republic governments.

Third, segmental institutions encourage leaders of segment-states to make more radical demands on behalf of their nation-state projects—that is, to demand a larger share of the decision rights of the common-state and ultimately to play the sovereignty card. Radicalization of segment-state leadership (at least on the nation-state issue) results from a change of leadership in some segment-states; leaders who are cross-pressured by the competing demands of the common-state and a segment-state often retreat to the sidelines of politics. Politicians with stronger objections to remaining within the common-state are likely to come to dominate political life. Yet even moderate leaders who remain in politics may press more radical nationalist demands, because in doing so they can externalize the costs of making everyone within the segment-state better off—at the expense of the common-state. Further radicalization of segment-state demands results from competition *among* segment-states. Once one segment-state has grabbed a greater share of the common-state powers, other segment-state leaders must also make power grabs. No leader wants to be the sucker left behind feeding the common-state that every other segment-state is milking dry. The ultimate radicalization of segment-state demands often takes place when segment-state leaders, frustrated by the multiplication of claims on the bargaining table, seek the unique advantages that come from playing the sovereignty card. Against a cacophony of competing demands, this is a nearly certain way to get heard: nothing momentarily silences the bargaining room and privileges the claims of a segment-state more than the assertion that these claims represent the sovereign prerogative of its people.

Fourth, segmental institutions increase the likelihood of dissolution because they foster divergent development among segment-states. Development along divergent trajectories makes it harder to find common policies and common institutions that can address the needs of all segment-states. In the late USSR, as the union republics developed in different directions, it became harder to identify a set of common-state institutions that could hold together a democratic Estonia and autocratic Turkmenistan and all the other republics in between. Moreover, the type of common-state that would reassure the Communist leadership of Belarus would be seen as threatening by a democratizing republic like Armenia, and vice versa. Previously acceptable compromises that at one time would have kept the common-state whole simply disappeared from the bargaining range as the union republics developed along diverging paths.

Fifth, segmental institutions increase the likelihood of dissolution because they empower the leaders of segment-states with means to make it too costly for the leaders of the common-state to try to hold on to the segment-state. The decision rights of segment-states become institutional weapons that give the leaders of segment-states leverage over the common-state leadership. In the late USSR, withholding funds from the all-union budget, imposing embargoes on the export of foodstuffs to other parts of the common-state, and mobilizing volunteer armed forces became means to increase the costs to Gorbachev, in hopes of inducing him to concede independence.

Sixth, in the extreme, segmental institutions can lead to weakening of the common-state government itself. Where segment-state governments are empowered within the common-state government, they can use this power to force deadlock in common-state deliberations and paralyze the common-state government. Where segment-state leaders induce the common-state leadership to devolve more powers onto the segment-state governments, the central government ceases to be a presence in the segment-states, or, as in the USSR, the central government may simply wither away.

Implications for Some Common Answers

As the previous section indicates, the segmental institutions thesis treats the most common explanations for the success of nation-state projects as intervening or endogenous factors affected by the presence and shape of segmental institutions. Studies of social movements, collective action, and violence—and the nationalist variants of each of these—have stressed the importance of identities, grievances and greed, mobilization of resources, political opportunities, and international recognition.[23] The segmental institutions thesis does not dismiss these factors but argues that normally they are conducive to the success of a nation-state project only in the presence of segmental institutions. That is, segmental institutions, such as the governments of autonomous homelands or self-governing colonies, come first in the causal chain of the thesis and align these other factors. In the creation of new nation-states, all these other factors are necessary in the sense that the misalignment of even one can pose an insurmountable obstacle to the success of a nation-state project; none alone is sufficient.[24] In the modern world, segmental institutions are almost always necessary for the creation of a new state, because usually these institutions alone have been able to align all these factors in a configuration that favors the success of a nation-state project.[25]

Political institutions have a profound effect in coordinating identities, framing and coordinating grievances, channeling ambition, distributing resources for collective action, creating opportunities to act effectively, and winning international recognition. Concerning identities, the hypotheses of the segmental institutions thesis identify the conditions under which one identity on the periphery is likely to coordinate and to achieve regional ascendance in political-identity hegemony.[26] Under this hegemony the political leadership identified with a segment-state and its nation-state project may not be able to mobilize extensive nationalist support, but it can block the expression of alternative projects.[27] Concerning grievance and greed, the hypotheses of the segmental institutions thesis identify institutional conditions under which grievances—such as those identified in relative deprivation theories—are likely to focus on independence as a solution, and ambition is channeled toward creation of an independent political system rather than seeking advancement within the existing political system.[28] The hypotheses of the segmental institutions thesis are consistent with many insights of the resource-mobilization approach to social movements

---

[23] Gurr (2000, 65–96) incorporates all of these in a process model. Also see McAdam, Tarrow, and Tilly 2001, 243–46, 252–55; Hechter and Okamoto 2001.

[24] Thus, partisans of approaches that seek to privilege one or the other of these factors must assume that the other factors are always favorable. See McCarthy and Zald 1987; Oberschall 1973.

[25] In addition to these mainstream explanations, political geographers privilege geography (Hartshorne 1936; M. Anderson 1996; Mellor 1989, 74–103; Parker and Dikshit, 1997) and sociobiologists privilege genetics in their explanations (Van den Berghe 1978).

[26] The emphasis on identities is particularly prominent in the work of Connor (1994), Geertz (1963), Haas (1993), and A. Smith (1981). Also see Nagel 1994.

[27] On the relative importance of language and religion in the genesis of nation-states, see A. Smith 1986; Armstrong 1982; Safran 1992.

[28] On grievances, see Gurr 1971. On greed and grievances, see Collier and Hoeffler 2000; Nagel and Olzak 1982; Ragin 1979; Rudolph and Thompson 1985.

as well. Specifically, the segment-state's superior organizational resources and its hierarchical rather than atomistic or corpuscular structure give it many advantages over its competitors in the competition to place claims on the bargaining table and to wring concessions from the central government.[29] According to the hypotheses of the segmental institutions thesis, segmental institutions are also essential to creating a political opportunity structure that makes it more likely that secessions will succeed.[30] For example, segmental institutions give some proponents privileged access to the leadership of the common-state; the leaders of autonomous homelands or colonies often become the officially sanctioned voice of every interest on the periphery before the common-state government. Segmental institutions also increase the likelihood that strong segment-state governments will confront a weakened common-state government. Finally, the segmental institutions thesis argues that segment-states are much more likely to gain international recognition as sovereign states than projects that lack segment-states. International recognition can determine whether a nation-state project achieves de jure status and can deter any attempt by the common-state government to reintegrate a secession state. Yet the segmental institutions thesis argues that these last steps are often only a ratification of a lengthy process of gestation of political-identity hegemony, focusing of greed and grievance on the solution offered by a nation-state project, empowerment of proponents of that project, and weakening of an existing common-state.

Nationalism

The most profound implication of the segmental institutions thesis may concern our understanding of the relationship between nationalism and nation-states. A usual story told about the creation of nation-states focuses on the political awakening of a people or the politicization of an ethnic group that galvanizes it into a nation, provides it a platform for nationalist mobilization, and finally empowers it with a state of its own. This is a common theme that unites scholars on both sides of their sectarian disputes between primordialists and constructivists. For primordialists such as Walker Connor, the demand for a nation-state and separatism arises from the awakening of ethnic self-awareness.[31] For constructivists such as Paul Brass, the process of nationality formation is "one in which objective differ-

---

[29] McCarthy and Zald 1987, 15–42; Oberschall 1973; McAdam 1982; Morris 1984; McAdam, McCarthy, and Zald 1988; also see Hardin 1995; Hechter and Okamoto 2001, 202–3.

[30] Tarrow 1977, 142; 1989, 32–38; Tilly 1978, 1984, 297–317. Also see Oberschall 1973; Rothschild 1981, 96, 99.

[31] Connor 1972; A. Smith 1986. Also see H. Seton-Watson 1977, 1–5.

ences between ethnic groups acquire increasingly subjective and symbolic significance, are translated into a consciousness of, and a desire for, group solidarity, and become the basis for successful political demands."[32] These are prominent themes in interpretations of the fourth phase of nation-state creation, from 1986 to 2000.[33] The story of many new nation-states in the fourth phase—and even many failed national projects—is widely told as the awakening or the failure of national identity.[34] For example, Ian Bremmer attributes the secession of union republics in 1991 to the failure of the USSR to create a Soviet nation that could bind its various peoples and to counter "the persistence of popular national feelings."[35] Gail Lapidus offers a compelling account of how the political liberalization called *glasnost* created the conditions for "cognitive liberation" in which cultural and intellectual elites began "to reshape and transform collective consciousness within the national republics." The subsequent mobilization of these communities—particularly by the popular fronts—and the political success of nationalists in the union republic elections of 1990 revealed "the emergence of mass nationalism as a major political force."[36]

In a similar way, Miroslav Hroch seeks to explain which nationalist movements among the "small nations" of Europe succeeded.[37] He defines the small nations as those peoples without states of their own that nevertheless challenged the existing states of Europe. For Hroch, the explanation of success lies with the development of a national movement. Hroch postulates that the fundamental phases of a national movement are growing cultural awareness of national distinctiveness among intellectuals, the development of a political program of independence, and mass mobilization on behalf of this program. Thus, for Hroch, the question is framed to exclude the role of statehood as a cause (rather than a consequence) of independence and to focus on nationalist mobilization as an essential step to statehood. Among his eight case studies, however, the two unambiguous successes are precisely cases of national revival with the aid of segment-states; thus, the Norwegian and Finnish movements were able to achieve sovereignty largely through their own efforts. The other movements that Hroch analyzes either failed to achieve independence (the Belgian Flemish and Schleswig Danes), or achieved independence only as part of another nation-state project (Czechs and Slovaks), or came to power not through their own efforts but as a result of great power intervention in wartime or in a peace settlement (Estonians, Lithuanians, and Czechoslovakians).

[32] Brass 1991, 22.
[33] Armstrong 1982; Breuilly 1994; Gellner 1983.
[34] Crowther 1991; Rutland 1994; Zaprudnik 1993.
[35] Bremmer 1997, 9–10.
[36] Lapidus 1992. Also see Beissinger 2002.
[37] Hroch 2000, xiii, 22–24, 177–91; also see Deutsch 1966, 86–106.

The segmental institutions thesis presents an alternative view: few nation-states actually resulted from such a process. Neither the national awakening stories nor the national mobilization stories can be generalized as a hypothesis that accurately identifies which nation-state projects have succeeded. In only a minority of successful nation-state projects was nationalism a strong popular force prior to statehood or independence. Dankwart Rustow notes that seldom in the founding of nation-states did national unity precede the creation of state authority; a rare exception is Japan. More typically, state authority came first, as in most of Western Europe.[38] Rupert Emerson argues that typically it was the state that was the "nation-maker" rather than nations creating states; this, he argues, was true almost everywhere—in Europe, the Americas, Africa, and much of Asia.[39] Indeed, in the story of new states created by decolonization, the crises of national identity typically followed independence.[40]

This is true of the so-called "new" nation-states of Eastern Europe created in the late nineteenth and early twentieth centuries. Hans Kohn, writing during World War II, contended that the process of nation-state creation was different in Eastern Europe because nationalism preceded statehood, and so nations "grew in protest against and in conflict with the existing state pattern."[41] In most new states of the region, however, national identity was not well developed prior to independence, and even less so before any statehood. As noted previously, before Bulgaria achieved autonomy and statehood at the Berlin Conference of 1878–a solution imposed on the Ottoman Empire by the European powers—Bulgarian elites had been divided on the issue of whether to seek political autonomy; popular support for this objective was sparse.[42] In Albania, which had neither statehood nor autonomy on the eve of independence (1912), indigenous leaders, according to Charles and Barbara Jelavich, "did not want the Ottoman Empire dismantled, nor did they seek an independent state."[43] In the western borderlands of the Russian Empire, according to Ronald Suny, independence "was not the result of a broad-based and coherent nationalist movement that realized long-held aspirations to nationhood."[44]

Even in the fourth phase of nation-state creation this ambiguity of nationalism prior to independence was common in Eastern Europe and Eurasia. Even autonomy and statehood in the form of a segment-state did not necessarily galvanize a single secessionist nationalism prior to indepen-

[38] Rustow 1967, 127–28.
[39] Emerson 1960, 114–19.
[40] Pye 1962, 1971.
[41] Kohn 1944, 329.
[42] Jelavich and Jelavich 1977, 134–47.
[43] Jelavich and Jelavich 1977, 222.
[44] Suny 1993b, 37, 81.

dence. For example, in the three countries that delivered the coup de grâce to the USSR in the Belovezhskii settlement in December 1991—Belarus, Russia, and Ukraine—popular sentiment was opposed to or ambivalent about secession. Even two years after the breakup of the USSR, John Dunlop could describe Russians as "a people in quest of an identity," because many Russians still clung to the idea that the USSR was their nation-state.[45] Similarly, Mark Beissinger attributes the continuing weakness of Russian identity to the ambiguity in the Russian mind concerning any distinction between the Russian nation and the Russian empire.[46] As late as 2000, a survey of 1,600 Russian citizens found that 55 percent "believe it is Russia's historical mission to incorporate various peoples into one state that would be a successor to the pre-1917 Russian Empire or the Soviet Union."[47] In Ukraine, citizens were divided in their national identities—Soviet and Ukrainian identities—and, as Alexander Motyl concludes, independence came "not because the [Ukrainian] nationalists tried harder or because they were stronger, but because the external conditions were right."[48] Belarusian popular nationalism was particularly weak, and support for the USSR remained high in Belarus even after the breakup.[49] In a national referendum on May 14, 1995, with a 65 percent turnout, 83.3 percent supported the restoration of Russian as an official language of the state and economic integration with Russia, and 75.1 percent supported restoration of the Soviet-era symbols of the Belorussian Soviet Socialist Republic.[50]

Similar observations have been made about the ambivalence of popular nationalism in the creation of some of the postcommunist nation-states in Eastern Europe. Indeed, the Czech and Slovak nation-states achieved sovereign independence even though a solid majority of the population apparently favored a united Czechoslovakia.[51] Martin Butora and Zora Butorova estimate that supporters of independence in Slovakia constituted less than a third of the population and that supporters in the Czech Republic constituted less than that. Even after separation, surveys in 1993 indicated that less than one-third of the combined Czech and Slovak populations would have voted for independence in a referendum and twice that number would have voted to retain Czechoslovakia.[52]

---

[45] Dunlop 1993–94, 603. Also see Dixon 1996; Solchanyk 1992, 31–45; Colton 2000, 158.

[46] Beissinger 1995, 149–84.

[47] *Interfax* December 26, 2000.

[48] Motyl 1993, 23; Solchanyk 1994; Pirie 1996, 1096; Barrington 1997; Kuzio 2000; Wilson 2000, 160–61.

[49] Jocelyn 1998, 73–83; Marples 1996, 124.

[50] See Olcott 2002, 24–50; Akiner 1995, 60; van der Leeuw 2000, 169; Roy 2000.

[51] Wolchik 1994, 177.

[52] Butora and Butorova 1993, 721–22; also see Hilde 1999.

The segmental institutions thesis supports the view that widespread popular nationalism seldom exists prior to statehood and typically does not precede independence, and thus does not provide an entirely satisfactory explanation for which nation-state projects succeed. In a minority of cases—and Israel and Pakistan present two of the clearest cases of this—nationalism preceded both statehood and independence. More frequently, successful claims on behalf of a nation-state have not been backed by extensive or intense popular nationalism because much of the population is parochial or cross-pressured. In a few instances, such as the United States, the creation of a nation occurred nearly simultaneously with the achievement of independence and statehood.[53] More frequently, states created nations and popular nationalism, and states created these after independence.

The absence of a coherent popular and elite nationalism has not been fatal to nation-state projects in the way that the absence of a segment-state has been. Yet the segmental institutions thesis argues that a successful claim does require something that sometimes resembles nationalism—political-identity hegemony. This describes a situation in which other ethnopoliticians cannot trump the nation-state project that supports segment-state independence by mobilizing the population on behalf of an alternative national claim. Thus, in the breakup of the USSR, Gorbachev's government largely failed in its attempt to trump the secessionist claims of union republic leaders by mobilizing the Soviet identity among members of titular nationalities.[54] According to the segmental institutions thesis, segment-states provide their leaders with unique opportunities to establish this political-identity hegemony. Segment-state leaders with political-identity hegemony are in a critical "switchman" role to determine when any national identity will be mobilized into political action.[55]

States Coordinate National Identities

In the absence of a state, either a nation-state or segment-state, that propagates a specific nation-state project, national identities seldom coordinate on a single alternative to the existing common-state. The state coordinates identities by serving as a unique focal point, but it reinforces this natural psychological tendency by rewarding supporters, suppressing proponents of alternative nation-state projects, and propagating the official project

---

[53] Kohn 1957; Morgan 1976.

[54] Alternatively, Moscow could trump the national claims of the leaders of provinces and second-order homelands with Russian majorities. See, for example, Muiznieks 1990, 19–24; Kirkow 1995, 932–33.

[55] Tarrow 1977, 4.

through public education, public ceremonies, and the many other tools a state uses to celebrate itself.[56]

The segmental institutions thesis argues that in the rare circumstances in which a strong nationalism exists prior to independence, it is usually the product of a segment-state. This provides the focal point for the coordination of imaginations and the political resources to privilege one project above others by hiring linguists, historians, and polemicists to embellish and propagate this project. In short, the segmental institutions thesis treats the role of nationalism in the creation of nation-states as largely an endogenous factor in the process that led from segment-states to nation-states, rather than a prior condition or cause. The heroes in the forging of nationalism are often not the romantic poets but politicians, humble bureaucrats, and the authors of dreadfully dull textbooks, who help shape each generation's knowledge of its world.[57] For example, many Soviet bureaucrats circulated and rose within the narrow nationalized hierarchies of their respective union republics. John Armstrong noted about these denizens of the governmental-administrative apparatus, or apparatchiks, that they "can scarcely fail to develop a certain amount of fellow-feeling with other officials in the area, perhaps even that feeling of 'local patriotism' which leads Party officials to endeavor to conceal the faults and the self-seeking of their associates from higher authorities."[58] At the union republic level this patriotism became a formal nationalism. Thus, as Roman Szporluk notes, "national awakeners" emerged from within "established power structures, power relationships, and the values upholding them."[59]

For almost two centuries, political leaders and apparatchiks have been the core of nation-state projects that succeeded. Benedict Anderson finds a similar pattern in the colonies of Latin America almost two hundred years ago in the phenomenon he labels Creole nationalism. This emerged within "administrative units" among bureaucrats who came to imagine these segments of the state as "fatherlands." These "absolutist functionaries" spread this sense of political solidarity to the broader population with the assistance of "provincial Creole printmen."[60]

In this way the histories of successful nationalisms are surprisingly uniform around the world. Students of nationalism have tended to view the type of nationalism that predominates in the region that is now the post-communist world as somehow different from the original nationalisms that emerged in Western Europe. The segmental institutions thesis suggests

[56] Schelling 1960.
[57] Compare A. Smith 1986; Connor 1994, 145–64.
[58] Armstrong 1959, 84.
[59] Szporluk 2000, 366–67.
[60] B. Anderson 1991, 53; also see Herbst 2000, 58–109.

that it is not fundamentally so. Hans Kohn first argued that Western nationalism, found in England, France, the Netherlands, Switzerland, and the United States, arose only after the formation of de facto nation-states. Eastern nationalism, found in Central and Eastern Europe as well as in Asia, arose among ethnic groups prior to the consolidation of nation-states.[61] In this now common view, Eastern European and Eurasian nationalisms frequently challenge existing states and seek "to redraw the political boundaries in conformity with ethnographic demands."[62] The segmental institutions thesis leads us to see Eastern nationalism as much more like Western nationalism than Kohn would have had us believe. Both originated as nationalism among political leaders and bureaucrats, which states—both sovereign states and segment-states—then propagated among ever-widening circles of the population.[63]

In France, for example, the conception of France emerged within the royal court, and as late as the early twentieth century the state was still turning peasants into Frenchmen. In less than a generation—in the brief span of time immediately before and during the French Revolution of 1789—many French elites outside the government began to think like nationalists. This was the surprising and unintended consequence of steps, such as public instruction, undertaken by the king's bureaucracy over the preceding century to form Frenchmen loyal to the Crown. It set the stage for the National Assembly to follow the lead of the Americans and announce that "the source of all sovereignty resides essentially in the nation."[64] The inculcation of a new nationalism in previously parochial peoples took the concerted efforts of the French state at least another century. Eugen Weber traces how French mentalities changed in the half century before World War I: "A lot of Frenchmen did not know that they belonged together until the long didactic campaigns of the later nineteenth century told them they did, and their own experience as conditions changed told them that this made sense." As Alexandre Sanguinetti summarizes, "France is a deliberate political construction for whose creation the central power has never ceased to fight."[65]

Similarly, in Great Britain, the reality of a new state formed in 1707 and the concerted effort of the Crown and civil service forged a new national identity. The latecomer, British nationalism, triumphed where older, narrower English and Scottish nationalisms had failed. As Linda Colley docu-

---

[61] Kohn 1944.
[62] Liebich 1995.
[63] Jocelyn 1998, 78–79; Roy 2000, x [sic], 107. Also see Pflanze 1996; Kuzio 2001.
[64] Bell 2001, 13–14.
[65] Weber 1976, 113. Also see Sahlins 1989, 286.

ments, the British identity was invented and deliberately propagated by the state through carefully staged royal visits, with the assistance of newspapers. British civil servants were among the first to develop an identity that transcended narrower identities as English, Scots, and Welsh. As elsewhere, the development of nationalism was linked with the popularization of politics: "Being a patriot was a way of claiming the right to participate in British public life, and ultimately a means of demanding a much broader access to citizenship."[66] Britishness did not replace or emerge from specific identities like Englishness; it did not emerge from integration or homogenization of cultures. "Instead, Britishness was superimposed over an array of internal differences" that in the nineteenth century did not become national identities in the sense of bringing rights to participate in political life in separate states.[67] By 1900 the British national identity had become widespread throughout the island.[68]

Even in the great unification projects of the mid-nineteenth century, nationalism was the project of a state. As the Risorgimento leader Massimo d'Azeglio proclaimed, "We have made Italy. Now we have to make Italians."[69] Similarly, in Germany, as Abigail Green stresses, German nationalism before unification was weak and had limited popular appeal. Even after 1871, "the German people themselves proved strangely unmoved by national unification."[70] This newly constructed identity to support the little German (*kleindeutsch*) nation-state that excluded Austria was propagated by the empire under Prussian leadership. Yet the German Empire also revealed the complications that arise in propagating a hegemonic nationalism in a segmented state. With the preservation of segment-states such as Württemberg and Bavaria until World War I, the public received conflicting messages about their fatherlands. German nationalism only slowly gained ascendance in the public.

The importance of the state in propagating nationalism in France, Britain, Italy, and Germany is underscored by the stark contrast with the late development of Austrian nationalism. As Peter Katzenstein noted in 1976, "in the last 150 years the concept of Austria has been disturbingly ambiguous."[71] Only after 1960 and decades of a separate independent state did a solid majority of Austrians favor the Austrian nation-state over alternative projects, such as unification with Germany.[72] Prior to the breakup of the

---

[66] Colley 1992, 5; also see 370.
[67] Colley 1992, 6.
[68] Davies 1999, 815.
[69] Quoted in Bell 2001, 198.
[70] Green 2001, 6, 298–99; also see 97–147, 268, 271, 312–37.
[71] Katzenstein 1976, 12.
[72] Katzenstein 1977.

Austro-Hungarian Empire in World War I, its German-speaking population divided among at least five different nation-state projects—the Greater Austria–Middle Europe project (*großösterreich-mitteleuropäische Lösung*), which would have united the entire Austro-Hungarian Empire with the German Empire; the Greater German project (*großdeutsche Lösung*), which would have abandoned the non-German-speaking areas of the Austro-Hungarian Empire and united the German-speaking areas with the German Empire; the Austro-Hungarian project, which would have kept the empire separate and whole but Germanize the empire; the German-Austria (*Deutschösterreich*) project, which would have separated the German-speaking parts of the empire in an independent state; and separate projects for provinces such as Tyrol. The failure of any single project to achieve hegemony was the consequence of the competing pressures from alternative state elites and institutions—the leaders of the Austro-Hungarian Empire, the leaders of "the Kingdoms and Lands Represented in the Parliament" (as the empire minus Hungary came to be styled), and the leaders of diets of separate provinces, such as Tyrol, Vorarlberg, Upper Austria, and Lower Austria. Missing was a pre-independence segment-state for Austria to privilege its nation-state project.

This challenge to the traditional narratives about nation-state creation begs the question of why these narratives are so common. The traditional view of the creation of nation-states that upholds the conventional sequence from national awakening to national independence has enjoyed currency because strong interests come to be associated with this interpretation after a nation-state project has achieved sovereign independence. Governments have an interest in propagating the view that their authority originates with the sovereign will of a people. The official stories of creation are akin to stork myths; both are told by the older generation to disguise many embarrassing facts from the next. (National myths, however, are more powerful than stork myths, because through persistent retelling they can actually create a national awakening.) The conventional sequence finds such resonance in the academy because the research methods of humanists, even when the scholars are not partisans of a particular nation-state project, privilege the story of successful nation-state projects. Most studies select on the dependent variable and seek to explain successful bids for independence.[73] Far fewer books have been published about the failures, with the possible exception of books about the Confederate States of America. With the outcome known, researchers tend to look for evidence

---

[73] "Selecting on the dependent variable" refers to the methodological problems that arise when a scholar attempts to explain variation in some outcome, such as success versus failure of nation-state projects, but selects only cases of success. The scholar has no evidence to ascertain whether the claimed causes of success were, in fact, absent from the cases of failure.

to explain the success. Scholars interpret ambiguous evidence through knowledge of the outcome. Often the easiest path to ordering history comes through reifying the vaporous connection of national identity that purportedly infuses the air prior to independence but leaves few tangible traces other than the outcome. What evidence that does exist for this official interpretation is collected and preserved in climate-controlled national libraries and archives, while evidence for alternative outcomes is often incinerated as inconsequential litter after a rally for a different nation-state project or as dangerous sedition.

"Ethnification" to Privilege One Nation

The segmental institutions thesis also challenges the common view that nationalism represents the politicization of ethnicity. As the Eurasian experience highlights, often ethnicity is the product of a nation-state project, not the other way around. The state creates an ethnic myth to privilege its nation against challengers. Ernst Renan once described the existence of a nation as "an everyday plebiscite." Yet no nation-states would remain stable if they rested on the shifting majorities that would emerge in daily plebiscites. In the extreme, this would lead to an endless cycling of nation-states as temporary majorities based on various cultural divides and various shared historic memories enjoyed their moments in the sun seriatim. So, not only do governments make it very difficult to hold such plebiscites, they expend enormous energy to privilege the nation-state project that favors the status quo. Among the most important ways to privilege the project is to "ethnify" the nation, that is, to propagate a myth of common origin.[74] (The term *myth*, following the tradition of Émile Durkheim, refers to a commonly held belief about origins that may be based on fact, fiction, or some combination of both.)

In short, the plebiscitary nature of the nation-state necessitates the ethnification of the nation. This is an attempt to constrain the present and future by a myth about the past. Nation-state projects concern the present and look forward by claiming that a people should have a state of its own from now on. Ethnic group myths look backward to identify the origins of the group in some remote seminal event and to memorialize their many generations of life together since that event.[75] To give stability to the future, nationalists often create ethnic myths that claim the nation is not simply the consequence of a momentary coordination in response to a plebiscite but the result of centuries that cannot be undone by a single vote.

---

[74] On alternative views of ethnic groups, see Burgess 1978.

[75] For example, see Schermerhorn 1970. There is a tendency to conflate these two very different concepts; see, for example, Dunn 1995.

This view of the origins of the most important ethnicities is consistent with the view of constructivists, who point out that ethnic groups are constructed,[76] yet it stresses that it is the nation-state that gives stability to ethnicity over time. That is, in an institution-free world, ethnic identities would themselves be constantly shifting, because they build on identities that are multiple and frequently intermittent, fluid, and changeable.[77] Moreover, they can be manipulated by strategic politicians.[78] To provide stability to the nation-state, political leaders must create ethnic groups, but the unique position of the nation-state in turn provides stability to the ethnic groups.

Nowhere are the deliberate act of ethnifying nations and the mutually reinforcing stability of ethnicity, nationalism, and states more apparent than in contemporary Eurasia. In the Soviet successor states, the existence of Tajiks and Moldovans, the division between Kazakhs and Kyrgyzes, the disappearance of Turkestanis and Sarts, and so forth are the consequences of segment-states creating or refashioning ethnicity. Soviet segment-states and now post-Soviet nation-states have provided a new stability to ethnic identities. The governments have reinforced this by creating official histories that explain the primordial roots of the titular nationality in the territory and its intergenerational unity as an ethnic group.[79] Thus, Kazakhstan's 1995 constitution and its new textbooks claim that the republic stands on the primordial homeland of the Kazakh people: "the emergence of the Kazakh Khanate in the fifteenth century is now being promoted as the birth of Kazakh statehood; the 540th anniversary of this event (which cannot, in fact, be attributed to a precise date) was celebrated in 1995."[80] Similarly, Uzbekistan's government has reified the Uzbek ethnic group with a myth that traces its continuity back to the Middle Ages.[81] Both governments lavishly reward scholars to embellish and propagate these ethnic myths.

Yet the ethnification of nation-states is much older. Indeed, Americans may have been among the first to invent an ethnic myth to privilege a nation-state project with a story of common origin, the immigrant myth. At the time of independence, the American population was divided among separate colonial segment-states, and many individuals were personally divided among multiple national identities as British, Americans, and colonials. According to Samuel Eliot Morison, only 40 percent of the population actively supported independence, while 10 percent continued to support

---

[76] Eriksen 1991, 263–64; C. Young 1976.
[77] Kasfir 1979; Rothschild 1981, 96, 99.
[78] Weinstein 1979, 360.
[79] Roy 2000, 15–18.
[80] Akiner 1995, 62, 69.
[81] Yalcin 2002, 61–66, 92–96.

the common-state (Britain).[82] The 40 percent supporting independence were further divided among proponents of competing nation-state projects such as a united states or separate independent states.[83] Perhaps even more inhabitants of the segment-states of North America were so cross-pressured by the competing demands of their multiple national identities that they were unable to choose among projects and simply remained neutral. Morison estimates that half of the colonists were indifferent or neutral among the competing nation-state projects.

Once one nation-state project was successful, however, Americans began to ethnify themselves. Much like other myths of ethnic origins, the story that Americans tell about themselves focuses on movement into the homeland from somewhere else. Its legends and icons celebrate this break with their previous separate experiences and stress the generations of common experiences ever since. Thus, the Pilgrims, one of the first to break with the Old World and settle in the New, became a symbol of all Americans. Many of the shrines to the nation celebrate the commonality of the Pilgrim experience, whether the break with the past existence began at Plymouth Rock or at Ellis Island. Despite their separate lives prior to the immigrant experience—and most myths of national origin recognize a prior period when the ethnic group was divided by or subsumed by other peoples—the migration and their subsequent lives together made them one. For many Americans raised on this mythology (as I was), this ethnic myth makes better sense of the disparate pieces of a family history than ethnic identities that would link us to peoples outside the United States who are simply foreign.[84] The challenge that our myth simplifies a more complex history and may even distort the facts a little is, of course, true; it is also trivial and irrelevant.

This ethnification of nations has been common throughout the old nation-states of Europe as well.[85] Ethnic myths constructed in the nineteenth century created histories of lengthy unity that could not be undone by a simple plebiscite. Thus, European nationalists, as Patrick Geary notes, "look to the moment of primary acquisition, when 'their people,' first arriving in the ruins of the Roman Empire, established their sacred territory and their national identity."[86] Yet the peoples of late antiquity and early medieval Europe that later nationalists identified as precursors were not cohesive cultural communities with common social patterns, language, or even identity. For example, the French people at the purported moment

---

[82] Morison 1965, 236.

[83] For examples of the competing nation-state projects in the American colonies, see Wood 1969, 356, 371.

[84] Hardin 1995, xi.

[85] Hobsbawm and Ranger 1992; also see Schulze 1998, 15.

[86] Geary 2002, 156.

of primary acquisition were actually diverse collections of Gauls, Romans, and Franks. (Moreover, they were only a fraction of the Franks, who also ruled kingdoms in southern Germany.) Waves of migration brought to this so-called homeland still more diverse social patterns, languages, and even identities. Thus, "the Franks 'born with the baptism of Clovis' are not the Franks of Charlemagne or those of the French people Jean Le Pen hoped to rally around his political movement."[87] It took an act of pure invention to overlook such anomalous facts and to celebrate Charlemagne as a Frenchman rather than yet another German seeking to submerge France in a larger Middle European state.

In Austria, majority support for the proposition that Austrians constitute an ethnic group (*Volk*) that is separate from the Germans emerged only in the decade after a majority of Austrians had concluded that they should have a state of their own. That is, ethnic identification followed political identification. By the mid-1960s most Austrians supported independence; it was only in the 1970s that a majority endorsed the proposition that they constituted a separate cultural community.[88] Similarly, in Latin America, most of the largest ethnic groups are the products of nation-states, not the other way around. The fact that we often distinguish Salvadorians, Argentineans, and Cubans and frequently dismiss as wrongheaded the attempts of bureaucrats in Washington, D.C., to bundle all together as Hispanics attests to the power of states to forge ethnicity.

International Recognition

Great powers attempt to influence which nations get states by selectively extending and withholding recognition. Yet the segmental institutions thesis stresses that early in the developments leading to a nation-state crisis between a segment-state and a common-state, the threat of withholding international recognition typically comes in a small, remote voice that has little influence on the participants. Once a nation-state crisis has fully developed, the threat of withholding recognition has little ability to reverse the crisis. Rather than assigning primacy to international constraints on domestic politics, the segmental institutions thesis stresses the constraints imposed by segmental institutions on the choices before foreign powers. This constraint of domestic institutions on international choices is mirrored in five patterns over the past century. First, although the international community has prevented de facto independence from becoming de jure independence—as in the cases of Abkhazia, Nagornyi Karabakh, South Ossetia, and Transdniestria in the Eurasian region—in most in-

---

[87] Geary 2002, 157.
[88] Katzenstein 1977.

stances the threat of nonrecognition has seldom blocked or reversed de facto independence. Second, the threat by great powers to withhold recognition has had little effect on reversing the course of nation-state crises unfolding in segmented states. For example, at the end of the cold war, the West European states withheld recognition from Lithuania in March 1990. On August 1, 1991, during his visit to Kiev, President George Bush urged the Ukrainians to reject "suicidal nationalism" and to negotiate with Moscow for reform of the USSR.[89] In neither case did nonrecognition stop the deterioration of the segmented state, and in the end, the great powers accepted the new nation-states created by the secession of segment-states. Third, recognition in most instances has not made independence happen without a prior domestic process created by segmental institutions. Forty years of recognition of the Baltic states by the United States and even the fiction of diplomatic relations did not make this a reality until domestic political processes in the Soviet segmented state made it happen. Similarly, the last-minute attempt to save Azerbaijan and Georgia in 1920 with diplomatic recognition could not preserve their independence. Fourth, international recognition typically comes only after the politics of segmented states have, in fact, made new sovereign states. In both 1919 and 1991 in the Eurasian region the international community was careful to withhold recognition from Finland, Ukraine, and other states until domestic political processes had legitimated their secession and independence. Fifth, international recognition can block the reversal of a successful secession by deterring the common-state government from attempting to reintegrate a former segment-state. Nevertheless, without extraordinary international support or even outright intervention—such as that which created the Democratic People's Republic of Korea and the German Democratic Republic—international recognition alone has usually done little more than ratify the outcomes created by segmental institutions.

The segmental institutions thesis challenges the view put forward by some students of international relations that the norms of international recognition explain why the major source of new nation-states since World War II has been decolonization rather than division of metropolitan cores. International relations scholars note that from 1941 to 2000, about 70 percent of new states had formerly been external rather than internal segment-states. According to the claim for the primacy of international norms in selecting among nation-state projects, the great powers and the international community more broadly have sought to limit disruption to existing states by limiting the right of national self-determination since World War II to the nation-state projects of external segment-states; for example, only

[89] Motyl 1993, 181.

these get the official label "decolonization" at the United Nations.[90] The segmental institutions thesis points up that the relationship between norms and outcome is spurious: at the beginning of the century (1901) at least 85 percent of segment-states, in the first years after World War II (1946) at least 77 percent of segment-states, and in each year until 1971 a majority of all segment-states were in fact external segment-states commonly called colonies or protectorates. It is no surprise that the majority of new states were created by decolonization. Moreover, any presumed norm did not end secession by internal segment-states; indeed, as figure 1.1 shows, in the fourth phase of nation-state creation, internal segment-states once again became the primary source of new nation-states.

The segmental institutions thesis also challenges the claim of international relations scholars that in effect characterizes the privileged access of segment-states to independence as itself the manifestation of an international norm that prohibits use of violence to change international boundaries. The special relationship between segment-states and successful nation-state projects actually predates the purported emergence of such an international norm. Moreover, the international community has refused to articulate any norm that would privilege segment-states for independence.[91] Thus, in the United Nations' *Declaration of Principles of International Law Concerning Friendly Relations and Cooperation Among States*, the rejection of violence to change borders is coupled with the additional stipulation that the principles of the declaration do not justify *any* action to facilitate secession or division of existing states.[92] Governments and the international community have, in fact, avoided articulating such a norm out of fear that this would unleash a wave of secessionist claims to dismantle states by declaring their segment-states independent. If the rejection of violence to change borders has favored segment-states, it is through two rather indirect consequences. First, the norm limits the only practice that in the early part of the twentieth century provided an alternative to segment-states as a source of new nation-states, great power intervention to redraw international borders. After this option was closed, almost all candidates for recognition have been segment-states, and the role of the international community has usually been limited to selecting which segment-

---

[90] Mayall 1999, 475; 1990, 50–69. The pressure to expand the right of self-determination to include indigenous peoples has created a contradictory theme since the collapse of the Soviet Union: according to Article 3 of the 1993 *Draft Declaration on the Rights of Indigenous Peoples*, "Indigenous peoples have the right of self-determination. By virtue of that right they freely determine their political status and freely pursue their economic, social, and cultural development." See UN, Doc.E/CN.4/Sub.2/1993/3/26 (1993).

[91] Finnemore and Sikkink 1998, 892.

[92] Compare Zacher 2001; UN General Assembly Resolution 2625 (1970). Also see Buchanan 1999.

states that are in fact already independent to give imprimaturs. Second, once international recognition gives this imprimatur to a segment-state, the norm deters the former common-state from attempting to reclaim its "lost" segment-state.

Research Strategy

In this book I generalize to the world at large and to the span of a century insights derived from closely following developments in the fourth phase of nation-state creation, 1986–2000. The juxtaposition of theory and empirical evidence that describe developments in many places and at many times permits tests of whether the segmental institutions thesis identifies a general pattern applicable to at least a century of nationalism around the world.

Overview

In the following chapters, to make sense of empirical observations, I develop the segmental institutions thesis. This thesis links institutions to bargaining within the segment-states and between segment-state and common-state leaders. The thesis then links this bargaining to the likelihood of common-state failure and the independence of new nation-states. The causal logic is strongly influenced by formal theories of bargaining developed originally in the field of economics. Key claims of cause and effect are, as far as possible, rooted in generalized findings that have been shown to be valid through rigorous formal proofs undertaken by others. Thus, claims about causation behind correlations are supported not only by process tracing through the narrative evidence but also by theory with deductive rigor.[93]

Much of the narrative evidence is drawn from the experience of the USSR and the Soviet successor states. My project began with close analysis of the politics between the union republics and the USSR, and then the politics between the new common-states, such as Russia, and the segment-states within them, such as Chechnya or Tatarstan. I began with interviews in the mid-Volga region during a six-month stay in Tatarstan. These interviews gave rise to many of the questions and hunches about bargaining within a segmented state that form the core of the segmental institutions thesis. I then turned to public documents and newspaper accounts to ascertain whether the politics of the mid-Volga region were duplicated in other Russian regions and in the other Soviet successor states. Where possible, I supplemented narrative evidence with statistical data from the USSR and

---

[93] Bates et al. 1998, particularly 3–22.

its successor states to test my interpretations of patterned relationships more rigorously. If, like many other studies of the origins of nation-states, this study had gone no farther, it might have fallen into the trap of selecting on the dependent variable, tracing backward to the preconditions for success, without asking whether these conditions were absent from or present in the cases that failed to lead to new nation-states. For this reason, I have taken care to compare nation-state projects that achieved sovereign independence, such as the Soviet successor states, and those that did not, such as Tatarstan or Turkestan.

And, had my study examined only the USSR and its successor states, it could be faulted for drawing conclusions applicable only to a narrow (though important) part of the world and a short period of time. So, to test whether the conclusions drawn from the late- and post-Soviet experience could be generalized beyond the last two decades of the twentieth century, I compared the experience of this period with the end of the Russian Empire and the creation of the USSR seventy years earlier. What I call the Eurasian cases constitute comparisons of four sets of cases associated with the breakup of the Russian Empire following the Russian Revolution of 1917, the recentralization of the Soviet segmented state during Stalin's consolidation of power in the 1920s, the disintegration and breakup of the USSR from 1988 to 1991, and the pattern of disintegration and recentralization in the fifteen Soviet successor states. This comparison across more than seventy years has a second methodological advantage: it permits quasi-experimental comparisons before and after the introduction of segment-states. Comparisons within a more limited time frame, even those of global reach, permit only correlational analysis when variations in segment-states occur only rarely. By carefully comparing Eurasian ethnic groups and nation-state projects over this longer period of time, it is possible to observe the effect of the introduction of segment-states associated with some ethnic groups and nation-state projects but not others.

I had still to test whether these generalizations drawn from the Eurasian region were applicable globally to the age of nationalism. For this I turned to statistical evidence, using three global data sets that I created for this book. The first contains observations of 658 different ethnic groups in 153 independent states for the forty-five years from 1955 to 1999. This data set permitted testing whether nation-state projects associated with segment-states are more likely than other nation-state projects to become parties to nation-state crises. The second data set contains observations on the 191 new sovereign states created after 1815, including data on their juridical status just prior to independence. The third data set contains observations on the 336 internal and external segment-states that existed in the twentieth century. The second and third data sets permitted testing the proposition that the segment-state is the common denominator in successful nation-state projects and refining this thesis with data on the conditions under which segment-states are actually likely to achieve sovereign independence.

The Contemporary Eurasian Cases

A central claim of this book is that the creation of the post-Soviet nation-states provides insight into why some nation-state projects and not others succeed at achieving sovereign independence. This is not to say that the late- and post-Soviet experience is identical in every detail to that of the nation-states that came before but rather to say that the common outcome does have common causes that many area specialists have long thought were unique maladies of their individual regions. This study shows, for example, that many patterns that Africanists have long lamented as a unique handicap of African statehood and that postcommunist specialists have seen as a distinctive malady of transitions from communism in multinational federations are actually common to almost all new nation-states. That is, the focus in this study on the emergence of new nation-states from the USSR and the politics of the Soviet successor states is useful because these are cases that underscore that the process of separation—whether it is the decolonization of dependencies or the breakup of the metropolitan cores themselves—conforms in important ways to a common pattern. The breakup of the USSR has been studied by scholars both as a case of the end of an empire (paralleling the end of the Austro-Hungarian and Ottoman Empires or the liberation of colonial peoples) and as a case of secession (paralleling the division of Pakistan or Ethiopia and potentially Canada).[94] It is both.

The Soviet transition is part of the process that also touched Yugoslavia and Czechoslovakia during the recent transformation of the Communist world. In 2000 there were twenty-eight nation-states where just a decade and a half earlier nine Communist countries had stood. This postcommunist transition constituted the major part of the fourth phase of nation-state creation and represented the second most intense burst of new states to enter the international system since 1815. In place of the USSR there are now fifteen independent states. The end of communism not only swept away a workers' state built on transnational appeals of proletarian and socialist internationalism, it also ended the attempt to create a new nation-state that transcended the boundaries of the individual segment-states. The USSR claimed to be the enactment of the Soviet people and to embody

---

[94] For examples of studies that treat the Soviet Union as an imperial or colonial relationship, see Barkey and von Hagen 1997; Beissinger and Young 2002; Carrère d'Encausse 1980; Gleason 1997; Spruyt 2005; Suny 1993b, 128–31; and Taagapera 2000.

"the state unity of the Soviet People."[95] All Soviet successor states jettisoned this mythology of a Soviet people or an ethnically indifferent working class; in their declarations of sovereignty, declarations of independence, and most constitutions they proclaimed their states to be the realization of their respective nation's will to statehood. In the preamble of Estonia's 1992 constitution, its authors proclaim that the state "is established on the inextinguishable right of the Estonian people to national self-determination . . . [and] shall guarantee the preservation of the Estonian nation and its culture throughout the ages."[96] The triumph of these fifteen successor states came at the expense of alternative nation-state projects that sought to draw the international boundaries of the region differently.

Organization of the Book

The organization of this book in four parts highlights the major elements of the segmental-institutions thesis: the book begins with the independent variables (segmental institutions), traces the consequences of these for political processes on the periphery and between center and periphery, and identifies the outcomes of these processes in nation-state crises and the creation of new nation-states. The first part introduces the institutional foundations and provides a theoretical and conceptual overview of the segmental institutions thesis. Following this introduction to the thesis, chapter 2 develops the concept of the segmented state more fully and provides an overview of the varieties of segmental institutions existing around the world over the past century. I devote particularly close attention to the segmental institutions of the Russian Empire (pre-1917), the former USSR (1922–92), and the USSR's fifteen successor states (1992 to the present).

The major part of the book investigates the political processes created by segmental institutions in two arenas: on the political periphery of an existing state and between the political center of that state and the periphery. Part 2 presents a theory of the conditions under which political-identity hegemony is likely to emerge within a candidate for nation-statehood on the periphery of an existing state. The focus is on bargaining among politicians pressing competing nation-state projects and cross-cutting interests. With political-identity hegemony a cohort of politicians associated with a specific nation-state project comes to dominate politics and control the expression of national identity within a people and their homeland. Part 3 presents a theory of the conditions under which nation-state crises between segment-state and common-state governments are likely to

---

[95] Constitution of the USSR (1977), Preamble and Article 70.

[96] Constitution of Estonia (adopted by referendum on June 28, 1992).

emerge. The focus in these chapters is on the political dynamic that emerges in center-periphery bargaining. Segmental institutions create motives, means, and opportunities for escalation of both the stakes and the means in this bargaining. This can escalate to a nation-state crisis—a turning point at which further escalation may bring about the failure of the existing state and the creation of new nation-states.

Part 4 turns to the outcomes of this bargaining on the periphery and between center and periphery. Chapters 9 and 10 present hypotheses, narrative evidence, and statistical tests that address the conditions under which nation-state crises are likely to occur, common-states are likely to fail, and new nation-states are likely to emerge. Chapter 11 turns to the implications of these findings for our understanding of the international system. The segmental institutions thesis identifies domestic political factors that explain why, despite enormous international pressures such as growing insecurity or globalization, the nation-state is likely to continue to be the primary building block of the international system. Proceeding still further, this thesis suggests effective ways to bring greater stability to the current configuration of nation-states and to minimize the likelihood of nation-state crises in the future.

TWO
Varieties of Segmented States

THE CREATION OF SEGMENT-STATES has accompanied the rise of popular sovereignty. The segmented state emerged soon after governments began to assert that they derived their powers from a people (the *nation*), for once the basis of a state's claims to legitimacy was the people, political leaders became very particular about who was included in the nation.[1] Segmental institutions provided a way for a state to incorporate within its jurisdiction diverse peoples who did not easily fit within a single nation. In one pattern, as the states of the North Atlantic region began to democratize, they could use segmental institutions to deny full citizenship to some peoples within their jurisdictions. For example, segmental institutions allowed the United Kingdom to continue to exclude American colonists from Parliament.[2] In a second pattern, as autocracies refused to embrace a notion of popular sovereignty for their own people, segmental institutions permitted autocrats to extend their jurisdiction to other peoples that already had their own institutions of self-governance. For example, the Russian Empire incorporated Finland as a grand duchy with its own parliament at a time that representative government was anathema in St. Petersburg. In a third pattern, particularly in the last decades of the twentieth century, segmental institutions have become a means to protect the rights of ethnic minorities, such as the Serbs in Bosnia, or to compromise with their demands for independence.

Yet segmental institutions have tended to be unstable. In the twentieth century, the life expectancy of segmental dyads—that is, the "age" at which half of the segment states had been dissolved or reconfigured—was forty-four years.[3] (The term segmental dyad refers to the relationship between a common-state and a segment-state such as the USSR–Turkmenistan or U.K.–Gold Coast dyads.) A quarter of segmental dyads had failed within sixteen years of creation. (A benchmark for comparison is the relatively greater stability of independent states: for even a quarter of the indepen-

---

[1] Rustow 1970, 350–51. Compare Jennings' (1958, 56) dismissal of self-determination.

[2] Also see Albertini 1982, 390; O'Donnell and Schmitter 1986, 7–8.

[3] These estimates are based on a statistical survival model that estimates survival times from the Kaplan-Meier product-limit estimate of the survivor function. It examines all segmental relationships that existed from 1901 to 2000 (omitting new segmental relationships created in the 1990s) and posits that the time at risk for independence and creation of new nation-states began with the age of nationalism (set at 1815 for statistical estimation).

dent states to fail it would have taken 104 years.)[4] Dissolution of segment-states often meant independence for the segment-state either as a completely sovereign state or as part of another sovereign state: within sixty-five years, half of the segment-states had become independent. The life expectancy of internal segmental dyads, such as the relationship between the Union of Soviet Socialist Republics (USSR or Soviet Union) and any of its union republics, was longer than that of external segmental dyads, such as the United Kingdom and its colonies, but not much longer. The time period before half of the external segmental dyads failed was thirty-nine years; for internal dyads it was fifty-five years. Many of the failures of external dyads resulted in reconfiguration of an empire, not independence for a segment-state; indeed, failure of an external dyad was only slightly more likely than failure of an internal dyad to result in independence. For external dyads, the time before half had "seceded" was fifty-seven years, and for internal dyads it was sixty-two years.[5]

This instability of segmental institutions and the differences in life expectancy of different types of segmental relationships set the stage for the question to be addressed in the next chapters: How do segmental institutions produce the instability that leads to nation-state crises and the independence of nation-states? In this chapter I develop this concept of the segmented state and introduce institutions that can push the segmented state toward failure and the independence of its segment-states. But not every segmented state fails, and so I introduce some variables to describe the different types of segment-states: I present descriptive data about the institutional variations in segmented states since the beginning of the twentieth century. The segmented states in Eurasia get particularly close attention. This description is at times tedious, but there is an analytic payoff. In this chapter I introduce the most important institutional foundations that are the building blocks of the answer provided by the segmental institutions thesis to the question, where do nation-states come from?

Constitutional Orders

The segmented state comprises both a *common-state*, which embraces the entire territory and population, and constituent *segment-states*, the smaller

---

[4] This is based on Gleditsch and Ward's (1999) list of independent states, using only those countries that were independent in the twentieth century, but not created after 1990. The rules for counting cases are explained in chapter 1, footnote 8.

[5] In log-rank and Wilcoxon tests for the equality of survivor functions, it is possible to reject at the .05 level the null hypothesis that internal and external segmental survival functions are equivalent. The survival functions are most dissimilar when segments with ambiguous status are classified as external segments. These are the estimates reported in the text.

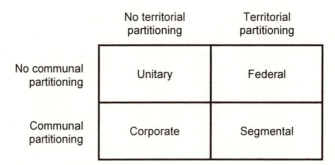

	No territorial partitioning	Territorial partitioning
No communal partitioning	Unitary	Federal
Communal partitioning	Corporate	Segmental

Figure 2.1 Constitutional orders.

territories and populations within the common-state.[6] Unlike the decentralized or simple federal state, the segmented state divides both its territory and its population into distinct political statuses, so that territories constitute separate jurisdictions and the peoples associated with those territories as homelands enjoy different rights. In the segmented state, peoples' political statuses are not simply a function of residence in a territorial jurisdiction as they are in a federal nation-state; the rights enjoyed by each people differ from the rights of other peoples within the common-state and vary as they move among the different segment-states. The rights of a segment-state and its population may be inferior to those of the rest of the common-state (as is commonly true with dependencies), superior to those of the rest (as sometimes happens with autonomous regions), or simply different (because the rights are associated with a specific homeland).

Segmental institutions represent one way in which constitutional designers allocate the decision rights of a state. The segmented state describes a particular arrangement of political institutions—a constitutional order—which adds a fourth category to the common distinction made among unitary, federal, and corporatist institutions (figure 2.1).[7] The differences among these alternative constitutional orders hang on their answers to the question, who gets to decide this type of issue?[8]

Unitary constitutions allocate all decision rights to the institutions of a common-state; that is, no powers of government are reserved to designated territorial administrations or communal governments. Governments under unitary constitutions need not be blind to the needs of minorities and regions and can protect these with special allocations of funds and extensive civil rights. What distinguishes the unitary constitution is the allocation of

[6] Moreno 1997, 69.

[7] This number and figure 2.1 could be expanded to include a third dimension for the allocation of rights between society and government.

[8] Coakley 1992; Horowitz 1985; Lijphart 1995; McRae 1975; Milne 1989; Rothschild 1981; Rudolph and Thompson 1985; Stanovcic 1992; Vetik 1993.

governmental decision rights: the governing institutions of the common-state can make policy for the whole territory and the entire citizenry; the constitutive rules reserve no governmental decisions to separate governmental agencies for specific territories or communities.

Federal constitutions partition the decision rights of government and allocate some to territorial administrations.[9] In a federal state, the population is not divided according to communal membership, and states within the common-state are the domains of their residents, not of specific communities such as ethnic or religious groups. Within the separate territorial jurisdictions all resident citizens enjoy equal rights regardless of their membership in different cultural communities. When citizens move into another jurisdiction they can become equal members; for example, as long as they leave their agricultural products at the border, other Americans can (and frequently do) become Californians.

Corporatist constitutions partition the decision rights allocated to government among agencies of communities—often but not exclusively cultural communities—that are not limited to specific territorial jurisdictions.[10] Ethnocorporatist constitutions, for example, typically assign specific policy realms to separate communal chambers or communal administrations for each ethnic group. For example, in Cyprus from 1961 to 1968, the constitution provided for communal legislative chambers that had exclusive law-making authority in matters of culture, education, religion, and personal status for the Greek and Turkish communities of the island. Corporatist bodies are organs of government, not voluntary associations; citizens must be enrolled in one or the other community and must submit to the compulsory jurisdiction of the agency once enrolled.[11] For the purposes of making common policy, corporatist constitutions may also provide for predetermined representation of the constituent groups in the government of the common-state. In Cyprus, the constitution assigned the presidency of the common-state to the Greek community and the vice presidency to the Turkish community, and each community held a separate election to fill its assigned post; furthermore, the Greek community elected 70 percent of the seats in the House of Representatives and the Turkish community elected 30 percent.[12]

Segmental constitutions differ from each of the foregoing because they partition the decision-making rights allocated to government and assign some of these rights to the governments of segment-states that are designated homelands of separate communities. Like federalism, segmentation

---

[9] Riker 1975.
[10] McRae 1975; Coakley 1994.
[11] See Hanf 1991, 38–40; S. Shaw 1976, 58–59, 151–53.
[12] Polyviou 1980, 13–25.

creates a distinction between the decision rights of the government of the common-state and those of the governments of the constituent states. Like federalism, segmentation may be asymmetrical in that the rights of the governments of the different constituent states can vary, and some exercise more decision rights than others.[13] This is most obvious within empires, in which the rights of the government of the metropolitan core, such as Belgium, differ from those of the governments in the colonies, such as the Belgian Congo.

Segmentation differs from federalism, however, in that segmentation simultaneously divides the population into separate communities or peoples and allocates members of these communities different decision rights. Segmentation differs from corporatism in that it links the rights of these communities to specific territories as their homelands. The rights of the members of these communities vary as they move from their segment-state to other parts of the same common-state; individuals do not freely enjoy the same rights of citizenship as they move among the jurisdictions of the segmented state. For example, Africans who lived in colonies or moved to Great Britain did not enjoy the full rights of citizenship to select the government of the empire. In the late Soviet period an ethnic Russian who moved to one of the non-Russian union republics did not enjoy the same rights to hold political office there as a fellow citizen of the USSR from the union republic's titular nationality.

Segmented States in the Twentieth Century

In the twentieth century there were a total of 368 segment-states within 43 segmented states at various times (table 2.1; see also the appendix).[14] The segment-states included 144 that by convention were classified at some time in the twentieth century as internal territories, including, for example, autonomous regions such as the Åland Islands in Finland, Val d'Aosta in Italy, Euskadi (Basque Country) in Spain, and Xinjiang in China; states or republics within ethnofederations, such as Jammu and Kashmir in India, the Northern Region within Nigeria, and the Armenian Soviet Socialist Republic in the USSR; and the Bantustans of South Africa during apartheid. Alternatively, 208 of the segment-states were classified at some time in the twentieth century as external or outlying territories, often designated by such statuses as colonies, protectorates (as in the British Em-

---

[13] Tarlton 1965, 861–74; also see Elazar 1994; Lapidoth 1997; Roessingh 1996, 30–31, 39, 41.

[14] The list of segment-states is constructed from all annual editions of the *Statesman's Yearbook* 1897–2001; *Europa World Yearbook* 1959–2001; Elazar 1994; Harding 1998; Henige 1970; *Linn's World Stamp Almanac* 1982; and Singer 2002.

TABLE 2.1

Numbers of internal and external segment-states worldwide, 1901–2000

	Terminal-year status[a]	Consistent status	Changing status
Internal segment states	140	137	
After status as:			
External segment state			2
After ambiguous status			1
Ambiguous status	39	18	
After status as:			
Internal segment state			4
External segment state			17
External segment states	189	189	0
Total	368		

[a] Terminal year refers to the final year before dissolution of the segment-state or to January 1, 2000 (for segment-states still present at the end of the century).

pire), commonwealths (as in the United States), or associated states. In between the internal and external territories were segment-states that defied easy categorization into internal or outlying territories. Many empires, such as the Japanese Empire, Ottoman Empire, Russian Empire, Italy under Mussolini, and Spain under Franco, blurred the distinction by designating their overseas possessions "provinces." Republics such as France granted many colonies from Algeria to Reunion the status of overseas departments, to keep their empires from falling apart or to administer parts of an empire that could not be easily divested (such as the Netherlands' Aruba). Four internal segment-states (Bophuthatswana, Ciskei, Transkei, and Venda) and another seventeen external segment-states moved to this ambiguous, in-between status during the century.

The total number of segment-states was equal at the start and end of the twentieth century, with 115 segment-states at the beginning of 1900 and 2000, but this total peaked mid-century with 173 segment-states in 1949 and 1954 (figure 2.2). More significantly, however, the longer-term trend over the century was growth in the share of internal segment-states as a consequence of granting independence to external segments, creating only a few new external segment-states after 1960, transferring external segment-states to internal status, and creating new internal segment-states. The proportion of segment-states that were classified as internal was a mere 4 percent in the first years of the century but began to rise after World War I, with a particularly rapid rise in the two decades immediately after each world war. Since 1971, internal segment-states have constituted a majority of all segments, reaching 74 percent of the total by 2000.

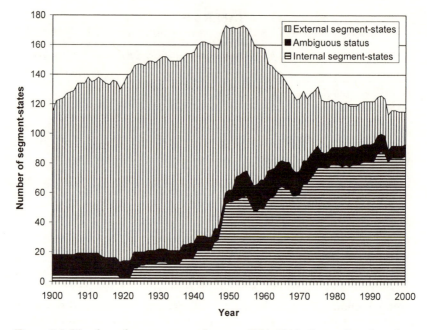

Figure 2.2 Number of segment-states by year, 1901–2000. *Sources:* Based on data in *Statesman's Yearbook* 1897–2001, *Europa World Yearbook* 1959–2001, Elazar 1994, Harding 1998, Henige 1970, *Linn's World Stamp Almanac* 1982, and Singer 2002.

More than 84 percent of the segmental dyads were culturally heterogeneous—that is, a majority within the segment-state either spoke a different language from the majority in the remainder of the common state or belonged to a different religion.[15] Internal and external segmental dyads were almost equally likely to be heterogeneous on at least one dimension—88.0 percent of the internal dyads and 82.3 percent of the external dyads were either linguistically or religiously heterogeneous (table 2.2). An important difference between internal and external segmental dyads, however, was the likelihood that the segment-state differed from the metropolitan core in its predominant "civilization." Samuel P. Huntington defines "civilization" as "the highest cultural grouping of people and the broadest level of cultural identity," and he identifies seven contemporary civilizations—Sinic, Japanese, Hindu, Islamic, Western, Latin American, and African.[16] More than half of the external dyads but only a third of the internal dyads

---

[15] In this context, linguistic difference means different languages even if within the same linguistic group; religious difference refers to a difference in what Huntington (1996) calls civilizations. Data on civilizations and language are from Bromlei 1988, Bruk and Apenchenko 1964, and Bruk 1986.

[16] Huntington 1996, 43.

TABLE 2.2

Cultural homogeneity and heterogeneity in segmental dyads worldwide, 1901–2000

	Internal segment-states (n = 142)		External segment-states[a] (n = 226)	
	Linguistic homogeneity	Linguistic heterogeneity	Linguistic homogeneity	Linguistic heterogeneity
Civilizational (religious) homogeneity	12.0%	54.2%	17.7%	24.8%
Civilizational (religious) heterogeneity	4.2%	29.6%	0%	57.5%
Civilizational (religious) homogeneity (prior to conversion)	12.0%	48.6%	15.9%	3.1%
Civilizational (religious) heterogeneity (prior to conversion)	4.2%	35.2%	1.8%	79.2%

[a] Includes segment-states of ambiguous status.

were civilizationally heterogeneous. This difference is even more pronounced if we exclude civilizational homogeneity that resulted from conversion by missionaries sent by the metropolitan core. For example, although a majority of the population of segment-states like Ruanda-Urundi might have been Roman Catholic, this resulted from conversion by German and Belgian missionaries, and many would contend that this conversion did not make Rwandans or Burundians members of the same civilization as Belgians.[17] By this second standard, which does not count converts made by the metropolitan core since the beginning of the age of nationalism as members of the metropolitan civilization, external segment-states were more than twice as likely as internal segment-states to be divided from the metropolitan core by civilization: less than two-fifths of the internal dyads but more than four-fifths of the external segmental dyads were civilizationally heterogeneous.

In Eurasia by the end of the seventeenth century, the Russian state had expanded to what some Russian ethnographers have described as its "natural" boundaries, which embraced "the scarcely settled lands fit for colonization, which were not parts of other states."[18] In the process, the Russian state incorporated significant Finnic-language and Turkic-language minorities. Administration of these diverse peoples was at first somewhat hap-

[17] This leaves open the possibility of prior conversion, such as the conversion of Samoans to Christianity by German missionaries prior to American control of the islands and Islamic conversion of the Sahel by North African missionaries prior to the French arrival.

[18] Matsyugina and Perepelkin 1996, 18.

hazard, but in 1775 the imperial government established a uniform administration for the entire state and divided Russia into forty provinces that showed little consideration for the cultural diversity within the empire—indeed, newly incorporated regions were divided among provinces to prevent crystallization of loyalties around such regions as Ukraine.[19] The expansion of Russia's boundaries continued, and over the course of the next century this uniform pattern was extended to more areas inhabited by non-Russians, such as the Caucasus and Poland. The acquisition of well-organized states such as Finland (1809), which was beginning to become a nation-state, led to the first segment-state. The eastern provinces of Poland, acquired at the end of the eighteenth century, enjoyed this status for almost a half century (1815–1864).[20] The Armenian oblast created by the tsarist regime after the capture of Erevan from the Persians lasted only about a decade; in 1840 the imperial administration abolished Armenia's special status and consolidated Transcaucasia into two provinces.[21] Bessarabia also enjoyed the status of a segment-state after its incorporation but lost this status in the mid-nineteenth century.[22] By 1900 only the Grand Duchy of Finland, the Khanate of Khiva, and the Emirate of Bukhara enjoyed local autonomy as internal segment-states (see figures 4.2 and 4.4).[23] In 1914 the empire added Tannu Tuva as an external protectorate.[24]

Alternatively, the USSR was a thoroughly segmented state. The Union of Soviet Socialist Republics began as a federation of four states—the Russian and Transcaucasian Soviet Federated Socialist Republics and the Belorussian and Ukrainian Soviet Socialist Republics. This number grew to eleven by 1937, peaked at sixteen from 1940 to 1956, and settled at fifteen union republics from 1956 until the breakup of the USSR.[25] Within these first-order segment-states were second-, third-, and fourth-order segment-states (the so-called autonomies). From 1961, when the USSR made the last change in its federal system by elevating Tuva to an autonomous republic, until the end of the USSR, fifty-three of the territorial administrations of the USSR were segment-states. Within the fifteen union republics (SSRs) were twenty autonomous republics (ASSRs), eight autonomous oblasts, and ten autonomous okrugs (figure 2.3). By 1988 segment-states

[19] Velychenko 1995, 189.
[20] Weeks 1996, 80–84.
[21] Hovannisian 1967, 9–11.
[22] Jussila 1989.
[23] Becker 1968.
[24] The USSR reestablished this protectorate in 1921 but annexed Tuva in 1944 (Mongush 1993, 47–52; Ballis 1941).
[25] Kelley 1924; Shabad 1946; Kaiser 1994. For a comparison with Eastern Europe's historical experience, see Mastny 2000.

existed for all twelve of the USSR's largest ethnic groups, ten of the twelve next largest ethnic minorities (only the Germans and Poles were excepted), nine of the twelve next largest minorities (only the Bulgarians, Greeks, and Koreans were excepted), and twenty-nine of the remaining sixty smaller ethnic groups.

The successor states created from the union republics of the USSR have retained most of the lower-order segment-states, abolishing only two, but have created three new segment-states (table 2.3). While still part of the USSR, Ukraine created the Autonomous Republic of Crimea on February 12, 1991.[26] After Chechnya seceded from the Russian Federation, Moscow recognized the separation of Ingushetia from the Chechen-Ingush ASSR on December 10, 1991. (In addition, the Russian Federation elevated four autonomous oblasts to republics—Adygeia, Altai, Khakassia, and Karachai-Cherkessia.) Moldova's 1994 constitution (Article 111) opened up the possibility of creating autonomous formations in Transdniestria and Gagauzia, but left the details to organic law.[27] On December 23, 1994, the Moldovan parliament passed organic legislation, the *Law on the Special Status of Gagauzia*, creating Gagauz Yeri, and on March 5, 1995, a referendum determined which communities would join the new Gagauz entity.[28] In amendments to the constitution added on July 25, 2003, under Council of Europe pressure, the Moldovan parliament inserted some of the law's provisions recognizing Gagauzia as an autonomous territorial unit into a new and expanded Article 111.

Alternatively, Azerbaijan abolished the Nagorno-Karabakh Autonomous Oblast on November 26, 1991,[29] and Georgia dissolved the South Ossetian Autonomous Oblast on December 11, 1990.[30] After independence, Azerbaijan eliminated the provisions concerning the Nagorno-Karabakh Autonomous Oblast from its constitution.[31] Georgia's first postindependence constitution (August 25, 1995) recognized Abkhazia and Ajaria but made no provision for South Ossetia, and now pointedly refers to this area in Article 1 as "the Former Autonomous Region of South Ossetia." According to the constitution, the issue of "the state-territorial organization of Georgia will be determined by constitutional law . . . after full restoration of

---

[26] Sergei Tsikora, "Krym poluchil avtonomiiu, no . . .," *Izvestiia* February 13, 1991, 2.

[27] All references are to the Constitution of the Republic of Moldova (adopted on July 29, 1994, as amended on July 25, 2003) in Blaustein and Flanz 2006.

[28] C. King 2000, 209–23.

[29] "Parlament Azerbaidzhana likvidiroval avtonomiiu Nagornogo Karabakha," *Izvestiia* November 28, 1991, 1; V. Samedov, "Baku," *Izvestiia* November 28, 1991, 1.

[30] A. Kochetkov, "Uprazdnena avtonomnaia oblast'," *Izvestiia* December 12, 1990, 3.

[31] All references are to the Constitution of the Azerbaijan Republic (adopted on November 12, 1995, as amended on August 24, 2002) in Blaustein and Flanz 2006.

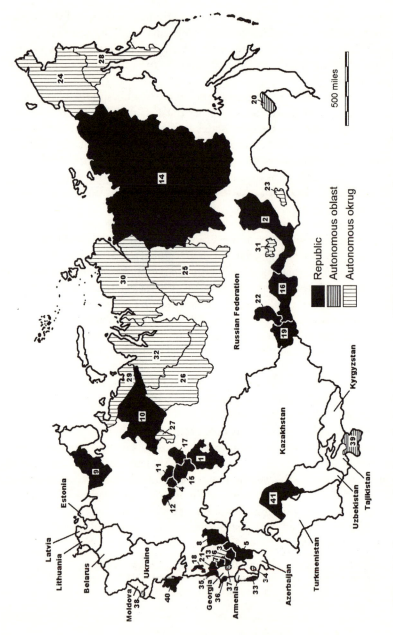

Figure 2.3 Segment-states in the Soviet successor states, 1991–2005. Numbers on the map refer to the list of segment-states in table 2.3.

Georgian jurisdiction in all the territory of the country" (Article 2).[32] More than a decade after independence, the future of the segment-states in Azerbaijan and Georgia is still unclear.

Origins of Segment-States

Some of the oldest segment-states that survived into the twentieth century evolved from medieval enfeudation (Andorra, 1278–1993; Guernsey, 1066–; Jersey, 1066–; Tibet, 1720–1914) or modern dynastic acquisitions (Hungary, 1867–1918; Iceland, 1380–1918; and Norway, 1814–1905), but most of the segmental relationships that existed in the twentieth century did not have long histories. As figure 2.4 shows, most external segment-states dated from the end of the nineteenth or the beginning of the twentieth century, and most internal segment-states that existed in the twentieth century dated from the post-World War I period.[33] Before World War I, most segment-states were created from newly conquered territories. After World War I, most segment-states were created through reorganization of territories and peoples already under the authority of the common-state. For example, the USSR created new segment-states such as the Uzbek SSR for peoples and territories without such status, and France shuffled the territories of West Africa among successive segment-states such as Upper Volta, which was first created in 1919 from territories and peoples previously included in the colony of Upper Senegal and Niger, then dissolved in 1932 and divided among Ivory Coast, Sudan, and Niger, but then recreated in 1947.

Only a minority of segment-states had previously been independent states.[34] Four of the segment-states that had been previously independent—the Estonian, Latvian, and Lithuanian SSRs and Zanzibar—had even maintained widespread diplomatic ties with great powers at some point after 1815 and just prior to annexation. Morocco (1912) and Hawaii (1898) were close to this status as sovereign members of the international community before instantiation as segment-states. Another twenty-nine entities—sultanates such as Johore, emirates such as Khiva, kingdoms such as Madagascar or Swaziland, or semi-independent republics such as Belorussia and

---

[32] All references are to the Constitution of Georgia (adopted August 24, 1995, as amended on July 1, 2004) in Blaustein and Flanz 2006.

[33] This figure treats the year of origin as the year the segmental relationship between a specific common-state and a first-order segment-state was established, even when the common-state was itself a segment. Thus, for example, the Russia-Bashkortostan segmental relationship dates from 1919 rather than 1992.

[34] Based on data in annual editions of the *Statesman's Yearbook* 1897–2001; *Europa World Yearbook* 1959–2001; Harding 1998; Henige 1970; and Singer 2002.

TABLE 2.3
Post-Soviet segment-states, 1991–2006

Segment-state	Status[a]	Territory[b]	Population[b]
Russian Federation	UR	1,7075.4	148,041
[1] Bashkortostan	AR	143.6	3,964
[2] Buryatia	AR	351.3	1,049
[3] Chechnya	AR[f]		
[4] Chuvashia	AR	18.3	1,340
[5] Dagestan	AR	50.3	1,823
[6] Ingushetia	AR[f]		
[7] Kabardino-Balkaria	AR	12.5	768
[8] Kalmykia	AR	76.1	325
[9] Karelia	AR	172.4	796
[10] Komi	AR	415.9	1,265
[11] Mari El	AR	23.2	754
[12] Mordovia	AR	26.2	964
[13] North Ossetia	AR	8.0	638
[14] Sakha	AR	3,103.2	1,099
[15] Tatarstan	AR	68.0	3,658
[16] Tyva	AR	170.5	314
[17] Udmurtia	AR	42.1	1,619
[18] Adygeia	AO[c]	7.6	436
[19] Altai	AO[bc]	92.6	194
[20] Jewish	AO[b]	36.0	218
[21] Karachai-Cherkessia	AO[bc]	14.1	422
[22] Khakassia	AO[bc]	61.9	573
[23] Aga Buryatia	AOk	19.0	77
[24] Chukotka	AOk	737.7	156
[25] Evenkia	AOk	767.6	25
[26] Khantia-Mansia	AOk	523.1	1,301
[27] Komi-Permyakia	AOk	32.9	160
[28] Koryakia	AOk	301.5	39
[29] Nenetsia	AOk	176.7	55
[30] Taimyria	AOk	862.1	55
[31] Ust-Orda Buryatia	AOk	22.4	137
[32] Yamalia	AOk	750.3	495
Azerbaijan	UR	86.6	7,131
[33] Nakhichevan	AR	5.5	300
[34] Nagornyi Karabakh[d]	AOb	4.4	192
Georgia	UR	69.7	5456
[35] Abkhazia	AR	8.6	538
[36] Ajaria	AR	3.0	382
[37] South Ossetia[d]	AOb	3.9	99

TABLE 2.3 (cont.)
Post-Soviet segment-states, 1991–2006

Segment-state	Status[a]	Territory[b]	Population[b]
Moldova	UR	33.7	4,362
[38] Gagauzia	—[e]		
Tajikistan	UR	143.1	5,248
[39] Gorno-Badakhshan	AOb	63.7	164
Ukraine	UR	603.7	51,839
[40] Crimea	AR	27.0	2,501
Uzbekistan	UR	447.4	20,322
[41] Karakalpakstan	AR	164.9	1,245
Armenia	UR	29.8	3,293
Belarus	UR	207.6	10,259
Estonia	UR	45.1	1,583
Kazakhstan	UR	2717.3	16,691
Kyrgyzstan	UR	198.5	4,367
Latvia	UR	64.5	2,687
Lithuania	UR	65.2	3,723
Turkmenistan	UR	488.1	3,622

Source: USSR, Gosudarstvennyi komitet po statistike 1990.

Notes: Numbers of segment-states correspond to labels in figure 4.3.

[a] Final Status in USSR: UR, union republic; AR, autonomous republic; AOb, autonomous oblast; AOk, autonomous okrug.

[b] On January 1, 1990 (territory in 1,000 km²; population in 1,000s).

[c] Autonomous oblast subsequently elevated to republic.

[d] Autonomous oblast dissolved by common-state.

[e] Created after 1991.

[f] Chechen-Ingush ASSR divided December 10, 1991.

Ukraine (1918–1922)—enjoyed some trappings of independent statehood just prior to their instantiation as segment-states.[35] For example, twenty segment-states created between 1861 and the end of World War I began as protectorates over states such as Annam (1862), Bahrain (1861), or Johore (1885) that preserved their statehood and their indigenous rulers—although now as segment-states within the jurisdiction of a common-state.

In recent years segmental institutions have become a means to cope with deep national divisions in countries such as Bosnia. Prior to this, in only a few instances did common-state governments create segment-states to tame national divisions. (It is important to underscore this previous history, because the segmental institutions thesis maintains that in those few instances where nationalism is strong and widespread by the time of independence, segment-states are typically the cause, not the consequence, of ris-

[35] In some instances (such as the Malay sultanates), this was statehood under the suzerainty of a foreign monarch (like the king of Thailand).

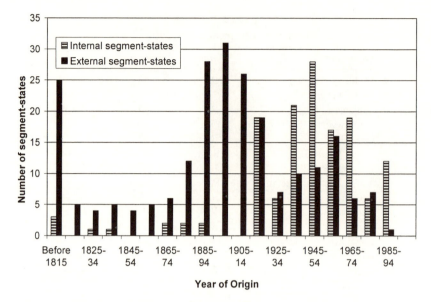

Figure 2.4   Year of origin of segmental dyads that existed between 1901 and 2000.
Sources: Based on data in *Statesman's Yearbook* 1897–2001, *Europa World Yearbook*
1959–2001, Harding 1998, Henige 1970, and Singer 2002.

ing nationalism.) In most instances the segmental arrangement predates
strong nationalism in the segment-state elites or public. Often common-
state governments created segment-states to exclude from full citizenship
a population that the common-state leaders viewed as so parochial that it
was not yet ready for independence or even self-government.[36] In other
instances the common-state sought to divide cultural communities that
the common-state government feared might eventually become bases of
nationalism and secessionism. But, most commonly, the segment-states
were drawn without any consideration for potential nationalism—either
they predated the era of nationalism or the common-state government
could not imagine that the purportedly benighted population would be
capable of generating its own nationalism.

In Eurasia, the Russian Empire preserved Finland, Bukhara, and Khiva
as segment-states until its end. By the Treaty of Frederikshamn, Finland
was incorporated within the empire in 1809, following Russia's victory over
Sweden. The empire preserved the Finnish Diet and developed a separate
administration for Finland that kept the grand duchy apart from the other
provinces.[37] The Central Asian protectorates had existed as states for four

[36] See Mill 1859 [1991], 14–15.
[37] Jussila 1989.

centuries—following the defeat of the Persians in 1511—and until 1598 were ruled by a common Shaibanid dynasty. Bukhara's Manghit dynasty ruled the emirate after 1785, but under a Russian protectorate after 1868. Khiva's Kungrat dynasty ruled from 1804, but under a Russian protectorate after 1873.[38]

The Communists introduced ethnofederalism immediately after the 1917 revolution. Developing a position taken prior to assuming power,[39] Vladimir Lenin insisted that the constitutional structure of the new Soviet state accommodate ethnic diversity through segmental incorporation of the homelands of ethnic minorities. The common-state would have full powers in "serious, major, basic matters" but would avoid "bureaucratic intervention into *purely* local (regional, national, et cetera) questions."[40] After the Communists seized power, the Third All-Russian Congress of Soviets in January 1918 proclaimed Russia to be "established on the basis of a free union of free nations, as a federation of Soviet national republics" and instructed the Central Executive Committee to draft principles for a constitution that would implement the resolution, "On the Federal Institutions of the Russian Republic." In July 1918, Russia's first constitution established it as the Russian Soviet Federated Socialist Republic (RSFSR), and Article 11 permitted soviets in areas "with a distinct mode of living and national composition" to unite in separate autonomous regions and to "enter the Russian Soviet Federated Socialist Republic on a federal basis" (Article 11).[41] Four years later this principle was extended with the creation of the USSR. On December 29, 1922, representatives of the RSFSR together with representatives of the new Ukrainian SSR, Belorussian SSR, and Transcaucasian SFSR signed a treaty of union.

The Soviet federal structure did not originate as a necessary compromise with nationalism, but for Lenin it quickly became a means to another end—controlling the rapidly expanding Soviet bureaucratic apparatus and its excessive "bureaucratic intervention" that he had warned against earlier. Within the RSFSR itself, where the original template of ethnofederalism was created, the homelands were not the result of spontaneous movement from below.[42] The national homelands that appeared spontaneously in 1917 and 1918, such as the Kuban–Black Sea Republic and the Terek Autonomous Socialist Republic, were short-lived. The only republic founded by agreement between the RSFSR and local nationalists was the Bashkir ASSR; the rest were creations of Moscow.[43] Furthermore, the accession to

---

[38] Becker 1968.

[39] Lenin 1913a [1980].

[40] Lenin 1913b. [1980], 146.

[41] Unger 1981, 25–41.

[42] Pipes 1968, 248.

[43] On the early history of the Bashkir ASSR, see Carr 1957; Pipes 1950; Schafer 2001.

the USSR by the other union republics was forced, not voluntary, and left the fate of the union republics completely in Moscow's hands. The Communists came to power in the other republics with the assistance of the Red Army. Where the Red Army did not hold power—in Finland, Poland, the Baltic states, and Bessarabia—the governments in these regions chose not to enter negotiations to create a common-state with Russia. Where the Red Army was in control—in Armenia, Azerbaijan, Belarus, Bukhara, Georgia, Khiva, and Ukraine—the non-Bolshevik governments had disappeared, and the leaders of the states that joined Russia in the USSR were dependent on the Red Army and had little leverage to press for a different type of constitutional order.[44]

In the Communist Party the proponents of federalism were numerically and politically weak and would have failed except for Lenin's support. A majority of the Bolsheviks, including many from the minority areas, in fact pressed for a unitary state rather than a segmented state; they sought to press forward with a revolution that would transform society in the interests of the proletariat without concessions to such atavisms of earlier epochs as nationalism. The voices of the nationalities within the decision-making centers in Moscow were very weak; most party organizations in Ukraine and elsewhere were dominated by ethnic Russians or Jews, who were suspicious of titular nationalism. Internationalists or Leftists such as Nikolai Bukharin objected to plans to give the republics autonomy, claiming that this would weaken the international solidarity of the proletariat.[45] Even among those Bolsheviks who accepted that there should be some accommodation with national diversity, such as Joseph Stalin, few were willing to grant the extent of autonomy implied by Lenin's federal plan.[46] Many of the leaders of the Communist parties outside Russia favored the "autonomization" plan, which would have incorporated their lands as autonomous republics within the RSFSR rather than uniting them in a new common-state alongside Russia.[47] Yet Lenin pushed his plan for a federal USSR against such resistance within his own party.[48]

Lenin had considered the alternatives to the segmented state and rejected these. On the one hand, he rejected the option of a unitary state, even though the tsarist period had shown this was viable in Russia and many of the more radical, internationalist Communists wanted to use such a state in order to construct communism quickly. In particular, he rejected the plan of the economic rationalizers in the State Planning Commission

[44] Sullivant 1962, 45–64.
[45] Sullivant 1962, 20–29, 96–105; Institut Marksa-Engel'sa-Lenina-Stalina, 1954, I:17.
[46] Lewin 1968, 43–63; Pipes 1968, 272–73.
[47] Suny 1988, 215; Sheehy 1990c, 18.
[48] Stalin 1917 and 1924 [1953]; Sullivant 1962, 89–96.

(*Gosplan*) to divide the country into twenty-one economic regions (raions) without consideration for the boundaries of nationalities.[49] On the other hand, Lenin rejected the various ethnocorporatist alternatives for nonterritorial autonomy for ethnic groups. Lenin anathematized the so-called Austrian plan authored by Karl Renner and Otto Bauer.[50] From 1903 to 1921 Lenin fought the Jewish Bund and criticized the ethnocorporatism that the Bund precedent represented; by 1921 the Bund was forced to submit to party hegemony.[51] Lenin rejected the demands for creation of separate Turkic and Russian Communist parties in Kazakhstan.[52] Similarly, in his defense of the design of the first constitution of the RSFSR in 1918, Lenin rejected the project of Professor Reisner for a nonterritorial "federation of social and economic organizations."[53] As a consequence, ethnocorporate entities were virtually unknown in the Soviet state; the USSR even failed to create officially sanctioned "public organizations" for ethnic groups without homelands. The first officially recognized all-union social organization for a national group—*Revival*, a political and cultural organization for Soviet Germans—was not created until the spring of 1989.[54]

The reasons for Lenin's insistence on the segmented state have puzzled analysts, who see little domestic-political or ideological necessity. Robert Conquest argues that Lenin's motivation was a desire to avoid diplomatic confrontation with those foreign powers that had established diplomatic relations with the briefly independent states.[55] Yet this advantage disappeared in 1922 once the republics became part of the USSR, and it was no longer a compelling factor when the constitution was adopted two years later. Richard Pipes claims that Lenin was motivated by the propaganda value of the segment-states in spreading revolution among the peoples of Asia and Africa.[56] But segmentation was applied to the European parts of the former Russian Empire first, and initially was not extended to Central Asia. A more compelling explanation, suggested by Moshe Lewin, argues that Lenin insisted on his plan in order to control the growing power of the party apparatus under Stalin—to curb its excessive "bureaucratic intervention." If Lenin's original opposition to Stalin's autonomization plan had succeeded, Lenin might have blocked the growth of the machine of party bureaucrats (apparatchiks) that Stalin cultivated as People's Commissar of Nationalities. Lenin's *Testament* criticized the autonomization proj-

---

[49] Morrison 1938.

[50] Pearson 1991, 20–22.

[51] Schapiro 1971, 227.

[52] Olcott 1987, 210.

[53] Borys 1960, 325–26.

[54] Barsamov 1997, 290–91.

[55] Conquest 1967, 36.

[56] Pipes 1968, 280; also see Fainsod 1963, 369.

ect as "unjust and premature" and urged building the bureaucracies of the union republics as counterweights to Stalin's centralizing tendencies.[57] Lenin won the battle to establish a segmented state based on ethnofederalism, but he was often incapacitated in his last years and did not live long enough to win the war that came with the implementation of his plan.

In establishing the borders of the new union republics, rather than compromising with the stronger nation-state projects, the designers of Soviet federalism drew lines to divide or submerge these in new segment-states. That is, these designers sought to control the nation-states most likely to foster centrifugal pressures in the future by dividing them and submerging them within new segment-states. The greatest potential for widespread nationalism existed in the segment-states that had enjoyed a measure of independence prior to 1922, particularly Georgia, Bukhara, and Khiva.[58] In March 1922, over strong objections from Georgian nationalists, Moscow united Armenia, Azerbaijan, and Georgia in what would be labeled the Transcaucasian Soviet Federated Socialist Republic (ZSFSR).[59] The three republics were divided by language, religious traditions, and animosities, however, which prevented the ZSFSR from becoming a nation-state that could threaten Moscow's control. To reduce the disruptive influence of the leaders of the Georgian opposition to the plan, the Russian Communist Party's Central Committee ordered them to leave Georgia.[60]

Similarly, strong opposition to incorporation within the USSR came from the Bukharan People's Soviet Republic, created in March 1921, and the Khorezmi (Khiva) Soviet People's Republic, created in September 1920.[61] To ease the transition in these previously autonomous monarchies, Moscow had created soviet people's republics that made them like protectorates, with considerable independence in their internal affairs. Facing the disruptive potential of these preexisting states within a state, however, in 1924 Moscow simply abolished the two Central Asian people's republics, divided them, and incorporated their parts within the newly created Tajik, Turkmen, and Uzbek republics.[62]

The Communists feared that the federal solution that was supposed to dilute nationalism in Transcaucasia by uniting disputatious nations in the same segment-state might have the opposite effect in Central Asia, where

[57] Lewin 1968, 62–63, 86–89. Also see Schapiro 1971, 272–75; Suny 1988, 216–17.

[58] Suny 1993b, 29–76. Robert Kaiser (1995, 427) claims that within Russia proper, only the Tatars and a few North Caucasus groups, such as the Ossetians, had forged a consciousness prior to 1917.

[59] Altstadt 1992, 119; Suny 1988, 214–16.

[60] Lewin 1968, 43–63; Pipes 1968, 273–75.

[61] Akiner 1997, 369.

[62] Becker 1968, 301–10; Pipes 1968, 255. The claim that borders were drawn to minimize nationalist threats is also made by Carley 1998 and by Menon and Fuller 2000, 35–36.

national distinctions were less well developed. The Turkestan Autonomous Republic was already becoming a focal point for some Central Asian nationalists soon after its creation in 1918 as part of the RSFSR. The amalgamation of Bukhara and Khiva with Turkestan might have provided the foundation for a nation-state that could threaten Moscow's control.[63] Indeed, the first organized indigenous opposition to the Soviet regime came with the declaration of an autonomous government in Kokand by a self-styled Turkestan Muslim Central Council.[64] The dangers of both Bukhara and Khiva, on one hand, and the Turkestan project, on the other, were demonstrated by the broad coalition of peoples in Central Asia, collectively known as the *Basmachis* (bandits), who conducted a guerrilla war against the Soviet-supported authorities.[65] Moscow had to navigate between the states that could become nations, such as Bukhara and Khiva, and the imagined nation that wanted to become a state, Turkestan. The solution came in dividing the territories of Bukhara and Khiva and combining these fragments with other regions in separate republics that divided Turkestan and its population. Thus, the Soviet state abandoned the Turkestan Autonomous Republic within two years of its creation. In 1920 Moscow began the so-called National Delimitation in Central Asia, peeling away new homelands with the creation of the Kirgiz (that is, Kazakh and Kirgiz) ASSR.[66] Although the professed reason was the redrawing of state boundaries to correspond to national boundaries, there were no nations to support these states, and the borders were highly contested.[67] In subsequent years, there was an iterative process in which both nations and territories were redefined, so that the creation of separate Kirgiz and Kazakh SSRs represented not only a recognition of the right of two populations to separate states but also a decision that these were indeed two different nations.[68] The decision to create some segment-states but not others was driven by Moscow's concern to prevent crystallization of nationalism around the most threatening nation-state projects. Although the Uzbeks were probably farthest along the road to developing a sense of nationalism (at least when compared with the other newly recognized nations of Central Asia), the Uzbek

[63] Allworth 1990, 189–209; Rywkin 1990, 33–43; Lipovsky 1996, 216–17; Alexander Park 1957, 70–87; Roy 2000, 66–68.

[64] Fierman 1991, 43; Allworth 1990, 179–80, 193–94; Alexander Park 1957, 14–18.

[65] Rywkin 1990, 33–43; Alexander Park 1957, 40–42, 49–58.

[66] Alexander Park 1957, 87–108. Four years later the Kirgiz ASSR was divided between a Kara-Kirgiz Autonomous Oblast and Kazakh ASSR. In 1924 rump Turkestan was divided among the Turkmen SSR, Uzbek SSR, and Tajik ASSR, which was subordinate to the Uzbek SSR; the following year a separate Karakalpak Autonomous Oblast (initially within the Kazakh ASSR) and Gorno-Badakhshan Autonomous Oblast (within the Tajik ASSR) were given third-order autonomous status.

[67] Akiner 1995, 36; 1997, 373–75; Rakowska-Harmstone 1970, 76–78; Fierman 1991, 45.

[68] J. Anderson 1999, 9.

SSR was far from a nation-state. According to Olivier Roy, "the concept of 'Uzbek' in 1924 was not that of a nationality conscious of itself: there was no Uzbek 'national movement', and what predominated were localist, tribal, and infra-ethnic identities."[69] The Soviet regime included within the Uzbek SSR a number of people that had ambiguous and sometimes hostile relations with peoples who were now dubbed fellow Uzbeks, yet by the late 1930s the Soviet regime had reclassified Bukharans, Kuramas, Kypchaks, and others as Uzbeks. Edward Allworth argues that the Uzbek SSR "began its existence as a theoretical framework into which the politicians of Moscow expected the leaders in Samarkand and the other principal cities to fit appropriate content."[70] Moscow had created new states that would be much easier to control than either a united Turkestan or separate Bukhara and Khiva.

In the North Caucasus and the mid-Volga regions, Moscow also abandoned early experiments with larger autonomous republics within the Russian Federation and created smaller states that would be easier to control. In the North Caucasus, the Mountain Autonomous Republic, created by Moscow on January 20, 1920, as Ronald Wixman notes, threatened to "be strongly conservative and anti-Russian in character."[71] Thus, between January 1921 and 1924, the Soviet regime peeled away homelands of more communities to create new, smaller segment-states, beginning with the Dagestan ASSR.[72] In the mid-Volga region the Soviet regime rejected plans for an Idel-Ural state that would unite Turkic (and perhaps Finnic) peoples. On November 19, 1917, the National Assembly of the Muslims of Inner Russia and Siberia had proclaimed an autonomous Idel-Ural state for Tatars and Bashkirs. On January 21, 1918, the Second Muslim Military Congress endorsed this decision, but the civil war soon swept away the first attempt to create such a republic. The following year Mirsaid Sultangaliev took up the cause and won endorsement from the Second All-Russian Congress of Communist Organizations of the Peoples of the East. Still, the Communist Party Politburo in Moscow rejected this plan. When Sultangaliev persisted and appealed the decision to the Central Committee, the Politburo came down hard. As Azade-Ayse Rorlich notes, "the Idel-Ural or the Tatar-Bashkir state had been divided up before it ever came into

[69] Roy 2000, 72.

[70] Allworth 1990, 210.

[71] Wixman 1980, 137, also see 126, 136–39.

[72] The Mountain Republic was divided into the Dagestan ASSR (January 1921); the Kabard Autonomous Oblast (September 1921), which was then incorporated into a new Kabard-Balkar Autonomous Oblast in January 1922; the Karachai-Cherkess Autonomous Oblast (January 1922); the Agygei-Cherkess Autonomous Oblast (July 1922); the Chechen Autonomous Oblast (November 1922); the Ingush Autonomous Oblast (July 1924); and the North Ossetian Autonomous Oblast (July 1924).

existence because its existence would have become a danger too real to be overlooked by the Soviet government." By sponsoring the formation of smaller republics, Moscow "fostered isolation and even nourished old jealousies and rivalries, thus facilitating its control over the peoples of the area."[73] The establishment of separate Bashkir (1919) and Tatar (1920) ASSRs, as well as the Chuvash (1920), Mari (1920), and Votyak (Udmurt) (1920) autonomous oblasts, emphasized their differences and cultivated political competition at the expense of unity among them.

Variation in Segmental Institutions

Segmented states are not all alike. Most fundamentally, they are based on varying notions of sovereignty—that is, their answers to the question, what population possesses the power to allocate and reallocate decision rights? Second, they vary in the ways their constitutions have actually allocated decision rights—specifically, the extent to which they empower the people of each segment-state to design their own political institutions, to select their own political leadership, to participate in the governance of the common-state, and to make policy. These institutional differences are important because the allocation of these powers is the substantive issue on which most nation-state crises focus. The powers given segment-state leaders can provide the advantage that permits them to establish political-identity hegemony on the periphery. These powers can be fashioned into institutional weapons that segment-state leaders use to coerce common-state leaders into relinquishing more decision rights. And these powers can create the political opportunities to weaken the common-state government through deadlock.

Complex Sovereignty

Segmented states typically raise complicated questions and intense political struggles over sovereignty. In this context the term *sovereignty* refers to the jurisdiction within which decision rights are allocated. That is, the sovereign state is distinguished from other jurisdictions by its authority to allocate and reallocate all decision rights within its borders.[74] These decision rights are never, except in fictional accounts of total regimes like George Orwell's *1984*, allocated only to government; the state's constitution—a set of rules-in-use that are both written and unwritten—allocates these decision rights, assigning some to government, others to society (in the

---

[73] Rorlich 1986, 137–38. Also see Alexander Park 1957, 92.
[74] Compare J. Thomson 1995, 214, 222–25; Krasner 1999, 1984.

form of civil rights), and prohibiting still other decisions to everyone.[75] The sovereign state may even delegate some decision rights to international organizations such as the European Union. Yet the sovereign state remains the jurisdiction where the decision to maintain or rescind any delegation of decision rights resides. Thus, in Alan James's formulation, the sovereign state is a territorial jurisdiction that is "constitutionally independent" and not "contained, however loosely, within a wider constitutional scheme."[76] In this sense of being "constitutionally apart," there is continuing relevance in the original formulations of Jean Bodin and Thomas Hobbes that sovereignty means both "internal supremacy and external independence."[77]

The rise of popular sovereignty represents the claim that this control over the allocation of decision rights resides with a people.[78] The concept of the *nation-state* is simply the attempt to give substance to popular sovereignty in specific cases; it identifies the specific population (the nation) that has resolved that it should make the decisions about the allocation of decision rights within a state of its own. Implementing popular sovereignty and creating real nation-states demand an answer to the inescapable boundary question of inclusion and exclusion: Who belongs to this nation that has a right to govern itself?[79] In the ideal formulation, the state belongs to one people and the people have one state—the nation and state are coextensive, undivided, and inseparable. The entire nation is empowered to participate in drafting and redrafting the constitution either directly through referenda or indirectly through their representatives in decisions concerning the allocation and reallocation of decision rights.

The *segmented state* can introduce fundamental amendments to this idea of popular sovereignty within a nation-state. In attempting to identify the locus of popular sovereignty, segmental constitutions have tended to provide five different answers that I will label common-state, metropolitan, pooled, partitioned, and segment-state sovereignty. *Common-state sovereignty* posits that the population of the country as a whole constitutes the sole sovereign collectivity, yet this is limited by the right of individual populations within it to have states, but not sovereign states of their own. In Eurasia, five of the seven Soviet successor states have adopted this concept of common-state sovereignty (table 2.4). The Russian Federation today

---

[75] James 1986, 37. As part of the allocation of decision rights constitutive rules may predetermine certain decisions, and so effectively place these decisions outside the competence of all—not only the governments of the common-state and segment-states, but also private citizens. See Heckathorn and Maser 1987; J. Knight 1992; North and Weingast 1988.

[76] James 1986, 24, 32–39.

[77] Philpott 2001, 316. Also see Fried 1968, 146.

[78] See Wood 1969, 344–89.

[79] R. Hall 1999, 51–72.

rests on the sovereignty of the people of Russia (*rossiiane*), not on the sovereignty of separate Russian (*russkii*), Tatar, Chuvash, Bashkir, and other peoples. According to Article 3 of Russia's 1993 constitution, "the multinational people of the Russian Federation shall be the vehicle of sovereignty and the only source of power in the Russian Federation."[80] The constitution does not recognize a right of secession by its segment-states or stipulate that their membership in the federation is voluntary. The only concession to what might be considered the sovereignty of the segment-states concerns changes in the statehood of the segment-states; these are subject to concurrent majorities insofar as all subjects of the federation—whether segment-states or provinces—are granted a veto in any decisions to change their status or to change their boundaries (Articles 66 and 67).[81] The jurisprudence of Azerbaijan, Georgia, Tajikistan, and Ukraine is even closer to the ideal of common-state sovereignty that resides solely with the people of the common-state. In neither Article 134 of Azerbaijan's 1995 constitution nor Article 81 of Tajikistan's 1994 constitution is the country's segment-state described as sovereign.[82] Under principles of common-state sovereignty, the segment-states of Azerbaijan and Tajikistan only exercise powers delegated by their common-state legislatures and cannot unilaterally reallocate decision rights; neither enjoys a right of secession. Tajikistan's constitution does guarantee that the territory of the Gorno-Badakhshan Autonomous Oblast cannot be changed without the consent of its *Majlis* (Article 81), but that right can be rescinded by constitutional amendments over which Gornyi Badakhshan has no veto. In Georgia, the constitution explicitly precludes the sovereign prerogative of secession, stipulating that "the alienation of the territory of Georgia is prohibited" (Article 2). Ukraine's constitution explicitly prohibits Crimea from secession or unification with Russia (Articles 92 and 157).

[80] All references are to the Constitution of the Russian Federation (adopted December 12, 1993) in Blaustein and Flanz 2006.

[81] Any proposal from a subject for a change in its status must have the consent of supermajorities in both chambers of the Federal Assembly (two-thirds of the total membership of the State Duma and three-quarters of the total membership in the Council of the Federation) plus the signature of the president. The rights of segment-states can be taken away by amendments to the Constitution, and such amendments do not require the concurrence of each segment-state. The ratification procedures require concurrence of two-thirds of the eighty-nine subjects of the federation, and so as few as two of the thirty-two segment-states need join the provinces and federal cities in ratifying the amendment as long as the non-segment-states stand together (Article 134). The exception to this is amendment of Article 5. Yet this merely stipulates that there are republics, autonomous oblasts, and autonomous okrugs in the federation; that republics can have their own constitutions rather than charters; and that all subjects of the federation are equal. Amendment to this requires a Constitutional Assembly.

[82] All references are to the Constitution of the Republic of Tajikistan (adopted on November 6, 1994, amended on September 26, 1999, and June 22, 2003) in Blaustein and Flanz 2006.

Metropolitan sovereignty posits that only the population associated with one territory possesses the sovereignty that constitutes the common-state. For example, in the British Empire after World War II, the Imperial Parliament was supreme throughout the king's dominions—a doctrine in force since the Declaratory Act of 1766, issued to put the American colonies in their place. This empowered Westminster to legislate directly for territories under the foreign jurisdiction of the crown (and, through orders in council, for the rest of the empire).[83] Yet only the citizens of the United Kingdom participated in the election of Parliament. For the rest of the subjects of the crown, there was only the hope, as Sir Ivor Jennings expressed it, that "the people of Hornsey, Huddersfield, Hertford, Pontypool, Gorbals, Hamilton, and Londonderry . . . can be persuaded that the people of the Gold Coast and Nigeria, British Honduras and Hong Kong, Basutoland and British North Borneo, are much like them and will 'reach a sensible decision' about their futures."[84] Any allocation of rights to a colony was a delegation of powers that the people of Hornsey and Huddersfield could take back, until they relinquished their sovereignty over the distant colony.

Pooled sovereignty posits that the population of the common-state and the populations of the separate segment-states each constitute collectivities with the prerogative to allocate decision rights, and so reallocation requires mutual consent. In the last years of the USSR as it democratized, both the union and the union republics styled themselves sovereign states. This pooled sovereignty had jurisprudential roots that went back as far as Article 7 of the 1924 constitution of the USSR, which made all individuals simultaneously citizens of their respective union republics and citizens of the union. In the 1977 constitution, the people of each union republic possessed the right of statehood (Article 76), and the union republics were defined as sovereign states that retained the right of secession (Article 4)—the right to retrieve the powers delegated to the union—as well as a veto over changes to their territories (Article 6).[85] Yet the union to which the union republics delegated authority was also a sovereign nation-state (Article 75), an expression of the sovereign prerogative of the Soviet people to constitute a state of its own. Over every part of the territory of the USSR two states exercised sovereignty, derived from two different, nested collectivities of peoples residing on that territory.[86] In the last years of Soviet

---

[83] Wight 1952, 88; Jackson 1987, 522–23.

[84] Jennings 1958, 58.

[85] Ponomarev et al. 1982, 225; also see Akademiia obshchestvennykh nauk 1984, 211–14.

[86] The jurisprudence of the late Soviet state clearly distinguished the sovereignty of the union republics from the dependence of the other autonomies. Nonetheless, the Soviet constitution granted the autonomous republics certain marks of statehood, including their own constitutions and state organs with a nomenclature (e.g., council of ministers) identical to the

jurisprudence, pooled sovereignty created a conceptual maze and provided justifications for competing claims to supremacy among these alternative sovereignties within the USSR. Of the Soviet successor states, only Uzbekistan and Moldova have maintained any doctrines of pooled sovereignty. In Uzbek jurisprudence the republic of Karakalpakstan is formally sovereign (Article 70) and shares its decision rights with Uzbekistan through concurrent decision making (mutual vetoes over decisions concerning Karakalpakstan).[87] According to the constitution, relations between Karakalpakstan and Uzbekistan are "regulated by treaties and agreements," and any disputes are "settled by way of reconciliation" (Article 78). Of course, as long as Uzbekistan remains a brutal autocracy, these doctrines are as formalistic as Soviet doctrines under Stalin. Karakalpakstan's right to secede (Article 74) is limited by the veto power of Uzbekistan's legislature (*Oliy Majlis*) over any decision to secede (Article 78), but at least on paper, Karakalpakstan can veto any changes in its boundaries voted by Uzbekistan's *Oliy Majlis* (Articles 69, 73). Moldova made a small step from common-state to pooled sovereignty in 1995: Gagauzia not only enjoys the right to symbols of statehood, such as an anthem, emblem, and flag, but by the *Law on the Special Status of Gagauzia* retains the right to secede if Moldova changes its legal status, such as unifying with Romania.[88] In this legal doctrine the reallocation of decision rights—that is, secession—resides with the segment-state, but only if the common-state decides to change its own legal status. Yet constitutional amendments adopted in July 2003, while inserting many provisions from the *Law on the Special Status of Gagauzia* into the constitution, omitted this provision for secession and described Gagauzia as "a constitutive and inalienable part of the Republic of Moldova" (Article 111).

Partitioned sovereignty posits that in distinct realms, the common-state and the segment-states have rights that cannot be taken from them. In the British relationship with so-called protected states such as Brunei, the Maldive Islands, or Tonga (but not the colonial protectorates), the protected state surrendered its rights in specific spheres such as foreign and defense affairs but retained a sovereign right in the remaining areas.[89] These relationships fell short of an international relationship between fully sovereign states because the segment-states did not retain the sovereign

---

all-union and union republic governments. See Akademiia obshchestvennykh nauk 1984, 253–54; also see "Avtonomiia" in *Bol'shaia Sovetskaia Entsiklopediia* 1970, 1:162; and "Suverenitet" in *Bol'shaia Sovetskaia Entsiklopediia* 1976, 25:26.

[87] All references are to the Constitution of the Republic of Uzbekistan (adopted on December 8, 1992) in Blaustein and Flanz 2006.

[88] Elena Druz', "Opredeleny granitsy Gagauzskoi avtonomii," *Segodnia* March 7, 1995, 5; also see C. King 2000, 217–20.

[89] Wight 1952, 2, 9–11, 64–67.

TABLE 2.4

Post-Soviet segmented states: Constitutional arrangements

| | Semidemocracies | | | | Autocracies | | |
| | Decentralized | | Centralized | | | | |
	Moldova	Russia	Georgia	Ukraine	Azerbaijan	Tajikistan	Uzbekistan
Freedom Score[a]							
Average 1992–2004	3.65	4.23	4.08	3.65	5.46	6.19	6.58
Range	(3.0–5.0)	(3.5–5.5)	(3.5–5.0)	(3.0–4.0)	(5.0–6.0)	(5.5–7.0)	(6.0–7.0)
Sovereignty	Pooled	Common	Common	Common	Common	Common	Pooled
Provisions for:							
Treaty relations	Yes	Yes	No	No	No	No	Yes
Right of secession	Yes	No	No	No	No	No	Yes
Segment constitution	Yes	Yes	No	Yes	Yes	No	Yes
Election/appointment of:							
Segment leadership	Local	Local	Local	Concurrent	Concurrent	Central	Local
Courts	Central	Central	—	Central	Central	Central	Local
Coöptation into:							
Executive	Yes	Yes	No	No	No	No	Yes
Legislative leadership	No	No	Yes	No	No	Yes	Yes
Second chamber	No	Yes	No	No	No	Yes	No

[a] Based on Freedom House (Gastil 1993–2005) annual scores of political liberties and civil liberties in each country, with 1 representing the most free and 7 representing the least free countries.

right to reclaim its powers over foreign policy; Britain had to decide to return these. Yet by the terms of partitioned sovereignty, the British government could not expand its rights into the area of domestic legislation in these protected states.

Segment-state sovereignty posits that the segment-states alone constitute collectivities with the prerogative to create states of their own, that segment-states become parts of the common-state by a delegation of powers from segment-states to the common-state, and that segment-states can rescind this delegation without approval from the common-state or other segment-states. This is frequently the arrangement that secessionist segment-states claim is the basis for the current common-state.

Segmental Self-Governance

The power of a segment-state to maintain its own governing institutions and its own indigenous leadership becomes the basis for one cohort to establish its predominance inside the segment-state with political-identity hegemony and to marshal the resources of the segment-state in a bid for independence from the common-state. Even where the indigenous leaders have not been elected democratically, they are likely to be privileged in both the politics on the periphery and the politics between center and periphery. Thus, it is significant that there was a secular trend in the twentieth century toward granting segment-states their own governing institutions and expanding participation of the segment populations in the selection of leaders of the segment-states. It is most useful to summarize these patterns by comparing the terminal years of a segmental dyad—the state of affairs on the first of January of the last year before a segmental dyad was terminated, or January 1, 2000, for ongoing dyads.

Only a few segment-states in the twentieth century were allowed to design their institutions of self-governance on their own.[90] At the time of initial establishment of a segmental relationship, twenty-seven of the new segment-states preserved existing indigenous institutions of segment-wide self-governance. These included protectorates over monarchies, such as Buganda, Bukhara, Cambodia, Qatar, Tonga, and Zanzibar, and annexation of territories that already had their own legislatures, such as Finland, Iceland, and Transvaal. Yet most of the institutions of self-governance in segment-states were creations of the common-state itself. Thus, Britain was more likely to foster development of parliaments and the USSR was more

---

[90] Information on governing institutions is from annual editions of the *Statesman's Yearbook* 1897–2001, *Europa World Yearbook* 1959–2001, and individual country studies in the Library of Congress's Country Study (previously the Department of the Army's Area Handbook) series.

likely to foster development of supreme soviets in each of their segment-states than to grant local people the right to concoct their own institutions.

The majority of segment-states in the twentieth century were allowed their own indigenous or locally constituted leadership with jurisdiction over the whole segment-state. In the terminal year, more than three-fifths (226) of the segmental dyads guaranteed the segment-state an opportunity for both indigenous executive and indigenous legislative authority. These included a variety of arrangements, however—not only locally elected legislative assemblies and executives but also hereditary kingships and emirates and indigenous leadership that rose to power within homelands under such authoritarian regimes as South Africa or the USSR. Another 18 percent had indigenous legislatures with segment-wide jurisdiction but not indigenous executives with segment-wide jurisdiction; the executive, such as a prefect or governor, was sent by the government of the common-state. Among the remaining segment-states, many had consultative councils of appointed or coöpted representatives or even local elective authorities with jurisdictions limited to a part of the segment-state, such as separate island legislatures or local chieftains, but no segment-wide indigenous leadership. These distinctions constituted a major difference between internal and external segment-states. As table 2.5 shows, by the terminal year almost all internal segment-states had both legislative and executive authorities that were indigenous. For example, Belgium's Flemish and Walloon regions, Italy's autonomous regions for German and French speakers, and India's states for linguistic minorities each had locally elected parliaments that selected their own executives. Alternatively, in the terminal years, less than half of the external segment-states had both indigenous executive and indigenous legislative authority.

In Eurasia, the Soviet segmented state imposed nearly identical institutions on the segment-states. From 1924 to 1989, each segment-state had identical state structures.[91] According to the 1977 Soviet constitution, a union republic was empowered to adopt its own constitution but was constrained by the requirement that this conform to the all-union constitution and the "general principles for the organization and activity of republic and local organs of state power and administration" adopted by the all-union Supreme Soviet (Article 73). From 1936 until 1989, each union republic had a supreme soviet formally elected by the public, a council of ministers (cabinet) formally elected by its supreme soviet, and a presidium of the supreme soviet (collective chief of state), also formally elected by the supreme soviet. All but the Russian SFSR also had identical party organs, with a Communist Party Congress composed of delegates from regional party organizations, a central committee formally elected by the congress,

---

[91] For details on Soviet institutions from 1924 to 1936, see Towster 1948; Unger 1981.

TABLE 2.5
Political institutions in segmented states worldwide, 1901–2000

	Terminal-year total[a]	Internal segment-states	Ambiguous status	External segment-states
Institutions within segment-state				
Indigenous legislative and executive authorities	226	121	14	91
Indigenous legislative, centrally appointed authorities	65	6	12	47
Centrally appointed legislative and executive authorities	74	10	13	51
Other	3	3	—	—
Legislative representation in common-state				
No legislative representation	202	19	21	162
Legislative representation, *including*:	163	118	18	27
Equal democratic representation	*76*	*66*	*6*	*4*
Inferior democratic representation	*15*	*1*	*1*	*13*
Formalistic nondemocratic representation	*72*	*51*	*11*	*10*
Other	3	3		
Total	368	140	39	189

[a] Terminal year refers to the final year before dissolution of the segment-state or to January 1, 2000 (for segment-states still present at the end of the century).

and a presidium and secretariat formally elected by the central committee.[92] The Soviet policy of indigenization (*korenizatsiia*) drew national cadres into the political and administrative posts of the Communist Party and Soviet state within their respective homelands.[93] In 1990, following Mikhail Gorbachev's call for contested elections and with the expanded autonomy of union republic leaders to decide how to respond to this call, in some union republics local populations were empowered to select leadership and to redesign their institutions, but in other union republics local elites took advantage of the new autonomy to close ranks against democratization and to redraw institutions according to their own designs.[94] Soon their institutions began to diverge.

Since 1991, the seven soviet successor states that are segmented states have fallen into three broad constitutional patterns that are defined by (1)

[92] Unger 1981; Roeder 1988, 171–232.
[93] Stalin 1920, 370–71.
[94] Roeder 2001.

the extent to which the common-state has democratized and (2) the extent to which the segment-states have been empowered by the constitution to design their own political institutions and select their own political leadership. The decentralized semidemocratic regimes (Moldova and Russia until 2005) give the segment-states extensive powers to select their own legislative and executive leadership (see table 2.4). In the Russian Federation until the late 1990s the republics also exercised extensive decision rights in the design of their own political institutions. In Moldova the design of the political institutions of Gagauz Yeri is a matter of Moldovan rather than Gagauz law.

The centralized semidemocratic states (Georgia, Ukraine, and Russia since 2005) have not only severely limited opportunities for segment-states to design their own political institutions, they have also given the common-state government the final say in the selection of segment-state leaders. In Georgia's current constitution the structure, election, and powers of any officials in Abkhazia and Ajaria are unspecified, but it is clear that the segment-state officials will be accountable to common-state officials (Article 73). In Ukraine's 1996 constitution, the Autonomous Republic of Crimea enjoys almost no discretion in the design of its governing institutions, which are specified in the Ukrainian constitution, and only limited discretion in electing its leadership (Article 135).[95] Although the Crimean legislature (*Verkhovna Rada*) selects and dismisses the head of its Cabinet of Ministers, this is subject to a veto by the Ukrainian president.[96] Russia joined the centralized successor states in 2005 with the introduction of presidential appointment of segment-state leaders, the threat of dissolution of any segment-state legislature that fails to confirm the president's nominee, and expanded presidential authority to remove those leaders that lose the president's trust.[97]

The authoritarian states (Azerbaijan, Tajikistan, and Uzbekistan) retain tight central control not only over the design of governing institutions but also over the selection of leadership in all parts of the common-state. Azerbaijan's 1995 constitution recognizes the Nakhichevan Republic as an autonomous state, possessing its own constitution, legislature (*Ali Mejlis*),

---

[95] All references are to the Constitution of Ukraine (adopted June 28, 1996) in Blaustein and Flanz 2006.

[96] In oblasts, by contrast, the president appoints and removes the heads of local state administrations upon the submission of the Ukrainian cabinet, although the popularly elected oblast councils can express no confidence by two-thirds vote.

[97] Federal'nyi zakon "O vnesenii izmenenii v Federal'nyi zakon 'Ob obshchikh printsipakh organizatsii zakonodatel'nykh (predstavitel'nykh) i ispolnitel'nykh organov gosudarstvennoi vlasti sub"ektov Rossiiskoi Federatsii' i Federal'nyi zakon 'Ob osnovnykh garantiiakh izbiratel'nykh prav i prava na uchastie v referendume grazhdan Rossiiskoi Federatsii" December 11, 2004, No. 159; available online at document.kremlin.ru.

and cabinet of ministers, yet Nakhichevan's institutions are specified in the common-state constitution, its constitution must be confirmed by the common-state government (Articles 134–140), and key executive appointments (prime minister and local executives) are made only with the concurrence of the common-state president (Articles 140–141). In Tajikistan's 1994 constitution the highly centralized, uniform constitutional structure that makes local authorities accountable to the president of Tajikistan is extended without modification to the Gorno-Badakhshan Autonomous Oblast (Articles 78 and 80). Uzbekistan's constitution formally grants Karakalpakstan extensive autonomy in creating and staffing its local institutions (Articles 93, 107, and 109), but constitutional prescriptions (Articles 71 and 73) and the reality of autocracy limit local discretion.[98]

Participation in the Common-State

The constitutions of segmented states also vary in the extent to which they permit segment-states to participate in the governance of the common state. Most important, this concerns whether the population of a segment-state is granted full citizenship rights in the common-state. Second, this concerns whether any segment-state government is guaranteed representation in the organs of the common-state government. Exclusion from full citizenship in the common-state often becomes a major grievance pressed by segment-state leaders seeking independence from the common-state. Coöptation of segment-state leaders into common-state organs gives these leaders privileged access over other spokespersons from the periphery. And this coöptation also gives segment-state leaders greater opportunity to weaken the common-state in its negotiations with segment-states.

Slightly less than half (163) of the segment-states that existed in the twentieth century enjoyed some form of elected representation in the common-state legislature in the terminal year.[99] This constitutes one of the major distinctions between internal and external segment-states. While 84 percent of the internal segment-states had representation in the common-state legislature, only 14 percent of the external segment-states had such representation. This representation may guarantee equal representation to all members of the common-state, whether members of a segment-state or not. For example, nonfederal states that maintain special autonomous segment-states, such as Italy's Val d'Aosta, Spain's Basque Country, and

---

[98] See Hanks 2000; Fane 1996, 280; Ismail Zhalilov, "Aral'skoe more umiraet," *Nezavisimaia gazeta* August 10, 1994, 3.

[99] Information on political institutions from all annual editions of the *Statesman's Yearbook* 1897–2001, *Europa World Yearbook* 1959–2001, and individual country studies in the Library of Congress's Country Study (previously the Department of the Army's Area Handbook) series.

the United Kingdom's Scotland, typically maintain a seamless citizenship that grants equal representation of the entire population in the common-state parliament, whether one resides inside or outside the segment-states. In a more complicated formula this representation may guarantee both equality among the segment-states and equality among citizens of the common-state. Ethnofederal states are more likely to maintain this more complex form of representation in which all citizens are equally represented in a lower chamber but are represented as members of a segment-state in an upper chamber. For example, seats in India's House of the People (*Lok Sabha*) are apportioned by population, but seats in its Council of States (*Rajya Sabha*) are filled by the state legislatures, with equal representation allotted to each state. Alternatively, some segment-states have had inferior citizenship rights in the common-state. For example, France has granted its overseas territories the right to elect representatives to the National Assembly, but the ratio of population to deputies is much lower in the metropolitan core. The United States grants residents of Puerto Rico citizenship but no vote for the president unless they migrate to the "mainland," and only a delegate in the lower chamber of Congress, who can vote in committees but not on the floor of the House of Representatives.

Coöptation of segment-state officials into the decision making of the common-state has been provided through a diverse set of institutional arrangements, but these take three broad forms. Most frequently, coöptation involves some form of formal representation within the executive organs of the government of the common-state. For example, the Netherlands provides that its colonies, which are not represented in the States-General, may participate in cabinet sessions (in the cabinet's role as the cabinet of the Kingdom of the Netherlands) when these address issues related to the colonies. Inclusion in cabinets may involve appointment of one minister within the cabinet to speak on issues sensitive to the community, such as the United Kingdom secretary of state for Scotland. Second, in the legislative branch coöptation may bring leaders of the segment-states or their representatives into an upper chamber, such as India's Council of States (*Rajya Sabha*). Third, coöptation into the decision making of the common-state but not its organs may take the form of requiring concurrent majorities between the common-state and segment-state governments for some decisions on common-state policy.

The Soviet ethnofederation combined seamless representation of all Soviet citizens in some common-state organs and segmental representation of each recognized segment-state population in other common-state organs. The latter directly coöpted segment-state leaders into the common-state organs.[100] The 1936 constitution established this formula and the 1977

---

[100] For details on coöptation from 1924 to 1936, see Towster 1948, 210, 284.

constitution reaffirmed it, but the direct representation of the citizenry remained formalistic until Mikhail Gorbachev began to democratize Soviet politics in the latter half of the 1980s. The bicameral Supreme Soviet included a lower chamber (Soviet of the Union) based on a seamless citizenship—deputies were formally elected from single-member districts based on equal population (in uncontested elections). Alternatively, seats in the upper chamber of the Supreme Soviet, the Soviet of Nationalities, were formally elected in single-member districts, but were apportioned among segment-states not according to population but according to a formula of twenty-five (later, thirty-three) deputies per union republic, eleven per autonomous republic, five per autonomous oblast, and one per national okrug.[101] Initially these were mechanisms to coöpt officials from the segment-states, but with time they lost their coöptational quality and became formalistic representation of the "working people" of each union republic.[102] Coöptation of the leaders of the segment-states into the executive-administrative organs of the Soviet common-state expanded with time, so that union republic officials sat on an ex officio basis on the collective presidency (Presidium of the Supreme Soviet), the collective executive (Presidium of the Council of Ministers), and the Supreme Court. Moreover, representatives from the corresponding union republic agencies sat within such all-union ministries as education and culture and such all-union state committees as the State Planning Committee (*Gosplan*) and State Construction Committee (*Gosstroi*).[103]

Most importantly, coöptation extended to the all-union organs of the Communist Party of the Soviet Union (CPSU). The CPSU organized its national congresses from delegations sent by the union republic, autonomous republic, and oblast party organizations, and these delegations included significant numbers of union republic and autonomous republic leaders. For example, in the Central Committee elected at the 1986 CPSU Congress, 38 percent of all delegates were officials of party or state organs of a union republic, autonomous republic, or oblast, and, with nearly mathematical precision to reflect the census, about half (49 percent) of these were from one of the non-Russian homelands. The CPSU Politburo itself routinely included the first secretary of the Ukrainian party organization as a full member beginning in the early 1960s and coöpted first secretaries from the Kazakh, Uzbek, and Belorussian party organizations as voting and nonvoting members at different times after that.[104]

---

[101] Feldbrugge 1979; Unger 1981.
[102] Hough and Fainsod 1979, 364.
[103] Ponomarev et al. 1982, 232–33.
[104] Laird 1986; Löwenhardt 1982; Löwenhardt, Ozinga, and van Ree 1992; *Konstitutsiia (osnovnoi zakon) Soiuza Sovetskikh Sotsialisticheskikh Respublik, Konstitutsii (osnovnye zakony) soiuznykh sovetskikh sotsialisticheskikh respublik* 1978; Feldbrugge 1979.

Since the breakup of the USSR, all seven successor states with segmental institutions maintain seamless representation of segment-state populations in at least one chamber of the legislature. All the segment-states have had the right of legislative initiative in the common-state legislature. Only Russia and Tajikistan maintain a second legislative chamber for regional representation (see table 2.4). Georgia in its constitution (Article 4) has promised an upper chamber once its segment-states return to Georgia (also see Articles 55 and 57). Concerning coöptation of segment-state leaders into the common-state, the successor states divide among three patterns of semidemocracies with coöptation, semidemocracies without coöptation, and autocracies. Among the semidemocracies, only Moldova and Russia have coöpted segment-state leaders into common-state organs. In Moldova, according to an organic law of December 1994, Gagauzia's elected leader (*bashkan*) should participate ex officio in the Moldovan government. In the Russian Federation from December 1993 until 2000 the executive and legislative leader of each segment-state sat ex officio in the upper legislative chamber—the Council of the Federation—alongside the leaders of the other subjects of the federation that were not segment-states. This was changed by law in 2000: the council now includes representatives of both branches of each subject. A new State Council now coöpts the chief executives of each subject into a consultative body in the executive branch under the chairmanship of the Russian president.[105] Georgia's and Ukraine's constitutions provide for no coöptation. Among the autocratic successor states, the constitutions of Tajikistan (Articles 53 and 89) and Uzbekistan (Articles 84 and 108) provide for extensive coöptation of segment-state leaders into common-state organs. Of course, these leaders have been appointed by the center. Alternatively, Azerbaijan has no constitutional provision for such coöptation.

Allocation of Policy-Making Powers

Beyond these constitutional rights, segmental constitutions vary in the ways they allocate decision-making rights to make policy.[106] These policy-making powers are important to the politics of the segmented state because

---

[105] Federal'nyi zakon "O poriadke formirovaniia Soveta Federatsii Federal'nogo Sobraniia Rossiiskoi Federatsii," *Rossiiskaia gazeta* August 8, 2000, 1; Ukaz Prezidenta Rossiiskoi Federatsii "O Gosudarstvennom sovete Rossiiskoi Federatsii," *Sobranie Zakonodatel'stva Rossiiskoi Federatsii* No. 36, Article 3633 (September 4, 2000), 7186–89.

[106] William Riker (1975, 102, 108) and Claire Palley (1979) have put forward very clear distinctions concerning the proportion of policy realms allocated to common-state and segment-state governments and whether this involves lawmaking, regulation making within laws, or administrative discretion in the implementation of laws or regulations. Also see Philipson 1992; Coakley 1992, 346–51; Hannum 1990, 458–68; McRae 1975, 44; Nordlinger 1972, 30–41; Rothschild 1981, 155–67; Stanovcic 1992; and Van Dyke 1974.

they can be forged into institutional weapons that common-state and segment-state governments use to coerce one another. Segmented states can lead to a less than clear delineation of decision rights, and this very murkiness of jurisdictions may be one of the most important initial sources of conflict in segmented states. For example, in defining the decision-making rights of its governments, the USSR Constitution divided decision-making rights among powers reserved to the common-state government, powers reserved to the segment-states (particularly, the union republics), and a broad intermediate realm of concurrent powers. Few decision-making rights fell within the exclusive prerogative of the common-state (or all-union) government, but according to the 1977 constitution, these did include decisions concerning the armed forces, war and peace, the Procuracy (public prosecutor's office), and the admission of new members to the union (Articles 73, 108, 121, and 164–168).[107] Still fewer decision rights fell within the exclusive jurisdiction of the union republic governments; indeed, the sole decision rights assigned exclusively to the union republics were the right to establish a second state language for the union republic and the right to secede (Article 72). In the Gorbachev era even these latter decision rights turned out to be subjects of concurrent jurisdiction, since all-union legislation required that the state language of the USSR, Russian, remain at least one of the state languages of each union republic and that a union republic decision to secede had to be ratified by the USSR.[108] Indeed, most decision-making rights in the Soviet segmented state were exercised concurrently.[109] Once the USSR began to democratize, these concurrent powers quickly became the first battlegrounds between common-state and segment-state governments.

The constitutions of the successor states that emerged within the union republics of the USSR limit the policy-making powers of their own segment-states. In particular, they limit concurrent powers that could become sources of coercion by a segment-state against the common-state government. The constitutions of Georgia, Moldova, and Tajikistan guarantee no policy-making realms to the segment-state governments and make these matters for subsequent legislation—a delegation of powers from the common-state government. The constitutions of Azerbaijan, Russia, Ukraine, and Uzbekistan are careful to limit the powers of segment-states (see the

---

[107] Feldbrugge 1979; Unger 1981.

[108] Zakon Soiuza Sovetskikh Sotsialisticheskikh Respublik "O poriadke resheniia voprosov, sviazannykh s vykhodom soiuznoi respubliki iz SSSR," *Pravda* April 7, 1990, 2; Zakon Soiuza Sovetskikh Sotsialisticheskikh Respublik "O iazykakh narodov SSSR," *Izvestiia* May 4, 1990, 1–2.

[109] These concurrent powers fell into four distinct patterns: concurrent powers with common-state preemption, segment-state decision making under common-state guidance, decentralized implementation, and concurrent decision making with mutual vetoes. See Ponomarev et al. 1982, 214–25.

constitutions of Azerbaijan, Articles 138–139; Ukraine, Articles 92, 118, 134, and 137; and Uzbekistan, Article 123), to establish the supremacy of common-state law and regulations (see the constitutions of Azerbaijan, Article 148; Russia, Articles 72, 76, and 77; Ukraine, Articles 138 and 139; and Uzbekistan, Articles 72 and 109), and to provide mechanisms for the common-state government to suspend executive and legislative actions by the segment-states (see the constitutions of Azerbaijan, Article 109; Russia, Articles 85 and 125; Ukraine, Articles 85, 106, 137, 144, and 150; and Uzbekistan, Articles 123, 109, 110, and 119).

PART TWO

PROCESSES: FORGING POLITICAL-IDENTITY HEGEMONIES

THREE

Hegemonies and Segment-State Machines

BEFORE INDEPENDENCE, each nation-state project proclaims the right of a nation to sovereign statehood. After independence, the usual historical narrative about successful nation-state projects begins with the formation of nations and ends in the achievement of statehood. Yet the causal chain implied in both projects and narratives confronts us with a paradox: a population is unlikely to become a nation with widespread consensus on its right to statehood until after the achievement of statehood. Before statehood, nations typically exist only in the minds of small circles of intellectuals and political activists, who often find themselves battling one another over competing visions of the future. The public at large is likely to be indifferent to the choice between the elite's projects and the status quo.

How do proponents of nation-state projects overcome this paradox of nation formation? The segmental institutions thesis argues that in most instances, the distinguishing attribute of a successful nation-state project is the presence of a segment-state that privileges its proponents and their project so that they can establish political-identity hegemony. On one hand, the proponents use the institutions of the segment-state to establish their own political hegemony within the "homeland" defined by the segment-state. On the other hand, the proponents use the segment-state to establish the hegemony of an official identity that defines "the nation" of the segment-state.

Without segment-states, proponents of nation-state projects are typically challenged by competing claims to some or all of the same people and territory. They are weakened by commanding few organizational resources to propagate their projects. And so proponents without segment-states seldom create more than parlor-nations—isolated circles of intellectuals who, despite the fervor with which they discuss their imagined communities among themselves, never fire many other imaginations. A few proponents garner a following beyond a parlor or two but still have little prospect for success, because they lack organizational resources to expand their nation and to press forward against the existing state. For example, in the United States in early 2004, more than a dozen shadowy movements for independence sought to create new nation-states, including Acadia (Francophone New Englanders), Alaska, Atzlán (Chicanos), California, the Confederacy, Dinétah (Navajos), Guam, Haudenosaunee (Iroquois),

Jefferson (Northern Californians), Puerto Rico, Texas, Vermont, and the Virgin Islands.[1] Few proponents of projects such as these command sufficient support and resources to provoke a nation-state crisis, let alone achieve sovereign independence.

The three chapters that constitute part 2 present an explanation for the emergence of *political-identity hegemony*, which consists of both the relative predominance of a national identity within "the people" and the relative empowerment of a cohort of politicians associated with that project within "the homeland." As *identity* hegemony, borrowing David Laitin's reformulation of Antonio Gramsci's concept, this means the institutionalization of "a dominant symbolic framework."[2] As *political* hegemony, it means the predominance of a cohort of politicians associated with this framework. This cohort controls access to political office within the territory they claim as their state to such an extent that they can bar from office politicians who would advance alternative nation-state projects. Political-identity hegemony does not require that the "dominant symbolic framework" has achieved the status of "common sense" among the public at large; a successful nation-state project does not require deep or broad nationalism. Nor does it require an extensive capacity to mobilize nationalist collective action. It does require that no other ethnopolitician is able to match or trump this project by mobilizing more members of the elite and public on behalf of an alternative national claim, particularly the nation-state project to preserve the common-state whole. For example, the late Soviet experience showed that union republic leaders could successfully press a nation-state project in at least three different configurations of national identities: first, where most of the population gave precedence to their segment-state identity over their common-state national identity (Georgia); second, where most of the population did not give precedence to either national identity (Ukraine); or third, where most of the population supported the common-state (Belarus and Russia). Only the first of these is the pattern identified by the usual stories of national awakening and nationalist mobilization. In the late Soviet experience, union republic leaders could successfully press a nation-state project even where they did not have the capacity to mobilize extensive nationalist protest on its behalf, as long as their political-identity hegemony empowered them to suppress mobilization on behalf of alternative nation-state projects such as the USSR.

According to the segmental institutions thesis, the leaders of segment-states are often in a unique position to establish political-identity hegemony. Concerning *identity* hegemony, the segmental institutions thesis does

---

[1] Many of these maintain active, if constantly shifting, web sites on the Internet that can be found by search engines. Also see Minahan 1996, 2002.

[2] Laitin 1986, 19.

not claim that existence of a segment-state foreordains success in focusing a national identity within the "titular" population of the segment-state but that prior to independence, a segment-state affords a much greater likelihood of success than attempts to focus national identity without a segment-state. The segment-state becomes the natural focal point for coordination of expectations about the most likely alternative to the existing common-state. Segment-states privilege one nation-state project with leadership that controls unparalleled organizational resources to propagate their imagined community. With these resources the leaders of the segment-state can make more credible claims about the likelihood of success of their project. They can offer immediate rewards to their followers, increase the obstacles in the path to success for alternative nation-state projects, and deprive opponents of much of the freedom needed to propagate their alternative projects. Concerning *political* hegemony, the segmental institutions thesis underscores that the very resources that permit segment-state leaders to privilege their nation-state project also empower them to establish their own hegemony within the territory of the segment-state. These leaders can anathematize their opponents, particularly opponents pressing alternative nation-state projects, as "enemies of the nation." They can offer rewards and threaten punishments to induce elites and publics to make more costly commitments to their rule. And they can place obstacles in the path of all political opposition. Segment-state leaders not only privilege a single nation-state project, they typically privilege their own role within the emerging nation-state.

The prevalence of political hegemonies within segment-states and their close association with identity hegemony have been observed around the world. For example, in the run-up to independence, political hegemony has emerged within many colonies as indigenous leaders came to define their political party and independence movement as the embodiment of the nation and their political monopoly as the only effective defense against enemies of the nation. As a government official from Dahomey on the eve of independence explained, "the evil of the party system"—by which he meant a competitive-party system—is "division which undermines our fighting forces and plays into the hands of the enemies, who, to perpetuate our subjection, dream only of hammering any attempt we make to achieve unity."[3] As Ruth Schachter Morgenthau observes, during the last years of segment-states "many Africans justified the existence of single-party states on grounds that a national emergency exists." The struggle to achieve the goals of their nation-state projects led segment-state leaders to brand politicians with alternative nation-state projects as quislings.[4] Around the

[3] von der Mehden 1964, 66.
[4] Morgenthau 1964, 354. Also see Kaviraj 2001, 313–14.

world, fully two-thirds or eighteen of the twenty-seven segment-states that gained independence in the explosion that began in 1960 began independence as single-party states.[5] Throughout the twentieth century more than two-thirds of the segment-states that became nation-states began independence as nondemocracies.[6]

Political-identity hegemony can coexist with competitive politics, but it is competition within a dominant cohort attached to a similar nation-state project; the cohort limits competition from outside the cohort so as to maintain the cohort's hegemony vis-à-vis politicians advancing alternative nation-state projects. In Estonia, for example, the politicians who advanced the nation-state project for an independent Estonia in 1990 competed among themselves over such issues as economic reform. Nevertheless, this cohort of Estonians established the hegemony of one national identity over competing national identities that might have kept Estonia within the USSR. This cohort also established its own hegemony over the ethnic Russians elites who backed the Joint Council of Labor Collectives and the *Interdvizhenie* movement to save the Estonian SSR; with independence, the dominant Estonian cohort stripped citizenship from many of the elites who had advanced these alternative nation-state projects.[7]

The three chapters that constitute part 2 of this book introduce the foundations of a larger theory of national identity formation to set the stage for addressing the following question: Which nation-state projects and which proponents are likely to emerge hegemonic prior to independence? These chapters about "bargaining on the periphery," however, are only the first part of the larger puzzle that explains which nation-state projects achieve sovereign independence. The present chapter begins with a summary of the chief causal claims that are elaborated and illustrated in the remainder of part 2. This chapter goes on to examine political hegemony in segment-states, arguing that segment-states create a nurturing environment for nationalist machines to emerge before independence. This relationship is illustrated with descriptions of the variety of political machines that developed within most of the segment-states of the USSR and the Russian Federation. Chapter 4 extends this discussion to the problem of creating identity hegemony, particularly the problem of focusing a national identity that is an alternative to an existing common-state. It argues that segment-state nationalist machines play a powerful role in this process. Although

[5] von der Mehden 1964. Also see Morgenthau 1964, 330–58; Coleman and Rosberg 1964, 3–4.

[6] This conclusion is based on ninety-five segment-states that became independent nation-states from 1901 to 2000, omitting the microstates. Using the Polity 4 data set, democracies are those countries with a Polity score of 6 or higher. See Marshall and Jaggers 2000.

[7] Kionka 1991; Dunlop 1993–94; Andrus Park 1994; Taagepera 1993; Vetik 1993; Hallik 1996.

these two chapters address each half of political-identity hegemony separately, both chapters stress the frequent fusion of both halves in a local hegemony that can threaten an existing common-state. Chapter 5 explores variation among segment-states and elaborates on the primary constraints that increase or decrease the likelihood that political-identity hegemony will emerge within a segment-state. The segmental institutions thesis stresses variations among segmental political institutions as primary constraints on the emergence of political-identity hegemony in segment-states. The traditional explanations for the rise of nationalism typically focus on cultural and economic constraints, but in the segmental institutions thesis these become important only in the context of politicians empowered by segmental institutions, which use the cultural and economic opportunities created by segmental institutions to privilege their nation-state projects and their own role within these projects.

The method of these three chapters is exploratory and the purpose is to generate hypotheses to be tested in statistical models that employ a large number of cases from around the world in part 4 of this book. Nevertheless, in these three chapters there are preliminary tests that look closely at cases from Eurasia. The comparisons of cases in these three chapters juxtapose the Russian Empire, the USSR, and the post-Soviet Russian Federation and seek to identify variation not only among but within each of these. This close-up examination of cases permits more careful tracing of the processes that lead from cause to effect and illustrates how political-identity hegemony is actually constructed within segment-states.

Constraints on Political-Identity Hegemony

The segmental institutions thesis stresses how much the presence of segment-states and the institutional arrangements that structure political life within the segment-states constrain the emergence of political-identity hegemony within them. The Eurasian experience suggests six propositions that explain when political-identity hegemony is likely to emerge. First, without a segment-state, a nation-state project is far less likely to achieve political-identity hegemony prior to independence. Nation-state projects associated with segment-states and proponents who lead segment-states enjoy unparalleled advantages over other projects and proponents in becoming hegemonic. Chapter 4 underscores this with the contrast between the pre-Soviet period, when segment-states and political-identity hegemonies were few, and the Soviet and post-Soviet periods, when they were seemingly ubiquitous.

Second, the regime of the common-state government constrains the development of political-identity hegemony. An autocratic common-state may have contradictory consequences. Segmented autocracies may enforce local hegemonies within each segment-state but are likely to limit the growth of this so that political identity hegemony is less likely to threaten the common-state. Democratic common-states typically lead to greater variation among segment-states: democratic common-states are less likely to guarantee local hegemonies in each segment-state, and so some segment-states may fail to develop political-identity hegemony. Yet the relaxation of autocratic control in a common-state also makes possible the development of political-identity hegemonies in segment-states that can challenge the common-state. In chapter 4 this second proposition is illustrated by the contrast between the union republics of the USSR prior to *perestroika*, on one hand, and the union republics after *perestroika* and the republics of the Russian Federation after the dissolution of the USSR, on the other.

Third, within both autocratic and democratic common-states, disunity in the common-state leadership expands the opportunities for segment-state leaders to use their decision rights to establish political-identity hegemony. In chapter 5 this relationship is underscored by two comparisons. The first is the contrast in the autonomy of Soviet-era union republic leaders during periods of succession crises and consolidated autocracy. When the USSR leadership was divided in a succession struggle, union republic leaders enjoyed greater autonomy than when the USSR leadership was dominated by an autocrat. The second comparison is between the autonomy of republics within the Russian Federation during the contested leadership of Boris Yeltsin prior to October 1993 and during the consolidated leadership of Vladimir Putin after 1999. During Yeltsin's struggles with the USSR leadership and then the Russian Congress of People's Deputies, republic leaders grabbed more decision rights than they could handle. Putin took back many of these decision rights.

Fourth, the more extensive the decision rights assigned to segment-state leaders, the greater the opportunities for them to establish political-identity hegemony. The pre-*perestroika* Soviet experience examined in chapters 3 and 4 illustrates that it takes only limited autonomy to begin establishing political and identity hegemony within segment-states. Yet with expansion of the segment-states' decision rights within the USSR under *perestroika* and within the post-Soviet Russian Federation—in particular, expansion of decision rights in the areas of designing political institutions, conducting elections, making appointments, and deploying mobilizational resources—came additional opportunities for the leaders of segment-states to establish political-identity hegemony. The importance of expanding decision rights to the establishment of political-identity hegemony is also underscored by the contrast between republics within the Russian Federation that had existed as autonomous republics in the Soviet period and those that were elevated to republic status only during the breakup of the USSR. Segment-state leaders in these newest republics, which had previously exercised significantly fewer decision rights, were far less likely to establish political-identity hegemony.

Other constraints such as demographic patterns and economic endowments within the segment-states affect the ability of segment-state leaders to establish political-identity hegemony, but only to make hegemony somewhat harder to establish, rather than posing absolute barriers to hegemony. Thus, a fifth proposition: Although it is harder to establish hegemony within a segment-state when the titular population constitutes only a minority of the population, extensive segment-state autonomy can nonetheless be used by segment-state leaders to establish political-identity hegemony. In chapter 5, comparisons among the republics within the Russian Federation underscore that even without a titular plurality in the population, segment-state institutions can empower titular leaders to establish political-identity hegemony. Sixth, the likelihood that political-identity hegemony will emerge depends less on the extent of resources within the region such as the availability of "lootable resources" and more on the extent to which available resources—even meager resources—are monopolized by the segment-state leaders.[8]

Illustration: The Tatarstan Machine

In the Russian Federation the strongest political-identity hegemony emerged in the Republic of Tatarstan under the leadership of Mintimer Shaimiev. The republic is located in the mid-Volga region, about 450 miles east of Moscow. It is the homeland of the Tatars, a people who traditionally spoke a Turkic language and adhered to Sunni Islam. Yet after 440 years within the Russian Empire and the USSR, the republic came to have a diverse population in which Tatars constituted 48.5 percent in 1989 and Russians constituted 43.3 percent. Shaimiev was born in 1932 in a village of what was then styled as the Tatar Autonomous Soviet Socialist Republic (ASSR), and he rose through the ranks of the republic's Communist Party organization and governmental administration in a typical Soviet career pattern. He completed his education as an engineer-mechanic at the agricultural institute in the republic's capital, Kazan. Eight years later, at the age of thirty, Shaimiev began his career in the Communist Party of the republic as an "instructor" (providing party guidance to subordinate organizations), but within two years he had become the republic's minister of land reclamation and water resources. In the 1980s he advanced rapidly to

[8] Fearon and van Houten 1998.

become first deputy chair of the Tatar ASSR council of ministers (1983), secretary of the party committee (*obkom*) for the republic (1983–1985), chairman of the republic's council of ministers (1985–1989), and first secretary of the obkom committee (1989–1990). As Russia democratized and the Communist Party disintegrated, the Tatarstan leadership elected Shaimiev to become chairman of the Supreme Soviet of the republic (1990–1991)—the de facto president of the republic. As Yeltsin began to consolidate his control in Moscow with his election as Russia's president, Tatarstan introduced its own presidency, and Shaimiev won the new post in an uncontested election in June 1991.[9] This set a pattern for Shaimiev's continuing dominance over politics. Prior to the March 1996 presidential elections, the Shaimiev machine intimidated or arrested all of the president's potential opponents, so that against no opposition and with 78 percent turnout, Shaimiev won 97.2 percent of the votes.[10] In his third presidential election, in March 2001, Shaimiev faced his first opponents. After vetting, four opponents were permitted to run. Shaimiev garnered 79.5 percent of the vote, outdistancing his closest competitor by 73 percentage points.[11]

Once in office, Shaimiev cultivated an indigenous Tatar machine and used it to consolidate his personal control over the republic's political life. In Kazan, Shaimiev cultivated a loyal republic leadership comprising subordinates who had served him in the Soviet period. At the time of his showdown with Yeltsin over the new constitutional order, in 1993, half of Shaimiev's cabinet was made up of holdovers from his 1988 council of ministers and another 36 percent had been local party or administration officials working under Shaimiev in 1988 or 1989. This continued to be true three and a half years later, when he appointed a cabinet for his second term following his overwhelming victory in the March 1996 presidential elections. Outside Kazan, Shaimiev extended his control throughout the republic by appointing the head of administration in each district (raion) and by relying on his trusted associates from the old party-state structures to fill these posts (figure 3.1). More than two-fifths of the raion heads in October 1993 had been district (raikom) party secretaries in 1988, and another fifth or more had been members of the district executive committee (raispolkom) or chairmen of the district council (raisovet) in 1988. Once in place, these raion heads of administration then established their control over local governments; in the late 1990s, more than half of the heads of administration served simultaneously as chairmen of the raion soviets, fusing executive and legislative leadership. Moreover, this was an ethnic ma-

[9] Kosov et al. 1993.

[10] Sh. Maratov, "Doverie naroda: M. Sh. Shaimiev izbran prezidentom Tatarstana na vtoroi srok," *Respublika Tatarstan* March 26, 1996, 1.

[11] *RFE/RL Newsline* February 21 and March 26, 2001.

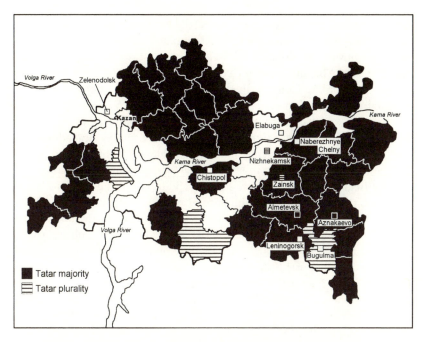

Figure 3.1 Tatarstan: cities and raions 1993. *Sources:* Based on data
in Mustafin and Kuzeev 1994.

chine: more than four-fifths of the cabinet members and raion heads in
1993 were Tatars, almost twice the proportion of Tatars in the adult population of the republic.[12] Six years later, 84 percent of the raion heads of
administration (all appointed by the president) were Tatars.[13]

This control over the administrative structure of the republic ensured
that the Shaimiev machine could control the republic's parliament (State
Council) through elections.[14] Legislative malapportionment was extreme so
that in the 1999 State Council elections the largest district had more than
a hundred times as many voters as the smallest. Malapportionment of seats
overrepresented rural constituents, and this in turn overrepresented Tatar
constituents. For example, in 1995, although people living in cities of more
than 25,000 population constituted 69 percent of Tatarstan's population,
they elected only half the deputies to the State Council. Although Tatars
constituted 49 percent of the population and Russians 43 percent, the Shaimiev machine allocated seats so that Tatars constituted a plurality in about
60 percent of the districts.[15] (Indeed, to leave little to chance, in 1990 and

[12] Mustafin and Khuzeev 1994; Kosov et al. 1993; interviews in Tatarstan.
[13] Zaznaev 2000, 215.
[14] Löwenhardt 1997; Löwenhardt and Verheul 2000.
[15] Russian Federation TsIK 1998; Mustafin and Khuzeev 1994.

1991 Tatarstan created four new, unusually small raions in Tatar-majority regions and gave each raion a territorial-administrative seat in the republic's Supreme Soviet.) Control of local electoral processes by raion heads ensured that the Shaimiev machine could secure election of its preferred candidates to the State Council. In the March 5, 1995, elections to the State Council, city and raion administrative heads themselves won forty-two of the forty-nine seats in territorial-administrative constituencies filled in the first round.[16] In the final count of the 130 elected deputies local administrators held fifty-two seats, members of the president's central administration held another eight, and members of legal agencies under the president's control held three more seats.[17] That is, about half of the legislators were executive or judicial officials appointed by the president. In the 1995–99 State Council, 42.3 percent of deputies worked in the executive branch; in the 1999–2003 State Council this figure rose to 50 percent. Political parties played virtually no role within the State Council: In the 1995–99 State Council, only five of 130 deputies had run with a party label—one each from the Tatar National Party *Ittifak* and the Equality and Law bloc and three from the Communist Party. The machine favored Tatars: according to Oleg Zaznaev, in the 1995–99 State Council, Tatars held 73 percent of the seats, and in the 1999–2003 State Council they held 75 percent.[18]

The Shaimiev machine carefully orchestrated the tools available to it to provide material incentives to its supporters and the public, to shape public opinion, and to intimidate or block opponents. The Tatarstan government controlled much of the countryside through the agro-industrial complex, owned significant segments of the republic's industrial economy, and maintained a welfare safety net, including subsidized food prices and food stamps. The administration's monopoly of local broadcasting, printing, and schooling provided it the instruments to cultivate an official nationalism based on the idealization of the Tatar motherland, loyalty to the republic and its government, and a small-scale cult of personality surrounding the president himself. Katherine Graney documents how the Shaimiev administration took control of the branch of the Russian Academy of Sciences in Kazan, expanded or created institutes within it to compose an official history and culture for the republic, and assigned its scholars the task of writing textbooks for an expanded curriculum of Tatar and Tatarstan studies in all grades. The expansion of the official historical and cultural apparatus was a boon for Tatar intellectuals, who found new lucrative and prestigious positions open to them if they were simply willing to sign on to the

[16] *OMRI Daily Digest* March 10, 1995.
[17] Russian Federation TsIK 1998.
[18] Russian Federation TsIK 1998; Zaznaev 2001, 3, 17.

president's nation-state project.[19] As Graney notes, the textbooks purveyed the message that Tatarstan is the "homeland to a multinational people known as 'Tatarstanis,'" but the ethnic "Tatars are . . . the ancient, indigenous, rightful owners of Tatarstan."[20] The Shaimiev administration did not claim that Tatars and Tatarstanis are not also Russians (*rossiiane*) but sought to assign to itself the authority to define the realms in which each identity was relevant and to control the mobilization of each into the public life of the republic.

Establishing the hegemony of its Tatarstan project and its own leadership within Tatarstan required that the Shaimiev machine domesticate those parts of the Tatar nationalist movement that emerged in competition and isolate those nationalists whom it could not coöpt. As moderate nationalists within the Tatar Public Center began to work closely with Shaimiev, more radical elements split in the autumn of 1991 to form *Ittifak* and *Azatlyk*. When the radicals convened a *Kurultai* (Congress of the Tatar People) in February 1992 to claim the mantle of Tatar nationalism and elect a shadow parliament (*Melli Majlis*), Shaimiev responded with his own convocation—but one backed with a massive outpouring of governmental resources.[21] In June 1992 Shaimiev's World Congress of Tatars overshadowed the *Melli Majlis*: More than 1,100 delegates attended the World Congress under the slogan proclaimed by Shaimiev at its opening, "Tatarstan is the cradle of the Tatar nation and its function is to unite the whole Tatar diaspora and so influence the national policy of Russia." The Shaimiev administration called to Kazan hundreds of "activists," whose trips were organized and financed by their employers on orders from the administration; participants received generous transportation allowances and the small enterprises, cooperatives, and foundations supporting the World Congress received tax exemptions and other compensation from the republic to cover their costs.[22]

When the nationalists of the Tatar Public Center began to attack the Tatarstan president, the Shaimiev administration intervened to remove the center's most militant leaders. In June 1993, criminal charges against the center's president Zinnur Agliullin accused him of illegal weapons possession, organization of an assault on a prosecutor's office, and slander against

---

[19] On Tatar historiography in the Soviet period, see Lazzerini 1981, Shnirelman 1996. On expansion of career opportunities, see Gorenburg 1999, 262–63.

[20] Graney 1999, 623.

[21] Leonid Tolchinskii, "Millimedzhlis glavnee parlamenta," *Nezavisimaia gazeta* January 29, 1992, 3; Al'ians Sabirov, "Kurultai provozglashaet nezavisimost' Tatarstana," *Izvestiia* February 3, 1992, 2.

[22] Matsyugina and Perepelkin 1996, 149.

the dignity of the president.[23] Five years later, when the center renewed its nationalist challenges to the president, the Shaimiev administration stepped up its pressure, removing another of the center's radical leaders in January 1998 and securing appointment of Fandas Safiullin, who allegedly would "make the center an instrument for implementing the policies of President Mintimer Shaimiev."[24] This pressure also hit *Ittifak*: on April 21, 1998, the Yar Chally municipal court suspended publication of *Ittifak*'s newspaper, *Altin Urda*, for violating the republic's law concerning the honor and dignity of the republic's president. In the 1999 elections to Tatarstan's State Council the radical nationalists in *Ittifak* won only one seat. The party's leader, Fauziya Bairamova, who lost her race in a Naberezhnye Chelny constituency, complained bitterly that "The Tatar people sold me out for packs of tea which were handed out by certain candidates."[25] Against the enormous advantages of the segment-state's leader it was difficult for other politicians to claim the nationalist mantle or to advance alternative nation-state projects. This was political-identity hegemony.

Segment-States and Nationalist Machines

Half of political-identity hegemony is the dominance of a cohort of politicians over their opposition and segment-states provide nurturing environments for political hegemony in the form of nationalist machines. The means to construct political hegemony and to disadvantage political competitors in segment-states are similar to the means employed by political machines in different jurisdictions around the world. Although the remainder of this chapter focuses on political hegemony, the development of each half of political-identity hegemony fosters the other and segment-states provide a particularly favorable environment for local officials to restrict competition from other identities as well as from other politicians. The autonomy granted the segment-state to foster and protect its distinct population within its homeland gives segment-state leaders access to a store of rewards and punishments to distribute within the segment-state—which they distribute much as any machine. Yet, because the segment-state constitutes simultaneously a homeland and a people with a separate political status, as segment-state leaders find unique opportunities to privilege their nation-state projects, these identity hegemonies facilitate con-

[23] Radik Batyrshin, "Krizis natsional'nogo dvizheniia respubliki," *Nezavisimaia gazeta* June 15, 1993, 3.

[24] *RFE/RL Newsline* June 19, 1998.

[25] Interfax March 10, 1995.

struction of political monopolies in the name of defending the local nation against its enemies.

Opportunities for political hegemony inhere in the allocation of decision rights to segment-states: as the segment-state's decision rights grow, so do the opportunities to construct political hegemony within its borders. Indirect rule, self-government, or indigenization of administration provide resources that can be used to establish hegemony within the segment-state. Advocates for creation or preservation of segment-states and expanded autonomy often wrestle with this problem. Will Kymlicka, in a forthright confrontation with this issue, acknowledges that autonomy often creates space for illiberal enclaves. Consistent with his defense of self-government rights he concludes that the common-state must avoid intervention to establish or restore liberal politics: "In these cases, members of the more liberal majority will have to sit down with the members of the national minority, and find a way of living together. Liberals have no automatic right to impose their views on non-liberal national minorities."[26] Kymlicka identifies the dilemma facing common-state governments: to the extent they allocate decision rights to segment-states they create opportunities for political hegemony, but attempts to break up this hegemony would limit the autonomy of segment-states.

The hypothesis that there is a propensity toward political hegemony within segment-states is supported by the pattern that emerges in a comparison of the republics within the Russian Federation and the other regions within the federation that were not segment-states (oblasts, krais, and federal cities). The republics had much greater autonomy to order their own affairs as homelands of their respective titular populations, and they developed far less democratically after 1990. Nikolai Petrov's study of regional and local elections from 1995 to 2002 in eighty-eight regions of the Russian Federation (excluding only Chechnya) shows that no republics ranked among the ten most democratic regions, and eight republics ranked among the ten least democratic. Indeed, the odds that a republic would rank among the bottom ten were nearly twenty-three times higher than the odds that an oblast, krai, or federal city would rank so low.[27] In the republics—particularly in those controlled by the machines discussed later in this chapter—incumbent executives were much less likely to lose elections. Grigorii Golosov's data on "executive power change by electoral means" shows that in eighteen republics, 27.8 percent of incumbent executives lost office in elections from 1995 to 1998; in the ten machine-controlled republics this figure was only 10 percent. By comparison, in all

---

[26] Kymlicka 1995, 171.

[27] Georgii Il'ichev, "Protsent demokratii: V kakom regione strany svobody bol'she," *Izvestiia* October 15, 2002, 4. Also see Moraski and Reisinger 2003; Moser 2001, 92–94.

TABLE 3.1
Russian Federation: Media freedom in regions, 1999–2000 (regression estimates)

	Coefficient	t-statistic
Republic	−18.32***	(−4.89)
Other segment-state	−14.96***	(−3.21)
Urbanization	0.49***	(4.01)
Disposable income	23.35	(1.80)
Constant	25.07**	(2.95)
Statistics:	$n = 87$	
	$F = 21.47$	
	$R^2 = 0.512$	

Source of media freedom data: *Russian Federation Report*, January 31, 2001.
Note: Media freedom varies from 0 to 100.
Significance: $*p < .05$; $** p < .01$, $*** p < .001$.

other subjects of the federation executives lost office in elections more than half (52.9 percent) of the time.[28]

The republics were much more likely to restrict the press and broadcast media, reflecting the particular importance of the media to creating and maintaining political-identity hegemony. The Glasnost Defense Fund conducted surveys of media freedom in eighty-seven of Russia's regions (Chechnya and Ingushetia were excluded) in autumn 1999 and spring–summer 2000. Its analysts developed an index of media freedom to measure the combined effects of restrictions on the press and broadcast media, such as bureaucratic interference in production and distribution.[29] Even after controlling for the relative size of the urban population and for disposable income in each region, the republics were significantly more likely to restrict freedom of the press. Indeed, if we calibrate the index of media freedom to range from 100 (the highest level, in Moscow City) to 0 (the lowest level, in Karachai-Cherkessia), an otherwise average oblast, krai, or federal city (setting urban population size and disposable income to the respective national means) stood at 45.9, but a republic with identical urbanization and income stood at only 27.7 (based on the regression equation in table 3.1).

Russia's republics, and particularly those republics controlled by machines, were much more likely to engage in undemocratic electoral practices. Boris Ovchinnikov's review of the results in the 1999 State Duma elections led him to conclude that eight regions experienced significant

[28] Golosov 1999, 1354–55.

[29] Russian Federation Report January 31, 2001. *RFE/RL Newsline* (February 28, 2000) reported that governments owned 45 percent of the press in Adygeia, 52 percent in Dagestan, 63 percent in Kalmykia, and 33 percent in Karelia.

falsification of vote totals in a majority of their territorial electoral commissions—seven of these eight were republics. Thus, 35 percent of the republics fell into this category, compared with less than 2 percent of the oblasts, krais, and federal cities. All the republics that exhibited extensive corruption were what I will identify later in this chapter as machine republics. Ovchinnikov claims that the most flagrant falsification in Russia took place in Bashkortostan and Tatarstan—two of these machine republics.[30] Similarly, in both the 1996 and the 2000 presidential elections for the Russian Federation, the machine republics—notably Kabardino-Balkaria and Tatarstan, but also Bashkortostan, Dagestan, and Ingushetia—were particularly effective at delivering votes for the incumbent president through a combination of high turnout plus high vote margin (table 3.2). Even more noteworthy was the "surge capacity" of these strongest machines to increase already high turnout to still higher levels, as was demonstrated in the rapid increase in turnout and vote margin between the first and second rounds of the 1996 presidential elections.[31]

Segment-State Machines in the Soviet Autocracy

Political-identity hegemony describes a relationship among competitors on the periphery and, according to the segmental institutions thesis, segment-states create a nurturing environment that facilitates the establishment of political hegemony by segment-state leaders over these other politicians. Even the narrow autonomy that might be found in an autocratic common-state or an empire can be used to create political hegemony. For example, an impressive feature of the Soviet segmented state was the emergence of segment-state machines, often called clans, within almost every union republic Communist Party organization.[32] These clans excluded other Communist clans from power and took control of the official expression of national identity within each union republic. The USSR government encouraged the growth of political-identity hegemony, but not the narrow clan-based political hegemony that actually emerged: Moscow mandated that there should be an indigenous administration in each segment-state, but urged these administrations to practice parity among the regions and subgroups of the titular population and not to discriminate against nontitular populations. Nevertheless, clan-based machines tended to emerge within each segment-state. In virtually every union republic

---

[30] Ovchinnikov 2001, 235–36.

[31] Also see Turovskii 2000.

[32] Willerton and Reisinger 1991. On the ethnic identity of leaders in the non-Russian homelands, see J. Miller 1977.

TABLE 3.2

Russian Federation: Republic machines in nationwide presidential elections, 1996–2000

	1996 Election			2000 Election	
	Turnout[a] round 1	Turnout round 2	Yeltsin margin	Turnout	Putin margin
Continuous autocracies					
Kabardino-Balkaria	76.0[b]	+6.18[b]	+30.8[b]	81.9[b]	55.2[b]
Tatarstan	73.8[b]	+3.46[b]	+29.9[b]	76.3[b]	48.8[b]
Later-developing machines					
Bashkortostan	78.1[b]	+1.55[b]	+8.0	76.2[b]	32.2
Buryatia	59.4	−2.08	−4.3	58.0	1.9
Kalmykia	68.2	−1.94	+44.0[b]	63.1	24.1
Mordovia	73.0[b]	+5.47[b]	−2.2	75.8[b]	29.2
Tyva	60.9	−0.43	+31.8[b]	60.5	35.0
Cartel machine					
Dagestan	69.8	+5.64[b]	+8.9	80.2[b]	65.2[b]
Challenged machines					
Adygeia	66.8	−1.75	−26.5	65.9	23.7
Chechnya					
Ingushetia			+65.2[b]		80.8[b]
North Ossetia	65.1	+2.31[b]	−10.0	66.4	36.2[b]
Sakha	61.1	−2.27	+35.3[b]	59.9	22.3
Competitive polities					
Altai Republic	68.9	−2.81	−8.8	66.8	−4.8
Chuvashia	65.5	+0.29[b]	−31.5	68.2	1.4
Karachai-Cherkessia	72.9[b]	+2.53[b]	+3.9	68.8	23.3
Karelia	65.5	−1.99	+40.2[b]	66.6	47.3[b]
Khakassia	59.0	−2.79	0.0	60.1	6.1
Komi	55.6	−2.44	+36.7[b]	62.0	38.1[b]
Mari El	68.5	−0.68	−12.2	68.8	4.5
Udmurtia	62.6	+0.37[b]	+12.2	68.7	36.2[b]
Oblast average	66.7	−1.75	+5.8	66.1	20.8
(Standard deviation)	(5.92)	(1.38)	(21.94)	(3.98)	(14.34)

Sources: Russian Federation TsIK 1996, 2000.

[a] Turnout is the proportion of the adult population, whether registered to vote or not.

[b] Indicates more than 1 standard deviation above oblast average.

local networks used the limited autonomy granted them to identify indigenous candidates for the career "fast track," and by a policy of indigenization of local administration the clan took control of the party and state apparatus within the segment-state.

In the Caucasus and Central Asia, these networks tended to draw together cadres who had shared common service in a specific geographic region and sometimes shared common kinship affiliations.[33] In Turkmenistan, although Moscow at first tried to implement a policy of tribal parity in allocation of seats, once an indigenous leadership was in place, it created a Communist Party machine based on the Tekke tribe around Ashkhabad.[34] In Kyrgyzstan, the party machine drew from kinship and regional patronage networks based in Naryn.[35] In Uzbekistan from 1937 until the late 1950s the Fergana-based faction dominated the union republic. After 1959, and particularly once Leonid Brezhnev rose to power in Moscow, the clan from the Jizak-Samarkand region rose to predominance in Uzbekistan: Sharaf "Rashidov was able to build a political machine resting upon personal associations mediated through nepotism, friendship, and shared region of origin." He cemented his machine with extensive patronage that showered favors on his clientele and protected them from harsh scrutiny. Yuri Andropov's purge of the Rashidov machine temporarily led to domination once again by the Fergana faction, but Islam Karimov brought the Samarkand faction back to power.[36] In Tajikistan, a machine drawn from the Pamiris of Gornyi Badakhshan dominated the Communist Party until 1937. After 1946, with the appointment of Babajan Ghafurov as first secretary, however, the Leninabad (Khojent) faction cemented its domination.[37] In Kazakhstan, the Communist Party machine relied on members of the Greater Horde to staff its elaborate political network.[38] In Azerbaijan, the Gaidar Aliev machine that began with his rise to first secretary in 1969 favored his associates from the Nakhichevan ASSR.[39] Georgia was dominated from 1931 by the political machine constructed by Lavrentii Beria, which drew disproportionately on Mingrelians from the western part of the republic, and then from 1953 until 1972 by the machine constructed by Vasilii Mzhavanadze, who purged the "Beria gang" and built on the Tblisi Georgians' resentment of Mingrelian dominance.[40]

In the western parts of the USSR, particularly after the World War II, these machines tended to be networks that had worked together in the 1930s or during the war. In Lithuania, according to Romuald J. Misiunas

---

[33] Luong 2002, 69–99.

[34] Edgar 2001, 278–88; Roy 2000, 13, 115.

[35] J. Anderson 1999 40–41, 43; Luong 2002, 79–80.

[36] Fane 1996; Gill and Pitty 1997, 72–80, 150–51; Roy 2000, 13, 104, 109–12; Luong 2002, 88; Critchlow 1992, 18–19.

[37] Roy 2000, 113–14; Juraeva 1996 255–70. On the continuing importance of these "clans" after independence, see Akbarzadeh 1996.

[38] Olcott 2002, 186; Gill and Pitty 1997, 87; Olcott 1987, 199–223. On the first decades of indigenization in Kazakhstan, see Cherot 1955; Lane 1975.

[39] Altstadt 1992, 181; Gill and Pitty 1997, 153; Swietochowski 1995, 182–84; Willerton 1992, 191–222.

[40] A. Knight 1993, 159, 163, 186–88; Suny 1988, 287, 301.

and Rein Taagapera, the "party had become its First Secretary's personal machine probably to a greater extent than that of any other Soviet Republic."[41] (This superlative claim is doubtful only because so many other union republic Communist parties developed machines that were every bit as personalistic.) Antanas Sniečkus had become the Lithuanian first secretary in 1936 while in exile in Russia, and he drew around him other so-called "Soviet" Lithuanians who had spent the interwar years in exile.[42] In Estonia and Latvia the Communist parties also drew their leadership from the small circles of Estonians and Latvians who had spent the interwar years in the USSR.[43] In Estonia, during a long tenure as first secretary (1950–78), Johannes Käbin created what one analyst called "a personal fiefdom."[44] In Moldavia even as late as 1988 the Communist Party was still dominated by secretaries born in the interwar USSR; the leaders of the segment-state had built an indigenous machine that favored Moldavians from Ukraine or Transdniestria—that is, from areas that had been part of the interwar Moldavian ASSR.[45] In Ukraine the "Partisan clan" formed through common service in World War II rose to dominance under Petro Shelest (until 1972).[46] In Belorussia the "Partisan faction," which had close ties dating from the members' common service during World War II, also came to dominate politics, particularly with the ascendance of Kirill Mazurov.[47]

Of course, in the Soviet period these machines were always limited by the power of the center to intervene in all appointments and remove the union republic leadership. Yet Moscow came to acquiesce in this prevalence of machines and relied on its ability to replace one clan or regional network by another—such as the alternation of Fergana and Samarkand factions in Uzbekistan—as a way of maintaining accountability to the center. This did not eliminate segment-state machines but simply chose among them.

Post-Soviet Segment-State Machines

Even in the more democratic politics of the Russian Federation, segment-states provided a more nurturing environment for political hegemony than other jurisdictions within the federation. Political machines were more likely to dominate in segment-states than in the neighboring provinces that

[41] Misiunas and Taagapera 1983, 196.

[42] Remeikis 1965, 122–23; also see Willerton 1992, 157–90.

[43] Misiunas and Taagapera 1983, 197–98; Taagepera 1993, 99–100; Raun 1987, 190–93.

[44] Pennar 1978, 117–18, 123; Raun 1987, 193–95.

[45] C. King 2000, 98–100.

[46] Krawchenko 1985, 242–48. On the removal of Shelest for "nationalistic excesses," see Tillett 1975.

[47] Urban 1989, 116–17; Urban and Reed 1989, 430–31; Marples 1999, 19–23.

were not segment-states. In the first decade of Russian independence, many republic leaders, such as Shaimiev of Tatarstan, used their special autonomy rights to rewrite the rules of local politics, to make appointments, to disseminate patronage, to deploy mobilizational resources, and to coerce opponents as a way of inducing other politicians to jump on the bandwagon and to isolate those who did not. Some machines, like that in Tatarstan, were holdovers from the Soviet period, but others, such as the Kirsan Iliumzhinov machine in Kalmykia, were new post-Soviet constructs that took advantage of the opportunities created by segment-states. Indeed, in the first decade after independence, political machines developed in a majority of the republics of the Russian Federation. As summarized in table 3.3, machines developed in three-fifths of the republics. A useful index of the progress of political hegemony in each republic is the length of time it took to introduce an elective chief executive: because each side feared the post would become the platform for the other to establish its hegemony, it took the republics with competitive polities about four times longer than machine-controlled republics. Moreover, in many competitive republics the creation of this post was actually forced by decisions made in Moscow. With these machines incumbents were much less likely to lose office. Indeed, in thirty-five elections completed between 1990 and 2003 in the republics with machines, incumbent presidents lost less than 9 percent of their bids for reelection. In seventeen elections in the republics with competitive politics, incumbents lost more than half their bids for reelection.

The republic machines tended—although not everywhere—to be ethnic machines and favored the republic's titular group, such as Tatars in Tatarstan, for political office. There was a sharp increase in the proportion of offices held by titulars in republics controlled by machines after 1991, leading to overrepresentation in the sense that the proportion of offices held by each titular nationality exceeded its proportion of its republic's population. For example, in 1990 Tatars were proportionately overrepresented by 20 percent in the Tatarstan parliament, Ossetians by 32 percent in the North Ossetian parliament, and Yakuts by 39 percent in the Sakha (Yakutia) parliament. Within five years this overrepresentation had jumped to over 50 percent in Tatarstan, 62 percent in North Ossetia, and 82 percent in Sakha.[48]

Kabardino-Balkaria and Tatarstan maintained stable autocratic regimes from 1990 to 2003. In both republics the Communist Party first secretaries—Valerii Kokov and Mintimer Shaimiev—combined the Soviet Party and state apparatuses in a coherent instrument of rule and with this support moved quickly to create a presidency before the USSR broke up. Both machines kept the former Communist Party first secretary in power

[48] Data from Robert Kaiser reported in Bahry 2002.

TABLE 3.3

Russian Federation: Types of political machines in republics, 1990–2003

	Titulars in population (%)	Months to first election	Incumbent[a]		Ultimate victor's[b]	
			Elected/Elections	Defeated/Bids	Average vote	Vote advantage
Continuous autocracies		*3.2*	*100%*	*0%*	*78.5%*	*72.9%*
Kabardino–Balkaria	48.2	6.3	3/3	0/3	74.8	65.7
Tatarstan	48.5	0.0	3/3	0/3	82.2	80.0
Later developing machines		*20.7*	*93.3%*	*6.7%*	*65.7%*	*49.4%*
Bashkortostan	21.9	30.0	3/3	0/3	61.0	40.7
Buryatia	24.0	36.0	3/3	0/3	59.3	43.3
Kalmykia	45.4	22.0	3/3	0/3	69.1	49.3
Mordovia	32.5	6.1	2/3	1/3	68.4	57.8
Tyva	64.3	9.1	3/3	0/3	70.7	55.7
Cartel-machine			—	—	—	—
Dagestan			0/0	0/0	0.0	0.0
Challenged machines		*11.4*	*66.7%*	*16.7%*	*62.3%*	*44.4%*
Adygeia	22.1	6.3	2/3	1/3	55.6	39.7
Chechnya[c]		4.5	2/2	0/2	74.9	53.5
Ingushetia		8.9	2/3	0/3	61.9	46.8
North Ossetia	53.0	31.2	2/3	1/3	66.0	42.7
Sakha	33.4	6.3	2/3	0/3	65.6	48.3

TABLE 3.3 (cont.)

Russian Federation: Types of political machines in republics, 1990–2003

	Titulars in population (%)	Months to first election	Incumbent[a]		Ultimate victor's[b]	
			Elected/Elections	Defeated/Bids	Average vote	Vote advantage
Competitive polities			47%	53%	41.7%	19.6%
Altai	31.0	56.8	0/2	2/2	23.2	4.2
Chuvashia	67.8	78.1	2/3	1/3	40.7	9.3
Karachai-Cherkessia	31.2	30.0	0/1	1/1	17.9	–22.2
Karelia	10.0	93.7	2/3	1/3	52.7	37.3
Khakassia	11.1	34.2	1/2	1/2	58.1	43.0
Komi	23.3	65.7	1/2	1/2	44.5	11.0
Mari El	43.3	5.9	1/3	2/3	40.5	28.6
Udmurtia	30.9	112.0	1/1	0/1	37.8	13.9

[a] Denominators are (respectively) the number of presidential (chief executive) elections and the number of attempts (bids) by incumbents to win reelection from 1990 to 2003.

[b] Vote in first-round election for candidate who became president even if a run-off had to be held.

[c] Chechnya is not included in group averages for challenged machines.

throughout the first decade of independence, suppressing opposition, so that the incumbent won presidential elections, often against no opponents, with an average vote of 78.5 percent on the first round, outdistancing any opponent by an average of 72.9 percentage points. Both presidents are titulars—Kokov is a Kabard and Shaimiev is a Tatar—and drew on an ethnic constituency that constitutes over 45 percent of the republic's population to staff an ethnic machine that dominates local administration and politics.

In five other republics—Bashkortostan, Buryatia,[49] Kalmykia, Mordovia,[50] and Tyva[51]—a machine under a boss came to dominate politics, but only after an initial transition struggle over control of the republic. In these later developing machines the bosses tended to win elections with lower vote totals (65.7 percent on the first round) than the autocrats and with narrower vote margins (49.4 percent on the first round). In many ways, these republics are more revealing than the continuous autocracies of the vulnerability of segment-states to illiberal political hegemony, because these elites had to use the resources of the segment-state to construct new monopolies rather than simply sustain a monopoly created in the autocratic Soviet period. Four of these bosses are titulars—Murtaza Rakhimov is a Bashkir, Kirsan Iliumzhinov is a Kalmyk, Nikolai Merkushkin is a Mordvin, and Sherig-Ool Oorzhak is a Tyvan; Leonid Potapov of Buryatia is a Russian, but made much of the fact that he had been raised by Buryat foster parents and is fluent in Buryat. Four of the bosses emerged from the republic's Communist Party secretarial apparatus; Iliumzhinov was an outsider who challenged the incumbent elite in the name of the titular nationality. In all five of these republics, divisions in the Soviet-era elite—often balanced between titular administrators in the Communist Party and governmental bureaucracies and Russian managers leading major enterprises with strong representation in the supreme soviets—delayed consolidation of control by the titular machine. Most important, this situation in turn delayed creation of a republic presidency, but after the creation of a presidency, one strong man and his machine came to dominate the republic's politics. In Bashkor-

---

[49] Boir Borboev, "U respubliki est' Konstitutsiia," *Nezavisimaia gazeta* February 24, 1994, 2; Elena Tregubova, "Vlast' v Buriatii, vozmozhno, pereidet k Sovetam," *Segodnia* June 16, 1994, 2; Elena Tregubova, "Buriatiia vybiraet prezidenta," *Segodnia* June 18, 1994, 2; Elena Tregubova, "Prezidentom Buriatii tozhe stal byvshii sekretar' obkoma," *Segodnia* July 2, 1994, 2.

[50] On the early conflicts that led to abolition of the presidency and Yeltsin's intervention in 1993 see Valentin Razboinikov, "V Mordovii uprazdnena dolzhnost' prezidenta," *Izvestiia* April 7, 1993, 2; Radik Batyrshin, ""V boi vvedena tiazhelaia artilleriia," *Nezavisimaia gazeta* April 9, 1993, 1; Zhanna Trofimova, "Mordovskii prezident uprazdnen," *Segodnia* June 4, 1993, 1; Natal'ia Gorodetskaia, "V S Mordovii vosstanovit raionnye i gorodskie sovety," *Segodnia* April 14, 1994, 2; ITAR-TASS April 20, 1993, June 3, 1993; Radio Rossii April 5, 1993, July 19, 1995; Radio Mayak August 21, 1993, September 20, 1995.

[51] On the transition period in Tyva, see Alatalu 1992.

tostan, Kalmykia, Mordovia, and Tyva, the presidents built their machines on the titular population even where this population constituted a small minority in the republic as a whole. For example, although Bashkirs constitute only 20 percent of Bashkortostan's population, Rakhimov consolidated a strong segment-state machine in which Bashkirs reportedly occupied more than 60 percent of the local executive posts and more than 60 percent of the republic's parliament.[52] In Mordovia, where Mordvins constituted only a third of the population in the 1990s, they constituted over half of the republic's Supreme Soviet and government.[53]

Bashkortostan represented the strongest of these machines dominated by an insider emerging from within an initially divided leadership. The rise of Murtaza Rakhimov's Bashkir machine is a textbook lesson for creating political hegemony within a segment-state even under difficult conditions. On the eve of Russia's democratization, divisions in the Bashkir ASSR elite led to brief paralysis. In February 1990, the republic's party committee (obkom) removed the first secretary, Ravmer Khabibullin, and all members of the obkom's bureau, and appointed a temporary bureau in the run-up to the elections to the republic's Supreme Soviet.[54] In April the Supreme Soviet elected Rakhimov, a Bashkir director of an oil refinery who could appeal to both Bashkir and economic interests, as Supreme Soviet chair— the de facto president of the republic. Rakhimov was unable to transform this post into an actual presidency in late 1991: although the republic's Supreme Soviet had adopted legislation creating the post in October and scheduled elections for December 15, the legislative body then voted to suspend all elections, including those for president of the republic. Nonetheless, Rakhimov used his post as de facto president to build a powerful machine. In November 1993, following the Yeltsin coup in Moscow, the Bashkortostan Supreme Soviet lifted its moratorium and scheduled presidential elections for December 12, 1993. Against a single, relatively insignificant opponent, Rakhimov won 64 percent of the vote. Over the next years the president's machine increasingly tightened its control over Bashkortostan politics through appointments to political offices, legislation to limit challenges from the opposition, and brute coercion. In his 1997 bid for reelection, Rakhimov won handily with 70 percent of the vote against a mere 9.3 percent for his forestry minister.[55] Rakhimov's bid for a third term in 2003 encountered stiff resistance from Moscow when the Rakhimov machine disqualified the president's major competitor, Sergei Vere-

---

[52] *RFE/RL Newsline* February 28, 2003.

[53] Taagepera 1999, 194.

[54] "Sostoialis' plenumy," *Pravda* February 11, 1990, 2.

[55] Svetlana Il'ina, "'Iabloko' prizyvaet prezidenta pokonchit s antidemokraticheskim proizvolom, tsariashchim v regionakh," *Nezavisimaia gazeta* June 19, 1998, 1, 3.

meenko. After Moscow's Central Electoral Commission threatened to dissolve the Bashkortostan Electoral Commission, the Bashkirs recanted. The first round of the election on December 7, 2003, gave Rakhimov only 46 percent of the vote against Veremeenko's 24 percent, forcing a run-off. Nonetheless, on December 21, with exceptionally high turnout, Rakhimov garnered 78 percent of the vote against only 16 percent for Veremeenko.[56]

Among these later developing machines the consolidation of the Kirsan Iliumzhinov machine in Kalmykia after April 1993 illustrates how outsiders used the special opportunities within a segment-state to purge the communists and create an alternative ethnic machine. From 1990 to April 1993, conflicts between the republic's executive and legislative leaders led to a stalemate: presidential elections in October 1991 resulted in no victor, and when the conflict between the leaders of the executive and legislative branches became particularly intense in the fall of 1992, both leaders were forced to retire. This stalemate left the republic's leadership vulnerable to an assault from the outside. Under pressure from the newly formed Extraordinary Congress of the People of Kalmykia, an unofficial nationalist organization, the Supreme Soviet scheduled presidential elections for April 11, 1993. In the three-way contest, the victor was Iliumzhinov—a wealthy businessman who promised to make Kalmykia another Kuwait, promised to give each citizen $100 from his personal fortune, and actually subsidized milk and bread prices in the capital (Elista) during the campaign. He won handily with 65 percent of the vote, a full 44 percentage points above his opponent.[57] Iliumzhinov moved quickly to consolidate his control over executive and legislative branches. The Iliumzhinov machine was personalistic and Kalmyk and relied on a constant flow of benefits, including a constant flow of rubles into the pockets of his lieutenants and supporters, to cement its support base. The Moscow-based newspaper *Nezavisimaia gazeta* complained that "the President's inner circle consists almost entirely of members of the titular nationality and they make up 76% of the leadership apparatus in federal agencies—although Kalmyks account for only about 46% of the republic's population." This extended even more thoroughly to the banking sector controlled by the Iliumzhinov administration and to higher education, where Kalmyks constituted more than 80 percent of the students admitted to Kalmyk State University.[58]

In Dagestan, a more complex oligarchic cartel machine restricted political competition. This arrangement has been called consociational, but more accurately it reflected the nondemocratic forms labeled "hegemonic

[56] *RFE/RL Newsline* December 23, 2003.

[57] ITAR-TASS February 22, 1993; Valerii Kornev, "Pervym prezidentom Kalmykii stal predprinimatel'-milliarder," *Izvestiia* April 13, 1993, 1.

[58] Vasilii Kindinov, "Iskhod Russkikh iz Kalmykii," *Nezavisimaia gazeta* March 21, 1997, 3.

exchange."[59] Dagestan is a multiethnic homeland of what are sometimes bracketed with the label "the nationalities of Dagestan," even though this grouping combines diverse Nakhko-Dagestani (Avars, Lezgins, Dargins, Laks, Tabasarans, Rutuls, Tsakhurs, and Aguls) and Turkic (Kumyks and Nogais) nationalities. In the Soviet period, as Edward Walker notes, "informal understandings arose about the ethnic distribution of appointments as mayors, procurators, chiefs of police, judges and so on at the republic, city/ town, and district (raion) level."[60] Even after the collapse of the USSR the Soviet-era leadership held on to power, but it was buffeted by conflicts among ethnic groups and infected by this to a certain extent. In March 1990 the republic's new Congress of Peoples Deputies reelected the incumbents Magomedali Magomedov, a Dargin, as chair of the Supreme Soviet, and Abdurazak Mirzabekov, a Kumyk, as chair of the Council of Ministers; both had served since 1987. (At the time, the republic's Communist Party first secretary was Mukhu Aliev, an Avar.) Its ethnic complexity paralyzed bold moves to reform institutions, particularly the introduction of a strong presidency. Twice, when the issue was submitted to a popular referendum, in June 1992 and December 1993, voters rejected introduction of a presidency by wide margins: 83 percent and 68 percent, respectively, voted against the proposal. Avar and Dargin leaders supported a presidency, expecting the president to be drawn from one of these ethnic groups; leaders of other ethnic groups tended to oppose a presidency that would strengthen the hand of Avar or Dargin leaders. Instead, the cartel agreed to create a collegial executive, the State Council, that would provide balanced representation of ethnic elites, and a new Constitutional Council that would comprise parliamentary deputies and representatives of local governments. Legislative authority would be vested in a People's Assembly. In July 1994 the Constitutional Council met and elected Magomedov as its chair and Mirzabekov as prime minister. Elections to the People's Assembly were held on March 5, 1995, and the new assembly elected Aliev (the former first secretary) as its chair. Thus, once again a Dargin, Kumyk, and Avar held the republic's three leadership posts.

In another four republics—Adygeia, Ingushetia, North Ossetia, and Sakha—elite divisions threatened the durability of the governing machine. These divisions led to the ultimate defeat or forced retirement of the republic's first boss, but the continued dominance of republic politics by the titular-led machine. In Adygeia, the former obkom first secretary, Aslan Dzharimov, had created a multiethnic machine in which posts were assigned on a proportional basis, but this was a fissiparous alliance—particularly as Russian industrial managers grew dissatisfied with Dzharimov's

[59] Rothchild 1986.
[60] Walker 1999–2000, 19.

policies favoring the Adygei.[61] This led to Dzharimov's defeat in his bid for a third term in January 2002. Although another Adygei, Khazret Sovmen, succeeded Dzharimov, within three years a stalemate had emerged between the representatives of the Russian elite in the State Council (legislature) and the president over a plan pressed by the Russians to dissolve the republic and join it to Krasnodar krai. In North Ossetia, Akhsarbek Galazov, former first secretary of the obkom, consolidated the leadership of the party machine within the republic, but faced growing opposition from defense industry managers within the republic.[62] In Galazov's bid for reelection in 1998, directors of North Ossetia's powerful military-industrial complex blamed Galazov for the republic's economic collapse, and many in Galazov's own administration blamed him for the continuing crisis with Ingush settlers in the republic. Together they threw their weight behind Galazov's predecessor as Communist Party first secretary of the republic, Aleksandr Dzasokhov, delivering a high turnout (68 percent) and a 66 percentage point vote margin to secure the comeback of a party boss from an earlier time to replace the incumbent.[63] In Sakha, Mikhail Nikolaev, formerly a secretary of the Yakut ASSR obkom, dominated the political institutions of his republic and captured the nationalist mantle, but mounting opposition from the Russian economic elite with backing from Moscow forced Nikolaev to step down at the end of his second term rather than seek a constitutional amendment that would permit him to remain in office. Nonetheless, Nikolaev negotiated to have Vyacheslav Shtyrov, a close ally, selected as his successor and victor in the presidential elections.[64]

Ingushetia represents a somewhat different type of challenged machine because the Ruslan Aushev machine, despite its hegemony in republic politics, remained so dependent on Moscow. Boris Yeltsin had sponsored the rise of Major General Ruslan Aushev as boss, but pressure from Vladimir Putin ended his rule and prevented him from seeking a third term. With the separation of the Ingush raions from Chechnya and the creation of a republic on June 4, 1992, Yeltsin appointed the decorated veteran of Afghanistan and leader of the Ingush national movement to head the temporary administration of Ingushetia. In the February 28, 1993, presidential elections Aushev stood as the sole candidate and garnered 99.94 percent of the vote. From this post Aushev established direct control over the government of the republic. On February 27, 1994, 97 percent of the voters approved Ingushetia's new constitution and 94 percent reelected Aushev,

---

[61] Orttung 2000, 6–7.

[62] "Provintsial'naia khronika," *Segodnia* November 11, 1993, 2; Liana Minasian, "Prezidentom stal Akhsarbek Galazov," *Nezavisimaia gazeta* January 18, 1994, 1.

[63] RIA-Novosti August 29, 1996; *RFE/RL Newsline* December 29, 1997, January 19, 1998.

[64] RFE/RL Newsline July 18, 2001; Russian Federation Report February 13, 2002.

who once again stood as the sole candidate.[65] Four years later Aushev's ability to win election had hardly diminished: on March 1, 1998, against eight opponents Aushev won 66.5 percent of the vote, outdistancing his closest opponent by 53 percentage points.[66] Yet Aushev's machine depended on special favors, such as the free trade zone, granted by the Russian president, and kept the Ingush elites on board by opportunities to skim enormous rents through black-market trade. When Moscow pressed Aushev not to run for a third term in 2002 and threatened to turn off the rent spigot, clan leaders withdrew their support from the Ingushetian president, and Aushev had little choice but to step down. On April 28, 2002, Moscow broke the Aushev machine by securing the election of Federal Security Service General Murat Zyazikov, the handpicked candidate of the Putin administration.[67]

Thus, in at least three-fifths of republics, segment-state leaders established political hegemony through a political machine. In only eight republics—Altai, Chuvashia, Karachai-Cherkessia, Karelia, Khakassia, Komi, Mari El, and Udmurtia—did the Communist Party autocracies fail to maintain their hold on power, and no new bosses emerged to create new machines.

[65] Georgii Ivanov-Smolenskii, "Ruslan Aushev izbran pervym prezidentom Ingushskoi Respubliki," *Izvestiia* March 2, 1993, 1–2; ITAR-TASS February 28, 1994.

[66] *RFE/RL Newsline* March 2, 1998.

[67] *RFE/RL Caucasus Report* January 3, 2002, May 3, 2002.

FOUR

Creating Identity Hegemony

THE SEGMENTAL INSTITUTIONS thesis identifies a paradox in the usual story of nation-state formation: although a state is supposed to be the expression of the will of a nation to have a state of its own, the focusing or coordination of national identity and suppression of alternatives necessary to create a nation are unlikely to take place in the absence of a state. The segmental institutions thesis identifies an answer to this paradox, however: a precursor to nationalism often emerges in a segment-state under the control of a nationalist machine, and this precursor is political-identity hegemony. This does not mean that a particular national identity is widespread in these segment-states; it means that this national identity trumps the alternatives in its ability to mobilize support. The leaders of the nationalist machine are uniquely positioned to entice or induce parts of the politically active members of "the people" to accept a nation-state project as their own, to persuade members of the elite, intelligentsia, and public to abandon alternative projects, and to suppress public expressions of support for these alternative projects.

The power of segment-states to create identity hegemony before independence has been observed around the world. For example, no more difficult environment for national identity hegemony exists than contemporary Africa. Yet most of the former colonies survived as independent states for more than four decades with few challenges from alternative nation-state projects, except for the very few independent states that contained segment-states such as Eritrea and Biafra. Crawford Young has argued that the borders of the colonies within which Africans conducted their decolonization struggles willy-nilly defined their national identities. As a consequence of their "common subjugation within a given territorial container a 'people' was constituted by the geographic frame of imperial rule."[1] William Miles notes the ability of the borders imposed by segment-states to create national identities that even divide tribes. From surveys conducted in Hausa villages on both sides of the Nigeria–Niger border, Miles concludes, "in partitioned Hausaland, where the aggregate population is united by ethnicity but divided by nationality . . . national distinctions not only come to assume greater prominence but tend to supplant ethnic ones in the construction of 'basic group identity.' "[2]

[1] Quoted in Englebert 2003, 17.
[2] Miles 1994, 58; also see Miles and Rochefort 1991.

In order to explain the process of creating identity hegemony, this chapter begins with an analytic model that defines the problem of coordinating national identities. The next three sections compare the coordination of national identities under three institutional constraints: in the absence of segment-states, in an autocratic segmented state, and in a democratizing segmented state. Where there is no segment-state, there is little prospect for identity hegemony in opposition to an existing common-state. The absence of segment-states leads to a proliferation of nation-state projects with competing claims to overlapping populations and territories; it results in what might be labeled coordination failure. Yet not all segment-states lead to identity hegemony, and not all identity hegemonies inside segment-states are identical. Autocratic segmentation establishes the hegemony of official nation-state projects in each segment-state, but typically limits this by the official nation-state project of the common-state. Democratic segmentation typically leads to much greater variation among segment-states, which tend to fall into two distinct patterns. Where a political machine takes control inside a segment-state, its leadership typically establishes identity hegemony uniting a predominant cohort of elites and intellectuals and rigidly controlling the propagation of alternative nation-state projects. Where no political machine takes control of a segment-state, it is more likely that there is no identity hegemony and the competing claims of different identity groups shape the segment-state's politics. The evidence for these patterns is drawn from the Eurasian region—the Russian Empire, the USSR, and the Russian Federation. It underscores that inside segment-states, political and identity hegemonies tend to grow together, each reinforcing the other.

Coordinating and Suppressing Identities

Segment-states help solve the paradox of nation formation before independence by providing a focal point, the incentives to coordinate identities, and the coercive resources to suppress public expressions of alternative national identities. This can be understood by beginning with a stylized picture of coordination failure in the absence of segmental institutions. This model, which is borrowed from the rational-choice institutionalists, highlights two problems that handicap any attempt to coordinate national identities among members of an elite and within the public at large: the proliferation of competing nation-state projects and the instability of any consensus.[3] The process by which one nation-state project emerges hege-

---

[3] Olson 1965; McKelvey 1976; Shepsle and Weingast 1981; Shepsle 1989; Cox 1997, particularly 159–61, 238–50.

monic is, thus, the solution to these problems of coordinating national identities among many individuals and giving this consensus greater stability over time. State institutions—a segment-state before independence and a nation-state afterward—typically are central to this process.

Segment-States and the Incentives for Coordination

For many members of the elite and public in the target population, the choice among nation-state projects entails complex calculations and trade-offs between the ideal and the achievable. Elites typically prefer nation-state projects in which they would become presidents, but often settle for one in which they are simply their leader's ministers—a second-best outcome that is, nonetheless, preferable in their eyes to the current state of affairs, in which they are mere subjects in "some other people's" nation-state.[4] In the absence of an institutional arrangement that privileges one nation-state project over the others, however, elites are likely to engage in competitive proliferation of more or less equally plausible projects. Intellectuals derive such unique rewards for advancing their own projects rather than following as a student of others that they have strong incentives to invent new imagined communities. Even if intellectual coordination around a nation-state project to challenge the existing state takes place, it may be short-lived, leading to alternation or even cycling of intellectual fads.[5] For publics, the contending nation-state projects offer a confusing array of equally plausible claims to their membership. If the projects demand only a relatively costless commitment, such as private professions of support or secret votes, publics may easily give their assent, but may just as easily give it simultaneously or seriatim to several projects.[6] This will further encourage the proliferation of nation-state projects and support the alternation of national fads.

For both elites and publics, the first problem of coordination is identifying a winner. Even if elites and publics are willing to make costly commitments to someone else's project, such as a public declaration of loyalty that costs them their place in another community, they are likely to do so only as long as they expect many other supporters of the project to do so as well. Although successful coordination raises the probability of success and lowers each individual's costs from retribution, before anyone has moved, everyone must try to guess which nation-state project will be the one that

[4] Rogowski 1985.

[5] On cycling and the role of institutions in providing stability, see Shepsle and Weingast 1981; Shepsle 1989. On the fluidity and malleability of national identities in post-Soviet Eurasia, see Suny 1999/2000.

[6] On multiple and situation-specific identities, see Kasfir 1986. On costless identities, see Waters 1990.

others will back with costly public commitments.[7] For example, before elites and intellectuals abandon their most favored nation-state projects for a second-best project and desist from offering up new projects for imagined communities, they must be convinced that one project stands so much above the others that it will pay to switch. In particular, the likelihood of success of the second-best project must be so much greater that elites and intellectuals will calculate that their expected payoff—that is, the probability of success times their payoff from a second-best outcome—exceeds their expected payoff from the first-best project. Thus, elites may bandwagon behind a project that promises to make them ministers and abandon the dream that would make them presidents, if the likelihood of becoming a minister is significantly greater than the likelihood of becoming president. For similar reasons, intellectuals may switch to projects that include some people and territory the intellectuals do not believe strictly belong to the nation-state or that omit some people and territory the intellectuals believe are legitimately part of the nation-state.

The second problem of coordination is ensuring that the payoff will be there once the nation-state project succeeds. Thus, before members of the elite, intelligentsia, and public are willing to make costly commitments in the form of time, contributions of resources, or public declarations that risk retribution, they may demand short-term private benefits as evidence that when the project succeeds the promised benefits will be distributed to supporters. In most instances, due to the limited resources that their proponents can use to offer particularistic inducements, national identities that begin to expand beyond a single parlor often fall into a trap—a local equilibrium—that keeps small the number of intellectuals, elites, and others who are willing to engage in costly action on its behalf. For the proponents, the pressure to expand membership in the nation comes from the hope that size will increase the chances for success. Yet the solidaristic benefits to individuals that come with membership in a community fall rapidly as membership expands beyond face-to-face contacts. Material benefits can only be shared among a few members before the inducement per member becomes insignificant.

According to the segmental institutions thesis, segment-states can solve these problems of coordination. The segment-state becomes a unique, stable focal point for expectations. Members of the elite, intelligentsia, and public are drawn to this focal point in part because they expect others to be drawn to its unique statehood. Members of the elite, intelligentsia, and public are also drawn to this nation-state project because the unique capabilities of the segment-state increase the likelihood that this nation-state project will succeed where projects without segment-states are likely to

[7] Schelling 1960; Downs 1957, 47–49.

fail. And the leaders of the segment-state are empowered to reward loyalists even before the project achieves its goal of independence. In short, in the competition among proponents of various nation-state projects to win a wider following among members of the elite, intelligentsia, and public and to establish identity hegemony on the periphery, the segment-state becomes a unique focal point for the convergence of expectations that is empowered in ways that competitors can seldom match.[8]

Suppressing Alternative Nation-State Projects

Establishing identity hegemony entails not only the constructive process of focusing a national identity but also the suppressive process of controlling the expression of alternative national identities. National identity hegemony does not require the absence of different national identities in the repertoire of individuals, only that these individuals are unlikely to make costly commitments to the alternatives. Leaders of segment-states are uniquely empowered to suppress such costly commitments to alternative nation-state projects, notably alternative projects that would reconfigure the titular population, that would separate parts of the people or homeland in yet smaller homelands, or that would bind the titular population to the common-state.

This capacity to suppress these alternatives is particularly important in segment-states: Seldom is secessionist nationalism widespread in the population before independence, and seldom is the nationalist attachment to the segment-state yet exclusive in the minds of the public at large. That is, segment-states often coordinate elite and public imaginations to focus national identities, but they typically create a dualistic national identity within many individuals and in the population at large.[9] Thus, it is critically important to the success of a nation-state project that segmental institutions often place segment-state leaders in a unique position with regard to their own population and these identities: segment-state leaders become the arbiters of public conflicts between these dueling dual identities. Segment-state leaders are often in a unique "switchman" position within the segment-state to choose the direction of political action by determining when one or the other identity will be salient to politics. This is contrary to the view that in secessionist conflicts identities are fixed and there are no identities that can keep the parties together. The segmental institutions thesis stresses the frequent presence of a common-state identity but the suppression of any costly commitments to the common-state within a segment-state, owing to the unique switchman role of segment-state leaders.

[8] Also see Verdery 1996.
[9] Akiner 1995, 48–50; Yemelianova 1999, 127–28. On Belarus, see Jocelyn 1998, 80.

The phenomenon of dueling dual national identities associated with segment-states has been encountered around the world. In the British Empire, for example, the term "British" applied to many, far-flung people of the Empire, such as Australians, Canadians, and New Zealanders, who were members of both the respective segment-state people and the British people. In Spain's cultural communities, including Catalonia and the Basque Country, Luis Moreno identifies the strength of what he calls "compound nationality."[10] The dual national identity typical of segment-states creates a mirror problem often observed within the population of the metropolis: they may be torn between competing claims that *their* state is both the metropolitan core and the common-state. For example, as Norman Davies notes, "the great majority of English people never learned to distinguish 'Britishness' from 'Englishness.' "[11]

This dualism and the switchman role of segment-state leaders became acute in Central Eurasia when segmental institutions existed. In the USSR, the union republic leaders propagated two imagined communities with a right to states of their own—the union republic's titular population and the Soviet people. The union republic leaders cultivated the myth of a Soviet people that made revolution, defended the socialist fatherland against the fascists, and were building communism together.[12] In a typical manifestation of this attempt to cultivate this Soviet identity,[13] *Moldova Socialista* on July 30, 1970, referred to Moscow's Red Square as "the heart of our motherland."[14] In many republics this had an enormous effect on popular identities. For example, "Kazakh soldiers fought alongside representatives of many other Soviet nationalities, united with them in the common cause of defending the 'Motherland,' a concept which embraced the national territory, but extended beyond that to include the broader Soviet identity."[15] As many authors have noted, this dual national identity also left many Russians uncertain whether the USSR or the RSFSR was their homeland.[16] This dual national identity has also been common within those Soviet successor states that maintained segment-states. In a survey conducted in Russia's republics two years after the breakup of the USSR, Timothy Colton and his research team found that a majority in each of twenty-one titular nationalities in sixteen republics—all but the Chechens of Chechnya—considered themselves representatives of both their republic

---

[10] Moreno 1997.
[11] Davies 1999, 815–16.
[12] Wilson 2000 140–48. Also see Weiner 1996.
[13] Marples 1996, 119–20.
[14] Dima 1991, 127.
[15] Akiner 1995, 48–49. Also see Olcott 2002, 55.
[16] See Brudny 1998, 7; Tolz 2001, 161–74, 237–38; Guroff and Guroff 1994; Szporluk 2000, 195–201.

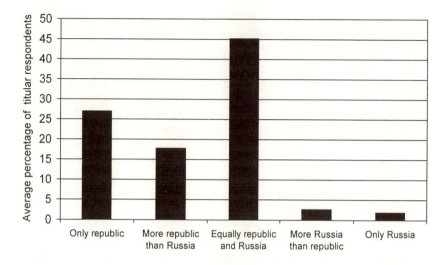

Question: Of what polity do you consider yourself a representative?

Figure 4.1 Russian Federation: national identities of titular populations in republics, 1993. *Source:* Based on data in Tishkov 1997, 261–64.

and Russia, although they varied in the priority they placed on the republic or Russia.[17] Most respondents—on average 65.6 percent of each nationality—considered themselves parts of both nations (figure 4.1).

These dueling dual national identities were manifest publicly in the last days of the USSR. For example, on March 17, 1991, Ukraine's citizens were asked to vote on two referenda, one endorsing a new Union Treaty and another endorsing Ukraine's state sovereignty within a Union of Soviet Sovereign States. Proponents and opponents presented the first to the voters as an affirmation of their membership in the Soviet people and the second as affirmation of their membership in the Ukrainian people. With 83.5 percent turnout, an overwhelming majority of these voters approved both questions, affirming their membership in both nations.[18] Dual national identities also created the opportunity for cycling of popular majorities when citizens of union republics were asked at different times which polity they endorsed. In different contexts, citizens who thought of themselves as belonging to both the Soviet common-state and a segment-state would respond with seemingly contradictory answers.

[17] Data from Tishkov 1997, 261–64.

[18] That is, the lowest double-positive percentage would be 50.4 percent voted for both, 29.8 percent of the participants voted for the first referendum and against the second, and 19.8 percent voted for the second and against the first. Also see Walker 2003, 117–18; Sheehy 1991a.

Most important, however, Soviet and post-Soviet segmental institutions privileged the segment-state leaders in the reconciliation of conflicts between each half of these dual national identities. In the USSR, for members of the titular nationalities of the union republics, and particularly for those who spoke Russian poorly or not at all, the primary point of contact with the Soviet state was through the indigenous cadres. Thus, Soviet policies placed the union republic leaders in the critical position to mediate between the halves of the dual national identities. Moscow's attempt to trump the national claims of the union republic leaders by mobilizing the Soviet identity among members of titular nationalities largely failed because these pan-Soviet claims often had to be mediated through the union republic leadership itself.[19]

Proliferation of Pre-Soviet Identities

According to the segmental institutions thesis, without a segment-state it is unlikely that national identities will coordinate around a single project that can challenge an existing common-state. The proliferation and general weakness of such nation-state projects and the alternation of national fads in the absence of segment-states are well illustrated by the Russian Empire on the eve of the Bolshevik Revolution. The leaders of the Russian Empire for the most part did not conceive of their state as a nation-state, for this would conjure radical ideas of popular sovereignty. Typically they tried to cultivate a sense of "regnal" loyalty to the tsar and his autocratic state.[20] In the twentieth century the empire gave no autonomy to segment-states—except Finland, Bukhara, Khiva, and briefly Tannu Tuva—and provided only limited support for separate cultural development for ethnic minorities.[21] As a consequence of this absence of prominent focal points for nationalist opposition to the empire, the intellectuals who developed nation-state projects tended to formulate competing projects, striving for prominence by the very originality of their imaginings. Many of these projects had short lives; intellectual fads for reforming the Empire and then dividing it and then again reforming it came into and fell out of fashion in small circles of intermittent nationalists. Some of the population at large was attached to the status quo of the Russian Empire; this empirical fact became "common sense" that framed their very conception of the givens of political life. Yet many inhabitants of the Russian Empire remained truly parochial: they not

---

[19] Muiznieks 1990.

[20] Weeks 1996, 3–4; Tolz 2001, 8, 100–101; also see S. Smith 2000, 320. For the concept of regnal loyalty, see Reynolds 1984.

[21] Also see Dowler 1995.

only lacked an identity that linked them to a people with a purported right to a state of its own, they lacked even the concept of a state.[22] To these villagers and nomads, the intellectuals who sought to propagate alternative nation-state projects in the name of the people were no less foreign than the leaders of the Russian Empire.

The empire did not foster a separate sense of nationhood within the population that we now know as ethnic Russians. Russian imperial authorities considered Ukrainians (Little Russians) and Belorussians (White Russians) alongside Great Russians to be parts of a common Russian ethnos. In the eyes of most intellectuals within what would become the narrower (Great) Russian national community, Vera Tolz observes, "the divisions between these subgroups were of little importance. Little Russians and Belorussians did not have their own languages, instead their peasants spoke farmyard dialects of Russian. In sum, Ukrainians and Belorussians were Russians."[23] Among peasants and workers, although forms of national identity began to sprout in a few places prior to 1917, most Russians tended to be parochials identifying with their villages and families. According to Tolz, "They did not regard any wide geographical areas of the Russian Empire, let alone the entire country with its non-Russian colonial domains, as their national homeland."[24]

Most intellectuals in what would become the other nations of the USSR, insofar as they talked about their membership in a state, belonged to the Russian nation on the eve of the Russian Revolution. They accepted their membership in the existing state, even though they often sought to reform it. Although they may have been Estonians or Turkestanis, they were also part of a common Russian (*rossiiskii*) nation in believing that Russia was their state—or, if they believed in the radical notion of popular sovereignty, that Russia should be their state. Alternative nation-state projects were typically "minority faiths," to use Andrew Wilson's apt phrase, vainly competing for the imaginations of more than a narrow circle of intellectuals.

Ukrainian and Belorussian nationalisms that might challenge the imagined nations of empire or Eastern Slavs were very limited within the Russian Empire prior to 1917. The region that would become Ukraine was divided among nine provinces—Chernigov, Ekaterinoslav, Kharkov, Kherson, Kiev, Podolia, Poltava, Taurida, Volynia—without Ukraine-wide governing institutions (figure 4.2). A Ukrainian nationalist project flourished in the Galician region of the Austro-Hungarian Empire, but this was not

[22] Kaiser 1995; Suny 1993b, 29–76; Seregny 2000; S. Smith 2000. See, for example, Rakowska-Harmstone 1970, 76–79; Snyder 2003, 130–31. Compare Mair 1977; Weber 1976, 95–114.

[23] Tolz 2001, 195, also see 12–18, 181–88; Weeks 1996, 64–66.

[24] Tolz 2001, 177.

the project that later triumphed in the Ukraine; Galicia was not even annexed to Ukraine until World War II, and so the creation of a Ukrainian state and the triumph of a nation-state project within the Ukrainian SSR were little informed by the Galician project.[25] Ukrainian intellectuals who imagined an independent nation-state were few and isolated on the eve of the Russian Revolution.[26] As Jurij Borys notes, in early 1917 "the supporters of separatism were generally regarded as scholastics, pure theorists, fanatical adherents of independence, or as neurotics hypersensitive on the question of nationality."[27] The larger population in the Ukrainian-speaking provinces was composed of peasants; literacy levels were well below 20 percent. According to Theodore Weeks, "From an admittedly limited data base, it would seem that these peasants were seldom conscious of their Ukrainian national identity. That is, they did not, on the whole, see themselves as Ukrainians as opposed to Russians. They were more likely to see themselves as Orthodox 'locals' as opposed to Catholic Poles or Jews."[28] Ukrainian villagers knew they were different from St. Petersburgers, from gentlemen (even those from Kiev), and from the heretical, and could reject all as alien, but they could not identify themselves as members of a nation with a right to a state of its own.[29]

Belorussian national identity was even less well developed before 1917. The small circle of intellectuals who championed an agenda of linguistic and literary development remained politically insignificant, marginal to the cultural life of the community, and profoundly divided among competing nation-state projects that might unite the lands inhabited by Belorussians with Russia, Poland, or Lithuania or establish a separate, sovereign Belarus state.[30] The absence of either a current segment-state or an unambiguous historic precedent permitted the proliferation of projects to continue with little restraint. In 1917 the region that would become the Belorussian SSR was divided among Grodno, Minsk, Mogilev, Vilna, and Vitebsk provinces without Belorussian-wide institutions (figure 4.2). The separate principalities that had existed briefly over one thousand years earlier and the fourteenth- to sixteenth-century Grand Duchy of Lithuania—which, according to some, was really Belorussian in its language—offered inspiration to some intellectuals.[31] Yet many, particularly socialists, saw themselves as parts of a seamless all-Russian movement, and for them Belorussian separatism had

[25] Snyder 2003, 122–53; Himka 1982.
[26] Motyl 1993, 30–31. Also see Reshetar 1952; Borys 1960.
[27] Borys 1960, 101.
[28] Weeks 1996, 125; Krawchenko 1985, 28, 34.
[29] Liber 1992, 4–7; Wilson 2000, 125. Contrast the view of Guthier 1979.
[30] Weeks 1996, 125–26; Zaprudnik 1993, 45–65; Vakar 1956, 75–92.
[31] Titarenko 1999, 156–58; Vakar 1956, 40–50.

Figure 4.2 European Russia in 1914: provinces. *Source:* Adapted from maps in Andree 1910, Bartholomew 1912, and Brokgauz and Efron 1899, 54:360–61.

little, if any, appeal.[32] In early 1918, when independence was forced on them by the Germans, Belorussian intellectuals divided among those who, like Anton and Ivan Luckevič, joined the German-backed Belorussian Assembly in Vilna that was to become part of a reestablished Grand Duchy of Lithuania; those who remained behind in Minsk to support creation of

[32] Lubachko 1972.

an independent Belarus state; those who rallied behind the Minsk Rada (Council) and insisted that any decision about the future of Belorussian lands must await an all-Russian Constituent Assembly; and those who joined the all-Russian Bolshevik movement.[33]

In the Baltic region, unlike the situation seventy years later, some intellectuals had advanced ethnic agendas of cultural rebirth, but few had rallied behind nationalist agendas of statehood and independence. The educated strata divided among imperialists, autonomists, nationalists, and international socialists.[34] The Baltic region was not organized by the Russian government into ethnic territories until the last days of World War I. In the empire, the region was divided among the provinces of Courland, Estonia, Kovno, Livonia, Vilna, and Vitebsk, and provinces of Poland; these divided each national group among multiple multinational provinces (see figure 4.2).[35] In much of the Baltic region the most fully developed nation-state projects came from the Balto-German nobility, which was highly placed in administration, universities, and intellectual circles. Defenders of the traditional order in this Balto-German community argued for restoration of such imagined states as the Grand Duchy of Livonia, based on German-Lutheran culture and the privileged status of the nobility. Modernizers among the Balto-German intelligentsia argued for a duchy uniting Livonia, Courland, Estonia, and Ösel (Saaremaa) and with a constitution guaranteeing the sort of self-government enjoyed in Finland.[36] Even in the first years of World War I, according to Georg von Rauch, Estonian and Latvian intellectuals "had not even considered the possibility of setting up independent states" and at most hoped for reorganization of the empire's administrative system along ethnic lines.[37] For the Estonian and Latvian peasants, "the question of independence simply did not arise."[38] In Latvia, even as late as November 1917 the first Latvian National Assembly continued to hold out for autonomy within the empire rather than independence, and many Latvian intellectuals were actively sympathetic to the Bolsheviks and joined the Russian Revolution.[39] Similarly, in Lithuania, the Russian declaration of war initially produced a patriotic rally behind the tsar.[40] By early 1917, Lithuanian leaders, who spoke a common language but were divided among prov-

[33] Vakar 1956, 93, 101–5. Also see Snyder 2003, 52–72.
[34] Von Rauch 1974, 13; Raun 1987, 99–104.
[35] See, for example, Hroch 2000, 83, which shows the Estonian national movement divided among the provinces of Estonia, Livonia, and Pskov.
[36] Jussila 1989, 94–96; Raun 1984.
[37] Von Rauch 1974, 25; Taagepera 1993, 31, 37. Compare Lieven 1993, 57–60.
[38] Von Rauch 1974, 25.
[39] Plakans 1995, 116–20; Pabriks 1999, 46; von Rauch 1974, 39–75.
[40] Senn 1959, 18–21.

inces of the Russian Empire, had a sense of ethnic unity, but had not associated this with a program of political-administrative organization.[41]

In the Transcaucasus, in the absence of segment-states, nationalism was also weak and unfocused, and alternative nation-state projects proliferated among small circles of intellectuals. The Transcaucasus was divided among Kutais, Tiflis, Erivan, Elizavetpol, and Baku provinces and Kars territory rather than ethnic republics (figure 4.3). In the absence of segment-states, advocates of projects for Azeri, Armenian, and Georgian states that would win the day seventy-five years later were overwhelmed by the advocates of projects for a Caucasian federation that would unite both slopes of the mountain range, for separate Transcaucasian and North Caucasian federations on each slope, as well as for a new Russian federation.[42] Intellectuals among what would become the Azeris were divided among projects for a Russian, pan-Turkic, or pan-Islamic state, and only a minority envisioned an independent Azerbaijan.[43] In 1914, Muslim deputies in the Duma and leaders from the regions inhabited by the people who would become Azeris greeted the war against the German and Austro-Hungarian empires with shows of patriotism and little dissent, but sentiments and divisions became more complex with the declaration of war against the Ottoman Empire.[44] The population that became Georgians included ethnic groups such as the Ajaris, Batsbis, Guris, Ingiloi, Imereli, Khevsurs, Mingrelians, Pshav, and Svans, whose spokespersons divided over whether they were part of a common Georgian nation. In the early twentieth century, according to Ghia Nodia, "Georgian national ambitions were still quite modest," and intellectuals directed most attention to cultural renewal, including preservation of the Georgian language.[45] Abkhazian leaders divided over whether they were part of the Georgian nation or the Russian nation, or constituted an independent Abkhazian nation with a right to a state of its own. Among Armenians what has subsequently been called "nationalism" tended prior to 1918 to stress cultural themes and strong loyalty to the Russian Empire. In 1914 the Armenian population enthusiastically supported the empire in its war with Turkey, and welcomed the February 1917 revolution. Even the *Dashnaktsutiun* at the time saw Armenia as part of a Russian state but hoped the liberal provisional government would redraw administrative borders in Transcaucasia and establish a federal state of ethnic cantons.[46] The idea of limited autonomy within the Russian Empire was not seriously

[41] Senn 1959, 2–16; Page 1948; White 1971.
[42] Van der Leeuw 2000, 108–115; Altstadt 1992, 50–87.
[43] Carley 1998, chap. 4. Also see Swietochowski 1995, 61–65; van der Leeuw 2000.
[44] Swietochowski 1985, 75–83
[45] Nodia, 1997–98, 19.
[46] Hovannisian 1967, 15–23, 40–68, 69–93.

debated by Armenian, Azeri, and Georgian intellectuals until Russia's 1905 revolution, and it remained a minority position until independence was actually thrust on all three peoples by the Ottoman Empire in 1918. Even with independence, intellectuals in all three republics remained divided over the configuration of their independent states.

In Central Asia, prior to 1917, intellectuals advanced competing projects for statehood on behalf of the Muslims as a single people, the Turkic Muslims, existing regional jurisdictions such as Turkestan or Bukhara, and imagined nationalities such as Kazakh-Kirgizes, Kirgizes, Kazakhs, or the Greater Horde within the Kazakhs. All these competed with those Central Asian intellectuals who argued for subordinating local differences in an all-Russian alliance of exploited classes or loyalty to the empire.[47] In this period of competing national projects, elite and popular identification with the groups that would eventually become nation-states tended to be weak.[48] The strongest candidates were those projects focused on the existing administrative jurisdictions—Bukhara, Khiva, and Turkestan (figure 4.4)— but even these were minority views. Alternatively, in 1917 Vladimir Lenin and Josef Stalin spoke as though the major national divide in Central Asia would be none of these but the then common and now somewhat obscure division between Sarts (settled peoples) and Kirgizes (all nomadic peoples).[49] When the Soviet regime proposed the national delimitation of Central Asia in the early 1920s, some intellectuals objected to the "parcellizing" of the existing segment states of Bukhara and Khiva and of Turkestan. Other intellectuals welcomed an opportunity to redraw geographic and human boundaries, but championed such nation-state projects as "Greater Kazakhstan," which would stretch from the Volga and Siberia to the Bukharan steppe, "Greater Kirgizia," and "Greater Uzbekistan." As Alexander Park notes, these alternative projects offered at the time of the national delimitation cross-cut one another in bewildering inconsistency: "Still others offered projects for the creation of 'separate autonomies,' 'unions of free tribes,' 'independent cities,' and other unworkable state structures."[50] Popular identities were decidedly parochial. Although most Central Asians probably recognized that they belonged to the community of Muslim believers (*umma*), as William Fierman observes, they "were probably not conscious of their Turkic roots. They identified themselves as members of particular tribes, inhabitants of certain villages, valleys, oases, towns, or

---

[47] Zenkovsky 1960. Also see Suny 1999/2000; Khalid 1996; Edgar 2001; and the discussion among Sanborn 2000, Seregny 2000, and S. Smith 2000.
[48] Olcott 1987, 135 138; Sabol 2003; Fierman 1991, 46.
[49] Allworth 1990, 178.
[50] Alexander Park 1957, 93.

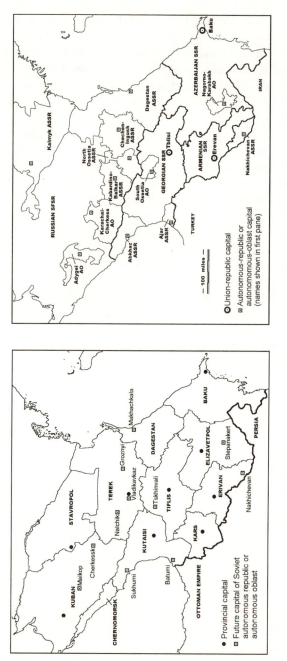

Figure 4.3 The Caucasus in 1914 and 1991: provinces and republics. *Source:* Adapted from maps in Andree 1910, Bartholomew 1912, and Brokgauz and Efron 1894, 26:824–25.

other small regions."[51] Within the broader population, Oliver Roy argues, "not only had no nation in the modern sense of the term even been created, but the meaning of the word 'national' itself (*milli*) referred to a religious and cultural community which had no territory and no state of its own."[52]

Soviet Political-Identity Hegemonies

The introduction of segment-states by the Soviet regime facilitated the coordination of identities around one set of these competing nation-state projects and relegated most of the others to the dustbin that is picked over by historians. Segment-states created the expectation among politicians and intellectuals with alternative nation-state projects that their best strategy would be to abandon these and to join the cohort of dominant politicians. For example, in Central Asia, intellectuals in the first years of the Soviet regime debated whether Tajiks constituted a nation, and if so, who should be included and excluded. The most common view rejected a separate Tajikistan and favored a united Turkestan. Yet the creation of the Tajik Autonomous Soviet Socialist Republic in 1924 shifted the terms of the debate decisively toward the project for a separate Tajik nation. As Guissou Jahangiri notes, the creation of the autonomous republic "encouraged a number of supporters of the Pan-Turkic argument to change their positions enough to take up jobs within the government of the new Republic. It also helped many institutions, such as universities, museums, and libraries, to spring up, which could underpin local identity."[53] For the population at large, the empirical reality of a state defined as their own and the actual incorporation of their villages into this state provided villagers their first sustained contact with a modern state and fostered new national identities among them. Similarly, at the other end of the USSR, among Ukrainians a decisive transformation began in the 1920s with creation of the Ukrainian SSR, an indigenous urban elite, a Ukrainian-language educational system, and mass media controlled by the new segment-state. Villagers entered into sustained contact with this state; "peasants became Ukrainians."[54]

In the Soviet period the coordination of identities was drawn to the new focal point of the segment-states, which were conspicuous among nation-state projects by virtue of their empirical reality. Individual members of the elite and public rallied around the new segment-states because each expected others to do so as well. Yet the psychological process of coordinating

---

[51] Fierman 1991, 40; Alexander Park 1957, 157–68.

[52] Roy 2000, viii–ix, 72.

[53] Jahangiri 1997, 33. See also Rakowska-Harmstone 1970, 76.

[54] Liber 1992, 120; Krawchenko 1985, 196–97. Also see Suny 1992.

Figure 4.4 Central Asia in 1914 and 1991: provinces, protectorates, and republics. *Source:* Adapted from maps in Andree 1910, Bartholomew 1912, and Brokgauz and Efron 1902, 67:200–201.

expectations was actively fostered by segment-state leaders using the unique opportunities they had to privilege their own nation-state project above alternatives. The segment-state leaders' advantages over competitors were significant: in crafting a nationality to fit the segment-state, union republic leaders enjoyed a political monopoly; no one else was permitted to speak on behalf of the titular nationality. The union republic leaders institutionalized this monopoly over the public expression of identity and used the indigenization of leadership posts in cultural institutions of the union republics to bring to power intellectuals who were willing to participate in the official nation-state project.[55]

The union republic leaders assigned to the official intelligentsia, who were organized in academies of sciences, institutes, and unions of writers, artists, and architects, the task of creating official cultures and official histories and, as much as possible, replacing alternative cultures and erasing other records of the past. For example, the creation of Azeri, Kazakh, Kirgiz, Tajik, Turkmen, and Uzbek segment-states required the development of separate, standardized languages and cultures for each.[56] The decision to reject pan-Turkic and Turkestan projects meant abandoning Tatar efforts to create a pan-Turkic language.[57] In Moldavia, the creation of a segment-state meant creating a Moldavian language and culture that would sustain its separation from Romania.[58] In Karelia this at first meant creating a Karelian language to separate Karelians from Finns, then, after World War II, as Moscow harbored hopes of annexing Finland, replacing Karelian by Finnish as the official language of the republic, and then, after a peace treaty with Finland in the mid-1950s, returning the Karelian language to its official status.[59] The creation of separate segment-states meant writing national histories that would sustain the myth that the official demarcation of boundaries among nationalities was simply the political recognition of a historical fact.[60]

The union republic leaders used their institutionalized monopoly of cultural life to silence intellectuals with competing nation-state projects and to erase records of paths that might have led to alternative nation-states.[61] They closed archives to all but the most reliable intellectuals; they culled books from library shelves to remove records of paths not taken. They punished severely those who attempted to articulate alternative nation-state projects.[62] Creative professionals who sought to spread alternative projects for nation-states could not gain access to public forums; thus, their alternative imagined communities might gain currency at most in dark corners of the country among small circles of acquaintances.[63] In many instances, serious discussion of these alternative projects simply ceased to be

[55] See Hodnett 1978, 90–91; Popovsky 1979, 118; Graney 1999; Verdery 1993; Slezkine 1994.

[56] Akiner 1995, 36–40; Fierman 1991; Allworth 1990, 219–23; Roy 2000, 78–82; Jahangiri 1997.

[57] Fierman 1991, 50; Swietochowski 1995, 108–15.

[58] Dima 1991, 94–100, 117–27; C. King 2000, 63–88. Also see C. King 1999.

[59] Austin 1992.

[60] Akiner 1995, 34.

[61] See, for example, Loeber 1968; Vakar 1956, 150–51; Inkeles 1950; Kenez 1985; Slezkine 1992.

[62] Alexeyeva 1985, 31.

[63] Kocaoglu 1983; Bennigsen 1984, 36–37; Alexeyeva 1985, 31.

politically significant. For example, after seventy years of Soviet power in Central Asia, alternative national projects such as Turkestan could not compete with the official nationalisms of Kazakhs, Uzbeks, and the other titular nationalities.[64]

One important addendum should be added to the Soviet story: the experience of independence after 1917—very brief, in some cases—could have a strong focusing effect. This is particularly true where the segment-state imposed on these "conquered nation-states" reinforced this nation-state project, which began to take shape during independence. This was most pronounced in the Baltic states, where the creation of nations was fostered by the policies of the new nation-state leaders during the period of independence. Between the wars, culture and education took on a very nationalistic tone, solidifying a national identity, particularly after the authoritarian coups of 1926, in Lithuania, and 1934, in Estonia and Latvia.[65] After they became segment-states, common-state identities that would have linked their populations to the USSR never developed as deeply in these three republics. The much briefer period of independence for the Transcaucasian republics (1918–21) also focused national identities. For example, the brief period of independence was very powerful in focusing Azeris' identity as a nation with a right to a state of their own, "and for most Azeris that period remains a pivotal point in their history and nationhood that they have not forgotten."[66] Yet this brief period of independence did not block the emergence of common-state identities—at least not to the same extent as in the Baltic republics—once they became segment-states within the USSR. Alternatively, where the segment-state worked at cross purposes with the experience of interwar independence, the nation-state project of the segment-state trumped the nation-state project of prior statehood. In Moldova, despite strong agitation from university faculty and students for reunification with Romania, the nation-state project forged within the Moldavian SSR trumped the project for a return to the interwar nation-state project of Greater Romania.[67]

Post-Soviet Political-Identity Hegemonies

Although the force with which the USSR imposed nation-state projects may have been extreme, it differed in degree, not in kind, from the force

---

[64] Lubin 1995, 18. Also see Olcott 1994, 549–65; Kubicek 1997.

[65] Taagepera 1993, 107; Plakans 1995, 137–38; Pabriks 1999, 68–73; Sabaliunas 1972, 25–40; Raun 1987, 118–23, 133–37.

[66] Carley 1998, chap. 4. Also see Swietochowski 1995, 61–65; Nodia 1997–98, 19.

[67] C. King 2000, 151–60.

with which segment-states within more democratic common-states typically privilege official nation-state projects over others. The experience of the Russian Federation highlights the opportunities that segment-states provide to establish local identity hegemonies even in more democratic common-states.[68] It also highlights the close, reciprocal connection between both halves of political-identity hegemony: political machines help focus national identity and suppress alternative nation-state projects, while identity hegemony in turn reinforces political hegemony. With Russia's experiment in democracy, the republics lost much of their centrally enforced cultural monopoly and had to rely on their own local resources from within the segment-states to maintain or reconstruct identity hegemony. The republics controlled by political machines were better able to privilege specific nation-state projects over their competitors and to marginalize ethnopoliticians who claimed to represent the segment-state project better or who advanced alternative nation-state projects (table 4.1). This relationship between political machines and identity hegemony is underscored in surveys conducted by Timothy Colton and his research team in sixteen of Russia's republics in November–December 1993; Dmitry Gorenburg reanalyzed these data to show the strength of national identities in the titular population of each republic.[69] The research team asked respondents the following questions concerning the nation-state projects of the republics:

> "How do you feel about the declarations of sovereignty by the former autonomous republics of the Russian Federation?" [Aggregated responses: support, no opinion, oppose]
> "Should all republics have the right of self-determination, including withdrawal from the Russian Federation?" [Aggregated responses: all or some republics, no opinion, no republics]
> "Should control of the army, police, and security be transferred to the jurisdiction of the sovereign republics of the Russian Federation?" [Aggregated responses: support, no opinion, oppose]

The respondents from the titular populations in republics controlled by machines (n = 12) were about twice as likely as respondents in the competitive republics (n = 5) to respond with support for the sovereignty declarations (57.4 percent versus 28.2 percent), to endorse the right of at least some republics to secede (59.4 percent versus 30.0 percent), and to support republican control over the power ministries (41.5 percent versus 17.6 percent) (Gorenberg 2003, 241–43).

[68] See Gorenburg 2003; Shnirelman 1996; Matveeva 1999.
[69] Gorenburg 2003, 241–43.

TABLE 4.1
Russian Federation: Political-identity hegemonies within republics[a]

	Machine republics	Competitive republics
Titular identity hegemony	Adygeia	
	Bashkortostan	
	Buryatia	
	Ingushetia	
	Kalmykia	
	Mordovia	
	North Ossetia	
	Sakha	
	Tatarstan	
	Tyva	
Multiethnic titular identity hegemony	Dagestan	
	Kabardino-Balkaria	
Competitive identities		Altai
		Chuvashia
		Karachai-Cherkessia
		Karelia
		Khakassia
		Komi
		Mari El
		Udmurtia

[a]Omits Chechnya.

Machine Republics

Like Shaimiev in Tatarstan (described in chapter 3), Presidents Aslan Dzharimov in Adygeia, Murtaza Rakhimov in Bashkortostan, Ruslan Aushev in Ingushetia, Kirsan Iliumzhinov in Kalmykia, Nikolai Merkushkin in Mordovia, Akhsarbek Galazov in North Ossetia, Mikhail Nikolaev in Sakha, and Sherig-ool Oorzhak in Tyva were all titulars who kept national identity closely associated with the existing segment-state and cast themselves as the best defenders of the national aspirations of the titular people.[70] These presidents captured the national mantle and made most of the nationalist movement dependent on the patronage of the republic; they also marginalized proponents of competing nation-state projects who

[70] On Sakha, see Balzer and Vinokurova 1996. On Chuvashia, see Igor' Lenskii, "Serye volki u okolitsy," *Pravda* December 11, 1992, 2. On Kalmykia, see Valerii Vyzhutovich, "Ulozhenie v step': Pokhorony kalmytskoi gosudarstvennosti Kirsanom Iliumzhinovym," *Izvestiia* April 13, 1994, 5; Andrei Pavlov and Sergei Sergienko, "Udarnye nochi brat'ev Iliumzhinovykh," *Komsomolskaia pravda* September 20, 1994, 3. On Tyva, see V. Danilenko, "Obostrilas' obstanovka," *Izvestiia* August 3, 1990, 2; Sheehy 1990d; Sullivan 1995.

claimed to represent the titular people better, or to represent at least parts of the titular population in alternative nation-state configurations. For example, in Bashkortostan, the Rakhimov administration moved decisively to coöpt or to clip the influence of the Bashkir nationalist movement that had organized before Rakhimov came to power. The Ural Bashkir People's Center, established in December 1989, created a widespread organization with separate front organizations such as the Bashkir Peoples' Party, Bashkir Women's Society, and Union of Bashkir Youth. The center championed the sovereignty of the republic and a special status for Bashkirs within Bashkortostan, demanding preferential treatment in privatization of property and assignment of political offices. At first the center assumed a harsh confrontational style with the republic's government, calling for creation of a Bashkir National Congress to serve as an alternative government. As Rakhimov consolidated his political machine and assumed the nationalist mantle, however, Bashkir nationalists increasingly rallied behind their republic's leadership as the best defender of Bashkir interests and penultimate manifestation of the Bashkirs' right to a sovereign state of their own.[71] The republic leaders marginalized those nationalists who would not join the official nation-state project. For example, the proponents of the Idel-Ural project that would unite Tatars, Bashkirs, and others in a single republic were forced underground, to become once again a parlor nation after a brief period as a fad among university professors and students. The Rakhimov administration also reined in proponents of nation-state projects on behalf of the republic's Tatar, Russian, Chuvash, Mari, and German minorities. For example, the outspoken newspaper *Otechestvo* (Fatherland), which defended the rights of Russians in the republic, was twice confiscated in October 1996 when it published articles critical of the republic's leadership and their declaration of sovereignty. Finally, on October 30, both its editor-in-chief and general manager reported that they had been told "that they would be killed if they continued publishing the paper"—allegedly by republican law enforcement officers.[72] Like Bashkortostan's leadership, Tyva's leadership under Oorzhak coöpted most nationalists and marginalized the more radical nationalists, such as the members of Free Tyva (*Khostug Tuva*), who pressed for independence.[73] In the other machine republics of Ingushetia, Kalmykia, Mordovia, and North Ossetia, opposition from proponents of alternative nation-state projects tended to be more limited and sporadic than in Bashkortostan, Tatarstan, or Tyva. Republic leaders offered patronage to cultural revival groups such as the recurring

---

[71] Gorenburg 1997, 18.
[72] OMRI Daily Digest October 31, 1996.
[73] Alatalu 1992; Anaiban and Walker 1996.

Congresses of Mordvin People, but cast the republic itself as the manifestation of the nation's right to a state of its own.[74]

In the machine republic of Buryatia, because President Leonid Potapov and many of his closest associates were not titulars, the task of establishing identity hegemony was more complicated. The Potapov machine claimed to represent legitimate Buryat nationalist aspirations but had a harder time at marginalizing nationalist opposition, such as the Buryat-Mongol People's Party and the Negedel National Unity Movement, which disputed the legitimacy of this claim.[75]

In the multiethnic republics of Dagestan and Kabardino-Balkaria the task of establishing hegemony of the multiethnic nation-state project that legitimated the existing republics was still more complicated. To stay in power the republic leaders relied on a coalition of elites from the different titular nationalities. Yet elites within one or more of the titular nationalities—frequently, these were raion and city leaders—were in a position to press alternative nation-state projects from below on behalf of these nationalities. Nevertheless, the machine of Valerii Kokov and the cartel machine in Dagestan contained these challenges and maintained not only their own monopoly control over power but also the official position of the multiethnic nation-state projects.

The Kabardino-Balkar Republic machine faced strong dissent from radical nationalists in both of its titular nationalities. Some Balkar ethnopoliticians demanded division of the republic in two, claiming that the current five-to-one advantage of Karachais over Balkars in the republic's population kept Balkars in a permanent minority. Reacting to the swift consolidation of control by the republic's leadership loyal to Kokov and the impending presidential elections, a self-proclaimed Congress of Balkars on November 17, 1991, proclaimed a separate Balkar Republic with the status of a subject of the Russian Federation; it designated the National Council of the Balkar People as its leadership council.[76] On the day of the republic's first presidential elections (December 29, 1991), urban, town, and village soviets within areas inhabited by Balkars held a referendum in which 94.9 percent of the voters purportedly affirmed their support for "the proclamation of a separate Balkar People's Republic." The fires of the Balkar nationalists were not cooled when a 1994 referendum conducted by the republic government showed that 96 percent of Balkars supported a unified Kabardino-Balkaria. On November 17, 1996, the Congress of Balkars issued yet another proclamation establishing a separate republic, suspending the laws

---

[74] *Russian Federation Report* October 20, 1999; Taagepera 1999.

[75] Iurii Vakhrin, "'Prishlye' v Rossiiskoi glubinke," *Rossiiskaia gazeta* February 24, 1993, 6.

[76] A. Kazikhanov, "Provozglashena novaia respublika—Balkariia," *Izvestiia* November 19, 1991, 2.

of Kabardino-Balkaria on its territory, and constituting itself as the governing authority until the Russian Federation could prepare for the creation of state organs and call elections.[77] In reaction to the Balkar demands, and fearing too many concessions would be made to the Balkars, a Congress of Kabards convened on January 10–12, 1992, and proclaimed a Kabard Republic. When protestors from this movement attempted to seize the local television center and the House of Soviets (parliament building) in the capital, Nalchik, in September 1992, the republic leadership imposed a state of emergency and called in Russian troops.[78] Swift action by the machine suppressed these challenges to the republic's machine and its official nation-state project.

In Dagestan, the republic's leadership confronted pressure from various radical nationalists, who rejected the official multiethnic nation-state project of the republic based on the so-called peoples of Dagestan and claimed that the cartel machine had failed to protect the interests of separate constituent nations. On November 19, 1989, the first National Congress of Kumyk People announced that its objectives included creation of a Kumyk autonomous republic within a new Dagestani confederation that would be part of the Russian Federation. The Lezgin National Council *Savdal* demanded creation of a Lezgistan within Russia, and on September 28, 1991, the Third National Congress of Lezgins proclaimed this republic. Dagestan's Nogai nationalists, led by their organization *Birlik* (Unity) and almost annual Congresses of the Nogai People, demanded unification of the Nogai lands scattered among Dagestan, Stavropol krai, and Karachai-Cherkessia into a new republic. The cartel machine was able to keep these challenges from threatening the hegemony of the machine and its nation-state project.

Competitive Republics

In the minority of republics in which a cohort of politicians failed to establish machine control, the consequence was a failure to establish identity hegemony, but once again, the failures of political hegemony and identity hegemony were reciprocal. In the competitive polities of Altai, Chuvashia, Karelia, Khakassia, Komi, Mari El, and Udmurtia, conflicts between titular elites claiming the republic as their own and ethnic Russian managerial elites fearing this would mean their own marginalization often defined a

---

[77] "Provozglashena suverennaia Balkariia," *Kommersant-Daily* November 19, 1996, 3; Petr Pliev, "Popytka raschleneniia Kabardino-Balkarii," *Nezavisimaia gazeta* November 19, 1996, 1.

[78] Ali Kazikhanov, "Chrezvychainoe polozhenie v Nal'chike ob"iavleno i tut zhe priostanovleno," *Izvestiia* September 28, 1992, 1–2; Ali Kazikhanov, "Nal'chik: 'Tret'ia sila,' kotoruiu nikto ne videl," *Izvestiia* September 30, 1992, 1; Igor' Terekhov, "Miting v Nal'chike okonchen," *Nezavisimaia gazeta* October 6, 1992, 3.

central dispute of the republics' politics. Competition between nation-state projects that privileged the titular people of the segment-state and the nation-state project that supported the sovereignty of the Russian Federation became a central issue that colored the political agenda of the segment-states. In some of these republics this confrontation over nation-state projects provoked a constitutional crisis over such issues as introduction of a presidency or the balance of powers between executive and legislative branches. The Russians within the republic often realized that the claim of the republic to greater autonomy and a greater share of resources than an oblast depended on its special national character. These were claims that could benefit everyone within the segment-state. At the same time these Russians often feared that on the basis of the special national character of the segment-state, the titular elites might lay special claim to power within the republic, such as monopolizing its presidency through language and residence requirements, and deny nontitulars their fair share of power. The introduction of such institutional innovations as a republic presidency was critical to establishing political-identity hegemony but was delayed as the supporters of the alternative nation-state projects fought over the details of control of institutions. For example, Chuvashia instituted a presidency on August 29, 1991, and scheduled elections for December 5. The first round of the elections, however, left the incumbent de facto president (Supreme Soviet chair) favored by the republic's Russian managerial elite in third place; the front-runner was the candidate of the Chuvash Party of National Rebirth. With the threat of a Chuvash victory in the run-off, the Supreme Soviet, which was dominated by Russian enterprise managers and their allies, voted to postpone the second round of elections. Chuvashia did not actually hold its first presidential elections until December 12, 1993.[79]

In the segment-states with competitive polities there could be a wide swing between attempts to indigenize government and the backlash from the Russian community as governments led by titulars and Russians alternated in office. In Mari El, where the two communities were evenly balanced in the population and in politics, this was the sad outcome. Following his victory in Mari El's first presidential elections in December 1991, Vladislav Zotin, a Mari, began constructing a national machine, appointing Maris to almost every executive position throughout the republic. He offered patronage to moderate nationalists, such as those within *Mari Ushem* (Mari Union), who were willing to work within his official nation-state project and direct their energies toward cultural projects; he marginalized radical nationalists, such as those in *Kugeze Mlande* (Ancestral Land), who

[79] "V Chuvashii priniat zakon o prezidente respubliki," *Izvestiia* November 26, 1993, 1; Irek Namyz, "Pervyi prezident Respubliki Nikolai Federov," *Nezavisimaia gazeta* December 28, 1993, 3.

continued to press for secession from Russia and for barriers to migration into the republic.[80] Yet the economic managers of industry and collective farms, who were overwhelmingly Russians, felt threatened by Zotin's pro-Mari policies. Five years later, in the republic's 1996 presidential elections Zotin's former subordinate, Vyacheslav Kislitsyn, won with 59 percent of the vote, but the strong showing of the Russian nationalist candidate, Leonid Markelov, in this election reflected Russian dissatisfaction with the Mari-first policies of Zotin's government.[81] In the December 2000 elections Markelov won in the second round with 58.2 percent of the vote over Kislitsyn's 33.4 percent. A former military prosecutor, backed by Vladimir Zhirinovsky's archnationalist Liberal Democratic Party of Russia, Markelov promised to undo the Mari-first policies and to strengthen Mari El's ties with Moscow.[82]

In the segment-states with competitive polities ethnic Russians were more successful in their attempts to capture the government and to privilege the nation-state project that supported the sovereignty of the Russian Federation over any local projects and to treat all residents of the republic as *rossiiane* (civic Russians) rather than titulars and nontitulars. In Altai, after introduction of a popularly elected chief executive in December 1997, a Russian, Semen Zubakin, narrowly defeated the Altai leader, Yurii Antaradonov. Afterward there was significant erosion of the special ethnic character of the republic and marginalization of Altai nationalist groups.[83] Similarly, in Khakassia, ethnic deadlock delayed introduction of a presidency until 1996. Khakasses had demanded guarantees that the presidency would go to one of their own, even though they constituted only 11 percent of the republic's population; leaders of the nontitular communities rejected any such guarantees. In the first elections for the republic's presidency, a Russian, Aleksei Lebed, won on the second round with 71 percent of the vote.[84] Khakass deputies also failed to win ethnic parity in the allocation of legislative seats between Khakasses and all other nationalities, and failed to win a constitutional provision to privilege Khakass culture within the republic.[85] In Udmurtia, the Supreme Soviet debated introduction of a

[80] Taagepera 1999, 240–52.

[81] Maksim Stepenii, "Byvshii prezident Marii El mozhet sest' na tri goda," *Kommersant-Daily* May 8, 1997, 2; *OMRI Daily Digest* December 23, 1996; ITAR-TASS December 31, 1996, January 5, 1997, January 29, 1997.

[82] *RFE/RL Newsline* July 11, 2001.

[83] Orttung 2000, 126.

[84] Irina Nagornykh, "Izbirkom Khakassii otkazalsia registrirovat' Alekseia Lebeda kandidatom na post glavy respubliki," *Segodnia* October 9, 1996, 2; Maksim Zhukov, "Lebed'-mladshchii oppozitsiei ne schitaetsia," *Kommersant-Daily* December 3, 1996.

[85] Sergei Fedorchenko, "Khakassiia reshila obzavestis' svoei konstitutsiei," *Segodnia* February 7, 1995, 3; Orttung 2000, 231; *RFE/RL Newsline* July 30, 1998.

presidency in October 1991, but stalemated over a requirement that candidates know the Udmurt language. A law on instituting a presidency was adopted only in January 1993, with the stipulation that the first president need not know the Udmurt language. But the conflict led the Supreme Soviet first to postpone the presidential elections until a new constitution could be adopted and then to dispense with a presidency entirely. Without a machine, the Udmurt role in politics rapidly declined; after the March 1995 elections Udmurts controlled only 16 percent of the legislative seats (down from 26 percent).[86] Yet according to the 1989 census, Udmurts constituted 55 percent of the republic's population.

In the multiethnic republic of Karachai-Cherkessia, the failure to consolidate a national machine based on the hegemony of a unifying nation-state project left the leadership vulnerable to secessionist opposition that paralyzed the republic's government. The roots of this crisis appear to have been the growing demands from Karachais to elevate their autonomous oblast to republic status, but this would remove the segment-state from the jurisdiction of Stavropol krai, which had maintained the internal inter-ethnic balance and protected Cherkess and other minority rights. The official nation-state project supporting a state that combined Karachais and Cherkesses was challenged by secessionist leaders within both titular groups. In October 1989 the first of a series of unofficial Karachai congresses and conferences convened to demand creation of a separate Karachai homeland (ultimately, to demand a Karachai Soviet Socialist Republic). In reaction, Cossacks in July 1990 convened the first of a series of Russian congresses to oppose inclusion of areas inhabited by ethnic Russians in any new Karachai republic. The task of creating institutions for the new Karachai-Cherkess Republic, which was elevated from the status of autonomous oblast in July 1991, raised the stakes and exacerbated competition among advocates of the alternative nation-state projects, and by March 1992 five committees were preparing plans for separate republics—Karachaisk, Cherkessk, Abazinsk (for Abazians), Batalpashinsk (for Cossacks and Russians), and Zelenchuk-Urup (for Cossacks and Russians). Nogais demanded separation of their lands from Karachai-Cherkessia and unification within an entirely new Nogai state. Even though on March 28, 1992, a referendum on the future of the republic showed that 78.6 percent of the voters supported a unified Karachai-Cherkessia, the republic's elites remained divided. These divisions led to a stalemate over fundamental constitutional issues within the republic, particularly the introduction of a

---

[86] Taagepera 1999, 288–93. The State Council (formerly the Supreme Soviet) finally authorized a referendum to create a presidency in 2000, but only after federal legislation mandated this. In the first presidential elections, on October 15, 2000, the chair of the State Council, Aleksandr Volkov, an ethnic Russian, won with 37.8 percent of the vote.

presidency that would likely go to a Karachai. Elections to a new republic Supreme Soviet were postponed indefinitely, and Boris Yeltsin intervened on January 13, 1992, to appoint Vladimir Khubiev, a Karachai, as head of administration until new elections could be called in 1999, but Khubiev was blocked in his attempt to consolidate a machine by the autonomous oblast soviet, which continued to sit as the republic legislature.[87] The 1999 elections for a republic president tore the republic apart with violent protest, street clashes between partisans of the leading Karachai and Cherkess contestants, a blockade of the government building, assassination attempts, bombings of homes and cafes, a grenade attack against the republic's Supreme Court chair, and renewed calls for separation of Cherkess, Russian, and Abazian regions from the Karachai core; this continued for more than a year.[88] The victor, elected under suspicious circumstances, was General Vladimir Semenov, a Karachai.

---

[87] Elena Viktorova, "Konstitutsiia Karachaevo-Cherkesii dorabatyvaetsia," *Segodnia* March 2, 1995, 2; Dmitrii Kamyshev, "V spore parlamenta i prem'era pobedila druzhba narodov," *Kommersant-Daily* April 1, 1995, 3; Radio Rossi June 12, 1995; ITAR-TASS September 12, 1995, March 15, 1996; *RFE/RL Newsline* October 10, 1997, January 24, 1998, February 5, 1998.

[88] Kozlov 2001, 133–34.

FIVE

Conditions for Political-Identity Hegemony

I **N IDENTIFYING THOSE NATION-STATE** projects that are likely to emerge hegemonic in the competition on the periphery, the segmental institutions thesis stresses, first of all, the association of successful projects with segment-states. Without a segment-state, political-identity hegemony prior to independence is unlikely. Yet what could explain why some but not other segment-state leaders establish political-identity hegemony? The segmental institutions thesis stresses that the configuration of political institutions in both segment-states and their respective common-states is a primary constraint in determining which segment-states develop political-identity hegemony. First, the greater their autonomy to design their own political institutions, fill political offices, make appointments to prestigious and lucrative positions in society, and control use of organizational resources for political action, the more opportunities that segment-state leaders have to create political-identity hegemony. That is, in establishing political-identity hegemony within segment-states, leaders use the decision rights assigned to the segment-state to make continued support of their project more attractive than support for an alternative.

Second, the institutional arrangements of the common-state also constrain the development of political-identity hegemony inside segment-states. In particular, autocratic and democratic common-states produce different patterns of political-identity hegemony in segment-states. The authoritarian common-state enforces the political-identity hegemony of segment-state leaders, but it also limits the ways in which segment-state leaders can turn this political-identity hegemony against the common-state. In democratic common-states there is typically greater variation among segment-states: there are more segment-states that fail to establish political-identity hegemony, but there are also more opportunities to establish political-identity hegemony strong enough to challenge the common-state. In both autocratic and democratic common-states, however, shifts in the consolidation of leadership within the common-state government produce fluctuations over time in the autonomy of segment-states.

In this chapter the evidence reported in the two previous chapters is gathered systematically to examine these patterns of variation. The relationship between common-state institutions and political-identity hegemony becomes clearly visible in two types of temporal comparisons—differences between the common-states of the autocratic USSR and semidemocratic

Russian Federation and variations within each of these as leadership consolidation in the common-state rose and fell. The importance of differences in the decision rights assigned to each segment-state is illustrated in cross-sectional comparisons among the segment-states of the USSR and among the segment-states of the Russian Federation. These relationships provide insights for hypotheses that are tested within a larger number of cases in part 4 of this book.

Autonomy and Intervention from the Center

The more that common-state leaders have the capacity to intervene against segment-state leaders, removing them or countermanding their decisions, the less likely it is that segment-state leaders will establish political-identity hegemonies—or at least hegemonies that can challenge the common-state. While the other constraints described in this chapter stress more stable allocations of decision rights, this first constraint points to fluctuation in the capacity of the common-state leadership to use its decision rights and the implications of this for the capacity of segment-state leaders to use their rights fully to build political-identity hegemony. The importance of this varying capacity of the common-state leaders to intervene is illustrated by two patterns of variation in Soviet politics and one in Russian politics. First, in the Soviet system the autonomy of union republic leaders varied with the succession cycle—the initial period of competition and then the period of consolidation that followed the Lenin-to-Stalin, Stalin-to-Khrushchev, and Khrushchev-to-Brezhnev successions.[1] The first union republic machines emerged in the initial wave of indigenization as Moscow was preoccupied with the succession to Vladimir Lenin.[2] Once Joseph Stalin consolidated autocratic control within the CPSU leadership, however, he purged the so-called bourgeois nationalists who had built local power bases in the republics.[3] During Nikita Khrushchev's struggle against Lavrentii Beria, Georgii Malenkov, and Vyacheslav Molotov, the first secretary at first made concessions of autonomy to union republic first secretaries in order to shore up his power base within the Communist Party. After 1957, however, Khrushchev became more interventionist, particularly in the area of personnel.

Second, in the autocratic Soviet common-state the opportunities to build nationalist machines grew over time as the union republic first secretaries enjoyed greater autonomy in making appointments and greater dis-

---

[1] Roeder 1984, 1988.
[2] T. Martin 2001, 125–81; Fierman 1991, 48; Gill and Pitty 1997, 159ff.
[3] See, for example, Liber 1992, 160–74; Dmytryshyn 1956, 151–62.

cretion in showering favors on loyalists. Stalin and Khrushchev tried to keep union republic monopolies from becoming nationalist machines through turnover of personnel, rotation of leading cadres among union republics, and the appointment to key posts of outsiders (nicknamed *variagi*, or Vikings) who would swoop down and shake things up.[4] Yet even in these most difficult conditions, "family circles" emerged within union republics "to protect the members from outside criticism and to see that they are provided with attractive positions"; machines developed in almost all union republics.[5] Nevertheless, there was a longer-term trend after Stalin's death in 1953 toward greater autonomy for union republic machines that culminated in the late 1970s. Leonid Brezhnev's policy of "respect for cadres" led to lengthening terms of office for the leaders of union republics as well as a reduction in the rotation of personnel among union republics, so that these leaders had more opportunities to cement loyalties within the republic's political elite.[6] As a consequence of this reduction in central interventions, the proportion of elite positions held by local patronage appointees grew in the Brezhnev years, the pace of indigenization accelerated, and overrepresentation of titulars in the political elites of most union republics became a worrisome problem for Moscow. In Estonia, where Estonians constituted about two-thirds of the population, by 1971 more than 80 percent of the Central Committee and close to 90 percent of the ministers on the Cabinet of Ministers were Estonians.[7] In Latvia, where Latvians constituted about 55 percent of the population, by 1975 the titulars held more than 70 percent of the seats on the Council of Ministers.[8] In Kazakhstan under Dinmukhamed Kunaev, Kazakhs, who constituted about 36 percent of the republic's population at the time, claimed a growing share of political posts, so that the proportion of seats on the Council of Ministers held by Kazakhs rose from 33 percent to 60 percent between 1964 and 1981.[9] In Kyrgyzstan, long tenure and growing autonomy permitted First Secretary Turdakun Usubaliev (1961–86) to indigenize the administrative apparatus "by simply increasing the total size of the administrative apparatus by around 150%, with most of the new posts occupied by members of the titular nationality."[10]

[4] Armstrong 1959, 52.

[5] Armstrong 1959, 82, 84.

[6] Gill and Pitty 1997, 126; Hodnett 1973, 1978, 63–65; United States CIA 1980; Beissinger 1988, 71–85; Cockburn 1989, 174–75; Suny 1988, 301–5; Moses 1985, 184–211; Olcott 1989, 77–81.

[7] Pennar 1978, 117–18, 123; Raun 1987, 193–95.

[8] Misiunas and Taagepera 1983, 197.

[9] Olcott 1987, 244–45. Also see Critchlow 1992, 27–29.

[10] J. Anderson 1999, 15.

Third, within the Russian Federation, the contrast between the contested presidency of Boris Yeltsin before October 1993 and the consolidated leadership of Vladimir Putin after 1999 highlights how the capacity
of the common-state government to intervene in the politics of its segment-states, which depended on the consolidation of common-state leadership, influenced the opportunities for segment-states leaders to develop
political-identity hegemony even in a semidemocracy. When Boris Yeltsin,
as chief executive of Russia, was locked in struggle with Mikhail Gorbachev
(before December 1991) and then the Congress of People's Deputies (until
October 1993), the republics enjoyed greater autonomy to order their internal affairs. Yeltsin's coup in late 1993 began a slow process of recentralization and in the latter half of the decade led to greater intervention from
Moscow to order the internal political arrangements within republics. Yeltsin's infirmity after 1996, however, limited the initiatives of his administration to control practices in the republics that violated the Russian Constitution. After Vladimir Putin succeeded Yeltsin as president and began to
consolidate his hold on power in Moscow, his government intervened more
extensively in the politics of the segment-states in order to limit the autonomy of republic leaders and to weaken local political-identity hegemony.

Autonomy to Design Institutions

The greater their control over the design of political institutions within
their respective segment-states, the greater are the opportunities for segment-state leaders to construct political-identity hegemonies. For example, the power to adopt language and residence requirements for political
offices in the segment-state not only permits segment-state leaders to so-
lidify the identification of the titular population with the segment-state as
their own, it also gives them the means to protect a nationalist machine
from challengers. Segment-state leaders are particularly interested in limiting challenges from the nontitular population within the segment-state,
such as non-Tatars within Tatarstan, and from members of the titular diaspora, such as Tatars outside Tatarstan. These two populations provide fertile recruiting ground, where the common-state leadership may find challengers to the segment-state leaders. Thus, in the USSR between January
1989 and October 1991, every union republic adopted a language law that
made the language of the titular nationality official in the union republic
and, according to Lawrence Robertson's tabulations, at least six of these
required knowledge of the titular language to hold political office in the
union republic.[11] In the Russian Federation, fourteen of the sixteen consti-

---

[11] Robertson 1995. Also see Anaiban and Walker 1996.

tutions adopted by republics between 1992 and 1996 provided for a popularly elected chief executive; nine of these constitutions required knowledge of the titular language and nine required residence of between five and fifteen years in order to qualify as a candidate for that office (table 5.1).

In the USSR the segment-states had few opportunities to deviate from the institutions specified in the Soviet constitution until the constitutional reforms that began in 1988.[12] After this the union republics gained expanding autonomy that began with the decision whether to introduce a congress of people's deputies in 1989, but then rapidly expanded to include whether to introduce presidential or parliamentary systems or retain the system of soviets.[13] For example, the introduction of a presidency by the RSFSR in 1991 created an opportunity for a cohort of politicians associated with a specific Russian nation-state project to establish their hegemony.[14] Most important was the autonomy to decide whether to democratize elections beginning in 1990 or to retain the autocratic control of the Soviet-era elite over access to political office.

In the Russian Federation, the autonomous republics, beginning in 1990, gained new decision rights to design their own political institutions. As the conflict between the RSFSR and USSR governments grew, Yeltsin acquiesced in the special rights to self-governance that the autonomous republics within Russia had claimed for themselves. In the fall of 1991, although he appointed heads of administration or "governors" in the Russian regions that were not segment-states (oblasts and krais) and even in the lower-order segment-states (autonomous oblasts and autonomous okrugs), he left in place the right of the autonomous republics to select their own chief executives.[15] In October 1993, when Yeltsin dissolved the provincial legislatures and suspended plans for gubernatorial elections in the oblasts and krais, he left in place the chief executives and legislatures within the autonomous republics (now simply called republics) and permitted the republics to conduct their own presidential elections.[16] Indeed, Yelt-

---

[12] *Konstitutsiia (osnovnoi zakon) Soiuza Sovetskikh Sotsialisticheskikh Respublik, Konstitutsii (osnovnye zakony) soiuznykh sovetskikh sotsialisticheskikh respublik* 1978; Feldbrugge 1979.

[13] Roeder 2001.

[14] Walker 2003, 78, 113–14.

[15] Ukaz Prezidenta Rossiiskoi Sovetskoi Federativnoi Sotsialisticheskoi Respubliki "O nekotorykh voprosakh deiatel'nosti organov ispolnitel'noi vlasti v RSFSR" August 22, 1991, in *Vedomosti S"ezda Narodnykh Deputatov RSFSR i Verkhovnogo Soveta RSFSR* 1991 No. 34, Article 1146. Also see the post-August 1991 presidential decrees removing chief executive officers in subjects of the federation, Presidium resolutions removing chairmen of soviets, presidential decrees appointing presidential representatives, and presidential decrees appointing heads of administration in oblasts, krais, federal cities, and autonomous okrugs, but not in republics (except for a presidential representative in Chechen-Ingushetia).

[16] Postanovlenie Verkhovnogo Soveta RSFSR "O glavakh ispolnitel'noi vlasti respublik v sostave RSFSR" October 11, 1991, in *Vedomosti S"ezda Narodnykh Deputatov RSFSR i Verkhov-*

sin gave the republics an additional incentive to introduce a presidency, if they had not already done so: he began to appoint "permanent representatives" in republics without presidents, to ensure "the single vertical hierarchy of executive power in Russia."[17]

After 1990, leaders of republics within the Russian Federation used their expanded opportunities to write the rules of political competition so as to disadvantage competitors and ensure their own survival in office. The most important prerogative they enjoyed that distinguished them from other subjects of the federation at the time was the right to write their own constitutions; the other subjects had to adopt charters that conformed to the institutional forms handed down from Moscow. Political machines used the power to rewrite their constitutions extensively in order to keep their leaders in office. For example, unable to run for a third term as president under Tyva's constitution, Sherig-ool Oorzhak proposed a new constitution. A vote taken forty minutes after the final draft of this document was delivered to Tyva's parliament (Supreme *Khural*) approved the draft and placed it before the public in a referendum. On May 6, 2001, 61 percent of the voters turned out, and 85.5 percent of these endorsed the constitution.[18] The constitution abolished the presidency and created a new post, that of head of government, with even wider powers than the presidency it replaced. On March 17, 2002, Oorzhak won election to a third term as Tyva's chief executive—but now only his first term under the title head of government rather than president. Similarly, in Bashkortostan, to help the incumbent president Murtaza Rakhimov win reelection, the parliament (State Council) rewrote the rules of presidential elections. By moving the elections forward from December 1998 to June 14, 1998, the State Council favored the incumbent: voters in cities, where his opposition was strongest, were more likely to be at their dachas away from their voting precincts for

---

nogo Soveta RSFSR 1991 No. 42, Article 1328. Also see Postanovlenia Prezidiuma Verkhovnogo Soveta RSFSR, "O vyborakh Prezidenta Mordovskoi SSR" November 18, 1991, in *Vedomosti S"ezda Narodnykh Deputatov RSFSR i Verkhovnogo Soveta RSFSR* 1991 No. 47, Article 1622; Postanovlenia Prezidiuma Verkhovnogo Soveta RSFSR "O vyborakh Prezidenta Mariiskoi SSR" November 18, 1991, in *Vedomosti S"ezda Narodnykh Deputatov RSFSR i Verkhovnogo Soveta RSFSR* 1991 No. 47, Article 162; Postanovlenia Prezidiuma Verkhovnogo Soveta RSFSR "O vyborakh Prezidenta Chuvashskoi SSR" November 18, 1991, in *Vedomosti S"ezda Narodnykh Deputatov RSFSR i Verkhovnogo Soveta RSFSR* 1991 No. 47, Article 1624; Postanovlenia Prezidiuma Verkhovnogo Soveta RSFSR "O vyborakh Prezidenta Iakutskoi-Sakha SSR" November 18, 1991, in *Vedomosti S"ezda Narodnykh Deputatov RSFSR i Verkhovnogo Soveta RSFSR* 1991 No. 47, Article 1625. On elections to the non-Russian regions in this early period, see Solnick 1998, 49–52. For the evolution of law concerning local self-government at the subregional level, see Kirkow 1997.

[17] *RFE/RL Daily Report* October 19, 1993; Radik Batyrshin, "Parlament Iakutii samoraspustilsia," *Nezavisimaia gazeta* October 13, 1993, 3.

[18] *Russian Federation Report* May 9, 2001.

TABLE 5.1

Russian Federation: Republic constitutions and political machines, 1992–1996

	Constitutional provisions for chief executive		Heads of administration in legislature[a]	Constitutional provisions for circular flow of power	
	Knowledge of titular language	Years of residency		Raions within presidential hierarchy[b]	President appoints head of administration[c]
Sakha (April 4, 1992)[d]	Yes	15	Yes	Yes	No
Tatarstan (November 30, 1992)	Yes	10	Yes	Yes	Yes
Tyva (October 21, 1993)	Yes	15	No	No	No
Bashkortostan (December 24, 1993)	Yes	10	Yes	Yes	Yes
Komi (February 17, 1994)	No	10	Yes	Yes	No
Buryatia (February 22, 1994)	Yes	10	Yes	Yes	No
Ingushetia (February 27, 1994)	Yes	None	Yes	Yes	Yes
Kalmykia (April 5, 1994)	No	None	Yes	Yes	No
Dagestan (July 26, 1994)	No chief executive	—	Yes	Yes	No
North Ossetia (November 12, 1994)	Yes	None	Yes	Yes	No
Udmurtia (December 7, 1994)	No chief executive	—	No	Yes	No

TABLE 5.1 (cont.)

Russian Federation: Republic constitutions and political machines, 1992–1996

	Constitutional provisions for chief executive		Heads of administration in legislature[a]	Constitutional provisions for circular flow of power	
	Knowledge of titular language	Years of residency		Raions within presidential hierarchy[b]	President appoints head of administration[c]
Adygeia (March 10, 1995)	Yes	10	No	Yes	No
Mari El (June 24, 1995)	Yes	None	Yes	No	No
Mordovia (September 21, 1995)	No	None	No	Yes	Yes
Khakassia (May 25, 1995)	No	7	No	Yes	Yes
Karachai-Cherkessia (March 5, 1996)	No	5	No	No	No

Sources: Russian Federation, Federal'noe Sobranie, Gosudarstvennaia Duma 1995, 1996; Parlamentarskaia biblioteka RF 1995; Karachaevo–Cherkesskaia Respublika 1996. (Omits March 12, 1992, constitution of Chechnya.)

[a] Heads of administration can sit in a republic's legislature.

[b] Raions are within the state power hierarchy of the republic chief executive.

[c] Republic chief executive nominates or appoints raion heads of administration.

[d] The date the constitution was adopted is in parentheses.

the summer.[19] As Rakhimov's second term as president came to an end, the State Council dealt with an inconvenient constitutional age limit of sixty-five years for presidential candidates and a constitutional prohibition on a third presidential term by simply adopting a new republic constitution on December 3, 2002.[20] A year later the sixty-nine-year-old Rakhimov won his third term.

The power to redesign republic institutions expanded opportunities for machines to dominate their republic's legislature and bureaucracy and use these to perpetuate the boss's rule. For example, upon taking office in Kalmykia Kirsan Iliumzhinov swiftly purged the government's ranks and reorganized it as a docile tool.[21] As *Komsomolskaia Pravda* reported a mere two and a half weeks after the election: "This week he broke up 40 ministries, leaving only five of the main ones. . . . He abolished all district administrative structures, putting all state farm directors directly under himself and appointing them personally."[22] By a combination of threats to Supreme Soviet deputies who were also administrative subordinates and financial incentives to other deputies, Iliumzhinov induced Kalmykia's Supreme Soviet to dissolve itself on April 30, 1993, in favor of a "professional parliament" composed of only 25 of the 130 Supreme Soviet deputies. The following year the Iliumzhinov machine further consolidated its position within the governmental structures when the rump Supreme Soviet of loyalists replaced the republic's constitution with a *Great Code of the Steppe*. A new legislature elected pursuant to the *Great Code of the Steppe* voted in August 1995 to extend the president's term until 2000, although it turned down an alternative proposal to make him president for life. The next day, on recommendations from Boris Yeltsin, Iliumzhinov declined the honor and modestly called for early presidential elections instead. On October 15, 1998, facing no opponents, Iliumzhinov won 85 percent of the vote for an unusual seven-year term.[23]

Dagestan's cartel machine was particularly adept at keeping itself in power through careful adjustments in its republic's constitution. In March 1996 the Constitutional Assembly voted to extend the term of the State Council for two years. When protesters on the streets pointed out that this violated the constitution, the People's Assembly voted to amend the constitution to give the Constitutional Assembly the power to extend the

[19] *RFE/RL Newsline* March 17, 1998, July 16, 1998.

[20] *RFE/RL Newsline* December 4, 2002.

[21] Andrei Pavlov and Sergei Sergienko, "Udarnye nochi brat'ev Iliumzhinovykh," *Komsomolskaia pravda* September 20, 1994, 3.

[22] Vladimir Ladnyi, "Chelovek, kupivshii respubliku," *Komsomolskaia pravda* April 30, 1993, 1.

[23] *OMRI Daily Report* October 16, 1995.

State Council's term.[24] A year later, when the term of Magomedali Magomedov, a Dargin, as chair of the State Council neared its end, Abudrazak Mirzabekov, a Kumyk, pointed out that the constitution prohibited Magomedov from a second term and argued that the office should rotate among leaders of the major ethnic groups. On August 20, 1997, the State Council dismissed Mirzabekov as a threat to the consociational allocation of posts and five days later appointed another Kumyk, Zhizri Shakhsaidov, to replace him.[25] On March 19, 1998, the State Council amended the constitution to permit a person to serve two consecutive terms as its chair, and on June 25 the Constitutional Assembly elected a new fourteen-person State Council with Magomedov as its chair.[26]

A poignant difference involving four of the republics of the Russian Federation underscores the consequences for political-identity hegemony when segment-states have fewer decision rights to design their own constitutions. Adygeia, Altai, Karachai-Cherkessia, and Khakassia began with significantly fewer decision rights because until mid-1991 each was an autonomous oblast—a lower-order jurisdiction that was subordinate to a province (krai) of the RSFSR. Until their elevation to the status of republics, these segment-states had no right to write a constitution and were forced to conform more closely to the mold of Russian provinces (oblasts and krais). From this weakened starting point, titulars in these four republics were less successful at building segment-state machines: while 71 percent of the other republics developed machines, only 25 percent of these latecomers developed a machine. The limited range of decision rights with which they began weakened the hands of the indigenous administration and made creating machines more difficult.[27]

Autonomy to Fill Political Offices

As with all machines, political-identity hegemony builds on the ability to fill key political positions with loyalists and in democracies to win elections; thus, the more extensive is the control of segment-state leaders over elections within the homeland, the more likely it is that they will build political-

[24] Radio Mayak March 21, 1996; ITAR-TASS, March 22, 1996.

[25] Il'ia Maksakov, "Prim'er-ministr otpravlen v otstavku," *Nezavisimaia gazeta* August 22, 1997, 3; ITAR-TASS August 25, 1997; Evgenii Krutinov, "Kavkazskii Vavilon na grani vzryva," *Segodnia* August 25, 1997, 2.

[26] Il'ia Maksakov, "Izmenena konstitutsiia Dagestana," *Nezavisimaia gazeta* March 20, 1998, 2; Il'ia Maksakov, "Brat'ia Khachilaevy trebuiut provedeniia priamykh vyborov prezidenta Dagestana," *Nezavisimaia gazeta* May 26, 1998, 1, 2; Il'ia Maksakov, "Magomedali Magomedov ostalsia rukovoditelem Dagestana," *Nezavisimaia gazeta* June 26, 1998, 1.

[27] Pustilnik 1995.

identity hegemony. In the USSR this was less difficult as long as the Communist Party of the Soviet Union (CPSU) banned opposition, but it called for increasing acumen once the USSR began to democratize in 1988. In the Russian Federation, the greater control exercised by political machines in its autonomous republics than in its regions that were not segment-states was manifest almost immediately in the far higher success rate of Communist Party first secretaries at winning elections in the autonomous republics—94 percent of the first secretaries in the sixteen autonomous republics won seats in the new USSR Congress of People's Deputies, but only 58 percent in the oblasts and krais. The two groups chose to run at approximately equal rates, but only those in segment-states won almost every time.[28]

Building a union republic machine loyal to its leader within the very centralized USSR did require considerable political skill. Throughout much of the Soviet period, appointments within segment-states were controlled by the *nomenklatura*—the lists of all important posts around the USSR—that determined that many appointments had to be made by or confirmed by the CPSU Central Committee departments in Moscow.[29] In appointments to lowest positions within the union republics, where careers began and the pool of titular candidates for promotion was formed, the union republic leadership enjoyed wide discretion, and this became the foundation of union republic machines. In promotions to intermediate positions within the segment-state, the Central Committee departments in Moscow had to confirm all appointments made by the union republic organization, but the machine was careful to put forward loyalists as candidates. Promotions to the highest posts within the union republic were made by the Central Committee organs, yet union republic leaders influenced even these appointments by identifying promising candidates within the homeland who would help "indigenize" the republic's administration.[30] Through skillful use of these opportunities, union republic leaders cultivated political patronage networks of loyalists sharing common origins or service.[31]

With the movement toward democracy in the Russian Federation, nationalist machines inside segment-states used the electoral commissions that the segment-state government appointed to prevent some opposition candidates from running for office and to ensure that the tally on election day favored the machine's candidates.[32] For example, in Bashkortostan's

[28] Embree 1991, 1076–77.

[29] Harasimyw 1969; Hough 1969, 114–15, 150–70; Theen 1980, 41–44; J. Miller 1983, 21.

[30] Sullivant 1962, 84–148; Dmytryshyn 1956, 57–90. Compare Newth 1963a, 1963b; S. Jones 1988.

[31] J. Miller 1983, 72–77; Suny 1993b, 118–19.

[32] On Adygeia, see Gleb Cherkasov, "V trekh regionakh vybrali glav ispolnitel'noi vlasti," *Segodnia* January 14, 1997, 2.

1998 presidential election, the republic's Electoral Commission revoked the candidacy of Aleksandr Arinin after more than 7 percent of those who signed his petitions subsequently disavowed their signatures during visits to their homes by the police.[33] After the republic's electoral commission then excluded the candidacy of the former prime minister Marat Mirgaziamov and a banker, Rafis Kadyrov, only Rakhimov's Minister of Forestry Rif Kazakkulov was left to contest the incumbent's presidency.[34] Even rulings by the Russian Federation Supreme Court ordering registration of disqualified candidates, including those not able to speak Bashkir, did not budge the republic's Electoral Commission, parliament, or the courts, which were all under the control of the Rakhimov machine.[35] In Mordovia, during the run-up to the February 15, 1998, elections for a republic president, the machine took no chances: seven would-be challengers to the incumbent president Nikolai Merkushkin were denied places on the ballot. The leading potential opponent complained that "his longtime supporters have been threatened and intimidated" and found himself called in for a criminal investigation. The only registered candidate other than Merkushkin was a little-known director of a local macaroni factory who announced during the campaign that he supported the president's policies. On election day, with turnout above 75 percent, Merkushkin scored a dazzling victory with 96.6 percent of the vote.[36] In Dagestan the cartel machine rested, in part, on a careful parceling of electoral districts to individual ethnic groups so that almost all districts either were drawn with ethnically homogeneous populations or were designated as "national electoral districts" (where the seat was assigned to an ethnic group even though the district's population was multiethnic).[37] Each member of the cartel machine wielded significant control over the electoral commission within his [sic] bailiwick to prevent opposition candidates from running and to ensure a favorable tally on election day.[38]

In the control of elections, Russia's segment-state machines often relied on the power of republic chief executives to appoint heads of administration in the cities and rural districts (raions). Indeed, most republic constitu-

---

[33] Aleksandra Poryvaeva, Irina Nagornykh, and Maksim Zhukov, "Deputata Dumy lishili prava ballotirovat'sia v prezidenty," *Kommersant-Daily* May 7, 1998, 5.

[34] Aleksandra Poryvaeva, "Rakhimov izbavliaetsia ot poslednikh konkurentov," *Kommersant-Daily* May 12, 1998, 5; Andrei Kamakin, "V Bashkirii vozmozhny povtornye vybory," *Nezavisimaia gazeta* July 25, 1998, 2.

[35] Igor' Timakov, "Verkhovnyi sud Rossii urezonil prezidenta Bashkirii," *Kommersant-Daily* March 28, 1998, 3; "Konstitutsionnyi sud razreshil prezidentam ne uchit' iazyki," *Kommersant-Daily* April 28, 1998, 2; *RFE/RL Newsline* June 15, 1998, July 29, 1998; *Vremia* July 22, 1998.

[36] *RFE/RL Newsline* February 5, 1998; ITAR-TASS February 16, 1998.

[37] Ware and Kisriev 1999, 2001.

[38] Orttung 2000, 112.

tions adopted between 1992 and 1996 placed the raions within the state power hierarchy controlled by the republican president so that the heads of raions were bureaucratic subordinates of the president (see table 5.1). Where the president appointed these, a form of circular flow of power resulted: the raion heads of administration conducted elections to all offices at the federal, republic, and local levels.[39] They ensured that the president won reelection and often secured their own election to the republic's legislature, from which they supported the president's legislative agenda. (Most of the republic constitutions adopted between 1992 and 1996 permitted heads of administration to hold legislative seats as well.) Thus, in the elections to seventy-two regional legislatures between 1995 and 1997, the proportion of seats won by executive branch officials was more than two times higher in the thirteen republics than in the forty-eight oblasts and krais: members of the executive branch held 24 percent of the seats in the republics but only 11 percent of the seats in oblasts and krais.[40] To ensure control of a republic's legislature by the raion heads of administration, a segment-state machine often had to malapportion seats so that electoral districts corresponded to administrative regions. Thus, in elections to regional legislatures conducted between 1995 and 1997, the disproportionality of electoral districts was significantly higher in the thirteen republics than in the forty-eight oblasts and krais: the proportion of districts with a population that was more than 10 percent above or below the average for the republic or province was 24 percent of the seats in the republics, but only 9 percent in the oblasts and krais.[41]

Using more extreme measures, political-identity hegemony may be built on control exercised by the machine over the police in order to conduct covert executive actions against its electoral opponents or to cover up such actions undertaken on its behalf. In preparation for the 1998 elections to the presidency of Bashkortostan, the authorities closed and threatened

[39] Hough and Fainsod 1979; Roeder 1993; Löwenhardt 1997; Löwenhart and Verheul 2000.

[40] The difference between republics and non-homelands is statistically significant at the .01 level in regression equations that control for proportion of population in rural areas. This excludes seats elected from autonomous okrugs within a krai. Source: Russian Federation TsIK 1998.

[41] The Russian law *On Basic Guarantees of Electoral Rights and the Right of Citizens of the Russian Federation to Participate in a Referendum*, Article 19, Section 3, requires "approximately equal number of voters in the electoral districts with an acceptable deviation from the average representation quota not more than 10 percent and for remote areas and areas of difficult access not more than 15 percent." Further, it permits deviations of up to 30 percent for districts that represent "indigenous, small peoples." Federal'nyi zakon No. 124-F3 "Ob osnovnykh garantiiakh izbiratel'nykh prav i prava na uchastie v referendume grazhdan Rossiiskoi Federatsii" September 19, 1997, in *Sobranie zakonodatel'stva Rossiiskoi Federatsii* 1997, No. 38, Article 4339.

newspapers critical of President Murtaza Rakhimov. By exerting pressure on printers, the authorities prevented publication of *Vechernii Neftekamsk*, which "no typesetter in Bashkortostan will print." After the editor began importing his newspaper from presses in neighboring Udmurtia, a city court in Neftekamsk on January 26, 1998, ordered the newspaper's editorial offices shut down on charges brought by the Bashkortostan minister of the press and mass media that "the newspaper was repeatedly publishing false information about the republic's leaders."[42] In the 1999 Duma elections, Bashkortostan's police received orders to confiscate campaign material of candidates not endorsed by the republic's leadership.[43] In Kalmykia in the late 1990s, only one nongovernmental paper survived—*Sovetskaia Kalmykia segodnia*. Denied access to printing presses within Kalmykia, the editors had to import copies printed in neighboring provinces. When intimidation did not silence the newspaper, assistants to the president apparently murdered the editor, Larisa Yudina.[44] In Tyva, one of the few candidates not scared into dropping out of the 2002 presidential elections, Vyacheslav Darzha, became the victim of an assassin's bullet after announcing on television that he possessed compromising materials about Oorzhak. Darzha survived to complete the election.[45]

Autonomy to Foster a National Culture

The opportunities to establish political-identity hegemony grow the more the decision rights of segment-states empower segment-state leaders to cultivate a cadre of national-cultural leaders who elaborate the segment-state's nation-state project, to mobilize resources in the campaign that propagates this project, and to deny alternative elites access to these resources. Political-identity hegemony is so common in segment-states because these powers are usually one hallmark of segment-states, even when segment-state leaders cannot design their own political institutions or control elections. Whether within an autocratic or a democratic common-state, segment-state leaders can build political-identity hegemony through artful use of powers to create research centers that develop and write national histories; to maintain archives, libraries, and museums that preserve

[42] Aleksandra Poryvaeva, "Bashkirskuiu gazetu sudiat na angliiskoe rugatel'stvo," *Kommersant-Daily* January 16, 1998, 4.

[43] See *Russian Federation Report* April 5, 2000, May 31, 2000. On Udmurtia's election see Cleave 2000.

[44] *RFE/RL Newsline* June 9, 1998, June 10, 1998; Interfax June 16, 1998; ITAR-TASS June 15, 1998; Vladimir Emel'ianenko, "Olimpiiskii vznoc Larisy Iudinoi," *Moskovskie novosti* June 14–21, 1998, 2–3.

[45] *RFE/RL Newsline* March 4, 2002, March 14, 2002.

and display the monuments of this history; and to establish ministries of education that design curricula for schools and universities to teach a myth of a common origin and a vision of a common future. Simultaneously, segment-state leaders can deny the authors of alternative nation-state projects access to these institutions and place high obstacles in the path of any attempt to mobilize support for these alternative projects through independent channels.

In the USSR, union republic leaders relied on their appointment powers to control the organizations that shaped the official nation-state project for the segment-state, to coöpt elites willing to sign on to the machine's nation-state project, to induce individuals to make more costly commitments to that nation-state project, and to suppress alternative mobilization. Policies to foster development of indigenous cultures toward socialism expanded the number of opportunities for union republic leaders to distribute prestigious and lucrative posts that tied individuals to the official nation-state project. The creation of universities and academies of sciences in many homelands dramatically expanded professional positions reserved for the minorities. Soon after the creation of the Belorussian Soviet Socialist Republic, for example, the new Soviet regime founded an Institute of Belorussian Culture in Minsk in 1921 and transformed this into the Belorussian Academy of Sciences in 1928 with departments in archeology, history, ethnography, folklore, music, fine arts, language, and natural resources, most of which were assigned the task of constructing a new Belorussian national culture and a national history. Creation of the Belorussian State University, State Publishing Office, National Theater, and other cultural institutions followed, and all needed staff. In a republic where prior to 1917 more than 90 percent of the population had been rural and engaged in agriculture, within eleven years (by 1928) there was a need for a native intelligentsia, including some 1,170 college professors to staff more than three dozen new postsecondary institutions.[46] Similarly, in Moldavia, the creation of the union republic in 1940 led to an explosion of career opportunities within the new official cultural establishment after World War II with the creation of Kishinev State University in October 1946 and more than a half-dozen other higher educational institutions in short order; these were followed by an Institute of Language and Literature in 1955, a Moldavian Academy of Sciences in 1961, more than 60 research centers, and dozens of segment-state performing groups such as the Moldavian State Dance Ensemble, the Moldavian Musical Drama Theater, and the Moldavian Opera and Ballet Theater.[47] The outcome of these Soviet policies was the creation of a national-cultural cadre that extended far be-

[46] Vakar 1956, 140–41.
[47] Dima 1991, 117–27; C. King 2000, 111.

yond the governmental and Communist Party organizations and owed their careers to the nation-state project of the segment-state leaders.[48]

The Communist Party's monopoly over such organizational resources as public spaces, meeting halls, printing presses, and broadcast facilities gave segment-state leaders enormous advantages over their opponents "on the periphery" who might want to propagate alternative nation-state projects.[49] In conducting its extensive agitation and propaganda efforts throughout the USSR, the CPSU relied on the coordinated efforts of an enormous mobilizational machine that included governmental agencies, party organizations, and so-called public organizations that reached into every workplace and neighborhood.[50] Union republic leaders enjoyed close to a monopoly over mobilizational resources in the cultural realm that defined and mobilized the titular nation. At the same time, the union republic elites established identity hegemony by blocking propagation of alternative nation-state projects, prohibiting independent associations, "decapitating" incipient dissident movements to deprive them of leadership, severing unofficial lines of communication between the intelligentsia and populace, and threatening, arresting, imprisoning, or executing exemplary figures in deterrent demonstrations of coercion.[51]

In the semidemocratic post-Soviet Russian Federation, the patronage used by segment-state leaders to build political-identity hegemony did not differ much in kind from that used in the autocratic state. As in Tatarstan, republic leaders used such institutions as academies of sciences, ministries of education, and cultural performance groups to elaborate and propagate their segment-states' nation-state projects. Republic leaders used their coercive powers to close down the offices of movements that propagated alternative nation-state projects, to arrest their leaders, to deny them access to printing presses within the republic, to prohibit public demonstrations by their supporters, and to burden their operations with a myriad of regulatory obstacles that slowed the opposition in every attempt to publicize their alternative nation-state projects.

In both autocratic and democratic common-states, because political hegemony and identity hegemony in segment-states are so closely intertwined, the suppression of alternative nation-state projects is inextricably intertwined with the nationalist machines' struggle to hold on to political power. In May 1998, for example, a month before Buryatia's presidential elections, the republic's administration sent in 100 troops to disperse pro-

---

[48] T. Martin 2001; Roeder 1991. Also see Akiner 1997, 376–78.

[49] On the importance of political parties to hold together federal states see Filippov, Ordeshook, and Shvetsova 2004.

[50] Friedgut 1979.

[51] See Olcott 1987, 253–57.

tests by Buddhist monks demanding greater support for traditional Buryat culture. The harsh treatment appears to have been based on the calculation that the protests might embarrass President Leonid Potapov in his bid for reelection. At the same time it was based on a calculation that if the Potapov machine did not clamp down on the monks, it risked losing control of the Buryat nation-state project.[52] In Tyva, during the campaign leading up to the March 17, 2002, elections for the newly created post of head of government of Tyva, the Oorzhak administration engineered a coup within the Buddhist religious community against the Xambo Lama. The preemptive strike against the spiritual leader expressed the government's growing agitation that the religious leader was pressing an alternative vision of Tyvan identity. The immediate spark, however, was the republic administration's anger that the Xambo Lama had failed to support Oorzhak for reelection. A new spiritual leader selected in time for the elections agreed to mobilize monks and religious voters behind Oorzhak.[53]

Primacy of Political Institutions

Each of the previous constraints underscores the primacy of political institutions that privilege segment-state leaders in the attempt to establish political-identity hegemony on the periphery: the more political institutions empower segment-state leaders to control access to leading positions in politics and culture, the more likely it is that segment-state leaders will create political-identity hegemony. The primacy of political institutions in the segmental institutions thesis runs counter to the usual emphasis in studies of nationalism on either primordial constraints (such as the ethnic divisions within a population) or economic constraints (such as the resource endowments of a region). According to the segmental institutions thesis, these other constraints do affect the ability of segment-state leaders to establish political-identity hegemony, but these constraints are shaped by segmental institutions.

Demographic Constraints

It is certainly harder to establish hegemony within a segment-state when the titular population constitutes only a minority of the population, but this is not an absolute barrier. Extensive segment-state autonomy can empower segment-state leaders to establish political-identity hegemony, even when the titular population is a minority. For example, in only nine republics of

---

[52] Orttung 2000, 64.
[53] *RFE/RL Newsline* March 19, 2002.

TABLE 5.2
Russian Federation: Cultural demography and republic machines

	Machine republics	Competitive republics	Total
Titular plurality that constitutes more than 45% of the population	89% Chechnya Dagestan Ingushetia Kabardino-Balkaria Kalmykia North Ossetia Tatarstan Tyva	11% Chuvashia	100%
Nontitular plurality or titulars that constitute less than 45% of the population	42% Adygeia Bashkortostan Buryatia Mordovia Sakha	58% Altai Karachai-Cherkessia Karelia Khakassia Komi Mari El Udmurtia	100%

the Russian Federation was the titular nationality the largest group; in twelve republics Russians constituted the largest group, and in nine of these Russians constituted an outright majority. Of the nine republics in which the titular nationality was the largest nationality and constituted at least 45 percent of the population, eight republics (89 percent) maintained or developed political identity machines (table 5.2). In the remaining twelve republics, five (42 percent) developed machines. The absence of a titular majority did not prevent segment-state leaders from building political identity hegemony, but a 9-in-10 chance of success in the titular-plurality republics declined to slightly less than even odds of success in the titular-minority republics. Nevertheless, even in Bashkortostan and Mordovia, where the titular populations constituted only a fifth and a third of their respective republics, the titular machines used the republic's powers to "favor their own," so that titulars held a majority of seats in the republic legislatures and a majority of posts in the republic governments.

Moreover, the demographic constraints on building political-identity hegemony are shaped, in the first instance, by institutional choices in the design of the segmented state. For example, in Bashkortostan the minority status of the Bashkirs in the republic is not only a consequence of decisions to draw its borders in a particular configuration that gave the republic a large Tatar population but also a consequence of the decision that Bashkirs and Tatars were two different nations with separate languages rather than one nation with two dialects. Among the most important consequences of these design decisions is the geographic and human borders of segment-states, because the borders define four peoples: the residents of the segment-state such as Tatarstanis, the resident titulars of the segment-state such as Tatars within Tatarstan, the nontitular population within the segment-state such as Russians and Chuvashes in Tatarstan, and the titular diaspora such as Tatars outside Tatarstan.[54] The borders limit the jurisdiction of the segment-state leaders' decision rights to the first three peoples. Although segment-state leaders may argue for revision of borders and (like Mintimer Shaimiev in Tatarstan) attempt to rally the diaspora, their powers fall off significantly among the diaspora titulars outside the geographic borders of their segment-state and more modestly among the nontitulars of their segment-state.

Designers of segmented states are typically aware of the importance of these institutional design decisions for the subsequent politics of a segment-state and draw borders so as to advantage some nation-state projects at the expense of others. The young Soviet regime was keenly aware that its decisions to draw the borders of segment-states in specific ways privileged some nation-state projects at the expense of others. Yet it was an inescapable choice. For example, in the initial creation of the segment-states in the Volga region in the 1920s, representatives of the common-state government decided that the Erzya and Moksha were one Mordvin nationality, the Kuryk Mari and Olyk Mari were one Mari nationality, and the Viryal and Anatri were one Chuvash nationality, but the Komis and Komi-Permyaks were two.[55] There were intellectuals who supported each of these competing nation-state projects, but there was no popular consensus; there were always critics on the losing side of a decision who were ready to claim that Moscow's choice among nation-state projects was wrong (and often to impute some sinister motive for the decision).[56] Moreover, the choices were seldom neat dichotomous choices between well-defined alternatives but cross-cutting and inconsistent alternatives.

The institutional designers used borders to disadvantage the nation-state projects such as Bukhara, Khiva, and Turkestan in Central Asia, Idel-Ural in the mid-Volga, and the Mountain Republic in the Caucasus that were most threatening to the unity of the young Soviet regime. Within the Russian Federation, the human and geographic borders of republics were set to divide or to subordinate alternative projects within official nation-state projects that the Soviets thought would pose less threat of secession. For

[54] Brubaker 1996.

[55] Taagepera 1999.

[56] Carley 1998, introduction. See Taagepera 1999, 149–51, 188–96, on whether there is really a Mordovian people or only separate Erzians and Mokshans.

example, the decision to constitute some republics as multinational republics introduced higher obstacles to political identity hegemony in Kabardino-Balkaria, necessitated a balanced cartel machine to manage conflict in Dagestan, and fueled instability and deadlock in Karachai-Cherkessia. Yet the unique empowerment of the leaders associated with the multinational project of each of these republics permitted them to establish political identity hegemony that has checked the authors of alternative nation-state projects, such as Balkaria and Cherkessia, that pose the greatest threat of secession. It is worth noting that even the alternative nation-state projects have been shaped by the segment-states. The idea of a Balkaria is itself a product of Soviet policies that brought a unity to the Balkar tribes that had not existed prior to the 1920s. The idea of a Cherkessia represents the triumph of Soviet policies to separate the constituents of the earlier pan-Circassian nation-state project by granting separate statehood to the Kabards and the Adygeis.[57]

The process of simultaneously redrawing borders and redefining nationalities ultimately converged on a rationalization of the Soviet segmented state, but it was a process in which peoples as well as homelands were transformed.[58] In 1936 Joseph Stalin explained the logic of the federal order when he defended the decision not to elevate more autonomous republics to union republic status: In contrast to autonomous republics, Stalin concluded, a union republic must (1) be "a border republic which is not surrounded on all sides by other territories of the U.S.S.R" so that it can exercise its right of secession, (2) be based on the territory of its titular nationality that represents "a more or less compact majority of that republic," and (3) comprise "not less but rather more than one million" people.[59] By 1939, with knowledge of the size of the population of an ethnic group, whether the ethnic group had an identifiable homeland within the USSR, and whether the homeland had an international boundary, one could predict the type of homeland accorded a nationality with 80 percent accuracy. By 1939, among the fifty-three homelands, forty had exactly the status that one would have predicted from Stalin's formula; only two homelands gave the ethnic group a higher status than its population would have warranted and eleven gave the ethnic group a lower status.

This rationalization was achieved, however, by redefining national communities to fit borders as well as by redrawing borders to accommodate national divisions. Stalin's logic was a specious justification for the status given individual segment-states, since Moscow could redefine not only homelands but also nationalities as a way to give or deny almost any one

---

[57] Wixman 1980, 1984.
[58] See Hirsch 1997.
[59] Stalin 1936, 25–26.

of them these three attributes. The USSR began in 1922 with four union republics, the first-order segment-states—the Russian Soviet Federative Socialist Republic, the Ukrainian Soviet Socialist Republic, the Belorussian Soviet Socialist Republic, and the Transcaucasian Soviet Federated Socialist Republic. Six more union republics were added by elevating the status of existing segments. Three—the Tajik SSR, the Kirgiz SSR, and the Kazakh SSR—were separated from the RSFSR and elevated from autonomous republics; the other three—the Armenian SSR, the Azerbaijan SSR, and the Georgian SSR—were created by dissolving the Transcaucasian SFSR. During World War II, five new union republics were added, three through annexation (the Estonian, Latvian, and Lithuanian SSRs) and two by elevating autonomous republics with the addition of annexed land (the Karelo-Finnish and Moldavian SSRs). (Moscow returned the Karelo-Finnish SSR to the status of an autonomous republic and gave it back its name of Karelian ASSR in 1956.) In addition, the status hierarchy of the second-, third-, and fourth-order autonomies was regularized. The proliferation of fifth-order autonomies ended: 250 national precincts (*uezdy*) and numerous autonomous villages had been established for smaller peoples and ethnic groups in 1920s. By the end of the 1930s these had been eliminated.[60]

Yet the iterative process that led to rationalization of the segment-states could only be achieved by redefining nationalities and by ad hoc adjustments in the definition of some of these as indigenous nationalities. Of the 107 ethnic groups with population over 5,000 in the 1926 census, twenty-eight did not have identifiable homelands within the USSR by 1939 because the majority of their population resided outside the USSR. Yet Moscow exercised considerable discretion in defining these populations as indigenous—as it did with the Volga Germans, Jews, and Moldavians—and granting them segment-states within the Soviet state. Among the other seventy-nine ethnic groups, rationalization of the segment-state was achieved by the end of the 1930s by reclassifying members of twenty-one ethnic groups as members of another ethnic group. Among the remaining fifty-eight ethnic groups only six did not have a segment-state of their own or participate in a multinational segment-state. When it was convenient to create or elevate differences within nationalities, Moscow could do this with abandon. For example, to back its irredentist claims on the Badakhshan region of Afghanistan, the Azerbaijani regions of Iran, the Kars and Ardahan regions of Turkey, Romanian Moldavia between the world wars, and parts or all of Finland in the first decade after World War II, Moscow created segment-states—the Gorno-Badakhshan Autonomous Oblast, the Nakhichevan Autonomous Soviet Socialist Republic, the Ajari Autonomous Soviet Socialist

---

[60] Matsyugina and Perepelkin 1996, 35; Shabad 1946. For more details on early institutional experiments see T. Martin 2001, 31–71.

Republic, the Moldavian Autonomous Soviet Socialist Republic (1924–40), and the Karelo-Finnish Soviet Socialist Republic (1940–55).[61] These segment-states were, however, based on the elevation of some ethnic divisions (such as that between Pamiris and Tajiks and between Ajaris and Georgians) that were simply anomalous, broke with its rule that homelands were not created for nationalities (like the Moldavians and Finns) with a homeland outside the USSR, or ignored the absence of an identifiable nationality as a basis for statehood (as in Nakhichevan).

Economic Constraints

According to the segmental institutions thesis, the presence or absence of economic assets such as lootable resources is less important than the institutions that determine who controls any resources—even meager resources—within the segment-state. In the Soviet and post-Soviet experience, political-identity hegemony developed in rich and poor segment-states without regard for whether these had lootable resources on their territory or not. In the Russian Federation, for example, machines were no more likely to emerge in richer than in poorer republics. Using Bert van Selm's ranking of economic performance in 1995, which combines indicators of nominal income, industrial and electrical output, and unemployment, the average rank of the eleven machine republics for which data are available was 40.3 (out of 78) and included the richest (Sakha) and poorest (Dagestan) subjects of the federation (table 5.3). The average rank for the eight competitive republics was 44.9, virtually the same as for the machine republics.[62] Certainly, several of the republics in which machines developed—for example, Sakha and Tatarstan—possessed lootable resources: diamonds in Sakha provided 80 percent of the republic's taxes as a result of an agreement with Yeltsin that established a joint federal-republic diamond

---

[61] Gornyi Badakhshan was established to accommodate the Pamiri subgroups among Tajiks and Ajaria to accommodate the Muslim Georgians called Ajars. Like the Moldavian ASSR and Karelo-Finnish SSR, these were also the core for possible annexation of territories in neighboring countries. The Badakhshan region had been divided with Afghanistan in 1895, when the Emir of Kabul Adgur Rahman conceded the right bank of the River Panj to the Emir of Bukhara (Centlivres and Centlivres-Demont 1997, 3). The USSR sought to annex the remainder of Badakhshan. Nakhichevan was the core for a brief attempt to create a people's republic in northern Iran after World War II. Ajaria was a remnant of the Kutaisi province, parts of which along with Kars region had been seized by Turkey during World War I. After the Second World War the USSR sought to retake Kars and Ardahan. The Moldavian ASSR became the core for a new Moldavian SSR after the annexation of Bessarabia from Romania. Karelia had been elevated to the status of a union republic as the Karelo-Finnish SSR in 1940 but was returned to the status of the Karelian ASSR as part of Khrushchev's attempt to improve relations with Finland in 1956.

[62] Van Selm 1998, 612–13.

TABLE 5.3

Russian Federation: Economic performance and republic machines.
Rank-order in economic performance, 1995[a]

Machine republics	Competitive republics
Sakha (1)	
	Khakassia (4)
	Karelia (13)
Tatarstan (21)	
Bashkortostan (22)	
Buryatia (31)	
	Komi (35)
	Udmurtia (45)
Adygeia (49)	
	Mari El (55)
	Altai (60)
North Ossetia (63)	
Tyva (65)	
	Chuvashia (72)
Mordovia (73)	
Kabardino-Balkaria (74)	
	Karachai-Cherkessia (75)
Kalmykia (76)	
Dagestan (78)	

Source: van Selm 1998, 612–13.
[a] Number indicates rank among seventy-eight subjects of the federation.

corporation. Tatarstan's possession of oil and gas resources and a controlling share in Tatneft, one of Europe's largest oil-drilling companies, gave it access to hard-currency income.[63] While the size of these resource endowments was important to the leverage these republics had over Moscow, within the segment-state it was relative control over any resources that was most important to the establishment of political-identity hegemony.

Where some resources are controlled by local elites who are not under the control of the segment-state leaders, these independent elites may use their economic resources to support alternative nation-state projects. For example, in the union republics of the USSR, political threats to political-identity hegemony varied with the extent to which centrally controlled or so-called all-union ministries directed the local economy, placing these outside the control of union republic leaders. Union republic leaders came closest to a monopoly in the rural-agricultural sector of the economy where state farms (*sovkhozy*), collective farms (*kolkhozy*), rural district party committees (*raikomy*), and rural district executive committees (*raispolkomy*)

[63] Kempton 1996; Stack 1999.

TABLE 5.4
Russian Federation: Soviet-era elite composition and republic machines

	Machine republics	*Competitive republics*	*Total*
Indigenous dominance or parity in late Soviet-era elite (Indicator: Indigenous obkom first secretary, summer 1990)	75% Adygeia Bashkortostan Chechen-Ingushetia Dagestan Kabardino-Balkaria North Ossetia Sakha Tatarstan Tyva	25% Altai Chuvashia Mari El	100%
Nonindigenous dominance in late Soviet-era elite (Indicator: Russian obkom first secretary, summer 1990)	29% Buryatia Kalmykia	71% Karachai-Cherkessia Karelia Khakassia Komi Udmurtia	100%
Unknown: Chuvashia, Mordovia			

were the dominant agencies of governance and political mobilization.[64] Appointments to these fell within the appointment jurisdiction (*nomenklatura*) of the union republic Communist parties. In all of the union republics (except Armenia, where all elites were so highly indigenized), agricultural managers constituted the single most "indigenized" elite of society. Alternatively, in the urban-industrial sector more institutions were under all-union control, more appointments were part of the all-union *nomenklatura*, and more outsiders from other union republics held leadership positions in these parts of the economy. All-union institutions typically circumvented the union republic leadership and reported directly to Moscow. Titular nationalities were particularly likely to be underrepresented in the management and labor force of heavy industry, construction, and transportation.[65] Thus, in the last years of the USSR, during the *perestroika* nation-state

[64] Gelman 1990, 19; Nove 1986, 124; Brovkin 1990, 16–17; Olcott 1987, 242–43; Roy 2000, 106.

[65] Data on indigenization from Hodnett 1978, 101–3, 377–78; Jones and Grupp 1984, 174; Helf 1988; USSR 1984. For long-term trends in indigenization within specific republics, see Armstrong 1959, 15–17; Burg 1979, 43–59; Lubin 1981, 283; Olcott 1987, 199–246; Parsons 1982, 554; Suny 1988, 209–318; USSR, 1972–73, II:12–75, IV:365–82. The last data on the ethnic composition of Soviet managerial elites by union republic in 1989 are available in USSR Gosudarstvennyi komitet SSSR po statistke 1992; Mal'tsev 1990, 8.

crisis, it was frequently the managers and labor collectives of heavy industry that mobilized the large-scale protests against the nation-state projects of the leaders in such union republics as Estonia, Latvia, and Moldova.

The transition to capitalism and democracy—particularly the privatization of enterprises previously under all-union control—left the new segment-states numerous patronage opportunities, but the common-state was no longer the primary alternative source of patronage within the segment-state. It was now the private sector—although often the managers in control of this sector were the same or similar ethnic Russians operating within segment-states. The influx of nontitular managerial elites due to heavy industrialization had been particularly pronounced in many republics within the Russian Federation. Where these nontitular managerial elites were particularly strong relative to the republic's titular elite, the nontitulars had a better chance to block establishment of political identity hegemony.[66] Perhaps the most important indicator of strong nontitular managerial elites in a republic prior to the end of Communist rule was the capture of the first secretary post by a nontitular. Even though titulars still controlled such posts as chairman of the local soviet (parliament), where nontitular managerial elites were particularly strong they could demand that the Communist Party obkom first secretary of the republic be one of their own. In those Russian republics for which the nationality of the Communist Party obkom first secretary in the summer of 1990 is known, seven fell into the category of nontitular dominance of the elite (the first secretary was not a titular). In contrast, in twelve republics there were more normal patterns of titular dominance or parity (the first secretary was a titular). This latter pattern supported the emergence of a national machine dominance; indeed, 75 percent of these became machine republics. The former became an obstacle to national machine domination: 71 percent of these became competitive polities after the end of Communist rule (table 5.4).

In short, the segmental institutions thesis does not deny the importance of economic constraints on building political-identity hegemony any more than it denies the importance of demographic and cultural factors. Yet, unlike the arguments advanced by political economists and political sociologists that privilege these other constraints, the segmental institutions thesis treats these as endogenous factors: their importance in the building of political-identity hegemony is shaped by segment-states.

[66] Compare Stoner-Weiss 2001, 2002.

PART THREE

PROCESSES: ESCALATION TO NATION-STATE CRISES

SIX

The Dynamics of Nation-State Crises

F OR PROPONENTS OF a nation-state project to achieve their objective of sovereign independence, they must force their claims onto the agenda of the government of their current state and induce the leaders of that government to surrender most if not all of their decision rights over the disputed people and territory. Most proponents of nation-state projects fail; they are simply ignored, fail to get the government to reallocate decision rights, or even suffer a diminution of decision rights through arrest or suppression. Part 3 offers an explanation for why a few succeed. The discussion in these chapters shifts from the horizontal bargaining on the periphery to the vertical or center-periphery bargaining between the proponents of nation-state projects and the leaders of existing sovereign states. The segmental institutions thesis stresses that in the competition to get access to common-state leaders and to influence their choices, segmental institutions typically privilege segment-state leaders over other claimants with nation-state projects by empowering these segment-state leaders with unique means to press their claims against the common-state leaders. Segmental institutions increase the likelihood of a *nation-state crisis*—a juncture at which there is the prospect of significant change in the configuration of nation-states. Segmental institutions also increase the likelihood that the outcome of such crises will be the breakdown of the existing common-state and the creation of new nation-states. Nation-state projects associated with segment-states are more likely than other nation-state projects to provoke nation-state crises and to achieve sovereign independence.

The three chapters that constitute part 3 explain why this is so. Moreover, they identify attributes that explain why some but not other segment-states achieve sovereign independence. The current chapter begins with an analytic model derived from formal theories of bargaining. It summarizes the major claims of the segmental institutions thesis concerning the consequences of segmental institutions for the vertical bargaining between leaders of a central government and various claimants with nation-state projects. This chapter continues with close inspection of the processes that lead to this instability through case studies of three Eurasian nation-state crises. The *perestroika* nation-state crisis of 1988–91 ended with the dissolution of the Union of Soviet Socialist Republics (USSR or Soviet Union). Segment-state leaders concluded that a common-state was not only unnecessary but possibly dangerous, and the common-state leader was unable to forestall the segment-states' withdrawal. Yet nation-state crises in segmented states may instead end in a loss of segment-state decision rights and in centralization. This alternative path and outcome are illustrated in two cases. The first is the nation-state crisis of the early USSR that began with the Union Treaty of 1922. This ended in extreme centralization under Stalin that took away many decision rights of republics to develop in diverging ways and forced all into a common mold of socialist construction after 1927. The second is the nation-state crisis within the Russian Federation during its transition to and in the first years of independence (1990–2004). The initial step toward centralization was the imposition of a new constitution in December 1993, but this was followed by an accelerating process of withdrawing concessions that had been made to the republics between 1990 and 1993.

The next two chapters of part 3 examine more closely the escalation of both claims and actions that characterizes nation-state crises and that increases the likelihood of failure of an existing common-state and independence for segment-states. Chapter 7 looks at the claims or stakes in segmental bargaining. The discussion explores the tendency for this agenda to focus on allocation of decision rights between common-state and segment-state governments and the incentives for segment-state leaders to escalate their demands for a greater share of the decision rights of the common-state and to play the sovereignty card. Chapter 8 looks more closely at the means used in segmental bargaining. It focuses on the leverage that segment-state leaders have over common-state leaders as a consequence of segmental institutions and the declining leverage of the common-state leaders that can result when the common-state government is weakened by devolution of power. Institutional weapons created by segmental institutions permit some segment-state leaders to make it too costly for common-state leaders to hold on.

Bargaining within Segmented States

When leaders of an existing state are challenged by claimants with alternative nation-state projects, the presence of segmental institutions increases the likelihood that center-periphery bargaining will escalate to a nation-state crisis and that this crisis will end in breakup of the existing common-state and the independence of new nation-states. In the context of this vertical bargaining, segmental institutions have six consequences—already introduced in chapter 1—that increase this likelihood of dissolution and independence for new nation-states. First, segmental institutions typically lead to a narrowing of the circle of participants in center-periphery bargaining to just the leaders of the common-state and segment-state governments. Segmental institutions privilege segment-state leaders over alternative politicians, empowering segment-state leaders with unique access to common-state policy-making and leverage over common-state leaders. Segment-state leaders muscle their way to the head of the queue and elbow aside the spokespersons for other interests and other nation-state projects seeking attention and favors from the common-state government. Spokespersons for cross-cutting interests that might moderate the differences between segment-states and the common-state find it particularly difficult to get a seat at the bargaining table.

The next three consequences concern the stakes or agenda of center-periphery bargaining. Second, segmental institutions typically lead the agenda of center-periphery bargaining to focus on a zero-sum conflict over the division of decision rights between common-state and segment-state governments. With time, other issues, such as environmental protection or political and economic reform, come to be subsumed under this agenda of fundamental constitutional issues, and it becomes harder to find joint policy gains through compromise as more issues are treated as parts of a zero-sum conflict. Third, segmental institutions create incentives for segment-state leaders to escalate the stakes in bargaining by pressing demands for more decision rights for their segment-states and ultimately by pressing sovereignty claims against the common-state.[1] Segmental institutions create incentives to frame progressively more claims as parts of the segment-state's nation-state project and, ultimately, to play the "sovereignty card" in order to get an advantage in center-periphery bargaining. Yet this escalation to the question of the location of sovereignty risks transforming bargaining into a simple dichotomous choice in which independence for the segment-state is one option. Fourth, segmental institutions lead to constriction in the bargaining range as more solutions that might keep segment-states within a common-state become unacceptable to one or the other party. Segmental institutions permit growing divergence among the cultural, economic, and political institutions of the segment-states and between those of some segment-states and the common-state. With divergent development, the types of common-state policies and institutions favored by some segment-state leaders or by the common-state leaders are increasingly seen as unnecessary, undesirable, or even threatening by the other side.

The last two consequences concern the means used to conduct bargaining. Fifth, segmental institutions typically empower the leaders of segment-states with the means to make it more costly for the leaders of the common-state to try to hold on to the segment-state. The decision rights

---

[1] Horowitz 1991, 452.

of segment-states can become institutional weapons that give segment-state leaders greater leverage over common-state leaders. Sixth, segmental institutions can weaken the common-state government itself. Where segment-state leaders are empowered within the decision-making processes of the common-state government, they can paralyze the common-state. Where the common-state response to escalating demands from segment-states is devolution of more powers, the common-state government may have little leverage to make secession a costly step for the segment-states. Indeed, in the extreme, the common-state, like the USSR, may simply wither away.

Together, the narrowing of participation, the conflation of agenda items into a zero-sum dispute over the allocation of decision rights, the escalation of demands to a conflict over the location of sovereignty, the disappearance of compromises and constriction of bargaining ranges due to divergent development, the increasing capacity of segment-states to impose losses on the common-state government, and the weakening of the common-state government make it more likely that common-state leaders will concede the sovereign rights claimed by the segment-state leaders.

Bargaining Leading to Nation-States

The segmental institutions thesis approaches nation-state crises through the conceptual lens offered by game-theoretic analyses of bargaining. The bargaining that leads to nation-state crises obviously includes formal negotiations, but this is only its smallest part. Bargaining is a game—a situation where the outcome from one side's choices also depends on the choices of others—but a game in which players seek to achieve their desired outcomes by inducing the others to choose in specific ways.[2] Bargaining may proceed through an idiom of actions as well as words. It may take place in paneled conference rooms with green-baize-covered tables and salty mineral water, but it also takes place in legislative chambers, on the streets, and on the battlefield.[3]

Nation-state crises emerge from bargaining in which politicians make demands on behalf of a community that they claim constitutes a nation with

---

[2] Schelling 1960, 5. Also see Schelling 1984.

[3] This bargaining model is implicit in much of the literature on ethnic conflict, such as Eriksen 1991; Esman 1992; Gurr 1993, 290–324; Milne 1989; D. Thomson 1992. This stands in sharp contrast with models that characterize ethnic conflict as direct confrontation between ethnic groups, such as Hewitt 1977; Horowitz 1985. A variant of the latter intergroup-conflict approach treats the common-state as, in effect, the executive committee of the dominant ethnic group; see Birch 1978; Coakley 1992; Hechter 1975; Rothschild 1981; A. Smith 1979.

a right to a state of its own.[4] The members of the purported nation identified by this nation-state project may consider themselves an ethnic group
with a myth of common descent, but few successful nation-state projects
have actually been pressed on behalf of an ethnically homogeneous nation.
They may be bound by common culture, such as language or religion, but
this is not necessary. They may already constitute, to use Benedict Anderson's term, an "imagined community" in whose minds "lives the image
of their communion."[5] More commonly, however, the nation-state project
imagines a community in a different sense: it is a prospective vision that
seeks to create both a nation and an independent state that do not yet exist.

In normal politics, prior to a nation-state crisis both the leaders of the
common-state and politicians who may with time come to press a nation-
state project conduct bargaining according to the constitutive rules of the
state. Although conflict is endemic to politics, this conflict is normally contained within these constitutive rules and does not call the allocation of
decision rights into question.[6] The stability of constitutional arrangements
depends on deterring the escalation of bargaining into constitutional crises,
such as nation-state crises, that threaten to change the existing allocation
of decision rights.

Escalation to nation-state crises can come from either the government
leaders of the common-state or politicians pressing alternative nation-state
projects. They may escalate either the stakes or the means of conflict (or
both).[7] With escalation in the stakes, the politicians demand a greater reallocation of decision rights. With escalation in means, the politicians increase the costs to the other side for not conceding these rights. Calculating
common-state leaders and claimants with nation-state projects that challenge the status quo decide to escalate conflict in this bargaining relationship when they expect a positive net payoff. That is, they consider the
decision rights they expect to keep or gain, when the other side finally gives
in, to be worth the losses that will be associated with escalating conflict.[8]
Alternatively, they are likely to be deterred from escalation when at least
one of the following is present: (1) they do not expect the other side to
concede or (2) they expect losses associated with conflict to exceed the
value of the decision rights.

[4] See, for example, Breuilly 1994, 453; Heisler 1977; Eriksen 1991; Mars 1995; Rothschild
1981, 4–5; Esman 1994, 216; R. Young 1997, 45–60.

[5] B. Anderson 1991, 6.

[6] Because the allocation of decision rights affects outcomes in many other games, cooperation is more difficult to achieve; see Behr 1981; Hirshleifer and Coll 1988, 390–94; Axelrod
and Keohane 1985; Stein 1990, 101.

[7] Smoke 1977, 14; Leatherman et al. 1998, 111–45.

[8] Ostrom 1990, 192–216.

Strategically minded bargainers need to look beyond their own immediate gains and losses. To choose prudently, each side must also attempt "to look into the minds" of the other side. For example, in estimating whether the common-state leaders will accede to a nation-state project, claimants must estimate the value the government leaders ascribe to the decision rights they would lose and the value the government leaders ascribe to the losses they would suffer in conflict. In addition, the common-state leaders and nation-state claimants must both attempt "to look ahead" (or "to look down the game tree") by anticipating the response of the other side, which may attempt to alter the first side's losses from conflict. For example, nation-state claimants know that common-state leaders may retaliate and that retaliation may so increase the claimants' losses that it is not worthwhile pressing their claim in the first place.

The failure to anticipate retaliation can be costly. For example, during the siege of the Russian legislature (Congress of People's Deputies) by President Yeltsin in September–October 1993, Kalmykia's president Kirsan Iliumzhinov sought to preserve the autonomy gained by Russia's segment-states while the common-state president and legislature were locked in a stalemate. Iliumzhinov thought Yeltsin lacked the will and might to prevail, and so Iliumzhinov joined the defenders of the legislature in the White House, announcing, "I declare in no uncertain terms that I will not leave it until the blockade of the White House, which disgraces the people of Russia before the whole world, is completely lifted and the military and police units, including the OMON, are withdrawn."[9] In retaliation for the Kalmyk president's opposition, once Yeltsin had eliminated the Congress of People's Deputies, the presidential administration began attacking Iliumzhinov's position within Kalmykia. Within a month the administration began leaking stories about the origins of Mr. Iliumzhinov's fortune and began investigations of misuse of commercial loans and governmental funds. In the face of mounting threats of a financial embargo of Kalmykia and criminal charges against him personally, Iliumzhinov capitulated and made the rather remarkable proposal to eliminate Kalmykia's status as a segment-state (republic), abolish its constitution, and rescind its rules on dual citizenship. He explained to his people: "Nobody is going to send us money here, and the republic's people will end up in dire straits. For this reason . . . we must repeal the Republic of Kalmykia's Constitution and dual citizenship and proclaim only Russian citizenship and the sole authority of the Russian Constitution on the territory of Kalmykia."[10] Iliumzhinov miscalculated when he looked into Yeltsin's mind and looked down the

---

[9] "Stop This Disgraceful Action," *Sovetskaia Rossiia* October 2, 1993, 2; translated in *Current Digest of the Post-Soviet Press* 45 (October 27, 1993), 15–16.

[10] Valerii Vyzhutovich, "Ulozhenie v step'," *Izvestiia* April 13, 1994, 5.

game tree before standing with the common-state legislature against Yeltsin; the retaliation against Iliumzhinov and his segment-state was very costly in terms of decision rights.

Common-state leaders and nation-state claimants try to influence the other side's calculations, but know the other side is doing the same. For example, nation-state claimants try to increase the government leaders' expectation of future losses if they do not accede to the claimants' nation-state project. Nation-state claimants also try to strengthen the common-state leaders' expectations that the claimants will not give in. Of course, nation-state claimants know that the common-state leaders are also attempting to influence the claimants' calculations at the same time so as to induce them to cry uncle.

Segmental Institutions and Bargaining

The presence of segmental institutions in this vertical bargaining increases the chances that proponents of nation-state projects empowered by segment states will escalate both stakes and means to provoke a nation-state crisis. When proponents of a nation-state project are leaders of a segment-state they are uniquely advantaged in bargaining with the common-state leadership—compared with other proponents of nation-state projects. Other proponents are less likely to have enough leverage to force their nation-state projects onto the bargaining table with the common-state leaders. Other proponents are unlikely to have enough leverage to induce the common-state leaders to concede sovereign rights within the segment-state. Yet not all segment-states are able to force a nation-state project to the point of a crisis. Nor do all segment-state leaders that try achieve sovereign independence. The likelihood that a nation-state crisis will end in dissolution of the segmental arrangement and the creation of new independent nation-states increases under the following conditions: as segment-state leaders consolidate political-identity hegemony, as segment-states develop in divergent directions (particularly in their political regimes), as there is growth in the capacity of segment-state leaders to back their demands for a greater share of decision rights with actions that inflict higher costs on the common-state leaders, and as the common-state leaders find the commitments they must make to appease the segment-state leaders too costly.[11]

These specific conditions highlight what might be called figuratively the balance of consolidation.[12] On one side of this balance, segment-state leaders who have consolidated political-identity hegemonies are better able than segment-state leaders who have not consolidated hegemony to press

---

[11] Axelrod 1984; Ellickson 1991; Dasgupta 1988, 50.
[12] Sutton 1986, 711, 714–15; McMillan 1992, 48–49.

their nation-state projects onto the bargaining table with the common-state leaders and to induce them to make more concessions. On the other side of this balance, the more divided are common-state leaders the more likely it is that segment-state leaders will be able to force a crisis and induce the common-state leaders to concede.[13] Of course, this is not strictly speaking a balance, since each proposition concerns variation among segment-states and among common-states, respectively, while the other is constant. In the true sense of a balance, it is the conjunction of strong political-identity hegemony in segment-states and a divided common-state government that creates the most favorable conditions for the independence of new nation-states.

These specific conditions also highlight what might be labeled the balance of leverage between segment-state and common-state leaders. This balance depends on the coercive resources and the institutional weapons at the disposal of common-state and segment-state leaders. The larger the share of decision rights assigned to segment-state governments and the smaller the share assigned to the common-state, the more likely it is that the segment-state leaders will be able to force a crisis and induce the common-state leaders to concede. This balance of leverage also explains how commonly cited factors such as demographic and economic constraints affect the likelihood of successful independence. The larger the population of the segment-state *relative* to that of the common-state the greater is the ability of segment-state leaders to force a nation-state crisis and to induce the common-state leaders to concede their sovereign rights in the segment-state. The greater the segment-state leaders' control over resources essential to the political survival of common-state leaders—resources such as arms, votes, or energy—the greater is the likelihood that segment-state leaders will be able to force a crisis and induce the common-state leaders to concede.[14]

The Dilemma of Instability in Segmented States

The bargaining model highlights an inherent instability in segmental institutions. A stable constitutional order allocates decision rights so that defenders of the existing constitutional order—a coalition that shifts from issue to issue—have an advantage in leverage over any challengers. This is more easily achieved in a pluralistic society where no single interest is strong enough to change the rules of the game and an overwhelming coali-

---

[13] Spruyt (2005, 6, 22–31) points up that divisions within a government (veto-gates) that do not weaken the common-state government in its bargaining with segment-states will reduce the likelihood that it will concede more decision rights to segment-states.

[14] Hanauer 1996; J. Knight 1992, 132.

tion of interests—which changes from issue to issue—forms to defeat any attempt by one group to change the rules in its favor. In this context the ambitions of challengers to the constitutional order are constrained by the knowledge they cannot possibly hope to win.[15]

Segmentation privileges the balance between the common-state and segment-state leaders above all other balances in politics whenever common-state policy that affects segment-states is on the table. This creates a dilemma for constitutional designers who attempt to stabilize the constitutional order. The designers of segmented states may attempt to check this instability in a delicate balance of leverage between common-state and segment-state governments, carefully balancing power against power and even creating a mutual hostage relationship. This knife-edge equilibrium is fragile and easily upset when the advantage shifts, even temporarily, to one side. William W. Kaufmann provides the key insight about stability in such situations that has survived to this day: stability requires that at any level of escalation, if one side has the option of escalation, the other side must be able and willing to match this.[16] Each side is deterred from escalation by knowledge that, even though "we" might escalate conflict, the other side can match this, and so our chances of gaining our objectives would not improve, but our costs would rise significantly. But it is difficult to design such institutional equilibria, and erring slightly in one direction or the other can be highly destabilizing. Any hobbling of the common-state government increases the prospects that segment-state leaders will use their powers against the common-state. Any weakening of segment-state governments increases the opportunities for predatory common-state leaders to steal segment-state rights. Where one side has an advantage observable by the other, then the predominant side can press for concessions of decision-making rights from the other, and the other is likely to concede. Knowing this, each side may develop a hair-trigger response to exploit any temporary inequalities that arise with periodic exogenous shocks.

Common-state and segment-state leaders must make their choices based on imperfect information. Because leaders on both sides know that the other side has an incentive to overstate its capabilities and resolve, any "objectively perfect" balance of leverage is the point at which tragic subjective errors of estimation are most likely to result.[17] The expectations of common-state and segment-state leaders about the outcome from escalating means predict outcomes as depicted in figure 6.1. Stability is likely where both expect the other side to win, both expect a draw, or one side

---

[15] Roeder 2005. For a similar insight into the more general problem of finding stability in federalism, see Figueiredo and Weingast 2001.

[16] Kaufmann 1956.

[17] Sutton 1986, 717; Fearon 1993, 4, 23.

Expectations in common-state

	Common-state victory	Draw	Segment-state victory
Common-state victory	Peaceful centralization (escalation of stakes, not means)	Stability (no escalation of stakes or means)	Stability (no escalation of stakes or means)
Draw	Escalation of conflict (escalaton of both stakes and means)	Stability (no escalation of stakes or means)	Stability (no escalation of stakes or means)
Segment-state victory	Escalation of conflict (escalaton of both stakes and means)	Escalation of conflict (escalaton of both stakes and means)	Peaceful devolution (escalation of stakes, not means)

Expectations in segment-state

Figure 6.1 Constitutional stability: expectations and outcomes.

expects the other to win but the other expects only a draw. In such cases neither side has an incentive to escalate the means, because it does not expect escalation will pay. (Ironically, two of these stable situations occur because at least one side is wrong in its expectations.) Alternatively, where both concur that the common-state is likely to prevail after escalation, the predicted outcome is peaceful centralization. Where both concur that the segment-state would prevail, the predicted outcome is peaceful devolution. Both sides know that resistance by the weaker side will be costly and ineffectual, and so, to avoid the costs of escalation in means, capitulation is the rational response. (There is an escalation in stakes, but not means.) Finally, where both sides expect to be victorious in a contest of escalating means, the prospects for mutual escalation in both stakes and means are greatest. Where one side expects victory and the other expects that it can at least fight to a draw, the prospects for mutual escalation in both stakes and means may be only slightly less.

Because they cannot measure leverage directly, participants in the bargaining process (just as analysts) must estimate leverage. Typically participants estimate this from the observable or "objective" indices of the capabilities and resolve of the other side, such as demonstrations of popular support in protests and elections or the accumulation of arms and training of troops on both sides. Yet each side knows that these indices are imperfect and can often be manipulated to create illusions of strength. Thus, there will be some variance in each side's estimates of leverage about the values of observable indices; further, there will be some variance in these observable indices about the "true balance of leverage," since what you see is not always what you get. Therein lie many opportunities for "subjective error" or incompatible expectations—where both expect to win, or one expects to win and the other expects a draw. Therein lie many opportunities for escalation of conflict to nation-state crises, even among rational politicians.[18] A significant body of theory and evidence in international relations supports the contention that power parity between polities increases the likelihood of escalating conflict.[19] Michelle Benson and Jacek Kugler argue and provide evidence that this same relationship holds inside polities as well: parity in the balance of leverage between government and opposition is associated with higher levels of violence.[20] According to the segmental institutions thesis, segment-states move proponents of nation-state projects closer to parity with the common-state government.

The *Perestroika* Nation-State Crisis and Dissolution

The story of the dissolution of the USSR has been told well in a number of places with considerable detail.[21] I will not attempt to retell this story one more time but to highlight three stages in the escalation of this crisis that unfolded between 1988 and 1991. From late 1988 until mid-1990, Mikhail Gorbachev introduced a series of constitutional reforms that in turn provoked a nation-state crisis over allocation of decision rights between common-state and segment-state governments. In late 1990 and early 1991 this nation-state crisis escalated to the point where all parties were negotiating whether the USSR would continue. After the failed August 1991 coup by hard-liners, negotiations between the common-state government under Gorbachev and the segment-state governments led by leaders of the fifteen union republics revealed that there was no consensus on new common-state institutions and that a majority of the union republic governments preferred dissolution to any single proposal on the bargaining table that would have kept the USSR common-state whole.

The nation-state crisis that brought the USSR to an end had its roots in 1988, when Mikhail Gorbachev began to implement his program for democratization. In his first speeches as general secretary to the April 1985 Central Committee Plenum and the 27th Congress of the Communist Party of the Soviet Union (CPSU) (February 25–March 6, 1986), Gorbachev's comments about democratization conformed to the threadbare formulas of mature socialism.[22] Yet less than a year later, in his report to the

---

[18] Blaney 1988, 108–9, 122; Gartzke 1999; Wagner 1993, 242–44, 252; Wittman 2001.

[19] Benson and Kugler 1998, 196–209; Organski 1958; Bueno de Mesquita and Lalman 1992; Kugler and Lemke 1996. Also see Collier 2000a, 10; McCord and McCord 1979, 428.

[20] Benson and Kugler 1998.

[21] See Hough 1997; McFaul 2001; Walker 2003.

[22] "O sozyve ocherednogo XXVII s"ezda KPSS i zadachakh, sviazannykh s ego podgotovkoi i provedeniem—Doklad general'nogo sekretaria Ts K KPSS M. S. Gorbacheva," *Pravda*

January 1987 Central Committee Plenum "On Perestroika and the Party's Personnel Policy," Gorbachev spoke at length of the need to introduce competitive elections in the selection of enterprise managers, people's deputies, and even Communist Party secretaries.[23] The resolution of the 19th CPSU Conference (June 28–July 1, 1988) "On Democratization and Political Reform" endorsed Gorbachev's commitment to offer voters more candidates than positions to be filled, but left the mechanisms for implementation unclear.[24]

Once the details of democratization were on the table, however, reactions from segment-state leaders (particularly union republic leaders) invoked a nation-state crisis over the allocation of decision rights between the segment-state and common-state (or "all-union") governments. Discussions of draft amendments to the Soviet constitution to implement these reforms in the fall of 1988 sparked heated criticism in Estonia and Latvia.[25] The Soviet constitutional amendments, which were, in fact, adopted on December 1, 1988, sought to introduce new congresses of people's deputies at all-union, union republic, and autonomous republic levels (Article 89). The amendments allocated one-third of the seats in these bodies to "social organizations" such as the CPSU, trade unions, cooperatives, the Komsomol (Communist Youth League), and women's and veterans' organizations (Article 95). The amendments extended the power to nominate candidates for the other two-thirds of seats (elected in districts) to labor collectives, social organizations, meetings of voters in residential areas, and units of the armed forces (Article 100).[26] It was the proposed changes in segment-state institutions threatening the political machines and the political-identity hegemony in some segment-states (particularly in the union republics) that provoked the strongest reaction, including the first declaration of sovereignty, the first claim of right of nullification, and the first moves in the "war of constitutions."

The proposed amendments were particularly threatening to the titular leadership within the Estonian Soviet Socialist Republic (SSR) and Latvian

April 24, 1985, 1–2; "Politicheskii doklad Tsentral'nogo Komiteta KPSS XXVII S"ezdu Kommunisticheskoi Partii Sovetskogo Soiuza—Doklad General'nogo Sekretaria Ts K KPSS tovarishcha Gorbacheva M S, 25 fevralia 1986 goda," *Pravda* February 26, 1986, 2–10.

[23] "O perestroike i kadrovoi politike partii—Doklad General'nogo Sekretaria Ts K KPSS M S Gorbacheva na plenume Ts K KPSS, 27 ianvaria 1987 goda," *Pravda* January 28, 1987, 1–5.

[24] "O demokratizatsii sovetskogo obshchestva i reforme politicheskoi sistemy," *Pravda* July 5, 1988, 2.

[25] Zakon Soiuza Sovetskikh Sotsialisticheskikh Respublik [Proekt] "Ob izmeneniiakh i dopolneniiakh Konstitutsii (osnovnogo zakona) SSSR," *Izvestiia* October 22, 1988, 1–2; Zakon Soiuza Sovetskikh Sotsialisticheskikh Respublik [Proekt] "O Vyborakh Narodnykh Deputatov SSSR," *Izvestiia* October 23, 1988, 1–3.

[26] Zakon Soiuza Sovetskikh Sotsialisticheskikh Respublik "Ob izmeneniiakh i dopolneniiakh Konstitutsii (osnovnogo zakona) SSSR," *Izvestiia* December 3, 1988, 1–2.

SSR, because these changes threatened the political machines they had constructed on the basis of overrepresentation of titulars in the state organs of their union republics. The proposed expansion of representation of social organizations, particularly labor collectives, and their special role in nominating candidates, would expand the role of nontitulars in the nomination of candidates even for leadership positions within the union republic. In these union republics the titular nationality held only a narrow margin in the population as a whole and was outnumbered in heavy industry, particularly in industrial management positions. These changes threatened to put Estonia and Latvia in the same position as the Kazakh SSR, where a Russian, Gennadii Kolbin, had become first secretary in December 1986 and had purged titulars from many positions of power.

The Estonian declaration "On the Sovereignty of the Estonian SSR," adopted on November 16, 1988, was a short document that briefly asserted the republic's sovereignty but devoted nearly half its text to the proposed amendments to the USSR Constitution and asserted that any such amendments would only apply on Estonian territory after ratification by the Estonian Supreme Soviet.[27] On the same day, the Estonian Supreme Soviet adopted a resolution accepting the creation of the Congress of People's Deputies at the common-state (all-union) level and even restating the Soviet-era formula that the legislative bodies at all levels would constitute a "unitary system of representative bodies of state power." The Estonian resolution, however, demanded that segment-states (specifically, union republics and autonomous republics) retain the right to choose whether to replace their own supreme soviets with new congresses of people's deputies and whether to change the method of election.[28] As Arnold Rüütel, chairman of the Presidium of the Estonian Supreme Soviet, explained to the all-union Supreme Soviet that adopted the constitutional amendments, "we would like to keep the [union] republic Supreme Soviet as the sole body of state power and not create another, higher body—the Estonian Republic Congress of People's Deputies—and we would also like to keep the [union] republic's right to determine the system of election of People's Deputies."[29]

At the common-state (all-union) level, democratization also threatened the special voice that the smaller union republics had enjoyed in authoritar-

---

[27] Deklaratsiia Verkhovnogo Soveta Estonskoi Sovetskoi Sotsialisticheskoi Respubliki "O suverenitete Estonskoi SSR," *Sovetskaia Estoniia* November 17, 1998, 1. Also see Hallik 1996, 87–108.

[28] Postanovlenie Verkhovnogo Soveta Estonskoi Sovetskoi Sotsialisticheskoi Respubliki "O predlozheniiakh po proektam Zakona SSSR Ob izmeneniiakh i dopolneniiakh Konstitutsii (osnovnogo zakona) SSSR i Zakona SSSR O vyborakh narodnykh deputatov SSSR," *Sovetskaia Estoniia* November 18, 1988, 1.

[29] "Zasedaniia Verkhovnogo Soveta SSSR—Rech' deputata A. F. Riuitelia," *Izvestiia* December 1, 1988, 6.

ian decision making that stressed elite consultation among union republic leaders in the Communist Party's Central Committee and Politburo. Democratization of the USSR's central governing institutions threatened to bring a shift in decision making from the Politburo and Central Committee to the Congress of People's Deputies, a body that would no longer privilege union republic leaders. The second declaration of sovereignty, Lithuania's, was issued on May 18, 1988, right after elections to the all-union body had been completed and just four days before the opening of the first all-union Congress of People's Deputies. Again, this was a short document that sought to protect the voice of Lithuania's Communist Party leadership in the legislative process, at least insofar as it bore on the union republic, by stipulating that only laws adopted by or ratified by the union republic's Supreme Soviet would be valid within Lithuania's borders and that relations between the Lithuanian government and the all-union government would be based on intergovernmental agreements.[30] This was a very conservative reaction from the Communist leaders of Lithuania, who sought to preserve the interelite bargaining of the segmented state from democratization of the common-state. The amendments to Lithuania's constitution adopted that same day stipulated that legislative and executive acts of the USSR would need to be ratified by Lithuania's Supreme Soviet to be valid within its borders and could be limited or suspended by the Lithuanian body (Article 70).[31] Estonia and Lithuania were followed in the latter half of 1989 by the Latvian SSR (July 23, 1989), Azerbaijani SSR (September 23, 1989), and Georgian SSR (November 18, 1989) in issuing declarations of sovereignty.

The nation-state crisis was engaged while the Communist Party monopoly was still in place in each segment-state, and the early actors in the crisis were the leaders of the segment-state political-identity hegemonies. After competitive elections brought new governments to power in several segment-states, the issue of independence was formally on the bargaining table with the common-state government; the nation-state crisis that began over allocation of decision rights escalated to disputes over sovereignty. All three Baltic states declared in the first half of 1990 that they had begun the process of restoring their independence—Lithuania on March 11, Estonia on March 30, and Latvia on May 4, 1990. Even Georgia, which was still under a Communist Party government, declared on March 9, 1990, that the treaties through which it came to join the USSR in 1921 and 1922 were illegal and invalid. Georgia's Communists announced that they would

---

[30] Deklaratsiia Verkhovnogo Soveta Litovskoi SSR "O gosudarstvennom suverenitete Litvy," *Sovetskaia Litva* May 19, 1989, 1.

[31] Zakon Litovskoi Sovetskoi Sotsialisticheskoi Respubliki "O vnesenii izmenenii Konstitutsiiu (Osnovnoi Zakon) Litovskoi SSR," *Sovetskaia Litva* May 19, 1989, 1.

begin talks to restore Georgian independence. The Georgians linked their announcement to the introduction of a common-state presidency, which, the Georgians claimed, had changed the balance of power between the common-state and segment-state governments. One year later, on April 9, 1991, under the new, democratically elected leadership of Zviad Gamsakhurdia, Georgia declared its independence.[32] These acts by the smaller republics were, nonetheless, a long way from bringing down the USSR. Indeed, Gorbachev simply played a waiting game with the Baltic states, expecting that this would bring them around.[33] It would require escalation of the crisis, bringing more segment-states to press for sovereignty and further weakening the common-state government, before the participants would agree to dissolution.

Nor was the so-called "parade of sovereignties" that began on June 12, 1990, with Russia's declaration of sovereignty the critical step that brought down the USSR. The texts of these declarations of sovereignty and the relative order in which the republics adopted them beginning in June 1990 are often treated as indicators of the growing distancing of individual republics from the center. Some declarations represented a significant escalation of the claims of segment-state governments in the nation-state crisis, yet most were only half-steps in an incremental escalation.[34] Most declarations copied the terms in the common-state (all-union) laws *On the Principles of Economic Relations between the USSR and the Union and Autonomous Republics* (April 10, 1990) and *On the Demarcation of Powers of the USSR and the Members of the Federation* (April 26, 1990). These laws allocated expanded decision rights to the segment-states (specifically, union republics and autonomous republics), authorized segment-states to suspend common-state (all-union) legislation pending resolution of the conflict in all-union organs, granted ownership of natural resources to the segment-states, and stipulated that relations among the common-state and segment-state governments would be defined in treaties.[35] The union republics' declarations in particular sought to expand their rights to suspend all-union legislation. Most declarations were adopted almost simultaneously because they were a necessary ticket for entering the negotiations over a new union treaty

---

[32] "Resolution of the Georgian Republic Supreme Soviet: On Guarantees of the Protection of Georgia's State Sovereignty," *Zarya Vostoka* March 12, 1990; translated in *Current Digest of the Soviet Press* 42 (April 11, 1990), 9; "Gruziia prinimaet Akt o vosstanovlenii nezavisimosti," *Izvestiia* April 9, 1991, 1. Also see Fuller 1990a, 1991d.

[33] Gorbachev 1995, II:505.

[34] Treisman 1997; J. Kahn 2000.

[35] Zakon Soiuza Sovetskikh Sotsialisticheskikh Respublik "Ob osnovakh ekonomicheskikh otnoshenii Soiuza SSR, soiuznykh i avtonomnykh respublik," *Izvestiia* April 16, 1990, 1–2; Zakon Soiuza Sovetskikh Sotsialisticheskikh Respublik "O razgranichenii polnomochii mezhdu Soiuzom SSR i sub"ektami federatsii," *Izvestiia* May 3, 1990, 1–2.

that Gorbachev officially initiated on June 11, 1990.[36] Indeed, Ukraine's declaration concludes, "the principles of the Declaration of Sovereignty of Ukraine will be used to lay the basis for the Union Treaty."[37] The adoption of a declaration and the speed with which they were adopted after June 11, 1990, were not good indicators of swelling nationalisms or impending secessions. Indeed, some of the last republics to pass such declarations, such as the Chechen-Ingush Autonomous Soviet Socialist Republic (ASSR) and Dagestani ASSR, which actually had to be pushed by both Gorbachev and Yeltsin into adopting a declaration, were precisely those republics where popular nationalism was potentially most threatening to the Communist Party elites still in power.

The nation-state crisis did escalate decisively in mid-1990 when the common-state (all-union) leadership split over political and economic reforms and Gorbachev reached out to segment-state (union republic) leaders for support against the conservative all-union officials with an offer of a renegotiated treaty of union. The decisive turn after June 1990 that escalated the nation-state crisis to a stage where all parties were aware that they were negotiating whether the USSR would survive came with the movement of negotiations over the future political structure of the USSR from the common-state legislature (the USSR Congress of People's Deputies) to the executive council, where leaders of the common-state and segment-state governments faced one another across the bargaining table (the Council of the Federation). As late as April 1990 the Congress of People's Deputies was still the forum for discussion and adoption of the laws on economic relations and demarcation of powers in the federation. Yet on June 11 Gorbachev called on the Council of the Federation to prepare a new union treaty. At the moment, this move seemed to be a clever démarche imposed to gain an advantage over the president's conservative opponents in the common-state (all-union) government, who stalled democratization and economic reform. In the new context, however, the bargaining increasingly entailed direct negotiations between the common-state and segment-state leaders that excluded other interests that might have cut across segment-state borders and knit together the USSR. In this new forum, negotiations increasingly focused on a single dimension of zero-sum conflict—allocating power (decision rights) between common-state and segment-state governments. With time, the council allocated a steadily growing share of decision rights to the segment-state (union re-

---

[36] "Soiuz gosudarstv: kontseptsiia Prezidenta," *Pravda* June 14, 1990, 4. Compare Teague 1994, 29–30; Treisman 1997. On the announcement of the drafting of a new union treaty, see Sheehy 1990c. Also see Hough 1997, 373–403.

[37] "Deklaratsiia 'O gosudarstvennom suverenitete Ukrainy' 16 iiuliia 1990" in Institut teorii i istroii sotsializma TsK KPSS 1991, 223–29.

public) governments, so that the common-state (all-union) government was progressively weakened.

After negotiations were moved to the Council of the Federation, the conflation of issues and narrowing of the circle of participants became more acute. Gorbachev initially sought to keep the negotiations within the council inclusive and to link them with parallel negotiations in other forums. In the summer of 1990, following confirmation of the Gorbachev initiative by the Council of the Federation,[38] the chair of the upper chamber of the common-state legislature (Rafik Nishanov, chairman of the USSR Council of Nationalities) began consultations with representatives of the republics in order to create a joint preparatory committee to draft a new union treaty to replace the 1922 document that had served as the basis of the USSR.[39] This preparatory work, however, was rejected and supplanted by the negotiations within the Council of the Federation, which included only leaders of union republics and autonomous republics as voting members. The union republic leaders objected to even the presence of the autonomous republics in the Council of the Federation, and by the spring of 1991 they had marginalized even these parties in the negotiation process. The circle of negotiators was limited to Gorbachev as leader of the common-state and the leaders of the union republics. On April 23, 1991, in an effort to negotiate a third draft treaty, Gorbachev asked the leaders of the union republics—nine leaders actually showed up—to meet in Novo-Ogarevo. This meeting would outline major issues in designing a new union, allocate decision rights between common-state and segment-state governments, and establish new institutions for the common-state.[40] The direct negotiation of representatives of the "9 + 1" circumvented the common-state (all-union) organs, such as the Congress of People's Deputies; the leaders of these all-union organs complained that they should at least be signatories to the treaty, alongside the union republic leaders.[41] The negotiations excluded the leaders of the autonomous republics, who also complained, but received only the right to sign the treaty after the union republics had hammered out the articles and signed.[42] Moreover, the Novo-Ogarevo pro-

---

[38] "Soiuz gosudarstv: kontseptsiia Prezidenta," *Pravda* June 14, 1990, 4.

[39] A. Stepovoi, "Poiski formuly soiuznogo dogovora," *Izvestiia* September 6, 1990, 1; A. Gorbatov, "Iskat' put' sblizheniia," *Pravda* September 6, 1990, 2; "Put' k soiuznomy dogovoru—Izlozhenie doklada R. N. Nishanova," *Izvestiia* September 26, 1990, 2.

[40] "Sovmestnoe zaiavlenie o bezotlagatel'nykh merakh po stabilizatsii obstanovki v strane i preodoleniiu krizisa," *Izvestiia* April 24, 1991, 1.

[41] A. Stepovoi and S. Chugaev, "Eshche raz o soiuznom dogovore," *Izvestiia* May 27, 1990, 1.

[42] "Vstrecha Prezidenta SSSR i Predsedatelia Verkhovnogo Soveta RSFSR s Predsedateliami Verkhovnykh Sovetov avtonomnykh respublik Rossiiskoi Federatsii," *Izvestiia* May 13, 1991, 1; G. Alimov, "Protivorechiia sniaty—k itogam vstrechi v Kremle," *Izvestiia* May 13, 1991, 1–2; Vera Kuznetsova, "Sud'ba '9 plius 1' eshche ne opredelena," *Nezavisimaia gazeta* June 15, 1991, 2.

cess became a central forum for the president to discuss with union republic leaders key issues of all-union policy, including economic, fiscal, and foreign policies—such as Gorbachev's pending trip to London to meet with the G-7 leaders.

Following the failed coup against Gorbachev in August 1991, the Novo-Ogarevo negotiations became virtually the only common decision-making forum for what remained of the USSR until its formal demise in December 1991. In early September this assembly of heads of union republics plus Gorbachev was dubbed the State Council and given superordinate authority above the common-state Supreme Soviet. Even this forum for joint decision making ended when the final assembly of now only 7+1 leaders in Novo-Ogarevo on November 25, 1991, failed to reach agreement on a new common-state.

As a consequence of the exclusion of other interests from the negotiations, successive drafts of the union treaty allocated more decision-making powers to the union republic governments and diminished the role of representatives of other interests.[43] Gorbachev published his first proposal for a new union treaty on November 24, 1990, but this received a chilly response from the union republic leaders and a threat of a coup from the conservatives within the common-state government. Gorbachev made a second offer in March 9, 1991, which received a similarly chilly response from seven of the union republics.[44] On July 23, 1991, the parties agreed to a third draft for a new union treaty, which was published on August 15 and was to be opened for signing on August 20, 1991.[45] The coup of August 19–22, 1991, sought to prevent this shift in decision making. The coup's Extraordinary Committee, which sought to establish its rule, included the leaders of those common-state (all-union) organs such as the USSR Council of Ministers that would lose the most in the reallocation of decision rights under the new union treaty. Yet the revolt and surrender of the members of the Extraordinary Committee decisively weakened the common-state government in the bargaining with the segment-state governments and, ironically, provided an opportunity for segment-state leaders to press for a still greater share of decision rights. The final drafts of the union treaty were put on the table on November 14 and 25, 1991.

The narrowing circle of parties, which excluded all but the union republic and all-union leaders from the bargaining table, was reflected in the

[43] "Proekt: Soiuznyi Dogovor," *Izvestiia* November 24, 1990, 3; "Proekt: Dogovor o Soiuze Suverennykh Respublik," *Izvestiia* March 9, 1991, 2; "Dogovor o Soiuze Suverennykh Respublik," *Izvestiia* March 15, 1991, 1–2; "Dogovor o Soiuze Suverennykh Respublik [Proekt]," *Izvestiia* November 26, 1991, 3; Sheehy 1990a, 1991b, 1991d, 1991e; Zacek 1997.

[44] "Dogovor o Soiuze Suverennykh Respublik [Proekt]," *Izvestiia* November 24, 1990, 1–2; "Proekt: Dogovor o Soiuze Suverennykh Respublik," *Izvestiia* March 9, 1991, 2.

[45] "Dogovor o Soiuze Suverennykh Gosudarstv," *Izvestiia* August 15, 1991, 1–2.

progressive shift in the terms of the four versions of the union treaty (tables 6.1 and 6.2). For example, the proposed upper legislative chamber (called the Council of Nationalities in the November 1990 draft, but the Council of Republics thereafter) at first permitted the legislatures of first-, second-, third-, and fourth-order segment-states (called union republics, autonomous republics, autonomous oblasts, and autonomous okrugs) to send delegations. Subsequent drafts, however, excluded the autonomous oblasts and okrugs (except as part of the union republic delegations), and finally excluded the autonomous republics as well.[46] The proposed voting rules within the legislature initially preserved the rule of one-representative-one-vote. Still later versions shifted to unit voting, in which each union republic cast one vote, and finally to a unanimity rule that gave each union republic one vote and a veto.

Similarly, in the proposed executive branch of the common-state government, the executive council (called the Council of the Federation initially, but then the State Council) at first included both union republic and autonomous republic leaders as ex officio members. The union republic leaders objected to sharing their privileged role in common-state decision making and in the July 1991 draft simply dispensed with the Council of the Federation. In the final version (November 1991) they created a new State Council that would include only the heads of the union republics and the common-state president. In the last version (November 25) the common-state president might not even be guaranteed the chairmanship of the State Council. Moreover, by the final draft, the union republic leaders were no longer willing to concede that the common-state president would be popularly elected—for many feared this would strengthen the common-state against the segment-states—and so they left the terms of selection for future negotiations.

As the stakes in the bargaining escalated, there was rapid devolution of more decision rights to the segment-state governments, which each draft of the union treaty sought to enshrine for the future (see table 6.2). With each draft the decision rights of the common-state government shrank, so that the final step to the elimination of the common-state was, indeed, a small one. Areas of exclusive common-state jurisdiction became fewer. In progressively more realms that had been the exclusive jurisdiction of the common-state government, such as national security and foreign affairs, policy would henceforth be formulated jointly by the common-state and segment-state (specifically, union republic) governments. By November 1991 in most substantive domestic policy areas the draft union treaty left all issues to subsequent multilateral agreements so that the common-state government had no guaranteed decision rights. With the shift in decision

---

[46] For a narrative history, see Walker 2003, chap. 5.

TABLE 6.1

USSR: Provisions for segmental representation in common-state organs in drafts of the Union Treaty, 1990–1991

Common-state organ	Draft Union Treaty, November 1990	Draft Union Treaty, March 1991	Draft Union Treaty, July 1991	Draft Union Treaty, November 1991
Legislature: Lower chamber	Council of the Union Popular election	Council of the Union Popular election	Council of the Union Popular election	Council of the Union Popular election
Legislature: Upper chamber	Council of Nationalities Legislative delegations from: Union republics Autonomous republics Autonomous oblasts Autonomous okrugs Also to include: [Other minorities]a	Council of Republics Popular election from: Union republics [Autonomous republics]b Also to include: [Autonomous oblasts]a [Autonomous okrugs]a	Council of Republics Legislative delegations from: Union republics (unit vote) Also to include: [Autonomous republics]a [Autonomous oblasts]a [Autonomous okrugs]a	Council of Republics Legislative delegations from: Union republics (unit veto) Also to include: [Autonomous republics]a [Autonomous oblasts]a [Autonomous okrugs]a
Executive council	Council of Federation Heads of state from: Union republics Autonomous republics	Council of Federation Heads of state from: Union republics Autonomous republics	None	State Council Heads of state from: Union republics
Council chair	Common-state president	Common-state president		[President]c Uncertain
President	Popular election	Popular election	Popular election	

a Representatives included within a delegation from a union republic.

b Not determined whether autonomous republics would send delegations or would be included within union republic delegations.

c The November 14 version designated the president as chair; the November 25 version did not.

TABLE 6.2

USSR: Provisions for common-state jurisdiction in drafts of the Union Treaty, 1990–1991

Common-state jurisdiction with respect to:	Draft Union Treaty, November 1990	Draft Union Treaty, March 1991	Draft Union Treaty, July 1991	Draft Union Treaty, November 1991
Constitution	Exclusive	Joint	Exclusive	Joint
National security	Exclusive	Formation joint Implementation exclusive[a]	Formation joint Implementation exclusive[a]	Joint
Foreign policy	Exclusive	Formation joint Implementation exclusive[a]	Formation joint Implementation exclusive[a]	Joint
Economic development	Joint	Joint	Joint	Joint
Fiscal and monetary policy	Exclusive	Joint	Joint	Joint
Infrastructure[b]	Joint	Joint	Joint	Joint
Federal taxation	Exclusive	Joint	Joint	No provision
Natural resources	Necessary to functions	Republic delegation	Republic delegation	No provision
Binding principles of legislation	Exclusive	Exclusive	Joint	None
Supremacy of federal laws	Yes, but republic nullification	Yes, but republic nullification	Yes, but republic nullification	None

[a] Formulation of policy jointly with republics; implementation of policy within exclusive federal jurisdiction.
[b] Energy, transportation, and communications.

rights to the union republic governments, the power of the common-state government to issue binding principles of legislation in its own areas of jurisdiction—that is, principles that would be repeated in union republic legislation—became something to be negotiated with the republics, and then simply disappeared from drafts of the treaty. Similarly, common-state tax rates became matters of negotiation, and then common-state taxes were simply eliminated and replaced by contributions from the segment-state (union republic) governments in the final version. Common-state property rights over land and natural resources ceased to extend automatically to all that were necessary to fulfill its functions and became a delegation of rights from the segment-state (union republic) governments that would be determined in future negotiated agreements.

In the end, the negotiations foundered on a central dilemma of segmented states. As autonomy permitted the segment-states (union republics) to grow more diverse, there were fewer bases on which they could agree to create a common-state government without also posing a significant threat to a large number of the segment-state (union republic) governments. The August 1991 coup against Gorbachev underscored the dangers to the union republic leaders from a common-state government. As President Nursultan Nazarbaev of Kazakhstan summarized, "the plan that had been worked out was now dangerous. . . . The USSR can no longer be a federation."[47] As the union republics became more diverse, they divided over the types of threats they needed to guard against. An agreement to guard against one type of threat might have held the union together, but only if the union republic governments agreed on the nature of the threat. There was no such agreement. For many reformist governments, the major threat was another hard-line coup to take control of the common-state government. As Armenia's President Levon Ter-Petrossyan warned, "the Union, as we see now, is a country where a neo-fascist coup is quite possible. We cannot be confident of our future in such a country."[48] For Communist governments that still held power in union republics, a more immediate threat was rapid decommunization pushed by the common-state government, which seemed to be on the horizon with Gorbachev's decree suspending the activities of the CPSU. In Belorussia, the hard-line leadership saw that only "one of two things was possible: Either Belorussia would remain in the Union and submit to Gorbachev's decree suspending the CPSU's activity, or it would declare independence and maintain all the Party structures."[49]

---

[47] Quoted in Zacek 1997, 86.

[48] Quoted in Fuller 1991d, 10.

[49] Igor Siniakevich, "Obyknovennoe chudo v V S Belorussii," *Nezavisimaia gazeta* August 27, 1991, 3; Stankievich 1991, 25–26.

For all governments except Russia's, the threat was also Russia. During the August 1991 coup Yeltsin decreed that pending a meeting of the common-state Congress of People's Deputies, the common-state executive organs, including the KGB, MVD, and Ministry of Defense, would be directly subordinate to Yeltsin's segment-state government in the Russian Soviet Federated Socialist Republic (RSFSR).[50] After the August coup, Yeltsin continued to exercise disproportionate influence over common-state agencies.[51] Ukraine's President Leonid Kravchuk complained on August 30 about Russia's usurpation, adding, "I have my doubts whether . . . representatives of one republic can defend the interests of other republics."[52] On November 26, in distinguishing the position of Ukraine and Russia on the union treaty, Kravchuk added, "I think B. Yeltsin assumes that Russia should continue to be the center around which the other planets, called states, will revolve as if it were the sun."[53] As the union republics diverged further in their development, finding a formula for a common-state that would both be responsive to the different segment-states and not threaten them became harder. Moreover, abandoning the now shriveled common-state government had become a less costly step. A commonwealth of independent states became the better, mutually agreeable option.

The Crisis of the Early USSR and Centralization

Not all nation-state crises proceed like the *perestroika* crisis. The nation-state crisis of the new Union of Soviet Socialist Republics in the 1920s underscores that nation-state crises in segmented states can be pressed by a predatory common-state government and can end in centralization of decision rights in the common-state government. The events of the early Soviet regime also are a twice-told story, and here I will only stress the nation-state crisis over decision rights. A stalemate between common-state and segment-state governments, which developed at a time of divisions within the common-state government (during the succession struggle after Vladimir Lenin's death), permitted segment-state (particularly union republic) leaders to exercise significant decision rights. Once a single common-state leader (Joseph Stalin) emerged predominant in Moscow, however, the common-state government began taking many of these decision rights and imposed a uniform rule within the segment-states. The first

[50] Hough 1997, 477–83.

[51] McFaul 2001, 107–8, 133; Thorson 1991, 16–17; Walker 2003, 141–42.

[52] Quoted in Hale 2001, 21. Also see Solchanyk 1991b, 15–16.

[53] N. Bondarnuk, "Leonid Kravchuk: Lider dolzhen podchinimaetsia vyboru naroda," *Izvestiia* November 26, 1991, 3. Vitalii Portnikov, "Ukraina progolosovala za nezavisimost'," *Nezavisimaia gazeta* December 3, 1991, 1. Also see Wilson 2000, 169–71.

half-decade from the signing of the Treaty of Union that created the USSR on December 30, 1922, until Stalin's victory over his opponents in 1927 afforded the union republic leaders, particularly in Ukraine, opportunities to build political machines, foster titular cultures, protect indigenous social patterns, and develop in diverging directions. In Moscow, Leon Trotsky, Grigorii Zinoviev, and their allies in the Left and United Oppositions criticized this autonomy and the nationalism they feared would threaten socialism in the republics. Stalin at first defended the autonomy of the republics against the attacks from his opponents. Yet by late 1927, once Stalin had eliminated the Left and United Oppositions and begun to consolidate his hold on power, he adopted many of their complaints about the union republic leadership and moved to centralize even more of the republics' decision rights in the common-state (all-union) government.

Although the constitution of the USSR adopted in 1924 placed most decision-making powers firmly in the common-state (all-union) government, Lenin's insistence had left segment-states (particularly union republics) enough autonomy to carry out extensive indigenization of personnel, social policies, and even some institutions. Decisions of the common-state organs were binding on segment-state organs, the common-state Central Executive Committee could suspend decisions taken in the segment-states, and the joint commissariats (or ministries) in the common-state and segment-state governments functioned as integrated administrative hierarchies directed from Moscow. Yet in such areas as personnel, education, culture, local administration, and even the armed forces, segment-state (and particularly union republic) leaders in the mid-1920s still had opportunities to develop in diverging directions through policies of Belorussianization, Ukrainianization, Tatarization, and so forth. Between 1924 and 1926, segment-state leaders pressed ahead by indigenizing Soviet institutions, by rapidly expanding indigenous membership in the governmental apparatus and Communist Party, by introducing the titular language in education, and by fostering growth of a titular literature, art, and historiography.[54] Thus, in Central Asia many traditional authorities, including village and clan leaders, were made chairmen of local soviets; traditional forms of economic life like nomadism were left in place; and even religious practices like *Sharia* courts were tolerated. In Belorussia, where the repartitional peasant commune had been less common prior to the revolution, individual private peasant farms at first flourished under the new Communist government.[55] In Ukraine, Robert S. Sullivant notes, the republic's leadership even sought to indigenize the armed forces assigned to the Ukraine Military District: by introducing a program of instruction and

[54] Krawchenko 1985, 46–112; Rorlich 1986, 142–56.
[55] Lubachko 1972, 73–76.

political lectures in the Ukrainian language, Ukrainianzation of the army "promised to increase the regional attachments of these important groups and to diminish their identification with the Union as a whole."[56]

In 1926 Stalin began to take a more critical tone toward the policies adopted in some republics.[57] Yet it was when Stalin began building socialism in one country with the collectivization of agriculture and the construction of socialist industry that he forced a rapid and extreme centralization of decision rights. For example, in Central Asia, Moscow began a direct assault on the divergent development in this region, banning *Sharia* courts and the veiling of women and forcing nomads onto collective farms.[58] The segment-state governments began to submit to the common-state government in Moscow. They adopted new laws on language usage that permitted wider use of Russian. They introduced the new all-union plan for agricultural production that would culminate a year later in the direct control by the common-state government over agriculture. They submitted to the authority of the State Planning Committee (Gosplan) in industrial and national economic policy.[59]

A few indigenous leaders in the segment-states initially argued against introduction of collectivization and the first five-year plan within their homelands. The resistors buttressed their defense of divergent development with claims that there was no need for an intensified class struggle in their segment-states because a bourgeoisie had not emerged in their countryside and their traditional villages already practiced a form of communism.[60] In 1928, however, a purge of national communists swept the country. By the fall of 1929 the Belorussian leadership had been imprisoned.[61] In Tatarstan the arrest of Mirsaid Sultangaliev was followed by a purge of the Tatar Communist Party organization, and in December 1928 a majority of the Tatar ASSR party committee (obkom) members were arrested, tried, and executed on charges of treason; a month later another purge of the obkom found still more Sultangalievists.[62] Until the end of 1929, some segment-state leaders continued to raise increasingly feeble protests against the rapid centralization of authority in such areas as the state budget and land-use policy.[63] Yet by the 16th CPSU Congress (July 1930), the segment-state leaders had become a claque for Stalin's policies.[64]

---

[56] Sullivant 1962, 114.
[57] Sullivant 1962, 128–34. Also see T. Martin 2001, 211–72.
[58] Roy 2000, 79; Massell 1974, 196–200.
[59] Sullivant 1962, 143.
[60] Olcott 1987, 212; Vakar 1956, 146; Lubachko 1972, 96; Massell 1974, 286–304.
[61] Vakar 1956, 146–47.
[62] Bennigsen and Wimbush 1979, 91.
[63] Sullivant 1962, 151–52; Rakowska-Harmstone 1970, 37–41.
[64] Rees 2002.

The decisive shift of decision rights to the common-state (all-union) government reduced the discretion of segment-state leaders to the minimum found in a unitary state.

The Russian Federation Crisis and Centralization

The nation-state crisis within the Russian Federation that began in 1990 continued for over a decade. It began, like the *perestroika* crisis, in a challenge to the common-state from the segment-states, but it ended, like the crisis of the early USSR, in centralization of many powers held by segment-states. Like the other two crises, the segment-state governments were able to challenge or resist the common-state government as long as Moscow was divided, but, as in the crisis of the early USSR, once a strong leader had reestablished consolidated leadership in Moscow, the segment-state leaders began conceding. The crisis began in 1990 as the segment-states inside Russia sought to claim a larger share of the decision rights and even to assert their sovereignty against the government of the RSFSR, at the time that Russia was itself a first-order segment-state or union republic within the USSR. With respect to its autonomous republics, autonomous oblasts, and autonomous okrugs—the second-, third-, and fourth-order segment-states of Soviet *matrioshka* federalism—the RSFSR was a common-state. The conflict between the Russian Federation common-state government and the governments of the segment-states within Russia reached a peak by the end of 1992 as differences over the segment-states' role in the common-state government and their powers at home prevented agreement on a new constitution for the now independent Russian Federation. Yet the segment-state leaders were never able to narrow the bargaining over the allocation of decision rights with Russia by excluding other participants or to conflate all issues, particularly cross-cutting issues like economic and political reform, in an overarching zero-sum conflict over allocation of decision rights between the common-state and segment-state governments. The establishment of presidential rule in the September–October 1993 coup stopped further devolution of powers to segment-states and began the process of recentralization.

Between 1991 and October 1993, many segment-states (particularly the republics) within Russia demanded that the Russian Federation recognize their sovereignty, grant the segment-states a collective legislative veto by assigning them half the seats in the upper chamber of the legislature, and establish ex officio representation of republics within the all-Russian executive.[65] This prevented agreement on both a federation treaty and a constitution for Russia. The negotiations over a federation treaty for Russia began when the Third (Extraordinary) Session of the Russian Congress of People's Deputies (March–April 1991) called for an agreement that would reform the nation-state structure of the RSFSR. The Congress created a Commission on the Nation-State Structure and Relations between Nationalities, and by March 13, 1992, the commission's negotiations with the republics had produced a *Treaty on Demarcating Objects of Jurisdiction between the Federal Bodies of Power of the Russian Federation and the Bodies of Power of the Republics within the Russian Federation.*[66] The treaty included a protocol that guaranteed continuation of the equal balance in the upper chamber of a future Russian parliament between representatives of segment-states (republics, autonomous oblasts, and autonomous okrugs) and representatives of other subjects of the federation that were not segment-states (oblasts, krais, and federal cities). It included a provision that the republics within the Russian Federation, unlike the other subjects of the federation, should be consulted *in advance* on legislation and government policies.[67] The Federation Treaty was supposed to become part of the Russian constitution. However, most leaders of the subjects of the federation that were not segment-state objected to the privileged status of republics, demanded equalization of rights among all subjects of the federation (whether segment-states or not), and refused to sign the draft Federation Treaty. In early 1992 the Yeltsin administration and the republics had to settle for not a single federation treaty, but multiple treaties—with different texts and separate protocols initialed by different groups of parties.[68] To allow republic leaders to sign a treaty that did not concede all the rights that many demanded, Moscow signed separate addenda with half of the republics—notably Bashkortostan, Karelia, and Sakha—granting each a separate set of prerogatives in such areas as control of resources, foreign trade, taxation, and legislative powers.[69]

Similarly, this dispute over the rights of segment-states was decisive in the deadlock that blocked adoption of a new Russian constitution prior to September–October 1993.[70] In the initial discussion of constitutional issues, even before the breakup of the USSR, the Russian Congress of

[65] Radik Batyrshin, "Sovet Federatsii kak umirotvoritel' parlamenta," *Nezavisimaia gazeta* August 27, 1993, 3.

[66] "Federativnyi Dogovor," *Rossiiskaia gazeta* March 18, 1992, 2.

[67] Slider 1994a, 247–48.

[68] See treaties in Konstitutsiia Rossiiskoi Federatsii, ofitsial'noe izdanie 1993.

[69] Radik Batyrshin, "Federativnyi dogovor podpisan," *Nezavisimaia gazeta* April 1, 1992, 1; Slider 1994a, 247–48; Teague 1994, 35; Balzer and Vinokurova 1996a, 1996b.

[70] Compare Remington 2001, 151–59; Andrews 2002.

People's Deputies at its third (extraordinary) session (March 30–April 5, 1991) deadlocked, with heated exchanges between representatives of the governments of segment-states and the other subjects of the federation.[71] The Congress had already agreed to create a presidency, schedule elections, and grant the executive branch significant powers to deal with the crisis in Russia.[72] The stalemate on the federation issue stood in stark contrast to the decisive action on other constitutional issues.

After the breakup of the USSR, the inner working body of the Russian Congress of People's Deputies (the Supreme Soviet) opened discussion of a draft constitution on February 14, 1992, but it too deadlocked over the federation issues relating to the privileged status of republics versus equalization of rights among all subjects of the federation. The Supreme Soviet successfully adopted provisions covering the distribution of power between executive and legislative branches within the common-state government. Indeed, as Josephine Andrews observes, "there was a stable majority in favor of reducing the president's powers."[73] When it came to provisions for representation of the subjects of the federation in the common-state organs, however, the differences within the Supreme Soviet were so deep that the body simply did not vote on these issues. Yet this inability to resolve the federation issue meant that the Congress of People's Deputies sent the draft constitution back to the Supreme Soviet without significant discussion. The Congress of People's Deputies had the constitutional authority (and probably the votes) to pass a new constitution by two-thirds majority without approval from other bodies. Yet the Congress could not secure approval of the republics, and the leaders of the Congress feared that this could lead to secession.[74] According to Nikolai Troitskii, the draft parliamentary (or "Rumiantsev") constitution had been "axed" by the upper chamber of the Supreme Soviet (the Council of Nationalities), where the segment-states had enough votes to block any proposals, and was "shelved precisely because it gave equal rights to the territories, provinces, and republics."[75] Radik Batyrshin concluded that "the republics virtually buried the official (parliamentary or Rumiantsev) draft of a new Russian

---

[71] I. Demchenko and G. Shipit'ko, "Rossiiskii s"ezd zavershil rabotu," *Izvestiia* April 6, 1991, 1, 3.

[72] I. Elistratov, "Deputaty ugovarivaiut drug druga nabrat'sia muzhestva," *Izvestiia* November 1, 1991, 2; I. Elistratov, "El'tsin poluchaet novye polnomochiia," *Izvestiia* November 2, 1991, 1.

[73] Andrews 2002, 51.

[74] "Obrashchenie Verkhovnogo Soveta Rossiiskoi Federatsii k narodu, Verkhovnomu Sovetu i Prezidentu Respubliki Tatarstan," *Rossiiskaia gazeta* March 7, 1992, 1.

[75] Nikolai Troitskii, "Conference Hit a Federal Impasse," *Megapolis-Ekspress* June 16, 1993, 20; translated in *Current Digest of the Post-Soviet Press* 45 (July 7, 1993), 11–12.

Constitution."[76] These complaints were not scapegoating; they reflected the harsh fears of late 1992 and 1993. The constitutional authority to adopt a new constitution rested with the Russian Congress of People's Deputies. Despite overwhelming support within the Congress of People's Deputies for a return of power from the president back to the Congress and for equalization of the status of subjects of the federation within the common-state, the Congress leaders feared that forcing a vote would lead to extra-constitutional moves such as secession or a decisive shift among republic governments to support a presidential coup against the Congress.[77] In the end, the Congress settled for continuing the constitutional ambiguity with which the Russian Federation had begun independence—the inconsistent rules contained in the much-amended 1978 RSFSR Constitution, a new law on legislative-executive relations to retract some of the emergency powers granted in 1991, and multiple versions of the Federation Treaty.

In the summer of 1993, President Yeltsin attempted to circumvent the Congress of People's Deputies through a Constitutional Conference, but this reached a similar impasse. Just prior to the convocation of the Constitutional Conference on July 5, 1993, Yeltsin's talks with the leaders of the republics and other subjects of the federation had failed to reach an agreement: "the sticking point, as many observers have surmised, is the question of equality for the members of the Federation."[78] In the Constitutional Conference itself, even though 82 percent of the participants endorsed the president's "Statement on the Draft of a New Constitution for the Russian Federation," the conference could not satisfy both the republics and the provinces (oblasts and krais) on this issue of the special status of republics within the common-state.[79] The "Statement on the Draft Constitution" dropped provisions from the Federation Treaty that defined the republics as sovereign and provisions for coöpting executive and legislative leaders from the subjects into an upper chamber of a federal assembly.[80]

[76] Radik Batyrshin, "Prezidentskii proekt i regional'nye interesy," *Nezavisimaia gazeta* May 15, 1993, 1. See also Teague 1994, 30–33.

[77] Teague 1994, 33.

[78] Vladimir Todres, "Pravo na vykhod: poslednii kozyr' bol'shoi igry," *Segodnia* June 4, 1993, 2.

[79] Lyubov Tsukanova, "Segodnia initsiativa v rukakh Prezidenta," *Rossiiskie vesti* June 15, 1993, 1; "Zaiavlenie narodnykh deputatov Rossiiskoi Federatsii," *Rossiiskie vesti* June 15, 1993, 1; Boris El'tsin, "Soglasie stanovit'sia mnogo mernym i vazhno sberech' opyt partnerstva dlia rossiiskii demokratii," *Rossiiskie vesti* June 17, 1991, 1; "Zaiavleniia o Proekte novoi Konstitutsii Rossiiskoi Federatsii," *Rossiiskie vesti* June 17, 1993, 1.

[80] Nikolai Troitskii, "The Titanic Work Breaks Off Until June 26," *Megapolis-Ekspress* June 23, 1993, 20; translated in *Current Digest of the Post-Soviet Press* 45 (July 14, 1993), 11; Sergei Parkhomenko, "Boris El'tsin otkladyvaet priznanie suvereniteta rossiiskikh avtonomii," *Segodnia* June 18, 1993, 2.

This produced an immediate negative response from republic leaders such as Tatarstan's President Mintimer Shaimiev, who threatened not to participate in ratification of the constitution. Ramazan Abdulatipov, speaker of the Council of Nationalities, warned ominously that "the Russian krais and oblasts alone will be responsible for the possible breakup of Russia."[81]

To appease the republics and bring them on board at the Constitutional Conference, the presidential staff tried various concessions that would paper over the disagreements with legal ambiguity. These concessions included treating the Federation Treaty as a document co-equal with the Constitution (despite inconsistencies between the documents), recognizing *both* the unique sovereignty of the republics *and* the equal rights of all subjects of the federation (despite the logical contradiction of these two principles), coöpting leaders of all subjects of the federation (whether they were segment-states or not) into an upper legislative chamber, and negotiating separate bilateral treaties with the republics that would grant them special prerogatives outside the provisions of the constitution (despite the legal supremacy of the basic law).[82] The leaders of the subjects of the federation that were not segment-states (that is, leaders of the oblasts, krais, and federal cities) made it clear they would not agree to these concessions. Viktor Ignatenko, chair of the Irkutsk Oblast Soviet, echoed their anger: "We are willing to leave [the republics] with the attributes of statehood: a state language, citizenship, an emblem, a flag, and an anthem. But everyone must have equal powers."[83] The legislatures of Arkhangelsk, Voronezh, Cheliabinsk, Kaliningrad, and Vologda oblasts and Krasnoiarsk and Primore krais, and an assembly of legislators from the oblasts of the Black-Earth Zone Association all threatened to proclaim themselves republics; Sverdlovsk oblast actually proclaimed itself the Urals Republic.[84]

---

[81] Vladimir Todres, "Mestnye sovety zhelaiut ratifitsirovat' konstitutsiiu," *Segodnia* July 13, 1993, 2. Radik Batyrshin, "Prezident Sakha (Iakutii)—za dosrochnye parlamentskie vybory v RF," *Nezavisimaia gazeta* August 17, 1993, 1, 3.

[82] Dmitrii Volkov, "Shakhrai nashel 'zolotuiu seredinu' federalizma," *Segodnia* June 18, 1993, 2; Petr Akopov, "Sovet Federatsii budet sozdan, Stanet li on instrumentom obnovleniia?" *Rossiiskie vesti* August 14, 1993, 1; Sergei Chugaev, "Sil'nyi khod prezidenta v Petrozavodske," *Izvestiia* August 17, 1993, 2.

[83] Vladimir Todres, "Mestnye sovety zhelaiut ratifitsirovat' konstitutsiiu," *Segodnia* July 13, 1993, 2. Also see Hughes 1994; Kirkow 1995.

[84] Radik Batyrshin, "Iuzhnoural'skaia respublika: davlenie na Moskvu, epidemiia ili zaiavka?" *Nezavisimaia gazeta* July 13, 1993, 3; Nikolai Efimovich, "Suverenitet uzhe pod Moskvoi," *Komsomolskaia Pravda* July 13, 1993, 1; Elena Matveeva, "Ot velikogo do smeshnogo," *Moskovskie novosti* July 18, 1993, A-9; Liubov Tsukanova, "Ural nachinaet, i vyigryvaet?" *Rossiiskie vesti* July 3, 1993, 1; Aleksandr Pashkov, "Eskalatsiia spora sub"ektov Federatsii: provozglashena Ural'skaia respublika," *Izvestiia* July 3, 1993, 1–2; Aleksandr Pashkov, "Ural'skaia respublika ukrepit Rossiiu," *Izvestiia* September 17, 1993, 2; *RFE/RL Daily Report* July 22, 1993; Easter 1997; Anna Efimova, "Voronezhskaia oblast' poka ne nazvala sebia respublikoi," *Segodnia* September 7, 1993, 3; Dmitrii Kuznets, "V tsentre Rossii sozdaetsia novaia res-

Although the president's Constitutional Conference reached agreement on almost all issues before it, as the *Izvestiia* correspondent Vasilii Kononenko observed, "The only question that it has not yet been possible to resolve within the framework of the constitutional process is the status of the members of the Federation."[85] Torn between competing demands for sovereign rights of republics and the equalization of the powers of the subjects of the federation, torn between competing threats of secession of republics and republicanization of oblasts, the Constitutional Conference ended in an impasse. As Nikolai Troitskii observed, "The Constitutional Conference has run aground on the same reef as the Congress' Constitutional Commission."[86]

Many segment-state governments within the Russian Federation were actually pleased with this deadlock. They found that their de facto autonomy and ability to wring de jure concessions had expanded with the stalemate at the center and weakening of the common-state government. Segment-state leaders sought to maintain the balance between the Russian Congress of People's Deputies and the Russian president. When the presidential coup of September–October 1993 cut through this impasse, leaders of many republics within the Russian Federation at first tried to forestall consolidation of power in a new common-state government. In response to Yeltsin's Decree No. 1400 (September 21, 1993) dissolving the Congress of People's Deputies and scheduling elections to a new State Duma, the supreme soviets of twelve of the nineteen republics with functioning legislatures officially denounced the decree (Table 6.3). Only Sakha endorsed Yeltsin's decree. Chechnya and Tatarstan remained aloof as officially disinterested sovereign states. Four republics remained silent.[87] On October 12, with Decree No. 1760 Yeltsin invited, but did not order, republics to dissolve their Soviet-era legislatures (supreme soviets) and elect new legislatures by March 1994. Thirteen of the nineteen republics with functioning supreme soviets initially rejected the call to reform. Only Sakha endorsed the decree. The remainder simply remained silent.

Yet when it became apparent in mid-October 1993 that a decisive shift in power toward the president had indeed taken place in Moscow, many

---

publika?" *Segodnia* August 31, 1993, 3; Aleksei Tarasov, "Obnarodovan proekt ustava Krasnoiarskogo kraia," *Izvestiia* May 21, 1993, 4; Viktor Filippov, "Volgogradskaia oblast' provozglashena gosudarstvom v sostave Rossii," *Izvestiia* May 18, 1993, 1–2; Viktor Filippov, "Volgogradskaia oblast' khochet stat' Volgogradskoi respublikoi," *Izvestiia* June 2, 1993, 4.

[85] Vasilii Kononenko, "The Constitutional Conference Approves the Draft of a New Constitution for Russia," *Izvestiia* July 13, 1993, 1–2, translated in *Current Digest of the Post-Soviet Press* 45 (August 11, 1993), 1.

[86] Nikolai Troitskii, "Conference Hit a Federal Impasse," *Megapolis-Ekspress* June 16, 1993, 20; translated in *Current Digest of the Post-Soviet Press* 45 (July 7, 1993), 11–12.

[87] Teague 1993.

TABLE 6.3

Russian Federation: Republic legislative responses to Yeltsin's coup, 1993

Republic	Response to Decree No. 1400[a]	Response to Decree No. 1760[b]	Actual Legislative Action		
Adygeia	Denounced	Silent	Reform	November 1993	No elections
Altai	Silent	Silent	Reform	December 1993	Elections
Bashkortostan	Denounced	Rejected	None		None
Buryatia	Denounced	Rejected	Reform	June 1994	Elections
Chechnya	Silent	Silent	None		None
Chuvashia	Denounced	Rejected	Reform	March 1994	Elections
Dagestan	Denounced	Rejected	None		None
Ingushetia	No legislature	No legislature	N/A		N/A
Kabardino-Balkaria	Denounced	Rejected	Reform	Fall 1993	No Election
Kalmykia	No legislature	No legislature	N/A		N/A
Karachai-Cherkessia	Silent	Silent	None		None
Karelia	Denounced	Rejected	Reform	April 1994	Election
Khakassia	Denounced	Rejected	None		None
Komi	Denounced	Rejected	None		None
Mari El	Silent	Rejected	Reform	December 1993	Elections
Mordovia	Denounced	Rejected	None		None
North Ossetia	Silent	Rejected	None		None
Sakha	Supported	Supported	Reform	October 1993	Elections
Tatarstan	Silent	Rejected	None		None
Tyva	Denounced	Rejected	Reform	December 1993	Elections
Udmurtia	Denounced	Silent	None		None

Sources: Teague 1993; Glubotskii, Mukhin, and Tiukov 1995.

[a] Presidential Decree No. 1400 (21 September 1993) dissolved the Russian Congress of People's Deputies.

[b] Presidential Decree No. 1760 (12 October 1993) invited republics to dissolve their supreme soviets, reform these legislatures, and call new legislative elections.

republics quickly adjusted their behavior.[88] By October 16, all but the supreme soviets of Komi and Mordovia had rescinded their denunciations of Yeltsin's Decree No. 1400. Nine of the republics reformed their legislatures, and seven of these held new popular elections before the March 1994 deadline. By June another two republics had followed with elections to new legislatures. Half of these republics had publicly proclaimed just weeks before that they would do no such thing.

With the consolidation of presidential authority against the legislature within the common-state government, the leadership under Boris Yeltsin used the so-called Yeltsin Constitution, adopted on December 12, 1993, to initiate the long-term process of equalization of the rights of segment-states with those of the other subjects of the federation and centralization of power by reallocating decision rights previously allowed to the segment-states. Compared to the arrangements negotiated with the republics in the Federation Treaty of 1992, the Yeltsin Constitution omitted any recognition of the sovereignty of the republics. It did not give the republics special representation within the legislative or executive branches. It allocated many more decision rights to the common-state government. It omitted any reference to republics' ownership of land or natural resources. It allocated republics no more decision rights than the provinces, except for the right to adopt constitutions (Article 66) and to institute their own state languages (Article 68). Moreover, in contrast to many other federations, the Yeltsin Constitution envisioned a highly centralized state.[89] Of course, in December 1993, the constitution was still more like a goal, or a plan to be fulfilled over multiple years, than a description of practices that would be implemented immediately. Temporary compromises, such as power-sharing treaties, were made to buy some republics' acceptance of the constitution, but the long-term objective with respect to the segment-states was equalization with the other subjects of the federation and centralization of decision rights in the common-state government. Important to the implementation of equalization and centralization, the 1993 constitution, unlike the Federation Treaty, granted the segment-states no veto points to block actions by the common-state government—except of constitutional legislation. Decisions of the upper legislative chamber (the Council of the Federation), the one place where segment-state leaders were coöpted into the common-state decision-making organs, could be taken without segment-state approval, since the segment-states held only 38 percent of the council seats and passage of legislation required a simple majority of the membership. A nearly unanimous block of segment-states could block fed-

[88] Payin 1998.
[89] Ordeshook 1995, 6.

eral action only when it came to federal constitutional laws, which required approval of three-fourths of the membership of the Council (Article 108), and constitutional amendments, which additionally required approval by two-thirds of all subjects of the federation (Article 136).

That the words of the Constitution of the Russian Federation provided legal grounds for equalization and centralization with respect to the segment-states—particularly the more independent-minded republics—became clear in cases brought before the Russian Constitutional Court.[90] The court decided a series of cases in which it reiterated that the constitutions of the republics, their treaties (including the Federation Treaty and specific power-sharing treaties), and their laws were subject to the provisions of the Russian Constitution and could be declared unconstitutional, null, and void on this basis (table 6.4). Thus, the Constitutional Court ruled, sovereignty resides solely with the population of the Russian Federation as a whole, and not with the separate populations of individual republics (Altai Republic: Sovereignty case, 2000).[91] In a June 27, 2000, advisory opinion (*opredelenie*), the court noted that provisions in six republican constitutions claiming sovereignty based on the Federation Treaty violated the federal constitution.[92] Contrary to the terms of the Federation Treaty, the court ruled, the natural resources of republics fell within the jurisdiction of the federation government (Karelia: Forest Code case, 1998).[93] And, even before adoption of the 1993 constitution, the court had ruled that republics do not have a right to secede (Tatarstan: Referendum case, 1992). In addition, the Constitutional Court decided a number of cases so as to limit the republics' discretion in designing their political institutions. These rulings and advisory opinions threatened the ability of republic leaders to maintain political machines. Thus, republics may not impose language or residence requirements for candidates (Khakassia: Residence requirement case, 1997; Bashkortostan: Presidential election case, 1998). The power to appoint heads of administration is limited by federal laws on self-government (Komi: Local government case, 1996). Executive officials may not sit as legislators (Komi: Executive officials case, 1998). Nor may republics malapportion seats within legislatures to give regions or titular groups extra seats (Tatarstan: Legislative electoral law case, 2002).

[90] Titkov 2001.

[91] Aleksandr Shinkin, "Altai perebral Suvereniteta," *Rossiiskaia gazeta* June 10, 2000, 3.

[92] "Opredelenie po zaprosu gruppy deputatov Gosudarstvennoi Dumy o proverke sootvetstviia Konstitutsii Rossiiskoi Federatsii otdel'nykh polozhenii konstitutsii Respubliki Adygeia, Respubliki Bashkortostan, Respubliki Ingushetiia, Respubliki Komi, Respubliki Severnaia Osetiia-Alaniia i Respubliki Tatarstan," *Vestnik Konstitutsionnogo Suda Rossiiskoi Federatsii* 5:59–80, 2000.

[93] Also see *RFE/RL Newsline* January 13, 1998.

TABLE 6.4

Russian Federation: Constitutional Court rulings involving republics, 1992–2003

Ruling	Date	Republics that were parties to the dispute	Issue
3	March 13, 1992	Tatarstan	Republic referendum on sovereignty
22	June 3, 1993	Mordovia	Republic executive-legislative relations
26	September 17, 1993	North Ossetia	Republic jurisdiction concerning refugees
27	September 30, 1993	Kabardino-Balkaria	Election/appointment of judges
36	July 10, 1995	Chuvashia	Republic legislature electoral law
41	November 24, 1995	North Ossetia	Republic legislature electoral law
57	May 30, 1996	Komi[a]	Appointment of local government
59	June 21, 1996	Bashkortostan	Republic president electoral law
66	January 24, 1997	Udmurtia	Election/appointment of local government
74	June 24, 1997	Khakassia	Residence requirement for office holders
76	July 2, 1997	Mordovia	Republic anticrime law
87	January 9, 1998	Karelia	Federal Forest Code
89	January 15, 1998	Komi	Election/appointment of local government
98	April 27, 1998	Bashkortostan	Republic president electoral law
102	May 29, 1998	Komi	Executive officials in legislature
105	June 16, 1998	Karelia, Komi	Competence of RF Constitutional Court
143	June 7, 2000	Altai	Sovereignty and local government
150	January 30, 2001	Chuvashia[a]	Taxation authority
167	January 22, 2002	Tatarstan	Republic legislature electoral law
173	April 4, 2002	Adygeia, Sakha	Federal intervention by Russian president
177	July 9, 2002	Sakha, Tatarstan	Republic president term limits
195	July 18, 2003	Bashkortostan, Tatarstan	Authority of federal Procuracy

Sources: All cases are available online at *www.ksrf.ru.*
[a] Parties also included at least one oblast or krai.

The power-sharing treaties signed by the common-state government with nine republics between March 1994 (Tatarstan) and May 1996 (Chuvashia) were an astute transitional arrangement that, in fact, facilitated equalization and centralization within the Russian Federation. The instrument of bilateral treaties minimized the total concessions made to the republics by making these concessions selectively rather than granting them to all republics. The instrument of bilateral treaties avoided institutionalizing these in the constitution, which would have given them greater permanence. Many analysts have complained that this form of "negotiated" fed-

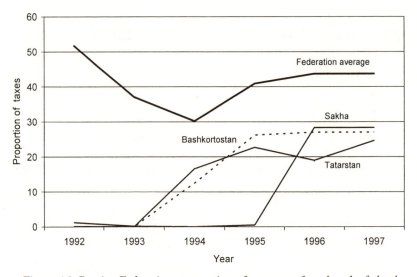

Figure 6.2 Russian Federation: proportion of taxes transferred to the federal budget, 1992–1997. *Source:* From data in Lavrov and Makushkin 2001, 60.

eralism led to inefficiencies in tax collection and policy. Yet, as figure 6.2 illustrates, the conclusion of treaties with Bashkortostan and Tatarstan in 1994 and with Sakha in 1995 was associated with a rise in the proportion of taxes collected within the borders of these republics that were transferred to the Russian Federation budget. Moreover, the inefficiencies sanctioned by these treaties were only transitional costs.[94] Indeed, the piecemeal dismantling of these special concessions to republics began in 1996, soon after Yeltsin's victory in the second round of presidential elections. The legal foundation for retrenchment was laid out in the law on power-sharing treaties (June 24, 1999).[95] Thus, the treaties and accompanying agreements are subordinate to the Russian Constitution, must operate within the Constitution's terms, and cannot change the terms of the Constitution, particularly the enumeration of powers within Articles 71 and 72. The State Duma refused to add its imprimatur by ratifying individual treaties, and so the power-sharing treaties became little more than ad hoc deals between President Yeltsin and individual chief executives of the republics to govern executive cooperation in areas of joint federal-republic jurisdiction.

After the 1996 presidential elections that returned Yeltsin to a second term, the pace of equalization and centralization began to pick up. As early

[94] Polishchuk 1996, 19.
[95] Federal'nyi zakon No. 119 "O printsipakh i poriadke razgranicheniia predmetov vedeniia i polnomochii mezhdu organami gosudarstvennoi vlasti Rossiiskoi Federatsii i organami

as mid-1997 Bashkortostan's president Murtaza Rakhimov complained with more than a bit of hyperbole that he feared his republic would soon be brought down to the level of a mere province (oblast).[96] Yet it was President Vladimir Putin's four-pronged assault, beginning soon after he was elected president in 2000, that actually made this a reality.[97] First, Putin improved the common-state government's monitoring and whistle-blowing capacity vis-à-vis the segment-states. In Decree No. 849 (May 13, 2000), Putin created seven federal districts, each under the direction of a presidential representative. Unlike Yeltsin's presidential representatives, these would have jurisdiction over all segment-states as well as the other subjects of the federation.[98] The representatives, backed by the military, security, and procuratorial agencies, would become monitors to identify and publicly denounce—and possibly help prepare legal actions against—instances in which the leaders of segment-states as well as other territorial jurisdictions failed to implement federal laws and directives. This was done with full endorsement of the courts. Indeed, in February 2000 the chief justice, Marat Baglai, had called on executive officials to use the Constitutional Court more actively "to review republic constitutions, bilateral treaties, as well as other important laws in force in the federation subjects."[99]

Second, Putin reduced the clout of segment-state leaders within the common-state government still further and stripped them of parliamentary immunity from prosecution. On August 5, 2000, Putin signed legislation that ended the ex officio coöptation of the leader of each region's executive and legislative branches to the Council of the Federation (upper chamber of the legislature). This stripped the regional leaders of their parliamentary immunity from prosecution.[100] To mollify regional leaders, Putin created by decree on September 1, 2000, a State Council within the executive branch that brought together the chief executives of the subjects of the federation—

---

gosudarstvennoi vlasti sub"ektov Rossiiskoi Federatsii" June 24, 1999 in *Sobranie Zakonodatel'stva Rossiiskoi Federatsii* 1999 No. 26, article 3176. Also see *OMRI Daily Digest* October 24,1996, October 30, 1996, December 5, 1996, December 30, 1996, January 7, 1997, March 25, 1997; *RFE/RL Newsline* May 20, 1997.

[96] Ilishev 1997, 6.

[97] For a fuller description, see Hyde 2001; Sharlet 2001. For a rather strong case, see Brown 2001, 49–51.

[98] Ukaz Prezidenta Rossiiskoi Federatsii No. 849 "O polnomochnom predstavitele Prezidenta Rossiiskoi Federatsii v regione Rossiiskoi Federatsii" May 13, 2000, *Rossiiskaia gazeta* May 16, 2000, 1. Also see V. Lysenko, "Istoriia povtoriaetsia trizhdy," *Rossiiskaia gazeta* May 16, 2000, 1, 4.

[99] Quoted in Sharlet 2001, 218. Also see *RFE/RL Newsline* June 1, 2000, April 5, 2001, April 11, 2001.

[100] Federal'nyi Zakon No. 113-FZ "O poriadke formirovaniia Soveta Federatsii Federal'nogo Sobraniia Rossiiskoi Federatsii" August 5, 2000, *Rossiiskaia gazeta* August 8, 2000, 4.

both segment-states and the other territorial jurisdictions—in a purely consultative role and under the chairmanship of the federation president.[101]

Third, Putin expanded the legal sanctions against segment-state leaders and segment-state legislatures for violating the Russian Constitution. On July 29, 2000, Putin signed a law authorizing the practice of "federal intervention," which permitted the president to take action against executive or legislative officials in any segment-state or other subject of the federation that violated the federal constitution or federal laws. The president could remove a segment-state chief executive upon a court order and corroboration from the Procuracy and could dissolve the segment-state's legislative body after approval from the State Duma.[102]

Fourth, on December 11, 2004, a new constitutional law of the Russian Federation gave the common-state president power to nominate the chief executives (called by such titles as president, governor, and so forth) in each subject of the federation. The constitutional law authorized regional legislatures to reject the president's nominee, but at the same time it empowered the common-state president to dissolve the legislature should it reject his nominee and to appoint his nominee as acting chief executive for a six-month term. The constitutional law also expanded the president's power to dismiss chief executives, so that the common-state president could dismiss a chief executive whenever the chief executive "loses his [the president's] trust."[103] This reallocation of decision rights transformed the balance of leverage between common-state and segment-state governments.

The more active common-state government brought results beginning in 1997. Progress was at first slow in narrowing the gap between practice and the constitutional goal, but the pace accelerated. Moscow first took on the weaker republic governments—those without machines that had failed to consolidate political-identity hegemony. On order of the Constitutional Court, Mari El permitted candidates who were not fluent in the Mari language to run for its presidency (1997).[104] Khakassia permitted candidates to run in the republic's presidential election even though they did not qual-

---

[101] Ukaz Prezidenta Rossiiskoi Federatsii "O Gosudarstvennom sovete Rossiiskoi Federatsii" September 1, 2000, in *Sobranie zakonodatel'stva Rossiiskoi Federatsii* No. 36, Article 3633 (September 4, 2000), 7186–89.

[102] Federal'nyi zakon No. 106 "O vnesenii izmenenii i dopolnenii v Federal'nyi zakon 'Ob obshchikh printsipakh organizatsii zakonodatel'nykh (predstavitel'nykh) i ispolnitel'nykh organov gosudarshvennykh vlasti sub"ektov Rossiiskoi Federatsii' " June 29, 2000, available online at document.kremlin.ru.

[103] Federal'nyi zakon No. 159 "O vnesenii izmenenii v Federal'nyi zakon 'Ob obshchikh printsipakh organizatsii zakonodatel'nykh (predstavitel'nykh) organov gosudarstvennoi vlasti sub"ektov Rossiiskoi Federatsii' i v Federal'nyi zakon 'Ob osnovnykh garantiiakh izbiratel'nykh prav i prava na uchastie v referendume grazhdan Rossiiskoi Federatstii" December 11, 2004; available online at document.kremlin.ru.

[104] *OMRI Daily Digest* January 2, 1997.

ify under the republic's seven-year residence requirement, and this permitted Aleksei Lebed to win the presidency (1997).[105] Yet in the late 1990s there was frequently stiff resistance even from some of the more competitive republic governments. A Constitution Court case to force Udmurtia's legislature (State Council) to rescind a law abolishing locally elected governments in the republic (1997) initially brought vociferous defiance from the republic. Only after a decree by Yeltsin threatened the republic did Udmurtia comply, grudgingly.[106] Komi caved in after much showy defiance that dragged on for over a year, holding elections to previously appointed posts in local government ("mayors").[107] Altai amended its constitution to remove a provision that required that the prime minister and legislative speaker be of different nationalities. Altai further rewrote the article that claimed Altai was a democratic state within Russia; Altai was henceforth to be an equal subject and inseparable part of the Russian Federation (2001).[108]

The consolidation of presidential authority within the common-state government under Putin tipped the "balance of consolidation" so that the common-state government was in a position to take on even the machine republics. After Putin's procurator general Vladimir Ustinov warned that regional leaders had one month to bring their legislation into line, many republics, including Tyva, Kalmykia, and Bashkortostan, acted quickly to revise their constitutions and laws in conformity with central standards.[109] Tyva amended its constitution to remove provisions claiming sovereignty and a right of secession (2001).[110] Sakha, despite its stiff resistance and delays, submitted to federal pressure to bar President Nikolaev from a third term (2001) and to amend parts of its constitution that conflicted with the federal Basic Law. (2002).[111] Most significantly, despite stiff resistance from Bashkortostan and Tatarstan, both agreed to relinquish the right of collecting taxes for the federal government and to permit all taxes collected on

---

[105] *RFE/RL Newsline* June 25, 1997.

[106] Irina Nagornykh, "Udmurtskii zakon oblasti obespokoil Moskvu," *Segodnia* October 16, 1996, 2; Konstantin Katanian, "Kto stoit blizhe k narodu," *Nezavisimaia gazeta* November 22, 1996, 3; Konstantin Katanian, "Zakoncheno Udmurtskoe delo," *Nezavisimaia gazeta* January 28, 1997, 2; Veronika Kutsyllo, "Boris El'tsin vyzval Udmurtiiu v Genprokuraturu," *Kommersant-Daily* February 22, 1997, 1; Vladislav Shuliaev, "Udmurtiia ustupaet prezidentu," *Kommersant-Daily* March 15, 1997, 2.

[107] *RFE/RL Newsline* January 20, 1998, February 3, 1998, March 2, 1998, March 31, 1998, June 2, 1998.

[108] *RFE/RL Newsline* February 15, 2001.

[109] *Russian Federation Report* June 21, 2000, June 22, 2000, June 23, 2000.

[110] *Russian Federation Report* May 9, 2001.

[111] *RFE/RL Newsline* July 18, 2001, September 26, 2001, October 9, 2001, October 25, 2001, October 26, 2001, October 30, 2001, November 1, 2001, November 6, 2001, November 21, 2001, November 29, 2001, December 13, 2001, January 17, 2001, May 18, 2001, May 4, 2001, June 26, 2001, March 8, 2002.

their territory to be sent directly to the federal treasury (2000).[112] Bashkortostan amended its constitution, after initial defiance, to remove any mention of sovereignty and such provisions as its language requirement for the presidency (2002).[113] Yet even the Putin administration encountered some stiff resistance from the machine republics with the strongest political-identity hegemony. Before it finally complied in 2002, Bashkortostan refused for four years to remove language and residence requirements for its president (1998–2002). Despite meeting most of Moscow's demands, Sakha kept in its constitution language requirements for its president and parliamentary speaker (2001). And Tatarstan, despite many amendments to its constitution in February 2002, fiercely refused for over a year to remove the sovereignty and citizenship provisions from its constitution.[114]

The early Soviet, *perestroika*, and Russian Federation nation-state crises highlight the instability of segmental arrangements. They show that both common-state and segment-state governments may be the first movers in a crisis. They also show that the outcome of such crises may be centralization as well as devolution of decision rights. With the assistance of the model of bargaining within a segmented state elaborated in the first section of this chapter, the next two chapters examine more closely the escalation of the stakes and means in nation-state crises to explain these different outcomes.

[112] *RFE/RL Newsline* March 24, 2000.

[113] *RFE/RL Newsline* December 4, 2002.

[114] *RFE/RL Newsline* March 4, 2002, March 5, 2002, April 3, 2002, June 18, 2002, July 2, 2002, September 27, 2002.

SEVEN

The Segmental Agenda and Escalation of Stakes

I **N BARGAINING BETWEEN** proponents of nation-state projects and leaders of existing states segmental institutions often shape the agenda in ways that make it harder to find compromises to keep the common-state whole. Segmental institutions focus the agenda and often lead to the conflation of many, potentially cross-cutting issues onto the single, zero-sum dimension of allocating decision rights between the segment-state and common-state governments. Segmental institutions create incentives for segment-state leaders to make more radical claims for a greater share of these decision rights. As the nation-state crisis grows more intense, the bargaining range that includes mutually acceptable compromises to keep the common-state whole may simply disappear. In the end all issues may become subsumed by a single, dichotomous choice whether to make the segment-state fully sovereign.[1] This chapter examines this escalation of stakes in nation-state crises and the role that segmental institutions play in fostering escalation.

The nation-state crises within the early USSR, during the *perestroika* period, and within the Russian Federation, discussed in chapter 6, illustrate how bargaining within segmented states typically pushes to the top of the agenda debates over two issues, the participation of segment-state leaders in common-state policy-making and the allocation of decision-making rights between common-state and segment-state governments. For example, following negotiations over a new Russian constitution during the summer of 1993, Sakha's president Mikhail Nikolaev outlined in the pages of *Nezavisimaia gazeta* the issues that divided the segment-state leaders from the common-state leaders. Nikolaev complained that the draft constitution emerging from the Constitutional Conference failed to recognize that "the Russian Federation is a federation of nation-states" that have rights to self-determination, rather than one nation-state based on the population of Russia. In particular, by failing to accept the republics within the Russian Federation as nation-states, Nikolaev objected, the draft Russian constitution moved common-state organs toward simple majority decision making and away from a voting rule that would protect the interests of republics in common-state policy. Nikolaev also complained that the draft dropped

---

[1] See Toft 2003 on the indivisibility of homelands and how this can lead to zero-sum conflicts.

provisions found in the Federation Treaty that had been signed with the segment-states within the Russian Federation that guaranteed the economic and legal independence of the republics; instead, the draft constitution privileged individualistic "human rights [such as property ownership] against the [collective] rights of people" such as the Yakuts of Sakha. Moreover, Nikolaev added, the document simply gave too many powers to the common-state government and too few to the segment-states.[2]

The demands that begin a nation-state crisis and initiate the escalation of stakes can come from either common-state or segment-state leaders, and, as the *perestroika* crisis shows, it is sometimes difficult to identify either as the first mover. Yet the evolution of nation-state crises toward dissolution and the creation of new nation-states almost always comes to involve escalating demands from segment-state leaders for a larger share of the decision rights previously exercised by the common-state government. Escalation of the stakes in a nation-state crisis often begins with conflicts over decision rights within a narrow realm of policy but leads to conflicts over ever more decision rights in more realms and, finally, to decision rights in all realms and the right to decide who decides.[3] Thus, the issues on the table in nation-state crises often escalate and simplify to the question of the location of sovereignty. A resolution adopted by the Transdniestrian legislature (Supreme Soviet), directing local authorities to begin creating a sovereign state, describes just such an escalation of its demands:

> The first thing the Left Bank [the Transdniestria region] wanted was economic independence. We were refused. The next proposal, which was based on an expression of the people's will, was that the eastern districts should be given the status of an autonomous republic. We were refused. Our third proposal—on a federal structure for Moldova—was also rejected. After the barbaric destruction of Bendery and broad-scale combat operations [by Moldova] that could only be conducted against a hated enemy, our people will never agree to be "under Moldova."[4]

Of course, the Transdniestrians' spin on events was self-serving, but it illustrates a history of escalating demands that culminated in a claim for independence from Moldova.

Many of the issues in nation-state crises are endemic in segmented states. In the USSR, when power was tightly concentrated in the hands of one man at the center, segment-state leaders were more likely to limit their

---

[2] Mikhail Nikolaev, "O novom proekte novoi konstitutsii," *Nezavisimaia gazeta* June 30, 1993, 2. Also see Balzer and Vinokurova 1996b.

[3] See Riker 1975.

[4] Leonid Kaneliushnyi, "Kakoi politicheskoi status ustroit Pridnestrov'e," *Izvestiia* June 27, 1992, 2.

claims concerning decision rights to such issues as their discretion in setting developmental objectives for their segment-states and selection of the
means to meet the central plan's objectives.[5] Yet when the Politburo members divided among themselves and sought the support of segment-state
leaders, the agenda expanded to include more discussion of the allocation
of decision-making rights between common-state and segment-state governments and, particularly, the control of segment-state leaders over the
political life of their respective homelands.

This chapter identifies the conditions under which this endemic bargaining over the allocation of decision rights escalates to a crisis and the
creation of new nation-states. It draws on the three Eurasian nation-state
crises. First, after the creation of the USSR in 1922, republic leaders resisted centralization of their decision rights: "Guided by Ukrainian Bolsheviks, they spoke out again and again at meetings of the Union parliament,
urging concessions to the localities and limitations on the powers of the
central government."[6] Second, more than six decades later the stakes in
segmental bargaining escalated once more to a nation-state crisis as soon
as Gorbachev's policy of openness (*glasnost*) permitted claimants to go public. The first methodical if still somewhat circumscribed listing of these
claims took place at the 19th Conference of the Communist Party of the
Soviet Union (CPSU), held from June 28 to July 1, 1988. Then the list
expanded and the stakes rapidly escalated as bargaining continued at the
CPSU Central Committee Plenum "On Improving Relations among Nationalities in the USSR," held on September 19–20, 1989. This escalation
continued in the declarations of sovereignty, associated constitutional
amendments adopted by union republics, and countermanding rulings of
the common-state's collective chief of state (the Presidium of the Supreme
Soviet) during the "parade of sovereignties" and "war of constitutions"
from 1988 to 1991. It reached its culmination in the final negotiations to
rewrite the Union Treaty from June 1990 to November 1991 that would
replace the 1922 treaty that created the USSR. Third, at about the same
time bargaining over the allocation of decision rights within the Russian
Federation—which was itself one of the segment-states of the USSR—
came into public view. The stakes escalated with attempts to write a federation treaty for Russia (April 1991–March 1992) and to rewrite the Russian
constitution of 1978 (April 1991–September 1993). This escalation continued in the claims to expanded decision rights made by republics inside the
Russian Federation in their declarations of sovereignty (July 1990–May
1991), which were reaffirmed in the republic constitutions adopted from
1992 to 1996.

[5] On politics of the plan see Berliner 1957; Nove 1986.
[6] Sullivant 1962, 80.

Focusing the Segmental Agenda

Within segmented states, the agenda of center–periphery bargaining comes to focus on constitutional issues concerning the reallocation of decision rights between common-state and segment-state governments. In particular, segmental institutions increase the opportunities and incentives for the leaders of segment-states to subsume all policy disputes within such constitutional issues and to eliminate cross-cutting issues that might moderate differences between segment-states and the rest of the common-state and that might build coalitions that cut across segment-state boundaries.[7] As underscored in the discussion of political identity hegemony, segmental institutions increase opportunities for segment-state leaders to play the "switchman" role that decides how issues relevant to their community and territory will be represented to the government of the common-state. These switchmen tend to direct negotiations toward issues that unite the population of their respective segment-states and reinforce the boundaries that separate the population from other groups, including the populations of the common-state, other segment-states, and cross-cutting interest groups. Segment-state leaders typically resist framing policy issues in terms that divide the members of their respective communities and unite some parts with other communities. Instead, segment-state leaders prefer that the only coalitions across segment-state lines are alliances of segment-state governments. Thus, policy divisions that are cumulative rather than cross-cutting reach the bargaining table between segment-state and common-state leaders, increasing the likelihood of conflict escalating to a nation-state crisis.[8] Politicians seeking attention and favors from the common-state government with agendas that might cut across segmental issues—for example, class-based issues—must reframe these issues in terms of segment-state interests in order to gain access to the centers of decision making.[9]

This is illustrated in the ways that most issues of the late USSR came to be framed in terms of the decision rights of segment-states. For example, environmental movements that sprang into public view in 1987 were co-öpted in the union republics by the movements dominated by the agendas of the union republic leaders. Jane Dawson notes how in the antinuclear movements in the non-Russian areas, "the shoddily constructed and carelessly operated nuclear power stations" were framed as "symbols of Mos-

---

[7] Karklins 1994, 42–64; Laitin 1986, 107; Suny 1993b; Verdery 1996, 79–83; Denitch 1990, 78.

[8] Rabushka and Shepsle 1982, 64, 66–74, 84; Haefele 1970, 74–90; Bélanger and Pinard 1991, 449.

[9] Wolchik 1994, 163. Also see Ishiyama 1999, 251–79.

cow's indifference to the welfare and even survival of the non-Russian nations of the Soviet Union."[10] Some of the shift in these movements was due
to what Dawson calls "movement surrogacy"—nationalists initially using
another issue to press their real agendas. Yet even where there was no
"movement surrogacy," this shift took place as a consequence of the process
by which the nation-state projects of segment-state leaders came to coöpt
and reframe virtually all other issues. In similar ways, issues of language
usage and economic development (discussed in this chapter) were coöpted
within, reframed by, subordinated to, or muscled aside by the segment-
state leaders' nation-state projects. The multidimensional issues of democratization and economic reform were trumped or subsumed by the issue
of the location of sovereignty in the people of the common-state or the
peoples of the segment-states. In the latter half of 1990 the Soviet Prime
Minister Nikolai Ryzhkov complained that discussions between Gorbachev's common-state government and Yeltsin's segment-state government
over the 500-Day Plan for much needed economic reform "quickly turned
to issues of Russian sovereignty, not economics."[11]

Segment-state leaders tend to share common concerns about (1) expanding the decision rights of their respective segment-state governments
relative to the common-state and (2) expanding the decision rights of their
segment-state governments relative to others within their respective segment-states. The issues are dear to segment-state leaders because they affect their own political fortunes. Reallocation of decision rights from common-state to segment-state governments gives segment-state leaders the
means to draft the rules of local politics, to make appointments to political
office, to distribute patronage among supporters, and to overwhelm, coöpt,
or suppress opponents inside the segment-state.[12] It would be a mistake to
accept without qualification the explanation for the conflict between the
common-state government of the Russian Federation and the segment-
state governments of Russia's republics offered by Nikolai Medvedev, director of President Yeltsin's Administration for Work with Geographic
Areas, but there is some truth to the observation that "it is not the republics' rights but the leaders' ambitions" that were at stake.[13] Nonetheless,
these ambitions, because they were associated with the political-identity
hegemony within individual segment-states, played an important role in
defining the decision rights demanded by segment-state leaders bargaining

[10] Dawson 1996, x [sic].

[11] McFaul 2001, 99–103.

[12] See A. Cherniak and A. Chernenko, "SSSR—Nash obshchii dom—Za 'Kruglym stolom
Pravdy'—chleny Ts K KPSS, deputaty Verkhovnogo Soveta SSSR," *Pravda* November 2,
1988, 1, 3.

[13] Pyotr Zhuravlyov, "Sergei Filatov: Lidery avtonomii 'budorazhat' MVD i armiiu,"
Segodnia December 9, 1993, 1.

with common-state leaders and in reframing many other issues as the rights of segment-states.[14] In the process the vertical bargaining increasingly came to focus on a single zero-sum conflict over who gets to decide.

Segment-State Powers in Common-State Governance

Segment-state leaders tend to push on to the bargaining table issues concerning their voice in the decisions of the common-state government. In the USSR, the union republics, the first-order segment-states, persistently pressed for expanded representation in the executive organs of the common-state and during periods of divided leadership in Moscow won de jure coöptation of the union republic officials into the USSR Council of Ministers, Presidium of the Supreme Soviet, and collegia of Gosplan and other ministerial agencies. As soon as *glasnost* permitted the complaints of segment-state leaders to be aired in public, this issue came into the open. For example, at the September 1989 "Nationalities" Plenum, the Tajik SSR first secretary Kakhar Makhkamov complained, "Tajikistan is almost completely unrepresented or else poorly represented in the apparatus of the CPSU Central Committee and the central Soviet, trade union, and Komsomol agencies, in foreign missions, in Union law-enforcement agencies, and so forth. . . . It is time . . . to create real conditions for ensuring that nations and nationalities are properly represented in all components of the country's administrative agencies."[15] During negotiations over a new union treaty and a new Soviet constitution, the union republic leaders pressed to expand the competence of the Council of the Federation, where the union republic chiefs of state had privileged representation, at the expense of the Presidential Council, which included key common-state (all-union) officials. In the negotiation of the first draft of a union treaty the union republics won the concession that the upper legislative chamber, the Soviet of Nationalities, would not be elected by the populace but would comprise delegations from the segment-state governments. They also won concessions that the collegia (collective leadership) of the ministries and Procuracy of the common-state government would include ex officio the corresponding union republic ministers and procurators.[16] In the design of a constitution for the new Russian Federation, the republics within Russia demanded additional representation in the parliament above that enjoyed by territorial jurisdictions that were not segment-states (the oblasts and krais): a Protocol attached to Russia's Federation Treaty and initialed by

---

[14] Tolz 1993, 7.

[15] " 'Na leninskikh printsipakh—k novomu kachestvu mezhdunarodnykh otnoshenii'—Diskussiia na Plenume Ts K KPSS," *Pravda* September 21, 1989, 1–7.

[16] Sheehy 1990e, 5.

the republics on March 13, 1992, stipulated that at least half the seats of an upper legislative chamber should be allocated to the segment-states within Russia (the republics, autonomous oblasts, and autonomous okrugs) so that they could block any legislation that would harm their interests.[17] During the debate within the Russian legislature (the Supreme Soviet) and the Constitutional Conference in 1992 and 1993, republic leaders proposed that, along with these provisions for the legislature, republic officials should become ex officio members of the Russian Security Council that would consult on foreign and domestic security policy, and that the republic chiefs of state themselves should form a Council of Heads of Republics to advise the president.[18]

Segment-State Powers Versus Common-State Powers

The more pervasive issue in bargaining between common-state and segment-state leaders, however, typically is the allocation of decision-making powers between the common-state and segment-state governments. In the USSR, the issue of the budgetary autonomy of union republics remained a mainstay of the debate over federalism. For example, in the discussions of a new constitution for the USSR that began in the late 1950s and continued until its adoption in 1977, Soviet politicians and constitutional experts debated whether the time had come to expand the autonomy of the union republics.[19] As Aryeh Unger notes, "federalism was the only area in which a genuine and protracted debate developed."[20] The debate was "sharply polarized" and raised issues of the allocation of decision-making powers between common-state organs and the union republics. Advocates of expanding the decision rights of the union republics proposed a bill of rights for the union republics that would "strengthen the guarantees of sovereignty of the union republics (the rights of secession from the USSR, the right of adopting their own constitutions, the rights of republic legislation, etc.)."[21] Alternatively, centralizers proposed circumscribing the rights of all segment-states, abolishing the union republics' right of secession, eliminat-

---

[17] "Protokol k Federativnomu Dogovoru," in *Konstitutsiia Rossiiskoi Federatsii, ofitsial'noe izdanie* 1993, 137.

[18] Vera Kuznetsova, "V Rossii sozdan eshche i sovet glav respublik," *Nezavisimaia gazeta* October 16, 1992, 1; Valerii Vyzhutovich, "Sovet glav respublik podderzhivaet Rossiiskogo Prezidenta," *Izvestiia* November 24, 1992, 1; Petr Akopov, "Sovet federatsii budet sozdan. Stanet li on instrumentom obnovleniia?" *Rossiiskie vesti* August 14, 1993, 1; Sergei Chugaev, "Sil'nyi khod prezidenta v Petrozavodske," *Izvestiia* August 17, 1993, 2; Matsyugina and Perepelkin 1996, 39.

[19] Hodnett 1978, 462–81.

[20] Unger 1981, 222.

[21] Hodnett 1978, 478.

ing the upper chamber of the legislature (the Council of Nationalities), which overrepresented segment-states, and even replacing all segment-states with administrative jurisdictions that would promote greater economic efficiency.

This issue was prominent in each of the three Eurasian nation-state crises. In the crisis of the early USSR, segment-state leaders, notably those from Ukraine, objected to and won minor revisions of the organic laws that had begun to centralize more decisions in Moscow.[22] Six decades later, as soon as *glasnost* permitted segment-state leaders to make their claims public once again, the issues of reallocating decision rights also became central to the agenda of the USSR. For months prior to the 19th CPSU Conference, in the Estonian, Latvia, and Lithuanian soviet socialist republics calls for "regional economic accountability," "territorial cost accounting," and "self-financing" supported the union republic leaders' attempts to eliminate centralized budgeting and to wrest control of industries from the centralized ministries.[23] At the 19th CPSU Conference itself the Estonian Communist Party first secretary complained that 90 percent of his republic's economy was under all-union administration and asserted that the union republic leaders must have greater control.[24] At the September 1989 Central Committee "Nationalities" Plenum, Communist Party first secretaries from even the most Sovietized republics, such as the Belorussian SSR, complained that common-state control over their union republics' economies was too extensive and that decisions in all but the essential areas should be handed over to the union republic governments.[25]

This tug of war over the allocation of rights soon became a debate over whether legislative supremacy resided in the common-state legislature (the Supreme Soviet of the USSR) or in the segment-state (union republic)

[22] Sullivant 1962.

[23] R. Kaarpere and L. Levitskii, "Khozraschet territorii—Beseda s Predsedatel'em Soveta Ministrov Estonii B. Saulom," *Izvestiia* September 11, 1988, 2; I. Litvinova, "Ekonomika bez absurdov—Predsedatel' Gosplana Latviiskoi SSR M. Raman razmyshlaet o printsipakh ekonomicheskoi samostoiatel'nosti respublik," *Izvestiia* August 3, 1989, 2; Valerii Badov, "Nuzhna li v Narve tamozhnia?" *Sovetskaia Industriia* March 2, 1989, 2. Also see "Sessii Verkhovnykh Sovetov soiuznykh respublik—Litovskaia SSR, Estonskaia SSR," *Izvestiia* May 19, 1989, 3; Deklaratsiia Verkhovnogo Soveta Litovskoi SSR "O gosudarstvennom suverenitete Litvy," *Sovetskaia Litva* May 19, 1989, 1; "Sessiia Verkhovnogo Soveta Latviiskoi SSR," *Pravda* July 30, 1989, 2; Bungs 1989; K. Girnius 1989; Moscow TASS, November 20, 1988, reported in FBIS, *Daily Report: Soviet Union* November 21, 1988, 42–43.

[24] Koroteeva, Perepelkin, and Shkaratan 1988.

[25] " 'Na leninskikh printsipakh—k novomu kachestvu mezhdunarodnykh otnoshenii'—Diskussiia na Plenume TsK KPSS," *Pravda* September 21, 1989, 1–7; "'O natsional'noi politike partii v sovremennykh usloviiakh'—Doklad General'nogo sekretaria TsK KPSS M. S. Gorbacheva na Plenume TsK KPSS 19 sentiabria 1989 goda," *Pravda* September 20, 1989, 2–3.

supreme soviets. In the Soviet "war of constitutions" as union republics began to introduce amendments to their constitutions that were at variance with articles of the USSR Constitution, claims to legislative supremacy became central to the bargaining. Estonia (November 16, 1988), Lithuania (May 18, 1989), and Latvia (July 29, 1989) were the first to amend their constitutions to claim that common-state (USSR) laws were only valid within their republics if ratified by their respective supreme soviets. Azerbaijan (September 23, 1989) followed, amending its constitution to declare invalid any all-union law that violated the union republic's sovereign rights.[26] The April 1990 USSR law on the principles of economic relations granted union republics the right to suspend acts of the common-state (all-union) Council of Ministers, pending resolution of the conflict by common-state procedures.[27] Yet in their sovereignty declarations, all fifteen union republics claimed a broader right to legislative review of any common-state laws that violated the sovereignty of their segment-states; ten union republics additionally included provisions claiming outright legislative supremacy for their segment-states (table 7.1).[28]

In the nation-state crisis within the Russian Federation, a similar tug of war over the allocation of decision rights took place.[29] The sovereignty declarations of autonomous republics (as the republics within the Russian Federation were labeled prior to the independence of Russia from the USSR) all claimed that the powers exercised by the USSR and the RSFSR within the autonomous republic's territory were the result of a voluntary delegation of powers from the autonomous republic. Five claimed that autonomous republic laws would be supreme (table 7.2). In the war of constitutions after the independence of Russia, if we include Chechnya in the count, seventeen of Russia's twenty-one republics adopted new constitutions within the first five years of Russian independence (table 7.3).[30] Eleven of these claimed to be sovereign states, including one (Chechnya) that claimed no relationship with the Russian Federation and six that claimed that the Russian Federation exercised powers over their population and territory only by virtue of a delegation of powers from the republic. For example, Tatarstan's constitution (Article 61) stipulated that it is "a sovereign state, a subject of international law, associated with the Russian Federation–Russia on the basis of a Treaty of mutual delegation of pow-

---

[26] "S zasedaniia Prezidiuma Verkhovnogo Soveta SSSR," *Izvestiia* November 13, 1989, 1, 3.

[27] Zakon Soiuza Sovetskikh Sotsialisticheskikh Respublik "Ob osnovakh ekonomicheskikh otnoshenii Soiuza SSR, soiuznykh i avtonomnykh respublik," *Izvestiia* April 16, 1990, 1–2.

[28] Robertson 1995.

[29] Hahn 1993, 84; Lapidus 1999, 78–79.

[30] Texts of constitutions from Karachaevo-Cherkesskaia Respublika 1996, Parlamentarskaia biblioteka RF 1995, and Respublika Altai 1996. Also see Safarova 1994.

TABLE 7.1
USSR: Union republic sovereignty declarations, 1988–1990

		Powers claimed by union republic		
	Date	Ownership of land/resources	Legislative review	Legislative supremacy
Estonian SSR	November 18, 1988	—	X	X
Lithuanian SSR	May 18, 1989	—	X	X
Latvian SSR	July 28, 1989	X	X	X
Azerbaijan SSR	September 23, 1989	X	X	—
Georgian SSR	November 18, 1989	—	X	—
Russian SFSR	June 11, 1990	—	X	—
Uzbek SSR	June 20, 1990	—	X	X
Moldavian SSR	June 23, 1990	X	X	X
Ukrainian SSR	July 16, 1990	X	X	X
Belorussian SSR	July 27, 1990	—	X	X
Turkmen SSR	August 22, 1990	X	X	—
Armenian SSR	August 23, 1990	X	X	X
Tajik SSR	August 25, 1990	X	X	—
Kazakh SSR	October 25, 1990	X	X	X
Kirgiz SSR	December 12, 1990	X	X	X

Sources: Robertson 1995; Institut teorii i istorii sotsializma TsK KPSS 1991.

ers." These claims were in conflict with the claims of both the 1978 and the 1993 Russian constitutions.[31] In the negotiations over the Russian constitution from 1990 to 1993, the republics demanded recognition as "sovereign states possessing full state (legislative, executive, and judicial) power on their territory, except for the powers that are voluntarily transferred (assigned) to the jurisdiction of the Russian Federation." Further, they demanded that on their territory "federal principles of legislation enter into force . . . after they are ratified . . . by the body of power in the member of the Federation."[32] Russian Deputy Prime Minister Boris Fedorov complained that during the Constitutional Conference in the summer of 1993, "Tatarstan, Bashkortostan, Sakha (Yakutia), Chechnya, and Karelia had made a series of unacceptable demands including the exclusive right to levy taxes and to launch their own currencies."[33] Tatarstan's vice president, Vasilii Likhachov, countered that the draft discussed by the Constitutional Conference "does not give due consideration to the problem of *equal* rights for the republics and the Center."[34]

[31] Parlamentarskaia biblioteka RF 1995, 7–14.

[32] Nikolai Troitsky, "Conference Hits a Federal Impasse," *Megapolis-Ekspress* June 16, 1993, 20; translated in *Current Digest of the Post-Soviet Press* 40 (July 7, 1993), 11–12.

[33] *RFE/RL Daily Report* June 4, 1993.

[34] Gleb Cherkasov, "Tatarstan trebuet ucheta ego spetsifiki," *Segodnia* June 29, 1993, 3, italics added.

Chief among the decision rights caught in the tug of war of segmental bargaining was control over the resources of the segment-state.[35] As an expression of the sovereignty of its people over their homeland, segment-state leaders claimed ownership of the resources of their territory. Yet this was also indispensable to establishment or maintenance of political-identity hegemony within the union republics, particularly when many managers of the segment-state economy were drawn from other ethnic groups. In the Soviet "war of constitutions" during the *perestroika* crisis, Estonia, Latvia, and Lithuania were the first to amend their constitutions to claim sole ownership of land, mineral deposits, waters, forests, and other natural resources.[36] The Baltic republics claimed the right to decide how and by whom these resources would be used. The April 1990 USSR law on the principles of economic relations conceded this by recognizing that the union republics and autonomous republics owned the land and other natural resources within their territory (Article 2.2). In the Russian nation-state crisis during drafting of the Federation Treaty, the list of demands from republics included, quite prominently, regional control over land and natural resources. The Federation Treaty, initialed by eighteen of the twenty republics in March 1992, in fact provided that "the land, minerals, water, flora, and fauna will belong (or be owned) by the national groups within the territory of the corresponding republics."[37]

A distinctive form of this tug of war over the allocation of decision rights between common-state and segment-state governments took place where the rights of segment-state governments were unequal—a conflict over each segment-state's *relative* status. In the Soviet system sometimes called *matrioshka* federalism, elevation of autonomous republics to union republic status was a persistent issue because union republic governments had more decision rights than the autonomous republics inside the union republics. In the 1920s, Tatar leaders objected to their republic's "second-class status" as an autonomous republic inside the Russian Soviet Federated Socialist Republic (RSFSR), which in turn was a union republic within the USSR.[38] In 1936, Stalin publicly defended his new constitution against proposals from the Tatar and Bashkir autonomous soviet socialist republics (ASSRs) to be elevated to union republic status.[39] And in the *perestroika* crisis, the

[35] Hahn 1993; McAuley 1992.

[36] "O nesootvetstvii nekotorykh zakonodatel'stvennykh aktov soiuznykh respublik Konstitutsii SSSR," *Izvestiia* November 13, 1989, 1, 3.

[37] Evgenii Panov and Vladimir Sluzhakov, "Spaset li na osobyi put'?" *Rossiiskaia gazeta*, March 14, 1991, 1; Nikolai Andreev, "'Dogovor sdelaet Rossiiu schastlivoi'—schitaet prezident Boris El'tsin," *Izvestiia* April 1, 1992, 1. Also see specific cases such as Sakha in Kempton 1996.

[38] Al'ians Sabirov, "Provozglashen nezavisimyi Tatarstan," *Izvestiia* August 31, 1990, 2.

[39] Stalin 1936. See Rakhimov's remarks in " 'Na leninskikh printsipakh—k novomu kachestvu mezhdunarodnykh otnoshenii'—Diskussiia na Plenume Ts K KPSS," *Pravda* September 21, 1989, 1–7.

TABLE 7.2

RSFSR: Autonomous republic sovereignty declarations, 1990–1991

			Claims made by autonomous republic[a]		
	Declaration of	Date	Republican supremacy	Budgetary independence	Elevated status
North Ossetia	State sovereignty	July 20, 1990	—	—	—
Karelia	State sovereignty	August 9, 1990	—	—	—
Komi	State sovereignty	August 29, 1990	X	X	SSR
Tataria	State sovereignty	August 30, 1990	X	—	SSR
Udmurtia	State sovereignty	September 20, 1990	—	X	Republic
Yakutia	State sovereignty	September 27, 1990	—	—	SSR
Buryatia	State sovereignty	October 8, 1990	—	—	SSR
Bashkiria	State sovereignty	October 11, 1990	X	—	SSR
Kalmykia	State sovereignty	October 18, 1990	—	—	SSR
Mari	State sovereignty	October 22, 1990	X	—	SSR
Chuvashia	State sovereignty	October 24, 1990	—	X	SSR
Chechen-Ingushetia	Republic	November 27, 1990	X	—	Republic
Mordovia	State	December 7, 1990	—	X	SSR
Tuva	State sovereignty	December 13, 1990	—	—	SSR
Kabardino-Balkaria	State sovereignty	January 30, 1991	—	X	SSR
Dagestan	Republic	May 13, 1991	—	—	—

[a]All declarations claimed ownership of land and resources within the borders of the autonomous republic. All declarations claimed that the USSR and RSFSR exercised authority over the autonomous republic by virtue of a voluntary delegation of powers from the republic.

TABLE 7.3

Russian Federation: Claims to decision rights in republic constitutions adopted 1992–1996

	Date of adoption	Relationship of the republic to the Russian Federation				Political institutions within the republic			
		Republic sovereign	Member of Russian Federation	Powers delegated from republic	Republic legislative supremacy	Official titular language	Language required for chief executive	Republic appoints judges	Republic appoints Procuracy
Sakha	April 4, 1992	X	X	X	—	X	X	X	d
Chechnya	May 5, 1992	X	a	a	X	—	—	X	X
Tatarstan	November 20, 1992	X	—	X	X	X	X	X	X
Tyva	October 21, 1993	X	—	X	X	X	X	X	X
Bashkortostan	December 24, 1993	X	—	X	X	—	X	X	X
Komi	February 17, 1994	—	X	X	—	X	—	—	d
Buryatia	February 22, 1994	X	X	X	—	X	X	X	d
Ingushetia	February 27, 1994	X	X	—	b	X	X	—	d
Kalmykia	April 5, 1994	—	X	—	—	X	—	X	d
Dagestan	July 26, 1994	X	X	—	—	—	c	X	d
North Ossetia	November 12, 1994	X	—	X	—	—	X	X	d
Udmurtia	December 7, 1994	X	X	—	—	—	—	X	d
Adygeia	March 10, 1995	—	X	—	—	—	X	X	d
Mari El	June 24, 1995	—	X	—	—	—	X	—	d
Mordovia	September 21, 1995	—	X	—	—	—	—	X	—
Khakassia	May 25, 1995	—	X	—	—	X	—	—	d
Karachai-Cherkessia	March 5, 1996	—	X	—	—	X	—	—	d

[a] No relationship with the Russian Federation.

[b] Federal authority extends only to areas outside sovereign prerogatives of Ingushetia.

[c] Dagestan requires rotation among major ethnic groups.

[d] Republic must approve Russian Federation appointments to procuracy.

issue was placed on the public agenda almost immediately.[40] At the September 1989 Central Committee "Nationalities" Plenum, the first secretaries of the Bashkir ASSR, Tatar ASSR, and Yakut ASSR all pressed the issue of raising their republics to union republic status. Ravmer Khabibullin of the Bashkir ASSR complained that "our unequal legal status infringes on the political rights of the autonomous republic's peoples" by underrepresenting them in common-state (all-union) institutions. Gumer Usmanov of the Tatar ASSR complained that as a result of Tatarstan's inferior status, "the field of lawmaking is narrowed and the rights and opportunities in the economy and social sphere are limited."[41] Similarly, in the Russian nation-state crisis, fifteen of the sixteen autonomous republics inside the RSFSR included in their sovereignty declarations the right to elevate the status of their republic within the USSR and RSFSR. Eleven actually declared the elevation of their autonomous republic to union republic status, making their governments equal to the government of the RSFSR in the segment-state status hierarchy of the USSR. Eleven justified this right to change their status as an expression of the right of their people to self-determination. As Peter Kirkow observed, however, elevation of status also provided "new privileges for top officials (ministerial posts, travel abroad, direct access to authorities in Moscow) ... [and] the right to control territorial resources and to set up their own legislation."[42]

Segment-State Powers at Home

In the Eurasian nation-state crises, bargaining over the allocation of decision rights also gave particular attention to the powers of segment-state leaders to shape the state and nation within their own borders—that is, the powers necessary for establishing or maintaining political identity hegemony. In the USSR, recurring issues in the debates between common-state (all-union) and segment-state (particularly but not exclusively union republic) leaders concerned the extent to which the latter should be empow-

[40] Rafael' Mustafin, "Razmyshleniia u geograficheskoi karty," *Pravda* January 25, 1989, 3.

[41] " 'Na leninskikh printsipakh—k novomu kachestvu mezhdunarodnykh otnoshenii'— Diskussiia na Plenume Ts K KPSS," *Pravda* September 21, 1989, 1–7; " 'O natsional'noi politike partii v sovremennykh usloviiakh'—Doklad General'nogo sekretaria Ts K KPSS M. S. Gorbacheva na Plenume Ts K KPSS 19 sentiabria 1989 goda," *Pravda* September 20, 1989, 2–3.

[42] Kirkow 1994, 1164–65. On a different tack, the cadres of other "subordinate" minorities—e.g., Nagornyi Karabakh, Abkhazia, and South Ossetia—demanded transfer from one union republic's control to another's control; see "Zasedanie Prezidiuma Verkhovnogo Soveta SSSR" and "Postanovlenie Prezidiuma Verkhovnogo Soveta SSSR 'O resheniiakh Verkhovnykh Sovetov Armianskoi SSR i Azerbaidzhanskoi SSR po voprosu o Nagornom Karabakhe," *Pravda* July 20, 1988, 1–4; "Nagornyi Karabakh: Programma razvitiia," *Izvestiia* March 25, 1988, 3; Fuller 1978, 1983, 1989; Karklins 1984, 278.

ered to design political institutions for the segment-states, to discriminate in favor of the titular nationality in political appointments, to privilege the titular language as a lingua franca in government, to control membership in the citizenry of the segment-states, and to establish superordinate authority over governmental agencies within the segment-states. This fight over the allocation of decision rights became one of the issues engaged in the nation-state crisis of the early USSR, when Stalin in 1926 attacked the excessive indigenization of personnel, language policy, and cultural policy in Ukraine.[43] Similarly, the *perestroika* nation-state crisis raised a tug of war over the allocation of the decision rights to set policy for the segment-states and to design their political institutions. In the Russian nation-state crisis, segment-states (particularly the republics) within the Russian Federation attempted to establish their right to craft their own political institutions in divergent ways, to privilege the titular language and population in political office, and to subordinate all government agencies within the segment-state to the sovereign authority of its leadership.

A free hand in designing the political institutions of the segment-state was both an expression of the sovereignty of the segment-state as well as a means for segment-state leaders to establish political-identity hegemony. In the USSR the "parade of sovereignties" and "war of constitutions" began in 1988 when Estonia's leaders sought to exempt their union republic from the constitutional changes that would create a congress of people's deputies in each union republic and autonomous republic. In Russia's "war of constitutions" the issues of republic control over federal agencies—particularly the courts and procuracy—operating within republic borders and republic control over city and rural district (raion) governments were repeatedly on the bargaining table. Thirteen of the seventeen constitutions adopted by the republics within the Russian Federation between 1992 and 1996 claimed that the republic would appoint judges within the republic, even though the federal authorities also claimed this power (table 7.3). Four republic constitutions stipulated that the republic would appoint the procuracy within the republic and all the others required republic approval of any appointments made within its borders by the common-state government. Many republics within the Russian Federation placed local governments under the authority of the republic's chief executives and, contrary to federal provisions, at least three republic constitutions claimed that city administrations also fell within this hierarchy. Some, such as Tatarstan, broke federal rules by placing local representative organs under the leadership of the local executive appointed by the republic's president.[44]

---

[43] Sullivant 1962, 126–34; Stalin 1926, 157–63.
[44] Safarova 1994, 25–26.

Since control over access to political office within the segment-state was critical to political-identity hegemony, there were frequent conflicts in center-periphery bargaining over who would control appointments and elections. For example, in the USSR a recurring conflict occurred over "the balance that should be maintained between local nationals and non-nationals in top leadership positions in the republics."[45] During the nation-state crisis of the early USSR, Stalin sent a sharp warning against excessive indigenization in an April 1926 letter to the leadership of the Ukrainian party that chastised the Ukrainian Commissar of Education (Oleksandr Shums'kyi) for pressing a speedy Ukrainianization of the proletariat that would favor Ukrainians at all levels, including appointments to the highest party and state posts within the union republic.[46] Early in the *perestroika* crisis—for example, at the September 1989 Central Committee "Nationalities" Plenum—party secretaries such as Kazakhstan's Nursultan Nazarbaev complained against the requirement of the *nomenklatura* system that segment-states seek common-state approval for appointments to offices nominally under the segment-state's control.[47] At stake for segment-state leaders in such conflicts over the allocation of decision rights were the very means by which they built their supporting clientele in a political machine.

Control over citizenship and residence within the segment-state defined the segment-state's very sovereignty, but for the segment-state leaders this was also essential to the creation or maintenance of political-identity hegemony, and so this issue frequently became part of the tug of war over decision rights between common-state and segment-state leaders. In the USSR this was often debated through indirect means: in many segment-states, rapid industrialization had become a magnet for workers of other nationalities. For the segment-state leaders this migration threatened the numerical predominance of the titular nationality on which their political power was based and increased pressures on the titular leaders of the segment-states to incorporate leaders of these other ethnic groups into the segment-state government. Thus, in the early nineteen-sixties Georgian and Latvian officials opposed Khrushchev's plans for further expansion of heavy industry in their union republics precisely because they feared it would bring still more Russian workers.[48] Armenian officials reportedly excluded Russian workers from permanent housing during the construc-

[45] Hodnett 1978, 458.
[46] Stalin 1926, 157–63.
[47] " 'Na leninskikh printsipakh—k novomu kachestvu mezhdunarodnykh otnoshenii'—Diskussiia na Plenume Ts K KPSS," *Pravda* September 21, 1989, 1–7; " 'O natsional'noi politike partii v sovremennykh usloviiakh'—Doklad General'nogo sekretaria Ts K KPSS M. S. Gorbacheva na Plenume Ts K KPSS 19 sentiabria 1989 goda," *Pravda* September 20, 1989, 2–3.
[48] Suny 1988, 213; Dreifelds 1977; Pennar 1968, 206.

tion of the Erevan subway as a way of preventing them from settling permanently. During the *perestroika* nation-state crisis these demands to control residence and citizenship in the segment-states became public and the methods to exclude "outsiders" became more direct. For example, through legislation that their titular languages would become the language of communication within their respective segment-states, titular leaders sought to strengthen indigenous control over political and economic institutions in the segment-states. Between 1988 and May 1990, eleven of the fifteen union republics adopted legislation establishing a state language. Even more extreme were the measures taken in the Soviet "war of constitutions" by Estonia and Latvia: they curtailed citizenship rights within their union republics, particularly voting rights and rights to hold office, by establishing language requirements for office holders and residence requirements (up to ten years) for voters as well as for office holders.[49]

Incentives for Focusing and Escalating Conflict

The tendency for bargaining between common-state and segment-state leaders to focus on the allocation of decision rights can transform this bargaining into raw, zero-sum conflict. If the stakes in this conflict escalate to a simple dichotomous choice of the location of sovereignty, the disappearance of mutually acceptable compromises that could keep the common-state together makes it more likely that segment-states will become independent nation-states. According to the segmental institutions thesis, both the focusing and escalation of stakes inhere in the structure of the segmented state. That is, segmental institutions create incentives for segment-state leaders to monopolize the agenda of center-periphery bargaining and to escalate their claims on behalf of their segment-states into more realms until these claims become demands for the sovereign independence of a nation-state. The Eurasian nation-state crises illustrate five major sources of incentives to focus and escalate the stakes of conflict: pressures to preserve political-identity hegemony, the temptation to externalize the costs of nationalistic outbidding, marginalization of moderates and activation of radicals, divergent development among the segment-states, and contagion or mimicry of escalatory actions. These incentives come from within indi-

---

[49] "Soobshcheniia iz Estonii," *Pravda* August 10, 1989, 2; Ideologicheskii otdel *Pravdy*, "Fakt i kommentarii: Iskat' kompromiss," *Pravda* July 29, 1989, 4. After this was nullified by the All-Union Supreme Soviet Presidium, Estonia adopted new legislation requiring that candidates for republic positions must be residents of Estonia for at least 10 years; "Na plenumakh i sessiiakh," *Pravda* November 18, 1989, 2. Also see Pigolkin and Studenikina 1991, 55–61; A. Pigolkin and M. Studenikina, "Iazyk i zakon—Opublikovannyi v Estonii proekt Zakona o iazyke s tochki zreniia uchenykh-iuristov," *Izvestiia* January 7, 1989, 3.

vidual segment-states, from the behavior of other segment-state leaders, and from the bargaining between segment-state and common-state leaders. Some of these are constants, others variables; that is, some of these sources of incentives are ever-present in segmental institutions, but others are more likely to be present under specific segmental arrangements, and still other sources of accelerating escalation emerge within segmental institutions only once escalation in the stakes has already begun.

Preserving Political-Identity Hegemony

A primary motivation for segment-state leaders to focus the agenda of center-periphery bargaining and to demand a greater share of the decision rights of the common-state arises from their desire to establish, expand, or protect their political-identity hegemony within their segment-states. The attempt by segment-state leaders to exclude cross-cutting issues from the agenda grows from their desire to minimize competition and to block political leaders with alternative agendas within the segment-state. The segmental institutions thesis stresses the persistent concern of politicians in holding on to power. This confronts a common sociological interpretation that explains the behavior of segment-state leaders by their nationalism. Yet in many cases, like the USSR's, it stretches credibility to argue that the indigenous leaders of segment-states were always crypto-nationalists but hid this by "preference falsification" or that previously loyal communists underwent an epiphany or change of consciousness in the 1980s.[50] It seems unlikely that first secretaries like Johannes Käbin of Estonia or Lavrentii Beria of Georgia were crypto-nationalists; it is also hard to believe that their successors who greedily gathered power, skimmed privileges, and suppressed nationalist dissent in the increasingly cynical and corrupt Brezhnev years underwent a conversion that then led to a nation-state crisis. It is still harder to believe that nationalists like Mintimer Shaimiev of Tatarstan who came out into the open or saw the light in the 1990s are now going back undercover or have undergone a reconversion so as to play the role of loyal members of Putin's common-state government once again. The Communist Party leaders in the segment-states who began the nation-state crisis seemed thoroughly Machiavellian and opportunistic during their terms of office. This instrumental behavior to hold on to power has made it possible for Moscow to cut deals and to expect previously rebellious leaders to comply with this compromise. Although some segment-state leaders are sincere nationalists, what unites both the sincere and cynical nationalists is their pursuit of power. The segmental institutions thesis explains their behavior by changes in the institutional constraints under

[50] Beissinger 1996, 116.

which they pursued power. An immediate "power" motive for escalation of the stakes of center-periphery bargaining was the growing threat to their political-identity hegemony within their segment-states.

In the last decades of the USSR some of this threat to political-identity hegemony grew with the very process of building hegemony within each segment-state.[51] As the machines within the segment-states grew stronger, so did three closely related problems associated with maintaining political-identity hegemony into the future. One mounting problem was controlling an ever larger indigenous professional elite and intelligentsia. The success of previous indigenization policies created a large titular professional class with the skills to constitute themselves as independent political entrepreneurs in opposition to the segment-state leaders. A second problem of mounting severity was the rising cost of providing rewards and mobility opportunities to a titular elite that already enjoyed high office within the segment-state. Given the size of the indigenous elite and its already high levels of material rewards, segment-state leaders had to find a still larger stock of material rewards to ensure their loyalty into the future. And a third problem was the limit on further expansion of mobility opportunities within the segment-states. The creation of a titular professional elite and intelligentsia within segment-states had brought rapid growth in the number of professional positions in segment-states, and with indigenization in the more developed segment-states it brought saturation of elite positions in many sectors within the segment-states with titular appointees. These problems threatened the segment-state leaders' capacity to continue showering the titular elite with rewards and expanding mobility opportunities for new aspirants to elite positions. This threatened the segment-state leaders' ability to keep the elite and most active members of the public from coalescing in opposition. In short, the last decades of Soviet power brought increasing threats to some of the very means by which the segment-state leaders had maintained their political-identity hegemony.

These problems were compounded over the last decades of the USSR by declining economic growth. The economic slowdown linked these concerns about the survival of political-identity hegemony within individual segment-states to divisive issues of common-state policy. As the economic pie ceased to grow, the leaders of the more developed segment-states felt more acutely the transfers of funds among segment-states made by the common-state government. Under tightening resource constraints, common-state policies that subsidized economic growth and expansion of mobility opportunities in the less developed segment-states had the unintended consequence of slowing growth of mobility opportunities in the more developed segment-states. As a consequence, in the *perestroika* na-

---

[51] Roeder 1991.

tion-state crisis, leaders of union republics with higher levels of socioeconomic attainment (particularly in the Baltic and Transcaucasian union republics) led the others in their demands for greater economic autonomy even before they faced the additional challenge of competitive elections, while leaders of less advanced union republics (notably in Central Asia) were less inclined to press these demands.[52]

Yet this slow accumulation of mounting threats to the position of union republic leaders was accelerated by an immediate threat—Gorbachev's democratization.[53] The introduction of democratic elections spurred the Communist Party leaders of Estonia to declare their sovereignty, the instantiation of the first elected common-state (all-union) Congress of People's Deputies led the Communist Party leaders of Lithuania to follow suit, and the introduction of the common-state (all-union) presidency led the Communist Party leaders of Georgia to renounce the 1922 Union Treaty.

In the *perestroika* nation-state crisis the grab for a greater share of common-state (all-union) decision rights by the first-order segment-state (union republic) governments complicated the problems of maintaining political-identity hegemony in many lower-order segment-states. The leaders of the autonomous republics, autonomous oblasts, and autonomous okrugs inside the union republics demanded a greater share of their respective union republic's decision rights. In some instances, these leaders of lower-order segment-states sought to remove their segment-states entirely from the authority of the union republic. In Georgia, for example, the escalation of South Ossetian demands to a formal declaration of secession from Georgia on December 11, 1990, came within days of the victory of the nationalist Georgian Round Table and the first session of the new Supreme Soviet that elected Zviad Gamsakhurdia as its chair with a promise to end Soviet-era minority rights within the republic. The South Ossetian Supreme Soviet resolved to subordinate all political institutions within South Ossetia directly to the USSR rather than to Georgia.[54]

Nationalistic Outbidding Externalities

Segmental institutions encourage even moderate segment-state leaders to make more radical demands because in the short term, escalation of demands for a greater share of decision rights permits segment-state leaders to shift to the common-state many of the costs of delivering more benefits

---

[52] Koroteeva, Perepelkin, and Shkaratan 1988; Moscow Television November 26, 1988, reported in FBIS, *Daily Report: Soviet Union* November 28, 1988, 50. Also see "Preniia po dokladu M. S. Gorbacheva—Rech' deputata R. N. Nishanova," *Izvestiia* November 30, 1988, 4.

[53] On the constraints on Gorbachev, see Roeder 1993.

[54] "Obrashchenie Prezidiuma Verkhovnogo Soveta SSSR k Verkhovnomu Sovetu Gruzinskoi SSR i oblastnomu sovetu Iugo-Osetinskoi avtonomnoi oblasti," *Izvestiia* December 15, 1990, 1. Also see Anaiban and Walker 1996, 183, 186.

to the segment-state elite and population.[55] As one Russian journalist observed after the segment-states within the Russian Federation began to demand more and more from the center in the name of national sovereignty: "After all, why stop shaking a tree from which more and more plums are falling?"[56]

For leaders of Soviet and post-Soviet segment-states, and particularly for leaders of a cohort of hegemonic politicians who hoped to satisfy the demands of indigenous elites and population for an expanding supply of rewards and opportunities, demands for a greater share of the decision rights of the common-state became an attractive short-term strategy for expanding the pie for everyone within the segment-state leaders' constituency. These politicians found that they could rally support with ever more extreme claims about what they would win for the segment-state in future bargaining with common-state leaders. For the leaders of political-identity hegemonies, this sometimes even permitted them to offer more to their followers without opening competition *within* the segment-state. For example, everyone within the segment-state could benefit if the segment-state leaders seized taxes collected within the segment-state but earmarked for the common-state budget. Many of the costs of the expanded rewards and opportunities for residents of the segment-state would come at the expense of the population living in other parts of the common-state; few costs would be borne by anyone within the segment-state. Indeed, segment-state leaders could promise that with expansion of the segment-state pie, both titular and minority groups within the segment-state would benefit.[57]

Playing the sovereignty card is the ultimate way to externalize the costs of a nation-state project. Michael McFaul and Edward Walker have observed that in the *perestroika* and Russian nation-state crises, segment-state leaders played the sovereignty card in order to rally their own populations behind a unifying theme that obscured the differences within the population. The sovereignty card promised a diverse set of interests that their specific objectives would all be achieved.[58] Communists as well as democrats could jump on board this bandwagon. Thus, Russian pressure for expanded sovereignty vis-à-vis the USSR—including expanded rights in economics, politics, and international affairs—initially came from the Russian Prime Minister Aleksandr Vlasov even before Yeltsin won election as chairman of the Supreme Soviet and became the official spokesperson for the Russian nation-state project.[59]

[55] Hislope 1997.

[56] Vladimir Todres, "Mestnye sovety zhelaiut ratifitsirovat' konstitutsiiu," *Segodnia* July 13, 1993, 2.

[57] Rabushka and Shepsle 1982.

[58] McFaul 2000, 196; Walker 2003, 61.

[59] O. Losoto and A. Cherniak, "Rossiia: shag v zavtra," *Pravda* May 12, 1990, 1–2.

The externalization of the costs of implementing the nation-state projects permitted union republic leaders to garner support even within the segment-state's minorities. Thus, in referenda for independence conducted in Estonia, Latvia, and Lithuania in early 1991 many Russians reportedly voted yes.[60] Ukraine's referendum on independence on December 1, 1991, which all but sealed the fate of the USSR, showed strong support for greater autonomy in all regions of the country, whether inhabited by Ukrainians or Russians.[61] As President Kravchuk informed President Yeltsin, much to the surprise of the latter, even the Don region adjacent to Russia voted for the Ukrainian referendum on December 1, 1991.[62] With promises that all boats would rise in a rusting tub filled with immediate concessions from the common-state, greater autonomy seemed to be good for all within the segment-state.

Radical Activism, Moderate Abstention

Once the policy agenda has come to focus on the allocation of decision rights between common-state and segment-state governments, and particularly once escalation in the stakes of segmental bargaining has begun, sincere moderates on these issues who do not succumb to the temptations of nationalistic outbidding may find themselves so cross-pressured that they withdraw from politics. Sincere radicals who previously abstained from participating in a collaborationist segment-state regime are likely to be drawn into politics and to play a proportionately larger role on the segment-state side of the bargaining table. Those who remain in politics or who are newly drawn to politics within the segment-states are increasingly likely to be individuals with more extreme nationalistic views than their predecessors in office and than the public at large.

In the Eurasian nation-state crises, as conflict focused on the allocation of decision rights between the common-state and segment-state governments, those moderates already in the segment-states who were indifferent or equally torn between the two sides were more likely to stand aside.[63] Moderates in the segment-states who had an "exit" option to flee from the periphery to the common-state had less incentive to voice their concerns or express their loyalty. For example, in Georgia the moderates who would ultimately turn to Eduard Shevardnadze were, until late 1991, more likely to stand on the sidelines as Zviad Gamsakhurdia and his radical nationalists

---

[60] Kionka 1991; Bungs 1991a, 1991b; S. Girnius 1991b.

[61] Vitalii Portnikov, "Ukraina progolosovala za Nezavisimost'," *Nezavisimaia gazeta* December 3, 1991, 1, 3.

[62] Wilson 2000, 169.

[63] See Aldrich 1983.

pushed the republic in an ever more extreme confrontation with external and internal enemies. Many Chechen moderates fled Chechnya for parts of Russia as the conflict between Chechen segment-state radicals and the Russian common-state government became more extreme. Alternatively, radicals within the segment-states who saw much greater distance between themselves and the common-state were more likely to become active. Radical nationalists who did not have an exit option—they had "nowhere to go" because they could not imagine a homeland other than the segment-state—were likely to become more vocal against the common-state.[64]

Within the Eurasian segment-states, those who became active in politics tended to be more radical than the median resident of the segment-state. As noted in previous chapters, residents in Belarus and Ukraine were less committed to secession than the politicians who led their republics into independence. Polls suggest that in the Baltic states, the titular populations were more willing to compromise with Moscow than the activists who dominated politics.[65] Similarly, although presidents Murtaza Rakhimov of Bashkortostan and Shaimiev of Tatarstan rejected the demands of the most extreme nationalist movements in their republics, they pressed platforms that were more nationalistic than the median voter of their republics, for in both republics the median voter (to the extent voters were grouped by nationality) was not even a member of the titular group.

Divergent Development

Diverging development in individual segment-states leads to the disappearance of compromise solutions that can keep the common-state whole. Diverging development becomes a fourth source of incentives for segment-state leaders to escalate their demands for a greater share of the decision rights of the common-state because their increasingly divergent needs cannot be addressed by common policies or by common institutions. In this way bargaining ranges that initially include mutually acceptable compromises over the shape of common-state policies and common-state institutions begin to narrow as more of these compromises cease to be acceptable to at least one party.

Expanding autonomy increases the likelihood that segment-states will develop in different directions, their resulting needs and preferences will also diverge, and common policies for all segment-states will become harder to find and increasingly irrelevant. The separate cultural development of different peoples—for example, the observance of different religious practices concerning marriage and divorce—can complicate the tasks

[64] Hirschman 1970, 69–70.
[65] Dunlop 1993–94.

of drafting a common civil law. This divergence can become particularly acute when political and economic reforms begin in the common-state or in some segment-states but do not progress evenly in all segment-states.[66] Charles D. Tarlton identified this problem in his discussion of asymmetrical federalism: When "the policies pursued and the conditions demanded by a single component state are importantly foreign to those of the overall system," the likelihood of conflict is higher. "When diversity predominates, the 'secession-potential' of the system is high."[67]

Even under the strict conformity of Soviet policies prior to *perestroika* union republics such as the Estonian SSR and the Tajik SSR developed within a common-state as two separate communities with little contact. For example, only 113 Tajiks lived in Estonia in 1989 and only 147 Estonians lived in Tajikistan. Only about a third of each population in its homeland spoke a common language—Russian—with which to speak to the other, and few Estonians spoke Tajik or Tajiks spoke Estonian. Within their respective republics they lived different lives: while 72 percent of Estonians lived in cities, where nuclear families with one child crowded into apartments, 68 percent of Tajiks lived in the countryside, where larger, often extended families with three times as many children lived on farms. Per capita GDP in Estonia, according to World Bank estimates, was over five times that in Tajikistan in 1989. Under *perestroika*, in a very short span of time the diverging political and economic development of each republic made it still more difficult to identify common policies that necessitated a common-state and that could address the needs of both an increasingly liberal and democratized Estonia as well as an illiberal, autocratic Tajikistan. Free speech and competition for office were common in Estonia's 1990 elections to its Supreme Soviet, but virtually absent from Tajikistan's elections that same year.[68] Economic liberalization proceeded much more rapidly in Estonia than Tajikistan.[69] With this diverging development in the USSR, as Soviet Prime Minister Nikolai Ryzhkov lamented, by late 1990 "no one needed the Center in any form."[70] Moreover, as noted in the previous chapter, by late 1991 many segment-state leaders saw the center as a threat to their distinctive developmental trajectory.

Divergent development also fueled the escalation of conflict in the Russian nation-state crisis once the USSR had broken apart. For example, in the privatization of state-owned enterprises the republics developed along divergent paths. Darrell Slider's data for privatization of small enterprises

---

[66] Bunce 1999, 87–88; Leff 1999, 212–13.
[67] Tarlton 1965, 870–71, 873.
[68] United States, Congress, Commission on Security and Cooperation in Europe 1990.
[69] USSR 1991, 58–59, 102.
[70] Quoted in Beissinger 2002, 94.

up to October 1993 show that this proceeded more slowly in the republics than in the subjects of the federation that were not segment-states (oblasts and krais).[71] Bashkortostan, Kabardino-Balkaria, Kalmykia, Mordovia, North Ossetia, Sakha, and Tatarstan were among the ten subjects with the lowest share of small enterprises privatized. Similarly, as the discussion of political-identity hegemony underscored, the republics and the subjects of the federation that were not segment-states were developing different political systems that demanded different common-state institutions. Diverging development, in the opinion of many republic leaders, made many common policies unnecessary; common policies became threats to their divergent path of political and economic development.

Outbidding, Mimicry, and Cascading Defections

Segmental institutions create a destructive dynamic of contagious radicalism or mimicry *among* segment-states. In a peculiar form of prisoners' dilemma the segmented state encourages leaders of each segment-state to seek to outbid one another. This constitutes a fifth source of incentives to escalate the stakes in center-periphery bargaining.

Institutionalized contagion of radicalism results when competition for precedence at the bargaining table with common-state leaders creates incentives for segment-state leaders to outbid or at least match the claims of leaders in other segment-states. Segment-state leaders compete with one another, as well as with spokespersons of other interests, for attention in common-state decision-making organs. One way to claim precedence in normal politics is to frame demands as claims to a greater share of decision rights. Once the leaders of one segment-state have muscled ahead of others by such claims, this increases the incentives for the leaders in other segment-states to escalate as well. In this way segmental institutions also create incentives for segment-state leaders to play the sovereignty card. In the competition for attention in common-state politics, segment-state leaders try to push to the head of the queue (as well as to trump common-state claimants) by framing their demands as claims on behalf of the sovereign rights of their respective "peoples." As the Russian correspondent Vladimir Todres observed during Russia's 1993 Constitutional Conference, "since the supreme dignitaries of the Russian Federation promised 'social and economic equality' to all Federation members, the republics, in order to preserve their primacy, have been forced to shift the discussion to the field of political rights." Once the center played what Todres called "the regional card"—that is, the claim that all subjects should be equal—the republics

---

[71] Slider 1994b, 380–81, 384–85. The percentage of small enterprises privatized was 46.7 in the republics but 65.5 in the oblasts and krais.

had but one option, to play the self-determination and "secession cards." And once one republic had played the sovereignty card, all the others had to follow. As U.S. Ambassador Jack Matlock observed about the *perestroika*-era "parade of sovereignties" that followed Russia's June 1990 declaration of sovereignty vis-à-vis the USSR: "Politically, the Russian action required the remaining republics to declare their own sovereignty if they were to be in a position to negotiate a new treaty of union as an equal."[72]

Once segment-state leaders play the "sovereignty card" the bargaining range of mutually acceptable outcomes threatens to narrow and focus on a single dichotomous choice over the location of sovereignty. Even though there are several complex formulas for joint sovereignty (as noted in chapter 2), in the rising heat of a nation-state crisis it becomes more difficult to agree to one of these compromises that would keep the common-state whole.[73] Playing the sovereignty card escalates conflict across a critical threshold. As Todres noted during the Russian nation-state crisis, once one segment-state has played the "sovereignty card," "The word has been spoken. . . . Once it is spoken, it takes on a life of its own. . . . One way or another, by playing their trump card, the former autonomous entities [that is, the segment-states within the Russian Federation] have started a very big game."[74] The central question on the bargaining table became whether the separate populations of the segment-states or the population of the common-state as a whole constituted a people with a sovereign right to an independent state of its own. It was a question on which compromise was difficult; complex formulas about partitioned sovereignty were just too obscure and complicated to serve as compromises in a rapidly evolving nation-state crisis. The *perestroika* and Russian nation-state crises resulted in simple answers to a dichotomous choice. In late 1991 the separate peoples of the union republics emerged sovereign; the sovereignty of the Soviet people simply ceased to exist. In late 1993 the multiethnic population of the Russian Federation emerged sovereign; the constitution adopted on December 12, 1993, rejected the sovereignty of the separate peoples within individual republics.

[72] Matlock 1995, 374.

[73] The bargaining begins to resemble an elimination tournament in which agreement is more difficult; see Hirshleifer and Coll 1988, 390–94. Also see Axelrod and Keohane 1985, 226–54; Stein 1990, 101.

[74] Vladimir Todres, "Pravo na vykhod: poslednyi kozyr' bol'shoi igry," *Segodnia* June 4, 1993, 2.

EIGHT

Escalation of Means in Nation-State Crises

PROPONENTS OF NATION-STATE projects are more likely to achieve sovereign independence when they possess the means to induce common-state leaders to listen and accede and when they are relatively secure against retaliation. In this respect, segment-states typically privilege the proponents of their nation-state projects over proponents without segment-states. Yet segment-states are not all alike, and differences among segmental institutions affect the ability of different segment-state leaders to grab the attention of common-state leaders and to press them to cede greater decision rights and, ultimately, sovereignty. The discussion in this chapter stresses three of these differences—whether segmental institutions empower segment-state leaders with a broader set of decision rights that can be turned into leverage against the common-state leaders, whether segmental institutions empower the segment-state leaders within common-state decision making in a manner that can weaken the common-state government, and whether segmental institutions empower segment-state leaders with political-identity hegemony. In the context of bargaining between common-state and segment-state leaders, these institutional differences are primary determinants of which segment-states are likely to become independent nation-states.

The discussion in this chapter emphasizes escalation in the means or leverage by which segment-state leaders and common-state leaders induce one another to listen to and to accede to their demands. Each side escalates the means in order to increase the losses of the other side and to increase the other's expectations of losses in the future. Each side may escalate, for example, from verbal declarations and denunciations to mass boycotts and strikes or from peaceful challenges to violence.[1] This type of escalation and threatened escalation was particularly prevalent in the *perestroika* and Russian Federation nation-state crises. For example, after electing their leader Vytautas Landsbergis as chairman of Lithuania's Supreme Soviet on March 11, 1990, the parliamentary majority from the pro-independence movement Sajudis moved quickly to escalate the pressure on Moscow so as to induce the common-state government of Mikhail Gorbachev to grant

---

[1] Shleifer and Treisman 2000, 162, 165.

full independence to their union republic.[2] The new Lithuanian government immediately limited the role of common-state (all-union) organs within the segment-state's (union republic's) borders. It authorized creation of a volunteer militia (territorial protection organizations) for the union republic as a signal that any brute force by Moscow might well encounter resistance that could be costly to Moscow. On March 21, 1990, Gorbachev responded by instructing the KGB (the Soviet security police) to enforce a ban on firearms within Lithuania and to reinforce border controls so as to restrict entry into Lithuania.[3] Landsbergis characterized the common-state moves as a "war of nerves and of psychological, political pressure on Lithuania."[4] Gorbachev's moves were exactly that—designed to counter the war of nerves conducted by Landsbergis. Common-state pressure was backed by a blockade on Lithuania from March 15 to June 20 that led to widespread shortages and threatened to shut down industry within the segment-state.[5] Moscow hoped that the suffering of the Lithuanian population (and the implied threat of further, mounting suffering in the future) would induce the Sajudis government to cry uncle. Gorbachev warned Landsbergis to back down because the common-state leadership would not: "I want to state once again that this path is disastrous, that it will lead only to an impasse."[6] In response the Lithuanian government encouraged demonstrations throughout the union republic in order to demonstrate the people's resolve to accept the pain inflicted by Moscow and to see the crisis beyond the brink of disaster in support of the Sajudis nation-state project. Moscow encouraged counterdemonstrations by its supporters to demonstrate that the population of Lithuania was divided and that many in the union republic supported the common-state government in the crisis. In late 1990 Sajudis followers began seizing control of state and Communist Party facilities in the union republic. In January 1991, Ministry of Defense forces sent by the common-state government intervened in Vilnius to take back these facilities, but encountered resis-

[2] "Na sessii Verkhovnogo Soveta Litvy," *Pravda* March 12, 1990, 2; "Sessiia Verkhovnogo Soveta Litvy," *Pravda* March 13, 1990, 3.

[3] Ukaz Prezidenta Soiuza Sovetskikh Sotsialisticheskikh Respublik "O dopolnitel'nykh merakh po obespecheniiu prav sovetskikh grazhdan, okhrane suvereniteta Soiuza SSR na territorii Litovskoi SSR," *Izvestiia* March 22, 1990, 1; "Zaiavlenie TASS," *Izvestiia* March 23, 1990, 1; M. S. Gorbachev, "Predsedatel'iu Verkhovnogo Soveta Litovskoi SSR Landsbergisu V. V.," *Izvestiia* March 23, 1990, 1.

[4] "K obstanovke v Litve," *Izvestiia* March 25, 1990, 2.

[5] "Blockade of Lithuania Begins to Hurt," *Current Digest of the Soviet Press* 42 (May 30, 1990), 16–18.

[6] "Obrashchenie Prezidenta SSSR k Verkhovnomu Sovetu Litovskoi SSR" and "Obrashchenie Prezidenta SSSR k narodu Litovskoi SSR," *Izvestiia* April 1, 1990, 1.

tance that ended in over a dozen deaths.[7] The Lithuanian parliament upped the ante still more by authorizing creation of a volunteer army for the segment-state, which sent a signal that further interventions by the common-state's armed forces would be still more costly to Moscow. It also scheduled a referendum on independence that Sajudis leaders hoped would convince Moscow that the opposition to Sajudis' nation-state project within the union republic was impotent and that Sajudis was the only party with whom Moscow could bargain over the future of Lithuania.[8] It was the ability to back their substantive demands with actions that were costly to the common-state government and to absorb the losses inflicted on them by the common-state government that made the Lithuanian segment-state leaders under Landsbergis such effective bargainers.

This chapter puts forth propositions about conditions that increase the ability of segment-state leaders to exercise leverage over common-state leaders and to withstand the pressures imposed by common-state leaders. These propositions are derived from the bargaining model and the three Eurasian nation-state crises introduced in chapter 6. These suggest that success in the form of a new sovereign nation-state is more likely when common-state leaders are weakened by division—particularly when segment-state leaders can exploit this division and produce deadlock in the common-state government—and when segment-state leaders have more decision rights and the ability to use these artfully as a consequence of political-identity hegemony within their segment-states. In part 4 of this book these propositions are reformulated as hypotheses to be tested in comparisons involving a larger number of cases.

The Balance of Leverage

The more that segmental institutions empower segment-state leaders with greater decision rights, the more opportunities these leaders have to escalate their conflict with the common-state leaders. These decision rights give segment-state leaders greater leverage over common-state leaders and thus become the means to press nation-state projects and to induce the leaders of the common-state to accede to their demands for still more decision rights—and ultimately for sovereignty. Yet constitutional orders, even

---

[7] "Lithuanian Violence: On Gorbachev's Orders?" *Current Digest of the Soviet Press* 43 (February 13, 1991), 1–10; S. Girnius 1991a.

[8] V. Okulov and Iu. Stroganov, "Kto sokhraniaet napriazhennost'?" *Pravda* January 18, 1991, 1; N. Lashkevich, "Litva naznachen referendum," *Izvestiia* January 21, 1991, 2; S. Girnius 1991b.

in segmented states, seldom are designed to give predominance to the segment-states, and the Eurasian segmented states certainly were no exception. Common-state leaders are normally better able than segment-state leaders to prevail in exchanges of pressure and retaliation.[9] The shift in the balance of leverage that leads to predominance of segment-states and to dissolution of the common-state emerges when the common-state government is weakened—often by internal divisions in the common-state leadership, but sometimes by coup, invasion, severe economic crisis, or other exogenous shock.

In this vertical bargaining, decision rights assigned to segment-state leaders are often weapons to be used against the leaders of the common-state. According to Philip Selznick, "institutional weapons" are powers that "are used by a power-seeking elite in a manner unrestrained by the constitutional order of the arena within which the contest takes place," and they are used to change that constitutional order.[10] For segment-state leaders, leverage over the government of the common-state is measured by their ability to back their claims with action that proves costly to the common-state leaders, such as delivering votes to the opposition, organizing strikes and boycotts, embargoing national taxes collected within the segment-state, initiating campaigns of terrorist violence, or conducting warfare.[11] At the same time, common-state leaders exercise leverage over segment-state leaders by such actions as withholding funds from the segment-state government, removing the segment-state leaders from office, or punishing, intimidating, and suppressing the supporters of segment-state leaders with physical coercion.[12]

Where the segmented state gives the common-state government a preponderance of decision rights, this imbalance increases the likelihood that the common-state government will simply impose recentralization of decisionmaking rights. Yet where this imbalance in leverage is seen by both sides there is not likely to be much escalation in means (figure 6.1). A significant body of formal theory on decentralization points in this same direction. First, in an environment of perfect information and no uncertainty, the typical advantage of the common-state in coercive capabilities should deter almost all threats of escalation from nation-state claimants. In these circumstances deterrence results because the segment-state leaders know that if they escalate means, the common-state leaders are able and willing to match this (and perhaps escalate further).[13] The segment-state

---

[9] J. Knight 1992, 132.

[10] Selznick 1960, 2.

[11] Treisman 1999, chap. 5; Boyd 1998, 42–55; Bebler 1993.

[12] See the discussion of a Gosplan memorandum planning all-union sanctions against union republics that failed to sign the Union Treaty in Hanson 1991. Also see Petrov 2001.

[13] Kaufmann 1956.

leaders must anticipate that, even though "we" might escalate conflict, the common-state leaders can match this, and so our chances of gaining our objectives will not improve, but our losses will rise significantly.[14] Second, where the balance of institutional weapons favors the leaders of the common-state, there is little to stop the common-state leaders from coercing the segment-state leaders to concede more decision-making rights. The common-state government is likely to believe that segment-state leaders will concede in order to avoid any costly losses from coercion.[15] Significant evidence from the experience of federations suggests that this type of imbalance makes the rights of cultural communities particularly vulnerable to common-state encroachment. More generally, Jenna Bednar, William Eskridge, and John Ferejohn observe about federations that "the national government will constantly be tempted to increase its own power relative to the provinces and to shift to the provinces some of the costs of national programs."[16]

Alternatively, as the *perestroika* crisis underscored, where segmental institutions give a preponderance of power to segment-states, devolution is more likely. Under these conditions segment-state leaders have greater ability to induce the common-state leaders to give in and to deter common-state retaliation.[17] Yet this imbalance favoring the segment-states was certainly not written into the Constitution of the Union of Soviet Socialist Republics (USSR) or the Rules of the Communist Party of the Soviet Union (CPSU)—as the very different outcome of the nation-state crisis of the early USSR underscores. This imbalance in favor of the segment-states was an unexpected outcome that was only a potentiality in the original design of institutions, but emerged with weakening of the common-state government. The weakened ability and resolve of the common-state government to insist on its rights under the existing constitutive rules invited probes by segment-state leaders to find the true limits of what powers could be taken. The common-state government's declining ability and resolve to defend its decision rights was signaled to segment-state leaders by the paralysis within the common-state (all-union) government and by offers of concessions from some members of the common-state leadership. Alternatively, as Henry E. Hale argues persuasively, a credible threat by Gorbachev to employ force against secessionist union republics might well have prevented the Soviet collapse.[18]

[14] Compare Zartman 1991, 516.

[15] Fearon 1994.

[16] Bednar, Eskridge, and Ferejohn 1999, 6–7.

[17] Tarlton 1965, 870–71; Wolchik 1994, 153–58; Butora and Butorova 1993, 709; R. Hill 1993.

[18] Hale 2001.

The Eurasian nation-state crises suggest that the likelihood of a breakdown in commitment to enforce the existing constitutive rules grows during a succession crisis, coup, foreign intervention, or other shock that introduces disunity into the common-state leadership on the issue of the constitutive rules of the segmented state and their enforcement.[19] The Soviet system was subject to vacillation in the relative leverage of the common-state (all-union) government over the segment-state (union-republic) governments with the alternation in the common-state government between periods of consolidated one-man rule and elite struggles that accompanied the successions from Vladimir Lenin to Joseph Stalin, Stalin to Nikita Khrushchev, Khrushchev to Leonid Brezhnev, and finally Brezhnev (via Yuri Andropov and Konstantin Chernenko) to Gorbachev.[20]

During all succession crises, the segment-state (union-republic) governments gained in bargaining power and extracted concessions. For example, in 1954 Khrushchev apparently transferred the Crimea from Russian to Ukrainian jurisdiction "to win favor with Ukraine's Party *aktiv*—future delegates to and participants in Congresses and plenary sessions [of the Central Committee]."[21] Three years later, as the leadership in the CPSU Politburo became locked in an increasingly bitter confrontation that culminated in the crisis of the so-called Anti-Party Group (June 1957), segment-state (particularly union republic) leaders received constitutional concessions to expand their role in the common-state (all-union) institutions: on February 12, 1957, the USSR Supreme Soviet amended the Soviet constitution to make the chairmen of the union republic supreme courts ex officio members of the USSR Supreme Court. On May 10, 1957, the USSR Supreme Soviet amended the Soviet constitution once again to make the chairmen of the union republic councils of ministers ex officio members of the USSR Council of Ministers.[22] They also received expanded decision rights at home. In February 1957 Khrushchev secured adoption of constitutional amendments that expanded the role of union republics in adopting

---

[19] To these cases we could add the nation-state crisis of the late Russian Empire during World War I. This ended in the secession of Finland, the Baltic states, Poland, and Bessarabia, as well as the temporary secession of Belarus, Ukraine, Armenia, Azerbaijan, and Georgia.

[20] Roeder 1993.

[21] Ol'ga Glezer, Nikita Khrushchev, and Vladimir Shevelen, "Krym v fevrale 1954 g.," *Moskovskie novosti* February 2, 1992, 10. Also see Szporluk 2000, 167.

[22] "Zakon o vnesenii izmenenii i dopolnenii v tekst Konstitutsii (Osnovnogo Zakona) SSSR," *Izvestiia* May 11, 1957, 2. On December 25, 1958, the Supreme Soviet further amended the Constitution to make explicit what had been de facto practice; the vice chairmen of the Presidium of the Supreme Soviet were drawn from each union republic; "Zakon o vnesenii izmenenii i dopolnenii v stat'i 48 i 83 Konstitutsii (Osnovnogo Zakona) SSSR," *Izvestiia* December 26, 1958, 7.

legal codes.[23] At the same time, a constitutional amendment transferred decisions to create territorial administrations to the jurisdiction of union republics and limited the common-state (all-union) organs to approval of new segment-states (specifically, autonomous republics and autonomous oblasts) within the union republics.[24] In the spring of 1957 Khrushchev initiated a dramatic reform in economic structure that abolished twenty-five common-state ministries and transferred decision-making power to regionally based economic councils (*sovnarkhozy*).[25] This enhanced the power of the union republic party secretaries, who had often felt at a disadvantage against the common-state ministries. The union republic supreme soviets drew the boundaries of the economic administrative regions and the union republic councils of ministers appointed the members of the respective *sovnarkhozy*.[26] Yet, much as Stalin had done three decades earlier, once Khrushchev had defeated his opponents in the common-state government, he tightened control over the segment-states.[27] As Khrushchev strengthened his position within the common-state Politburo, he introduced new centralizing policies and removed segment-state leaders in Azerbaijan (1959), Latvia (1959), Uzbekistan (1959), Kirgizia (1961), Tajikistan (1962), and Turkmenistan (1963). Furthermore, in 1962 he established a new Central Asian *Sovnarkhoz* and new party bureaus for Central Asia and Transcaucasia to stand above and to supervise the party organizations of these union republics.[28]

Only two of the four Soviet succession crises led to nation-state crises, however, and only one led to breakdown of the common-state and creation of new independent nation-states. If we add to this list the divided leadership in the Russian Federation, only three of five periods of divided leadership led to nation-state crises, and only one led to successful creation of new sovereign nation-states. Thus, division in the common-state leadership alone is inadequate to explain the shift in the balance of leverage that leads to common-state failure and the creation of new sovereign nation-states. In the three Eurasian nation-state crises two additional elements

[23] "Zakon ob utverzhdenii Polozheniia o Verkhovnom Sude SSSR i o vnesenii izmenenii i dopolnenii v stat'i 104 i 105 Konstitutsii (Osnovnogo Zakona) SSSR," *Izvestiia* February 13, 1957, 1; "Zakon ob otnesenii k vedeniiu soiuznykh respublik zakonodatel'stva ob ustroistve sudov soiuznykh respublik, priniatiia grazhdanskogo, ugolovnogo i protsessual'nykh kodeksov," *Izvestiia* February 12, 1957, 1.

[24] "Zakon ob otnesenii k vedeniiu soiuznykh respublik razresheniia voprosov oblastnogo, kraevogo administrativno-territorial'nogo ustroistva," *Izvestiia* February 12, 1957, 1; Ponomarev et al. 1982, 237.

[25] Löwenhardt 1981, 40–43.

[26] Swearer 1959, 45–61; Lydolph 1958, 293–301; Laskovsky 1958, 47–58.

[27] Krawchenko 1985, 200, 246.

[28] Hodnett 1967, 458–59.

pushed the balance of leverage in favor of the segment-states once division in the common-state leadership created an opening for segment-state leaders to press their nation-state projects. First, in the *perestroika* and Russian Federation nation-state crises many segment-state leaders had consolidated political-identity hegemony to such an extent that they could escalate their claims to the point of a nation-state crisis. Second, segmental institutions in the *perestroika* but not the Russian nation-state crises empowered the segment-state leaders to push the division in the common-state leadership to the point of deadlock. Only in the *perestroika* nation-state crisis was the common-state government weakened enough and the segment-states strong enough to induce failure in the common-state and to enable segment-state leaders to create sovereign nation-states.

Segment-States in Common-State Policy-Making

The more that segmental institutions give the leaders of segment-states privileged access to common-state policy-making—particularly where that access permits the segment-state leaders to weaken the common-state government—the better able these leaders are to press a nation-state project to a crisis and to induce common-state leaders to concede sovereign independence. As already emphasized, this privileged access to common-state policy-making means that the claims of segment-state leaders are likely to be heard before and above those of competitors, including other politicians making claims on behalf of segment-states, politicians making claims on behalf of other peoples or territories without the status of a segment-state, and politicians making claims on behalf of identities and interests that cut across the official segment-state boundaries. For example, in the USSR during the *perestroika* crisis the movements to restore the largely forgotten Donetsk-Krivoi Rog Republic of early 1918 or an autonomous Novorossiia remained on the sidelines of nation-state conflicts because their proponents did not control segment-states and they could find few patrons among the regional administrations.[29] The claim that the so-called Novorossy of the Black Sea littoral from the Crimea to Transdniestria constitute a distinct ethnos deserving autonomy within Ukraine or the USSR was advanced by Professor Oleksii Surylov of Odessa State University, but this, like many other professorial projects, remained a parlor or campus nation—imagined only among a small circle of intellectuals largely found on university campuses—and not a major issue on the bargaining table as a nation-state crisis. Similarly, the campaign to restore the Crimean Tatars' autonomy within Ukraine or the USSR was disadvantaged because the

[29] Harris 1994.

government of the Autonomous Republic of Crimea, controlled by Russians and Russophone Ukrainians, was unwilling to champion the Crimean Tatars' cause. The governments in Moscow and Kiev deferred to the Crimean administration rather than the social movement. Concurring in the Crimean legislature's condemnation of the actions of the Tatar *Majlis*, President Leonid Kravchuk of Ukraine proclaimed, "We . . . came to the conclusion that in the future, as before, Ukraine, its bodies of power, and the President will have relations and dealings only with Crimea's legitimately elected bodies of power and the structures of authority created by them."[30] The Crimean Tatars were unable to make it in the president's interest to deal with the Crimean Tatar project, and they could not convince the Crimean government to champion their project before the government of Ukraine.

Yet, access to common-state policy-making is particularly important to the outcome of nation-state crises when the access permits segment-state governments to shift the balance of leverage in their favor by weakening the common-state government through deadlock within it. The special role of segment-states in common-state government is particularly likely to weaken the common-state government when institutions assign the segment-states real or potential vetoes in common-state decision making. The differences in the outcomes of the *perestroika* and Russian Federation nation-state crises underscore the way in which institutions shape the outcome.

Deadlock in USSR Decision Making

The *perestroika* nation-state crisis, in particular, underscores that the more common-state institutions privilege segment-states in common-state decision making by granting them effective vetoes over policy, the more likely it is that the segment-state leaders will succeed in pressing their project to a nation-state crisis and will induce the common-state leaders to concede independence. As more policy-making shifted to forums that gave the heads of union republics exclusive voice in policy-making and as decision making shifted to a unit-vote and then unit-veto rule, the ability of union republic leaders to paralyze Gorbachev's common-state government grew. Their veto in decisions of the common-state gave union republic leaders the power to paralyze the common-state decision making process, and so threaten mutual disaster, as a way of inducing the common-state government to give in. In the end, Gorbachev's common-state government was so weakened that it simply acquiesced, with virtually no independent say, in the decision of the union republics to end the USSR.

---

[30] Vladimir Skachko, "Kravchuk-Bagrov: pozitsii sovpali," *Nezavisimaia gazeta* October 14, 1992, 1.

Even before the *perestroika* nation-state crisis in the USSR, the hierarchy of segment-states (union republics, autonomous republics, autonomous oblasts, and autonomous okrugs) was mirrored in a hierarchy of access to common-state (officially called "all-union") institutions. Moreover, the segmented state virtually disfranchised national communities without segment-states, such as the Crimean Tatars. This was formalized in the common-state governing organs of the USSR through coöptation of union republic leaders into the common-state's Presidium of the Supreme Soviet, Council of Ministers, and Supreme Court. More significantly, it was mirrored in the informal allocation of seats in the real common-state decision-making centers of the Communist Party of the Soviet Union (CPSU): by the end of the Nikita Khrushchev era in 1964 it had become the norm to coöpt four of the fourteen union republic first secretaries into the CPSU Politburo.[31] Under Leonid Brezhnev this proportion grew, so that the last Politburo under Brezhnev in the early 1980s coöpted six of the fourteen union republic first secretaries—those from Ukraine, Belarus, Azerbaijan, Georgia, Kazakhstan, and Uzbekistan. This was a privilege unique to union republics: no first secretaries of the lower-order segment-states were coöpted, and no first secretaries to represent ethnic groups without segment-states existed. This hierarchy of access to the central decision-making councils was also reflected in the election of segment-state first secretaries to the common-state Central Committee of the CPSU. In 1986, all fourteen union republic first secretaries but only 60 percent of the autonomous republic first secretaries and none of the autonomous oblast or autonomous okrug first secretaries were elected to the all-union Central Committee. In addition, four of the fifteen union republic chairmen of councils of ministers were elected, but none of the chairmen from the autonomous republics.[32] A similar pattern of access characterized participation in the CPSU congresses. As Howard L. Biddulph notes, "A speech at a Party Congress is more than a symbolic honor for an obkom or republic first secretary. Access to the 'high podium' gives such leaders the chance to place on the public record a proposal that otherwise would have to be made through less visible channels."[33] According to Biddulph's count, in the four congresses held under Brezhnev from 1966 to 1981, leaders of first-order segment-states (union republics) were more than ten times as likely to speak from the "high

[31] The fifteenth union republic (the RSFSR) did not have a separate party organization or first secretary.

[32] This difference in access was shown starkly when the Karelo-Finnish union republic was demoted to the status of an autonomous republic in July 1956: while both the first secretary and chairman of the Supreme Soviet Presidium of the Karelo-Finnish SSR sat in the Central Committee elected earlier that year, neither from the newly demoted Karelian ASSR was elected to a term in the Central Committee in 1961.

[33] Biddulph 1983, 32.

podium" as leaders of second-order segment-states (autonomous republics) and more than fourteen times as likely as the leaders of second-order jurisdictions that were not segment-states (oblasts and krais).[34]

Under Gorbachev, the beginning of the constitutional reform process heightened concerns among union republic leaders that they maintain their privileged access to the shifting centers of decision making. Thus, they worked to ensure that constitutional provisions for the new common-state Congress of People's Deputies and Supreme Soviet, which were to assume a real role in lawmaking and in constitutional reform, guaranteed that a third of the seats in the Congress would be allocated by federal status— thirty-two seats per union republic, eleven per autonomous republic, five per autonomous oblast, and one per autonomous okrug. The Congress elected the working legislature, the Supreme Soviet, as two equal chambers based on population and on federal status, respectively; in the upper chamber (Soviet of Nationalities) the norm was eleven deputies per union republic, four per autonomous republic, two per autonomous oblast, and one per autonomous okrug.[35] As the *perestroika* nation-state crisis escalated, however, the venue that became the primary decision-making center was a council of the presidents of the union republics plus the president of the USSR. This was originally constituted as the Council of the Federation: in creating a USSR presidency on March 14, 1990, the Congress of People's Deputies also created the Council of the Federation (Article 127.4 of the USSR Constitution).[36] The leaders of lower-order segment-states could participate in meetings during relevant discussions, but the heart of the council was the meeting of fifteen union republic presidents and the president of the USSR. After just nine months the council was strengthened with further amendments to the Constitution, transforming the body so that, in the words of Gorbachev, "the council will consider all major questions of all-union [common-state] significance, ensure coordination of the activities of Union [common-state] and republic [segment-state] bodies of power, and facilitate the resolution of disputes and the settlement of conflict situations."[37]

---

[34] These are based on the number of speeches by officials from each type of administrative division divided by the total number of such territorial administrations in that year. These numbers were 1.6 speeches per union republic, 0.15 per autonomous republic, and 0.11 per oblast or krai.

[35] Zakon Soveta Sovetskikh Sotsialisticheskikh Respublik "Ob izmeneniiakh i dopolneniiakh Konstitutsii (Osnovnogo Zakona) SSSR," *Izvestiia* December 3, 1988, 1–2.

[36] Zakon Soiuza Sovetskikh Sotsialisticheskikh Respublik "Ob uchrezhdenii posta Prezidenta SSSR i vnesenii i dopolnenii v Konstitutsiiu (Osnovnoi Zakon) SSSR," *Pravda* March 16, 1990, 3.

[37] S. Chugaev, "Predlozheniia Prezidenta SSSR podderzhany," *Izvestiia* December 5, 1990, 1–2. Also see "Prezident predlagaet svoiu programmu—Vystuplenie M. S. Gorbacheva na sessii Verkhovnogo Soveta SSSR 17 noiabria 1990 goda," *Izvestiia* November 17, 1990, 1;

As the stakes in bargaining over the constitutional structure of the USSR escalated, it became harder to decide all-union issues without privileging the union-republic leaders in the decision process still more. With further escalation in the nation-state crisis this special access by union-republic leaders became a collective veto power over the most fundamental constitutional issues. The union-republic leaders worked hard to exclude other voices from these negotiations. For example, in creating a Constitutional Committee to draft a new USSR Constitution, the Congress of People's Deputies in June 1989 had carefully balanced the committee's membership so that half—52 of its 105 members—came from an official institution of a union-republic or lower-order segment-state, so that every union republic had representation, and so that the union republics held the overwhelming majority of the segment-state seats—45 of the 52 seats.[38] Yet by the latter half of 1990 the presidents of the union republics had supplanted this body with the Council of the Federation, where they were the only voice beside the USSR president.[39] When Gorbachev raised the possibility that autonomous republics might sign the new Union Treaty as equal parties, the leaders of union republics adamantly objected and declared that they alone would be parties. In the final months of negotiations over a Union Treaty for a renewed USSR, the decisions that only heads of union republics would participate, that these heads had to reach decisions by consensus and not simply majority vote, and that any head could opt out of the Union Treaty made it difficult to reach an agreement that would keep the USSR whole.

Balance among Russian Institutions

Within the Russian Federation there was an important difference in the segment-states' role in common-state policy-making during the critical transition period immediately before and after the breakup of the USSR. The republics and other segment-states inside the Russian Federation en-

"Perekhodit' ot slov k delu, reshitel'no dvigat'sia vpered—Doklad M. S. Gorbacheva na IV S"ezde narodnykh deputatov SSSR," *Izvestiia* December 18, 1991, 1–2; Zakon Soveta Sovetskikh Sotsialisticheskikh Respublik "Ob izmeneniiakh i dopolneniiakh Konstitutsii (Osnovnogo Zakona) SSSR v sviazi s sovershenstvovaniem sistemy gosudarstvennogo upravleniia," *Izvestiia* December 27, 1990, 1–2.

[38] Among the representatives from the union republics and autonomies, half (27) were officials in the party or state organs and another quarter (15) were officials in one of the union republic academies or state universities; Postanovlenie S"ezda narodnykh deputatov Soiuza Sovetskikh Sotsialisticheskikh Respublik "Ob obrazovanii Konstitutstionnnoi komissii," *Izvestiia* June 10, 1989, 3.

[39] "Vstrecha Prezidenta SSSR i Predsedatelia Verkhovnogo Soveta RSFSR s Predsedateliami Verkhovnykh Sovetov avtonomnykh respublik Rossiiskoi Federatsii," *Izvestiia* May 13, 1991, 1; G. Alimov, "Protivorechiia sniaty—k itogam vstrechi v Kremle," *Izvestiia* May 13, 1991, 1–2. Also see Solchanyk 1991a, 16–17; Sheehy 1991c, 1991d, 18.

joyed special access to common-state legislative and executive decision making that privileged them relative to other subjects of the federation, other peoples, and other interests. Yet Russian legislative and executive bodies never gave Russia's segment-states an effective veto over common-state policy, even when this policy was directed at the segment-states. Thus, they could never transform all policy debates into discussions of the allocation of decision rights and create stalemate on this all consuming issue. This institutional balancing of segment-states against other interests resulted in large part because the Russian Federation was not a thoroughly segmented state—that is, the majority of its first-order jurisdictions (55 of 89 subjects of the federation) were not segment-states. The only trump that segment-states exercised throughout this period of the nation-state crisis was an extraconstitutional threat to follow the example of Chechnya and secede—a bluff that the Yeltsin administration finally chose to call in late 1993.

The Russian legislative bodies during the critical transition period prior to the adoption of the Yeltsin Constitution in December 1993 overrepresented the segment-states, but did not give them a majority of votes or even a collective veto. Like the corresponding Soviet organ, the Russian Congress of People's Deputies elected not only a lower chamber of the Supreme Soviet based on population but also an upper chamber composed of deputies from so-called national territorial districts. Yet even the latter were distributed in equal number between the segment-states and the other subjects of the federation that were not segment-states.[40] The two chambers of the Supreme Soviet actually met as a single body, and so the addition of the seats allocated by national territorial district to the seats allocated on the basis of population did lead to overrepresentation of segment-states in that body: Even though they comprised only 18 percent of Russia's population, the segment-states were guaranteed about a third of the Supreme Soviet seats. Yet this did not protect the segment-states from unfavorable constitutional amendments, since those were taken in the Congress of Peoples' Deputies, where the segment-states held much less than a third of the seats and adoption of a new constitution required only a two-thirds majority.

In the executive branch, Boris Yeltsin in mid-October 1992 created the Council of Heads of Republics in the Russian Federation "to work on political, economic, and social problems."[41] This new council, however, was an advisory body alongside other such advisory bodies as the council of

[40] Remington 2001, 115.
[41] Vera Kuznetsova, "V Rossii sozdan eshche i sovet glav respublik," *Nezavisimaia gazeta* October 16, 1992, 1; Valerii Vyzhutovich, "Sovet glav respublik podderzhivaet Rossiiskogo Prezidenta," *Izvestiia* November 24, 1992, 1.

governors for the oblasts and krais and did not supplant the real executive branch decision-making organs of the Cabinet and Security Council. Indeed, like many of his more autocratic predecessors, President Yeltsin was a master at balancing one of these bodies against the others as a way of maximizing his personal control over the policy agenda.

Despite the division among common-state leaders the segment-states were simply not strong enough in common-state policy-making to block adoption of a federation treaty and or constitution that were unfavorable to their interests. The Yeltsin Constitution of 1993 was, in fact, adopted by a simple majority of the Russian voters. The segment-states within the Russian Federation (unlike the union republics of the USSR) could not prevent this referendum, which became an end-run around their obstructionism, since more than three-fifths of the subjects of the federation were not segment-states and over 80 percent of the population of Russia lived in these other subjects. In both the Federation Treaty and the new Russian constitution the republics within the Russian Federation had to settle for separate agreements with the Yeltsin administration, including a different federation treaty than the text signed by the oblasts and krais and separate power-sharing treaties to modify the application of the common-state constitution to individual segment-states.

Segment-State Hegemonies and Center-Periphery Bargaining

The balance of leverage is more likely to favor segment-states when this division and stalemate within the common-state government over the issue of preventing secession is challenged by segment-states that have consolidated political-identity hegemony. This strengthens the bargaining position of segment-state leaders vis-à-vis common-state leaders in at least four ways: political-identity hegemony increases the segment-state leaders' leverage over the common-state, buffers segment-state leaders so that they can withstand greater pressure from common-state leaders, eliminates alternative offers from the segment-state's side of the table, and permits segment-state leaders to keep information private or release it strategically.

The balance of leverage between common-state and segment-state leaders in a sense depends on the *relative* consolidation in common-state and segment-state governments, which varies over time more than formal institutional arrangements. Thus, Soviet succession crises at times when segment-state leaders had not fully consolidated political-identity hegemony did not lead to a nation-state crisis. In the post-Stalin and post-Khrushchev successions, the previous period of consolidated autocracy in Moscow had left the union republic leaders too weak to press their claims to the point of a nation-state crisis. Alternatively, the post-Lenin and post-Brezhnev succession crises occurred at times when segment-state leaders had consolidated political-identity hegemony that was strong enough to permit them to press their demands or resist the common-state government, but only as long as common-state leadership was divided. The nation-state crisis of the early USSR ended in centralization: although the segment-state leaders were strong enough to put up a fight while the common-state leadership was divided by the succession struggle, they were too weak to prevent Stalin from consolidating his leadership in the common-state government and to sustain their resistance against Stalin. The last succession of the USSR (the *perestroika* crisis) resulted in devolution because the union republic leaders had consolidated political-identity hegemonies and the common-state leaders became and remained too divided to confront these hegemonies.[42]

Even in the absence of a deadlocked common-state leadership, segment-state leaders are more likely to gain more decision rights when the segment-state leaders have consolidated political-identity hegemony within their segment-states. This is illustrated by the nine power-sharing treaties signed by the Yeltsin government with Russia's republics between February 1993 and the 1996 presidential elections.[43] The first six were signed with republics governed by machines that had established political-identity hegemony rather than republics with competitive politics (table 8.1). Five of these power-sharing treaties stand out for the concessions in decision rights wrenched from the federation by machine republics—the treaties with Tatarstan, Kabardino-Balkaria, Bashkortostan, North Ossetia, and Sakha. For example, the treaties with the first three were styled treaties of mutual delegation of powers between the republics and the Russian Federation rather than simply treaties of the delimitation of powers. The first five treaties recognized the statehood of the republics; Tatarstan's treaty even recognized that its status was more like an independent state in voluntary association with Russia. The treaties with strongest concessions omitted reference to the supremacy of federal law in areas of joint jurisdiction and gave the republics joint responsibility with the common-state government in such vital areas as the delimitation of state property, coordination of price and monetary policy, management of the economic infrastructure, and coordination of foreign relations (including foreign economic relations).

Common-state and segment-state leaders typically recognize this relationship between consolidation on each side and bargaining outcomes between sides and so they often engage in competitive attempts to prevent or undermine the consolidation on the other side. For example, in the Russian Federation's nation-state crisis throughout 1992 and 1993, but

---

[42] On two-level games, see Putnam 1988.

[43] This analysis is based on the texts of Dogovor 1994, 1995a, 1995b, 1995c, 1996a, 1996b, 1996c, 1996d, 1996e.

TABLE 8.1

Russian Federation: Power-sharing treaties with republics concluded prior to the 1996 presidential elections

Republic: Date of agreement:	Tatarstan February 15, 1994	Kabardino-Balkaria July 1, 1994	Bashkortostan August 3, 1994	North Ossetia March 23, 1995	Sakha June 29, 1995
Delimitation of powers and mutual delegation of powers	X	X	X	—	—
Status relative to federation					
United by mutual delegation	X	—	—	—	—
Sovereign state within federation	—	—	X	—	—
State within federation	—	X	—	X	X
Republic citizenship	X	X	X	X	—
Jurisdiction					
Federal preemption[a]	—	—	—	—	X
Joint delimitation of state property	X	X	X	X	X
Joint coordination of price-monetary	X	X	X	X	—
Joint management of infrastructure	X	X	—	X	X
Joint coordination of foreign relations	X	X	X	X	X

TABLE 8.1 (cont.)

Russian Federation: Power-sharing treaties with republics concluded prior to the 1996 presidential elections

Republic: Date of agreement:	Buryatia August 29, 1995	Udmurtia October 17, 1995	Komi March 20, 1996	Chuvashia May 27, 1996
Delimitation of powers and mutual delegation of powers	—	—	—	—
Status relative to federation				
United by mutual delegation	—	—	—	—
Sovereign state within federation	—	—	—	—
State within federation	X	—	—	—
Republic citizenship	—	—	—	—
Jurisdiction				
Federal preemption[a]	X	X	X	X
Joint delimitation of state property	—	—	—	—
Joint coordination of price-monetary	—	—	—	—
Joint management of infrastructure	—	—	—	—
Joint coordination of foreign relations	—	—	—	—

Sources: Dogovor 1994, 1995a, 1995b, 1995c, 1996a, 1996b, 1996c, 1996d, 1996e.

Note: X = Provision in agreement.

[a] Federal preemption: republic can legislate in areas of shared jurisdiction until federal laws are passed; republic will implement federal laws through republic legislation; republic legislation that contradicts federal law will have no effect.

particularly during the September–October 1993 showdown between President Yeltsin and the Russian Congress of People's Deputies, many segment-state leaders within the Russian Federation sought to prevent the consolidation of power in the common-state government and to maintain the balance and even stalemate in Moscow. The Council of Heads of Republics refused to endorse calling a referendum on April 25, 1993, fearing this would shift the balance in Moscow toward the president.[44] After the presidential coup, a joint statement signed on September 28, 1993, by the leaders of Adygeia, Altai, Bashkortostan, Buryatia, Chuvashia, Dagestan, Kalmykia, Karachai-Cherkessia, Karelia, Khakassia, Mordovia, Sakha, Tyva, and Udmurtia declared "the Russian Federation's Supreme Soviet, as the supreme body of legislative power, provides an essential balance of forces that society must have in the relationship among the legislative, executive, and judicial branches. We are convinced that maintaining the existing separation of powers is an extremely important condition for preserving Russia as an integral state."[45] Yet common-state leaders also attempt to introduce competition within segment-states so as to shift the balance at the bargaining table. For example, after 1999 the Putin administration very carefully linked its campaign to change the terms of power-sharing treaties and so shift the balance toward the center with its campaigns to end practices that had permitted machines to flourish in republics. Thus, the Putin administration used the Constitutional Court and pressure on republic leaders to end such practices as appointment of city heads of administration in segment-states, malapportionment of segment-state legislatures, and language requirements for office holding.

Hegemony and Segment-State Leverage

As the bargaining literature stresses, if a bargainer is able to inflict greater losses on the other side, the bargainer is in a better position to induce the other side to concede more.[46] Consolidation of political-identity hegemony within a segment-state increases the segment-state leader's ability to increase pressure on the common-state leaders. For example, political-identity hegemony gives segment-state leaders resources to organize sustained, collective action among the local population against the government of the common-state.[47] Segment-state leaders are better able than the proponents

---

[44] Vasilii Kononenko, "Prezident gotov otkazat'sia ot referenduma, esli s"ezd primet konstitutsionnoe soglashenie," *Izvestiia* March 10, 1993, 1.

[45] Radik Batyrshin, "Chetvertaia sila v Rossiiskoi politike," *Nezavisimaia gazeta* September 29, 1992, 3.

[46] The general claims about the bargaining literature are drawn from Sutton 1986; McMillan 1992; J. Knight 1992; Binmore, Osborne, and Rubinstein 1992.

[47] Collier 2000a, 2000b. Also see Leites and Wolf 1970; Hardin 1995, 150–53.

of nation-state projects without segment-states to solve three problems commonly identified by theories of collective action. Consolidation of political-identity hegemony by segment-state leaders magnifies these advantages. First, in confronting the free-rider problem in the local population, leaders with machine control over a segment-state are better able to offer protection from common-state punishment to any citizen who joins the segment-state sponsored protest or resistance to the common-state, to offer particularistic rewards for the joiners, and to sanction free-riders who seek to enjoy the benefits of the protest without contributing to its success. Second, in confronting the coordination problem among potential protesters, the segment-state leaders who have consolidated political-identity hegemony and previously demonstrated their capacity to mobilize collective action in other areas are better able to convince supporters that the critical mass for success will be crossed in the current action against the common-state. Third, in addressing the time-inconsistency problem, the segment-state leaders with political-identity hegemony are in a better position to overcome the credible-commitment problem associated with mere promises of rewards for success of a nation-state project by distributing rewards to supporters and beginning to implement the reform program within the segment-state even before independence.[48]

The ability of segment-state leaders that have consolidated political-identity hegemony to organize collective action so as to reward or sanction common-state leaders is illustrated by the manipulation of federal elections in the Russian Federation's republics. Segment-state leaders used their control over the electoral process within their segment-states to induce concessions from the common-state leaders by threats to withhold (and promises to deliver) votes in common-state referenda and elections. From 1991 to 1996 the Russian president was greatly concerned with maintaining voter support in order to win referenda (1991 and 1993) that would strengthen his position and to win two presidential elections (1991 and 1996).[49] Republic leaders who had consolidated machine control over local politics exercised significant leverage over the Russian president by withholding votes or delivering them on election day. For example, in 1991 Tatarstan's leader Mintimer Shaimiev pressed for high turnout for the all-union referendum on the continuation of the USSR held on March 17, but urged a boycott of the Russian presidential election held on June 13. In the March vote, turnout reportedly reached 77.1 percent, but three months later it fell by more than half, to 36.6 percent. In a populous republic such

---

[48] Brass 1991, 48–49.

[49] Petr Zhuravlev, "Sergei Filatov: Lidery avtonomiii 'budorazhat' MVD i armiiu," *Segodnia* December 9, 1993, 1. Earlier in 1993 the republics had demonstrated in the April referendum ability to deliver votes for or against the president; see Lyubarsky 1993.

as Tatarstan, this amounted to withholding or delivering over a million votes. Two years later, in the December 1993 referendum on the Yeltsin Constitution, turnout in Tatarstan was only 13.4 percent; if turnout had been closer to the levels that Shaimiev subsequently delivered in the 1996 presidential elections, Tatarstan would have delivered another 1.6 million votes to the Russian totals, and nationwide turnout for the vote on the Russian Constitution might have been closer to the 50 percent of the electorate required to validate the referendum results.

Alternatively, in 1996, backing from the segment-state leaders with political-identity hegemony contributed to the Russian president's spectacular electoral success (see table 3.2). In Tatarstan, President Shaimiev reportedly threatened dismissal of a dozen heads of administration in rural districts (raions) where the Communists had done well in the first round of presidential voting; Shaimiev threatened dismissal if the heads of administration failed "to influence voters' preferences" in the run-off. After this threat failed to yield the desired results, Shaimiev apparently ordered his republic electoral officials simply to falsify the reported vote totals.[50] Shaimiev was not alone in using a heavy hand to deliver votes in the 1996 elections. Between the first and second rounds of balloting, Yeltsin's total vote doubled in five subjects of the Russian Federation, all of them republics—Dagestan (+102 percent), Ingushetia (+104 percent), Karachai-Cherkessia (+100 percent), Mordovia (+104 percent), and North Ossetia (+131 percent). The total vote for Yeltsin's primary opponent (Gennadii Zyuganov) actually fell in six subjects; once again, all six were republics—Kabardino-Balkaria (−3 percent), Tatarstan (−11 percent), North Ossetia (−12 percent), Karachai-Cherkessia (−14 percent), Dagestan (−24 percent), and Ingushetia (−25 percent).[51] All but one of these were republics under the control of machines that had consolidated political-identity hegemony. The exception, Karachai-Cherkessia, was under special administration headed by an appointee of Yeltsin. Alternatively, in Chuvashia, a republic with competitive politics, President Nikolai Fedorov failed to deliver his republic's votes to Yeltsin in 1996 and feared that this would bring retaliation in the form of a loss of Moscow's financial support. And so Fedorov prudently made a public show of his regret and offered to step down if he was found to be at fault for the low vote.[52]

In the extreme, political-identity hegemony permits segment-state leaders to organize still more hurtful forms of pressure on common-state lead-

---

[50] *OMRI Daily Digest* July 15, 1996.

[51] See also Dmitrii Oreshkin and Vladimir Kozlov, "Odin prezident—dve strany," *Segodnia* July 10, 1996, 5; Elena Tregubova, "Leonid Smirniagin: mestnye vlasti po-prezhnemu manipuliruiut mneniem grazhdan," *Segodnia* November 21, 1995, 2.

[52] Elena Dikun, "Red Tornado Strikes Chuvashia," *Obshchaia gazeta* July 11–17, 1996, 1; translated in *Current Digest of the Post-Soviet Press* 48 (August 7, 1996), 15.

ers. For example, Eurasian segment-state leaders with political-identity hegemony were in a better position to organize boycotts or embargoes of the common-state. This is illustrated by the leverage that Bashkortostan, Sakha, and Tatarstan exercised over Moscow by withholding taxes and threatening to withhold valuable natural resources. Bashkortostan and Tatarstan were major suppliers of gas and oil and Sakha was a major supplier of diamonds and gold. Political-identity hegemony within these segment-states empowered their leaders to use these resources to back their political demands on Moscow. In the summer of 1992 Russia's republics and the common-state government bargained over the rights of republics to control taxation and budgets. It began with a war of laws as republics staked their claim to taxation and spending powers. Bashkortostan, Sakha, and Tatarstan escalated the conflict by refusing to send to Moscow taxes collected on their territory. In response, and as a shot across the bow, the Russian Supreme Soviet, at the request of Boris Yeltsin's government, declared these republic decisions null and void and adopted a law, *On the Budget System of the Russian Federation for 1992*, declaring the acts of these republics illegal. When this did not bring the republics into line, the Russian government then began to withhold all funds as well as Central Bank credits in order to starve the republic governments into submission. In response, as summer waned and winter approached, Bashkortostan's leader Murtaza Rakhimov escalated one step further by threatening to shut off the flow of oil and gas from his republic to the rest of Russia.[53] Rakhimov's threat was clear: more Russians would shiver in the dark if Moscow did not relent. The three republics had their way for at least another year.

Hegemony and Surviving Losses

Bargainers are more likely to get better terms in an agreement if they can absorb losses associated with bargaining, including losses inflicted by the other side.[54] Where segment-state leaders have consolidated political-identity hegemony, they are better able to withstand higher losses in center–periphery conflicts with less fear for their own political survival. In the *perestroika* crisis, strongly consolidated political-identity hegemony improved the segment-state leaders' ability to hold out for a better deal even as the losses inflicted on the people of the segment-state mounted with embargoes or even violence from the center. In particular, segment-state leaders who had consolidated political-identity hegemony had less fear of

---

[53] Radik Batyrshin, "Kazan', Ufa, i Iakutsk ob"edinilis' protiv parlamenta Rossii," *Nezavisimaia gazeta* August 15, 1992, 1.

[54] Binmore, Osborne, and Rubinstein 1992, 182–88, 191; J. Knight 1992, 132; McMillan 1992, 49; Sutton 1986, 711.

losing office as pressures from the common-state leaders intensified. For example, Tatarstan's Mintimer Shaimiev proved such a formidable bargainer precisely because he was fairly confident and had reason to believe Moscow also shared the view that the common-state government could not remove him except by brute force. Stated somewhat differently, the segment-state leadership that is hegemonic is better able to limit the audience costs that might otherwise favor compromise. The segment-state may include a significant population that favors the status quo or resists escalation of conflict.[55] This often includes minority groups not part of the segment-state's "titular" population (such as Chuvashes in Tatarstan) or even members of the common-state's largest population living on the territory of a segment-state (such as Russians in Tatarstan).[56] Consolidation of political-identity hegemony permits the segment-state leaders to limit the pressure from these audiences for compromise at the bargaining table.[57] Even in a segment-state like Bashkortostan, where the titular population constituted a minority (22 percent in 1989), the Tatars outnumbered Bashkirs (28 percent in 1989), and the Russians outnumbered both of these (39 percent in 1989), the political-identity hegemony crafted by Rakhimov protected the Bashkir president against opposition and permitted him to stand tough against Boris Yeltsin.

Hegemony and Elimination of Better Offers

Bargainers strengthen their hand when they can convince the other side that no better offers will come from the bargainer's side of the table—now or in the future.[58] With political-identity hegemony Eurasian segment-state leaders were in a better position to convince common-state leaders that there were no credible opposition leaders with better offers, that the present dominant politicians were not likely to be replaced soon by politicians with more attractive offers, and that the current dominant politicians themselves were unlikely to make such offers in the near or distant future.

---

[55] Bear F. Braumoeller (1997, 380, 389) finds in surveys of Russian and Ukrainian elites and publics that publics are in fact less likely than elites to advocate use of violence to resolve disputes.

[56] For example, see Vetik's (1993, 271–72) comparison of support for independence in Estonia's Estonian and Russian communities. Nevertheless, consolidation can also exact a price in the bargaining strength of a leader. Where domestic constituencies are more extreme than the leader or the constituencies will see backing down from any claim as a humiliation, there the unconsolidated leadership may have a bargaining advantage compared to the consolidated leadership, with an ability to tie their hands. See Fearon 1994. In this situation the common-state leaders know that segment-state leaders cannot back down and that the alternatives to the segment-leaders are likely to demand more and escalate further.

[57] J. Knight 1992, 132.

[58] McMillan 1992, 48; Sutton 1986, 714–15.

Thus, signaling the consolidation of political-identity hegemony and the impotence of the opposition was an essential part of the artistry of the bargaining process. For example, on March 24, 1996, Tatarstan's President Shaimiev staged presidential elections in which he alone stood as a candidate. Early in the campaign, potential candidates were convinced that it would be unwise to run "if they wished to continue to live in Tatarstan." When the Communist Party candidate, Ramil Gabrakhmanov, director of the Kazan Vinegar Factory, could not be dissuaded in this manner, he was arrested (but released after the election) for the murder of the former chief of Kazan's criminal police.[59] The ballot, consistent with Soviet practice, contained only the president's name, requiring those who wished to vote against Shaimiev to enter the voting booth, but permitting those who wished to vote for the president simply to deposit the ballot in the urn. The margin of victory was dazzling: Shaimiev claimed 97.2 percent of the vote with 77.9 percent turnout.[60] Why undertake this charade? Few believed that Shaimiev would lose a competitive election; he was apparently quite popular.[61] Certainly Moscow was not deceived, nor were the voters of Tatarstan. The hollowness of this exercise as a true measure of Shaimiev's popularity was immediately apparent in Moscow, which had its own independent measures of Shaimiev's popularity. Nonetheless, the mobilization of voters and suppression of opposition did have an important demonstration effect that was targeted at Moscow: in center–periphery bargaining there were no alternatives to Shaimiev on the Tatarstan side of the table through much of the 1990s.

Hegemony and Controlling Information

Since bargaining outcomes depend to a significant extent on expectations about the future behavior of the other side, a bargainer who can control the release of information from her or his side of the table is likely to get a better deal.[62] Consolidation of political-identity hegemony increases the opportunities for segment-state leaders to keep information private—notably, information about the compromises that they might accept, differences of opinion within their own governments, their capabilities, risks they might face from conflict, and their resolve. Hegemony puts segment-state

---

[59] Interviews with Tatarstanis during the campaign; Interfax, January 18, 1996. Gabrakhmanov and his close associates claimed that the dead police chief had in fact been a friend of Gabrakhmanov, making the charges even more bizarre in their view.

[60] Sh. Maratov, "Doverie naroda: M. Sh. Shaimiev izbran prezidentom Tatarstana na vtoroi srok," *Respublika Tatarstan* March 26, 1996,1; Vera Postnova, "Mintimer Shaimiev snova izbran prezidentom," *Nezavisimaia gazeta* March 26, 1996, 3; Russian Federation TsIK 1997.

[61] Interfax, January 31, 1996; author's interviews.

[62] Binmore, Osborne, and Rubinstein 1993, 210; Sutton 1986, 717.

leaders in a better position to use clever signaling that creates expectations among common-state leaders—particularly expectations that the segment-state leaders will not accept compromises and are able and willing to incur short-term decision losses and even risks of longer-term losses until the common-state leaders give in.

One of the great advantages enjoyed by Tatarstan's President Shaimiev in bargaining with Moscow was his ability to keep Moscow guessing whether he would actually follow the lead of Chechnya and formally press the secession of his republic. From late 1991 through early 1994, Shaimiev permitted the nationalists in *Ittifak* and the Tatar Public Center to stage protests for immediate independence and to convene an unofficial National Assembly (*Milli Majlis*) that declared independence.[63] As a truly artful bargainer, the Tatar president kept his silence so as to permit many in Moscow to draw the conclusion that the "spontaneous" demonstrations of the Tatars' nationalism tied Shaimiev's hands. Tatarstan's decision to hold a referendum on sovereignty on March 22, 1992—which brought 81.6 percent turnout and 61.4 percent of voters supporting sovereignty for the republic—and then the announcement that Tatarstan would not sign the Federation Treaty led to hysterical conjectures from members of Boris Yeltsin's presidential administration and the Moscow press that secession was imminent.[64]

The session of Tatarstan's Supreme Soviet that opened on October 28, 1992, had only one agenda item, a new constitution for the republic, and the failure of that document to mention Tatarstan's place in the Russian Federation fed a new round of hysteria in Moscow. The opening of parliamentary debate brought a stream of visitors from Moscow to urge amendments that would bring the document into line with Russia's constitution. The debate prompted Oleg Rumiantsev, Executive Secretary of the Russian Supreme Soviet's Constitutional Commission, to warn that "the adoption of the Tatarstan Constitution in its present form would legally codify Tatarstan's detachment as a state from Russia."[65] Yurii Yanov, Vice Chair-

---

[63] N. Morozov, "Vzgliad iz regiona—Tatarstan: Sozdaetsia narodnoe opolchenie," *Pravda* October 16, 1991, 1, 3; "Iz goriachikh tochek—Tatarstan: Burlit ploshchad' Svobody," *Pravda* October 17, 1991, 1; A. Putko, "Kak tataram predlagaiut osvobodit'sia ot 'russkogo iga,'" *Izvestiia* November 26, 1991, 4; Vitalii Portnikov, "Kreml' pod polumesiatsem," *Nezavisimaia gazeta* November 26, 1991, 3; Evgenii Skukin, "Obyknovennyi ittifashizm?" *Rossiiskaia gazeta* November 28, 1991, 3; Al'ians Sabirov, "Kurultai provozglashaet nezavisimost' Tatarstana," *Izvestiia* February 3, 1992, 2; J. Kahn 2000, 68–71.

[64] Sergei Chugaev, "Referendum v Tatarstane—popytka gosudarstvennogo perevorota v masshtabakh vsei Rossiiskoi Federatsii, schitaet vitse-prem'er Rossii Sergei Shakhrai," *Izvestiia* March 17, 1992, 2; Al'ians Sabirov and Konstantin Eggert, "Otvety referenduma v Tatarstane staviat voprosy pered Rossiei," *Izvestiia* March 23, 1992, 1; Vitalii Marsov, "Tatarstan ne podpishet federativnogo dogovora s Rossiei," *Nezavisimaia gazeta* March 24, 1992, 1.

[65] Tagir Agliullin, "Konstitutsiia Tatarstanu daetsia nelegko," *Nezavisimaia gazeta* October 30, 1992, 1, 3; Vladimir Todres, "Moskovskie strasti po kazanskoi konstitutsii," *Nezavisimaia gazeta* November 4, 1992, 2.

man of the Russian Supreme Soviet, told Russian deputies to the Tatarstan parliament that "right now is the time when it must be clearly ascertained whether or not Tatarstan is leaving the Russian Federation."[66] It brought appeals and pressure from the Yeltsin administration and the Russian Congress of People's Deputies and wild claims from the Moscow media that the end of Tatarstan's long union with Russia was within sight.

Shaimiev's decision to accept only observer status within the Russian Council of the Federation, because his republic had not signed the Federation Treaty, and then his boycott of the December 1993 referendum on the Yeltsin Constitution kept Moscow uncertain about his true intentions. In the words of one correspondent, "whether the republic is 'a region of the Russian federation' or not is something that no one today can say for certain."[67] Shaimiev created the impression that Russia and Tatarstan stood on the brink of a break and that Moscow had to "blink." As a result of his artful control of information about his true intentions Shaimiev received better terms from Moscow: in the very first power-sharing treaty with a republic (February 15, 1994) Russian conceded far more to Tatarstan than to any other republic in subsequent treaties.[68] For over a decade, Shaimiev so effectively controlled information released from his segment-state government that outsiders continued to debate whether he would actually have attempted to take his republic out of the Russian Federation.

Alternatively, competitive politics in a segment-state reveals information about alternative offers that different politicians would make. In the Russian nation-state crisis the terms in the powersharing treaties signed with the governments of republics with competitive polities were less favorable to the republics than the terms extracted by Shaimiev and the other hegemonic segment-state leaders.

Cascading Defections that Weaken the Common-State

In a segmented state, bargaining between common-state and segment-state leaders can set in motion a process of cascading preemptive acts by segment-state leaders that weaken the common-state government. The power of the common-state government over segment-states may simply wither away. This process is set in motion because segmental institutions create

---

[66] Radik Batyrshin and Tagir Agliullin, "Na sessii V S Respubliki sokhraniaetsia traditsionnoe protivostoianie," *Nezavisimaia gazeta* October 29, 1992, 1; Radik Batyrshin, "Parlament budet prinimat' novuiu konstitutsiiu," *Nezavisimaia gazeta* October 27, 1992, 3.

[67] Dmitrii Mikhailin, "Tatarstan vybral voinu konstitutsii?" *Rossiiskaia gazeta* November 11, 1992, 2.

[68] Radik Batyrshin, "Tatarstan ob"edinilisia s Rossiei," *Nezavisimaia gazeta* February 16, 1994, 1; Vladimir Todres, "Federativnyi dogovor otsluzhil svoe," *Segodnia* February 16, 1994, 1.

incentives for leaders of each segment-state to exploit the cooperation of the leaders of other segment-states—what is commonly called "free-riding."[69] That is, while other leaders observe the rules of the game, the defector or free-rider can pay less for (and/or extract a larger share of) the benefits created by the compliant behavior of others. Segment-state leaders face strong incentives to reduce their respective contributions to the provision of common goods and increase their shares of the benefits while others observe the rules and pay the price of maintaining the union.[70] For example, in the *perestroika* and Russian Federation nation-state crises some republic leaders sought to free-ride by withholding tax revenues owed to the common-state budget and by seizing control of common-state institutions generating rents on their territory. These segment-state leaders often used this income to ensure that common-state programs like public transportation and public health on their territory would be fully funded as overall expenditures were declining throughout the common-state.

Those who do not follow suit by also free-riding are suckers who continue to pay the price of maintaining the common-state while their benefits from the common-state decline, while the others, who do not contribute, nevertheless draw above-average benefits.[71] In this way each such preemptive act affects the incentives and opportunities of the other segment-states to defect or free ride as well. Each of the "law-abiding" segment-state leaders has a tipping point at which the benefits of escalating actions exceed the benefits of continued law-abiding behavior; at this point the leader shifts from a strategy of acquiescing in the current allocation of decision rights to grabbing powers.[72] Each defection, which raises the costs and lowers the benefits of maintaining the union and lowers the costs of leaving, moves yet another segment-state government past its "tipping point."[73]

In the Eurasian nation-state crises, three types of defections from the existing allocation of decision rights worsened the position of those segment-state governments left behind upholding the existing constitutional order. First, in the purest sense of free-riding, some segment-states reduced their contributions to common policy while continuing to "consume" this public good. This increased the costs of maintaining the union and reduced the benefits for all who did not defect. For example, by withholding taxes collected on its territory, Tatarstan reduced the resources available in Moscow for national security, control of epidemics in the mid-Volga region, and environmental protection along the Volga River, but Tatarstan contin-

---

[69] Rabushka and Shepsle 1982, 76.

[70] Tedstrom 1991, 3.

[71] Sheehy 1990e; Treisman 1999, 203.

[72] Goldstein 1991.

[73] Schelling 1978, 101–2, 137–66; Kuran 1989; Hardin 1995, 146–47; Laitin 1998, 21–29; Rose-Ackerman 1981, 152–65.

ued to enjoy the public goods produced by these common-state policies. Second, some segment-states grabbed powers to set policy for the entire common-state, claiming decision rights that had previously been exercised in common. For example, Yeltsin's takeover of all-union institutions, including many remaining common-state ministries, in October and November 1991 came at the expense of the decision rights of other union republic leaders who had previously had a say in the all-union government. The third type of defection adversely affected some but not all who remained behind—the defection of allies in the policy process of the common-state. For example, when reformist segment-states stopped participating in all-union decision making, the position of the remaining reformers became untenable in the more conservative common-state forums. The withdrawal of the reformist Baltic republics from negotiations over a new union in late 1991 left reformist governments such as Russia in a minority facing a coalition of more conservative union republics, particularly those in Central Asia.

Such cascading defections weaken the government of the common-state. In the *perestroika* crisis Gorbachev responded to early preemptive grabs for power by allowing more decision rights to devolve onto the segment-states, but at some point the common-state government no longer had the means to enforce its will throughout the territory and population that were now only nominally within its jurisdiction.[74] By December 1991 Gorbachev found it easier to agree to the segment-state leaders' nation-state projects because this final step represented only a small marginal loss of decision rights; Gorbachev had little left to lose in decision rights by conceding sovereign independence to the segment-states. Moreover, Gorbachev no longer had the leverage to resist—and everyone knew this. The common-state government had allowed more decisions to devolve onto the segment-states, but at some point the common-state government no longer had the means to enforce its will against secessionist segment-state governments. Indeed, this is what the Belovezhskii Agreements, signed by Russia, Ukraine, and Belarus, ratified in December 1991; these did not dissolve the USSR government but simply confirmed that for all intents and purposes it had already mostly disappeared.

Ironically, Communism did not cause the common-state to wither away; segmentation did. The Soviet segmented state unraveled through a domino effect or cascading defections as each segment-state reduced its contribution and grabbed for more powers at the expense of the common-state; each defection and grab for power inspired still other segment-states to

---

[74] Michael Hechter (2000) argues that it is the imposition of direct rule after a period of indirect rule that produces nationalist revolt. Yet in all three communist federations the demand for sovereignty came after movement toward greater indirect rule.

reduce their contributions and grab as much or more. The defection of first the Baltic states and then Georgia and Moldova made it harder for Belarus, Russia, and Ukraine to remain within a Soviet Union that would be dominated by Gorbachev and the Central Asian union republics. The secession of the three Slavic union republics meant that even the Central Asian states found it more attractive to leave the USSR. Even if no leader had chosen to dissolve the USSR, the cumulative effect of each following this logic of defection led to exactly that.

PART FOUR

Outcomes: Crises and Independence

NINE

Which Nation-State Projects Create Crises?

P**REVIOUS CHAPTERS REFRAME** the question with which this book began. The question implied in the title, where do nation-states come from? becomes two questions that empirical social science can address. First, which nation-state projects are likely to reach the bargaining table with leaders of an existing state and to become the focus of a nation-state crisis? Second, which of these nation-state projects are likely to succeed at creating a sovereign nation-state? The answers offered up to this point have emphasized that some nation-state projects are set apart and above others because segment-states empower their proponents with the means to coordinate national identities, coöpt or suppress competitors, and coerce common-state governments. The development of the segmental institutions thesis up to this point has focused on politics within segment-states and between segment-state and common-state governments, but has stopped just short of a systematic accounting of the outcomes of this politics—particularly in nation-state crises and new independent nation-states. In part 4 the discussion turns to these outcomes. This chapter introduces hypotheses that are derived from the propositions in previous chapters and explain which nation-state projects reach the bargaining table with the leaders of existing states and become the focus of nation-state crises. It also includes the results of statistical tests of these hypotheses. Chapter 10 introduces hypotheses and statistical tests that explain which of the projects succeed at becoming sovereign nation-states.

Up to this point the evidence has been limited, for the most part, to the Eurasian states. This chapter begins with a systematic overview of the patterns of nation-state crises in Central Eurasia from 1987 to 1997. Yet data from the Eurasian cases at the end of the twentieth century inevitably raise the question of whether these findings "travel"—whether this pattern applies to other decades of the age of nationalism and to other parts of the world. The Eurasian data for the last two decades of the twentieth century in particular handicap any analysis that stresses the presence or absence of segment-states because there was such saturation of the USSR and its successor states by segmental institutions; few indigenous ethnic groups did not have a segment-state. Thus, the discussion in this chapter draws on two additional sets of comparisons to broaden the analysis. The first is a temporal comparison of these post-Soviet cases with pre-Soviet cases in the same Eurasian region. The second includes global comparisons involving all major ethnic groups in the independent countries of the world throughout the latter half of the twentieth century.

The present chapter distinguishes nation-state projects that succeed in creating nation-state crises. The task of devising a list of cases for comparison—a list that includes not only nation-state projects that get heard but also nation-state projects that fail to get heard—poses a thorny problem. Many of the projects that are not heard remain as invisible to the analyst as to the leaders of governments. Thus, in the tests in this chapter I will follow a common convention—as inadequate as it might be—and begin with ethnic groups as candidates for nation-state projects. Many analysts, both primordialists who see ethnicity as an inherited identity and instrumentalists who see ethnicity as a chosen identity, begin from the assumption that ethnic groups are the bases for nations. Thus, Walker Connor describes nations as "self-differentiating ethnic groups."[1] Paul Brass defines a nation "as a particular type of ethnic community, or, rather, as an ethnic community politicized."[2] It is probably true that within almost every ethnic group except the most isolated there are dreamers who imagine the group as a nation with a state of its own. Thus, analysis of which ethnic groups create nation-state crises is a good first cut at answering the central question of this chapter. It is, however, important to keep in mind two caveats: nation-state projects are often made on behalf of people, such as the Mountain-People project in the North Caucasus, that are today considered multiethnic; indeed, many successful nation-state projects are made on behalf of multiethnic nations. And in the past, the invention of an ethnic myth that brought ethnic homogeneity to the nation typically followed rather than preceded the creation of the nation-state. With these caveats the purpose of this chapter is not to identify all the factors that lead to nation-state crises involving ethnic groups but to treat ethnic groups as only one type of candidate for nation-state projects, and to assess the role of segment-states in their genesis.

Hypotheses

The segmental institutions thesis begins from the observation that our fertile imaginations have spawned many more nation-state projects than the few hundred that have claimed the attention of leaders of existing states and created nation-state crises. Normally in their appeals to common-state leaders, proponents lack the means and opportunity to press their nation-state projects onto the bargaining table. Most authors of nation-state proj-

---

[1] Connor 1972, 327–28, 334.
[2] Brass 1991, 20.

ects remain pathetically obscure and ignored by almost all. Those claimants may be even more passionate about their causes and they may press claims that would change even more than the projects that get heard, but their inability to gain access to the bargaining table with the common-state leaders means their voices go unheard in the redesign of state institutions.

The bargaining model used to analyze the Eurasian nation-state crises focuses our attention on the impact of institutions on the relationship between the leaders of the common-state and the proponents of various nation-state projects. The segmental institutions thesis identifies segmental institutions as an important factor in creating the motive, means, and opportunity to press nation-state projects onto the bargaining table with common-state leaders. The segmental institutions thesis leads to the expectation that we should observe a simple but overwhelming pattern: the nation-state projects for populations with segment-states are far more likely to result in nation-state crises. The simple counterfactual claim implied by this is that if they had been empowered by segment-states, the authors of nation-state projects that did not get heard would have been much more likely to provoke nation-state crises. Hence,

Hypothesis 1. The likelihood that bargaining between proponents of nation-state projects and common-state leaders will escalate to a nation-state crisis rises when the proponents control a segment-state.

On one hand, these institutions create means, motive, and opportunity for claimants to escalate the *stakes* in bargaining with common-state leaders (see chapter 7). In particular, segmental institutions create an incentive for segment-state leaders to privilege their claims by playing the "sovereignty card," so that these leaders come to demand the right to allocate all decision rights that pertain to their segment-state. On the other hand, segmental institutions also empower the leaders of segment-states with the *means* to back up their rising demands with rewards and punishments (see chapter 8). Of course, the incentive to escalate means is closely linked to the incentive to escalate stakes: the greater the ability of the segment-state leaders to inflict losses on the common-state leaders and the greater the ability of the segment-state leaders to accept losses from retaliation, the more the segment-state leaders can demand in concessions.

Alternative Forms of Statehood

State formations that are similar to segment-states in creating political identity hegemony should also increase the likelihood that a nation-state project will get to the bargaining table and create a nation-state crisis. Independent statehood prior to incorporation of an ethnic group in a new common-state, such as Estonian independence between 1918 and 1940, can coordinate identities and create institutions for the mobilization of collective action that survive subsequent rule by others, a situation that might be called "the conquered nation-state syndrome." The resemblance of the conquered nation-state to the segment-state is particularly strong when statehood was recent rather than a remote historic event and the prior state had created political-identity hegemony and institutional resources (such as churches or social networks) that survived conquest. Hence,

> *Hypothesis 1a.* The likelihood that bargaining between proponents of a nation-state project and common-state leaders will escalate to a nation-state crisis rises when the nation-state imagined by the project existed immediately prior to incorporation into the common-state.

Alternatively, the existence of a nation-state elsewhere, such as Norway for Norwegians living in the United States, is likely to reduce pressure for a second nation-state and reduce the willingness of common-state leaders to accede to such demands. Hence,

> *Hypothesis 1b.* The likelihood that bargaining between the proponents of a nation-state project and common-state leaders will escalate to a nation-state crisis declines when the nation has a remote state of its own outside the common-state.

The latter hypothesis does not address the problem of adjacent nation-states that might become the source of irredentism. It also leaves open the prospect that proponents of a nation-state project may attempt to distinguish their nation from the homeland population, such as distinguishing the Moldovan nation-state project from the Romanian nation-state project or the Kosovar nation-state project from the Albanian nation-state project.

Weakened Common-State Governments

Where the common-state government is weakened by division and turmoil or by constitutional transitions, bargaining between proponents of nation-state projects and common-state leaders is much more likely to escalate to a nation-state crisis (see chapter 8). Hence,

> *Hypothesis 1c.* The likelihood that bargaining between proponents of nation-state projects and common-state leaders will escalate to a nation-state crisis rises when the common-state government is weakened by political turmoil or constitutional transition.

A weak extension of this proposition is that regime type may affect the strength or weakness of the common-state. Strong autocracies deprive politicians outside the central leadership of organizational resources and give common-state leaders severe sanctions to use against opponents. In strong autocracies, bargaining between proponents of nation-state projects and common-state leaders is less likely to escalate to a nation-state crisis.[3] Hence,

Hypothesis 1c'. The likelihood that bargaining between proponents of nation-state projects and common-state leaders will escalate to a nation-state crisis is lower under a strong autocratic common-state government.

There is, however, reason to be skeptical that regime type alone is a consistent predictor of the balance of leverage. Many autocracies, particularly personalistic regimes, are not institutionally strong. Institutionalized democracies, such as France or the United Kingdom, have some of the strongest common-state governments.

Socioeconomic Constraints on Leverage

Other constraints that interact with these institutional constraints and affect the likelihood of escalation to a nation-state crisis include the demographic balance and cultural distance (see chapter 8). First, as the size of the population mobilized by the nation-state project rises relative to the size of the population mobilized by the common-state, the balance of leverage becomes more favorable for the claimants and the likelihood of a nation-state crisis rises. Second, cultural differences between the ethnic group and the rest of the population of the common-state increase the likelihood of divergent development and the likelihood that the issues on the bargaining table associated with the nation-state project will come close to a zero-sum conflict, with few if any mutually acceptable compromises. Of course, favorable demographic or cultural constraints cannot be mobilized without organizational capabilities; the backing of a segment-state should magnify the affect of favorable demographic and cultural factors. Hence,

Hypothesis 1d. The likelihood that bargaining between proponents of a nation-state project and common-state leaders will escalate to a nation-state crisis rises as the population of the imagined nation grows relative to the population of the rest of the common-state.

Hypothesis 1d'. The growing likelihood of escalation as the bargaining partners approach demographic parity is significantly steeper when the proponents of the nation-state project are empowered with a segment-state.

[3] Compare Riggs 1995.

Hypothesis 1e. The likelihood that bargaining between proponents of a nation-state project and common-state leaders will escalate to a nation-state crisis rises when the imagined nation is culturally separated from the rest of the population of the common-state.

Hypothesis 1e'. The likelihood of escalation between culturally heterogeneous bargaining partners is greater still when the proponents of the nation-state project are empowered with a segment-state.

These hypotheses describe patterns that should be observable when we look at many cases side by side. In the next three sections I use three different data sets to see whether these patterns do indeed appear. The startling finding is the overwhelming and consistent strength of the statistical relationship between segment-states and the occurrence of nation-state crises.

Post-Soviet Patterns, 1987–1997

The ways in which segment-states come to dominate ethnic politics is illustrated by the patterns of nation-state crises in the USSR and its successor states during the decade from July 1987 through June 1997. The proponents of nation-state projects who controlled segment-states had a clear advantage in getting their demands on the public agenda. Segment-state leaders became the dominant spokespersons for the ethnic groups and exercised unique control over the expression of nation-state agendas within the borders of their territories. The issues they pressed to the bargaining table with their common-state leaders stressed the decision rights allocated to the segment-states.

Model Specification

I turn to a statistical procedure called logit analysis to test the previous hypotheses and to estimate the impact of segmental institutions on the likelihood that nation-state projects on behalf of an ethnic group will become the focus of a nation-state crisis. This enables me to estimate the probability that bargaining between ethnic group and common-state leaders will escalate to a nation-state crisis, and to estimate the influence on this probability of such constraints as the empowerment of the leaders of an ethnic group with a segment-state.

The unit of analysis (that is, a case or observation) is the dyadic relationship between the state and an ethnic group (such as the Russian Federation–Bashkir dyad). The data set includes all those dyads in which the ethnic group had at least 5,000 members within the state; this is the equivalent of a small city or several villages and represented between 0.003 percent of the total population of the Russian Federation and 0.3 percent of the population of Estonia in 1989.[4] Bargaining between an ethnic group and the USSR government and bargaining between the same ethnic group and its union republic government are recorded as separate observations; nation-state crises often emerged in one bargaining relationship but not the other.[5] In total, the database includes 349 dyads.

The dependent variable is a dichotomous indicator of the existence of a nation-state crisis in a dyad, begun by either the common-state government or proponents of nation-state projects. The issues in these crises include all statehood issues such as creation of a new segment-state, elevation of an existing segment-state, and demands for autonomy, irredentism, or secession. This includes only conflicts that escalated into public view and claims by one side that brought a response from the other. It excludes conflicts that were so minor that they remained private affairs and claims by one side that were ignored by the other, such as appeals by isolated intellectuals for their pet nation-state projects. This also excludes communal conflicts, such as the violence between villages of different ethnic groups in the Fergana Valley or private pogroms against Armenians in Kazakhstan. The data are drawn from more than 50,000 Radio Free Europe news reports and Foreign Broadcast Information Service transcriptions.[6] It is unlikely that nation-state crises that engaged both common-state leaders and ethnopoliticians escape this data set.

The model to be operationalized and estimated is of the following form:

$$C_{pe} = \theta \, (S_{pe}, \, M_{pe}, \, A_{pe}, \, P_{pe}, \, U_{pe}),$$

where

C_{pe} indicates a nation-state crisis between the government of polity p and ethnic group e,
S_{pe} indicates whether ethnic group e had a segment-state within polity p,
M_{pe} indicates that ethnic group e was a cultural minority in polity p,
A_{pe} indicates acculturation of ethnic group e within polity p,

---

[4] This excludes observations for each of the fifteen titular nationalities within its respective union republic, but includes these nationalities in other union republics and in the USSR. That is, there is no Armenia–Armenian dyad, but there are Azerbaijan–Armenian and USSR–Armenian dyads.

[5] Another ten dyads for particularly small ethnic groups are dropped owing to missing information that was not reported in the 1989 census.

[6] The data are posted at weber.ucsd.edu/~proeder. The data for dependent variables were checked against Ted Robert Gurr's (2001) Minorities at Risk project, James Minahan's (1996, 2002) encyclopedias of contemporary nationalist movements, and Peter Wallensteen and Margaret Sollenberg's (1998; SIPRI 1987–1997) data on armed conflicts.

P_{pe} is the proportionate size of the population of ethnic group e within polity p, and

U_{pe} is the proportion of ethnic group e in polity p living in urban areas.[7]

In this model two separate dichotomous variables (the operationalizations of S_{pe}) indicate whether the ethnic group had a segment-state (union republic, autonomous republic, autonomous oblast, or autonomous okrug) in the specific polity and whether the ethnic group was a subordinate group within a multiethnic segment-state. Two separate dichotomous variables for cultural distance (the operationalizations of M_{pe}) indicate whether the ethnic group and the majority of the polity spoke languages that belong to different linguistic groups (such as Romance versus Slavic groups) and whether they traditionally practiced religions that belong to different civilizations as defined by Samuel P. Huntington.[8] Acculturation is estimated by the proportion of the ethnic group in the polity claiming to be fluent in the language of the majority (A_{pe}).[9] Because the dependent variable is dichotomous, I use the estimation procedure of logit analysis.

Estimation Results

Throughout the decade from July 1987 through June 1997, escalation of bargaining between state leaders and ethnopoliticians into a public nation-state crisis took place in 95 of the 349 dyads. Of these crises, thirteen involved some violence, yet only three (Azerbaijan-Armenians, Georgia-Abkhazians, and Russia-Chechens) reached the magnitude that international relations scholars typically classify as a civil war—that is, 1,000 battle-related deaths in a single year. Another four (Georgia-Ossetians, Moldova-Russophones, USSR-Armenians, and USSR-Azeris) had at least twenty-five battle-related deaths in a single year, qualifying as one of the scholars' "minor armed conflicts."[10]

The statistical model in table 9.1 is quite successful. It correctly classifies more than 89 percent of the dyads, with mistaken predictions of crises in 3.4 percent of the cases and mistaken predictions of no crises in 7.2 percent of the cases. The coefficient estimates for segment-states and relative population size are particularly strong. The probabilities of a nation-state crisis in a state–ethnic group dyad under different constraints appear in table

---

[7] The data for ethnic group populations in each segment-state, urbanization of ethnic group populations in each segment-state, and rate of fluency in the titular language of the segment-state are from the 1989 Soviet census; see USSR 1992.

[8] Huntington 1996. Data are from Tishkov 1994; Wixman 1984.

[9] There appears to be no collinearity among independent variables; no two independent variables are correlated above 0.50.

[10] Wallensteen and Sollenberg 1998.

TABLE 9.1
Soviet and post-Soviet nation-state crises with ethnic groups,
1987–1997 (logit estimates)

	Coefficient	(z)
Segment-state	4.968***	(7.87)
Secondary in multiethnic segment-state	−2.318***	(−4.05)
Ethnic group's relative population size	13.861***	(3.69)
Urbanization of ethnic group population	0.077	(0.08)
Linguistically remote ethnic group	1.334	(1.81)
Religiously remote ethnic group	−1.620**	(−2.89)
Acculturation of ethnic group	−0.777	(−1.16)
Constant	−3.035**	(−3.12)
Statistics:	$N = 349$	
	$\chi^2 = 213.17$	
	Pseudo-$R^2 = 0.522$	

Significance: ** $p < .01$; *** $p < .001$.

9.2. (These are derived by the Clarify procedure of King, Tomz, and Wittenberg [2000] from the estimation results reported in table 9.1.) The table shows how this probability of a nation-state crisis varied depending on whether the dyad was divided by culture and whether the ethnic group had a segment-state. In each of these probabilities the ethnic group is otherwise "average"—that is, the ethnic group's relative population size, urbanization, and acculturation are set at the mean level for each variable. In dyads in which the ethnic group was similar in language and religion to the rest of the common-state population and the group had no segment-state, the probability of a nation-state crisis was only .048 (table 9.2).[11]

The impact of segmental institutions dwarfed other constraints, highlighting the prediction in hypothesis 1. The otherwise average ethnic group with a segment-state was five to twenty-seven times as likely to be engaged in a nation-state crisis as a similar ethnic group without a segment-state (compare the second column of probabilities with the first in table 9.2).

Cultural distance had only a small impact on the escalation of conflict to a nation-state crisis. Linguistic distance increased the likelihood of nation-state crises, as predicted by hypothesis 1e, yet this relationship is not statistically significant at the .05 level (table 9.1). Linguistic acculturation of an ethnic group to the language of the majority had no statistically significant effect on the likelihood of a nation-state crisis. Alternatively, reli-

---

[11] To estimate these probabilities I use the procedure Clarify developed by G. King, Tomz, and Wittenberg 2000. In these equations for "otherwise average ethnic groups" all variables are set to the mean values.

TABLE 9.2

Probabilities of Soviet and post-Soviet nation-state crises, 1987–1997

Cultural distance of ethnic group from majority in common-state	Ethnic group without segment-state (probability)	Ethnic group with segment-state (probability)
Culturally proximate	.048	.824
	(.010–.141)	(.518–.970)
Linguistically but not religiously remote	.141	.949
	(.080–.226)	(.854–.988)
Both linguistically and religiously remote	.034	.807
	(.012–.080)	(.656–.912)

Note: The probabilities are derived from the equation in table 9.1 using Clarify (King, Tomz, and Wittenberg 2000). Figures in parentheses represent the 95 percent confidence interval.

gious difference had a statistically strong relationship with nation-state crises, but just the opposite of what culturalist theorists might predict. Ethnic groups that had a pre-Soviet religious tradition that belonged to a different civilization than the majority's tradition were less, not more, likely than culturally proximate ethnic groups to be parties to a nation-state crisis (table 9.1). This may reflect other (particularly institutional) factors that are not included in the equation but are correlated with religious traditions. The tighter controls that remained in place in most Islamic regions and the loyalty of their Communist Party leaders limited the independent mobilization of this cultural difference that could have threatened the segment-state leaders. When mobilization of religious constituencies took place it tended not to present a new nation-state project, but to seek control of an existing nation-state. When taken together with the results for linguistic proximity, these results underscore the importance of segmental institutions in deciding which cultural differences are mobilized into nation-state crises—a finding that is consistent with hypothesis 1e'.

There was power in numbers, as predicted in hypothesis 1d. In the absence of a segment-state, the likelihood of a crisis rose rapidly with the ethnic group's proportion of the state's population once it was above 20 percent (figure 9.1): for the average-size ethnic group—1.6 percent of the common-state population—this probability was .011, but for an ethnic group that constituted 33 percent of the population, this probability was .468.

Discussion

The statistical findings concerning the likelihood of nation-state crises involving ethnic groups with segment-states are consistent with a substantial body of scholarship on the transition from communism. Since the begin-

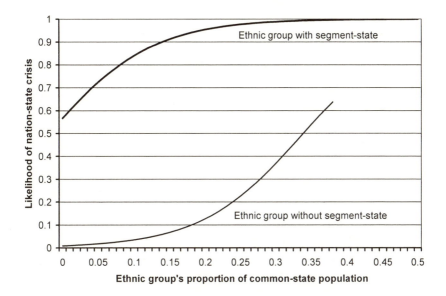

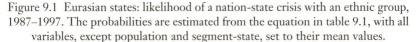

Figure 9.1 Eurasian states: likelihood of a nation-state crisis with an ethnic group, 1987–1997. The probabilities are estimated from the equation in table 9.1, with all variables, except population and segment-state, set to their mean values.

ning of nationalist challenges to Moscow, a recurring theme has been the importance of what have been labeled here as segment-states. For example, in a 1991 article that is, in a sense, the beginning of the present book, I argued that in the early *perestroika* period, union republic leaders exercised such decisive control over mobilizational resources that they could determine whether protest would be large-scale and sustained or simply sporadic.[12] In a splendid juxtaposition, Valerie Bunce gives these segmental arrangements the apt label *subversive institutions*.[13] Looking beyond the Soviet experience, Bunce demonstrates how ethnonational federations generated similar patterns of nation-state crises in the other socialist federations of Yugoslavia and Czechoslovakia. In an article the same year I presented statistical data that showed a pattern similar to that reported above, but for ethnic groups in all twenty-eight postcommunist states: segmental institutions were associated with significantly more and more intense ethnopolitical crises. Relative population size was also important, but segmental institutions made even relatively small ethnic groups political giants.[14]

More recently, in a superb analysis of demonstrations and protests in the USSR and its successor states between June 1987 and December 1992,

[12] Roeder 1991, 1998.
[13] Bunce 1999.
[14] Roeder 1999.

Mark Beissinger reported results that confirm the power of segmental institutions. He found, for example, that union republic status increased the likelihood of separatist mobilization within an ethnic group by over 1,800 percent. He notes that relative population size was also important alongside this.[15] (Interestingly, he finds that linguistic assimilation was important, but this may be due to the smaller number of ethnic groups in his analysis.) He cautions that ethnofederalism "was much more likely to structure elite rather than mass behavior," but adds that mass mobilization was often associated with major elite conflicts such as republican-union confrontations over legislation or elections.[16]

Despite this strong confirming evidence from earlier research, two caveats are in order. First, as important as nationalist mobilization is in its own right, it offers only limited insight into the question of which nation-state projects within the USSR achieved sovereign independence. Not all nation-state crises ended in a new sovereign state, and the successful nation-state projects were not necessarily those that mobilized the most extensive or intense collective action. In addition, as Beissinger's data show quite starkly, there was actually a secular decline in participation in demonstrations from its peak in 1988.[17] As the crisis became more intense, mass mobilization became less common. Nor can demonstrations be very good indicators of a rise in secessionist consciousness, since as demonstrations were declining, a secessionist consciousness was apparently rising in 1990 and 1991. Rather than relying on Beissinger's formulation that demonstrations led to the "institutionalization of secessionist consciousness in new republican governments," the segmental institutions thesis argues that demonstrations were an early technique used by some segment-state leaders to support their bargaining with common-state leaders, but soon segment-state leaders found more effective means to escalate their pressure. Second, the Soviet and post-Soviet cases are too limited in time for there to have been much variation in segmental institutions over time that permit a test whether the introduction of the institutions was the cause rather than simply a covariate of the nation-state crises. Further, as Beissinger prudently warns, in any analysis of the Soviet cases we are limited because ethnofederal structure was closely associated with other variables: "Thus, a perspective which emphasized the influence of the ethnofederal system on mobilization without taking into consideration the impact of these other factors would be misleading."[18] An analysis that is limited to the Soviet cases in this short time frame cannot untangle these factors. We need to expand

[15] Beissinger 2002, 209–14; also see Beissinger's results on 110–11, 114–15.
[16] Beissinger 2002, 122, 136–41, 235.
[17] Beissinger 2002, 77–78, 105, 160, 165, 254ff.
[18] Beissinger 2002, 120.

our analysis to other cases with a longer time frame and more independent variation among independent variables. That is the purpose of the next two batteries of tests in this chapter.

Before Segmentation, 1917–1921

One way to expand the analysis temporally is to compare the pattern of nation-state crises and ethnic conflict found in 1987–97 with that found seventy years earlier before the establishment of the Soviet segmented state. The critical causal role of segmentation in privileging some nation-state projects over others is illustrated by three comparisons between 1917–21 and 1987–97. The first highlights nation-state projects that were not prominent in the earlier years but became prominent in the later years after being privileged by segment-states. The second highlights nation-state projects that were prominent in the earlier years but were not heard again after seventy years of segment-states that disfranchised these projects in favor of others. The third identifies ethnic candidates that simply failed to develop nation-state projects over the seventy years in which they were disfranchised by segmental institutions.

Projects before Segment-States, 1917–1921

The first comparison highlights nation-state projects that were successful at getting their claims on the bargaining table after 1987, after they had been privileged for decades as segment-states, but failed to mobilize significant support before the creation of segment-states, particularly during the Russian Revolution in 1917. The evidence presented in chapter 4 reveals an important pattern: in the earlier years, authors of the nation-state projects without segment-states were typically isolated intellectuals with far less popular support than in 1987–97. Authors of nation-state projects had to compete with the authors of other projects to unite and divide the population in various ways. In 1917–21 the proponents of nation-state projects that were ultimately heard after 1987 but that lacked segment-states prior to 1917 were usually drowned out by the cacophony of proliferating projects.

The limited role of nationalism in the public at large is manifested in the patterns of protest within the stratum that romantic nationalists typically saw as the reservoir of distinctive national traditions, the peasantry. The pattern of peasant revolutionary activity after the fall of the imperial regime and before the victory of the Bolsheviks in Petrograd shows very little connection to ethnic differences. This becomes apparent in a simple statistical test.[19] The dependent variable is the number of incidents of collective revolutionary action (I_p)—or, as the Provisional Government authorities categorized them, "transgressions of the law" (*pravonarusheniia*)—by peasants in each of forty-seven provinces in European Russian between March and September 1917 (figure 9.2).[20] The raw data include incidents of forced renting of land to peasants; forced dismissal of hired and war-prisoner labor working noble lands; peasant prohibitions on the cutting and removal of forests by landowners; confiscations of harvests, agricultural inventories, forests, meadows, arable land, or whole estates; and arson and destruction of estates. To estimate these incidents, the administration in Petrograd collected regular reports from the provisional government's provincial and county commissars, supplemented by sporadic complaints from landowners, factory managers, and other private citizens. The total number of incidents recorded in the forty-seven provinces is 3,370; this ranged from one in Olonets province to 233 in Kazan province.

The model to be estimated by statistical procedures is of the following form:

$$I_p = \theta \ (W_p, N_p, M_p, D_p, P_p),$$

where

I_p is the number of incidents of peasant revolutionary action in province p,
W_p is peasant household wealth in province p,
N_p is inequality in landholding in province p,
M_p is the proportion of the rural population of province p that belongs to various minority cultural groups,
D_p is the cultural division of labor in the countryside of province p, and
P_p is the rural population of province p.

The estimation procedure is simple OLS regression. The dependent variable is the natural logarithm of the number of incidents, so that the predicted number of incidents is never negative and each additional incident in a province is less significant than the previous. Because the administration was still in formation in March and data collection was therefore somewhat erratic, I use only the figures for the six months from April to September 1917. The measure of peasant household wealth (W_p) is the ratio of the average peasant household's landholding allotment (*nadel'*) to the amount of land necessary to produce a subsistence minimum for a house-

---

[19] Roeder 1982.

[20] This omits three European provinces (Courland, Grodno, and Kovno) for which the data are incomplete due to the war. These data are drawn from Iakovlev 1927.

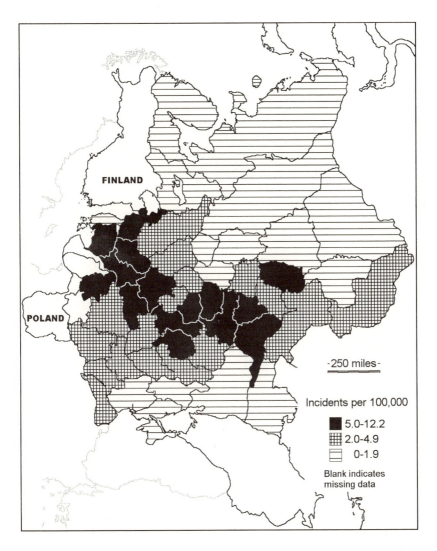

Figure 9.2 European Russia: incidents of peasant violence per 100,000 rural residents, April–September 1917. Figure based on data in Iakovlev 1927.

hold.[21] The measure of landholding inequality (N_p) is the proportion of all private and allotment land (*chastnaia i nadel'naia zemlia*) owned by members of the nobility or clergy.[22] The indicators of the presence of minority cultural groups (M_p) include, first, the proportion of the rural population belonging to each of the following ethnic groups—Ukrainians, Belorussians, Baltic peoples, or Turkic-Tatars. Each of these was a major player in the nation-state crises 70 years later. In an alternative formulation, the indicators of minority cultural groups include the proportion of the rural population belonging to each of the following minority religious communities—Roman Catholicism, Protestantism, and Islam. These were not major players seventy years later. The cultural division of labor in the countryside (D_p) is measured by differences in the ethnic composition of the peasantry and nobility in each province.[23]

The segmental-institutions thesis leads us to expect that in the absence of segment-states ethnic differences should not be strong predictors of the level of peasant revolutionary activity. Indeed, for the most part the proponents of nation-state projects failed to induce peasants to coordinate their claims in a common challenge to the Russian Empire. The major ethnic groups that were so prevalent seventy years later were virtually invisible in the pattern of peasant revolutionary activity in 1917.

The usual explanation for variation in the levels of peasant revolutionary activity focuses on the peasants' economic rather than ethnic grievances. In the statistical models this does a very good job indeed: the two measures of peasant wealth and inequality of landownership account for a significant

---

[21] The numerator is a measure of allotment production potential (in *puds*; 1 American ton = 55.38 puds) calculated by $a_p\Sigma(c_{ip}y_{ip})$, where a_p is the average peasant allotment size (in *desiatinas*; 1 = 2.26997 acres) in province p in 1905, c_{ip} is the proportion of sown area under crop i in province p (crops included are winter rye, spring wheat, barley, buckwheat, oats, potatoes, corn, peas, flax, and hemp from 1911 to 1915, so that $\Sigma c_{ip} = 1$); and y_{ip} is the average yield by weight (in puds) per unit of allotment land from crop i in province p from 1911 to 1915. The denominator is the subsistence minimum (in puds) estimated by $28.8f_p$, where 28.8 is the estimated weight (in puds) of produce necessary to feed one peasant, feed the livestock and poultry per head of rural population, and provide the coming sowing per head of rural population and f_p is the average family size in province p in 1897. Sources of data are Chuprov 1897; Russian Empire 1899–1905; Russian Empire 1916.

[22] Data from Russian Empire 1907.

[23] The index of cultural division of labor is calculated according to the formula: $\Sigma(n_{ep} - p_{ep})$, if $n_{ep} > p_{ep}$, where n_{ep} is the proportion of the nobility in province p belonging to ethnic group e and p_{ep} is the proportion of the peasantry in province p belonging to ethnic group e. Source of data is Russian Empire 1899–1905. The only severe collinearity ($r > 0.6$) is found in the correlation of ethnic composition of the population with religious composition of the population and so I do not include these in the same equations. Strong correlations do exist between the Baltic and Protestant regions, on one hand, and higher peasant wealth ($r = 0.584$ with Baltic and 0.574 with Protestant) and larger proportion of land held by the nobility ($r = 0.588$ with Baltic and 0.544 with Protestant) on the other hand.

part of the variance among provinces (table 9.3). The two economic variables yield significant coefficient estimates and account for much of the variance (R^2 = 0.602). Consider the otherwise average province—that is, one where the size of the rural population and the proportion of land held by the nobility are at the mean values. In this otherwise average province, as peasant wealth increased from its lowest to highest levels, the expected number of incidents rose from 6.4 to 70.2 incidents. As the proportion of land held by the nobility increased from its lowest to highest percentage in the otherwise average province, the expected number of incidents rose from 51.3 to 150.3 incidents.

Adding variables to account for the strength of minority populations in the countryside does not improve on this simple model. Adding to the previous equation the four variables for the proportion of the province's rural population that was Ukrainian, Belorussian, Baltic, or Turkic-Tatar does not yield any additional significant variables (table 9.3).[24] It is important to note that the Baltic provinces had unusually high levels of nobility ownership of land and, as a consequence, high levels of landlessness among peasants, so that there is potential for collinearity (r = 0.574). The other three coefficients associated with ethnicity are noteworthy for their low magnitude. This suggests that peasants from minority ethnic groups, such as Ukrainians and Belorussians or even Tatars and Bashkirs, were little different from ethnic Russian peasants in propensity to engage in revolutionary violence, when their economic conditions were similar.

This absence of coordination on nation-state projects to challenge the Russian state was particularly apparent in the reactions of the public at large to the attack on their homeland in World War I. Not only did much of the population rally behind the tsarist regime at the start of the war, but when war came to the Baltic region, for example, much of the population sought refuge deeper within the empire. An estimated 2.6 to 3.0 million refugees fled Latvia, Lithuania, and Polish territories for Russia proper. Lithuania was depopulated. By March 1917 more than two-thirds of the Latvian population had fled.[25] Rather than staying to fight for independent nation-states, they took refuge more deeply within what they believed was their homeland, the Russian Empire.

The third equation in table 9.3 shows that religious difference may have been somewhat more likely than ethnic difference to be associated with peasant revolutionary activity.[26] There is a hint that Roman Catholics (Poles, Lithuanians, and western Ukrainians) as well as Protestants (Estonians, Finns, Germans, and Latvians) were more likely to engage in revolu-

[24] Source of data is Russian Empire 1899–1905.

[25] Plakans 1995, 115–16; Pabriks 1999, 46.

[26] Source of data is Russian Empire 1899–1905.

TABLE 9.3

Russian peasant violence, April–September 1917 (regression estimates)

	Economics only		Economics and ethnicity		Economics and religion		Economics and cultural division of labor	
	Coefficient	t	Coefficient	t	Coefficient	t	Coefficient	t
Peasant wealth	−0.112***	(−3.78)	−0.134***	(−3.86)	−0.128***	(−3.55)	−0.117***	(−3.62)
Nobility landholdings	2.262**	(2.93)	1.088	(0.84)	0.700	(0.59)	2.070*	(2.29)
Rural population (ln)	0.814***	(4.01)	1.047***	(4.51)	1.049***	(4.12)	0.797***	(3.81)
Ukrainian population			0.521	(−1.28)				
Belorussian population			0.708	(1.10)				
Baltic population			1.219	(1.35)				
Turkic-Tatar population			0.264	(0.30)				
Roman Catholic population					2.256	(1.47)		
Protestant population					1.576	(1.42)		
Muslim population					−0.068	(−0.06)		
Peasant vs. noble ethnicity							0.237	(0.42)
Constant	−7.765 *	(−2.60)	−10.751**	(−3.26)	−10.828**	(−2.99)	−7.522*	(−2.45)
Statistics:	$n = 47$		$n = 47$		$n = 47$		$n = 47$	
	$R^2 = 0.602$		$R^2 = 0.654$		$R^2 = 0.629$		$R^2 = 0.604$	

Significance: $^*p < .05$; $^{**}p < .01$; $^{***}p < .001$.

tionary violence, but neither coefficient is statistically significant at the .05 level. Moreover, as the segmental institutions thesis stresses, even if religious difference was important in 1917, religious groups were not the major players and religious difference was not a primary divide in the nation-state crises after seventy years of segment-states. In the fourth equation a variable for the cultural division of labor in the countryside fails to yield a significant coefficient. Indeed, this is the weakest of the coefficients associated with any of the ethnicity variables.[27]

In short, the nation-state projects that were so powerful seventy years later played a minor role in shaping patterns of political action prior to the establishment of segment-states. Elites were typically fragmented by competing nation-state projects. Peasants were typically quite parochial in their concerns. Without segment-states to focus and coordinate identity and provide resources for mobilization, few of the nation-state projects that reached the bargaining table after 1987 were able to muscle their way to the head of the queue in 1917. (The exceptions to this are addressed in chapter 10.) This stands in contrast to the pattern after 1987, when the claims of nation-state projects dominated the demands of public protest. For example, according to Beissinger's categorization of 6,663 Soviet and post-Soviet demonstrations from January 1987 to December 1992, at least two-thirds of the demonstrations, which mobilized nine-tenths of all demonstrators, involved nationalist claims.[28] Beissinger finds very few revolting peasants seizing the lands of their oppressors. What a difference seventy years of segmentation could make.

Forgotten and Failed Projects

The second temporal comparison highlights nation-state projects that were prominent in 1917, often based on administrative structures that existed in the Russian Empire, were subsequently disfranchised in the Soviet state, and were unable to get their projects onto the bargaining table after 1987. These are not "dogs that didn't bark" after 1987, as it was common to refer to more passive ethnic groups, but dogs that by 1987 apparently had disappeared (although one must always qualify such judgments, because seemingly dead dogs may yet come back to bite).

As stressed elsewhere in this book, there were few strong nation-state projects in 1917 and even fewer that did not receive either independent states (Finland and Poland) or segment-states within the USSR. Central Asia provides three examples of exceptions—failed projects that were

---

[27] On the cultural division of labor, see Hechter 1975; Rogowski 1985.
[28] Beissinger 2002, 75–79.

largely forgotten after seventy years. The leading contenders for nation-hood prior to the Soviet period—Bukhara, Khiva, and Turkestan—did not become the focal point of nation-state crises after 1987. This is testimonial to the power of segment-states to empower some and disfranchise other nation-state projects. Interestingly, the Turkestan project in 1917 had flourished within an existing jurisdiction of the Russian Empire, but after its dismemberment in 1924, the Turkestan nation-state project became a "minority faith." In the 1990s, as Shirin Akiner notes, "There are some individuals who espouse the creation (or recreation) of a united Turkestan, but they have no organized infrastructure."[29] Similarly, the nation-state projects that kept alive the memory of Bukhara and Khiva remained as only the precious possessions of a few isolated intellectuals after the elimination of the segment-states. Regionalism, such as the localism found in Bukhara and Khorezm (Khiva) oblasts, continues in Uzbekistan, but since 1987 this has not come to focus on alternative nation-state projects.[30]

More profoundly, however, the third temporal comparison draws our attention to the far more numerous (and probably uncountable) candidates for nation-state projects that never moved beyond parlors and university classrooms, either in 1917 or after 1987. The segmental-institutions thesis implies the counterfactual claim that if the boundaries of segmental institutions had been drawn differently then these parlor and campus nations might have assaulted common-states. These are not simply "dogs that didn't bark," but "dogs that were never born"—or at least were born in such small litters of runts that they were overlooked. For example, the last imperial census, conducted in 1897, recorded thirty-nine Turkic and Muslim ethnic groups living within the Russian Empire.[31] These were all potential candidates for nation-state projects and nation-state crises, but those that were not empowered with segment-states were much more likely to be forgotten. Among the twenty-three Turkic or Muslim ethnic groups subsequently recognized in a segment state in the USSR, nineteen (83 percent) became parties to nation-state crises after 1987. Among the seven groups that were not empowered with segment-states but continued to be recognized as ethnic groups only two (28.6 percent) became parties to nation-state crises after 1987. Among the nine Turkic or Muslim groups that lost their official recognition as nationalities and were reclassified as parts of some other titular nationality within a recognized ethnic group only one (11.1 percent), the Talysh, became a party to a nation-state crisis. Although some dreamer may have advanced nation-state projects for the Karapa-pakhs, Kipchaks, Mishars, Sarts, Teptyars, and other largely forgotten peo-

[29] Akiner 1995, 66, 369. Also see Ritter 1985.
[30] Luong 2002, 51–101.
[31] Russian Empire 1899–1905.

ples, they failed to draw enough attention to provoke a crisis. By stark contrast, an additional five Turkic and Muslim nationalities were identified by the Soviet authorities after 1917 and empowered with segment-states; all of these became parties to nation-state crises after 1987.

In subsequent years there were countless other parlor and campus projects that would have recombined these Muslim and Turkic ethnic groups in various ways. Without segment-states these also went nowhere. In the Mid-Volga region, for example, these included the Idel-Ural project, which would unite Tatars, Bashkirs, and Chuvashes, or a project to divide the Chuvashes between Viryal (Northern Chuvash) and Anatri (Southern Chuvash) states. Among the Muslim and Turkic populations of the Caucasus a bewildering number of projects bubbled up and burst under the pressure of segment-states, including the project to unite all in a Mountain Republic; to unite Adygeis, Cherkesses, and Kabards in a Circassian nation; or to unite Balkars and Karachais in a larger Karachai-Balkar nation. A myriad of smaller, tribal groups were candidates for nation-state projects but never developed these because they were absorbed into larger segment-states that forged new nations. For example, the Malkar, Baksan, Byzygny, Chegem, and Kholam had not considered themselves one people before 1917 but were nevertheless classified as one Balkar nationality and placed within a Balkar segment-state in the 1920s; after seventy years of segmental institutions these smaller candidates failed to develop separate nation-state projects, but the Balkar nation did.[32] Lists of failed and forgotten projects could be multiplied many times over. All would point to the common conclusion that these alternative imagined communities failed to become the focus of nation-state crises after 1987 as a consequence of the decision to include their members within other nation-state projects empowered with segment-states.

Global Patterns

The evidence drawn from just the Eurasian space and even comparisons with other postcommunist regimes or with the pre-Soviet past raise the question whether these patterns are unique to ethnic politics in that one part of the world. Does close examination of the Eurasian experience identify global patterns that explain which nation-state projects for ethnic groups are likely to get to the bargaining table as nation-state crises? To answer this question I turn to a data set that covers almost all independent states of the world for forty-five years. On one hand, this permits examination of variation in many more variables (that were constants or correlated

[32] Wixman 1984, 126, 174.

with segmental institutions in the Eurasian cases). On the other hand, because the time period is limited, these data permit only correlational analysis rather than a quasi-experimental analysis of politics before and after introduction of segment-states. (For the latter, the close historical studies in the previous section are better.) Nonetheless, the data show a strong relationship between segment-states and nation-state crises.

Model Specification

The cases to be analyzed and compared are once again dyads that link governments and ethnic groups. The ethnic groups include all that constituted at least 1 percent of the country's total population or, in the largest countries, with a population over 20 million, that consisted of at least 200,000 members. (Because of limited data, this does not include the ethnic groups of colonies until they became independent states.) The observations for a dyad cover up to nine five-year periods beginning with January 1, 1955; a dyad is omitted from a time period if the country was not independent on the first day of the period. (An example of an observation is the Spain–Basques dyad in the 1960–64 time period.) The total number of observations in this analysis is 8,074. The 1,296 dyads include 658 ethnic groups around the globe within 153 independent states between 1955 and 1999.[33] Throughout this time period 238 dyads (18.4 percent of the 1296 dyads) experienced a nation-state crisis in at least one time period. This is a large enough population to test whether the conclusions about the consequences of segmental institutions can be generalized.[34]

[33] Twenty-five of these ethnic groups constitute aggregations of smaller indigenous groups, such as indigenous peoples in a few Latin American countries where the populations of individual groups are very small, Berbers in North African states, and Pygmies in Congo. To construct the list and populations of ethnic groups I used census data where available, but where census data were unavailable I relied on anthropologists' estimates of ethnic groups and their populations. The list of ethnic groups and their populations is derived from Bromlei 1988; Bruk 1986; Bruk and Apenchenko 1964; Levinson 1991; Minority Rights Group 1997; Moseley and Asher 1994; United Nations 1980, 1985, 1986, 1990, 1995; and individual country studies in the area handbook series commissioned by the Federal Research Division of the United States Library of Congress. The number of dyads in a single five-year period ranges from 508 for 1955–59 to 1,134 for 1995–99. To illustrate the selection process, looking at the 1980–84 period, the 1,042 dyads are a subset of 4,027 identified by these sources. Dropping countries that were not independent or that comprised fewer than 1 million people reduces the number to 3,682 dyads. Dropping ethnic groups that constituted less than 1 percent of the country's population or comprised fewer than 200,000 people in the largest countries reduces the number to 1,042 dyads. These 1,042 dyads that cross the size threshold accounted for an estimated 97.3 percent of the world's population in 1983.

[34] These data are posted on weber.ucsd.edu/~proeder.

The dependent variable is a nation-state crisis (C_{pe})—a public dispute between the central government and members of an ethnic group over the latter's claim to rights of self-governance (statehood).[35] The model is of the form:

$$C_{pe} = \theta\ (S_{pe}, I_{pe}, H_{pe}, T_p, R_p, P_{pe}, M_{pe}, G_p),$$

where

C_{pe} is a nation-state crisis between the government of polity p and ethnic group e,

S_{pe} indicates whether ethnic group e had a segment-state within polity p,

I_{pe} indicates whether ethnic group e had an independent state immediately prior to incorporation within polity p,

H_{pe} indicates whether members of ethnic group e had a nation-state or segment-state outside, but not adjacent to, polity p,

T_p indicates whether the government of polity p was in turmoil,

R_p indicates the regime type of polity p,

P_{pe} is the proportionate size of the population of ethnic group e within polity p,

M_{pe} indicates whether ethnic group e was a cultural minority in polity p, and

G_p is the gross domestic product per capita of polity p.

The statistical procedure I employ to estimate this model is once again logit analysis.

In this model three dichotomous indicators designate segmental institutions (S_{pe}): an ethnic group with a first-order segment-state (such as a union republic), an ethnic group with a second-order segment-state (such as an autonomous republic in the USSR), and a disfranchised ethnic group that is denied a segment-state within a common-state that grants other ethnic groups such status.[36] The variable for prior statehood (I_{pe}) indicates whether immediately prior to its incorporation or reincorporation within the current state the ethnic group had enjoyed statehood in the form of an independent state (e.g., Lithuanians in the USSR), wartime puppet state (e.g., Slovakians in Czechoslovakia), a protectorate (e.g., Tyvans in the USSR), a semistate during a civil war (e.g., Ukrainians in the USSR), or proto-state (e.g., Ashanti in Ghana).[37] The remote homeland variable (H_{pe}) indicates

---

[35] Sources of data are *Facts on File* 1955–2000; Gurr 2001; *Keesing's Record of World Events* 1955–2000; Minahan 1996, 2002; SIPRI 1987–2001; Wallensteen and Sollenberg 1998.

[36] Sources of data are Elazar 1994; *Europa World Yearbook* 1959–2001; *Statesman's Yearbook* 1955–2001.

[37] Sources of data are *Statesman's Yearbook* 1897–2001; *Encyclopaedia Britannica* 1910–22; Harding 1998.

whether the ethnic group had a nation-state or segment-state outside the common-state and not contiguous with the common-state during the time period. The variable for regime turmoil (T_p) is a dichotomous indicator: whether the common-state was in political turmoil or constitutional transition at the beginning of the time period.[38] Regime type (R_p) is two dichotomous indicators: whether the regime was an autocracy and whether the regime was a democracy at the beginning of the time period.

To estimate the impact of demographic, cultural, and economic constraints, the equations include three other independent variables. The equation includes the ethnic group's proportion of the country's total population (P_{pe}).[39] The cultural minority status variable (M_{pe}) indicates either linguistic or religious difference between the ethnic group and the country's majority: whether the ethnic group spoke a language that belongs to a different linguistic group (the first-order division of a linguistic phylum such as the Romance versus the Slavic language groups) or the ethnic group practiced a religion that belongs to a different civilization (e.g., Islam versus Orthodox Christianity) or a different sect (e.g., Shiite versus Sunni Islam).[40] To control for the possibility that the crises are all driven by problems of economic poverty, the equation also includes the country's gross domestic product per capita (natural logarithm) (G_p).[41]

The nature of the data in these equations leads to the suspicion that they violate the assumption of independence of observations in the logit model. That is, a nation-state crisis in one time period is likely to continue or recur in the same dyad in the next time period and a crisis in one dyad within a country is likely to occur in other dyads within the same country.[42] The models therefore incorporate two common remedies for dependence across time and within countries. First, the equations include eight panel dummy variables for time periods, as suggested by Nathaniel Beck, Jonathan Katz, and Richard Tucker.[43] (The separate dummy variables are omitted from the report of results in the tables.) Second, the estimation proce-

---

[38] Turmoil and regime type at the beginning of a five-year period are operationalized with data from the Polity scores in Marshall and Jaggers 2000. Polities in political turmoil or undergoing constitutional change have codes of −66, −77, or −88 in the year before the beginning of the time period. Democracies on the eve of a period have a polity score of 6 or higher in the year before the beginning of the period; autocracies have a score of −6 or lower.

[39] Sources of data are Bromlei 1988; Bruk 1986; Bruk and Apenchenko 1964. Data are interpolated and extrapolated at five-year intervals.

[40] The sources of data on the cultural practices of ethnic groups are Bruk 1986; Levinson 1991.

[41] The economic data are measured in U.S. dollars at 1990 prices and are taken from World Bank 2002 and supplemented by United Nations and CIA indicators where data are missing.

[42] For example, a Cook-Weisberg test for heteroskedasticity reinforces this concern; we can reject the null hypothesis of constant variance at the .001 level.

[43] Beck, Katz, and Tucker 1998.

TABLE 9.4

Nation-state crises with ethnic groups in 153 countries, 1955–1999 (logit estimates)

	Coefficient	$(z)^a$
First-order segment-state and prior state	2.41***	(4.34)
First-order segment-state, no prior state	1.64***	(4.79)
Prior state, no first-order segment-state	1.52**	(2.86)
Second-order segment-state	−0.59	(−0.98)
Disfranchisement	1.27*	(2.29)
Remote homeland	−3.12***	(−4.06)
Turmoil at beginning of period	0.37	(1.21)
Autocracy at beginning of period	−0.51	(−1.80)
Democracy at beginning of period	0.03	(0.09)
Proportion of population	4.44***	(3.33)
Cultural minority	1.12***	(4.72)
GDP per capita (*ln*)	1.17	(1.48)
Constant[b]	−4.22***	(−7.45)
Statistics:	$n = 8{,}074$	
	Wald $\chi^2 = 358.81$	
	Pseudo-$R^2 = 0.168$	

Significance: * $p < .05$, ** $p < .01$, *** $p < .001$.
[a] Based on Huber-White robust estimator of variance with clustering on country.
[b] Eight panel dummy variables for time periods t_2 to t_9 are omitted from this report.

dure uses the Huber-White robust estimates of variance with the assumption that observations cluster within countries. One problem for which there is no simple statistical solution is the endogeneity problem. Since most segment-states predate the first time period of this data set, it is not possible to engage in meaningful comparisons of the dyads before and after introduction of segmental institutions, as I have done in the close-up studies of the Central Eurasian cases. Alternative solutions, such as instrumental variables, are likely to introduce more new problems into the estimation, and so I have not turned to these.

Estimation Results

Around the globe segmental institutions were associated with a substantially greater likelihood of nation-state crises, as predicted by hypothesis 1. (See the estimation results in table 9.4.) The model correctly predicts 87 percent of the cases, but it has a bias toward overpredicting crises. That is, while the model's predictions of no nation-state crisis are 88 percent correct, its predictions of crises are only 54 percent correct.

Ethnic groups with segment-states were at least twice as likely as those without segment-states to be engaged in nation-state crisis. First, consider

TABLE 9.5
Probabilities of nation-state crises, 153 countries, 1955–1999

	Ethnic group without segment-state (probability)	Ethnic group with segment-state (probability)
Ethnic group (not a cultural minority) *without* prior statehood	.063 (.053–.075)	.254 (.204–.306)
Ethnic group (not a cultural minority) *with* prior statehood	.234 (.157–.329)	.421 (.331–.510)
Cultural minority *without* prior statehood	.171 (.150–.193)	.510 (.446–.572)
Cultural minority *with* prior statehood	.481 (.369–.589)	.689 (.612–.757)

Note: The probabilities are derived from equations identical to those in table 9.4 using Clarify (King, Tomz, and Wittenberg 2000), but without the panel dummy variables. Figures in parentheses represent the 95 percent confidence interval.

the case of bargaining that involved the "otherwise average" ethnic group that was not a cultural minority and had not had its own state immediately prior to its incorporation into its current common-state.[44] (See the probabilities in table 9.5, which are derived from equations identical to those reported in table 9.4, but without the panel dummy variables.) The likelihood of a nation-state crisis for an otherwise average ethnic group without its own segment-state was .063 in a five-year period, but for an otherwise similar ethnic group with a segment-state this probability was .254—that is, a one-in-four likelihood of a crisis. Second, consider the case of bargaining that involved the "otherwise average" ethnic group that was a cultural minority but had not had its own state immediately prior to its incorporation into the current state. The probability of a nation-state crisis in a five-year period was .171 for the ethnic group that did not have a segment-state, but it was .510—slightly better than even odds—for the ethnic group that had a segment-state. Third, consider the case of bargaining with cultural minorities with both a segment-state and prior statehood. The odds of a crisis at least once in a five-year period were better than two to one (.688).

These three conclusions are underscored by closer examination of the probabilities in table 9.5. First, creating a segment-state was like bringing a conquered country into the heart of the common-state. Bargaining with a segment-state was in every instance as likely as bargaining with a conquered nation-state to escalate to a nation-state crisis—probabilities of .254 versus .234 for the ethnic group that was not a cultural minority and .510

[44] The estimates of probabilities are derived with the Clarify procedure developed by G. King, Tomz, and Wittenberg 2000.

versus .481 for the cultural minority. In tests of the difference of the probabilities for prior statehood and present segment-state the null hypothesis
cannot be rejected; the probabilities for conquered nation-states and segment-states are probably identical.[45] Second, annexing a state and then preserving it as a segment-state compounds the risk of a nation-state crisis. In
bargaining between a common-state government and a cultural minority
that preserved its previous statehood through a segment-state, the likelihood of escalation to a nation-state crisis was .688, compared to.481 for
minorities that lost their statehood upon annexation. (This difference is
statistically significant at the .05 level.)

Another type of statehood that had just the opposite effect was the existence of a remote (nonadjacent) segment-state or nation-state, as predicted
in hypothesis 1b. Ethnic groups with such remote homelands were significantly less likely to become involved in nation-state crises with their new
common-state governments. The likelihood of a nation-state crisis for an
ethnic group that was a cultural minority but had a remote homeland was
near zero (.009).

The results once again show that there was also power in numbers, as
predicted by hypotheses 1d and 1d' (figure 9.3.) There was a significant
rise in the likelihood of a nation-state crisis associated with ethnic groups
that constituted a larger share of the country's population. As the ethnic
group approached half the country's population, the balance of numbers
in the bargaining relationship approached parity. Even in bargaining with
a cultural minority without a segment-state or previous statehood, as the
proportionate size of the ethnic groups grew, the probability of a nation-
state crisis rose to more than .500. The statistical results provide reason to
question the claim of hypothesis 1d' that there was an interaction effect
between population and segmental institutions that accelerated the effect
of relative population size on the likelihood of a nation-state crisis. Instead,
results of a reestimation suggest that segmental institutions and relative
population size are independent, additive effects on the balance of leverage.
The reestimation of both equations in table 9.4 introduced two variables
for relative population size, one for ethnic groups with segment-states and
the other for the ethnic groups without segment-states. In the equation for
the likelihood of a nation-state crisis, there is no difference between the
two coefficient estimates; the presence of segment-states does not acceler-
ate the effect of greater relative population size. Nonetheless, the presence
of segment-states is a substitute for small relative population size. Seg-

---

[45] These probabilities are estimated by the Clarify procedure from equations in which relative population size and gross domestic product are set to their mean values and all other
values are set to zero except for the variables under consideration, which are set to one.

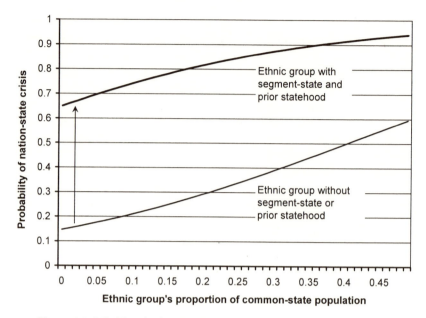

Figure 9.3 Likelihood of a nation-state crisis with an ethnic group, 153 independent countries, 1955–1999. The probabilities are estimated from the equation in table 9.4, with cultural minority set to 1, GDP per capita set to its mean value, and all other variables, except population, segment-state, and prior state, set to zero.

ment-states make even demographic Lilliputians into political giants in their power to provoke nation-state crises.

The major alternative hypotheses in the study of nation-state crises have long concerned the role of identity and cultural factors in the escalation of ethnonational conflicts. The segmental institutions thesis recognizes the importance of these factors (hypothesis 1e) but stresses the role of segmental institutions not only in the focusing of national identity, but also in the mobilization of identity groups (hypothesis 1e'). Although we cannot measure identities in any practical sense, the observable cultural markers of membership in language and religious communities give us some purchase on this sometimes vaporous issue. In table 9.4 a single cultural minority-status variable is positive and statistically significant at the .001 level. Yet the contradictory findings concerning the impact of religion and language in Eurasia and the lack of significant findings in the pre-Soviet cases suggest this needs closer examination. In table 9.6 the equations in table 9.4 are duplicated, but with two important changes. First, separate variables disaggregate the cultural minority variable into linguistic minority and religious minority status, and further disaggregate the latter into what have become known as civilizational divides (after Samuel P. Huntington's land-

TABLE 9.6
Influence of cultural difference and segmental institutions on the likelihood of
nation-state crises, 153 countries, 1955–1999 (logit estimates)

	Coefficient	$(z)^a$
Civilizational minority	0.55	(1.08)
With segment-state	3.59***	(7.93)
Sectarian minority	1.31***	(3.20)
With segment-state	c	
Ethnolinguistic minority	0.74**	(2.58)
With segment-state	2.02**	(2.96)
Civilizational and linguistic minority	1.20***	(3.39)
With segment-state	2.74***	(5.78)
Sectarian and linguistic minority	0.98*	(2.24)
With segment-state	3.08***	(4.81)
Not autonomous, but segmented state	1.05*	(2.17)
Second-order autonomy for group	−0.16	(−0.31)
Remote nation-state	−3.29***	(−4.44)
Country in turmoil on eve of period	0.39	(1.27)
Country autocratic on eve of period	−0.48	(−1.63)
Country democratic on eve of period	0.26	(0.77)
Proportion of country's population	4.61***	(3.63)
GNP per capita (*ln*)	0.72	(0.75)
Constant[b]	−3.69***	(−5.38)

Statistics:	$n = 8065$
	Wald $\chi^2 = 832.84$
	Pseudo-$R^2 = 0.148$

Significance: *$p < .05$, **$p < .01$, ***$p < .001$.
[a] Based on Huber-White robust estimator of variance with clustering on country.
[b] Eight panel dummy variables for time periods t_2 to t_9 are omitted from this report.
[c] All cases of sectarian difference with segment-state resulted in crisis.

mark work) and sectarian religious divides within civilizations.[46] The results
show that each dimension of cultural minority status increases the likelihood of a nation-state crisis. Second, the interaction of cultural minority
status and segmental institutions is tested by dividing each of these groups
of cultural minorities between those with segment-states and those without
segment-states. Consistent with hypothesis 1e', segmental institutions
magnified the effect of each cultural divide—and in every instance more
than doubled the coefficient. Returning to the probabilities shown in table
9.5, in bargaining with ethnic groups with no previous or current statehood
the likelihood of a nation-state crisis increased from .063 to .171 when
cultural-minority status difference is introduced. Yet it jumped to around

[46] See Roeder 2003.

TABLE 9.7

Summary of results: Predictors of nation-state crises

Hypotheses			Findings[a]			
	Constraint	Prediction	Post-Soviet cases		Worldwide	
1	Segment-state	+	+	.001	+	.001
1a	Prior statehood	+			+	.01–.001
1b	Remote statehood	−			−	.001
1c	Weak common-state	+			0	
1c'	Autocracy	−			0	
1d	Relative population	+	+	.001	+	.001
1d'	Interaction of 1 and 1d	+			0	
1e	Cultural difference	+	0/—[b]	.01	+	.001
1e'	Interaction of 1 and 1e	+			+	.001

[a] Pluses, minuses, and zeroes indicate positive, negative, or no statistically significant relationship; numbers indicate level of significance.

[b] Different results are found for linguistic and religious difference.

.500 when either previous statehood or current segment-state is also present. In short, the effect of segmental institutions appears to dwarf that of cultural divides.

Patterns in the Results

Around the world segmental institutions are linked to nation-state crises. The statistical tests in this chapter are consistent with most expectations in the hypotheses derived from the bargaining model and the Eurasian experience. These expectations and results are summarized in table 9.7. The presence of segment-states, as predicted by hypothesis 1, had a consistently strong, positive relationship with the occurrence of nation-state crises. Statehood immediately prior to incorporation in the current state, as predicted by hypothesis 1a, similarly increased this likelihood of crisis. Indeed, these first two variables indicating statehood tended to dwarf the other variables. Weakness in the government of the common-state had the relationship predicted in hypothesis 1c, but the statistical results were not significant. Regime type had an uncertain relationship with nation-state crises: the results are all in the expected directions but none is significant at the .05 level. Finally, the demographic and cultural constraints were strongly related to the likelihood of nation-state crises, as predicted by hypotheses 1d and 1e. Yet the impact of cultural difference varied with institutional environment, as predicted by hypothesis 1e'. Around the world the presence of segment-states was associated with significantly higher likelihood that common-state governments and ethnic groups divided by language or religion would be parties to a nation-state crisis.

Despite results that show a strong relationship between the presence of segment-states and the escalation of bargaining to nation-state crises, this moves us only part way to answering the question where nation-states come from. After all, few nation-state crises led to establishment of new states for the ethnic groups, and still fewer led to independence. In the period covered by the global data (1955–99), 238 dyads experienced a nation-state crisis at least once, yet only twenty-five new independent states were created by secession of territory from the metropolitan territory of an existing state.[47] Clearly, we need to look beyond nationalist mobilization of ethnic groups to explain where nation-states come from.

---

[47] In addition, sixty new first-order segment-states were created either by creating new states or by elevating existing jurisdictions.

TEN

Which Segment-States Become Nation-States?

IN THE SEARCH FOR ANSWERS to the question of where nation-states come from, the segmental institutions thesis stresses that it is not ethnic groups that become nation-states; it is segment-states. Thus, the thesis directs attention away from the usual focus on ethnic groups and their mobilization and toward circumstances under which segment-states are more likely to secede and become new, independent nation-states. More than 47 percent of the segment-states that existed between 1900 and 1990 became independent before 2000. Almost 80 percent of these segment-states that gained independence were simply elevated to independence without significant reconfiguration—for example, East Pakistan became Bangladesh. The remaining 20 percent were either combined into unions (as Cape Colony became part of the Union of South Africa in 1910) or adjoined to existing independent states (as Bosnia-Herzegovina was joined to Serbia in the formation of Yugoslavia in 1918). The segmental institutions thesis focuses our attention on the question, what conditions increase the likelihood that segment-states will become independent nation-states?

This chapter begins with hypotheses derived from the bargaining model and case studies in parts 2 and 3. It reexamines the Eurasian cases with a more systematic comparison of the pattern of outcomes for Soviet and post-Soviet segment-states, including successful independence, de facto and thwarted secessions, and continued inclusion in a common-state. The pattern in the Soviet and post-Soviet cases is so overdetermined, however, that in order to distinguish the effect of individual constraints, it becomes necessary to focus on the marginal cases. Even that approach leaves some ambiguity, and so it is necessary to expand the comparison set. A comparison between the segment-states of the late Soviet period and the segment-states of the Russian Empire seventy years earlier permits us to begin narrowing our focus to those conditions that have been most important in explaining the successful elevation of segment-states to independent nation-states. Nonetheless, a still wider comparison of cases is necessary to derive more precise estimates of the relative importance of the different constraints on the secession and independence of segment-states. Thus, a third comparison goes one step further to include all segment-states that existed around the world between 1900 and 1990. Of course, such a broad comparison permits less careful attention to the details of each individual case.

The patterns that are revealed by these comparisons underscore the importance of the balance of leverage between segment-state and common-state governments. In particular, they highlight the role of political-identity hegemony within segment-states and the weakening of the common-state government in bringing about a shift in this balance. They underscore that inclusion of segment-state populations in the politics of their segment-states but exclusion from the politics of the common-state can be a particularly explosive combination when it empowers segment-state leaders as autonomous "switchmen" who mediate between the segment-state population and the common-state. These patterns in the evidence also point to the role that outside allies can play in shifting the balance of leverage to one side or the other within the bargaining relationship between common-state and segment-state leaders, but this is a role that is more important in preventing a reversal of a bid for independence than in initiating the bid in the first place.

Hypotheses

In the bargaining model a primary change leading to the elevation of some segment-states to independence is a shift in the balance of leverage between common-state and segment-state leaders toward the latter. That is, the likelihood that segment-state leaders will press nation-state projects onto the bargaining table and the likelihood that common-state leaders will accede both rise with growth in the ability of segment-state leaders (1) to inflict losses on the common-state leaders, (2) to accept losses from conflict, including retaliatory losses inflicted by the common-state leaders, and (3) to control the release of information from their side of the bargaining table. The probability of achieving independence also rises with a decline in the ability of the common-state leaders to inflict losses, to accept losses, and to control information. This is a primary conclusion in part 3 of this book. Reformulated as a hypothesis, this should account for both cross-sectional and longitudinal variation. Hence,

> *Hypothesis 2.* When and where segmental institutions give greater leverage to segment-states there are (a) greater incentives and means for segment-state leaders to press for independence from the common-state and (b) greater incentive for common-state leaders to accede to independence.

The segmental-institutions thesis identifies political-institutional constraints as preeminently, but not exclusively, important in shaping this balance of leverage.

Political-Identity Hegemony and Common-State Consolidation

With political-identity hegemony, segment-state leaders are typically better able to mobilize any advantages, such as a favorable demographic balance, as leverage against the common-state leadership. In the absence of this hegemony, these advantages are more likely to go unexploited. More broadly, political-identity hegemony in a segment-state permits segment-state leaders to be better bargainers who can hold out for a better agreement by inflicting greater losses on the common-state government with more effective use of institutional weapons, by withstanding more retaliatory losses—in particular, by reducing the losses to the segment-state leaders from losses inflicted on the segment-state population—and by successfully manipulating release of information about their capabilities and intentions through strategic signaling. Hence,

Hypothesis 3. When and where segment-state leaders have consolidated political-identity hegemony there are (a) greater incentives and means for segment-state leaders to press for independence from the common-state and (b) greater incentive for common-state leaders to accede to independence.

The balance of leverage also depends on the consolidation of political leadership in the common-state government. United and secure common-state leaders are in a better bargaining position: they can hold out for a better agreement by inflicting greater losses on the segment-state government with more effective use of institutional weapons, by withstanding more retaliatory losses inflicted by segment-state leaders, and by successfully manipulating release of information about their capabilities and intentions through strategic signaling. United common-state leaders are also in a stronger position to remove segment-state leaders and deprive them of many means to consolidate political-identity hegemony within their segment-states. Hence,

Hypothesis 4. When and where the unity and security of common-state leaders decline there are (a) greater incentives and means for segment-state leaders to press for independence from the common-state and (b) greater incentives for common-state leaders to accede to independence.

It is, however, the interaction of the unity and security of leadership in the common-state with political-identity hegemony in the segment-states that affects bargaining between them. Common-state leaders are most disadvantaged when they are divided and insecure in their posts—for example, during a succession or reform crisis—and they confront segment-state leaders who have consolidated political-identity hegemony. This is the conjunction of events—the balance of consolidation, so to speak—most likely to lead to the end of the segmented state and the creation of new, independent nation-states. Alternatively, a segmented state in which vulnerable common-state leaders face vulnerable segment-state leaders is less likely to fail.

Disunity or insecurity in the common-state government may come from within the common-state leadership, from the deadlock and cascading defections created by segment-state leaders, or from exogenous shocks. First, extreme political conflicts within the common-state leadership that cannot be attributed directly to segment-states, such as a succession crisis, coup, or constitutional reform crisis, can weaken common-state leaders in their bargaining with segment-state leaders. Second, deadlock in the common-state government created by segment-state leaders or defection of some segment-states from the common-state can weaken the common-state government in its bargaining with segment-state governments. Third, exogenous shocks that weaken the common-state government include international pressures that tie the hands of the common-state government in its relations with the segment-state or direct invasion and occupation of the metropolitan core of the common-state. All three of these situations shift the balance of leverage toward the segment-state leaders. Weakness in the common-state government not only creates an opportunity for segment-state leaders by weakening common-state governments. As the Eurasian cases revealed, political instability in the common-state also creates incentives for segment-state leaders to declare independence as a way of insulating themselves from the uncertainty and potential threats to their own political positions.

Constraints on the Balance of Leverage

The concentration of more institutional weapons in the hands of segment-state leaders, such as vetoes that can force deadlock in common-state decision making, increases the likelihood that segment-state leaders will escalate conflicts. Many decision rights can be turned into institutional weapons, and so many forms of devolution of decision rights to segment-state leaders expand the means available to them to alter the strategic calculations of common-state leaders by inflicting losses. In the extreme, these losses outweigh the losses in decision rights that the common-state leaders expect from agreeing to the demands of the segment-state leaders.[1] Hence,

Hypothesis 2a. When and where segmental institutions allocate a greater share of decision rights to segment-state leaders there are (a) greater incentives and means for segment-state leaders to press for

---

[1] Blaney 1988.

independence from the common-state and (b) greater incentives for common-state leaders to accede to independence.

This balance of leverage between common-state and segment-state leaders is also constrained by such factors as the demographic balance, cultural divisions between the common-state and segment-state populations, and resource endowments of the segment-states. Nonetheless, the segmental institutions thesis stresses the centrality of the institutional arrangements that enable segment-state leaders to use demographic, cultural, and resource advantages. For example, in the bargaining between common-state and segment-state leaders, the relative ability of each side to inflict losses on the other depends in part on the demographic balance.[2] As the balance between the population of the common-state and that of the segment-state shifts toward the latter, the balance of leverage shifts toward the segment-state as well. Not only are nationalist challenges more likely from segment-states with relatively larger populations, but they are more likely to succeed. Hence,

> *Hypothesis 2b.* When and where the demographic balance shifts toward segment-states there are (a) greater incentives and means for segment-state leaders to press for independence from the common-state and (b) greater incentives for common-state leaders to accede to independence.

Cultural unity within the segment-state population (horizontal homogeneity) gives segment-state leaders greater leverage over common-state leaders. Cultural divisions that separate the segment-state population from the common-state population (vertical heterogeneity) make it more likely that mutually acceptable compromises to hold the common-state together will begin to disappear. The combination of horizontal homogeneity and vertical heterogeneity increases both the motive and the means for segment-state leaders to press nation-state projects and the willingness of common-state leaders to accede. Cultural institutions that unify the segment-state population and separate it from the rest of the common-state population may provide additional bases for collective action that segment-state leaders can use to pressure the common-state leaders. Under these conditions it becomes harder for segment-state and common-state leaders to identify common policies that can address the needs of both the segment-state population and the rest of the common-state population, and even harder to agree on common decision-making institutions that can legislate and implement such common policies. Alternatively, a culturally divided segment-state population in which many are tied to the common-state population by culture subverts the leverage of segment-state leaders. Hence,

---

[2] Roeder 2003.

Hypothesis 2c. When and where cultural institutions divide segment-state and common-state populations and cultural institutions unify the segment-state population there are (a) greater incentives and means for segment-state leaders to press for independence from the common-state and (b) greater incentives for common-state leaders to accede to independence.

Control of resources and independent revenue streams may empower segment-state leaders to reward or punish the common-state leaders, and may enable segment-state leaders to withstand sanctions from the common-state leaders.[3] Hence,

Hypothesis 2d. When and where the segment-state leaders independently control more resources and revenue streams there are (a) greater incentives and means for segment-state leaders to press for independence from the common-state and (b) greater incentives for common-state leaders to accede to independence.

The ability of segment-state leaders to inflict losses or withstand losses until their terms are met can be strengthened by the support of outside powers. This alliance may also deter the common-state's retaliation against the segment-state. Hence,

Hypothesis 2e. When and where segment-state leaders enjoy support for independence from external allies there are (a) greater incentives and means for segment-state leaders to press for independence from the common-state and (b) greater incentives for common-state leaders to accede to independence.

Variation in Segmental Institutions

Segment-states are more likely to achieve independence when and where institutional arrangements foster the growth of political-identity hegemony, as hypothesis 3d predicts. These institutional arrangements are particularly likely to favor segment-state leaders in their bargaining with common-state leaders the more these arrangements place segment-state leaders in a unique switchman role between the common-state government and the segment-state population. Segment-state leaders become switchmen in the sense that they can direct the political action of the segment-state population to support or challenge the common-state. Two institutional arrangements are particularly important in privileging segment-state leaders as switchmen: (1) the extent to which the tenure of segment-state leaders does not depend on the common-state leadership (autonomy versus

[3] See Collier 2000a, 2000b.

dependence) and (2) the extent to which the segment-state population is empowered to participate in the governance of the common-state (inclusion versus exclusion). The most explosive combination is an autonomous segment-state leadership—particularly an elected leadership within the segment-state—and exclusion of the segment-state population from participation in common-state politics. In this arrangement, the only contacts between the segment-state population and the common-state government are likely to be channeled through the segment-state leaders. At the other extreme, the least explosive combination is a segment-state leadership that is dependent on the common-state government and total exclusion of the segment-state population from segment-state and common-state politics. This arrangement denies the segment-state population any leadership that can stand up to the common-state leaders. In between these two extremes are various mixtures that can be summarized as the ratio of autonomy to inclusion:

> *Hypothesis 5.* The more the political empowerment of the segment-state population within the segment-state exceeds their empowerment within the common-state (a) the greater are the incentives and means for segment-state leaders to press for independence from the common-state and (b) the greater is the incentive for common-state leaders to accede to independence.

By extension of this hypothesis, the nature of the common-state regime should make a difference in the propensity for segment-states to become independent. In an autocracy, the segment-state leaders are more likely to be dependent agents of the common-state leadership and so less able to press nation-state projects against common-state leaders. These agents are likely to take control of the segment-state's nation-state project, eliminate alternative leaders within the segment-state, and direct the political activities of the segment-state population away from disloyalty to the common-state. Hence,

> *Hypothesis 5a.* In an autocratic common-state there are (a) few incentives and means for segment-state leaders to press for independence from the common-state and (b) few incentives for common-state leaders to accede to independence.

The likelihood of secession may be somewhat higher in a fully inclusive democratic common-state in which the segment-state leadership and population participate with full citizenship rights to run for office and to vote for leaders or representatives in the common-state government. A fully inclusive democracy that makes almost no distinctions in the political statuses of populations—thus, segment-states are nearly formalistic—provide few incentives for independence. The extent to which segment-state leadership is autonomous from the common-state government will determine the extent to which segment-state leaders have the means (and so some more incentive) to mobilize publics and to use institutional weapons to press for independence. Hence,

Hypothesis 5b. In a fully inclusive democratic common-state with autonomous segment-state leadership there are (a) few incentives but modest means for segment-state leaders to press for independence from the common-state and (b) few incentives for common-state leaders to accede to independence.

In between these two unmixed patterns of full inclusion and full exclusion are more volatile combinations. First, in a discriminatory democracy, the public of the metropolitan core participates in the selection of the common-state government, but the segment-state leadership cannot rise to common-state leadership except as leaders of the segment-state, and the segment-state population does not have full citizenship rights to participate in selection of the common-state leadership or to send representatives to the common-state legislature. Where the segment-state nonetheless has autonomous political leadership, the combination of motivation and means increases the likelihood of secession. Where common-state leaders refuse to grant full citizenship rights to the population of the segment-state, acceding to independence may be preferable to a costly conflict. Hence,

Hypothesis 5c. In a discriminatory democratic common-state with autonomous segment-state leadership there are (a) strong incentives and many means for segment-state leaders to press for independence from the common-state and (b) moderate incentives for common-state leaders to accede to independence.

Second, in an anocracy—a piece of political science jargon that describes the weakly institutionalized, imperfectly competitive, and less than fully inclusive polities between autocracy and democracy—the leadership selection process of the common-state does not permit the segment-state leadership or population to participate fully, and common-state leaders typically are too weak to control segment-state leaders. The autonomy of segment-state leaders from the common-state government increases their ability to resist counterpressures once they have begun to press for independence. Where the segment-state population is enfranchised within the segment-state, the contrast between their limited political incorporation within the political life of the common-state and their empowerment within the politics of the segment-state increases the segment-state leaders' incentives to press for independence. The weakness of the common-state leaders in an anocracy increases their vulnerability to pressure from the segment-state leaders and so their inclination to grant independence. Hence,

Hypothesis 5d. In an anocracy there are (a) strong incentives and means for segment-state leaders to press for independence from the common-state and (b) strong incentives for common-state leaders to accede to independence.

These hypotheses concerning variation in regime-type and segmental institutions are summarized in figure 10.1. The axes correspond to the two dimensions of enfranchisement of the segment-state population within common-state politics and autonomy of the segment-state leaders from the common-state government. The highest probability of secession and independence occurs closer to the lower right corner, with autonomy of the segment-state leadership and exclusion of the segment-state population from the common-state. The placement of the five specific segmental institutional arrangements identified by the hypotheses ranks each relative to the others with regard to the exclusion-inclusion and dependency-autonomy dimensions (shown on the two axes) and with regard to the probabilities of secession and independence (shown by the curve). This figure describes a somewhat different relationship than the categories proposed by David Laitin to describe patterns of elite incorporation in multiethnic societies, but the two taxonomies are complementary. In his theory of assimilation and identity formation, Laitin distinguishes the most-favored-lord, colonial, and integralist models by the extent to which elites on the periphery find political opportunities in the power establishment at the center.[4] This corresponds in part to variation along the enfranchisement dimension, but only in part, and Laitin's categories do not vary along the second dimension of autonomy of segment-state leaders.

Constraints on Hegemony

To the extent that the balance of leverage depends on the consolidation of political-identity hegemony within segment-states, as hypothesis 3 predicts, the constraints on political-identity hegemony identified in part 2 will have an indirect but real influence on this balance. Not surprisingly, these constraints on political-identity hegemony include many of the political-institutional factors, as well as demographic, cultural, and economic factors that influence the balance of leverage directly. The allocation of decision rights to segment-state governments, which can become institutional weapons in bargaining with the common-state government, affects the opportunities for consolidation of political-identity hegemony. The ability to write the rules of local politics can privilege the dominant cohort

[4] Laitin 1998, 59–82.

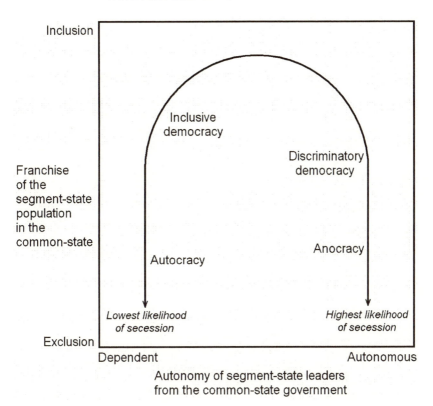

Figure 10.1 Segmental institutions and the likelihood of secession by segment-states.

of politicians against competitors. Cultural institutions that unite the segment-state population can provide segment-state leaders mobilizational resources to consolidate political-identity hegemony. Monopolistic control
of resource endowments to reward supporters can help in building political
monopolies. Hence,

Hypothesis 3a. When and where segment-state governments possess a
greater share of the decision rights to constitute their own political
leadership there is a greater likelihood that political-identity hegemonies will emerge within the segment-states.

Hypothesis 3b. When and where segment-state populations are culturally separated from the common-state population and culturally unified within the segment-state there is a greater likelihood that political-identity hegemonies will emerge within the segment-states.

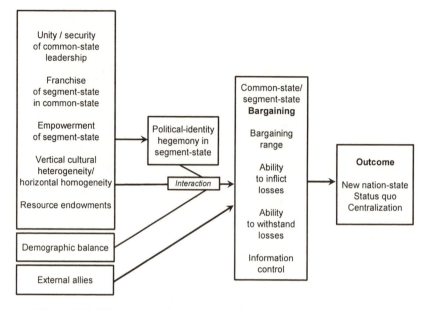

Figure 10.2 The segmental-institutions thesis: schematic representation
of hypothesized relationships.

Hypothesis 3c. When and where segment-state governments monopolize control over resource endowments and revenue streams within
the segment-state there is a greater likelihood that political-identity
hegemonies will emerge within the segment-states.

Overview of Hypotheses

Thus, these hypotheses expand upon the simple relationship shown in figure 1.2, which can now be elaborated as shown in figure 10.2. The hypotheses describe a relationship in which the relative unity of the common-state
leadership, the allocation of decision rights, the demographic balance, the
pattern of cultural divisions, relative resource endowments, and external
allies have a direct impact on the balance of leverage between segment-
state and common-state leaders. These factors all affect the *means* available
to segment-state leaders to press their claims.

The availability of these means also increases *incentives* for independence. In addition, exclusion from the political life of the common-state
increases incentives in segment-states to press for independence. Turmoil
and constitutional changes in the common-state regime that pose a threat
to the power and even the survival of segment-state leaders create still more
incentives for segment-state leaders to press for independence. Vertical

cultural heterogeneity that leads many compromises to disappear from the bargaining range increases the incentives on both sides to part ways.

In the absence of consolidated segment-state leadership with political-identity hegemony, however, these constraints are likely to have far less influence. Once again this is a matter of means. Institutional weapons, local political empowerment, demographic balances, and resource endowments are more likely to be effective when there is an autonomous segment-state leadership with political-identity hegemony to mobilize these resources as leverage against the common-state leaders. Hence, there is an interaction effect indicated in figure 10.2. The development of this political-identity hegemony within segment-states depends on the allocation of decision rights to the segment-states, the pattern of cultural divisions, control over the resource endowments of the segment-state, and weakness in the common-state leadership. In other words, these constraints not only affect the balance of leverage directly, they also have an indirect effect on the bargaining between common-state and segment-state leaders through their effect on the politics within the segment-states and the consolidation of political-identity hegemony within them.

None of these causal relationships is deterministic; none is a sufficient cause. We need comparative analysis, including statistical methods, to begin estimating the relative importance of each constraint in increasing the likelihood of independence of segment-states as new nation-states.

Post-Soviet Patterns

The post-Soviet pattern conforms almost perfectly to the expectations of the segmental institutions thesis. In particular, it underscores the importance of the conjunction of division in the common-state leadership and political-identity hegemony in the segment-states. Yet if we examine just the fifteen union republics of the USSR, the outcome is so overdetermined that it is difficult to disentangle the effect of institutions from demographic, cultural, resource, and international constraints. We can gain greater purchase on individual causes by expanding our comparison to include all Soviet and post-Soviet segment-states, to compare not only cross-sectional differences among segment-states but also temporal changes in their relationship to their respective common-states from 1988 to 2005, and to examine attempts at secession that fell short of de jure independence.

In the last months of the USSR there were fifty-four segment-states. As table 10.1 shows, from 1988 to 2005 there were fifteen successful secessions of segment-states that were recognized as sovereign states by the international community. All new independent states had been union republics, and no union republic failed to achieve de jure independence. In addition, there were three de facto secessions of segment-states that remained out-side the control of a common-state until at least the end of 2005.[5] Abkhazia had been an autonomous republic; Nagornyi Karabakh and South Ossetia had been autonomous oblasts. One more de facto secession of a segment-state subsequently failed: Chechnya had been an autonomous republic as the Chechen-Ingush ASSR. Finally, three ambiguous threats of secession by segment-states were not implemented and were later withdrawn. These included two autonomous republics (Crimea and Tatarstan) and one auton-omous oblast (Gornyi Badakhshan). Particularly useful insights can be gained by focusing on the variation among the lower-order autonomies and among the cases on the margins of secession and independence—the de facto and thwarted secessions.

Cross-Section Variations

The correspondence between these outcomes and the status of the first-, second-, third-, and fourth-order segment-states within the Soviet system of *matrioshka* federalism is very neat. As table 10.2 shows, 100 percent of first-order segment-states (union republics) ended in de jure independence, 13.8 percent of the autonomous republics and autonomous oblasts ended in de facto independence and another 6.9 percent made ambiguous threats of independence, but none of the autonomous okrugs attempted to secede. Status within the federal system was closely correlated with the decision rights and institutional weapons in the hands of the segment-state leaders. Thus, this seems to confirm the simple institutionalist expectation in hypotheses 2 and 2a that the greater the institutional weapons in the hands of segment-state leaders, the greater the likelihood of successful secession and creation of new nation-states. Yet caution is in order in these cross-sectional comparisons since, as table 10.2 also shows, this status and the decision rights were highly correlated with other constraints mentioned in the previous hypotheses.

First, higher status and secession were associated with a demographic balance more favorable to segment-states, confirming the pattern pre-dicted by hypothesis 2b. Indeed, as the ranges in table 10.2 show, only among the union republics did any segment-state comprise over 50 percent of the common-state population; a second union republic comprised al-most 18 percent. Closer examination of the lower-order segment-states reveals that the six cases of de facto or thwarted secession tended to involve the segment-states that were largest relative to their common-states. Among twenty-one autonomous republics Abkhazia had the highest, Cri-mea the fourth highest, and Tatarstan the sixth highest population ratios.

[5] For additional information on the de facto states, see Lynch 2004.

TABLE 10.1
Real and imaginary post-Soviet nation-states, 1991–2005

De jure independence	Status[a]	Independence proclaimed	Transition began
Armenia (USSR)	UR	1991: September 23	1990: August 23
Azerbaijan (USSR)	UR	1991: August 30	
Belarus (USSR)	UR	1991: August 25	
Estonia (USSR)	UR	1991: August 20	1990: March 30
Georgia (USSR)	UR	1991: April 9	1990: April 9
Kazakhstan (USSR)	UR	1991: December 17	
Kyrgyzstan (USSR)	UR	1991: August 31	
Latvia (USSR)	UR	1991: August 21	1990: May 4
Lithuania (USSR)	UR	1990: March 11	
Moldova (USSR)	UR	1991: August 27	
Russia (USSR)	UR	1991: December 12	
Tajikistan (USSR)	UR	1991: September 9	
Turkmenistan (USSR)	UR	1991: October 22	
Ukraine (USSR)	UR	1991: August 24	
Uzbekistan (USSR)	UR	1991: August 31	

De facto independence		Independence proclaimed	Transition began
Abkhazia (Georgia)	AR	1992: July 23	1990: August 25
Nagornyi Karabakh (Azerbaijan)	AOb	1991: December 10	1988: July 12
South Ossetia (Georgia)	AOb	1991: December 22	1990: September 20
Transdniestria (Moldova)	None	1991: December 1	1990: September 2

De facto independence that failed		Independence proclaimed	Terminated
Chechnya (Russia)	AR	1991: November 1	2003: October 5
Gagauzia (Moldova)	None	1990: August 19	1995: March 5
Talysh-Murgan (Azerbaijan)	None	1993: c. June 15	1993: August 23

Threatened, not implemented		Crisis began	Ended
Badakhshan (Tajikistan)	AOb	1992: April 11	1993: June 20
Crimea (Ukraine)	AR	1992: May 5	1995: September 23
Poles (Lithuania)	None	1990: May 23	1991: c. September 9
Russophones (Estonia)	None	1993: July 16	1993: October 17
Russophones (Kazakhstan)	None	1990: c. October	[b]
Russophones (Latvia)	None	1990: c. May 16	1991: c. October
Tatarstan (Russia)	AR	1990: September 2	1994: February 15
Transcarpathia (Ukraine)	Ob	1991: December 1	[b]

Note: A few dates (indicated by c [circa]) are imprecise because the date of the initiating action is disputed or the date of the end of a crisis that had no formal announcement of termination is difficult to fix.

[a] Status: UR, union republic; AR, autonomous republic; AOb, autonomous oblast; Ob, Oblast.

[b] Threat not repeated in a public crisis.

TABLE 10.2

Constraints affecting the likelihood of independence of Soviet segment-states, 1988–2005

	Union republics	Autonomous republics	Autonomous oblasts	Autonomous okrugs
Outcomes				
De jure independence	100%	0%	0%	0%
De facto independence	0%	4.8%	25.0%	0%
Failed independence bid	0%	4.8%	0%	0%
Threat without implementation	0%	9.5%	0%	0%
Segment-state population as percentage of common-state population				
Average	6.7	2.2	1.1	.001
Median	1.8	0.9	0.3	.0006
Range	0.5–51.2	0.2–9.8	0.1–3.1	.0001–.0076
Ratio of titular to common-state majority within segment-state[a]				
Average	9.3	1.4	1.0	0.5
Median	5.9	0.9	0.4	0.2
Range	0.0–58.3	0.0–8.68	0.0–3.58	0.0–1.7
Titular percentage of segment-state				
Average	68.8	47.7	42.7	22.0
Median	71.4	45.4	36.0	13.6
Range	39.7–93.3	10.0–95.9	4.2–89.5	1.4–60.2
Percentage of segment-states with titular predominance plus cultural difference				
Civilization and language	60.0	28.6	12.5	10.0
Language difference only	20.0	9.5	12.5	10.0
n =	15	21	8	10

Sources: USSR Gosudarstvennyi komitet SSSR po statistike 1990, 1991, 1992; Tishkov 1994.

[a] In Ajaria, Gornyi Badakhshan, Nakhichevan, and Russia the titular nationality is the same as that of the common-state and so is assigned a value of zero in the numerator.

Among eight autonomous oblasts Nagornyi Karabakh and South Ossetia were the second and third largest relative to their common-states. Although these figures seem to confirm the demographic balance hypothesis, some anomalies suggest that caution is in order. Much of Abkhazia's population, which was overwhelmingly Georgian, fled to Georgia during the brief civil war. Chechen-Ingushetia ranked as only the median case among autonomous republics.

Second, higher status and secession were also associated with numerical predominance of the titular nationality within the segment-state population, confirming the pattern predicted by hypotheses 2c and 3b. In all of the union republics except Kazakhstan the titular nationality constituted a majority of the population. By contrast, in ten of the twenty-one autonomous republics, five of the eight autonomous oblasts, and eight of the ten autonomous okrugs the titular nationality of the common-state living

within the borders of the segment-state outnumbered the titular nationality of the segment-state. Looking more closely at the lower-order segment-
states reveals a close link to the pattern predicted in hypotheses 2c and 3b.
The six cases of de facto or thwarted secession tended to involve segment-
states with the highest titular presence. There were almost 3.6 times as
many Armenians as Azeris in Nagornyi Karabakh, more than three times
as many Chechens and Ingushes as Russians in the Chechen-Ingush ASSR,
2.6 times as many Russians as Ukrainians in Crimea, and 2.3 times as many
Ossetians as Georgians in South Ossetia. These accounted for the second
and third highest ratios among autonomous republics (only Dagestan's
multiethnic majority was higher) and the first and second highest ratios
among the autonomous oblasts. But, the correlation is not perfect, and an
important anomaly suggests that caution is in order: in Abkhazia, prior to
the growing violence Georgians outnumbered Abkhazians by more than
2.5 times.

Third, with higher institutional status there was a greater likelihood of
a fatal combination of titular predominance within a segment-state (horizontal homogeneity) and cultural separation from the common-state majority (vertical heterogeneity)—a combination highlighted by hypothesis
2c. Table 10.2 shows the proportion of segment-states of each status in
which, first, the segment-state titulars residing in the segment-state outnumbered the common-state titulars residing in the same segment-state,
and second, the two populations shared neither traditional civilization nor
language group, or shared only traditional civilization. There appears to
be a relationship to the likelihood of secession. Nonetheless, this does not
produce an airtight explanation for the different outcomes. The six segment-states involved in de facto or thwarted secessions were typically separated from their common-states by language group and civilization, but no
more so than other segment-states that did not attempt to secede. Nagornyi Karabakh (an autonomous oblast) was divided from Azerbaijan and
both Chechen-Ingushetia and Tatarstan (autonomous republics) were divided from Russia by both civilization and language group, but so were
eight other autonomous republics. Abkhazia (an autonomous republic) and
South Ossetia (an autonomous oblast) were divided from their common-
state majority (Georgians) by language group but not civilization; so were
seven other autonomous republics.[6] Crimean Russians shared both religious tradition and language group with the Ukrainians.

---

[6] Contrary to the claims made by Georgians, who tried to characterize their conflict with
Abkhazia as a clash of civilizations, many Muslim Abkhazians had fled the Russian Empire in
the 1860s, leaving Orthodox Christians in the majority; see Wixman 1984, 3.

Fourth, higher status and secession were also associated with greater control over the local economy and natural resources, confirming the pattern predicted by hypotheses 2d and 3c. Data for systematic comparisons of resource endowments and revenue streams that cover all segment-states prior to 1991 are not available, but patterns among subsets of these cases do suggest that these constraints were important. Control over resources was correlated with federal status, but resource endowments were unequally distributed. Thus, among segment-states of similar status, resource endowments were a major constraint on the ability to fund political monopolies that could be used to exercise leverage against the common-state. Within the Russian Federation claims to autonomy came from regional leaders who sat atop valuable resource bases, particularly in Sakha and Tatarstan. Support was significantly lower where the homeland economy was heavily dependent on subsidies from the center. For example, in Tyva (called Tuva by the Russians), local party leaders swept the March 4, 1990, elections and eased out non-Tyvans. According to Toomas Alatalu, "in this situation the local party leaders acted emphatically as nationalists. . . ." Nonetheless, "at the same time the local party leaders continue[d] reiterating to the public that the republic is a backward one and unable to cope without the Soviet Union."[7] Subsequently, leaders of Tyva resisted the demands of the Tyvan Popular Front for a referendum on independence. As a Moscow newspaper explained, "The overwhelming majority of deputies [opposing independence] pointed out that 90 percent of Tuva's budget comprised subsidies from Moscow. None of the leaders of Tuva supported the republic's secession."[8]

Fifth, international support was also closely correlated with prior federal status and secession, confirming the pattern in hypothesis 2e. Foreign powers drew a sharp line between secessions by first-order and lower-order segment-states and between secessions recognized by or rejected by the existing common-state (such as the USSR). Closer examination, however, suggests that the key role of external allies came later, in preserving the secession of some segment-states. Outside support was not critical in the initial decision for secession by Nagornyi Karabakh, South Ossetia, and Abkhazia, but it was critical in sustaining this decision against common-state pressure to reintegrate these regions. The weakness of outside support may account for the failure to sustain Chechnya's secession and for the decision by Crimea and Tatarstan to withdraw key provisions of their declarations of sovereignty. Alternatively, threats posed by external

---

[7] Alatalu 1992, 891.

[8] Aleksei Tarasov, "V Tuve reshili iz Rossii poka ne vykhodit'," *Izvestiia* September 18, 1992, 2. Also see Kirkow 1994, 1164–65.

actors may have encouraged the leaders of Gornyi Badakhshan to submit to reintegration.

The correlation of so many causes in the cross-sectional comparison of post-Soviet cases—collinearity, in the vocabulary of statistical analysis—leaves us unable to estimate the relative contribution of each variable to the outcomes. However, a closer examination of temporal variations in the timing of secessions, reversals, and withdrawals of secession threats gives us insight into the critical role of some constraints. These temporal comparisons hold constant many attributes of individual cases and permit us to highlight what changed.

Timing of Secessions

The clustering of secessions in time points to the critical importance of the conjunction of a weakened common-state leadership and political-identity hegemonies in segment-states to the initiation of bids for secession and their initial success, a pattern emphasized in hypotheses 3 and 4. Where weak common-state governments faced segment-state leadership that had consolidated political-identity hegemony, the result was often secession. Outside allies became critical only later, when newly consolidated common-state leadership tried to reverse these secessions. This was, of course, the pattern at the all-union level after the failed August 1991 coup. It was also the pattern in those successor states immediately after independence in 1991 that experienced secessions or threats of secession by subordinate segment-states. The patterns of disunity in the central government of the USSR; temporary disunity in the governments of Azerbaijan, Georgia, Russia, Tajikistan, and Ukraine; but continuing unity in Uzbekistan account for much of the variation in outcomes. During the periods of disunity within the common-state governments, the balance of leverage shifted toward the respective segment-states. This provided the critical moment for independence not only for the fifteen union republics of the USSR but also for Abkhazia, Chechnya, Nagornyi Karabakh, and South Ossetia. It was also the occasion for threats of secession by Crimea, Gornyi Badakhshan, and Tatarstan. Alternatively, in Uzbekistan, where union republic leaders maintained a relatively tighter monopoly over politics throughout the transition to independence, a secession attempt from Karakalpakstan did not emerge. Reestablishment of unity in the common-state leadership led to a reversal of de facto secession by Chechnya and the withdrawal of threats to secede from Crimea, Gornyi Badakhshan, and Tatarstan. Yet even a reunified common-state government, such as Azerbaijan under Gaidar Aliev or Georgia under Mikhail Saakashvili, could be blocked from reintegrating the segment-states if the latter, such as Nagornyi Karabakh, Abkhazia, or South Ossetia, had acquired powerful outside allies. This suggests an amendment to hypothesis 2c: external allies are less important in the incentives to secede in the initial stages of a nation-state crisis than in the deterrence of the common-state government from retaliating in the later stages of a crisis.

Disunity, turmoil, and constitutional change in the common-state governments created the dangerous combination of opportunity and incentives for secession. These sources of weakness in the common-state also created growing threats to segment-state leaders, who feared that changes in the constitutional order of the common-state would come at the expense of segment-states, particularly where common-state nationalists and reformers threatened to end segmental institutions that divided the nation or subverted democracy and economic efficiency. For example, in the Autonomous Republic of Crimea, as Denis J. B. Shaw notes, the threat of secession "concerned the preservation of the local political elite; as former members of the communist partocracy, the positions of Mykola Bahrov (Nikolay Bagrov) and other local leaders might certainly be threatened by forced democratization as well as by assimilation to Ukraine."[9] In the last years of the USSR, moves by new union republic leaders to assert their dominance provoked reactions from the leaders of lower-order segment-states within the union republics. A significant escalation in demands from leaders of the autonomous republics, autonomous oblasts, and autonomous okrugs followed the union republics' declarations of sovereignty and independence. The union republics' declarations of sovereignty implied that the leaders of the union republics would no longer be restrained by the USSR leadership in the old checks and balances of *matrioshka* federalism in their relations with the lower-order segment-states. As one newspaper correspondent from *Izvestiia* summed up the motivations for secession in South Ossetia: When asked "What are the Ossetians upset about?" South Ossetians responded, "The Georgians want to secede from the USSR . . . but first of all they want to take away our autonomy."[10] The lower-order segment-state officials reacted to the threat to their decision-making power from union republic officials with claims for expanded autonomy or even independence. Znaur Gassiev, former first secretary of the Communist Party organization in South Ossetia, explained to a *Pravda* reporter the strategic calculation that led to secession: "We have calculated the development of events into the future and see that it promises nothing good for the people of the South Ossetian Republic if we remain in Georgia."[11]

[9] D. Shaw 1994, 227. Also see Solchanyk 1994, 51.

[10] V. Arsen'ev, "Iuzhnaia Osetiia: dni trevog i nadezhd," *Izvestiia* October 28, 1989, 4.

[11] Georgii Ovcharenko, "Goriachaia tochka—Puchina bezzakoniia," *Pravda* January 6, 1992, 1–2.

External Deterrence of Common-State Retaliation

The three de facto secessions of segment-states that remained independent after a decade—Abkhazia, Nagornyi Karabakh, and South Ossetia—highlight the importance of outside allies that prevented the common-state government from reversing the secessions even after new unified common-state leadership had consolidated power. This outside support compensated for weaknesses on the segment-state's side, such as numerical weakness or even divided segmental leadership.[12]

Georgia and Abkhazia became parties to a nation-state crisis after March 18, 1989, when Abkhazian deputies from the autonomous republic's soviets at all levels, including the first secretary of the republic's Communist Party organization, adopted a letter to the USSR leadership calling for "Restoring to Abkhazia the Status of a Soviet Socialist Republic, As It Was Recognized in 1921 During the Lifetime of V. I. Lenin."[13] Fifteen months later the conflict with the Georgian SSR escalated further when the Abkhaz Supreme Soviet adopted a declaration of sovereignty on August 25, 1990; it unilaterally elevated the autonomous republic to union republic status, making it co-equal with Georgia, and declared that henceforth its relations with Georgia would be defined by treaties.[14] Abkhaz concern grew after the nationalist Georgian Round Table swept Georgia's first free elections in November and the first session of the new Georgian Supreme Soviet elected Zviad Gamsakhurdia as its chair, with a clear commitment to terminate the segment-states within Georgia. Growing disunity within the Georgian leadership after August 1991 that led to a coup against Gamsakhurdia in January 1992 and a civil war among Georgian armies provided Abkhazia the opportunity to press its independence. By June 1992 Abkhazia had proclaimed itself a sovereign republic under its 1925 constitution.[15] Yet without backing from Russia, Abkhazia probably could not have sustained its independence. The Abkhaz crisis heated up after August 12, 1992, when Georgian troops crossed into Abkhazia and occupied much of the republic.[16] Only with help from volunteers mobilized by the Confeder-

---

[12] See Cornell 2001.

[13] T. Chanturiia, "Sessii Verkhovnykh Sovetov soiuznykh respublik—Gruzinskaia SSR," *Izvestiia* March 31, 1989, 2. Also see Vl. Arsen'ev, "Obstanovka v Abkhazii," *Izvestiia* July 17, 1989, 3; Otyrba 1994; T. Pachkoriia, "Rabotaiut sessii," *Pravda* August 26, 1990, 2; B. Urigashvili, "Resheniia Verkhovnogo Soveta Abkhazii priznany nepravomochnymi," *Izvestiia* August 28, 1990, 1.

[14] "Deklaratsiia o gosudarstvennom suverenitete Abkhazskoi Sovetskoi Sotsialisticheskoi Respubliki," *Sovetskaia Abkhaziia* August 28, 1991, 1.

[15] Fuller 1990c, 1991a, 1993, 91; Tengiz Pachkoriia, "Federativnoe gruzino-abkhazskoe gosudarstvo?" *Nezavisimaia gazeta* July 25, 1992, 1.

[16] Nodar Broladze, "Novyi konflikt na zapade Gruzii," *Nezavisimaia gazeta* August 15, 1992, 1; Besik Urigashvili, "Vystrely v Sukhumi eshche zvuchat, no do Novogo Saraevo delo

ation of Mountain Peoples and from the Russian armed forces were the Abkhaz leaders able to plan and implement a coordinated yearlong counteroffensive to expel the Georgian army. The Abkhaz army reached the republic's border with Georgia on September 30, 1993.[17] The war produced over 2,500 casualties and 300,000 Georgian refugees from Abkhazia. The introduction of Russian peacekeepers along the border between Abkhazia and Georgia not only prevented a resumption of war, it also prevented further attempts by Georgia to reverse the secession, and so sustained the secession for more than a decade. On November 26, 1994, the Abkhaz Supreme Soviet adopted yet a new constitution that proclaimed the republic's sovereignty based on "the people's right to free self-determination" and reaffirmed that Abkhazia was a subject of international law.[18] Neither Georgia nor any other sovereign state was willing to recognize this new status.[19]

Similarly, sustaining the South Ossetian secession from Georgia depended on Russian backing, even though such backing had not been critical in the initial decision to secede. The South Ossetian crisis began on November 10, 1989, when the legislature (soviet) of the South Ossetian Autonomous Oblast called on the USSR and Georgian SSR governments to elevate their oblast to the status of an autonomous republic.[20] Failing to convince either common-state government of this, on September 20, 1990, the soviet simply proclaimed their oblast the South Ossetian Soviet Demo-

---

ne doidet," *Izvestiia* August 17, 1992, 1–2; "Gortsy vstupaiut v voinu na storone Abkhazii," *Izvestiia* August 26, 1992, 1–2; Vasilii Kononenko, "5 sentiabria, 12.00—vremia prekrashcheniia ognia v Abkhazii," *Izvestiia* September 4, 1992, 1–2; Besik Urigashvili, "Shevardnadze obviniaet abkhazskuiu storonu v sryve dogovorennostei," *Izvestiia* September 9, 1992, 1.

[17] Besik Urigashvili, "Ataka na Gagru: Panenye i ubitye ischisliaiutsia desiatkami," *Izvestiia* October 2, 1992, 2; "Kavkazskii region na grani krupnomasshtabnoi voiny," *Izvestiia* October 5, 1992, 1–2; "Posle sdachi Gantiadi i Leselidze gruziny ozhidaiut ataki na Sukhumi," *Izvestiia* October 7, 1992, 1; Besik Urigashvili, "Abkhazskie voiska shturmuiut Sukhumi," *Izvestiia* March 17, 1993, 1; Besik Urigashvili, "Gruziia nastaivaet na otvetstvennosti Rossii za zhertvy i razrusheniia v Sukhumi," *Izvestiia* March 18, 1993, 1; Besik Urigashvili, "Ataka abkhaztsev na Sukhumi: zhertvy s obeikh storon ischisliaiutsia sotniami," *Izvestiia* July 6, 1993, 1; Georgii Ivanov-Smolenskii, "Polozhenie v Gruzii deistvitel'no chrezvychainoe: voina idet na dva fronta," *Izvestiia* September 17, 1993, 1; Besik Urigashvili, "Sanktsii Rossii ne ostanovili voinu, V Sukhumi po-prezhnemu l'etsia krov,'" *Izvestiia* September 22, 1993, 1–2; Besik Urigashvili, "Padenie Sukhumi mozhet vyzvat' nachalo bol'shoi kavkazskoi voiny," *Izvestiia* September 28, 1993, 1; Guga Lolishvili, Tengiz Pachkoriia, and Liana Minasian, "Abkhazskie formirovaniia nastupaiut," *Nezavisimaia gazeta* July 3, 1993, 3; Guga Lolishvili, "Sukhumi pal, voina prodolzhaetsia," *Nezavisimaia gazeta* September 29, 1993, 1; Guga Lolishvili, "Abkhazskie formirovaniia vyshli k Inguri," *Nezavisimaia gazeta* October 2, 1993, 1.

[18] "Parlament prinial novuiu konstitutsiiu," *Segodnia* November 19, 1994, 4.

[19] Mikhail Vignanskii, "SB OON vidit Abkhaziiu tol'ko v peredelakh gruzinskogo gosudarstva," *Segodnia* July 17, 1996, 9.

[20] Aleksandr Mineev, "Stoianie u Tskhinvali," *Moskovskie novosti* December 3, 1989, 2; Tat'iana Nedashkovskaia, "Gruziia: poliarizatsiia sil," *Izvestiia* January 2, 1991, 4.

cratic Republic. Soon after this declaration a reported 200 busloads of Georgian activists loyal to Gamsakhurdia flooded into the oblast's capital, Tskhinvali, followed by Georgian troops, and for the next two months a small civil war raged in the region. Intervention by the USSR government forced the Georgians to retreat. The decisive step toward secession came after the seating of the Gamsakhurdia majority in the Georgian Supreme Soviet in November 1990 and its vote to annul all acts of the self-proclaimed South Ossetian republic.[21] On November 28, 1990, South Ossetia's soviet declared their autonomous oblast the South Ossetia Soviet Republic, thereby elevating itself to a status equal to that of Georgia, and on December 11 it declared that henceforth it would be directly subordinate to the USSR government and not Georgia. On December 11, 1990, the Georgian Supreme Soviet countered with legislation that dissolved the South Ossetian Autonomous Oblast.[22] The next day the Presidium of the Georgian Supreme Soviet declared a state of emergency in the South Ossetian capital and adjacent countryside and ordered units of the republic's MVD and KGB troops to establish control over the oblast, but the USSR government once again blocked reintegration. With the dissolution of the USSR, the South Ossetian soviet declared South Ossetia's independence on December 22, 1991, and a referendum the next month confirmed this.[23] On April 17, 1992, the South Ossetian soviet called on Russia to admit their territory to the Russian Federation.[24] The military standoff began to ease after the removal of Gamsakhurdia in January 1992, but, when Georgian forces tried to take advantage of disunity in the South Ossetian government of Torez Kulumbekov in order to reconquer South Ossetia, the fighting resumed in the summer.[25] Without Russian backing at this point, South Ossetia might have been reintegrated within Georgia. Russian armed support tipped the balance in favor of South Ossetia. The war produced at least 2,000 casualties and 30,000 refugees from South Ossetia. The presence of a Russian peacekeeping force after July 1992 kept South

---

[21] G. Lebanidze, "V Gruzii—novoe pravitel'stvo," *Pravda* November 24, 1990, 2.

[22] Nelson and Amonashvili 1992, 688; "Urazdnena avtonomnaia oblast,'" *Izvestiia* December 12, 1990, 3; "Obrashchenie Prezidiuma Verkhovnogo Soveta SSSR k Verkhovnomu Sovetu Gruzinskoi SSR i oblastnomu sovetu Iugo-Osetinskoi avtonomnoi oblasti," *Izvestiia* December 15, 1990, 1; Ukaz Prezidenta Soiuza Sovetskikh Sotsialisticheskikh Respublik "O nekotorykh zakonodatel'nykh aktakh, priniatykh v dekabre 1990 goda v Gruzinskoi SSR," *Izvestiia* January 8, 1991, 1; A. Semeniaka, "Razrushenie—Iuzhnaia Osetia: vystrelov net, no poka ne legche," *Pravda* August 16, 1991, 6.

[23] *RFE/RL* Daily Report January 10, 1992, January 31, 1992.

[24] *RFE/RL* Daily Report May 1, 1992.

[25] Besik Urigashvili, "Gruziia-Iuzhnaia Osetiia: za oshibki politikov narody rasplachivaiutsia krov'iu," *Izvestiia* June 12, 1992, 1, 3. Also see Liana Minasian, "Nekakikh kompromissov s Gruziei," *Nezavisimaia gazeta* April 10, 1992, 3; Mikhail Shevelev, "Voina idet s ioga," *Moskovskie novosti* June 21, 1992, 4.

Ossetia independent in fact, if not in the eyes of Georgia or the international community.[26]

The importance of Russia's support to deter Georgia became apparent in the very different outcomes of the nation-state crises in the summer of 2004. Georgia's new nationalist government, led by Mikhail Saakashvili, sought to reintegrate South Ossetia and Abkhazia. In May 2004 Saakashvili's ultimatum to Ajaria had brought Russian mediation and an offer of asylum in Russia for Ajaria's president; without Russian support, Ajaria's segment-state government capitulated. Alternatively, when Saakashvili turned to South Ossetia in June, Russian backing for the South Ossetian regime permitted it to stand up against superior Georgian armed forces and deter the attempt at reintegration. Saakashvili was keenly aware of the Russian military presence and warned that this "will be a conflict between Georgia and Russia." The prospect of confronting Russia and the warnings from Georgia's allies to pull back kept Georgia from reintegrating either South Ossetia or Abkhazia and kept Saakashvili complaining that it was Russian presence that blocked the solution that he sought.

In Nagornyi Karabakh it was the armed forces of Armenia that deterred the Azerbaijan common-state from reversing the secession. The Karabakh nation-state crisis was engaged on February 20, 1988, when the legislature (soviet) of the Nagorno-Karabakh Autonomous Oblast adopted an appeal to the Presidium of the USSR Supreme Soviet to transfer the oblast to the jurisdiction of Armenia. Failing to elicit a favorable response from the USSR, the oblast soviet voted on July 12, 1988, to secede from Azerbaijan and join Armenia on its own.[27] Immediately after the failed coup against Gorbachev in August 1991, deputies from all soviets within the oblast and the neighboring raion of Shaumianovskii assembled to declare an independent Nagorno-Karabakh Republic.[28] On November 26 the Azerbaijan Supreme Soviet voted to revoke the autonomous status of the oblast, but troops from Armenia prevented forceful reintegration of the Karabakh by

[26] Besik Urigashvili, "Shevardnadze prizyvaet mirovuiu obshchestvennost' ne dopustit' agressii protiv Gruzii," *Izvestiia* June 20, 1992, 1; Viktor Litovkin, "Rossiiskie desantniki voshli v Iuzhnuiu Osetiiu," *Izvestiia* July 14, 1992, 1; Alan Kasaev, "Pora pechal'nykh iubileev," *Nezavisimaia gazeta* November 28, 1995, 3; Mikhail Vignanskii, "Reshenie o prezidentskikh vyborakh v Iuzhnom Osetii vyzvalo ozabochennost' Tblisi," *Segodnia* September 17, 1996, 3; Mikhail Vignanskii, "Liudvig Chibirov izbran prezidentom Iuzhnoi Osetii," *Segodnia* November 12, 1996, 1.

[27] Ukaz Prezidiuma Verkhovnogo Soveta SSSR "O vvedenii osoboi formy upravleniia v Nagorno-Karabakhskoi avtonomnoi oblasti Azerbaidzhanskoi SSR," *Izvestiia* January 15, 1989, 1; "V Prezidiume Verkhovnogo Soveta respubliki," *Izvestiia* September 3, 1989, 1; Rutland 1994, 843.

[28] V. Byrkin, "Oblast' vyrosla iz shtanishek," *Pravda* September 4, 1991, 1; "Parlament Azerbaidzhana likvidiroval avtonomiiu Nagornogo Karabakha," *Izvestiia* November 28, 1991, 1.

Azerbaijan: the Armenian invasion of Azerbaijan in January 1992 led to the occupation of Nagornyi Karabakh, and by mid-1992 Armenia's armed forces controlled the Karabakh and the Lachin corridor that linked it with Armenia. A firm response from Azerbaijan beyond solemn pronouncements was hampered by the growing instability in its central government and a near civil war among Azerbaijan warlords with private armies. A coup against the Communists in May 1992 and a counter-coup in June 1993 that brought former first secretary Gaidar Aliev back to power kept the common-state government in turmoil. Even after Aliev consolidated his leadership, however, Armenia's armed forces (and the possibility of Russian support) deterred any attempts to reverse the de facto secession. A cease-fire on May 12, 1994, left the Armenian armed force in place and kept Nagornyi Karabakh outside the jurisdiction of the Azerbaijan common-state government. Within Nagornyi Karabakh the State Defense Committee under the chairmanship of Robert Kocharyan assumed effective control.[29] On December 22, 1994, the Nagornyi Karabakh parliament elected Kocharyan the republic's president.[30]

International Isolation and the Reversal of Secession

By contrast, where the secessionist governments remained isolated from outside allies, and particularly where external powers posed a threat to the survival of the secessionist regime, the initiation and reversal of secession tracked closely the shifting unity of leadership on each side of the bargaining table. In particular, establishment of unified common-state governments within the Soviet successor states, after the initial contested authority during and after the breakup of the USSR, brought reversal of the de facto secession of Chechnya and withdrawal of threats to secede by Crimea, Gornyi Badakhshan, and Tatarstan.

In Chechnya, continuing international isolation meant that the fate of the secession tracked shifts in the balance of consolidation, particularly shifts in the division and unity of the common-state leadership of the Russian Federation. Division in 1991 created the occasion for secession. The subsequent restoration of strong common-state leadership under Putin almost a decade later brought reintegration of Chechnya within the federation, reversing the de facto secession.[31]

---

[29] *RFE/RL Daily Report* August 28, 1992; Liana Minasian, "Vsia vlast' komitetu oborony," *Nezavisimaia gazeta* August 18, 1992, 3.

[30] Dmitrii Zhdannikov, "V Nagornom Karabakhe izbran prezident," *Segodnia* December 24, 1994, 4.

[31] See Gall and de Waal 1998; Lieven 1998; Evangelista 2002.

A festering conflict between the leadership of the Chechen-Ingush ASSR and Boris Yeltsin's reformist government of the Russian Federation became a nation-state crisis after the Chechen National Congress (CNC) staged a successful coup in Groznyi. Ironically, Yeltsin had encouraged the coup against the Communist Chechen leaders who, he alleged, had supported the Moscow coup against Mikhail Gorbachev's government in August 1991.[32] Elections coordinated by the CNC elected its leader Dzhokhar Dudaev as president of the republic, but on October 27, 1991, much to Yeltsin's consternation, Dudaev declared the republic's independence.[33] Only after nine years, on its third attempt, was Russia able to reassert control over most of Chechnya for an extended period.

The failure of the first two attempts at reintegration came as the common-state leadership of the Russian Federation was weakened, first by division in Moscow and then by Yeltsin's physical incapacitation. The first attempt at reversal, Yeltsin's declaration of a state of emergency on November 9, 1991, led to a badly muddled attempt to use troops of the Russian Ministry of Internal Affairs (MVD) to secure the airport in Groznyi and other strategic points around Chechnya. Yeltsin's hands were tied by his conflict with Gorbachev in the last days of the USSR, while Chechnya's leadership was initially united in its opposition to Yeltsin. Yet divisions in the Chechen leadership soon surfaced. Dudaev's opponents attempted a coup in the spring of 1992. Conflicts between Dudaev and his parliament led the Chechen president to prorogue the legislative body in the summer of 1993. The republic seemed ripe for reconquest once Yeltsin had eliminated his opponents in the Congress of Peoples Deputies in late 1993 and once he had settled his dispute with Tatarstan in February 1994. In the summer of 1994 the Russian government began providing more active and open support to the Chechen opposition to the Dudaev regime.

Russia's second direct attempt to regain Chechnya began on December 9, 1994, when Yeltsin authorized the use of all means to disarm all sides of the expanding conflict within Chechnya. Two days later Russian armed forces entered Chechnya. The result was an indecisive and bloody war that continued for two years, dragging on into the presidential election year of 1996. Under increasing regional and parliamentary pressure to wind up the war, Yeltsin initiated new peace talks during the late summer of 1996. The common-state government pressed for a quick end to the conflict after the 1996 presidential elections. These talks led to a compromise permitting the Chechens to claim that their republic was independent—although no foreign government recognized this—and Moscow to claim that Chechnya

[32] Deklaratsiia "O gosudarstvennom suverenitete," *Golos Checheno-Ingushetii* November 30, 1990, 1.

[33] Ali Kazikhanov, "Pervye ukazy Dudaeva," *Izvestiia* November 6, 1991, 2.

remained a subject of the Russian Federation. The Chechen government under Dudaev's successor, Aslan Maskhadov, showed increasing internal division and had only limited control over the many armed rebel forces located in the republic's villages and towns. In the summer of 1999 sporadic raids by these forces into the neighboring republic of Dagestan threatened the tenuous cease-fire with Russia.[34] Russian armed forces expelled the Chechen forces from Dagestan, but beginning in late August the Chechen rebels escalated their conflict with Russia by spreading it into the heart of Russia itself with terrorist attacks against civilian targets.[35]

The third and most successful Russian attempt to reverse the de facto secession of Chechnya began as Vladimir Putin took more responsibility for leading the government in Moscow and culminated as Putin consolidated his hold on power as Russia's president: In late September 1999 Russian air forces began bombing strategic targets within Chechnya. Russia massed 50,000 troops along the Chechen borders. On October 1, Prime Minister Putin announced that Russia would commence ground operations, and by the beginning of February 2000 Russian troops had taken control of the last rebel strongholds within Groznyi. Despite continuing terrorist attacks, the Russian government conducted elections for a Chechen president on October 5, 2003, and its candidate, Akhmad Kadyrov, won handily. This was only a partial victory: terrorists assassinated Kadyrov seven months later, and new presidential elections had to be held in August 2004.

In Tatarstan, the political-identity hegemony of the Shaimiev machine was not challenged, but international support was not forthcoming; these were constants. Thus, the outcome in the dispute with the common-state government of the Russian Federation tracked shifts in the common-state government. The crisis arose when the common-state government was divided but ended once it became clear that a more unified common-state leadership had emerged. The dispute escalated to a crisis on August 31, 1990, when Tatarstan adopted a declaration of sovereignty proclaiming itself to be a union republic, placing it outside the jurisdiction of Russia.[36] Despite a desperate search for links to the international community, President Shaimiev found that even Turkey was unwilling to engage in much more than business and cultural relations. Moreover, Tatarstan remained vulnerable to Russian threats to shut off all economic and communications links with the outside world. Despite these vulnerabilities, Shaimiev played

---

[34] See *Current Digest of the Post-Soviet Press* 51 (September 8, 1999), 9–12.

[35] See *Current Digest of the Post-Soviet Press* 51 (October 20, 1999), 6.

[36] N. Morozov, "Pozitsiia Tatarstana," *Pravda* May 18, 1991, 2. Also see Al'ians Sabirov, "Provozglashen nezavisimyi Tatarstan," *Izvestiia* August 31, 1990, 2; N. Morozov, "Tatariia sdelala vybor," *Pravda* September 1, 1990, 3.

the game of threatened secession well—as long as Moscow was divided between president and the Congress of People's Deputies. The shift began once Yeltsin eliminated the Russian Congress of People's Deputies, successfully conducted elections for a new parliament, and secured de facto popular ratification of a new federal constitution in December 1993. Shaimiev soon announced that Tatarstan and Russia would sign a treaty of mutual delegation of powers. The treaty followed on February 15, 1994. The shift culminated in the thorough reintegration of Tatarstan in the Russian Federation under the consolidated rule of President Putin.

In Tajikistan, the Gorno-Badakhshan Autonomous Oblast made ambiguous threats to secede in 1992 and 1993, but once a strong common-state leadership reemerged in Tajikistan and Gornyi Badakhshan's leaders weighed the dangers of independence in a hostile international environment, they accepted reintegration of their segment-state within the Tajikistan common-state. With the move to withdraw Tajikistan from the USSR, demonstrators in Khorog, the capital of Gornyi Badakhshan, demanded that their autonomous oblast be elevated to the status of an autonomous republic, but they made it clear that Gornyi Badakhshan would remain within Tajikistan. After the central government refused to grant the demand, Gornyi Badakhshan's legislature (soviet) on April 11, 1992, unilaterally declared an autonomous republic.[37] The ambiguous threat of secession came during Tajikistan's civil war. Gornyi Badakhshan established self-defense forces to maintain order within its borders but found itself involved in conflicts with the forces of the common-state government.[38] With the consolidation of Imomali Rakhmonov's control as leader of Tajikistan during the first months of 1993, fears of Gornyi Badakhshan's secession at first increased, but the central government was able to reach a shaky agreement with Gornyi Badakhshan's leaders to reestablish common-state control within the region.[39] Gornyi Badakhshan's leadership was in a precarious position, with independent armies prowling its mountains and valleys, some apparently in alliance with the Taliban regime across the border in Afghanistan's Badakhshan province. After they had received assurances from the new Tajik government that the segment-state leaders would retain

---

[37] *RFE/RL Daily Report* May 1, 1992.

[38] Andrei Borodin, "Gornyi Badakhshan oboroniaet pereval Khaburobad ot voisk dushanbinskogo rezhima," *Segodnia* August 10, 1993, 1; Aleksandr Karpov, "Tadzhikistan: pereval Khaborabad bezopasen," *Izvestiia* August 11, 1993, 1; Oleg Panfilov, "Dushanbe prodolzhaet voennoe davlenie na Badakhshan," *Nezavisimaia gazeta* August 11, 1993, 3; Margolian 1995; Zviagelskaia 1998.

[39] *RFE/RL Daily Report* January 8, 1993, January 15, 1993, March 5, 1993, March 15, 1993, March 19, 1993, April 7, 1993, June 13, 1993, June 16, 1993, June 21, 1993, July 2, 1993, July 21, 1993, August 4, 1993, August 5, 1993; K. Martin, 1993; United States Institute of Peace 1995, 7.

their positions, officials of the autonomous oblast publicly announced on June 20, 1993, that they would no longer seek independence and would integrate their "self-defense forces" within the command structure of the Tajik army. In 1994, following a referendum on a new Tajikistan constitution, Gornyi Badakhshan confirmed its status as a segment-state (autonomous oblast) within the common-state.

In the Crimean nation-state crisis, disunity in the common-state government of Ukraine was never as extreme as in Russia, Azerbaijan, Georgia, or Tajikistan—and certainly not on the issue of dealing with the segment-state government. Crimea's threat of secession was commensurately guarded. The Crimean threat of secession first became a crisis in May 1992 when the Crimean Supreme Soviet issued a declaration of independence pending a referendum to be held August 2, but the Crimean leaders soon relented by suspending the declaration.[40] The nation-state crisis peaked during a brief period of strong leadership in the segment-state government of Crimea. Yurii Meshkov, leader of the pro-Russia party, won election on January 30, 1994, as president of the Crimean Republic, with the promise that Crimea would become a part of Russia and that relations between Crimea and Ukraine in the future would be governed by treaties.[41] In the early stages of the crisis, conflicting signals from the legislative and executive branches of the Russian government in Moscow to both sides of the Ukrainian crisis left the role of this powerful external actor uncertain, but Yeltsin's victory over the Congress of People's Deputies in late 1993 eliminated the most important source of hope that Crimea might receive support from outside. The threat of secession receded, however, only after the Crimean leaders became deeply divided over how far to press their confrontation with Kiev and how far the Crimean Supreme Soviet would support President Meshkov in building political-identity

[40] Iurii Orlik and Inga Prelovskaia, "Samostoiatel'nost' Kryma provozglashena ego parlamentom, no dolzhna byt' podtverzhdena referendumom," *Izvestiia* May 6, 1992, 1; "Priniata Konstitutsiia Respubliki Krym," *Izvestiia* May 7, 1992, 1; "Parlament Kryma otmenil akt o gosudarstvennoi samostoiatel'nosti respubliki," *Rossiiskaia gazeta* May 22, 1992, 1.

[41] Konstantin Parishkura, "Pervyi krymskii prezident gotov vstupat' v SNG," *Segodnia* February 1, 1994, 1; Mikhail Leont'ev, "Krym vybiraetsia iz-pod oblomkov ukrainskoi ekonomiki," *Segodnia* February 1, 1994, 1; Aleksandr Pilat, "Poluostrov kak most," *Nezavisimaia gazeta* February 2, 1994, 3; Vladimir Skachko, "Kiev dal poniat' Simferopoliu, chto tot slishkom mnogo o sebe vozomnil," *Nezavisimaia gazeta* February 26, 1994, 1; Nikolai Semena, "L. Kravchuk otmenil dve treti spornogo ukaza Iu. Meshkova," *Izvestiia* March 17, 1994, 2; Dmitrii Zhdannikov, "I nikakikh referendumov!" *Segodnia* March 23, 1994, 4; Nikolai Semena, "Kadrovye stressy potriasaiut Krym," *Izvestiia* April 6, 1994, 2; Aleksandr Pilat, "Novyi vitok konfrontatsii mezhdu Simferopolem i Kievom," *Nezavisimaia gazeta* May 20, 1994, 1; Nikolai Semena, "Krym: voina ukazov pererastaet v silovye deistviia," *Izvestiia* May 21, 1994, 2; Aleksandr Pilat, "Krymskie parlamentarii vosstanovili konstitutsiiu 1992 goda," *Nezavisimaia gazeta* May 21, 1994, 1, 3.

hegemony based on his nation-state project. Final agreement between Ukraine and Crimea came in 1995 when a confrontation between the Crimean executive and legislative leaders over competing attempts to consolidate a republic machine left the autonomous republic leaders completely at the mercy of Kiev.[42]

Pre-Soviet Segment-States

The problems of overdetermination in the Soviet and post-Soviet cases limits our ability to distinguish the impact of individual causes in the absence of the others. Moreover, since these cases are limited to a single decade, they beg the question of whether the patterns travel across time to earlier decades in the age of nationalism. For this reason we turn to the pre-Soviet period. Indeed, the very different fates of the three segment-states within the Russian Federation—the Grand Duchy of Finland, the Emirate of Bukhara, and the Khanate of Khiva—confirm the pattern that emphasizes the consolidation of political-identity hegemony in the segment-state, alternating weakness and unity in the common-state leadership, and external allies as deterrents of reversal but not instigators of secession. All three segment-states seceded, but only Finland remained independent after three years. In explaining the temporal variation that ended in very different outcomes, the three factors previously stressed once again emerge as most important, but with one further amendment. Secession by all three began while the common-state leadership of Russia was weakened. Finland had consolidated political-identity hegemony even before secession, but Bukhara and Khiva remained internally divided. Finland gained admission to the international community and support from Euro-

[42] Aleksandr Pilat, "Iurii Meshkov okonchatel'no passorilis' s parlamentom," *Nezavisimaia gazeta* September 9, 1994, 1,3; Aleksandr Pilat, "Parlament progolosoval za votum nedoveriia pravitel'stvu," *Nezavisimaia gazeta* September 17, 1994, 3; Viacheslav Savchenko, "Krym: osen' prezidenta," *Moskovskie novosti* September 11–18, 1994, 1,4; Viachevslav Savchenko, "Krym: skhvatka za absoliutnuiu vlast'," *Moskovskie novosti* October 2–9, 1994, 10; Nikolai Semena, "Krym: Politicheskii shturm v Barkhatnyi sezon," *Izvestiia* September 13, 1994, 1–2; Nikolai Semena, "Meshkov stremitsia k 'nulevomu' variantu, parlament Kryma eto ne ustraivaet . . ." *Izvestiia* September 24, 1994, 2; Nikolai Semena, "V Krymu dva pravitel'stva no ot etogo ne legche," *Izvestiia* October 8, 1994, 2; Viktor Iadukha, "Prezident Meshkov ostanetsia vysshim dolzhnostnym litsom, no ot vlasti fakticheski budet otstranen," *Segodnia* September 30, 1994, 1; Viktor Iadukha, "V S Kryma otmenil reshenie o referendume," *Segodnia* June 1, 1995, 1; Viacheslav Savchenko i Sergei Tikhii, "Krym: Kanun dvoevlastie," *Moskovskie novosti* September 3–10, 1995, 9; Viktor Iadukha, "Krymskie parlament prinial proekt konstitutsii," *Segodnia* September 23, 1995, 4; Mark Agatov, "Revizor s rasshirennymi polnomochiiami," *Kommersant-Daily* February 8, 1996, 4; Vladimir Skachko, "Ukrainskii parlament prinial konstitutsiiu," *Segodnia* June 29, 1996, 1.

pean allies after secession, but the Central Asian emirates remained isolated. Once the Bolsheviks established unified leadership within the RSFSR common-state by beating back the White Armies, the Bolsheviks could take advantage of the Central Asian vulnerabilities, but found no opening to regain Finland. All this suggests the preeminent importance of common-state strength in the initiation of secession, but the importance of political-identity hegemony and external allies to sustain secession against common-state retaliation and reintegration.

On November 15, 1917, a little over a week after the Bolshevik seizure of power in Petrograd, the Finnish parliament (*Eduskunta*) declared that sovereignty had passed to it from the Russian government, and on December 6 it ratified what was subsequently dubbed the Finnish declaration of independence. The new Soviet government acquiesced, and on December 31 the Russian Council of People's Commissars handed to the Finnish government delegation a written message recognizing this independence. On January 4, 1918, the Petrograd Soviet of Workers' and Soldiers' Deputies ratified the grant of independence. Finland's civil war in the first months of 1918 provided the Bolsheviks some hope of recovering Finland, but the Russian government was too preoccupied with other crises to exploit this opportunity fully. With little support from the embattled Red Army, the Finnish Reds were no more successful in Finland than the Tashkent Communists were in Bukhara or Khiva in early 1918.

The fate of the Central Asian segment-states initially paralleled that of Finland, but within three years both had lost their independence, and within seven years both had ceased to exist even as segment-states. The Turkestan Soviet that sought to establish Communist rule in Central Asia tacitly recognized Bukhara's independence on November 29, 1917. After a failed military campaign to reverse this and to reclaim Bukhara the next February and March (at the same time as the Finnish civil war), the Tashkent Soviet formally recognized the independence of both Bukhara and Khiva in May 1918. Yet less than two years later the Red Army invaded Khiva, on December 25, 1919, capturing the Khivan capital on February 1, 1920. In late April 1920 the First All-Khorezmi (Khivan) Congress of Soviets abolished the khanate and proclaimed the Khorezmi People's Soviet Republic. Four months later the Red Army launched an assault on Bukhara and captured the emir's capital by September 2, 1920. On October 6, 1920, the First All-Bukharan Congress of Soviets abolished the 400-year-old emirate and declared the Bukharan People's Soviet Republic. In the 1924 national delimitation, both people's republics were dissolved and divided among the new Central Asian soviet socialist republics.

Which of the factors identified in the hypotheses might explain these different outcomes? First, the relative size of the segment-states may explain the success of Finland where Bukhara and Khiva failed, as predicted by hypothesis 2b. On the eve of World War I, Finland's population of 3.6 million was two-and-a-half times as large as Bukhara's population (1.25 million) and over five times as large as Khiva's population (0.65 million). Yet this seems a less than compelling comparison, since all three populations were miniscule relative to the 130 millions residing in Russia at that time. Second, the vertical cultural divide that separated all three segment-states from the empire's majority contributed to their desire to secede from the empire. All three segment-states were divided from the Orthodox Slavic majority of the empire both by civilization (Islam in Central Asia, Lutheranism in Finland) and by language family (Turkic and Iranian languages in Central Asia, a Finnic language in Finland). This similarity among the segment-states, however, cannot explain their very different fates after three years. Third, each segment-state had preserved or developed political institutions that provided political leadership with institutional weapons to use against local opponents and against Petrograd, as predicted by hypothesis 2a. These local institutions distanced the segment-states from the empire and made the policies of a common-state increasingly irrelevant and even threatening to the segment-state leaders, particularly after the Bolsheviks took power in Petrograd. This similarity may explain the secession of the segment-states, but it cannot explain the different outcomes.

Fourth, and more compelling as an explanation for these different outcomes, is the horizontal cultural heterogeneity of the Central Asian republics that contributed to their weakness in the face of the 1919–20 Red Army offensives, as predicted by hypotheses 2c and 3b. The population of the Central Asian segment-states was divided among Uzbeks, Turkmen, Sarts, and Tajiks, plus Kirgizes in Bukhara and Karakalpaks in Khiva. In contrast, there was significantly greater unity in Finland: in 1917 Finns constituted more than 80 percent of the grand duchy's population. This difference constrained politics within each segment-state. Fifth, and closely related to this cultural diversity, Finland differed from the Central Asian emirates in that its politicians established political-identity hegemony—leading to the outcome predicted by hypothesis 3. As the Finnish historian Osmo Jussila notes in explaining what set the grand duchy apart from regular provinces, "Finland had acquired an identifiable profile as an embryonic state even before the outbreak of the war."[43] The Finnish estates (Diet) had met since the incorporation of Finland into the Russian Empire in 1809, and a separate administration had developed to deal with Finnish affairs that distanced the grand duchy from the direct control of Russian ministries. Among the bureaucrats of this administration a "Finland concept" emerged, and with scholarships, titles, and decorations they privileged

[43] Jussila 1989, 85.

writers and authors who propagated this nation-state project. The strengthening of the Finnish Diet and Senate in the 1856 reform set the stage for the subsequent conflicts over Finland's status that became framed as an interstate conflict—a "conflict between the Finnish 'government' (the Senate and Diet) and the Russian government (the Tsar and his ministers)."[44] The transformation of the four-estate Finnish Diet into a unicameral parliament elected by universal suffrage of both men and women set the stage for an increasingly intense disagreement between this parliament and the Tsarist government after 1910 over the allocation of decision rights, a conflict that was cut short by World War I. As Jussila notes, when sovereign independence for the nation-state came, it was more an administrative upgrade than an act of creation de novo: "What happened on 6 December 1917 was that Finland ceased to be merely an internally independent state [segment-state], and became an externally independent state [nation-state]."[45]

Alternatively, neither the Khan nor the Emir used their political monopolies before the Russian Revolution to create political-identity hegemony that would silence alternative leaders with very different visions of their political future. Both Central Asian dynasties faced recurring revolts from local warlords and Turkmen tribes and increasingly faced a challenge in their cities from reformers (Jadidists) inspired by the Tatars' pan-Turkic program. At the last minute, leaders of both segment-states attempted to impose political-identity hegemony, but it was too late. Khiva's indigenous leadership, which was under the control of Djunaid-khan, the power behind the khan's throne, used the weakening of Petrograd's control after the 1917 revolution to consolidate control by expelling, arresting, and executing modernist reformers and establishing a network of military commanders in each locality, but Khiva could not end the recurring revolts of Turkmen tribes that threatened this unity and drained military resources. Similarly, Bukhara's Emir Alim mobilized a wave of religious zealotry that forced many modernist reformers to flee, and arrested and executed not only reformers but many westernized Bukharans as well, who were identified simply by their education or the fact that they read newspapers.[46] The failure to consolidate political-identity hegemony that would back their autocratic rule and the internal turmoil arising from their last-minute effort to consolidate their hold left both rulers much weaker than the Finnish government once the Soviet leadership had consolidated its hold on power and sought to reverse the secessions.

[44] Jussila, Hentilä, and Nevakivi 1995, 61; also see 39, 88.
[45] Jussila 1989, 100.
[46] Becker 1968, 269–70, 276, 281–84.

Once the Bolshevik government had defeated the White Armies within European Russia, it could turn to reincorporating the segment-states. By 1920, however, the Russian Soviet Federated Socialist Republic faced very different circumstances in each secessionist segment-state. The differences grew not solely from their relative success at establishing political-identity hegemony; they also reflected the quick international recognition of Finland and its access to outside support through ports and shared borders, and, in contrast, the diplomatic, economic, and communications isolation of the Central Asian segment-states. Finnish leaders had been aware for decades before 1917 that "it was important for Finland's future that the country should be ranked as a state in international opinion."[47] Yet in 1917, international recognition did not increase the incentive to initiate a bid for secession. No state was willing to recognize the independence of Finland until the Russian government granted it, and the Nordic countries advised the Finns to lose no time in seeking this recognition from Lenin's Council of People's Commissars. Russian ratification of Finland's independence opened the door to recognition: On the same day, France and Sweden extended recognition, followed by other European states, which only then were willing to support Finland in its struggle to keep independence.[48] By late 1920, reconquest of Finland would have been inordinately costly for the new Soviet state: the Finnish population was united by political-identity hegemony in defense of Finnish independence, particularly after the brutal suppression of the Reds two years earlier, and European powers had made it clear to the Bolsheviks that they would help in the defense of Finnish independence against any westward expansion of Bolshevism.

Alternatively, Bukhara and Khiva had not established their claims to statehood in the world community. Russian recognition of their independence had not brought links to the larger international community. Both Bukhara and Khiva depended on Russia for railroad and communication links with the outside world, and Bukhara even depended on Russia for its water supply. Bukhara needed Russian markets for its only major commercial crop, cotton, and found that the closure of these markets and the absence of alternatives deprived the emir of critical tax revenues he needed to maintain his army.[49] The British operating from India had sent troops to Transcaspia, the Russian province just south and west of Khiva, but were unwilling to provide more than token armed support. The evacuation of British troops by April 1919 left the Bukharans and Khivans isolated except for sporadic contacts across desert and mountains with the new Afghanistan regime.

[47] Jussila 1989, 90.
[48] Jussila, Hentilä, and Nevakivi 1995, 102–8.
[49] Becker 1968, 275, 283.

In short, the opportunity for all three segment-states to assert their independence was the turmoil in the common-state government of the Russian Empire that brought down the Tsarist regime and then the Provisional Government. Under conditions of complete collapse of central control in 1917, even segment-states without political-identity hegemony could claim their independence. Yet the success of Finland at building political-identity hegemony before secession and its success at building links to the international community during the brief period that followed secession permitted Finland to fend off any attempt to reintegrate the former segment-state once the Bolsheviks began to consolidate power in the new Soviet common-state. Alternatively, the failure to establish political-identity hegemony before secession or international diplomatic ties in the brief period after secession left Bukhara and Khiva internally weakened and internationally isolated. Once the Bolsheviks established control over the Volga and Urals regions and over the railway in Central Asia, the balance shifted decisively back toward the common-state government, and both Bukhara and Khiva lost not only their independence but, in 1924, their very existence as states.[50]

Global Patterns

The high correlation of status and decision rights with demographic and cultural factors in the post-Soviet cases makes it difficult to estimate the relative importance of each constraint on the survival of segmental institutions. The closer examination of secessions, de facto secessions, reversals, and withdrawn threats begins to unravel one cause from the other. Yet these cases leave open the possibility that these findings are limited in time and space to one set of events that never have been or will be repeated. The comparison with the pattern of success and failure among pre-Soviet segment-states does confirm the continuing central importance of political-identity hegemony within segment-states, the unity and security of leadership within the common-state, and the role of external allies in deterring reversal of secession. Still to be determined is the question of whether these patterns hold with equal strength in other parts of the world. To answer this question, we must expand the cases we compare.

Model Specification

To estimate the relative importance of each constraint identified in the hypotheses and to test the universality of these hypotheses, I again turn to statistical analysis with a global data set. This analysis uses all segmental

---

[50] Mandel 1942.

relationships in the twentieth century, as discussed in chapter 2 and identified in the appendix. In the statistical analysis, new segmental relationships that were established after 1990 are dropped because the span of time before the end of the century is so short. The resulting data set includes 336 segmental dyads, each of which links a common-state government and a segment-state (such as the Russian Empire–Bukhara dyad). There are separate observations on a dyad for each year that it existed between 1901 and 2000. There are, thus, 13,644 observations.

The dependent variable is a measure of institutional failure (F_{cy})—all secessions of segment-states from common-states that elevated the segment-state itself to the status of an independent nation-state. (A secondary dependent variable is simply all secessions. This second equation is estimated to check whether there is a different pattern in this larger group of failed segmented states.) Of the 336 segmental dyads, 194 (57.7 percent) failed because of secession, termination and centralization, or reconfiguration within a new segment-state during the century. Failure that ended with secession of the segment-state accounted for 159 of the failures. These include 127 cases that elevated the segment-state into a sovereign state such as Estonia in 1991 and Samoa in 1962 without significant change in territory or population. The other 32 secessions resulted in partition of the segment-state (such as, Palestine in 1947 and Ruanda-Urundi in 1962) or unification with another sovereign state (such as, Bosnia-Herzegovina in 1918 and British Somaliland in 1960).

To test the hypotheses presented in the first part of this chapter concerning the likelihood that segmental arrangements will survive or fail, I use the statistical technique of survival analysis.[51] This is a method that analyzes the expected length of time until failure; it also estimates the impact of different constraints on this failure rate. (It is a technique most often associated with clinical trials where medical researchers attempt to estimate the life expectancy of patients after administration of various procedures.) It is preferable to linear regression for the analysis of this type of data, because it makes more reasonable assumptions about the distribution of time to failure. In particular, it does not require the assumption of a normal distribution of error terms.

Constraints on Survival

The constraints on survival (or covariates) that we can test with available data include many of the institutional, demographic, and cultural factors identified in previous hypotheses as bearing on the balance of leverage

---

[51] See Box-Steffensmeier and Jones 1997.

between segment-state and common-state leaders.[52] The model is of the form:

$$F_{csy} = \theta \, (W_{cy}, \, E_{sy}, \, S_s, \, D_{csy}, \, P_{csy}, \, C_{cs}, \, Y_y),$$

where

F_{csy} indicates the failure of a segmental relationship linking common-state c with segment-state s that resulted in the secession (independence) of s in year y,

W_{cy} indicates weakness in the government of common-state c due to turmoil or constitutional change at the beginning of year y,

E_{sy} indicates empowerment of the population of the segment-state s within its borders through self-government at the beginning of year y,

S_s indicates that segment-state s had been an independent state immediately prior to its incorporation within common-state c,

D_{csy} indicates disfranchisement of the population of the segment-state s (that is, exclusion) from the government of common-state c at the beginning of year y,

P_{csy} is the population balance between segment-state s and the metropolitan core of common-state c at the beginning of year y,

C_{cs} indicates cultural division between the population of segment-state s and the population of the metropolitan core of common-state c, and

Y is a count variable for the number of years since 1900.

The indicator of empowerment of the population of the segment-state (E_{sy}) is whether the segment-state had a locally constituted legislature at the beginning of the year—that is, whether the segment-state was at least minimally self-governing. These segment legislatures included not only assemblies with a majority elected by the local population (or the enfranchised portion of that population) but also assemblies of local oligarchs or nobles.[53] They do not include purely coöpted bodies that were appointed by the common-state government.[54]

Consistent with the segmental institutions thesis, most of the institutional variables indicate interaction in politics of both the common-state and the segment-state. For example, to test whether the weakening of the common-state government affected the likelihood of institutional failure

---

[52] Unfortunately, I have been unable to identify a data source for variables that would permit a test of the hypothesis about external allies. Existing data sets for external involvement in extrasystemic and intrastate wars that cover the entire century—for example, the Correlates of War project—only code formal, publically acknowledged commitments of troops. Thus, fewer than five external alliances are identified for the cases examined here.

[53] Data are from *Statesman's Yearbook* 1900–2001.

[54] The chief executive or administrative officer, such as the governor, may have been constituted locally or appointed by the common-state government.

and secession, common-state weakness (W_{cy}) indicates regime change or constitutional turmoil in the common-state government as it entered the new year.[55] Segment-states with their own political leadership are in a better position to take advantage of this, so the survival model includes two variables based on the interaction of political turmoil with the previous indicator of segment-state self-governance—turmoil in the presence of self-governance and turmoil in the absence of self-governance.

The primary institutional patterns in the common-state concern disfranchisement or exclusion of the segment-state's population from the politics of the common-state (D_{cy}) and the interaction of this with segment-state self-government. Five variables indicate political arrangements that range from the fully exclusive common-state autocracy to the fully inclusive common-state democracy. These variables capture the interaction among three factors: the inclusiveness of the common-state government, the role of the segment-state population within that government, and the availability of empowered leadership within the segment-state. Specifically, the variables are (1) common-state autocracy, (2) common-state anocracy with segment-state self-governance, (3) common-state anocracy without segment-state self-governance, (4) democracy within the metropolitan core but exclusion of the population of a self-governing segment-state, and (5) democracy within the metropolitan core but exclusion of the population of a non-self-governing segment-state.[56] The baseline or comparison group—that is, the omitted category—against which the hazard rates are compared is the set of fully inclusive democracies.

Statehood immediately prior to incorporation as a segment-state may be associated with stronger political-identity hegemony within segment-states, as note in chapter 9. Four of the segment-states had previously been states with recognition from the great powers and another thirty-two had resembled independent states—some examples of the latter are, Hawaii, the sultanates of the Malay peninsula, Madagascar, and Tibet—but were not integrated within the international system through state-level diplomatic relations with more than one great power.[57] Yet the examples of Bukhara and Khiva suggest that traditional leaders in segment-states may be unwilling to embrace the form of populist politics necessary for strong political-identity hegemony. Thus, the survival model includes two indicators of prior statehood (S_s). The thirty-six cases of prior statehood are divided between those in which the executive—usually a traditional monarch

[55] Data are from Marshall and Jaggers 2000; all cases coded –66, –77, or –88 are coded as turmoil or change.

[56] Data are from Marshall and Jaggers 2000. Democracies are polities that have a Polity Score of 6 or higher; semicompetitive polities have scores from –5 to 5.

[57] Data are from *Statesman's Yearbook* 1900–2001; Singer 2002; K. Gleditsch and Ward 1999; Harding 1998.

such as a king, emir, or sultan—was retained as at least a figurehead for the segment-state and those in which the traditional leadership was abolished.

The population balance (P_{cy}) is measured by the ratio between the populations of the segment-state (numerator) and metropolitan core (denominator).[58] This varies from 0.000055 for Palau and the United States in 1981 to 9.5 for India and the United Kingdom in 1947.

Vertical cultural heterogeneity (C_{cs}) in a segmental dyad is indicated by three variables for religion and language: simultaneous religious and linguistic difference, religious difference only, and linguistic difference only.[59] Using Samuel P. Huntington's distinction among civilizations, the variables for religious differences indicate whether the dominant religion of the segment-state population belonged to a different civilization than the dominant religion of the common-state population. This codes segment-state populations by their religions prior to establishment of control by the metropolitan core. Thus, extensive conversions to the religion of the metropole, as took place among the Tongans or Rwandans, do not change the "civilizational" divide between metropolitan core and segment-state populations. Linguistic difference indicates that the language of segment-state and common-state populations belong to different language groups (such as Romance versus Germanic languages). In total, 208 (61.6 percent) of the segmental dyads were divided by both religion and language; 70 (20.8 percent) were divided only by language.

The survival model also includes a variable counting the number of years since 1900 (Y). This permits estimation of changes in the failure rate over the century.

Estimation Results

In these statistical models the primary purpose is to estimate the effect of each constraint on the likelihood that a segment-state will be elevated to the status of an independent nation-state. (The second dependent variable for all secessions is only a check that the larger category of secessions does not turn up contradictory results.) The estimation procedure is a Cox proportional hazard model. This does not directly estimate the hazard rate but instead estimates hazard ratios, which show how much higher or lower the hazard rate is when some constraint is present. When this hazard ratio is greater than 1 it indicates a proportionate increase in the rate of failure

---

[58] For internal segments the denominator is the remainder of the population after subtraction of the segment population. Data are from *Statesman's Yearbook* 1900–2001; Mitchell 1998a, 1998b, 1998c; United States Bureau of the Census 1998.

[59] Sources are *Statesman's Yearbook* 1900–2001; Bromlei 1988; Bruk 1986; Bruk and Apenchenko 1964; Levinson 1991.

(in this case, secession and independence); for example, a hazard ratio of 1.5 would indicate a 50 percent higher failure rate when a dichotomous condition like cultural heterogeneity was present or a continuous variable, such as the population ratio had increased by one unit. A hazard ratio below 1 indicates a proportionate decline in the rate of failure; for example, a hazard ratio of 0.67 indicates a 33 percent lower failure rate when a dichotomous condition is present or the independent variable is one unit higher.

The hazard ratios associated with secession and elevation of a segment-state to independence appear in the first column of figures in table 10.3. The likelihood that a segment-state would be "elevated" to independence rose over the course of the twentieth century—and at an escalating rate. As the Year variable indicates, each year from 1900 brought a 3.9 percent increase in the independence rate—an increase that was compounded. Thus, by 1950 the independence rate was about 6.87 times as high as in 1900.[60] This does not mean that the average age of the segmental relationship at the point of failure and independence was falling, however. Although the average age at death in a few years shows the affect of a few outliers, such as Cuba (4 years old) in 1902 and Andorra (715 years old) in 1993, there is no long-term trend. Similarly, despite fluctuations in a few years with bursts of independence, the average age of surviving segment-states is remarkably steady across the century—74.14 years in 1901 and again in 2000. Both old and new segmental relations were failing across the century at roughly the same rate, but both were failing at a higher rate in the latter half of the century.

Political institutions had a profound effect on the likelihood of failure that led to independence of new nation-states. The interaction of segment-state institutions and the common-state political regime was of overwhelming importance. By arranging the relative failure rates, as in table 10.4, there is an apparent progression from exclusive autocracy with the least likelihood of secession to open and competitive politics with higher likelihood of secession—a pattern predicted by hypotheses 5a, 5b, and 5c. A democracy that gave separate political status to segment-state populations, by excluding them from politics ran roughly triple the risk of secession that led to a new nation-state as a fully inclusive democracy. When this separate political status was further reinforced by separate locally constituted political authority in the segment-state, the risk was about 17 times greater than in a fully inclusive democracy. Anocracies, in the absence of segmental self-governance, were no more likely than exclusionary democracies to experience secession that led to a new nation-state, but the introduction of self-

---

[60] The compounding rate is estimated by 1.039298^n, where n is the number of years since 1900.

TABLE 10.3

Constraints affecting the likelihood of independence of segment-states worldwide, 1901–2000 (Cox proportional hazard ratios)

	Outcome: Independent nation-state		Outcome: All secessions	
	Hazard ratio	z	Hazard ratio	z
Common-state anocracy:				
Self-governing segment-state	39.365***	(7.26)	33.095***	(7.60)
Non-self-governing segment-state	3.067	(0.99)	6.022*	(2.42)
Democratic metropole, exclusion of:				
Self-governing segment-state	17.204***	(5.90)	14.098***	(6.05)
Non-self-governing segment-state	3.103*	(1.96)	3.693**	(2.63)
Common-state transition:				
Segment-state self-government	49.271***	(5.93)	37.931***	(5.88)
Non-self-governing segment-state	16.595***	(3.68)	27.454***	(5.62)
Autocracy	a		0.560	(−0.88)
Prior statehood with coöptation of pre-incorporation leadership	0.493*	(−2.00)	0.400**	(−2.69)
Prior statehood with abolition of pre-incorporation leadership	1.635	(1.14)	1.584	(1.23)
Population ratio	1.265**	(2.68)	1.205*	(2.27)
Religious plus linguistic heterogeneity	2.732***	(3.51)	3.305***	(4.45)
Religious heterogeneity only	0.298	(−1.85)	0.330	(−1.73)
Linguistic heterogeneity only	0.477	(−1.89)	0.436*	(−2.16)
Year	1.039***	(7.67)	1.034***	(7.82)
Statistics:				
n = 336	$\chi^2 = 320.74$		$\chi^2 = 323.90$	
Time at risk = 13,675	p < .0000		p < .0000	
Observations = 13,644	Failures = 129		Failures = 161	

Significance: *p < .05, **p <. 01, *** p <. 001.
[a] Approaches zero (1.77e–20).

government in the segment-state raised the likelihood over 39 times compared to a fully inclusive democracy.

Weakness in the common-state government reflected in or due to political transition increased the likelihood of secession and independence even in the absence of segment-state self-government. With this weakness the likelihood of secession leading to a new independent nation-state was over 16 times higher than the base rate. Turmoil together with segment-state self-governance had a devastating effect: the likelihood of secession and independence was over 49 times higher than in the fully inclusive democracy. This is consistent with hypothesis 4.

TABLE 10.4

Relative likelihood of independence under alternative institutional arrangements worldwide, 1901–2000 (Cox proportional hazard ratios)

	Segment-state	
Common-state	Non-self-governing	Self-governing
Turmoil	16.60***	49.27***
Anocracy	3.07	39.37***
Democracy, exclusion of segment-state	3.10*	17.20***
Inclusive democracy[a]	1.0	1.0
Autocracy	—[b]	—[b]

Significance: *$p < .05$, **$p < .01$, ***$p < .001$.

[a] The baseline against which all other hazard ratios are compared.

[b] Failure under autocracy approached zero.

In each of these instances it was the empowerment of the segment-state with its own locally constituted political authority that had a larger effect than differences in the common-state regime.[61] The differences among common-state regimes (moving upward along the first column of table 10.4) were associated with less dramatic increases in the likelihood of secession than the difference between non-self-governing and self-governing segment-states (moving from the first to the second column of hazard ratios). The only exceptions were autocratic common-state governments, which virtually eliminated the chances of successful secession as long as the common-state regime remained stable. This pattern is consistent with the predictions of hypotheses 5, 5a, 5b, 5c, and 5d.

As in the differences between Finland and the Central Asian protectorates, it was the development of self-government that empowered a broader elite (not just a narrow autocratic elite, as in a traditional protectorate) and increased the likelihood of secession and independence. Indeed, many traditional elites in protectorates, such as Bukhara and Khiva, were reluctant to champion political-identity hegemony or a nation-state project that would empower the public at large. Thus, the hazard ratio for coöpted pre-incorporation leadership actually indicates a much lower likelihood of independence.

The rate at which segment-states became independent nation-states was significantly affected by the other constraints on the balance of leverage. The population ratio is significant, but not an overwhelming constraint on the independence rate. The segment-state that approached parity with the common-state—that is, where the population ratio approached 1—had an approximately 26.5 percent greater likelihood of independence than a seg-

---

[61] Compare the results in Strang 1990, 853–56.

ment-state that was significantly smaller than the common-state, where the ratio approached 0. This is consistent with hypothesis 2b.

Vertical cultural heterogeneity was also important, but only simultaneous religious and linguistic difference between the segment-state and common-state populations was statistically significant. Segment-states divided from the metropolitan core by both religious and linguistic traditions were more than 2.5 times as likely to become independent nation-states as segment-states that shared a common religion and linguistic tradition with the common-state. This is consistent with hypothesis 2c. Neither religious nor linguistic difference alone was significant, however.

Where Else Did Nation-States Come From?

The focus on dynamics within segment-states to explain where nation-states come from does overlook the experience of those few independent states that were not created from segment-states. Do these exceptions show a pattern that challenges the segmental institutions thesis? Of the 177 nation-states created between 1901 and 2000, only twenty-four (13.6 percent) could be counted as exceptions to the segmental institutions thesis. Two of these new nation-states resulted from incorporation of territory previously outside the international system (Afghanistan in 1919, Saudi Arabia in 1932).[62] Six resulted from postwar occupations that divided existing states but were supposed to be temporary (the two Koreas in 1948, the two Germanies in 1949, the two Vietnams in 1954). Four new nation-states resulted from unification of segment-states (South Africa in 1910), segment-states with existing independent states (Yugoslavia in 1918), or the divided states created by postwar occupation (unified Vietnam in 1975, unified Germany in 1990).[63] The remaining twelve resulted from secessions of territories and peoples that were not segment-states—Panama in 1903, Albania in 1912, Poland in 1918, Czechoslovakia in 1919, Estonia in 1919, Latvia in 1919, Lithuania in 1919, Yemen in 1919, Pakistan in 1947, Israel in 1948, and Burundi and Rwanda in 1962. These are the most important anomalies for the segmental institutions thesis. Yet, closer examination reveals two reasons that these anomalies are less troubling for the thesis. First, anomalies have become fewer with time. Two-thirds of the twelve anomalies took place by the time of the peace treaties that ended World War I. Only the separation of Pakistan in 1947, Israel in 1948, and Rwanda and Burundi in 1962 came later. Anomalies accounted for more than 36 percent of all new

[62] The core of Saudi Arabia had been part of the Ottoman Empire until 1918, but for the next decade the successor states of Asir, Hejaz, and Nejd were not recognized as sovereign states until united in the Saudi Kingdom.

[63] On unification as a path to new nation-states, see Ziblatt 2006.

nation-states created through secession prior to World War II but less than 4 percent of those created after World War II. Second, with closer examination, it becomes apparent that many of these anomalies looked much like segment-states prior to independence. The anomalies fall into three patterns (table 10.5). Four of these—Estonia, Latvia, Lithuania, and Poland—were actually segment-states just prior to independence but were created in the heat of World War I and on the very eve of independence. Another four cases—Panama, Yemen, Burundi, and Rwanda—represent marginal cases with weak formal institutions and strong informal institutions, so that classifying them as segment-states or not remains ambiguous. The remaining four cases are unambiguously anomalies that thoroughly contradict the expectations of the segmental institutions thesis. Albania and Czechoslovakia represent clear-cut cases of international intervention to impose a solution without strong support from segmental institutions. Israel and Pakistan stand out as extremely rare instances in which the romantic story of a newly awakened, impatient nation insisting on the creation of an entirely new state is closer to the mark.

In the Baltic and Polish provinces of the Russian Empire, the reorganization of administrations along ethnic lines came during World War I. In a last-minute effort to hold on to power against the Germans in the Baltic provinces, the Russian Provisional Government created segment-states to reorganize its administration in the areas it still controlled, to undermine the occupying German forces in the other regions, and to weaken German allies among the Baltic nobility in Livonia and Courland. On March 30, 1917, the Russian Provisional Government created an Estonia from Estland and northern Livland and temporarily instituted a new provincial assembly.[64] In the remainder of the unoccupied areas of Courland and Livland a local administration emerged and pressed Petrograd to recognize its ambition to constitute itself as an autonomous Latvian unit within a future democratic Russia.[65] With the German decision to recreate a Lithuanian state, three segment-like states were nearly accomplished facts before the war was over. Yet the fate of the new divisions quickly came to depend on the German occupation and Western intervention. In the Estonian lands that Germany occupied from late February 1918 until the November armistice, the Germans suppressed the nationalists and pushed forward with plans for a personal union of the lands with the German emperor. After the German surrender in November, however, the Western powers cultivated Estonia as a bulwark against the Bolsheviks.[66] In Latvia, the German Empire did not cultivate the new national administration, since the Germans

---

[64] Browder and Kerensky 1961, 300–1; Raun 1987, 100.
[65] Page 1949.
[66] Raun 1987, 105–11; Page 1948.

TABLE 10.5
Origins of new states worldwide, 1901–2000

Origin	Examples	Number of States
Segment-states		153
Newly incorporated territory	Afghanistan 1919	2
	Saudi Arabia 1932	
Occupation and division of states	South Korea 1948	6
	North Korea 1948	
	East Germany 1949	
	West Germany 1949	
	North Vietnam 1954	
	South Vietnam 1954	
Unification of segment-states or existing states	South Africa 1910	4
	Yugoslavia 1918	
	Vietnam 1975	
	Germany 1990	
Last-minute segment-states	Poland 1918	4
	Estonia 1919	
	Latvia 1919	
	Lithuania 1919	
Ambiguous institutional arrangement	Panama 1903	4
	Yemen 1919	
	Burundi 1962	
	Rwanda 1962	
Great-power division of empires	Albania 1912	2
	Czechoslovakia 1919	
National awakening without segment-state and not imposed by great powers	Pakistan 1947	2
	Israel 1948	
Total		177

sought to restore the Baltic German nobility in an extension of the empire. After the Armistice of November 1918, however, German policy changed. Latvians, with continuing protection from the German troops that remained in occupation and with entente support, declared their independence and, with a joint German-Latvian force, expelled the Bolsheviks from Riga and eastern Latvia.[67] In Lithuania, the German occupation was more supportive of a declaration of independence: the German commander-in-chief authorized creation of a Lithuanian Council on June 2, 1917, and the Lithuanians created an independent republic under the patronage of the Reich authority.[68]

---

[67] Plakans 1995, 116–20; von Rauch 1974, 39–75. Also see Hiden 1970.
[68] Von Rauch 1974, 40–43; Sužiedėlis 1965, 7–19; Senn 1959, 28–46; Misiunas and Taagapera 1983, 9.

Poland became a segment-state just prior to independence. The Kingdom of Poland had been a segment-state within the Russian Empire after 1815 but lost its constitution and institutions of self-governance in 1832.[69] After the 1863 Polish insurrection it lost its separate administrative status. The Polish state that attained independence in late 1918 was actually a reconstitution of the earlier segment-state by the German and Austrian Empires as part of their war effort to detach Poland from the Russian Empire. On November 5, 1916, the German and Austrian emperors proclaimed a new Kingdom of Poland as a state with a constitution of its own. On September 12, 1917, the two emperors sanctioned creation of a Polish Regency Council that would serve as a collective chief of state and began ceding legislative, judicial, and administrative powers to the Poles. On June 22, 1918, the emperors empowered a national *Sejm* (Parliament). The emperors were cultivating a segment-state that they hoped would serve as a buffer against Russia once the war ended. Once the defeat of Germany and Austria seemed imminent, however, this last-minute segment-state seceded. Other contemporaneous attempts to create an independent Poland without a segment-state failed, including Pilsudski's attempt in 1914 to fight for independence, the Polish National Committee's attempt to rally the governments in Paris, London, and Washington behind their own Poland project, and the socialists' attempt to create a people's state with a coup in Lublin in November 1917. All had to come to terms with the kingdom. As Hans Roos observes, this project was privileged above the others by creating a real proto-state prior to independence: "all the Poles' efforts could scarcely have been successful had the Austro-German proclamation of the State not created the fundamental presuppositions for independence. The manifestos of November 5, 1916, not only founded an independent administration, which was there ready to be used when the Central Powers collapsed, but it also set the Polish question in motion on the diplomatic level both among the Entente Powers and in Russia."[70]

Four of the anomalies are borderline cases in which weak formal institutions and strong informal institutional arrangements made de facto segment-states. Panama was a province but not a segment-state when it seceded from Colombia in 1903. Yet for more than sixty years prior to constitutional changes in 1885, Panama was close to a segment-state with extensive self-rule. Panama had even enjoyed a constitutional right to secede, which it exercised in 1840–42 and 1857–63.[71] This put in place an identity and institutional network that was mobilized by provincial leaders in 1903. Prior to independence in 1918, Yemen had been a province (*vil-*

[69] Porter 1992.

[70] Roos 1966, 46. Also see Leslie et al. 1980, 112–38; Lundgreen-Nielsen 1979.

[71] H. Hill 1965, 30–68; McCain 1965, 11–18.

layet) within the Ottoman Empire under the direct rule of a Pasha appointed as governor from Istanbul, but in the Treaty of Da'an (1913), Istanbul gave Imam Muhammad ibn Yahya autonomy within the Zaydi community in the highlands. Northern Yemen quickly came close to being a segment-state under the Imams and, as Manfred W. Wenner notes, "the Imam had established a strong legal precedent for his assumption of power once the Porte abandoned the Wilayat [*villayet*]."[72] Burundi and Rwanda became independent in 1962 by dividing the segment-state of Ruanda-Urundi, despite continuing United Nations pressure to preserve the unity of the trust territory into independence. Yet Ruanda-Urundi was more a legal fiction than a reality of administration: the Belgians created few common institutions for Ruanda-Urundi and relied on the separate kingships of the two territories for the development of indigenous administration and participatory politics. In the 1940s and 1950s, when the Belgians developed councils for self-government from the local level up, self-government terminated at the two kingships without a council for the Trust Territory as a whole. The two halves of the Trust Territory diverged in their political development as political parties to contest elections developed separately in each, and then in 1961 a coup toppled the king (*mwami*) of Rwanda and declared a republic, while Burundi remained a kingdom. Each half looked more like a segment-state than the trust territory that combined them. As René Lemarchand observes, "lacking a central institutional focus around which a common political consciousness could be developed, there were ample grounds for questioning the prospects of a durable union between the two states. Now that their recent political evolution had drawn them further apart from each other, their unification into a single independent state seemed even more improbable."[73]

More clearly anomalous for the segmental institutions thesis were the two cases in which the newly independent nation-states had not had a unified administration to provide a basis for statehood. Albania and Czechoslovakia were the results of great power politics around the time of World War I. Albania was the creation of an international Conference of Ambassadors that on July 29, 1913, proclaimed Albania to be a sovereign state. Prior to this, what would become Albania was divided among four distinct provinces (*villayet*) of the Ottoman Empire. The majority of the provincial elites had favored remaining part of the empire, and even as the empire began to collapse around them and after Montenegro invaded with the objective of annexing some of these provinces, the provincial elites could not reach consensus on a nation-state project.[74] As J. Swire laments, Albania

[72] Wenner 1967, 48. Also see Dresch 2000, 1–27; Farah 2002, 212–73.
[73] Lemarchand 1970, 86. Also see Nyrop et al. 1969, 13–24; McDonald et al. 1969, 12–20.
[74] Skendi 1967, 438–63.

was a product of Austrian and Italian diplomacy and "was created of expediency, not of spontaneity, and her vital interests were sacrificed that the peace of Europe might be preserved."[75] The creation of Czechoslovakia resulted from the conjunction of two factors—expulsion of the Czech regions from Austria and the commitment during World War I to the Czechoslovak nation-state project by the Entente Powers. The solid support of the American, British, and French governments for the Czechoslovak project was the result of able diplomacy by Professor Tomás Masaryk. Yet there was remarkably little activism to support this project in the Czech and Slovak lands. Victor Mamatey notes that "on the eve of World War I the Czechs, though deeply frustrated in the Hapsburg Empire, could not conceive of living outside it" and that "the Czechs and Slovaks had no plans to seek independence and unity before World War I."[76] R. W. Seton-Watson explains this lack of separatism in terms that sound like the segmental institutions thesis: "there was no Czech state outside the Monarchy towards which they could gravitate."[77] The de facto independence of the Czech lands was the curious consequence of Austria's decision to dissolve the last of its empire on October 21, 1918. The Czechs were forced to be free, but it took them another seven days to acknowledge their own independence.[78] Creation of a Czechoslovak state followed after the Entente Powers pressed Hungary to surrender the Slovak lands.

Although the stories of the creation of Israel and Pakistan have provided templates through which many scholars have attempted to account for the origins of nation-states more generally, the story of each is exceptional.[79] In broad strokes the creation of Israel resembles the story of national awakening, mobilization, and creation of new states told in conventional accounts of where nation-states come from. Jews kept alive the idea of nationhood and a homeland for centuries. Through the masterful efforts of Theodor Herzl, an Austrian journalist, and the first Zionist Congress in 1897, this took political form in the age of nationalism with an actual project for a Jewish nation-state. The propagation of this nation-state project through newspapers like Herzl's *Die Welt*, pamphlets, and orators focused support among Jews. Among the unusual accomplishments of a movement without a segment-state were the coordination of unofficial immigration into Palestine, the organization of paramilitary groups to defend settlers and press their cause, the unofficial diplomacy that kept pressure on the British government through nearly three decades of its Palestine Mandate,

---

[75] Swire 1971, 148.
[76] Mamatey 1973, 5, 10.
[77] R. Seton-Watson 1965, 285.
[78] Mamatey 1973; R. Seton-Watson 1965, 284–312; Kovtun 1985.
[79] See A. Smith 1986, 1998; Armstrong 1982.

and the pressure that placed this nation-state project on the bargaining table of the United Nations.[80] The national awakening, mobilization, and birth of the nation-state of Pakistan had a similar but much shorter gestation. The poet-philosopher Muhammad Iqbal, by the time of his Allahabad Address to the Muslim League in December 1930, had formulated a vision of statehood for the Muslim regions of British India. This idea spread rapidly among Indian Muslim intellectuals, including the student at Cambridge who concocted the acronym Pakistan from the provinces that would make up this entirely new imagined state. The conversion of Mohammed Ali Jinnah to this nation-state project and abandonment of the Union of India project culminated after the 1937 provincial assembly elections. On March 22, 1940, Jinnah presented his own plan for independence before the Muslim League, and the following day the league adopted this in its Lahore Resolution. Through artful propagation of this nation-state project by journalists and through compromises with vested interests in the provinces that would constitute Pakistan, the Muslim League emerged as the leading party among India's Muslims in time for the 1947 provincial assembly elections. Despite continuing opposition from the British authorities and Congress Party leaders, who devised various plans after World War II to keep the Union of India whole, the firm stance of the Muslim League, its Direct Action program of 1946, and the spread of Hindu-Muslim communal violence convinced the British authorities and Congress Party leaders that an attempt to save the Union of India project might lead to a full civil war. On June 3, 1947, the British Viceroy Louis Mountbatten relented and announced the beginning of the transfer of power to separate states of India and Pakistan—a transfer that was completed within two and a half months when independence came on August 15, 1947.[81]

Patterns in the Results

The comparisons using qualitative and quantitative evidence reveal a pattern that is consistent with the hypotheses presented at the opening of this chapter (table 10.6). The evidence highlights variation in political institutions within the segmented state, which affected the incentives and distribution of means to escalate conflict. First, the empowerment of the leadership within the segment-state was most important in the initiation of secessions and the successful achievement of independence, as predicted by hypotheses 2a and 3a. This empowerment provided greater *means* for segment-state leaders to create political-identity hegemony, to mobilize

---

[80] Fraser 1984, 130–59; Gilbert 1998, 3–249; Lucas 1975.
[81] Symonds 1950, 49–88; Fraser 1984, 68–129; Burki 1986, 9–25; Hussain 1997, 418–61.

TABLE 10.6

Summary of results: Predictors of segment-state independence

Hypotheses		Findings[a]		
Constraint	*Prediction*	*Post-Soviet cases*	*Pre-Soviet cases*	*Worldwide*
2 *Segment leverage*				
2a Segment decision rights	+	+		
2b Demographic parity	+	+		+ .05–.01
2c Cultural heterogeneity	+	+		+ .001
2d Segment revenue stream	+	+		
2e Segment external allies	+	+	+	
3 *Political-identity hegemony*	+		+	+
3a Segment decision rights	+	+		
3b Cultural separation-unity	+	+	+	+ .001[b]
3c Revenue stream	+	+		+
3d Prior independence	+			
4 *Common-state weakness*	+	+	+	+ .001
5 *Relative incorporation*				
5a Segment disfranchised	–			–
5b Disfranchised/empowered	+			+ .001
5c Fully enfranchised	–			–

[a] Pluses, minuses, and zeroes indicate positive, negative, or no significant relationship in the pattern of variation. Only the global comparisons use statistical tests; the numbers indicate the level of significance.
[b] Results for simultaneous linguistic and religious difference only.

the segment-state population behind a nation-state project, and to pressure the common-state government. Second, particularly promising for the independence of empowered segment-states was weakness in the common-state government due to political turmoil or constitutional change, as predicted by hypothesis 4.

Strong support for these institutional hypotheses is apparent in the patterns of successful achievement of sovereign independence by the union republics, the varying fortunes of de facto secessions both among the lower-order autonomies within the Soviet successor states and among the pre-Soviet segment-states, and the elevation of segment-states to sovereign independence around the world for the past century. Indeed, in the Eurasian cases both segment-state hegemony and common-state weakness were usually present when a segment-state initiated its bid to achieve independence. Complete collapse of the center, as during the Russian Revolution, might permit even segment-states without political-identity hegemony to claim independence, but that extreme balance of consolidation has been unusual. The absence of political-identity hegemony may very soon prove fatal to a bid for independence. The reversal of the secessions of Bukhara, Chechnya, and Khiva all took place when their leaders failed to establish political-identity hegemony and they could not hold off a newly unified common-state leadership. The withdrawal of Crimea's threat of secession came as its leadership divided over attempts to create political-identity hegemony in the segment-state. The complete absence from the list of secessionist regimes of any republics identified as having competitive polities in chapter 3 reinforces this conclusion.

Turmoil or constitutional change in the common-state that threatened the survival of segment-state leaders was a particularly powerful source of incentives to escalate pressure for independence. This was a reason behind the first challenges from the Baltic states as they confronted Gorbachev's democratization reforms. It led the South Ossetian and Abkhazian leaders to conclude that they could not remain within Georgia. In addition, the exclusion of empowered segment-states from common-state governance was a powerful motive to escalate pressure for independence and had a devastating effect on the survival of segmental institutions, as predicted by hypotheses 3 and 5. Globally the combination of empowerment within the segment-state but disfranchisement from the common-state government led to a manifold increase in the likelihood of secession and independence of segment-states.

The pre- and post-Soviet comparisons suggest the importance of external allies, as predicted by hypothesis 2e. Yet this was important only in a very specific institutional context. External allies were opportunistic. They entered conflicts defined by segmental institutions; they took sides by throwing weight behind either the common-state or segment-state leaders. These Johnny-come-latelies did not play a critical role at the initiation of the secession but could be decisive in preventing (or facilitating) a reversal. The absence of external allies did not prevent secessions by segment-states, and there is little evidence that the presence of an external ally made a difference in initial decisions to secede in most instances. Yet the presence of external allies—particularly for Abkhazia, Nagornyi Karabakh, and South Ossetia, and possibly for Finland—blocked the reversal of secession; the absence of external allies left Bukhara, Khiva, Chechnya, and Tatarstan unable to resist Moscow's pressures for reintegration.

Horizontal cultural unity within the segment-state gave the leaders additional institutional bases for leverage against the common-state leaders, as predicted by hypothesis 3b. The cultural disunity in the pre-Soviet Central Asian segment-states weakened them in the confrontation with the new Soviet common-state government. Vertical cultural heterogeneity in segmental relationships created incentives to escalate because this made it harder to find acceptable compromises that would keep the common-state whole, as predicted by hypothesis 2c. Yet, this was not an overwhelmingly powerful constraint. In the post-Soviet cases the extent of vertical cultural division only weakly distinguished the segment-states that successfully seceded from those that failed or never tried. In the global data the simultaneous presence of civilizational and linguistic divides was a significant factor in the secession and independence of segment-states, but the magnitude of the effect was small compared to the effect of the institutional variables.

ELEVEN

Nation-States and the International System

THIS PROJECT BEGAN with the question, where do nation-states come from? That is, why have some nation-state projects achieved sovereign independence, while a much larger number have failed? According to the segmental institutions thesis, the essential precondition for a successful nation-state project is a *segment-state*. In the final analysis it is not multiethnic societies or simple federations that are torn apart, but segmented states. It simplifies the evidence that I present in this book to say "no segment-state, no nation-state," but the correlation between segment-states and independent nation-states is overwhelming. Of the 177 sovereign states that joined the international community between 1901 and 2000, more than 86 percent had been segment-states immediately prior to independence (table 10.5). Independence represented an administrative upgrade of a jurisdiction that was already in existence.

The segmental institutions thesis highlights the profound effects that developments inside states can have on the structure of the international system, on international relations, and on changes in each of these. Indeed, the changes in Central Eurasia in the last decade of the twentieth century not only altered the configuration of nation-states but also transformed the polarity of the international system, ended the cold war, and redesigned the agenda of international politics. So, in this conclusion I turn to three implications of the segmental institutions thesis for international relations, the ways we study change in the international system, and the ways we manage nation-state crises. First, I begin with a discussion of the relationship of the segmental institutions thesis to the scholarly debates over the sources of change in the international system. Second, the discussion then turns to implications of the segmental institutions thesis for the longer-term evolution of the international system. The segmental institutions thesis provides additional reasons why we should expect the nation-state to persist as the central structuring feature of the modern international system, even in the face of the enormous international pressures of insecurity and globalization. The segmental institutions thesis sees nationalism and the nation-state as unseverable consequences of a development in domestic politics—the spread of the principle of popular sovereignty—that is unlikely to disappear soon. Indeed, pressures for the fulfillment of the ideal that all subjects should become citizens of their states have made the issue of nationalism and the nation-state even more relevant than ever before.

Third, the discussion turns to the more immediate foreign policy issue of managing nation-state crises. The segmental institutions thesis warns of dangers in the current international practice of fostering segmental institutions. Segmental institutions may be the perfect transitional arrangement to facilitate the partition of states, but in most instances they are the wrong formula for holding together ethnically divided societies. A lesson of the last hundred years is that once segmental institutions gestate nation-state projects and empower these against the common-state, it becomes much harder to keep the common-state whole.

Implications for the Study of International Change

With so many scholars coming to the phenomenon of nation-state creation from different analytic perspectives, it is no surprise that the questions we have asked and the answers we have offered diverge widely—and with considerable opportunity for misunderstanding among us. The most significant analytic alternative to the segmental institutions thesis comes from the field of international relations. Among these specialists it has become common to argue that the choice among nation-state projects is made not by processes inside existing states but by international selection mechanisms that favor some projects, particularly projects that can demonstrate superior economic efficiency or military prowess. This is not simply a difference between alternative answers to the same question but a more fundamental difference between two levels of analysis that seem to address many of the same phenomena but ask profoundly different questions. In this debate, the segmental institutions thesis speaks of the need to rediscover the ways in which domestic political processes constrain and even constitute the modern international system. In the discussion of the triumph of nation-states we may have come full circle as we see the limits of international constraints to explain outcomes within states. For example, the segmental institutions thesis casts the role of external actors as largely opportunistic, cameo appearances and typically as Johnny-come-latelies rather than as primary instigating causes of nation-state crises. For the most part, over the past century the willingness and ability of external actors to forestall nation-state crises was very limited and actually waned. External actors have been particularly reluctant to intervene early, well before a nation-state crisis, to shape the menu of their options for granting recognition to sovereign states later. Yet the outcome of domestic processes has affected the shape of the international system profoundly.

In academic circles this debate is reflected in the diverging perspectives of international relations specialists who focus on forces outside states shaping their internal development and comparative politics specialists who stress the importance of forces inside states for the international system. The first view Peter Gourevitch calls "the second-image reversed"[1]; the second we might label somewhat mischievously "the second-image set right." A quarter-century ago Gourevitch wrote of the need for students of comparative politics to study the ways in which international developments in ideas, social patterns, economics, and political institutions constrain developments within individual states. The segmental institutions thesis underscores the need to make the second-image face forward more often and highlights the role of domestic political developments inside countries such as the USSR in constituting the international system.

Much of the most important work that might bear on the question of which nations get states of their own has developed in the field of international relations but has focused on a different level of analysis, where the question being asked concerns changing attributes of the international system.[2] For scholars in this field, the dependent variables are often the nature of the dominant political unit that characterizes each international system and changes in the central tendencies in the number and average size of these units.[3] Thus, Robert Gilpin asks why the "the predominant feature of modern international relations has been the emergence of the nation-state as the dominant form of political organization."[4] At other times and in specific corners of the world, this dominant form has been the empire or the city-state. These authors attribute the triumph of the modern state to international selection mechanisms that selected out the alternatives and left states surviving. Thus, according to Gilpin, "the nation-state succeeded because it was the most efficient form of political organization for the set of environmental conditions that developed in early modern Europe."[5] In his magisterial account of the dominance of the (prenational) state over its early modern alternatives Hendrik Spruyt identifies two potential advantages of the state—its war-making potential and its economic efficiency.[6]

These explanations for system-level outcomes are not intended to explain why some but not other nation-state projects succeeded,[7] and this may be their weakness: the major system-level approaches claim to explain

[1] Gourevitch 1978.

[2] For example, see Strang 1991.

[3] Spruyt 1994, 2005.

[4] Gilpin 1981, 116.

[5] Gilpin 1981, 116.

[6] Spruyt 1994, 153–80; also see Spruyt 2005, 39–87.

[7] Moreover, these explanations focus on the early state prior to nationalism. The rise of the modern state (circa fourteenth to sixteenth centuries) predates the propagation of the idea of the modern nation-state (circa eighteenth to nineteenth centuries) by at least two centuries and as much as four centuries. The original state was a dynastic possession. The early nation-state was a competitor with the dynastic state, as the vigilant war on nationalism in the early nineteenth century by the Neo-Holy Alliance attests.

macrohistorical shifts such as the historic shift to the state as the predominant political form in Europe, but they have a hard time explaining any of the specific changes that constituted this shift. The states that have triumphed are typically neither economically nor militarily superior to those they replaced or to all the many alternative projects on the table at the time. Indeed, after tracing processes of change in individual cases, it is difficult to show that international selection mechanisms were the causal factors in the creation of many new nation-states. The segmental institutions thesis contends that new nation-states have been fashioned not by the invisible hand of the international system but by the very real hands of politicians within segmented states.[8]

Military Prowess

The international system, in one rendering, selects among competing nation-state projects through warfare. Nation-states, according to Gilpin, represented an optimal mix of expanded resource base and intense popular loyalty that is necessary for modern warfare. Empires fielded larger armies and city-states commanded more intense loyalty from their soldiers, but the nation-state trumped both by an optimal mix of size and loyalty found in mass, citizen armies.[9] Charles Tilly adds that their homogeneous population gave nation-states a firmer civilian base during international conflicts: "a homogeneous population was more likely to remain loyal to a regime of its own kind, just as it was more likely to mount a successful rebellion against foreign domination."[10] In warfare, alternative forms of political organization were selected out. The revolution in warfare that Robert Osgood and Robert Tucker label the "popularization of military power" dates from the wars of the French Revolution and made the nation-state a superior form of political organization on the battlefield. With this, as Marshal Foch observed, "The wars of Kings were at an end; the wars of peoples were beginning."[11]

The attempt to extend this logic to explain which nations get states—that is, to move to a different level of analysis—does not meet with much success.[12] Warfare has been implicated in the independence of only a small minority of new nation-states. And where warfare has been involved, it has tended to be the war-making capacity of outside powers, such as the European states' role in the independence of Bulgaria and Bosnia, not the

---

[8] I have shamelessly appropriated this turn of phrase from Downing 1992, 14.

[9] Gilpin 1981, 117–18.

[10] Tilly 1975, 79.

[11] Osgood and Tucker 1967, 52. Also see Bean 1973; Dudley 1990; Quester 1977.

[12] Geopoliticians have attempted to develop strategies for individual states based on this logic (see Haushofer 1927).

war-making capacity of the new states themselves. In addition, most new states have not been better at defending themselves or maintaining domestic law and order than the predecessor states they replaced. The inability of central governments to exercise effective control throughout their territories has earned many African countries the label "quasi-states."[13] Jeffrey Herbst has suggested that in Africa the inability of regimes to extend their power throughout their territory should lead us to ask whether boundaries should be redrawn by "decertifying" old states, recognizing new nation-states, and fostering the growth of institutions to supplant the existing pattern of sovereign statehood.[14] Similar questions could be asked about other postcolonial states such as Myanmar or post-secession states such as Bosnia or Georgia.

According to the segmental institutions thesis, where relative military prowess has been important to the success of one nation-state project over another it has been as an endogenous factor within the dynamics of a segmented state. In those few instances in which states emerged from civil conflicts, such as the independence of Croatia, the war-making capacity of the secessionists depended on their control of a segment-state.

Economic Efficiency

Political economists have argued that international selection mechanisms pick among competing political forms such as empires and states on the basis of their contribution to relative economic efficiency. For example, Spruyt attributes the triumph of the (prenational) sovereign state to the changed economic conditions of early modern Europe, which gave kings an incentive to rationalize the economies of their realms and so gave their states a competitive advantage in trade and finance over empires, city-states, and trading leagues.[15] Alberto Alesina and Enrico Spolaore bring this logic to the analysis of the size and shape of states: they argue that states are shaped by "the trade-off between the benefits of large jurisdictions and the costs of heterogeneity of large and diverse populations."[16] Thus, individual states will divide or merge in order to maximize wealth, or at least the wealth of rulers, subject to the twin constraints of greater economies of scale with increasing market size (favoring larger states) and more costly heterogeneity of preferences with increasing population size (favoring smaller states). Larger states promise a myriad of economic benefits—larger markets, greater division of labor, economies of scale, lower

[13] Jackson 1987.
[14] Herbst 2000, 258–72.
[15] Spruyt 1994, 153–80.
[16] Alesina and Spolaore 1997, 1027; Bolton and Roland 1997; North 1981, 66.

per capita cost of nonrival public goods, greater efficiency in taxation, less duplication of government costs (notably for defense and law enforcement), coordination of public goods (including transportation, communications, and standards), and lower per capita cost from uninsurable shocks. Alternatively, more homogeneous nation-states promise greater economic efficiency because their governments can more easily apply uniform policies throughout society. Their governments have less need for either costly schemes to compensate or wasteful duplication of bureaucracies to administer distinct cultural communities. More homogeneous nation-states are more likely to nurture the trust and solidarity that early sociologists such as Émile Durkheim and J. S. Furnivall claimed are necessary for the contracting and exchange of the modern market and that contemporary political economists claim leads to greater willingness to invest in public goods like education, roads, and other infrastructure essential to economic growth.[17]

Yet it is difficult to identify the causal mechanisms that lead to the failure of economically inefficient states and their replacement by alternatives. For example, it is difficult to show that the search for improved efficiency has been a motivation among the key actors in the creation of new nation-states. Indeed, confronted with the case for economic efficiency, nationalists have often responded with wishful thinking about the economic promise of their imagined nation-states or with the dismissive sentiment of Sékou Touré that "it is better to have poverty in freedom than richness in slavery."[18] Moreover, contrary to the national efficiency hypothesis, it is difficult to demonstrate that the configuration of nation-states is an improvement over the configuration of states they replaced. Division of the market typically comes at a high price. For example, in addition to the problems of economic transition found in most postcommunist states, the division of the USSR market meant that the slide of the Soviet successor states tended to be deeper and the recovery tended to be slower. In addition, it is difficult to demonstrate that the successful nation-state projects have been superior to the many other projects on the table at the moment of breakup. Indeed, around the world at the moment of independence there have often been competing attempts to unite the candidates for statehood in federations or confederations precisely because the individual candidates were likely to be economically inefficient on their own. In a few instances these proposals for federation succeeded, including Australia (1901) and the Union of South Africa (1910).[19] Yet many more federations cobbled

---

[17] Alesina, Baqir, and Easterly 1999; Alesina and Spolaore 1997; Alesina, Spolaore, and Wacziarg 1997; Bolton and Roland 1997; Dallago and Uvalic 1998; Friedman 1977; Furnivall 1944; D. Miller 1994; Tilly 1975, 79; Wittman 1991, 126–29.

[18] Zartman 1991, 515.

[19] For the logic that may explain unification, see Ziblatt 2006.

together for the sake of greater efficiency failed, including at least four different West Indies federations (from the 1950s to the 1970s), the Federation of Rhodesia and Nyasaland (1953–63), the Mali Federation (1959–61), the Malaysia that included Singapore (1963–65), and the Commonwealth of Independent States (1991–).

The segmental institutions thesis argues that insofar as improvements in the economic efficiency of existing states play an independent role it is as a secondary, endogenous factor in the process that led from segmental institutions to the creation of new nation-states. Economic inefficiency may become particularly acute as a consequence of the political dynamics created by the segmented state. The bargaining between segment-state and common-state leaders may lead each side to erect barriers to trade that vitiate many of the gains from larger markets. Complaints about the economic inefficiency of the existing structure of states are seldom foremost at the beginning of a nation-state crisis leading to state failure, but once the crisis creates inefficiencies—such as those that arise from internal boycotts and embargoes—economic inefficiencies may become ammunition in the case against the existing common-state. In short, the institutions and political dynamics of segmented states can create peculiar economic inefficiencies that help bring down the old order, so that while the independent states are often not more efficient than the old common-state, they can be an improvement over the inefficiencies of a segmented state in its death throes. But this is all ancillary to the nation-state crises that engage common-state and segment-state leaders.

Continuing Centrality of the Nation-State

The segmental institutions thesis highlights reasons that the nation-state is likely to remain the dominant structuring feature of the international system for some time to come. The reasons have much to do with domestic sources of the nation-state that defy international pressures of insecurity or globalization that many claim will lead to its demise.[20]

The evidence provided in previous chapters speaks to the near universality and the continuing vitality in the modern world of the institution of the nation-state. The pace of creating new nation-states accelerated in the latter half of the twentieth century; the last decade of the century saw a new explosion. Thus, by the early twentieth-first century almost every square

---

[20] Bracketing the many years of this scholarship and diverse analytic perspectives that have predicted the demise of the nation-state are such notable works as Herz 1957 and Guéhenno 1995. Also see Barber 1995; Deudney 1995; Fukuyama 1992; Ohmae 1995; Powell 1999; Spruyt 2002.

inch of soil from Slovakia to Palau and back again—with the exception of Antarctica—has been shoe-horned into the sometimes pinching form of a nation-state. Moreover, nation-states have been remarkably durable over the past century. While 177 new nation-states were created between 1901 and 2000, few disappeared. From 1901 to 2000 only twelve independent states disappeared and did not reappear by the end of the century: the Orange Free State (1910), Transvaal (1910), Korea (1910), Serbia (1915), Montenegro (1915), Austro-Hungary (1918), Zanzibar (1964), South Vietnam (1975), East Germany (1990), South Yemen (1990), the USSR (1991), and Czechoslovakia (1992). (And by 2006 this count was down to ten.) Another five disappeared for more than a decade, but reappeared: Morocco, Haiti, Estonia, Latvia, and Lithuania.[21]

Almost all new states claim to derive their sovereignty from a nation that is coextensive with the population within its boundaries. To a remarkable extent, in the early twenty-first century this claim to nationhood is actually true; that is, most inhabitants at least acquiesce in the status quo and do not even imagine, let alone actively support, an alternative nation-state project to which they would rather belong. For example, in Europe, repeated waves of Eurobarometer surveys show most inhabitants of the European Union's member states remain primarily or solely attached to their separate nation-state communities.[22] In Africa, attachments to nation-state projects reveal the near monopoly of the status quo; there are few active alternatives to the existing nation-states.[23]

The claim that nation-states are increasingly weakened derives in part from two misapprehensions. One is that the threat to existing commonstates from secessionist movements and even terrorism represents a challenge to the nation-state. Yet movements such as the Irish Republican Army, the Basques' ETA, and the Tamil Eelam challenge not the nation-state as a way of organizing political life but specific nation-states. Indeed, these movements affirm the nation-state system in that they seek nation-states of their own. The second misapprehension sees the emergence of larger political unions—particularly the European Union—that are associated with the phenomenon of globalization as a threat to the nation-state. It is premature to predict that the European Union will replace Europe's existing nation-states. Yet even the most ambitious plans for Europe imagine the continent as either a segmented state or a new nation-state within a world of other nation-states. Rather than a challenge to the nation-state

[21] Based on K. Gleditsch and Ward 1999.

[22] Based on data presented by Ramiro Cibrian, "The Future of National Identities in the European Union" (a presentation at the conference titled "Identity and Nationalism in Europe and Eurasia," Claremont McKenna College, Claremont, Calif., 8 April 2004).

[23] Englebert 2003. Also see Miles 1994, 42–59.

system, this transformation of Europe would represent yet another reaffirmation. Much as the union of Germans subsumed individual nationalisms associated with such states as Saxony, Württemberg, and Bavaria, today's dreamers see Europeans as a larger nation. Already a nationalism has emerged among the Eurocrats, who have used their enormous resources to attempt to privilege their nation-state project. Aided by professors in European universities and polemicists in the press, they propagate this nation-state project among students and the public at large.

There have been real alternatives to the nation-state, and not all of these are atavisms from the prenationalist age. Those that have arisen since the beginning of the age of nationalism, however, have so far failed. The Communist vision of a world in which the state would wither away and the proletariat would have no nation was the most thoroughgoing alternative, yet it succumbed to the nation-state: Communists fell in love with their states, and workers with their nations. The USSR quickly reconciled itself by attempting to become a nation-state built on the sovereign right of the Soviet people, but at the same time it created segment-states based on the simultaneous right of peoples within the Soviet people to have separate states of their own. In the end, the segment-states triumphed, freed from the frayed myth of a proletariat that would eventually sunder nations and states. Religious movements espousing universalistic claims have similarly challenged the nation-state system. Yet these too have tended with time to accept the nation-state system and accept the nation-state as at least the vessel in which to institutionalize the community of believers.[24] Protestant and Orthodox Christianity embraced separate nation-states early and enthusiastically. Although at first critical of nationalism—as attested as late as 1864 in the Syllabus of Errors—the Roman Catholic Church with its own universalistic, transnational ambitions reached a truce with the nation-state in the twentieth century. Most fundamentalist Buddhist and Islamic movements do not challenge the current configuration of nation-states, but want to cleanse existing nation-states from within. Current challengers to the nation-state system within these movements, much like the earlier radicals in the Comintern, are a small if often violent fringe.

The continued relevance of the nation-state is due to its unseverable link to the nearly universalistic ideal of popular sovereignty based on the claim that states derive their just powers from a people.[25] Once politicians make this claim, they must answer the questions, "Who are the people? Who is in? And who is not?" In short, the nation-state is the inevitable concomitant of citizenship.

[24] A. Gill 2001, 126–68.
[25] Schumpeter 1976, 247; Wood 1969, 344–89. Also see O'Leary 2001.

In this sense the age of nationalism opened in 1776, when a few men had the audacity to assert that the people were the repository of the sovereign prerogative to create a state and could "dissolve the Political Bands which have connected them with another" (U.S. Declaration of Independence). It was a difficult choice for these men who had wrestled with the multiple national identities common in segment-states: once they asserted this principle of national self-determination, they had to decide whether the people to which they belonged and which had a right to create a state of its own was the British people, the American people, or the people of separate colonies, such as Virginians. They claimed to be part of a common ethnic group with their "British Brethren" to whom they were bound "by the Ties of our common Kindred." Yet, because their attempts to appeal for support on this basis fell on deaf ears, out of "Necessity" they chose separation. This made the British like "the rest of Mankind"—foreigners. The conclusion of the signers of the Declaration of Independence was to proclaim their segment-states' sovereignty—they assumed decision rights that previously had been the prerogative of the common-state government in London and elevated themselves to "Free and Independent States." The rest of their declaration was a list of justifications for this first successful act of nationalism—"the causes which impel them to the Separation."

Prior to 1776, many people had begun to develop a sense of community; for example, Englishness had begun to develop as early as the eighth century.[26] Moreover, ties to a monarch—a form of "regnal" identity, as Susan Reynolds labels it—had begun to develop among some political classes. What was truly revolutionary about 1776 was the formulation of a doctrine, and the first successful implementation of it, that simultaneously identified a community as a people, granted the people sovereign rights previously held by monarchs, and explicitly stressed that this sovereignty included the right to change the boundaries of states and create new sovereign states. Other times and other peoples may have supplied some of the building blocks, but the idea of a nation as a people with a right to a state of its own and the implementation of this in a doctrine and act of national self-determination takes place on a large scale for the first time in that summer in Philadelphia.[27]

It is this link to popular sovereignty that makes the boundaries of the nation-state an issue worth fighting for. In an age when individuals are participants and not simply subjects or parochials that sit on the sidelines of the politics of the state, the configuration of the nation-state determines how individuals will be empowered. The sovereign nation-state is the jurisdiction within which all decision rights are allocated, whether that alloca-

[26] Hastings 1997, 36–37.
[27] Reynolds 1984. Also see Strang 1991, 432.

tion is determined by democratic or autocratic means. It is at the level of the nation-state that individuals acquire the rights to participate in common-state decision making. More than this, it is at the level of the nation-state that decision rights are allocated among government, civil society, and individuals and so it is determined whether individuals will have the right to decide for themselves whether to attend particular religious ceremonies, how to dispose of private property, and when and where to express unorthodox views. Change the boundaries of the nation-state and the outcomes in these decisions are likely to change. For these reasons, individuals invest great significance in nation-state projects and, like the Founding Fathers in 1776, are willing to fight for one project over others.

Until the doctrine of popular sovereignty is replaced by some other principle for constituting government or until a global state ends the division of populations and their lands into separate independent jurisdictions, nation-states will remain the basic structure of both domestic and international politics. Changes that would make the nation-state irrelevant are, in present circumstances, remote and unwelcomed.

Implications for Foreign Policies

The segmental institutions thesis is principally a scholar's tool for making sense of a complex historical record. Yet it has implications for the real world in which foreign policy analysts must make sense of contemporary events, forecast likely futures, and design responses. In forecasting likely candidates for membership in the international community or likely challenges to existing nation-states, the segmental institutions thesis adds a critical perspective that has been overlooked by culturalists and political economists. Even in the forecasting of which nationalist movements are likely to have staying power and which potential nationalist movements are most likely to create nation-state crises, the segmental institutions thesis improves our predictive powers. The segmental institutions thesis provides the single best betting rule for making predictions about changes in the configuration of states in the international system. More specifically, in situations where leaders of the international community must design responses to ethnic conflicts and civil strife, the segmental institutions thesis points up an opportunity and a danger in institutional arrangements commonly called power sharing or consociationalism in societies deeply divided by ethnicity.[28] Segmental institutions can facilitate the transition to secession and independence, but they can worsen the problems of holding states together.

[28] Roeder 2004; Roeder and Rothchild 2005.

In situations in which great powers individually or collectively seek to facilitate the independence of peoples, segmental institutions can expedite secession and a transition to independence. Thus, for example, if the United States hopes to expedite the process by which Kosovo and Kurdistan achieve independence as sovereign states, the most important step would be to reinforce the special status of the Kosovar segment-state created by the Yugoslavs and the Kurdish segment-state that began to take shape in northern Iraq under the American protectorate after the first Gulf War. This is a risky strategy, however, because the commitment of the common-state governments (e.g., Serbia and Iraq) to the objective of independence must be credible. To this end, the timetable for independence must be public and the steps taken to implement each stage must be unambiguous and on time. Otherwise segmental institutions create the very dangerous combination of an empowered political elite in the segment-state and uncertainty about the credibility of the commitment by the common-state to elevating the segment-state to sovereign independence.

Alternatively, the segmental institutions thesis warns that institutional arrangements that provide ethnic groups states of their own—often bracketed under the label "autonomy arrangements"—are very poor institutions for keeping a common-state together. The very process of negotiating a power-sharing arrangement that creates segment-states typically reinforces the twin dangers that the circle of participants at the bargaining table will narrow and the agenda will focus exclusively on allocating decision rights between common-state and segment-state governments. Cross-cutting interests that might knit society together will be excluded. One zero-sum conflict will frame all policy issues. Particularly dangerous in these autonomy arrangements is the emergence of political-identity hegemony in the segment-states. Advocates of power sharing have called this "structured predominance" of segmental elites and have claimed that it is necessary for the success of power-sharing arrangements. For example, Eric Nordlinger argues that the "structured predominance of elites" is a necessary condition for conflict regulation in divided societies.[29] Arend Lijphart lists among favorable conditions for consociationalism "a high degree of internal political cohesion" within segment-states.[30] Within ethnic communities, this purportedly permits elites to enforce the compromise on their populations, and it protects the elites from radicals.[31] Yet the segmental institutions thesis points up that this political-identity hegemony transforms the capabilities and incentives of segment-state leaders and may shift the balance of leverage to the disadvantage of the common-state. Structural predomi-

---

[29] Nordlinger 1972, 73–87.
[30] Lijphart 1969.
[31] Fearon and Laitin 1996, 715–35; Nordlinger 1972, 65.

nance gives segment-state leaders greater means to press a nation-state project and increases incentives to play the sovereignty card. Structured predominance expands the segment-state leaders' ability to extort further concessions from the leaders of the common-state. Contrary to the argument of the power-sharing literature, the leaders who control segment-states are often not characterized by what Eric Nordlinger calls "strong, salient conflict regulating motives."[32] Indeed, there is a tendency for segment-state leaders to become more radical than the public at large. Policing capability gives the leaders of a segment-state the ability to silence moderates who favor compromise. Segmentation erodes the incentive to regulate conflict with the government of the common-state. In short, segment-states become like hostile conquered nations in the heart of the common-state.

Despite these dangers, segment-states have become part of the international community's preferred solution to ethnic conflicts. In the aftermath of severe conflicts such as the civil war in Bosnia, the United States and its allies have created new segment-states. Ironically, unless the segmental institutions thesis suddenly ceases to hold true, the preferred solution may in the longer term prove to be the worst enemy of unity. Not only will segmental institutions create new incentives for division, they will magnify incentives already present from the severe conflict. Perhaps this is good news for the segmental institutions thesis. It means that the segmental institutions thesis will be an even better betting rule in the twenty-first century.

[32] Nordlinger 1972, 42.

APPENDIX

Segment-States, 1901–2000

Metropole	Segment-State[a]	Period[b]
	Internal segment-states	
Austro-Hungary	Hungary	1867–1918
Azerbaijan	Nagornyi Karabakh	1992–
Belgium	Flanders	1970–
Belgium	Wallonia	1970–
Bosnia	Bosnia and Herzegovina	1995–
Bosnia	Republika Srpska	1995–
Cameroon	Eastern Cameroon	1961–72
Cameroon	Southern Cameroon	1961–72
Canada	Quebec	1867–
China	Guangxi Zhuang AR	1958–
China	Ningxia Hui AR	1958–
China	Sinkiang	1881–
China	Tibet AR	1951–
Czechoslovakia	Czech Republic	1969–92
Czechoslovakia	Slovakia	1948–92
Denmark	Faroe Islands	1948–
Ethiopia	Eritrea	1952–93
Finland	Åaland Islands	1922–
France	Corsica	1982–
Georgia	Abkhazia	1992–
Georgia	Ajaria	1992–
Georgia	South Ossetia	1992–
India	Andhra Pradesh	1953–
India	Arunachal Pradesh	1987–
India	Assam	1947–
India	Gujurat	1960–
India	Hyderabad	1948–56
India	Karnataka	1956–
India	Kashmir	1947–
India	Madhya Bharat	1948–56
India	Maharashtra	1960–
India	Manipur	1972–
India	Meghalaya	1972–

Metropole	*Segment-State*[a]	*Period*[b]
	Internal segment-states (*cont'd*)	
India	Mizoram	1986–
India	Mysore	1947–56
India	Nagaland	1963–
India	Orissa	1948–
India	Patalia and EPSU	1948–56
India	Punjab	1947–
India	Rajasthan Union	1949–56
India	Saurashtra Union	1948–56
India	Tamil Nadu	1956–
India	Travancore-Cochin/Kerala	1949–
India	Tripura	1972–
India	West Bengal	1947–
Italy	Friuli-Venezia Giulia	1963–
Italy	Sardinia	1948–
Italy	Trentino-Alto Adige	1948–
Italy	Valle d'Aosta	1948–
Malaysia	Singapore	1963–65
Moldova	Gagauz Yeri	1995–
Myanmar	Chin State	1974–
Myanmar	Kachin State	1948–
Myanmar	Karen State	1948–
Myanmar	Kayeh State	1948–
Myanmar	Mon State	1974–
Myanmar	Rakhine State	1974–
Myanmar	Shan State	1948–
Nigeria	Eastern Region	1960–67
Nigeria	Mid-Western Region	1963–67
Nigeria	Northern Region	1960–67
Nigeria	Western Region	1960–67
Pakistan	Baluchistan	1947–55
Pakistan	Baluchistan	1970–
Pakistan	East Bengal	1947–73
Pakistan	Northwest Frontier Agencies	1947–55
Pakistan	Northwest Frontier Agencies	1970–
Pakistan	Northwest Frontier Province	1947–55
Pakistan	Northwest Frontier Province	1970–
Pakistan	Punjab	1970–
Pakistan	Punjab and Bahawalpur	1947–55
Pakistan	Sindh	1970–
Pakistan	Sindh and Khairpur	1947–55

Metropole	Segment-State[a]	Period[b]
	Internal segment-states (*cont'd*)	
Philippines	Moslem Mindanao	1990–
Russia	Adygeia	1992–
Russia	Bashkortostan	1992–
Russia	Buryatia	1992–
Russia	Chechnya	1992–
Russia	Chuvashia	1992–
Russia	Dagestan	1992–
Russia	Ingushetia	1992–
Russia	Kabardino-Balkaria	1992–
Russia	Kalmykia	1992–
Russia	Karachai-Cherkessia	1992–
Russia	Karelia	1992–
Russia	Khakassia	1992–
Russia	Komi	1992–
Russia	Mari El	1992–
Russia	Mordovia	1992–
Russia	North Ossetia	1992–
Russia	Sakha (Yakutia)	1992–
Russia	Tatarstan	1992–
Russia	Tyva	1992–
Russia	Udmurtia	1992–
Saudi Arabia	Hejaz	1926–32
South Africa	Gazankulu	1973–94
South Africa	KaNgware	1984–94
South Africa	Kwandebele	1977–94
South Africa	Kwazulu	1973–94
South Africa	Lebowa	1972–94
South Africa	Qwaqwa	1974–94
Spain	Catalunya	1978–
Spain	Euskadi	1978–
Spain	Galiza	1978–
Sudan	Southern Region	1972–83
Sweden	Norway	1814–1905
Tajikistan	Gornyi Badakhshan	1992–
Tanzania	Zanzibar	1964–
Uganda	Baganda	1962–67
Ukraine	Crimea	1992–
United Kingdom	Northern Ireland	1922–
United Kingdom	Scotland	1707–
United Kingdom	Wales	1999–

Metropole	*Segment-State*[a]	*Period*[b]
\multicolumn{3}{c}{Internal segment-states (*cont'd*)}		
USSR	Armenia	1936–91
USSR	Azerbaijan	1936–91
USSR	Belorussia	1922–91
USSR	Estonia	1940–91
USSR	Georgia	1936–91
USSR	Karelo-Finland	1940–56
USSR	Kazakhstan	1936–91
USSR	Kyrgyzstan	1936–91
USSR	Latvia	1940–91
USSR	Lithuania	1940–91
USSR	Moldavia	1940–91
USSR	Russia	1922–91
USSR	Tajikistan	1929–91
USSR	Transcaucasia	1922–36
USSR	Turkmenistan	1924–91
USSR	Ukraine	1922–91
USSR	Uzbekistan	1924–91
Uzbekistan	Karakalpakstan	1992–
Yugoslavia	Bosnia	1945–92
Yugoslavia	Croatia	1945–91
Yugoslavia	Macedonia	1945–91
Yugoslavia	Montenegro	1945–
Yugoslavia	Serbia	1945–
Yugoslavia	Slovenia	1945–91
\multicolumn{3}{c}{Internal segment-state after periods of ambiguous status}		
China	Inner Mongolia	1924–
\multicolumn{3}{c}{Internal segment-states after periods as external segment-states}		
Austro-Hungary	Bosnia-Hercegovina	1878–1918
India	Sikkim	1950–
\multicolumn{3}{c}{Ambiguous status after periods as internal segment-states}		
South Africa	Bophuthatswana	1972–94
South Africa	Ciskei	1972–94
South Africa	Transkei	1963–94
South Africa	Venda	1973–94
\multicolumn{3}{c}{Ambiguous status}		
China	Mongolia	1691–1924
China	Tibet	1720–1914
France	Algeria	1845–1963
Japan	Chosen	1906–45
Japan	Formosa	1895–1945

Metropole	Segment-State[a]	Period[b]
	Ambiguous status (*cont'd*)	
Japan	Karafuto	1905–45
Japan	Pacific Islands Mandate	1919–45
Ottoman Empire	Bulgaria	1878–1908
Ottoman Empire	Crete	1898–1913
Ottoman Empire	Samos	1832–1913
Russia / USSR	Bukhara	1868–1924
Russia	Finland	1809–1917
Russia / USSR	Khiva	1873–1924
Spain	Fernando Poo	1960–68
Spain	Rio Muni	1960–68
United Kingdom	Guernsey	1066–
United Kingdom	Jersey	1066–
United Kingdom	Man	1828–
	External segment-states after periods of ambiguous status	
Denmark	Greenland	1814–
France	French Guiana	1817–
France	Guadeloupe	1775–
France	Martinique	1650–
France	Reunion	1638–
France	St. Pierre-Miquelon	1816–
Italy	Libya	1928–43
Portugal	Angola	1926–75
Portugal	Cape Verde Islands	1587–1975
Portugal	Macao	1849–
Portugal	Mozambique	1926–75
Portugal	Portuguese Guinea	1879–1974
Portugal	Portuguese India	1538–1961
Portugal	Portuguese Timor	1896–1975
Portugal	Sao Tomé e Principe	1648–1975
Spain	Spanish Guinea	1855–1960
Spain	Spanish Sahara	1939–75
	External segment-states	
Australia	New Guinea	1914–45
Australia	Papua	1906–45
Australia	Papua–New Guinea	1945–75
Belgium	Belgian Congo	1908–60
Belgium	Ruanda-Urundi	1916–62
Denmark	Iceland	1380–1918
Denmark	West Indies	1754–1917
France	Annam	1862–1949

Metropole	*Segment-State*[a]	*Period*[b]
	External segment-states (*cont'd*)	
France	Cambodia	1863–1954
France	Cameroon	1916–60
France	Chad	1920–60
France	Cochin China	1867–1949
France	Comoro Archipelago	1947–75
France	Dahomey	1894–1960
France	French Guinea	1893–1958
France	French India	1816–1954
France	French Polynesia	1903–
France	French Somaliland	1888–1977
France	French Sudan	1920–60
France	Gabon	1886–1960
France	Grand Comoro	1886–1912
France	Ivory Coast	1893–1960
France	Jebel Druze	1930–42
France	Laos	1897–1949
France	Latakia	1930–42
France	Lebanon	1920–46
France	Madagascar	1896–1960
France	Mauritania	1903–60
France	Mayotte	1841–1914
France	Mayotte	1974–
France	Middle Congo	1897–1903
France	Middle Congo	1906–25
France	Middle Congo	1929–32
France	Middle Congo	1941–60
France	Morocco	1912–56
France	New Caledonia	1853–
France	Niger	1920–60
France	Senegal	1890–1960
France	Syria	1919–46
France	Togo	1914–60
France	Tonkin	1884–1949
France	Tunisia	1881–1956
France	Ubangi-Shari	1920–60
France	Ubangi-Shari and Chad	1906–20
France	Upper Senegal–Niger	1904–20
France	Upper Volta	1919–32
France	Upper Volta	1947–60
France	Vietnam	1949–54

Metropole	Segment-State[a]	Period[b]
	External segment-states (*cont'd*)	
France	Wallis and Futuna	1961–
France/Spain	Andorra	1278–1993
France/Turkey	Hatay	1937–39
France/UK	New Hebrides	1906–80
Germany	German East Africa	1885–1918
Germany	German New Guinea	1885–1914
Germany	German Samoa	1900–14
Germany	German Southwest Africa	1884–1915
Germany	Kamerun	1884–1916
Germany	Togo	1884–1914
India	Bhutan	1949–71
Israel	Gaza	1967–
Israel	West Bank	1967–
Italy	Cyrenaica	1912–28
Italy	Dodecanese	1923–47
Italy	Eritrea	1890–1936
Italy	Italian East Africa	1936–41
Italy	Somaliland	1905–36
Italy	Somaliland	1950–60
Italy	Tipolitania	1911–28
Japan	Manchukuo	1932–45
Netherlands	Aruba	1986–
Netherlands	Netherlands Antilles	1845–
Netherlands	Netherlands East Indies	1816–1949
Netherlands	Netherlands New Guinea	1949–62
Netherlands	Surinam	1814–75
New Zealand	Cook Islands	1901–
New Zealand	Western Samoa	1919–62
Russia / USSR	Tannu Tuva	1911–17
Russia / USSR	Tannu Tuva	1921–44
South Africa	Southwest Africa	1920–90
Spain	Morocco	1912–56
United Kingdom	Aden Colony	1839–63
United Kingdom	Aden Protectorate	1939–63
United Kingdom	Anguilla	1980–
United Kingdom	Antigua	1956–81
United Kingdom	Bahama Islands	1717–1973
United Kingdom	Bahrain	1861–1971
United Kingdom	Barbados	1885–1966
United Kingdom	Basutoland	1884–1966

Metropole	*Segment-State*[a]	*Period*[b]
	External segment-states (*cont'd*)	
United Kingdom	Bechuanaland	1885–1966
United Kingdom	Bermuda	1684–
United Kingdom	Bhutan	1910–49
United Kingdom	British Guiana	1831–1966
United Kingdom	British Honduras	1884–1981
United Kingdom	British New Guinea	1888–1906
United Kingdom	British Somaliland	1884–1960
United Kingdom	British Virgin Islands	1956–
United Kingdom	Brunei	1888–1984
United Kingdom	Burma	1937–48
United Kingdom	Cape Colony	1806–1910
United Kingdom	Cayman Islands	1962–
United Kingdom	Ceylon	1802–1948
United Kingdom	Cyprus	1878–1960
United Kingdom	Cyrenaica	1942–51
United Kingdom	Dominica	1960–78
United Kingdom	Eastern Aden Protectorate	1959–63
United Kingdom	Egypt	1882–1922
United Kingdom	Ellice Islands/Tuvalu	1975–78
United Kingdom	Eritrea	1941–52
United Kingdom	Federated Malay States	1896–1948
United Kingdom	Federation of South Arabia	1959–67
United Kingdom	Fiji	1874–1970
United Kingdom	Gambia	1894–1965
United Kingdom	Gibraltar	1713–
United Kingdom	Gilbert and Ellice Islands	1892–1975
United Kingdom	Gilbert Islands/Kiribati	1975–79
United Kingdom	Gold Coast	1906–57
United Kingdom	Grenada	1960–74
United Kingdom	Hong Kong	1841–1997
United Kingdom	India	1818–1947
United Kingdom	Iraq	1914–32
United Kingdom	Jamaica	1655–1962
United Kingdom	Johore	1885–1948
United Kingdom	Kedah	1909–48
United Kingdom	Kelantan	1909–48
United Kingdom	Kenya	1895–1963
United Kingdom	Kuwait	1904–61
United Kingdom	Lagos	1886–1904
United Kingdom	Leeward Islands	1833–1956

Metropole	Segment-State[a]	Period[b]
	External segment-states (*cont'd*)	
United Kingdom	Malaya	1948–57
United Kingdom	Maldive Islands	1887–1965
United Kingdom	Malta	1814–1964
United Kingdom	Mauritius	1814–1968
United Kingdom	Montserrat	1956–
United Kingdom	Natal	1843–1910
United Kingdom	New Zealand	1840–1907
United Kingdom	Newfoundland	1855–1949
United Kingdom	Nigeria	1914–60
United Kingdom	North Borneo	1888–1963
United Kingdom	Northeastern Rhodesia	1900–11
United Kingdom	Northern Nigeria	1900–14
United Kingdom	Northern Rhodesia	1911–64
United Kingdom	Northwestern Rhodesia	1900–11
United Kingdom	Nyasaland Protectorate	1891–64
United Kingdom	Oman	1763–1971
United Kingdom	Orange River Colony	1902–10
United Kingdom	Palestine	1920–48
United Kingdom	Perlis	1909–48
United Kingdom	Qatar	1916–71
United Kingdom	Sarawak	1886–1963
United Kingdom	Seychelles	1903–76
United Kingdom	Sierra Leone	1896–1961
United Kingdom	Singapore	1946–59
United Kingdom	Solomon Islands	1893–1978
United Kingdom	Somaliland	1941–50
United Kingdom	Southern Nigeria	1900–14
United Kingdom	Southern Rhodesia	1894–1965
United Kingdom	St. Kitts-Nevis	1956–83
United Kingdom	St. Lucia	1960–79
United Kingdom	St. Vincent	1960–79
United Kingdom	Straits Settlements	1867–1945
United Kingdom	Sudan	1899–1956
United Kingdom	Swaziland	1907–68
United Kingdom	Tanganyika	1916–61
United Kingdom	Tonga	1900–70
United Kingdom	Transjordan	1921–46
United Kingdom	Transvaal	1902–10
United Kingdom	Trengganu	1909–48
United Kingdom	Trinidad and Tobago	1889–1962

Metropole	*Segment-State*[a]	*Period*[b]
	External segment-states (*cont'd*)	
United Kingdom	Tripolitania	1942–51
United Kingdom	Trucial States	1892–1971
United Kingdom	Turks and Caicos	1962–
United Kingdom	Uganda	1914–62
United Kingdom	Winward Islands	1885–1960
United Kingdom	Zanzibar	1891–1963
United States	Alaska	1867–1959
United States	American Samoa	1900–
United States	Canal Zone	1903–75
United States	Cuba	1898–1902
United States	Guam	1898–
United States	Hawaii	1898–1959
United States	Marshall Islands	1979–91
United States	Micronesia	1979–91
United States	Northern Mariana Islands	1978–
United States	Pacific Trust Territories	1946–81
United States	Palau	1981–94
United States	Philippines	1898–1946
United States	Puerto Rico	1898–
United States	Ryuku Islands	1952–72
United States	Virgin Islands	1917–

Note: Excluded from this list: Australia (Nauru, Norfolk Island), Czechoslovakia (Ruthenia), France (Cilicia, Fezzan), Italy (Fiume), New Zealand (Niue), Spain (Ceuta and Melilla) , Uganda (Ankoli, Bunyoro, Busoga, Toro), and the United Kingdom (Cameroons, Falkland Islands, Pitcairn, Saint Helena, Togo).

[a] Only first-order segment-states are listed.

[b] The date of origin is the year of creation of a first-order segment-state of an independent common-state or the year of elevation to that status, even if the segment-state existed previously as a second-order segment-state (such as Abkhazia within the Georgian SSR until 1991). Years of termination and origin may overlap (such as that between the end of German East Africa and the beginning of Ruanda-Urundi and Tanganyika) where contending authorities simultaneously attempted to administer the same jurisdiction.

REFERENCES

Akademiia obshchestvennykh nauk pri TsK KPSS. Kafedra sovetskogo gosudar-stvennogo stroitel'stva i prava. 1984. *Sovetskoe gosudarstvennoe stroitel'stvo i pravo: Uchebnik dlia vysshikh partiinykh shkol.* Moscow: Mysl'.

Akbarzadeh, Shahram. 1996. "Why Did Nationalism Fail in Tajikistan?" *Europe-Asia Studies* 48 (November), 1105–29.

Akiner, Shirin. 1995. *The Formation of Kazakh Identity: From Tribe to Nation-State.* London: Royal Institute of International Affairs.

———. 1997. "Melting Pot, Salad Bowl—Cauldron? Manipulation and Mobiliza-tion of Ethnic and Religion Identities in Central Asia." *Ethnic and Racial Studies* 20 (April), 362–98.

Alatalu, Toomas. 1992. "Tuva—A State Reawakens." *Soviet Studies* 44, 881–95.

Albertini, Rudolf von. 1982. *Decolonization.* New York: Holmes and Meier.

Aldrich, John H. 1983. "A Downsian Spatial Model with Party Activism." *American Political Science Review* 77 (December), 974–90.

Alesina, Alberto, Reza Baqir, and William Easterly. 1999. "Public Goods and Eth-nic Divisions." *Quarterly Journal of Economics* 114 (November), 1243–84.

Alesina, Alberto, and Enrico Spolaore. 1997. "On the Number and Size of Na-tions." *Quarterly Journal of Economics* 112 (November), 1027–56.

Alesina, Alberto, Enrico Spolaore, and Romain Wacziarg. 1997. "Economic Inte-gration and Political Disintegration." NBER Working Paper Series, No. 6163. Cambridge, MA: National Bureau of Economic Research.

Alexeyeva, Ludmilla. 1985. *Soviet Dissent.* Middletown, CT: Wesleyan University Press.

Allworth, Edward A. 1990. *The Modern Uzbeks: From the Fourteenth Century to the Present. A Cultural History.* Stanford: Hoover Institution Press.

Alstadt, Audrey L. 1992. *The Azerbaijani Turks: Power and Identity Under Russian Rule.* Stanford: Hoover Institution Press.

Anaiban, Zoia V., and Edward W. Walker. 1996. "On the Problem of Interethnic Conflict: The Republic of Tuva." In *Ethnic Conflict in the Post-Soviet World: Case Studies and Analysis,* ed. Leokadia Drobizheva, Rose Gottemoeller, Catherine McArdle Kelleher, and Lee Walker, 179–94. Armonk, NY: M. E. Sharpe.

Ancel, Jacques. 1938. *Geographie des frontiers.* Paris: Gallimard.

Anderson, Benedict. 1991. *Imagined Communities: Reflections on the Origins and Spread of Nationalism,* rev. ed. London: Verso.

Anderson, John. 1999. *Kyrgyzstan: Central Asia's Island of Democracy?* Amsterdam: Harwood Academic Publishers.

Anderson, Malcolm. 1996. *Frontiers: Territory and State Formation in the Modern World.* Cambridge: Polity Press.

Andree, Richard. 1910. *Allgemeiner Handatlas in 139 Haupt- und 161 Nebenkarten nebst vollständigem alphabetischem Namenverzeichinis.* Bielefeld: Velhagen and Klasings.

Andrews, Josephine T. 2002. *When Majorities Fail: The Russian Parliament, 1990–1993.* New York: Cambridge University Press.

Armstrong, John A. 1959. *The Soviet Bureaucratic Elite: A Case Study of the Ukrainian Apparatus*. New York: Praeger.

———. 1982. *Nations Before Nationalism*. Chapel Hill: University of North Carolina Press.

Austin, Paul M. 1992. "Soviet Karelian: The Language That Failed." *Slavic Review* 51 (Spring), 16–35.

Axelrod, Robert. 1984. *The Evolution of Cooperation*. New York: Basic Books.

Axelrod, Robert, and Robert O. Keohane. 1985. "Achieving Cooperation Under Anarchy: Strategies and Institutions." *World Politics* 38 (October), 226–54.

Bahry, Donna. 2002. "Ethnicity and Equality in Post-Communist Economic Transition: Evidence from Russia's Republics." Manuscript. Department of Political Science, Vanderbilt University, Nashville, TN.

Ballis, William. 1941. "Soviet Russia's Asiatic Frontier Technique: Tana Tuva." *Pacific Affairs* 41 (March), 91–96.

Balzer, Marjorie Mandelstam, and Uliana Alekseevna Vinokurova. 1996a. "Nationalism, Interethnic Relations and Federalism: The Case of the Sakha Republic (Yakutia)." *Europe-Asia Studies* 48 (January), 101–20.

———. 1996b. "Ethnicity or Nationalism? The Sakha Republic (Yakutia)." In *Ethnic Conflict in the Post-Soviet World: Case Studies and Analysis*, ed. Leokadia Drobizheva, Rose Gottemoeller, Catherine McArdle Kelleher, and Lee Walker, 157–78. Armonk, NY: M. E. Sharpe.

Banfield, Edward, and Daniel Patrick Moynihan. 1975. *Ethnicity: Theory and Experience*. Cambridge, MA: Harvard University Press.

Barber, Benjamin. 1995. *Jihad vs. McWorld*. New York: Time Books.

Barkey, Karen, and Mark von Hagen, eds. 1997. *After Empire: Multiethnic Societies and Nation-Building (The Soviet Union and the Russian, Ottoman, and Habsburg Empires)*. Boulder, CO: Westview Press.

Barrington, Lowell. 1997. "The Geographic Component of Mass Attitudes in Ukraine." *Post-Soviet Geography and Economics* 38 (December), 601–14.

Barsamov, Vladimir. 1997. "Kazakhstan: How Long Can Ethnic Harmony Last?" In *Managing Conflict in the Former Soviet Union: Russian and American Perspectives*, ed. Alexei Arbatov, Abram Chayes, Antonia Handler Chayes, and Lara Olson, 273–331. Cambridge, MA: MIT Press.

Bartholomew, J. G. 1912. *The Citizen's Atlas of the World*. Edinburgh: J. Bartholomew and Co.

Bates, Robert H., Avner Greif, Margaret Levi, Jean-Laurent Rosenthal, and Barry R. Weingast. 1998. *Analytic Narratives*. Princeton: Princeton University Press.

Bean, Richard. 1973. "War and the Birth of the Nation State." *Journal of Economic History* 33 (March), 203–22.

Bebler, Anton. 1993. "Yugoslavia's Variety of Communist Federalism and Her Demise." *Communist and Post-Communist Studies* 26 (March), 72–86.

Beck, Nathaniel, Jonathan N. Katz, and Richard Tucker. 1998. "Taking Time Seriously: Time-Series—Cross-Section Analysis with a Binary Dependent Variable." *American Journal of Political Science* 42 (October), 1260–88.

Becker, Seymour. 1968. *Russia's Protectorates in Central Asia: Bukhara and Khiva, 1865–1924*. Cambridge, MA: Harvard University Press.

Bednar, Jenna, William N. Eskridge, Jr., and John Ferejohn. 1999. "A Political Theory of Federalism." In *Constitutional Culture and Democratic Rule*, ed. John Ferejohn, Jack N. Rakove, and Jonathan Riley, 223–67. New York: Cambridge University Press.

Behr, Roy L. 1981. "Nice Guys Finish Last—Sometimes." *Journal of Conflict Resolution* 25 (June), 289–300.

Beissinger, Mark R. 1988. "Ethnicity, the Personnel Weapon, and Neo-Imperial Integration: Ukrainian and R.S.F.S.R. Provincial Party Officials Compared." *Studies in Comparative Communism* 21 (Spring), 71–85.

———. 1995. "The Persisting Ambiguity of Empire." *Post-Soviet Affairs* 11 (April–June), 149–84.

———. 1996. "How Nationalisms Spread: Eastern Europe Adrift on the Tides and Cycles of Nationalist Contention." *Social Research* 63 (Spring), 97–146.

———. 2002. *Nationalist Mobilization and the Collapse of the Soviet State*. Cambridge: Cambridge University Press.

Beissinger, Mark R., and Crawford Young. 2002. "Convergence to Crisis: Pre-Independence State Legacies and Post-Independence State Breakdown in Africa and Eurasia." In *Beyond State Crisis? Post-Colonial Africa and Post-Soviet Eurasia in Comparative Perspective*, ed. Mark R. Beissinger and Crawford Young, 19–50. Baltimore: Johns Hopkins University Press.

Bélanger, Sarah, and Maurice Pinard. 1991. "Ethnic Movements and the Competition Model: Some Missing Links." *American Sociological Review* 56 (August), 446–57.

Bell, David A. 2001. *The Cult of the Nation in France: Inventing Nationalism, 1680–1800*. Cambridge, MA: Harvard University Press.

Bennigsen, Alexandre A. 1984. "Mullahs, Mujahidin, and Soviet Muslims." *Problems of Communism* 33 (November–December), 28–44.

Bennigsen, Alexandre A., and S. Enders Wimbush. 1979. *Muslim National Communism in the Soviet Union*. Chicago: University of Chicago Press.

Benson, Michelle, and Jacek Kugler. 1998. "Power Parity, Democracy, and the Severity of Internal Violence." *Journal of Conflict Resolution* 42 (April), 196–209.

Berliner, Joseph S. 1957. *Factory and Manager in the USSR*. Cambridge, MA: Harvard University Press.

Biddulph, Howard L. 1983. "Local Interest Articulation at CPSU Congresses." *World Politics* 36 (October), 28–52.

Binmore, Ken, Martin J. Osborne, and Ariel Rubinstein. 1992. "Noncooperative Models of Bargaining." In *Handbook of Game Theory*, vol. 1, ed. Robert J. Aumann and Sergiu Hart, 179–225. Amsterdam: Elsevier Science Publishers.

Birch, Anthony H. 1978. "Minority Nationalist Movements and Theories of Political Integration." *World Politics* 30 (April), 325–44.

Blaney, Geoffrey. 1988. *The Causes of War*, 3rd ed. London: Macmillan Press.

Blaufarb, Douglas S. 1977. *The Counterinsurgency Era: U.S. Doctrine and Performance, 1950 to the Present*. New York: Free Press.

Blaustein, Albert P., and Gisbert H. Flanz. 2006. *Constitutions of the Countries of the World*, 20 vols. Dobbs Ferry, NY: Oceana Publications.

Blaustein, Albert P., Jay Sigler, and Benjamin R. Beede, eds. 1977. *Independence Documents of the World*, 2 vols. Dobbs Ferry, NY: Oceana Publications.

Bol'shaia Sovetskaia Entsiklopediia. 1970–1978. Volumes 1–30. Moscow: Sovetskaia Entsiklopediia.

Bolton, Patrick, and Gerard Roland. 1997. "The Breakup of Nations: A Political Economy Analysis." *Quarterly Journal of Economics* 112 (November), 1057–90.

Borys, Jurij. 1960. *The Russian Communist Party and the Sovietization of Ukraine: A Study in the Communist Doctrine of the Self-Determination of Nations.* Westport, CT: Hyperion Press.

Box-Steffensmeier, Janet M., and Bradford S. Jones. 1997. "Time is of the Essence: Event History Models in Political Science." *American Journal of Political Science* 41 (October), 1414–61.

Boyd, Charles G. 1998. "Making Bosnia Work." *Foreign Affairs* 77 (January–February), 42–55.

Brass, Paul R. 1991. *Ethnicity and Nationalism: Theory and Comparison.* New Delhi: Sage.

Braumoeller, Bear F. 1997. "Deadly Doves: Liberal Nationalism and the Democratic Peace in the Soviet Successor States." *International Studies Quarterly* 41 (September), 375–402.

Bremmer, Ian. 1994. "Nazarbayev and the North: State-building and Ethnic Relations in Kazakhstan." *Ethnic and Racial Studies* 17 (October), 619–35.

———. 1997. "Post-Soviet Nationalities Theory: Past, Present, and Future." In *New States, New Politics: Building the Post-Soviet Nations*, ed. Ian Bremmer and Ray Taras, 3–26. Cambridge: Cambridge University Press.

Breuilly, John. 1994. *Nationalism and the State*, 2nd ed. Chicago: University of Chicago Press.

Brokgauz, F. A., and I. A. Efron, publishers. 1890–1904. *Entsiklopedicheskii Slovar'*, 82 vol. St. Petersburg.

Bromlei, Iu. V., ed. 1988. *Narody mira: Istoriko-etnograficheskii spravochnik.* Moscow: Sovetskaia Entsiklopediia.

Brovkin, Vladimir. 1990. "First Party Secretaries: An Endangered Species?" *Problems of Communism* 39 (January–February), 15–27.

Browder, Robert Paul, and Alexander F. Kerensky. 1961. *The Russian Provisional Government 1917*, 3 vols. Sanford: Stanford University Press.

Brown, Archie. 2001. "Vladimir Putin and the Reaffirmation of Central State Power." *Post-Soviet Affairs* 17 (January–March), 45–55.

Brubaker, Rogers. 1996. *Nationalism Reframed: Nationhood and the National Question in the New Europe.* Cambridge: Cambridge University Press.

Brudny, Yitzhak M. 1998. *Reinventing Russia: Russian Nationalism and the Soviet State, 1953–1991.* Cambridge, MA: Harvard University Press.

Bruk, S. I. 1986. *Naselenie mira: Etnodemograficheskii spravochnik*, 2nd rev. ed. Moscow: Izdatel'stvo Nauka.

Bruk, S. I., and V. S. Apenchenko. 1964. *Atlas narodov mira.* Moscow: Glavnoe Upravlenie Geodezii i Kartografii Gosudarstvennogo Geologicheskogo Komiteta SSSR, Institut Etnografii im. Miklukho-Miklaia Akademii Nauk SSSR.

Buchanan, Allen. 1999. "Secession and State-Breakdown." Paper presented at a meeting sponsored by the Carnegie Corporation of New York, "The Conflicting Norms of Self-Determination and the Sanctity of Borders," Washington, DC, 30 September.

Bueno de Mesquita, Bruce, and David Lalman. 1992. *War and Reason: Domestic and International Imperatives.* New Haven: Yale University Press.

Bunce, Valerie. 1999. *Subversive Institutions: The Design and the Destruction of Socialism and the State.* Cambridge: Cambridge University Press.

Bungs, Dzintra. 1989. "A Comparison of the Baltic Declarations of Sovereignty." *Report on the USSR* 1 (15 September), 13–16.

———. 1991a. "Poll Shows Majority in Latvia Endorses Independence." *Report on the USSR* 3 (15 March), 22–25.

———. 1991b. "Voting Patterns in Latvian Independence Poll." *Report on the USSR* 3 (22 March), 21–24.

Burant, Stephen R. 1993. "International Relations in a Regional Context: Poland and Its Eastern Neighbours—Lithuania, Belarus, Ukraine." *Europe-Asia Studies* 45, 395–418.

Burg, Steven L. 1979. "Russians, Natives, and Jews in the Soviet Scientific Elite: Cadre Competition in Central Asia." *Cahiers du Monde Russe et Soviétique* 20 (January–March), 43–59.

Burgess, M. Elaine. 1978. "The Resurgence of Ethnicity: Myth or Reality?" *Ethnic and Racial Studies* 1 (July), 265–85.

Burki, Shahid Javed. 1986. *Pakistan: A Nation in the Making.* Boulder, CO: Westview Press.

Butora, Martin, and Zora Butorova. 1993. "Slovakia: The Identity Challenges of the Newly Born State." *Social Research* 60 (Winter), 705–36.

Callahan, David. 2002. *The Enduring Challenge: Self-Determination and Ethnic Conflict in the 21st Century.* New York: Carnegie Corporation of New York.

Carley, Patricia. 1998. *Nagorno-Karabakh: Searching for a Solution.* United States Institute of Peace Roundtable Report. Washington, DC: USIP.

Carment, David. 1994. "The Ethnic Dimension in World Politics: Theory, Policy, and Early Warning." *Third World Quarterly* 15, 551–82.

Carr, E. H. 1957. "Some Notes on Soviet Bashkiria." *Soviet Studies* 8 (January), 217–35.

Carrère d'Encausse, Hélène. 1980. *Decline of an Empire: The Soviet Socialist Republics in Revolt.* New York: Newsweek Books.

Catlin, G. E. G. 1927. *Science and Method of Politics.* New York: Macmillan.

Centlivres, Pierre, and Micheline Centlivres-Demont. 1997. "Tajikistan and Afghanistan: The Ethnic Groups on Either Side of the Border." In *Tajikistan: The Trials of Independence,* ed. Mohammad-Reza Djalili, Frédéric Grare, and Shirin Akiner, 3–13. New York: St. Martin's Press.

Chamberlin, William Henry. 1944. *Ukraine: A Submerged Nation.* New York: Macmillan.

Cherot, Romeo A. 1955. "Nativization of Government and Party Structure in Kazakhstan, 1920–1930." *American Slavic and East European Review* 14 (February), 42–58.

Chuprov, A. I., ed. 1897. *Vliianie urozhaev i khlebnykh tsen na raznye storony ekonomicheskoi zhizni.* St. Petersburg.

Cleave, Jan. 2000. "Controversy Dogs Election for Russia's Newest President." *Russian Federation Report* 2 (11 October 2000).

Coakley, John. 1992. "The Resolution of Ethnic Conflict: Towards a Typology." *International Political Science Review* 13 (October), 343–58.

———. 1994. "Approaches to the Resolution of Ethnic Conflict: The Strategy of Non-territorial Autonomy." *International Political Science Review* 15 (July), 297–314.

Cockburn, Patrick. 1989. "Dateline USSR: Ethnic Tremors." *Foreign Policy* 74 (Spring), 168–84.

Coleman, James S., and Carl G. Rosberg. 1964. *Political Parties and National Integration in Tropical Africa*. Berkeley and Los Angeles: University of California Press.

Colley, Linda. 1992. *Britons: Forging the Nation 1707–1837*. New Haven: Yale University Press.

Collier, Paul. 2000a. *Economic Causes of Civil Conflict and Their Implications for Policy*. Washington, DC: World Bank.

———. 2000b. "Doing Well Out of War: An Economic Perspective." In *Greed and Grievance: Economic Agendas in Civil Wars*, ed. Mats Berdal and David Malone, 91–111. Boulder, CO: Lynne Reiner.

Collier, Paul, and Anke Hoeffler. 2000. "Greed and Grievance in Civil War." Washington, DC: World Bank.

Colton, Timothy J. 2000. *Transitional Citizens: Voters and What Influences Them in the New Russia*. Cambridge: Harvard University Press.

Connor, Walker. 1972. "Nation-Building or Nation-Destroying?" *World Politics* 24 (April), 319–55.

———. 1994. *Ethnonationalism: The Quest for Understanding*. Princeton: Princeton University Press.

Conquest, Robert. 1967. *Soviet Nationalities Policy in Practice*. New York: Praeger.

Cornell, Svante E. 2001. *Small Nations and Great Powers: A Study of Ethnopolitical Conflict in the Caucasus*. Surrey, England: Curzon Press.

Cox, Gary W. 1997. *Making Votes Count: Strategic Coordination in the World's Electoral Systems*. Cambridge: Cambridge University Press.

Crawford, James. 1988. "The Rights of Peoples: 'Peoples' or 'Governments'?" In *The Rights of Peoples*, ed. James Crawford, 55–67. Oxford: Clarendon Press.

Critchlow, James. 1989. "How Solid Is Uzbekistan's Support for Moscow?" *Report on the USSR* 1 (10 February).

———. 1992. *Nationalism in Uzbekistan: A Soviet Republic's Road to Sovereignty*. Boulder, CO: Westview Press.

Crowther, William. 1991. "The Politics of Ethno-National Mobilization: Nationalism and Reform in Soviet Moldavia." *Russian Review* 50 (April), 183–202.

Dallago, Bruno, and Milica Uvalic. 1998. "The Distributive Consequences of Nationalism: The Case of Former Yugoslavia." *Europe-Asia Studies* 50 (January), 71–90.

Dasgupta, Partha. 1988. "Trust as a Commodity." In *Trust: Making and Breaking Cooperative Relations*, ed. Diego Gambetta, 49–72. New York: Blackwell.

Davies, Norman. 1999. *The Isles: A History*. New York: Oxford University Press.

Dawson, Jane I. 1996. *Eco-Nationalism: Anti-Nuclear Activism and National Identity in Russia, Lithuania, and Ukraine*. Durham: Duke University Press.

Denitch, Bogdan. 1990. *Limits and Possibilities: The Crises of Yugoslav Socialism and State-Socialist Systems*. Minneapolis: University of Minnesota Press.

Deudney, Daniel. 1995. "Nuclear Weapons and the Waning of the Real-State." *Daedalus* 124 (Spring), 209–31.

Deutsch, Karl W. 1966. *Nationalism and Social Communication: An Inquiry into the Foundations of Nationality.* Cambridge: MIT Press.

Dima, Nicholas. 1991. *From Moldavia to Moldova: The Soviet-Romanian Territorial Dispute.* Boulder, CO: East European Monographs.

Dixon, Simon. 1996. "The Russians and the Russian Question." In *The Nationalities Question in the Post-Soviet States,* ed. Graham Smith, 47–74. New York: Longman.

Dmytryshyn, Basil. 1956. *Moscow and the Ukraine, 1918–1953: A Study of Russian Bolshevik Nationality Policy.* New York: Bookman Associates.

Dogovor. 1994. Dogovor Rossiiskoi Federatsii i Respubliki Tatarstan 'O razgranichenii predmetov vedeniia i vzaimnom delegirovanii polnomochii mezhdu organami gosudarstvennoi vlasti Rossiiskoi Federatsii i organami gosudarstvennoi vlasti Respubliki Tatarstan.' 15 February 1994. Kazan: Kazan State University, Department of Law.

———. 1995a. Dogovor o razgranichenii predmetov vedeniia i polnomochii mezhdu organami gosudarstvennoi vlasti Rossiiskoi Federatsii i organami gosudarstvennoi vlasti Udmurtskoi Respubliki. 17 October 1995. *Rossiiskie vesti* 17 February 1996, 5.

———. 1995b. Dogovor o razgranichenii predmetov vedeniia i polnomochii mezhdu organami gosudarstvennoi vlasti Rossiiskoi Federatsii i organami gosudarstvennoi vlasti Respubliki Buriatiia. 29 August 1995. *Rossiiskie vesti* 22 February 1996, 3.

———. 1995c. Dogovor o razgranichenii predmetov vedeniia i polnomochii mezhdu organami gosudarstvennoi vlasti Rossiiskoi Federatsii i organami gosudarstvennoi vlasti Respubliki Severnaia Osetiia-Alaniia. 23 March 1995. *Rossiiskie vesti* 29 February 1996, 3.

———. 1996a. Dogovor o razgranichenii predmetov vedeniia i polnomochii mezhdu organami gosudarstvennoi vlasti Rossiiskoi Federatsii i organami gosudarstvennoi vlasti Chuvashskoi Respubliki. 27 May 1996. *Rossiiskie vesti* 25 July 1996, 6.

———. 1996b. Dogovor o razgranichenii predmetov vedeniia i polnomochii mezhdu organami gosudarstvennoi vlasti Rossiiskoi Federatsii i organami gosudarstvennoi vlasti Respubliki Komi. 20 March 1996. *Rossiiskie vesti* 28 March 1996, 3.

———. 1996c. Dogovor o razgranichenii predmetov vedeniia i polnomochii mezhdu organami gosudarstvennoi vlasti Rossiiskoi Federatsii i organami gosudarstvennoi vlasti Respubliki Sakha (Iatkutiia). 29 June 1995. *Rossiiskie vesti* 14 March 1996, 3.

———. 1996d. Dogovor Rossiiskoi Federatsii i Kabardino-Balkarskoi Respubliki 'O razgranichenii predmetov vedeniia i vzaimnom delegirovanii polnomochii mezhdu organami gosudarstvennoi vlasti Rossiiskoi Federatsii i organami gosudarstvennoi vlasti Kabardino-Balkarskoi Respubliki'. 1 July 1994. *Rossiiskie vesti* 29 February 1996, 3.

———. 1996e. Dogovor Rossiiskoi Federatsii i Respubliki Bashkortostan 'O razgranichenii predmetov vedeniia i vzaimnom delegirovanii polnomochii mezhdu organami gosudarstvennoi vlasti Rossiiskoi Federatsii i organami gosudarstvennoi vlasti Respubliki Bashkortostan.' 3 August 1994. *Rossiiskie vesti* 22 February 1996, 3.

Dowler, Wayne. 1995. "The Politics of Language in Non-Russian Elementary Schools in the Eastern Empire, 1865–1914." *Russian Review* 54 (October), 516–38.

Downing, Brian. 1992. *The Military Revolution and Political Change: Origins of Democracy and Autocracy in Early Modern Europe.* Princeton: Princeton University Press.

Downs, Anthony. 1957. *An Economic Theory of Democracy.* New York: Harper and Row.

Dreifelds, Juris. 1977. "Latvian National Demands and Group Consciousness since 1959." In *Nationalism in the USSR and Eastern Europe in the Era of Brezhnev and Kosygin,* ed. George Simmonds, 136–56. Detroit: University of Detroit Press.

Dresch, Paul. 2000. *A History of Modern Yemen.* Cambridge: Cambridge University Press.

Dudley, Leonard. 1990. "Structural Change in Interdependent Bureaucracies: Was Rome's Failure Economic or Military?" *Explorations in Economic History* 27 (April), 232–48.

Dunlop, John B. 1993–94. "Russia: Confronting a Loss of Empire, 1987–1991." *Political Science Quarterly* 108 (Winter), 603–34.

Dunn, John. 1995. "Introduction: Crisis of the Nation State?" In *Contemporary Crisis of the Nation-State?* Ed. John Dunn, 3–15. Oxford: Blackwell.

Easter, Gerald. 1997. "Redefining Centre-Regional Relations in the Russian Federation: Sverdlovsk *Oblast'*." *Europe-Asia Studies* 49 (June), 617–35.

Edgar, Adrienne L. 2001. "Genealogy, Class, and 'Tribal Policy' in Soviet Turkmenistan, 1924–1934." *Slavic Review* 60 (Summer), 266–98.

Eisinger, Peter. 1973. "The Conditions of Protest Behavior in American Cities." *American Political Science Review* 67 (March), 11–28.

Elazar, Daniel J. 1994. *Federal Systems of the World: A Handbook of Federal, Confederal, and Autonomy Arrangements.* London: Longman.

Ellickson, Robert C. 1991. *Order without Law: How Neighbors Settle Disputes.* Cambridge: Harvard University Press.

Embree, Gregory J. 1991. "RSFSR Election Results and Roll Call Votes." *Soviet Studies* 43, 1065–84.

Emerson, Rupert. 1960. *From Empire to Nation: The Rise to Self-Assertion of Asian and African Peoples.* Boston: Beacon Press.

Encyclopaedia Britannica. 1910–22. Eleventh ed., 32 vols. New York: Encyclopaedia Britannica.

Englebert, Pierre. 2003. "Let's Stick Together: Understanding Africa's Secessionist Deficit." Paper presented at the annual meeting of the African Studies Association, Boston, 30 October–2 November 2003.

Eriksen, Thomas Hylland. 1991. "Ethnicity versus Nationalism." *Journal of Peace Research* 28 (August), 263–78.

Esman, Milton J. 1992. "The State and Language Policy." *International Political Science Review* 13 (October), 381–96.

———. 1994. *Ethnic Politics.* Ithaca: Cornell University Press.

Europa World Year Book [earlier *Europa Year Book*]. 1959–2001. London: Europa Publications.

Evangelista, Matthew. 2002. *The Chechen Wars: Will Russia Go the Way of the Soviet Union?* Washington, DC: Brookings Institution Press.

Facts on File. 1955–2000. New York: Facts on File News Service.

Fainsod, Merle. 1963. *How Russia Is Ruled*, rev. ed. Cambridge: Harvard University Press.

Fane, Daria. 1996. "Ethnicity and Regionalism in Uzbekistan: Maintaining Stability through Authoritarian Control." In *Ethnic Conflict in the Post-Soviet World: Case Studies and Analysis*, ed. Leokadia Drobizheva, Rose Gottemoeller, Catherine McArdle Kelleher, and Lee Walker, 271–301. Armonk, NY: M. E. Sharpe.

Farah, Caesar E. 2002. *The Sultan's Yemen: Nineteenth-Century Challenges to Ottoman Rule.* London: I. B. Tauris.

Fearon, James D. 1993. "Cooperation and Bargaining Under Anarchy." Paper presented at the 1993 meeting of the Public Choice Society, New Orleans, 19–21 March.

———. 1994. "Domestic Audience Costs and the Escalation of International Disputes." *American Political Science Review* 88 (September), 577–92.

Fearon, James D., and Pieter van Houten. 1998. "The Politicization of Cultural and Economic Difference." Paper presented at the annual meeting of the American Political Science Association, Boston, 3–6 September.

Fearon, James D., and David D. Laitin. 1996. "Explaining Interethnic Cooperation." *American Political Science Review* 90 (December), 715–35.

Feldbrugge, F. J. M., ed. 1979. *The Constitution of the USSR and the Union Republics: Analysis, Texts, Reports.* Alphen aan den Rijn, The Netherlands: Sijthoff and Noordhoff.

Fierman, William. 1991. *Language Planning and National Development: The Uzbek Experience.* New York: Mouton de Gruyter.

Figueiredo, Rui J. P. de, Jr., and Barry R. Weingast. 2001. "A Model of Self-Enforcing Federalism." Manuscript. Department of Political Science, University of California, Berkeley; Department of Political Science, Stanford University, Stanford.

Filippov, Mikhail, Peter C. Ordeshook, and Olga Shvetsova. 2004. *Designing Federalism: A Theory of Self-Sustaining Federal Institutions.* Cambridge: Cambridge University Press.

Finnemore, Martha, and Kathryn Sikkink. 1998. "International Norm Dynamics and Political Change." *International Organization* 52 (Fall), 887–917.

Fraser, T. G. 1984. *Partition in Ireland, India, and Palestine: Theory and Practice.* London: Macmillan.

Fried, Morton H. 1968. "State: The Institution." *International Encyclopedia of the Social Sciences*, ed. David L. Sills, 15, 143–50. New York: Macmillan.

Friedgut, Theodore H. 1979. *Political Participation in the USSR.* Princeton: Princeton University Press.

Friedman, David. 1977. "A Theory of the Size and Shape of Nations," *Journal of Political Economy* 85 (February), 59–77.

Fukuyama, Francis. 1992. *The End of History and the Last Man.* New York: Free Press.

Fuller, Elizabeth. 1978, "Kapitonov on Nationality Problems in Georgia." *Radio Liberty Research Bulletin* RL 125/78 (9 June).

———. 1983, "How Serious Are Inter-Nationality Tensions in Georgia?" *Radio Liberty Research Bulletin* RL 444/83 (25 November).

———. 1989. "Abkhaz-Georgian Relations Remain Strained." *Report on the USSR* 1 (10 March), 25–27.

———. 1990a. "Georgia Edges towards Secession." *Report on the USSR* 2 (1 June), 14–18.

———. 1990b. "Zviad Gamsakhurdia Proposes Abolition of Adzhar Autonomy." *Report on the USSR* 2 (30 November), 13–14.

———. 1990c. "Georgian Parliament Votes to Abolish Ossetian Autonomy." *Report on the USSR* 2 (21 December), 8–9.

———. 1991a. "South Ossetia: Analysis of a Permanent Crisis." *Report on the USSR* 3 (15 February), 20–22.

———. 1991b. "Georgia Declares Independence." *Report on the USSR* 3 (19 April), 11–12.

———. 1991c. "What Lies Behind the Current Armenian-Azerbaijani Tensions?" *Report on the USSR* 3 (24 May), 12–15.

———. 1991d. "Armenia Votes Overwhelmingly for Secession." *Report on the USSR* 3 (27 September), 18–20.

———. 1993. "Mediators in Transcaucasia's Conflicts." *The World Today* 49 (May), 89–92.

Furnivall, J. S. 1944. *Netherlands India: A Study of Plural Economy.* Cambridge: Cambridge University Press.

Gall, Carlotta, and Thomas de Waal. 1998. *Chechnya: Calamity in the Caucasus.* New York: New York University Press.

Gartzke, Erik. 1999. "War Is in the Error Term." *International Organization* 53 (Summer), 567–87.

Gastil, Raymond. 1993–2005. *Freedom in the World*, annual eds. New York: Freedom House.

Geary, Patrick J. 2002. *The Myth of Nations: The Medieval Origins of Europe.* Princeton: Princeton University Press.

Geertz, Clifford. 1963. *Old Societies and New States.* New York: Free Press.

Gellner, Ernst. 1983. *Nations and Nationalism.* Ithaca: Cornell University Press.

Gelman, Harry. 1990. *Gorbachev's First Five Years in the Soviet Leadership: The Clash of Personalities and Remaking of Institutions.* RAND Report R-3951-A. Santa Monica: RAND Corporation.

Gerth, H. H., and C. Wright Mills. 1958. *From Max Weber: Essays in Sociology.* New York: Oxford University Press.

Gilbert, Martin. 1998. *Israel: A History.* New York: Murrow.

Gill, Anthony. 2001. "Religion and Comparative Politics." *Annual Review of Political Science* 4, 117–38.

Gill, Graeme, and Roderic Pitty. 1997. *Power in the Party: The Organization of Power and Central-Republican Relations in the CPSU.* New York: St. Martin's Press.

Gilpin, Robert. 1981. *War and Change in World Politics.* Cambridge: Cambridge University Press.

Girnius, Kestutis. 1989. "The Lithuanian Communist Party and Calls for Sovereignty." *Report on the USSR* 1 (17 February), 18–20.

———. 1989. "Unofficial Groups in the Baltic Republics and Access to the Mass Media." *Report on the USSR* 1 (5 May), 16–19.

———. 1991a. "Lithuania's Struggle with the USSR." *Report on the USSR* 3 (1 February), 1–3.

———. 1991b. "Lithuanian Votes for Independence." *Report on the USSR* 3 (22 February), 24–25.

———. 1993. "Lithuania's Foreign Policy." *RFE/RL Research Report* 2 (3 September), 23–30.

Gleason, Gregory. 1997. *The Central Asian States: Discovering Independence*. Boulder, CO: Westview Press.

Gleditsch, Kristian D., and Michael D. Ward. 1999. "A Revised List of Independent States Since the Congress of Vienna." *International Interactions* 25, 393–413.

Gleditsch, Nils Petter, Peter Wallensteen, Mikael Eriksson, Margareta Sollenberg, and Håvard Strand. 2002. "Armed Conflict 1946–2001: A New Dataset." *Journal of Peace Research* 39 (September), 615–63.

Glubotskii, A., A. Mukhin, and N. Tiukhov. 1995. *Organy vlasti sub"ektov Rossiiskoi Federatsii: Obzory, biografii, telefony*. Moscow: Panorama.

Goldstein, Avery. 1991. *From Bandwagon to Balance-of-Power Politics: Structural Constraints and Politics in China, 1949–1978*. Stanford: Stanford University Press.

Golosov, Grigorii V. 1999. "From Adygeia to Yaroslavl: Factors of Party Development in the Regions of Russia, 1995–1998." *Europe-Asia Studies* 51 (December), 1333–65.

Gorbachev, Mikhail. 1995. *Zhizn' i reformy*. Moscow: Novosti.

Gorenburg, Dmitry. 1997. "Organizing Nationalists in Russia's Republics: The Effect of Political Context." Paper presented at the annual meeting of the American Political Science Association, Washington, DC.

———. 1999. "Regional Separatism in Russia: Ethnic Mobilisation or Power Grab?" *Europe-Asia Studies* 51 (March), 245–74.

Gorenburg, Dmitry P. 2003. *Minority Ethnic Mobilization in the Russian Federation*. Cambridge: Cambridge University Press.

Gourevitch, Peter. 1978. "The Second Image Reversed: The International Sources of Domestic Politics." *International Organization* 32 (Autumn), 881–911.

Graney, Katherine E. 1999. "Education Reform in Tatarstan and Bashkortostan: Sovereignty Projects in Post-Soviet Russia." *Europe-Asia Studies* 51 (June), 611–32.

Green, Abigail. 2001. *Fatherlands: State-Building and Nationhood in Nineteenth-Century Germany*. Cambridge: Cambridge University Press.

Guéhenno, Jean-Marie. 1995. *The End of the Nation-State*, trans. Victoria Elliot. Minneapolis: University of Minnesota Press.

Guroff, Gregory, and Alexander Guroff. 1994. "The Paradox of Russian National Identity." In *National Identity and Ethnicity in Russia and the New States of Eurasia*, ed. Roman Szporluk, 78–100. Armonk, NY: M. E. Sharpe.

Gurr, Ted Robert. 1971. *Why Men Rebel*. Princeton: Princeton University Press.

———. 1993. *Minorities at Risk: A Global View of Ethnopolitical Conflicts*. Washington, DC: United States of Institute Press.

Gurr, Ted Robert. 2000. *Peoples Versus States: Minorities at Risk in the New Century.* Washington, DC: United States Institute of Peace.

———. 2001. *Minorities at Risk Project* (Web site), http://www.bsos.umd.edu/cidcm/mar

Guthier, Steven L. 1979. "The Popular Base of Ukrainian Nationalism in 1917." *Slavic Review* 38 (March), 30–47.

Haas, Ernst B. 1986. "What is Nationalism and Why Should We Study It?" *International Organization* 40 (Summer), 707–44.

———. 1993. "Nationalism: An Instrumental Social Construction." *Millenium* 22 (Winter), 505–45.

Haefele, Edwin T. 1970. "Coalitions, Minority Representation, and Vote-Trading Probabilities." *Public Choice* 8 (Spring), 74–90.

Hahn, Jeffrey. 1993. "Attitudes Toward Reform Among Provincial Russian Politicians." *Post-Soviet Affairs* 9 (January—March), 66–85.

Hale, Henry E. 2001. "Ethnofederalism and Theories of Secession: Getting More from the Soviet Case." Manuscript. Department of Political Science, Indiana University, Bloomington.

Hall, Peter A., and Rosemary C. R. Taylor. 1996. "Political Science and the Three New Institutionalisms." *Political Studies* 44 (December), 936–57.

Hall, Rodney Bruce. 1999. *National Collective Identity: Social Constructs and International Systems.* New York: Columbia University Press.

Hallik, Klara. 1996. "Ethnopolitical Conflict in Estonia." In *Ethnic Conflict in the Post-Soviet World: Case Studies and Analysis,* ed. Leokadia Drobizheva, Rose Gottemoeller, Catherine McArdle Kelleher, and Lee Walker, 87–108. Armonk, NY: M. E. Sharpe.

Hanauer, Laurence S. 1996. "Tatarstan's Bid for Autonomy: Tatarstan as a Model for the Devolution of Power in the Russian Federation." *Journal of Communist Studies and Transition Politics* 12 (March), 63–82.

Hanf, Theodor. 1991. "Reducing Conflict Through Cultural Autonomy: Karl Rener's Contribution." In *State and Nation in Multi-ethnic Societies: The Breakup of Multinational States,* ed. Uri Ra'anan et al., 33–52. New York: Manchester University Press.

Hanks, Reuel R. 2000. "A Separate Space? Karakalpak Nationalism and Devolution in Post-Soviet Uzbekistan." *Europe-Asia Studies* 52 (July), 939–53.

Hannum, Hurst. 1990. *Autonomy, Sovereignty, and Self-Determination: The Accommodation of Conflicting Rights,* rev. ed. Philadelphia: University of Pennsylvania Press.

Hanson, Philip. 1991. "The Union Treaty: Embargoes or Surrender?" *Report on the USSR* 3 (28 June), 15–16.

Harasimyw, Bohdan. 1969. "Nomenklatura: The Soviet Communist Party's Leadership Recruitment System." *Canadian Journal of Political Science* 2 (November), 493–512.

Hardin, Russell. 1995. *One for All: The Logic of Group Conflict.* Princeton: Princeton University Press.

Harding, Les. 1998. *Dead Countries of the Nineteenth and Twentieth Centuries: Aden to Zululand.* Lanham: Scarecrow Press.

Harris, Chauncy D. 1994. "Ethnic Tensions in the Successor Republics in 1993 and Early 1994." *Post-Soviet Geography* 35 (April), 185–203.

Hartshorne, Richard. 1936. "Suggestions on the Terminology of Political Boundaries." *Annals of the Association of American Geographers* 26 (March), 56–57.

Hastings, Adrian. 1997. *The Construction of Nationhood: Ethnicity, Religion, and Nationalism*. Cambridge: Cambridge University Press.

Haushofer, Karl. 1927. *Grenzen in ihrer Geographischen und politischen Bedeutung*. Berlin: K. Vowinckel.

Hechter, Michael. 1975. *Internal Colonialism: The Celtic Fringe in British National Development 1536–1966*. London: Routledge and Kegan Paul.

———. 2000. *Containing Nationalism*. New York: Oxford University Press.

Hechter, Michael, and Margaret Levi. 1979. "The Comparative Analysis of Ethnoregional Movements." *Ethnic and Racial Studies* 2 (July), 260–74.

Hechter, M., and D. Okamoto. 2001. "Political Consequences of Minority Group Formation." *Annual Review of Political Science* 4, 189–215.

Heckathorn, Douglas D., and Steven M. Maser. 1987. "Bargaining and Constitutional Contracts." *American Journal of Political Science* 31 (February), 142–68.

Heisler, Martin O. 1977. "Ethnic Conflict in the World Today: An Introduction." *Annals of the American Academy of Political and Social Science* 433 (September), 1–5.

Helf, Gavin, comp. 1988. *A Biographical Directory of Soviet Regional Party Leaders*, 2nd ed. Munich: Radio Free Europe/Radio Liberty.

Henige, David P. 1970. *Colonial Governors from the Fifteenth Century to the Present*. Madison: University of Wisconsin Press.

Herbst, Jeffrey. 2000. *States and Power in Africa: Comparative Lessons in Authority and Control*. Princeton: Princeton University Press.

Herz, John H. 1957. "The Rise and Demise of the Territorial State." *World Politics* 9 (July), 473–93.

Hewitt, Christopher. 1977. "Majorities and Minorities: A Comparative Survey of Ethnic Violence." *Annals of the American Academy of Political and Social Science* 433 (September), 150–60.

Hiden, J. W. 1970. "The Baltic Germans and German Policy towards Latvia after 1918." *Historical Journal* 13 (June), 295–317.

Hilde, Paal Sigurd. 1999. "Slovak Nationalism and the Break-up of Czechoslovakia." *Europe-Asia Studies* 51 (June), 647–65.

Hill, Howard D. 1965. *Roosevelt and the Caribbean*. New York: Russell and Russell.

Hill, Ronald J. 1993. "Managing Ethnic Conflict." *Journal of Communist Studies* 9 (March), 57–73.

Himka, John-Paul. 1982. "Young Radicals and Independent Statehood: The Idea of a Ukrainian Nation-State, 1890–1895." *Slavic Review* 41 (Summer), 219–35.

Hirsch, Francine. 1997. "The Soviet Union as a Work-in-Progress: Ethnographers and the Category *Nationality* in the 1926, 1937, and 1939 Censuses." *Slavic Review* 56 (Summer), 251–78.

Hirschman, Albert O. 1970. *Exit, Voice, and Loyalty: Responses to Decline in Firms, Organizations, and States*. Cambridge: Harvard University Press.

Hirshleifer, Jack, and Juan Carlos Martin Coll. 1988. "What Strategies Can Support the Evolutionary Emergence of Cooperation?" *Journal of Conflict Resolution* 32 (June), 367–98.

Hislope, Robert. 1997. "Intra-Ethnic Conflict in Croatia and Serbia: Flanking and the Consequences for Democracy." *East European Quarterly* 30 (January), 471–94.

Hobsbawm, Eric, and Terence Ranger. 1992. *The Invention of Tradition.* Cambridge: Cambridge University Press.

Hodnett, Grey. 1967. "The Debate over Soviet Federalism." *Soviet Studies* 18 (April), 458–81.

Hodnett, Grey. 1973. *Leaders of the Soviet Republics, 1955–1972.* Canberra: Australian National University.

———. 1978. *Leadership in the Soviet National Republics: A Quantitative Study of Recruitment Policy.* Oakville, ON: Mosaic Press.

Horowitz, Donald L. 1985. *Ethnic Groups in Conflict.* Berkeley and Los Angeles: University of California Press, 1985.

———. 1991. "Making Moderation Pay: The Comparative Politics of Ethnic Conflict Management." In *Conflict and Peacemaking in Multiethnic Societies,* ed. Joseph V. Montville, 451–75. New York: Lexington Books.

Hough, Jerry F. 1969. *The Soviet Prefects.* Cambridge, MA: Harvard University Press.

———. 1997. *Democratization and Revolution in the USSR, 1985–1991.* Washington, DC: Brookings Institution Press.

Hough, Jerry F., and Merle Fainsod. 1979. *How the Soviet Union Is Governed.* Cambridge, MA: Harvard University Press.

Hovannisian, Richard G. 1967. *Armenia on the Road to Independence, 1918.* Berkeley and Los Angeles: University of California Press.

———. 1974. "Dimensions of Democracy and Authority in Caucasian Armenia, 1917–1920." *Russian Review* 33 (January), 37–49.

Hroch, Miroslav. 2000. *The Social Preconditions of National Revival in Europe: A Comparative Analysis of the Social Composition of Patriotic Groups among the Smaller European Nations.* New York: Columbia University Press.

Hughes, James. 1994. "Regionalism in Russia: The Rise and Fall of Siberian Agreement." *Europe-Asia Studies* 46, 1133–61.

Huntington, Samuel P. 1996. *The Clash of Civilizations and the Remaking of World Order.* New York: Simon and Schuster.

Hussain, J. 1997. *A History of the Peoples of Pakistan: Towards Independence.* Karachi: Oxford University Press.

Hutchinson, John. 1987. *The Dynamics of Cultural Nationalism.* London: Allen and Unwin.

Hutchinson, John, and Anthony D. Smith, eds. 1994. *Nationalism.* New York: Oxford University Press.

Hyde, Matthew. 2001. "Putin's Federal Reforms and Their Implications for Presidential Power in Russia." *Europe-Asia Studies* 53 (June), 719–43.

Iakovlev, Ia. A. 1927. *Krest'ianskoe dvizhenie v 1917 godu.* Moscow.

Ilishev, Ildus G. 1997. "Tightening in the Federation: Will Russia's Autonomies Disappear?" *Analysis of Current Events* 9 (July), 6–8.

Inkeles, Alex. 1950 *Public Opinion in Soviet Russia: A Study in Mass Persuasion.* Cambridge, MA: Harvard University Press.

Institut Marksa-Engel'sa-Lenina-Stalina. 1954. *Kommunisticheskaia Partiia Sovet-skogo Soiuza v Rezoliutsiiakh i Resheniiakh s"ezdov, konferentsii, i plenumov TsK*, 3 vols. Moscow: Gosudarstvennoe Izdatel'stvo Politicheskoi Literatury.

Institut teorii i istorii sotsializma TsK KPSS. 1991. *K soiuzu suverennykh narodov: Sbornik dokumentov KPSS, zakonodatel'nykh aktov, deklaratsii, obrashchenii i prezident-skikh ukazov, posviashchennykh probleme natsional'no-gosudarstvennogo suvereniteta*. Moscow.

Ishiyama, John T. 1999. "Representational Mechanisms and Ethnopolitics: Evidence from Transitional Democracies in Eastern Europe." *East European Quarterly* 33 (June), 251–79.

Jackson, Robert H. 1987. "Quasi-States, Dual Regimes, and Neoclassical Theory: International Jurisprudence and the Third World." *International Organization* 41 (Autumn), 519–49.

Jahangiri, Guissou. 1997. "The Premises for the Construction of a Tajik National Identity, 1920–1930." In *Tajikistan: The Trials of Independence*, ed. Mohammad-Reza Djalili, Frédéric Grare, and Shirin Akiner, 14–41. New York: St. Martin's Press.

James, Alan. 1986. *Sovereign Statehood: The Basis of International Society*. London: Allen and Unwin.

Jelavich, Charles, and Barbara Jelavich. 1977. *The Establishment of the Balkan National States, 1804–1920*. Seattle: University of Washington Press.

Jennings, Ivor. 1958. *The Approach to Self-Government*. Cambridge: University Press.

Jocelyn, Ed. 1998. "Nationalism, Identity, and the Belarusian State." In *National Identities and Ethnic Minorities in Eastern Europe*, ed. Ray Taras, 73–83. New York: St. Martin's Press.

Jones, Ellen, and Fred W. Grupp. 1984. "Modernisation and Ethnic Equalisation in the USSR." *Soviet Studies* 36 (April), 159–84.

Jones, Stephen. 1988. "The Establishment of Soviet Power in Transcaucasia: The Case of Georgia 1921–1928." *Soviet Studies* 40 (October), 616–39.

Juraeva, Gavhar. 1996. "Ethnic Conflict in Tajikistan." In *Ethnic Conflict in the Post-Soviet World: Case Studies and Analysis*, ed. Leokadia Drobizheva, Rose Gottemoeller, Catherine McArdle Kelleher, and Lee Walker, 255–70. Armonk, NY: M. E. Sharpe.

Jussila, Osmo. 1989. "Finland from Province to State." In *Finland: People, Nation, State*, ed. Max Engman and David Kirby, 85–101. Bloomington: Indiana University Press.

Jussila, Osmo, Seppo Hentilä, and Jukka Nevakivi. 1995. *From Grand Duchy to a Modern State: A Political History of Finland since 1809*, trans. David and Eva-Kaisa Arter. London: Hurst.

Kahn, Jeff. 2000. "The Parade of Sovereignties: Establishing the Vocabulary of the New Russian Federalism." *Post-Soviet Affairs* 16 (January—March), 58–59.

Kaiser, Robert J. 1994. *The Geography of Nationalism in Russia and the USSR*. Princeton: Princeton University Press.

———. 1995. "Prospects for the Disintegration of the Russian Federation." *Post-Soviet Geography* 36 (September), 426–35.

Karachaevo-Cherkesskaia Respublika. 1996. *Konstitutsiia Karachaevo-Cherkesskoi Respubliki.* Cherkessk: Karachaevo-Cherkesskoe Gosudarstvennoe Respublikanskoe Knizhnoe Izdatel'stvo.

Karklins, Rasma. 1984. "Ethnic Politics and Access to Higher Education: The Soviet Case." *Comparative Politics* 16 (April), 277–94.

———. 1994. *Ethnopolitics and Transition to Democracy: The Collapse of the USSR and Latvia.* Washington, DC: Woodrow Wilson Center Press.

Kasfir, Nelson. 1979. "Explaining Ethnic Political Participation." *World Politics* 31 (April), 365–88.

———. 1986. *The Shrinking Political Agenda: Participation and Ethnicity in African Politics.* Berkeley and Los Angeles: University of California Press.

Katzenstein, Peter J. 1976. *Disjoined Partners: Austria and Germany since 1815.* Berkeley and Los Angeles: University of California Press.

———. 1977. "The Last Old Nation: Austrian National Consciousness since 1945." *Comparative Politics* 9 (January), 147–71.

Kaufmann, William W. 1956. "Limited Warfare." In *Military Policy and National Security,* ed. William W. Kaufmann. Princeton: Princeton University Press.

Kaviraj, Sudipta. 2001. "In Search of Civil Society." In *Civil Society: History and Possibilities,* ed. Sudipta Kaviraj and Sunil Khilnani, 287–323. Cambridge: Cambridge University Press.

Keesing's Record of World Events (earlier *Keesing's Contemporary Archives*). 1955–2000. London: Longman's.

Kelley, Robert F. 1924. "The Territorial Organization of the Soviet Power, 1924." *Geographical Review* 14 (October), 615–21.

Kempton, Daniel. 1996. "The Republic of Sakha (Yakutia): The Evolution of Center-Periphery Relations in the Russian Federation." *Europe-Asia Studies* 48 (June), 587–613.

Kenez, Peter. 1985. *The Birth of the Propaganda State: Soviet Methods of Mass Mobilization, 1917–1929.* Cambridge: Cambridge University Press.

Khalid, Adeeb. 1996. "Tashkent 1917: Muslim Politics in Revolutionary Turkestan." *Slavic Review* 55 (Summer), 270–96.

King, Charles. 1993. "Moldova and the New Bessarabian Questions." *The World Today* 49 (July), 135–39.

———. 1999. "The Ambivalence of Authenticity, or How the Moldovan Language Was Made." *Slavic Review* 58 (Spring), 117–42.

———. 2000. *The Moldovans: Romania, Russia, and the Politics of Culture.* Stanford: Hoover Institution Press.

King, Gary, Michael Tomz, and Jason Wittenberg. 2000. "Making the Most of Statistical Analyses: Improving Interpretation and Presentation." *American Journal of Political Science* 44 (April), 341–55.

Kionka, Riina. 1991. "Estonia Says 'Yes' to Independence." *Report on the USSR* 3 (15 March), 25–26.

Kirkow, Peter. 1994. "Regional Politics and Market Reform in Russia: The Case of the Altai." *Europe-Asia Studies* 46, 1163–87.

———. 1995. "Regional Warlordism in Russia: The Case of Primorskii *Krai.*" *Europe-Asia Studies* 47 (September), 923–47.

Kitschelt, Herbert P. 1986. "Political Opportunity Structures and Political Protest: Anti-Nuclear Movements in Four Democracies." *British Journal of Political Science* 16 (January), 57–85.

Knight, Amy. 1993. *Beria: Stalin's First Lieutenant*. Princeton: Princeton University Press.

Knight, Jack. 1992. *Institutions and Social Conflict*. Cambridge: Cambridge University Press.

Kocaoglu, Timur. 1983. "Muslim Chain Letters in Central Asia." *Radio Liberty Research Bulletin*, RL 313/83 (18 August).

Kohn, Hans. 1944. *The Idea of Nationalism: A Study in Its Origins and Background*. New York: Macmillan.

———. 1957. *American Nationalism: An Interpretative Essay*. New York: Macmillan.

Kolstø, Pål, Andrei Edemsky, and Natalya Kalashnikova. 1993. "The Dniester Conflict: Between Irredentism and Separatism." *Europe-Asia Studies* 45, 973–1000.

Kolstø, Pål, and Boris Tsilevich. 1997. "Patterns of Nation-Building and Political Integration in a Bifurcated Postcommunist State: Ethnic Aspects of Parliamentary Elections in Latvia." *East European Politics and Societies* 11 (Spring), 366–91.

Konstitutsiia (osnovnoi zakon) Soiuza Sovetskikh Sotsialisticheskikh Respublik, Konstitutsii (osnovnye zakony) soiuznykh sovetskikh sotsialisticheskikh respublik. 1978. Moscow: Iuridicheskaia literatura.

Konstitutsiia Rossiiskoi Federatsii, ofitsial'noe izdanie. 1993. Moscow: Iuridicheskaia literatura.

Koroteeva, V., L. Perepelkin, and O. Shkaratan. 1988. "Ot biurokraticheskogo tsentralizma k ekonomicheskoi integratsii suverennykh respublik." *Kommunist* 15 (October), 22–33.

Kosov, Iu., E. Lisin, R. Mingazov, and D. Khairullina. 1993. *Kto est' kto v Respublike Tatarstan*. Kazan: Tatarskoe gazetno-zhurnal'noe izdatel'stvo.

Kovtun, George J. 1985. *The Czechoslovak Declaration of Independence*. Washington, DC: Library of Congress.

Kozlov, Vladimir. 2001. "Vybory glav ispolnitel'noi vlasti regionov." In *Regiony Rossii v 1999g.*, ed. Nikolai Petrov, 130–39. Moscow: Carnegie Center.

Krasner, Stephen D. 1984. "Approaches to the State: Alternative Conceptions and Historical Dynamics." *Comparative Politics* 16 (January), 223–46.

———. 1999. *Sovereignty: Organized Hypocrisy*. Princeton: Princeton University Press.

Krawchenko, Bohdan. 1985. *Social Change and National Consciousness in Twentieth-Century Ukraine*. London: Macmillan.

Kubicek, Paul. 1997. "Regionalism, Nationalism, and Realpolitik in Central Asia." *Europe-Asia Studies* 49 (June), 637–55.

Kugler, Jacek, and Douglas Lemke, eds. 1996. *Parity and War: Evaluations and Extensions of the War Ledger*. Ann Arbor: University of Michigan Press.

Kuran, Timur. 1989. "Sparks and Prairie Fires: A Theory of Unanticipated Political Revolution." *Public Choice* 61 (April), 41–74.

Kuzio, Taras. 2000. "The National Factor in Ukraine's Quadruple Transition." *Contemporary Politics* 6, 143–64.

Kuzio, Taras. 2001. "'Nationalising states' or nation-building? A critical review of the theoretical literature and empirical evidence." *Nations and Nationalism* 7, 135–54.

Kymlicka, Will. 1995. *Multicultural Citizenship.* New York: Oxford University Press.

Laird, Roy D. 1986. *The Politburo: Demographic Trends, Gorbachev, and the Future.* Boulder, CO: Westview.

Laitin, David D. 1986. *Hegemony and Culture: Politics and Religious Change among the Yoruba.* Chicago: University of Chicago Press.

———. 1998. *Identity in Formation: The Russian-Speaking Populations in the Near Abroad.* Ithaca: Cornell University Press.

Lalman, David, Joe Oppenheimer, and Piotr Swistak. 1993. "Formal Rational Choice Theory: A Cumulative Science of Politics." In *Political Science: The State of the Discipline—II*, ed. Ada W. Finifter. Washington, DC: American Political Science Association, 1993.

Lane, David. 1975. "Ethnic and Class Stratification in Soviet Kazakhstan, 1917–39." *Comparative Studies in Society and History* 17 (April), 165–89.

Lapidoth, Ruth. 1997. *Autonomy: Flexible Solutions to Ethnic Conflicts.* Washington, DC: United States Institute of Peace Press.

Lapidus, Gail W. 1992. "From Democratization to Disintegration: The Impact of Perestroika on the National Question." In *From Union to Commonwealth: Nationalism and Separatism in the Soviet Republics*, ed. Gail W. Lapidus, Victor Zaslavsky, and Philip Goldman, 45–70. Cambridge: Cambridge University Press.

———. 1999. "Asymmetrical Federalism and State Breakdown in Russia." *Post-Soviet Affairs* 15 (January–March), 74–82.

Laskovsky, Nicholas. 1958. "Reflections on Soviet Industrial Reorganization." *American Slavic and East European Review* 17 (February), 47–58.

Lavrov, Alexei M., and Alexei G. Makushkin. 2001. *The Fiscal Structure of the Russian Federation: Financial Flows Between the Center and the Regions.* Armonk, NY: M. E. Sharpe.

Lazzerini, Edward J. 1981. "Tatarovedenie and the 'New Historiography' in the Soviet Union: Revising the Interpretation of the Tatar-Russian Relationship." *Slavic Review* 40 (Winter), 625–35.

Leatherman, Janie, William DeMars, Patrick Gaffney, and Raimo Väyrynen. 1998. *Pursuing Peace in the Shadow of War: Strategies for Early Warning and Conflict Prevention.* South Bend: University of Notre Dame, Joan Kroc Institute for International Peace Studies.

Leff, Carol Skalnik. 1999. "Democratization and Disintegration in Multinational States: The Breakup of the Communist Federations." *World Politics* 51 (January), 205–35.

Leites, Nathan, and Charles Wolf, Jr. 1970. *Rebellion and Authority: An Analytic Essay on Insurgent Conflicts.* Chicago: Markham.

Lemarchand, René. 1970. *Rwanda and Burundi.* New York: Praeger Publishers.

Lenin, V. I. 1913a [1980]. "Tezisy po natsional'nomu voprosu." In *Polnoe sobranie sochinenii*, 5th ed., 23, 314–22. Moscow: Politicheskaia Literatura.

———. 1913b [1980]. "Kriticheskie zametki po natsional'nomu voprosu." In *Polnoe sobranie sochinenii*, 5th ed., 24, 113–50. Moscow: Politicheskaia Literatura.

Leslie, R. F., et al. 1980. *The History of Poland since 1863*. Cambridge: Cambridge University Press.

Levinson, David, ed. 1991. *Encyclopedia of World Cultures*, 10 vols. Boston: G. K. Hall.

Lewin, Moshe. 1968. *Lenin's Last Struggle*. New York: Monthly Review Press.

Liber, George O. 1992. *Soviet Nationality Policy, Urban Growth, and Identity Change in the Ukrainian SSR 1923–1934*. Cambridge: Cambridge University Press.

Liebich, Andre. 1995. "Nations, States, Minorities: Why Is Eastern Europe Different?" *Dissent* 42 (Summer), 313–17.

———. 1996. "Getting Better, Getting Worse." *Dissent* 43 (Summer), 84–89.

Lieven, Anatol. 1993. *The Baltic Revolution: Estonia, Latvia, Lithuania and the Path to Independence*. New Haven: Yale University Press.

———. 1998. *Chechnya: Tombstone of Russian Power*. New Haven: Yale University Press.

Ligachev, Yegor. 1993. *Inside Gorbachev's Kremlin*. New York: Pantheon Books.

Lijphart, Arend. 1969. "Consociational Democracy." *World Politics* 21 (January), 207–25.

———. 1995. "Multiethnic Democracy." In *The Encyclopedia of Democracy*, ed. Seymour Martin Lipset, 3:853–65. Washington, DC: Congressional Quarterly.

Linn's World Stamp Almanac. 1982. Sidney, OH: Amos Press.

Lipovsky, Igor P. 1996. "Central Asia: In Search of a New Political Identity." *Middle East Journal* 50 (Spring), 211–23.

Loeber, Dietrich A. 1968. "Administration of Culture in Soviet Latvia." In *Res Baltica*, ed. Adolf Sprudz and Armin Rusis, 133–45. Leyden: A. W. Sijthoff.

Löwenhardt, John. 1981. *Decision Making in Soviet Politics*. New York: St. Martin's Press.

———. 1982. *The Soviet Politburo*. Edinburgh: Canongate.

———. 1997. "The 1996 Presidential Elections in Tatarstan." *Journal of Communist Studies and Transition Politics* 13 (March), 132–44.

Löwenhardt, John, James R. Ozinga, and Eric van Ree. 1992. *The Rise and Fall of the Soviet Politburo*. New York: St. Martin's Press.

Löwenhardt, John, and Ruben Verheul. 2000. "The Village Votes: The December 1999 Elections in Tatarstan's Pestretsy District." *Journal of Communist Studies and Transition Politics* 16 (September), 113–22.

Lubachko, Ivan S. 1972. *Belorussia Under Soviet Rule, 1917–1957*. Lexington: University Press of Kentucky.

Lubin, Nancy. 1981. "Assimilation and Retention of Ethnic Identity in Uzbekistan." *Asian Affairs* 12 (October), 277–85.

———. 1995. *Central Asians Take Stock: Reform, Corruption, and Identity*. Washington, DC: United States Institute of Peace.

Lucas, Noah. 1975. *The Modern History of Israel*. New York: Praeger.

Lukianov, A. I. et al. 1984. *Sovety Narodnykh Deputatov*. Moscow: Politicheskaia Literatura.

Lundgreen-Nielsen, Kay. 1979. *The Polish Problem at the Paris Peace Conference: A Study of the Policies of the Great Powers and the Poles, 1918–1919*. Odense, Denmark: Odense University Press.

Luong, Pauline Jones. 2002. *Institutional Change and Political Continuity in Post-Soviet Central Asia: Power, Perceptions, and Pacts*. Cambridge: Cambridge University Press.

Lustick, Ian. 1990. "Becoming Problematic: Breakdown of a Hegemonic Conception of Ireland in Nineteenth Century Britain." *Politics and Society* 18 (March), 39–73.

Lydolph, Paul E. 1958. "The Soviet Reorganization of Industry." *American Slavic and East European Review* 17 (October), 293–301.

Lynch, Dov. 2004. *Engaging Eurasia's Separatist States: Unresolved Conflicts and De Facto States*. Washington, DC: United States Institute of Peace Press.

Lyubarsky, Kronid. 1993. "Referendum—Likes and Dislikes." *New Times International* No. 19 (May), 6–7.

MacFarlane, S. Neil. 1999. *Western Engagement in the Caucasus and Central Asia*. London: Royal Institute of International Affairs.

Mair, Lucy. 1977. *Primitive Government: A Study of Traditional Political Systems in Eastern Africa*. Bloomington: Indiana University Press.

Mal'tsev, V. 1990. "Territorial'nyi khozraschet: ot raspredeleneiia k obmenu." *Vestnik statistiki*, 1:3–10.

Mamatey, Victor S. 1973. "The Establishment of the Republic." In *A History of the Czechoslovak Republic, 1918–1948*, ed. Victor S. Mamatey and Radomír Luža, 3–38. Princeton: Princeton University Press.

Mandel, William M. 1942. "Soviet Central Asia." *Pacific Affairs* 15 (December), 389–409.

Mann, Michael. 1995. "A Political Theory of Nationalism and Its Excesses." In *Notions of Nationalism*, ed. Sukumar Periwal, 44–54. Budapest: Central European University Press.

Margolian, M. 1995. *The Conflict in Tajikistan*. Ottawa, Canada: Department of National Defence, Operation Research and Analysis, Directorate of Strategic Analysis, Research Note 95/2.

Marples, David R. 1996. *Belarus: From Soviet Rule to Nuclear Catastrophe*. New York: St. Martin's Press.

———. 1999. *Belarus: A Denationalized Nation*. Amsterdam: Harwood Academic Publishers.

Mars, Perry. 1995. "State Intervention and Ethnic Conflict Resolution: Guyana and the Caribbean Experience." *Comparative Politics* 27 (January), 167–186.

Marshall, Monty, and Keith Jaggers. 2000. "Polity IV: Political Regime Characteristics and Transitions, 1800–1999." Available online at http://www.cidcm.umd.edu/inscr/polity

Martin, Keith. 1993. "Tajikistan: Civil War Without End?" *RFE/RL Research Report* 2 (20 August), 18–29.

Martin, Terry. 2001. *The Affirmative Action Empire: Nations and Nationalism in the Soviet Union, 1923–1939*. Ithaca: Cornell University Press.

Massell, Gregory J. 1974. *The Surrogate Proletariat: Moslem Women and Revolutionary Strategies in Soviet Central Asia, 1919–29*. Princeton: Princeton University Press.

Mastny, Vojtech. 2000. "The Historical Experience of Federalism in East Central Europe." *East European Politics and Societies* 14 (Winter), 64–96.

Matlock, Jack F., Jr. 1995. *Autopsy of an Empire: The American's Ambassador's Account of the Collapse of the Soviet Union.* New York: Random House.

Matsyugina, Tatiana, and Lev Perepelkin. 1996. *An Ethnic History of Russia: Pre-revolutionary Times to the Present.* Westport, CT: Greenwood Press.

Matveeva, Anna. 1999. *The North Caucasus: Russia's Fragile Borderland.* London: Royal Institute of International Affairs.

Mayall, James. 1990. *Nationalism and International Society.* Cambridge: Cambridge University Press.

———. 1999. "Sovereignty, Nationalism, and Self-determination." *Political Studies* 47 (Special Issue), 474–502.

McAdam, Doug. 1982. *Political Process and the Development of Black Insurgency 1930–1970.* Chicago: University of Chicago Press.

McAdam, Doug, John D. McCarthy, and Mayer N. Zald. 1988. "Social Movements." In *Handbook of Sociology*, ed. Neil J. Smelser, 695–737. Newbury Park, CA: Sage.

McAdam, Doug, Sidney Tarrow, and Charles Tilly. 2001. *Dynamics of Contention.* Cambridge: Cambridge University Press.

McAuley, Mary. 1992. "Politics, Economics, and Elite Realignment in Russia: A Regional Perspective." *Soviet Economy* 8 (January–March), 46–88.

McCain, William D. 1965. *The United States and the Republic of Panama.* New York: Russell and Russell.

McCarthy, John D., and Mayer N. Zald. 1987. "Resource Mobilization and Social Movements: A Partial Theory." In *Social Movements in an Organizational Society*, ed. Mayer N. Zald and John D. McCarthy, 15–42. New Brunswick, NJ: Transaction Books.

McCord, Arline, and William McCord. 1979. "Ethnic Autonomy: A Socio-Historical Synthesis." In *Ethnic Autonomy: Comparative Dynamics*, ed. Raymond L. Hall, 426–36. New York: Pergamon Press.

McDonald, Gordon, et al. 1969. *Area Handbook for Burundi.* Washington, DC: United States Government Printing Office.

McFaul, Michael. 2000. "The Sovereignty Script: Red Book for Russian Revolutionaries." In *Problematic Sovereignty*, ed. Stephen Krasner, 194–223. New York: Columbia University Press.

———. 2001. *Russia's Unfinished Revolution: Political Change from Gorbachev to Putin.* Ithaca: Cornell University Press.

McKelvey, Richard. 1976. "Intransitivities in Multidimensional Voting Models, and Some Implications for Agenda Control." *Journal of Economic Theory* 2, 472–82.

McMillan, John. 1992. *Games, Strategies, and Managers.* New York: Oxford University Press, 1992.

McRae, Kenneth D. 1975. "The Principle of Territoriality and the Principle of Personality in Multilingual States." *Linguistics* 158, 33–54.

Mellor, Roy E. H. 1989. *Nation, State, and Territory: A Political Geography.* New York: Routledge.

Menon, Rajan, and Graham E. Fuller. 2000. "Russia's Ruinous Chechen War." *Foreign Affairs* 79 (March–April), 32–44.

Miles, William F. S. 1994. *Hausaland Divided: Colonialism and Independence in Nigeria and Niger.* Ithaca: Cornell University Press.

Miles, William F. S., and David A. Rochefort. 1991. "Nationalism versus Ethnic Identity in Sub-Saharan Africa." *American Political Science Review* 85 (June), 393–403.

Mill, John Stuart. 1859 [1991]. *On Liberty*. In *On Liberty and Other Essays*, ed. John Gray, 1–128. Oxford: Oxford University Press.

Miller, David. 1994. "The Nation State: A Modest Defense." In *Political Restructuring in Europe*, ed. Chris Brown, 137–62. London: Routledge.

Miller, John H. 1977. "Cadres Policy in Nationality Areas: Recruitment of CPSU First and Second Secretaries in Non-Russian Republics of the USSR." *Soviet Studies* 29 (January), 3–36.

———. 1983. "*Nomenklatura*: Check on Localism?" In *Leadership Selection and Patron-Client Relations in the USSR and Yugoslavia*, ed. T. H. Rigby and Bohdan Harasymiw, 62–97. London: George Allen and Unwin.

Milne, R. S. 1989. "The Relevance of Ethnicity." *Political Science* 41 (December), 30–50.

Minahan, James. 1996. *Nations Without States: A Historical Dictionary of Contemporary National Movements*. Westport, CT: Greenwood Press.

———. 2002. *Encyclopedia of the Stateless Nations: Ethnic and National Groups Around the World*. Westport, CT: Greenwood Press.

Minority Rights Group. 1997. *World Directory of Minorities*. London: Minority Rights Group International.

Misiunas, Romuald J., and Rein Taagepera. 1983. *The Baltic States: Years of Dependence, 1940–1980*. Berkeley and Los Angeles: University of California Press.

Mitchell, Brian R. 1998a. *International Historical Statistics: Africa, Asia, and Oceania, 1750–1993*. New York: Stockton Press.

———. 1998b. *International Historical Statistics: The Americas, 1750–1993*. New York: Stockton Press.

———. 1998c. *International Historical Statistics: Europe, 1750–1993*. New York: Stockton Press.

Mongush, Mergen. 1993. "The Annexation of Tannu-Tuva and the Formation of the Tuvinskaya ASSR." *Nationalities Papers* 21 (Fall), 47–52.

Moraski, Bryon J. 2001. "Political Competition and Democratic Development in Russia's Regions." Paper presented at the 2001 annual meeting of the American Political Science Association. San Francisco, 30 August–2 September.

Moraski, Bryon, and William M. Reisinger, 2003. "Explaining Electoral Competition across Russia's Regions." *Slavic Review* 62 (Summer), 278–301.

Moreno, Luis. 1997. "Federalization and Ethnoterritorial Concurrence in Spain." *Publius: The Journal of Federalism* 27 (Fall), 65–84.

Morgan, Edmund S. 1976. *The Meaning of Independence: John Adams, George Washington, and Thomas Jefferson*. Charlottesville: University of Virginia Press.

Morgenthau, Ruth Schachter. 1964. *Political Parties in French-Speaking Africa*. Oxford: Clarendon Press.

Morison, Samuel Eliot. 1965. *The Oxford History of the American People*. New York: Oxford University Press.

Morris, Aldon. 1984. *The Origin of the Civil Rights Movement*. New York: Free Press.

Morrison, J. A. 1938. "The Evolution of the Territorial-Administrative System of the USSR." *American Quarterly of the Soviet Union* 1 (October), 25–46.

Moseley, Christopher, and R. E. Asher, eds. 1994. *Atlas of the World's Languages*. New York: Routledge.

Moser, Robert G. 2001. *Unexpected Outcomes: Electoral Systems, Political Parties, and Representation in Russia*. Pittsburgh: University of Pittsburgh Press.

Moses, Joel. 1985. "Regionalism in Soviet Politics: Continuity as a Source of Change, 1953–82." *Soviet Studies* 37 (April), 184–211.

Motyl, Alexander J. 1993. *Dilemmas of Independence: Ukraine After Totalitarianism*. New York: Council on Foreign Relations.

Muiznieks, Nils R. 1990. "The Pro-Soviet Movement in Latvia." *Report on the USSR* 2 (24 August), 19–24.

Musgrave, Thomas D. 1997. *Self-Determination and National Minorities*. Oxford: Clarendon Press.

Mustafin, M. P., and R. G. Khuzeev. 1994. *Vse o Tatarstane: Ekonomiko-geograficheskii Spravochnik*. Kazan: Tatarskoe knizhnoe izdatel'stvo.

Nagel, Joane. 1994. "Constructing Ethnicity: Creating and Recreating Ethnic Identity and Culture." *Social Problems* 41 (February), 152–76.

Nagel, Joane, and Susan Olzak. 1982. "Ethnic Competition in New and Old States: An Extension of the Competition Model." *Social Problems* 30 (December), 127–43.

Nahaylo, Bohdan. 1989a. "Baltic Echoes in the Ukraine." *Report on the USSR* 1 (13 January), 18–20.

———. 1989b. "Confrontation over Creation of Ukrainian 'Popular Front.' " *Report on the USSR* 1 (3 March), 13–17.

Nelson, Lynn D., and Paata Amonashvili. 1992. "Voting and Political Attitudes in Soviet Georgia." *Soviet Studies* 44, 687–97.

Nevitte, Neil, and Charles H. Kennedy, eds. 1986. *Ethnic Preference and Public Policy in Developing States*. Boulder, CO: Lynne Reiner.

Newth, J. A. 1963a. "The 'Establishment' in Tajikistan, I." *Soviet Studies* 14 (April), 408–20.

———. 1963b. "The 'Establishment' in Tajikistan, II." *Soviet Studies* 15 (July), 72–81.

Nodia, Ghia. 1997–98. *Causes and Visions of Conflict in Abkhazia*. Berkeley Program in Soviet and Post-Soviet Studies, Working Paper Series. Berkeley: University of California.

Nordlinger, Eric A. 1972. *Conflict Regulation in Divided Societies*. Occasional Papers in International Affairs No. 29. Cambridge, MA: Harvard University, Center for International Affairs.

North, Douglass C. 1981. *Structure and Change in Economic History*. New York: Norton.

North, Douglass C., and Barry R. Weingast. 1988. "Constitutions and Commitment: The Evolution of Institutions Governing Public Choice in 17th Century England." Working Papers in Political Science P-88–11. Stanford: Hoover Institution.

Nove, Alec. 1986. *The Soviet Economic System*, 3rd ed. Boston: Allen and Unwin.

Nyrop, Richard F. et al. 1969. *Area Handbook for Rwanda*. Washington, DC: United States Government Printing Office.

Oberschall, Anthony. 1973. *Social Conflict and Social Movements.* Englewood Cliffs: Prentice-Hall.

O'Donnell, Guillermo, and Philippe C. Schmitter. 1986. *Transitions from Authoritarian Rule: Tentative Conclusions and Uncertain Democracies.* Baltimore: Johns Hopkins University Press.

Ohmae, Kenichi. 1995. *The End of the Nation State: The Rise of Regional Economies.* New York: Random House.

Olcott, Martha Brill. 1987. *The Kazakhs.* Stanford: Hoover Institution Press.

———. 1989. "Gorbachev's Nationalities Policy and Soviet Central Asia." In *Limits to Soviet Power*, ed. Rajan Menon and Daniel N. Nelson, 69–91. Lexington: Lexington Books.

———. 1994. "The Myth of 'Tsentral'naia Aziia'." *Orbis* 38 (Fall), 549–65.

———. *Kazakhstan: Unfulfilled Promise.* Washington, DC: Carnegie Endowment for International Peace.

O'Leary, Brendan. 2001. "The Elements of Right-Sizing and Right-Peopling the State." In *Right-Sizing the State: The Politics of Moving Borders*, ed. Brendan O'Leary, Ian S. Lustick, and Thomas Callaghy, 15–73. London: Oxford University Press.

Olson, Mancur, Jr. 1965. *The Logic of Collective Action: Public Goods and the Theory of Groups.* Cambridge: Harvard University Press.

Ordeshook, Peter C. 1995. *Constitutions for New Democracies: Reflections on Turmoil or Agents of Stability?* Social Science Working Paper 924. Pasadena: California Institute of Technology, Division of Humanities and Social Sciences.

Organski, A. F. K. 1958. *World Politics.* New York: Alfred Knopf.

Orttung, Robert W., ed. 2000. *The Republics and Regions of the Russian Federation: A Guide to Politics, Policies, and Leaders.* Armonk, NY: M. E. Sharpe.

Osgood, Robert E., and Robert W. Tucker. 1967. *Force, Order, and Justice.* Baltimore: Johns Hopkins University Press.

Ostrom, Elinor. 1990. *Governing the Commons: The Evolution of Institutions for Collective Action.* Cambridge: Cambridge University Press.

———. 1992. *Crafting Institutions for Self-Governing Irrigation Systems.* San Francisco: ICS Press.

Otyrba, Gueorgui. 1994. "War in Abkhazia: The Regional Significance of the Georgian-Abkhazian Conflict." In *National Identity and Ethnicity in Russia and the New States in Eurasia*, ed. Roman Szporluk, 281–309. Armonk, NY: M. E. Sharpe.

Ovchinnikov, Boris. 2001. "Parlamentskie vybory—1999: Statisticheskie anomalii." In *Regiony Rossii v 1999 g*, ed. Nikolai Petrov, 225–37. Moscow: Carnegie Center.

Pabriks, Artis. 1999. *From Nationalism to Ethnic Policy: The Latvian Nation in the Present and in the Past.* Berlin: Berliner Interuniversitäre Arbeitsgruppe "Baltische Staaten."

Page, Stanley W. 1948. "Lenin, the National Question and the Baltic States, 1917–19." *American Slavic and East European Review* 7 (February), 15–31.

———. 1949. "Social and National Currents in Latvia, 1860–1917." *American Slavic and East European Review* 8 (February), 25–36.

Palley, Claire. 1979. "The Role of Law in Relation to Minority Groups." In *The Future of Cultural Minorities*, ed. Antony E. Alcock, Brian K. Taylor, and John M. Welton, 120–60. London: Macmillan.

Pape, Robert. 2003. "The Strategic Logic of Suicide Terrorism." *American Political Science Review* 97 (August), 343–61.

Park, Alexander G. 1957. *Bolshevism in Turkestan, 1917–1927*. New York: Columbia University Press.

Park, Andrus. 1994. "Ethnicity and Independence: The Case of Estonia in Comparative Perspective." *Europe-Asia Studies* 46, 69–87.

Parker, Geoffrey, and Ramesh Dutta Dikshit. 1997. "Boundary Studies in Political Geography: Focus on the Changing Boundaries in Europe." In *Developments in Political Geography: A Century of Progress*, 170–201. New Delhi: Sage.

Parlamentarskaia biblioteka RF. 1995. *Konstitutsii respublik v sostave RF.* Moscow: Manuskript.

Parsons, J. W. R. 1982. "National Integration in Soviet Georgia." *Soviet Studies* 34 (October), 547–69.

Payin, Emil A. 1998. "Ethnic Separatism." In *Conflict and Consensus in Ethno-Political and Center-Periphery Relations in Russia*, ed. Jeremy R. Azrael and Emil A. Payin. Santa Monica: RAND Corporation.

Pearson, Raymond. 1991. "The Historical Background to Soviet Federalism." In *Soviet Federalism: Nationalism and Economic Decentralisation*, ed. Alastair McAuley, 13–32. Leicester: Leicester University Press.

Pennar, Jaan. 1968. "Nationalism in the Soviet Baltics." In *Ethnic Minorities in the Soviet Union*, ed. Erich Goldhagen, 198–217. New York: Praeger.

———. 1978. "Soviet Nationality Policy and the Estonian Communist Elite." In *A Case Study of a Soviet Republic: The Estonian SSR*, ed. Tönu Parming and Elmar Järvesoo, 105–27. Boulder, CO: Westview Press.

Petrov, Nikolai. 2001. "Knut i prianik." In *Rossiia v izbiratel'nom tsikle*, ed. M. Makfol, N. Petrov, and A. Riabov, 510–16. Moscow: Gendal'f.

Pflanze, Otto. 1996. "Nationalism in Europe, 1848–1871." *Review of Politics* 28 (April), 129–43.

Philipson, Tomas. 1992. "The Exchange and Allocation of Decision Power." *Theory and Decision* 33 (November), 191–206.

Philpott, Daniel. 2001. "Usurping the Sovereignty of Sovereignty?" *World Politics* 53 (January), 297–324.

Pigolkin, Albert S., and Marina S. Studenikina. 1991. "Republican Language Laws in the USSR: A Comparative Analysis." *Journal of Soviet Nationalities* 2 (Spring), 38–76.

Pipes, Richard E. 1950. "The First Experiment in Soviet National Policy: The Bashkir Republic, 1917–1920." *Russian Review* 9 (October), 303–19.

———. 1968. *The Formation of the USSR*, rev. ed. New York: Atheneum.

Pirie, Paul S. 1996. "National Identity and Politics in Southern and Eastern Ukraine." *Europe-Asia Studies* 48 (November), 1079–1104.

Plakans, Andrejs. 1995. *The Latvians: A Short History*. Stanford: Hoover Institution Press.

Polishchuk, Leonid. 1996. *Russian Federalism: Economic Reform and Political Behavior.* Social Science Working Paper 972. Pasadena: California Institute of Technology, Division of the Humanities and Social Science.

Polyviou, Polyvios G. 1980. *Cyprus: Conflict and Negotiation, 1960–80*. London: Duckworth.

Ponomarev, B. N., et al. 1982. *Konstitutsiia SSSR: Politiko-pravovoi kommentarii.* Moscow: Izdatel'stvo Politicheskaia Literatura.

Popovsky, Mark. 1979. *Manipulated Science.* Garden City, NJ: Doubleday.

Porter, Brian A. 1992. "Who Is a Pole and Where Is Poland? Territory and Nation in the Rhetoric of Polish National Democracy before 1905." *Slavic Review* 51 (Winter), 639–53.

Powell, Robert. 1999. *In the Shadow of Power: States and Strategies in International Politics.* Princeton: Princeton University Press.

Pustilnik, Marina. 1995. "Caucasian Stresses." *Transition* 1 (15 March), 16–18.

Putnam, Robert D. 1988. "Diplomacy and Domestic Politics: The Logic of Two-Level Games." *International Organization* 42 (Summer), 427–60.

Pye, Lucian W. 1962. *Politics, Personality, and Nation Building: Burma's Search for Identity.* New Haven: Yale University Press.

Quester, George H. 1977. *Offense and Defense in the International System.* New York: John Wiley and Sons.

Rabushka, Alvin, and Kenneth A. Shepsle. 1982. *Politics in Plural Societies: A Theory of Democratic Instability.* Columbus: Charles E. Merrill.

Ragin, Charles C. 1979. "Ethnic Political Mobilization: The Welsh Case." *American Sociological Review* 44 (August), 619–35.

Rakowska-Harmstone, Teresa. 1970. *Russia and Nationalism in Central Asia: The Case of Tadzhikistan.* Baltimore: Johns Hopkins University Press.

Ratzel, Friedrich. 1903. *Politische Geographie.* Munich: Oldenbourg.

Raun, Toivo U. 1984. "The Revolution of 1905 in the Baltic Provinces and Finland." *Slavic Review* 43 (Autumn), 453–67.

———. 1987. *Estonia and the Estonians.* Stanford: Hoover Institution Press.

Rees, E. A. 2002. "The Changing Nature of Centre-Local Relations in the USSR, 1928–36." In *Centre-Local Relations in the Stalinist State, 1928–1941,* ed. E. A. Rees, 9–36. New York: Palgrave Macmillan.

Remeikis, Thomas. 1965. "The Administration of Power: The Communist Party and the Soviet Government." In *Lithuania Under the Soviets: Portrait of a Nation, 1940–65,* ed. Stanley Vardys, 111–40. New York: Praeger.

Remington, Thomas F. 2001. *The Russian Parliament: Institutional Evolution in a Transitional Regime, 1989–1999.* New Haven: Yale University Press.

Renan, Ernest. 1882 [1994]. "Qu'est-ce qu'une nation?" Lecture delivered at the Sorbonne, 11 March 1882. Excerpt reprinted in *Nationalism,* ed. John Hutchinson and Anthony D. Smith, 17–18. London: Oxford University Press.

Reshetar, John S. 1952. *The Ukrainian Revolution, 1917–1920: A Study in Nationalism.* Princeton: Princeton University Press.

Respublika Altai. 1995. "Konstitutsiia Respubliki Altai (Osnovnoi Zakon) [proekt]." *Zvezda Altaia* 16 June 1995.

Reynolds, Susan. 1984. *Kingdoms and Communities in Western Europe, 900–1300.* Oxford: Clarendon Press.

Riggs, Fred W. 1995. "Ethnonational Rebellions and Viable Constitutionalism." *International Political Science Review* 16, 375–404.

Riker, William H. 1975. "Federalism." In *Handbook of Political Science,* ed. Fred I. Greenstein and Nelson W. Polsby, 5:93–172. Reading, MA: Addison-Wesley.

Ritter, William S. 1985. "The Final Phase in the Liquidation of Anti-Soviet Resistance in Tadzhikistan: Ibrahim Bek and the Basmachi, 1924–31." *Soviet Studies* 37 (October), 484–93.

Robertson, Lawrence Rutherford. 1995. "The Political Economy of Ethnonationalism: Separatism and Secession from the Soviet Union and the Russian Federation." Dissertation. University of California, Los Angeles.

Roeder, Philip G. 1982. "Rational Revolution: Extensions of the 'By-Product' Model of Revolutionary Involvement." *Western Political Quarterly* 35 (March), 5–23.

———. 1984. "Soviet Policies and Kremlin Politics." *International Studies Quarterly* 28 (June), 171–93.

———. 1988. "Do New Soviet Leaders Really Make a Difference?: Rethinking the 'Succession Connection'." *American Political Science Review* 79 (December), 958–76.

———. 1988. *Soviet Political Dynamics: Development of the First Leninist Polity.* New York: Harper and Row.

———. 1991. "Soviet Federalism and Ethnic Mobilization." *World Politics* 43 (January), 196–232.

———. 1993. *Red Sunset: The Failure of Soviet Politics.* Princeton: Princeton University Press.

———. 1998. "Liberalization and Ethnic Entrepreneurs in the Soviet Successor States." In *The Myth of "Ethnic Conflict": Politics, Economics, and "Cultural" Violence,* ed. Beverly Crawford and Ronnie D. Lipschutz, 78–107. University of California, Berkeley, International and Area Studies.

———. 1999. "Peoples and States after 1989: The Political Costs of Incomplete National Revolutions." *Slavic Review* 58 (Winter), 854–82.

———. 2001. "The Rejection of Authoritarianism." In *Postcommunism and the Theory of Democracy,* by Richard D. Anderson, Jr., M. Steven Fish, Stephen E. Hanson, and Philip G. Roeder, 11–53. Princeton: Princeton University Press.

———. 2003. "Clash of Civilizations and the Escalation of Ethnopolitical Conflicts." *Comparative Political Studies* 36 (June), 509–40.

———. 2004. "National Self-Determination and Postcommunist Popular Sovereignty." In *Nationalism after Communism,* ed. Alina Mungiu-Pippidi and Ivan Krastev. Budapest: Central European University Press.

———. 2005. "Power Dividing as an Alternative to Ethnic Power Sharing." In *Sustainable Peace: Power and Institutions after Civil Wars,* ed. Philip G. Roeder and Donald Rothchild, 51–82. Ithaca: Cornell University Press.

Roeder, Philip G., and Donald Rothchild, eds. 2005. *Sustainable Peace: Power and Institutions after Civil Wars.* Ithaca: Cornell University Press.

Roessingh, Martijn A. 1996. *Ethnonationalism and Political Systems in Europe.* Amsterdam: Amsterdam University Press.

Rogowski, Ronald. 1985. "Causes and Varieties of Nationalism: A Rationalist Account." In *New Nationalisms of the Developed World: Toward Explanation,* ed. Edward A. Tiryakian and Ronald Rogowski, 87–107. Boston: Allen and Unwin.

Rokkan, Stein, and Derek W. Urwin. 1983. *Economy, Territory, Identity: Politics of West European Peripheries.* Beverly Hills, CA: Sage.

Roos, Hans. 1966. *A History of Modern Poland: From the Foundation of the State in the First World War to the Present Day*. New York: Alfred A. Knopf.

Rorlich, Azade-Ayse. 1986. *The Volga Tatars: A Profile in National Resilience*. Stanford: Hoover Institution Press.

Rose-Ackerman, Susan. 1981. "Does Federalism Matter? Political Choice in a Federal Republic." *Journal of Political Economy* 89 (February), 152–65.

Rothchild, Donald. 1970. "Ethnicity and Conflict Resolution." *World Politics* 22 (July), 597–616.

———. 1986. "Hegemonial Exchange: An Alternative Model for Managing Conflict in Middle Africa." In *Ethnicity, Politics and Development*, ed. Dennis L. Thompson and Dov Ronen, 65–104. Boulder, CO: Lynne Reiner.

Rothschild, Joseph. 1981. *Ethnopolitics: A Conceptual Framework*. New York: Columbia University Press.

Roy, Olivier. 2000. *The New Central Asia: The Creation of Nations*. New York: New York University Press.

Rudenshiold, Eric. 1992. "Ethnic Dimensions in Contemporary Latvian Politics: Focusing Forces for Change." *Soviet Studies* 44, 609–39.

Rudolph, Joseph R., Jr., and Robert Thompson. 1985. "Ethnoterritorial Movements and the Policy Process: Accommodating Nationalist Demands in the Developing World." *Comparative Politics* 17 (April), 291–311.

Russian Empire. 1899–1905. Tsentral'nyi statisticheskii komitet. *Pervaia vseobshchaia perepis' naseleniia Rossiiskoi Imperii, 1897 g.* St. Petersburg.

———. 1907. Tsentral'nyi statisticheskii komitet. *Statistika zemlevladeniia 1905 g.: Svod dannykh po 50–ti guberniiam Evropeiskoi Rossii*. St. Petersburg.

———. 1916. Glavnoe upravlenie zemleustroistva i zemledeliia (Ministerstvo zemledeliia). Otdel sel'skoi ekonomii i selskokhoziaistvennoi statistiki. *Sbornik statistiko-ekonomicheskoi svedenii po sel'skomu khoziaistvu Rossii i inostrannykh gosudarstv*, IX. Petrograd.

Russian Federation. Federal'noe Sobranie. Gosudarstevennaia Duma. 1995. *Konstitutsii respublik v sostave Rossiiskoi Federatsii*, vypusk 1. Moscow: Izdanie Gosudarstvennoi Dumy "Izvestiia".

———. Federal'noe Sobranie. Gosudarstevennaia Duma. 1996. *Konstitutsii respublik v sostave Rossiiskoi Federatsii*, vypusk 2. Moscow: Izdanie Gosudarstvennoi Dumy "Izvestiia".

———. Tsentral'naia Izbiratel'naia Komissiia Rossiiskoi Federatsii (TsIK). 1996. *Vybory Prezidenta Rossiiskoi Federatsii: Elektoral'naia statistika*. Moscow: Ves Mir.

———. Tsentral'naia Izbiratel'naia Komissiia Rossiiskoi Federatsii (TsIK). 1997. *Vybory Glav Ispolnitel'noi Vlasti Sub"ektov Rossiiskoi Federatsii: Elektoral'naia statistika*. Moscow: Ves Mir.

———. Tsentral'naia Izbiratel'naia Komissiia Rossiiskoi Federatsii (TsIK). 1998. *Vybory v zakonodatel'nye (predstavitel'nye) organy gosudarstvennoi vlasti sub"ektov Rossiiskoi Federatsii: Elektoral'naia statistika*. Moscow: Ves Mir.

———. Tsentral'naia Izbiratel'naia Komissiia Rossiiskoi Federatsii (TsIK). 2000. *Vybory Prezidenta Rossiiskoi Federatsii*. Available online at www.cikrf.ru.

———. Tsentral'naia Izbiratel'naia Komissiia Rossiiskoi Federatsii (TsIK). 2001. *Vybory v organy gosudarstvennoi vlasti sub"ektov Rossiiskoi Federatsii, 1997–2000: Elektoral'naia statistika*. 2 vols. Moscow: Ves Mir.

Rustow, Dankwart A. 1967. *A World of Nations: Problems of Political Modernization.* Washington, DC: Brookings Institution, 1967.

———. 1970. "Transition to Democracy: Toward a Dynamic Model." *Comparative Politics* 2 (April), 337–65.

Rutland, Peter. 1994. "Democracy and Nationalism in Armenia." *Europe-Asia Studies* 46, 839–61.

Rywkin, Michael. 1990. *Moscow's Muslim Challenge: Soviet Central Asia*, rev. ed. Armonk, NY: M. E. Sharpe.

Ryzhkov, Nikolai. 1992. *Perestroika.* Moscow: Novosti.

Sabaliunas, Leonas. 1972. *Lithuania in Crisis: Nationalism to Communism, 1939–1940.* Bloomington: Indiana University Press.

Sabol, Steven. 2003. *Russian Colonization and the Genesis of Kazak National Consciousness.* New York: Palgrave.

Safarova, M. P., et al. 1994. "Analiticheskii obzor konstitutstii respublik, vkhodiashchikh v sostav Rossiiskoi Federatsii." *Rossiiskaia federatsiia* No. 21, 18–27.

Safran, William. 1992. "Language, Ideology, and State-Building: A Comparison of Policies in France, Israel, and the Soviet Union." *International Political Science Review* 13 (October), 397–414.

Sahlins, Peter. 1989. *Boundaries: The Making of France and Spain in the Pyrennes.* Berkeley and Los Angeles: University of California Press.

Sanborn, Josh. 2000. "The Mobilization of 1914 and the Question of the Russian Nation: A Reexamination." *Slavic Review* 59 (Summer), 267–89.

Schafer, Daniel E. 2001. "Local Politics and the Birth of the Republic of Bashkortostan, 1919–1920." In *A State of Nations: Empire and Nation-Making in the Age of Lenin and Stalin*, ed. Ronald Grigor Suny and Terry Martin, 23–66. Oxford: Oxford University Press.

Schapiro, Leonard. 1971. *The Communist Party of the Soviet Union*, rev. ed. New York: Vintage Books.

Schelling, Thomas C. 1960. *The Strategy of Conflict.* Cambridge, MA: Harvard University Press.

———. 1966. *Arms and Influence.* New Haven: Yale University Press.

———. 1978. *Micromotives and Macrobehavior.* New York: Norton.

———. 1984. "What Is Game Theory?" In *Choice and Consequence: Perspectives of an Errant Economist*, ed. Thomas C. Schelling, 213–34. Cambridge, MA: Harvard University Press.

Schermerhorn, Richard A. 1970. *Comparative Ethnic Relations: A Framework for Theory and Research.* New York: Random House.

Schulze, Hagen. 1998. *Germany: A New History.* Cambridge, MA: Harvard University Press.

Schumpeter, Joseph. 1976. *Capitalism, Socialism and Democracy*, 3rd ed. London: Allen and Unwin.

Selden, Mark. 1969. "The Yenan Legacy: The Mass Line." In *Chinese Communist Politics in Action*, ed. A. Doak Barnett, 99–151. Seattle: University of Washington Press.

Selznick, Philip. 1960. *The Organizational Weapon: A Study of Bolshevik Strategy and Tactics.* Glencoe: Free Press.

Senn, Alfred Erich. 1959. *The Emergence of Modern Lithuania*. New York: Columbia University Press.

Seregny, Scott J. 2000. "Zemstvos, Peasants, and Citizenship: The Russian Adult Education Movement and World War I." *Slavic Review* 59 (Summer), 290–315.

Seton-Watson, Hugh. 1977. *Nations and States: An Enquiry into the Origins of Nations and the Politics of Nationalism*. London: Methuen.

Seton-Watson, R. W. 1965. *A History of the Czechs and Slovaks*. Hamden, CT: Archon Books.

Shabad, Theodore. 1946. "Political-Administrative Divisions of the U. S. S. R., 1945." *Geographical Review* 36 (April), 303–11.

Sharlet, Robert. 2001. "Putin and the Politics of Law in Russia." *Post-Soviet Affairs* 17 (July–September), 195–234.

Shaw, Denis J. B. 1994. "Crimea: Background and Aftermath of Its 1994 Presidential Election." *Post-Soviet Geography* 35 (April), 221–46.

Shaw, Stanford J. 1976. *History of the Ottoman Empire and Modern Turkey*. Vol. 1. *Empire of the Gazis: The Rise and Decline of the Ottoman Empire, 1280–1808*. Cambridge: Cambridge University Press.

Shaw, Stanford J., and Ezel Kural Shaw. 1977. *History of the Ottoman Empire and Modern Turkey*. Vol. II. *The Rise of Modern Turkey, 1808–1975*. Cambridge: Cambridge University Press.

Sheehy, Ann. 1990a. "Moves to Draw Up New Union Treaty." *Report on the USSR* 2 (6 July), 14–17.

———. 1990b. "Russians the Target of Inter-ethnic Violence in Tuva." *Report on the USSR* 2 (14 September), 13–17.

———. 1990c. "Sidelights on the Union Treaty of 1922." *Report on the USSR* 2 (28 September), 17–20.

———. 1990d. "Fact Sheet on Declarations of Sovereignty." *Report on the USSR* 2 (9 November), 23–25.

———. 1990e. "A Draft Union Treaty: A Preliminary Assessment." *Report on the USSR* 2 (21 December), 1–6.

———. 1991a. "Fact Sheet on Questions in the Referendum of March 17 and Later Referendums." *Report on the USSR* 3 (22 March), 4–6.

———. 1991b. "Revised Draft of the Union Treaty." *Report on the USSR* 3 (22 March), 1–3.

———. 1991c. "Council of the Federation to Be Abolished?" *Report on the USSR* 3 (21 June), 1–4.

———. 1991d. "A Progress Report on the Union Treaty." *Report on the USSR* 3 (12 July), 17–8.

———. 1991e. "The Union Treaty: A Further Setback." *Report on the USSR* 3 (6 December), 1–4.

Shepsle, Kenneth A. 1989. "Studying Institutions: Some Lessons from the Rational Choice Approach." *Journal of Theoretical Politics* 1 (April), 131–47.

Shepsle, Kenneth A., and Barry R. Weingast. 1981. "Structure-Induced Equilibrium and Legislative Choice." *Public Choice* 37, 503–19.

Shleifer, Andrei, and Daniel Treisman. 2000. *Without a Map: Political Tactics and Economic Reform in Russia*. Cambridge, MA: MIT Press.

Shnirelman, Victor A. 1996. *Who Gets the Past? Competition for Ancestors among Non-Russian Intellectuals in Russia.* Washington, DC: Woodrow Wilson Center Press.

Singer, J. David. 2002. "The Correlates of War Project." Ann Arbor: University of Michigan. Available online at www.umich.edu/~cowproj

SIPRI (Stockholm International Peace Research Institute). 1987–2001. *SIPRI Yearbook: World Armaments and Disarmament,* annual editions. New York: Oxford University Press.

Skendi, Stavor. 1967. *The Albanian National Awakening, 1878–1912.* Princeton: Princeton University Press.

Slezkine, Yuri. 1992. "From Savages to Citizens: The Cultural Revolution in the Soviet Far North, 1928–1938." *Slavic Review* 51 (Spring), 52–76.

———. 1994. "The USSR as a Communal Apartment, or How a Socialist State Promoted Ethnic Particularism." *Slavic Review* 53 (Summer), 414–52.

Slider, Darrell. 1994a. "Federalism, Discord, and Accommodation." In *Local Power and Post-Soviet Politics,* ed. Theodore H. Friedgut and Jeffrey W. Hahn, 239–69. Armonk, NY: M. E. Sharpe.

———. 1994b. "Privatization in Russia's Regions." *Post-Soviet Affairs* 10 (October–December), 367–96.

Smith, Anthony D. 1979. "Towards a Theory of Ethnic Separatism." *Ethnic and Racial Studies* 2 (January), 21–37.

———. 1981. *The Ethnic Revival.* Cambridge: Cambridge University Press.

———. 1986. *The Ethnic Origins of Nations.* London: Blackwell.

———. 1998. *Nationalism and Modernism: A Critical Survey of Recent Theories of Nations and Nationalism.* London: Routledge.

Smith, S. A. 2000. "Citizenship and the Russian Nation during World War I: A Comment." *Slavic Review* 59 (Summer), 316–29.

Smoke, Richard. 1977. *War: Controlling Escalation.* Cambridge: Harvard University Press.

Snyder, Timothy. 2003. *The Reconstruction of Nations: Poland, Ukraine, Lithuania, Belarus, 1569–1999.* New Haven: Yale University Press.

Socor, Vladimir. 1990. "Gagauz in Moldavia Demand Separate Republic." *Report on the USSR* 2 (7 September), 8–13.

Solchanyk, Roman. 1991a. "The Draft Union Treaty and the 'Big Five'." *Report on the USSR* 3 (3 May), 16–18.

———. 1991b. "Ukraine and Russia: Before and After the Coup." *Report on the USSR* 3 (27 September), 13–17.

———. 1992. "Ukraine, The (Former) Center, Russia, and 'Russia'." *Studies in Comparative Communism* 25 (March), 31–45.

———. 1994. "The Politics of State Building: Centre-Periphery Relations in Post-Soviet Ukraine." *Europe-Asia Studies* 46, 47–68.

Solnick, Steven L. 1998. "Gubernatorial Elections in Russia, 1996–1997." *Post-Soviet Affairs* 14 (January–March), 48–80.

Spruyt, Hendrik. 1994. *The Sovereign State and Its Competitors.* Princeton: Princeton University Press.

———. 2002. "The Origins, Development, and Possible Decline of the Modern State." *Annual Review of Political Science* 5, 127–49.

Spruyt, Hendrik. 2005. *Ending Empire: Contested Sovereignty and Territorial Partition.* Ithaca: Cornell University Press.

Stack, Graham. 1999. "Neoinstitutionalist Perspectives on Regionalisation in Russia." Arbeitspapiere des Osteuropa-Instituts der Freien Universität Berlin, No. 21. Berlin: Free University of Berlin.

Stalin, Josef. 1917 and 1924 [1953]. "Against Federalism." In *Works* 3:25–33. Moscow: Foreign Languages Publishing House.

———. 1920 [1953]. "The Policy of the Soviet Government on the National Question in Russia." In *Works* 4:363–376. Moscow: Foreign Languages Publishing House.

———. 1926 [1954]. "To Comrade Kaganovich and the Other Members of the Political Bureau of the Central Committee, Ukrainian C. P. (B.) [26 April 1926]." In *Works* 8:157–63. Moscow: Foreign Languages Publishing House.

———. 1936. *Stalin on the New Soviet Constitution.* New York: International Publishers.

Stankievich, Walter. 1991. "The Events behind Belorussia's Independence Declaration." *Report on the USSR* 3 (20 September), 24–26.

Stanovcic, Vojislav. 1992. "Problems and Options in Institutionalizing Ethnic Relations." *International Political Science Review* 13 (October), 359–79.

Statesman's Yearbook. 1897–2001. New York: St. Martin's Press.

Stein, Arthur A. 1990. *Why Nations Cooperate: Circumstance and Choice in International Relations.* Ithaca: Cornell University Press.

Stoner-Weiss, Kathryn. 2001. "The Russian Central State in Crisis: Center and Periphery in the Post-Soviet Era." In *Russian Politics: Challenges of Democratization,* ed. Zoltan Barany and Robert G. Moser, 103–34. Cambridge: Cambridge University Press.

———. 2002. "Central Governing Incapacity and the Weakness of Political Parties: Russian Democracy in Disarray." *Publius* 32 (November), 125–46.

Strang, David. 1990. "From Dependency to Sovereignty: An Event History Analysis of Decolonization 1870–1987." *American Sociological Review* 55 (December), 846–60.

———. 1991. "Global Patterns of Decolonization, 1500–1987." *International Studies Quarterly* 35 (December), 429–54.

Sullivan, Stefan. 1995. "Interethnic Relations in post-Soviet Tuva." *Ethnic and Racial Studies* 18 (January), 64–88.

Sullivant, Robert S. 1962. *Soviet Politics and the Ukraine 1917–1957.* New York: Columbia University Press.

Suny, Ronald Grigor. 1988. *The Making of the Georgian Nation.* Bloomington: Indiana University Press.

———. 1992. "State, Civil Society, and Ethnic Cultural Consolidation in the USSR: Roots of the National Question." In *From Union to Commonwealth: Nationalism and Separatism in the Soviet Republics,* ed. Gail W. Lapidus, Victor Zaslavsky, and Philip Goldman, 22–44. Cambridge: Cambridge University Press.

———. 1993a. *Looking Toward Ararat: Armenia in Modern History.* Bloomington: Indiana University Press.

———. 1993b. *The Revenge of the Past: Nationalism, Revolution, and the Collapse of the Soviet Union.* Stanford: Stanford University Press.

———. 1999/2000. "Provisional Stabilities: The Politics of Identities in Post-Soviet Eurasia." *International Security* 24 (Winter), 139–78.

Sutton, John. 1986. "Non-Cooperative Bargaining Theory: An Introduction." *Review of Economic Studies* 53 (October), 709–24.

Sužiedėlis, Simas. 1965. "Lithuania from Medieval to Modern Times: A Historical Outline." In *Lithuania Under the Soviets: Portrait of a Nation, 1940–65*, ed. Stanley Vardys, 3–19. New York: Praeger Publishers.

Swearer, Howard. 1959. "Khrushchev's Revolution in Industrial Management." *World Politics* 12 (October), 45–61.

Swietochowski, Tadeusz. 1985. *Russian Azerbaijan, 1905–1920: The Shaping of National Identity in a Muslim Community*. Cambridge: Cambridge University Press.

———. 1995. *Russia and Azerbaijan: A Borderland in Transition*. New York: Columbia University Press.

Swire, Joseph. 1971. *Albania: The Rise of a Kingdom*. New York: Arno Press.

Symonds, Richard. 1950. *The Making of Pakistan*. London: Faber and Faber.

Szporluk, Roman. 2000. *Russia, Ukraine, and the Breakup of the Soviet Union*. Stanford: Hoover Institution Press.

Taagepera, Rein. 1993. *Estonia: Return to Independence*. Boulder, CO: Westview Press.

———. 1999. *The Finno-Ugric Republics and the Russian State*. New York: Routledge.

———. 2000. "Should Russia Break Up." Paper presented at the annual meeting of the American Political Science Association, Washington, DC, 31 August–3 September.

Tarlton, Charles. 1965. "Symmetry and Asymmetry as Elements of Federalism: A Theoretical Speculation." *Journal of Politics* 27 (November), 861–74.

Tarrow, Sidney. 1977. *Between Center and Periphery: Grassroots Politicians in Italy and France*. New Haven: Yale University Press.

Tarrow, Sidney. 1988. "National Politics and Collective Action: Recent Theory and Research in Western Europe and the United States." *Annual Review of Sociology* 14, 421–40.

———. 1989. *Struggle, Politics, and Reform: Collective Action, Social Movements, and Cycles of Protest*. Western Societies Program, Occasional Paper No. 21. Ithaca, NY: Cornell University, Center for International Studies.

Teague, Elizabeth. 1993. "North-South Divide: Yeltsin and Russia's Provincial Leaders." *RFE/RL Research Report* 2 (26 November), 7–23.

———. 1994. "Center-Periphery Relations in the Russian Federation." In *National Identity and Ethnicity in Russia and the New States of Eurasia*, ed. Roman Szporluk, 20–57. Armonk, NY: M. E. Sharpe.

Tedstrom, John. 1991. "Soviet Fiscal Federalism in a Time of Crisis." *Report on the USSR* 3 (2 August), 1–5.

Theen, Rolf H. W. 1980. "Party and Bureaucracy." In *Public Policy and Administration in the Soviet Union*, ed. Gordon B. Smith, 16–52. New York: Praeger.

Thomson, Dennis L. 1992. "Comparative Policy Towards Cultural Isolationists in Canada and Norway." *International Political Science Review* 13 (October), 433–49.

Thomson, Janice E. 1995. "State Sovereignty in International Relations: Bridging the Gap between Theory and Empirical Research." *International Studies Quarterly* 39 (June), 213–33.

Thorson, Carla. 1991. "The Collapse of the Constitutional Order." *Report on the USSR* 3 (18 October), 15–18.

Tillett, Lowell. 1975. "Ukrainian Nationalism and the Fall of Shelest." *Slavic Review* 34 (December), 752–68.

Tilly, Charles. 1975. "Reflections on the History of European State-Making." In *The Formation of National States in Europe*, ed. Charles Tilly, 3–83. Princeton: Princeton University Press.

———. *From Mobilization to Revolution.* Reading, MA: Addison-Wesley Publishing Co.

———. 1984. "Social Movements and National Politics." In *Statemaking and Social Movements: Essays in History and Theory*, ed. Charles Bright and Susan Harding, 297–317. Ann Arbor: University of Michigan Press.

Tishkov, Valerii A. 1994. *Narody Rossii: Entsiklopediia.* Moscow: Nauchnoe izdatel'stvo Bol'shaia Rossiiskaia Entsiklopediia.

———. 1997. *Ethnicity, Nationalism, and Conflict in and after the Soviet Union: The Mind Aflame.* London: Sage.

Titarenko, Larissa G. 1999. "Globalisation, Nationalism, and Ethnic Relations in Belarus." In *Ethnicity and Nationalism in Russia, the CIS and the Baltic States*, ed. Christopher Williams and Thanasis D. Sfikas, 150–83. Brookfield: Ashgate.

Titkov, Aleksei. 2001. "Konstitutsionnyi sud v otnosheniiakh Tsentra s regionami." In *Regiony Rossii v 1999 g.*, 259–65. Moscow: Carnegie Center.

Toft, Monica Duffy. 2003. *The Geography of Ethnic Violence: Identities, Interests, and the Indivisibility of Territory.* Princeton: Princeton University Press.

Tolz, Vera. 1993. "Regionalism in Russia: The Case of Siberia." *RFE/RL Research Report* 2 (26 February), 1–9.

———. 2001. *Inventing the Nation: Russia.* New York: Arnold.

Towster, Julian. 1948. *Political Power in the U.S.S.R., 1917–1947.* New York: Oxford University Press.

Treisman, Daniel S. 1997. "Russia's 'Ethnic Revival': The Separatist Activism of Regional Leaders in a Postcommunist Order." *World Politics* 49 (January), 212–49.

———. 1999. *After the Deluge: Regional Crises and Political Consolidation in Russia.* Ann Arbor: University of Michigan Press.

Turovskii, Rostislav. 2000. "Pozitsii regional'nykh elit." In *Rossiia v izbiratel'nom tsikle*, ed. M. Makfol, N. Petrov, A. Riabov, 506–9. Moscow: Gendal'f.

Unger, Aryeh L. 1981. *Constitutional Development in the USSR: A Guide to the Soviet Constitutions.* London: Methuen.

United Nations. 1980, 1985, 1986, 1990, 1995. Department of Economic and Social Information and Policy Analysis. Statistical Division. *Statistical Yearbook*, annual editions. New York: United Nations.

United States. Bureau of the Census. 1998. "International Data Base." Washington, DC. Available online at http://www.census.gov/ipc/www/idbprint.html

———. Central Intelligence Agency. 1980. *Directory of Soviet Officials: Republic Organizations.* Washington, DC.

———. Congress. Commission on Security and Cooperation in Europe. 1990. *Elections in the Baltic States and Soviet Republics: A Compendium of Reports on Parliamentary Elections Held in 1990.* Washington, DC: US Government Printing Office.

————. Library of Congress. "Country Studies." Available online at http:// lcweb2.loc.gov/frd/cs/cshome.html

United States Institute of Peace. 1995. *The War in Tajikistan: Three Years On*. Special Report. Washington, DC: United States Institute of Peace.

Urban, Michael E. 1989. *An Algebra of Soviet Power: Elite Circulation in the Belorussian Republic, 1966–86*. Cambridge: Cambridge University Press.

Urban, Michael E., and Russell B. Reed. 1989. "Regionalism in a Systems Perspective: Explaining Elite Circulation in a Soviet Republic." *Slavic Review* 48 (Fall), 413–31.

USSR. Gosudarstvennyi komitet SSSR po statistike. 1990. *Narodnoe khoziaistvo SSSR v 1989 g.: statisticheskii ezhegodnik*. Moscow: Finansy i statistika.

————. Gosudarstvennyi komitet SSSR po statistike. 1991. *Narodnoe khoziaistvo SSSR v 1990 g.: statisticheskii ezhegodnik*. Moscow: Finansy i statistika.

————. Gosudarstvennyi komitet SSSR po statistike. 1992. *Itogi vsesoiuznoi perepisi naseleniia 1989 goda* (microform). Minneapolis: East View Publications.

————. Tsentral'noe statisticheskoe upravlenie. 1972–73. *Itogi vsesoiuznoi perepisi naseleniia 1970 goda*. Moscow: Statistika.

————. Verkhovnyi Sovet SSSR. 1984. *Deputaty verkhovnogo soveta SSSR, odinatsatyi sozyv*. Moscow: Izvestiia.

Vakar, Nicholas P. 1956. *Belorussia: The Making of a Nation, A Case Study*. Cambridge: Harvard University Press.

Van den Berghe, Pierre L. 1978. "Race and Ethnicity: A Sociobiological Perspective." *Ethnic and Racial Studies* 1 (October), 401–11.

van der Leeuw, Charles. 2000. *Azerbaijan: A Quest for Identity, A Short History*. New York: St. Martin's Press.

Van Dyke, Vernon. 1974. "Human Rights and the Rights of Groups." *American Journal of Political Science* 18 (November), 725–41.

Van Selm, Bert. 1998. "Economic Performance in Russia's Regions." *Europe-Asia Studies* 50 (June), 603–18.

Velychenko, Stephen. 1995. "Identities, Loyalties and Service in Imperial Russia: Who Administered the Borderlands?" *Russian Review* 54 (April), 188–208.

Verdery, Katherine. 1993. "Nationalism and National Sentiment in Post-socialist Romania." *Slavic Review* 52 (Summer), 179–203.

————. 1996. "Nationalism, Postsocialism, and Space in Eastern Europe." *Social Research* 63 (Spring), 77–95.

Vetik, Raivo. 1993. "Ethnic Conflict and Accommodation in Post-Communist Estonia." *Journal of Peace Research* 30 (August), 271–80.

von der Mehden, Fred R. 1964. *Politics of the Developing Nations*. Englewood Cliffs: Prentice-Hall.

von Rauch, Georg. 1974. *The Baltic States: The Years of Independence (Estonia, Latvia, Lithuania, 1917–1940)*, trans. Gerald Onn. London: C. Hurst.

Wagner, Robert Harrison. 1993. "The Causes of Peace." In *Stopping the Killing: How Civil Wars End*, ed. Roy Licklider, 235–68. New York: New York University Press.

Walker, Edward W. 1999–2000. "Russia's Soft Underbelly: The Stability of Instability in Dagestan." Working Paper Series. Berkeley: University of California, Berkeley Program in Soviet and Post-Soviet Studies.

Walker, Edward W. 2003. *Dissolution: Sovereignty and the Breakup of the Soviet Union.* Lanham: Rowman and Littlefield.

Wallensteen, Peter, and Margareta Sollenberg. 1998. "Armed Conflict and Regional Conflict Complexes, 1989–97." *Journal of Peace Research* 35 (July), 621–34.

Ware, Robert Bruce, and Enver Kisriev. 1999. "Political Stability in Dagestan: Ethnic Parity and Religious Polarization." Paper presented at the 1999 annual meeting of the American Political Science Association, Atlanta.

———. 2001. "Ethnic Parity and Democratic Pluralism in Dagestan: A Consociational Approach." *Europe-Asia Studies* 53 (January), 105–31.

Waters, Mary C. 1990. *Ethnic Options: Choosing Identities in America.* Berkeley and Los Angeles: University of California Press.

Weber, Eugen. 1976. *Peasants into Frenchmen: The Modernization of Rural France, 1870–1914.* Stanford: Stanford University Press.

Weeks, Theodore R. 1996. *Nation and State in Late Imperial Russia: Nationalism and Russification on the Western Frontier, 1863–1914.* De Kalb: Northern Illinois University Press.

Weiner, Amir. 1996. "The Making of a Dominant Myth: The Second World War and the Construction of Political Identities within the Soviet Polity." *Russian Review* 55 (October), 638–60.

Weinstein, Brian. 1979. "Language Strategists: Redefining Political Frontiers on the Basis of Linguistic Choices." *World Politics* 31 (April), 345–64.

Wenner, Manfred W. 1967. *Modern Yemen, 1918–1966.* Baltimore: Johns Hopkins University Press.

Wheeler-Bennett, John W. 1956. *Brest-Litovsk: The Forgotten Peace, March 1918.* New York: Macmillan.

White, J. D. 1971. "The Revolution in Lithuania 1918–19." *Soviet Studies* 23 (October), 186–200.

Wight, Martin. 1952. *British Colonial Constitutions 1952.* Oxford: Clarendon Press.

Willerton, John P. 1992. *Patronage and Politics in the USSR.* Cambridge: Cambridge University Press.

Willerton, John P., and William Reisinger. 1991. "Troubleshooters, Political Machines, and Moscow's Regional Control." *Slavic Review* 50 (Summer), 347–58.

Wilson, Andrew. 2000. *The Ukrainians: Unexpected Nation.* New Haven: Yale University Press.

Wittman, Donald. 1991. "Nations and States: Mergers and Acquisitions; Dissolutions and Divorce." *American Economic Review* 81 (May), 126–29.

———. 2001. "War or Peace?" Manuscript. University of California, Santa Cruz, Department of Economics.

Wixman, Ronald. 1980. *Language Aspects of Ethnic Patterns and Processes in the North Caucasus.* Research Paper No. 191. University of Chicago, Department of Geography.

———. 1984. *The Peoples of the USSR: An Ethnographic Handbook.* Armonk, NY: M. E. Sharpe.

Wolchik, Sharon L. 1994 "The Politics of Ethnicity in Post-Communist Czechoslovakia." *East European Politics and Societies* 8 (Winter), 153–88.

Wood, Gordon. 1969. *The Creation of the American Republic, 1776–1787.* Chapel Hill: University of North Carolina Press.

World Bank. 2002. *World Development Indicators* (CD-Rom version). Washington, DC: World Bank.

Yalcin, Resul. 2002. *The Rebirth of Uzbekistan: Politics, Economy, and Society in the Post-Soviet Era.* Reading, UK: Ithaca Press.

Yemelianova, Galina. 1999. "Ethnic Nationalism, Islam and Russian Politics in the North Caucasus (with special reference to the autonomous Republic of Dagestan." In *Ethnicity and Nationalism in Russia, the CIS and the Baltic States*, ed. Christopher Williams and Thanasis D. Sfikas, 120–47. Brookfield: Ashgate.

Young, Crawford. 1976. *The Politics of Cultural Pluralism.* Madison: University of Wisconsin Press.

Young, Robert A. 1997. "How Do Peaceful Secessions Happen?" In *War in the Midst of Peace: The International Politics of Ethnic Conflict*, ed. David Carment and Patrick James, 45–60. Pittsburgh: University of Pittsburgh Press.

Zacek, Jane Shapiro. 1997. "Reorganizing Intergovernmental Relations in the USSR." In *Legacy of the Soviet Bloc*, ed. Jane Shapiro Zacek and Ilpyong J. Kim, 73–90. Gainesville: University Press of Florida.

Zacher, Mark W. 2001. "The Territorial Integrity Norm: International Boundaries and the Use of Force." *International Organization* 55 (Spring), 215–50.

Zaprudnik, Jan. 1993. *Belarus as a Crossroads in History.* Boulder, CO: Westview Press.

Zartman, I. William. 1991. "Negotiations and Prenegotiations in Ethnic Conflict: The Beginning, the Middle, and the Ends." In *Conflict and Peacemaking in Multiethnic Societies*, ed. Joseph V. Montville, 511–33. New York: Lexington Books.

Zaznaev, Oleg. 2000. "Respublika Tatarstan: Regional'nye osobennosti vybory-99." *Konstitutsionnoe Pravo: Vostochnoevropeiskoe Obozrenie* No. 1 (30), 213–15.

———. 2001. "The Implications of Federal Reforms for Russia's Regions." Paper presented at the 2001 annual meeting of the American Political Science Association. San Francisco, 30 August–2 September.

Zenkovsky, Serge A. 1960. *Pan-Turkism and Islam in Russia.* Cambridge, MA: Harvard University Press.

Ziblatt, David. 2006. *Structuring the State: The Formation of Italy and Germany and the Puzzle of Federalism.* Princeton: Princeton University Press.

Zviagelskaya, Irina. 1998. "The Tajikistan Conflict." In *Armaments, Disarmament, and International Security*, 63–75. Oxford: Oxford University Press.

INDEX

Tables and figures are indicated with *italic* type, e.g., *56t, 89f*